CORPORATE GOVERNANCE IN JAPAN

Corporate Governance in Japan

in Japan

Institutional Change and Organizational Diversity

Edited by

MASAHIKO AOKI

GREGORY JACKSON

HIDEAKI MIYAJIMA

OXFORD

UNIVERSITY PRESS

OXFORD
UNIVERSITY PRESS

Great Clarendon Street, Oxford OX2 6DP

Oxford University Press is a department of the University of Oxford.
It furthers the University's objective of excellence in research, scholarship,
and education by publishing worldwide in

Oxford New York

Auckland Cape Town Dar es Salaam Hong Kong Karachi
Kuala Lumpur Madrid Melbourne Mexico City Nairobi
New Delhi Shanghai Taipei Toronto

With offices in

Argentina Austria Brazil Chile Czech Republic France Greece
Guatemala Hungary Italy Japan Poland Portugal Singapore
South Korea Switzerland Thailand Turkey Ukraine Vietnam

Oxford is a registered trade mark of Oxford University Press
in the UK and in certain other countries

Published in the United States
by Oxford University Press Inc., New York

British Library Cataloguing in Publication Data

Data available

Library of Congress Cataloging in Publication Data

Data available

Typeset by SPI Publisher Services, Pondicherry, India
Printed in Great Britain
on acid-free paper by
Biddles Ltd., King's Lynn, Norfolk

ISBN 978–0–19–928451–1

1 3 5 7 9 10 8 6 4 2

Contents

Preface

This volume grew out of a study group on corporate governance at the Research Institute of Economy, Trade and Industry (RIETI) in 2002. The project was motivated by a concern to take stock of the changes underway in corporate governance in Japan. Our feeling was that the conventional understanding about the Japanese firm was increasingly becoming outdated. At the same time, both popular and academic commentators seemed all too often to either over claim that little had changed in Japan, or to portray those changes in terms of an inevitable process of convergence toward the model of "shareholder value" found in the United States. To bring this debate forward, we felt that a third perspective was needed that was both empirically comprehensive and theoretically grounded. While some of this empirical work was becoming available in Japanese language publications, our secondary goal was to bring together these contributions and fill out the picture of contemporary Japanese business in a single English-language volume.

This type of long-term and inter-disciplinary project would not have been possible without the unique support of RIETI. Founded in 2001 by the Ministry of Economy, Trade and Industry (METI), RIETI has established a unique position to facilitate lively exchange between independent social science research and the formulation of public policy in Japan. RIETI was also able to host international scholars such as Mari Sako and Ronald Dore as visiting fellows to support their contributions to this book. For this, we are very grateful and hope this volume reflects the aim of bringing academic research to bear on contemporary policy issues.

This publication has taken a long time to realize, having outlived our study group in Tokyo and turning into a collaborative effort across different continents. Gregory Jackson took a new position at King's College London in August 2004. Hideaki Miyajima spent time as a fellow of the Reischauer Institute at Harvard University from April 2004 to August 2005, and Masahiko Aoki returned to Stanford after ending his tenure as President and Chief Research Officer of RIETI in March 2004. We must thank all those involved for their patience and belief that the project would come to fruition.

We would like to thank the participants in the RIETI Policy Symposium in October 2004 for useful comments and suggestions, especially Yuji Hosoya, Hideshi Itoh, Juro Teranishi, and Masaru Yoshitomi. We are also grateful to a number of people who kindly provided useful comments and suggestions on various drafts of individual chapters: Kee Hong Bae, Simon Chadwick, Jenny Corbett, Katsuyuki Kubo, Curtis Milhaupt, Mitsuharu Miyamoto, Masao Nakamura, Hiroshi Osano, Han Shin, and Yishay Yafeh. Special thanks must be extended to Hirohiko Nakahara from METI and Hiroyuki Yanai from the Japan Association of Corporate Directors, both of whom were ongoing members of our study group and brought important practical and intellectual insights to this project. We thank Jennifer Wilkinson and Andrew Schuller at Oxford University Press for their support and patience throughout the project.

Gregory Jackson would like to thank all the past and present staff at RIETI for their support. Their patience and friendship during my stay at RIETI from 2002 to 2004 was beyond the call of duty and made it an unforgettable experience. Special thanks go to Yukiko Yamazaki, for her excellent research assistance, talented translation, and friendship throughout this project. My original interest in Japan (and in corporate governance for that matter) was inspired by my experience of working for Ronald Dore back in 1992, and it's a particular honour to complete this circle by including his contribution in this book. Turning this interest into actual research in Japan would have not been possible without the strong personal encouragement of Masahiko Aoki and Kozo Yamamura to whom I owe my immense personal gratitude. Most of all, I would like to thank Nicola, Henri, and Ella for their loving support. It's been an adventure!

Hideaki Miyajima would like to thank Michael Cutler for his intensive help for editing several chapters. Michael suggested various points to make the chapters much more readable. Thanks go to Fumiaki Kuroki and Keisuke Nitta, who were instrumental in helping to construct the micro databases of Japanese firms used in parts of this book. Yurie Otsu provided excellent research support. Finally, special thanks also go to Susan Pharr, Mary Brinton, and other members of Reischauer Institute for Japanese Studies and US–Japan programs at Harvard University. I benefited a lot from their comments and, more generally, the intellectual atmosphere at Harvard during the final phase of writing and editing this book.

Finally Masahiko Aoki would like to thank my co-editors, Gregory Jackson and Hideaki Miyajima. Although the project was initially conceived and organized by myself at the inception of RIETI, the actual development and management of the project in all aspects and throughout the period are mainly due to them, as I was compelled to be occupied with many other duties as President of RIETI between 2001 and 2004 and in other capacities thereafter. However, my interests in corporate governance institution in general, and that in Japan in particular, has remained acute and I am particularly happy that our initial, intuitive beliefs in the "third perspective" has now been theoretically and empirically shaped in tangible form as presented in this volume for academic and public scrutiny. For this I am extremely thankful for all the contributors of this volume. I would like to note my personal gratitude to two institutions: the Economics Department of Stanford and the Graduate School of International Corporate Strategy of Hitotsubashi University. The former was generous enough to grant me a long leave of absence during my tenure at RIETI and the latter has been providing an excellent visiting environment for continuing my research in corporate governance after that.

Stanford, CA, London, and Tokyo
Masahiko Aoki, Gregory Jackson, and Hideaki Miyajima

1

Introduction: The Diversity and Change of Corporate Governance in Japan[1]

Gregory Jackson and Hideaki Miyajima

This book addresses the evolving patterns of corporate governance among Japanese corporations since the early-1990s. Since the collapse of the so-called Bubble economy, the Japanese economy suffered from a long-term economic slump. Alongside this, the Japanese firm entered a period of fundamental challenge to its post-war corporate governance institutions. Well-known features of the Japanese firms, such as the main bank system, cross-shareholding, boards dominated by insiders, and lifetime employment have undergone significant crises. Meanwhile, new patterns of corporate governance emerged through legal reforms, as well as innovations in corporate finance and the organizational architecture of business firms. Many changes suggest a step toward more market-oriented corporate governance as found in countries like the United States or Britain. However, less agreement exists over the underlying significance of these changes and the extent to which they imply a departure from the past Japanese model of corporate governance. Understanding the current process of institutional continuity and change is the central task of this book.

Empirically this book examines how various elements of corporate governance have changed, and the inter-relationships between those changes. Corporate governance is often defined narrowly in terms of agency problems between owners and managers. This book reflects a broader view of corporate governance as involving relations among multiple stakeholders, such as individual shareholders, institutional investors, banks, employees, unions and various groups of managers. Corporate governance is also viewed as being embedded within various institutional rules and beliefs that shape how these stakeholders interact in corporate decision-making—including corporate law, the financial system,

[1] The authors thank Christine Ahmadjian, Masahiko Aoki, Gerald Curtis, Virginia Doellgast, Ron Dore, Howard Gospel, Yuji Hosoya, Hideshi Itoh, Ricardo Peccei, Juro Teranishi, Steven Vogel, Darrell Whitten, Peng Xu, and Masaru Yoshitomi for useful comments and suggestions. We also thank the Research Institute of Economy, Trade and Industry (RIETI) for supporting this research. All errors are our own.

labor law, industrial relations the prevailing career patterns and ideologies of management, or the political economy regime, just to name a few.

Corporate governance also has qualities of a "system" or "regime" where configurations of different elements or institutions interact (Aoki 1994; Aguilera and Jackson 2003).[2] These interdependencies are particularly important for understanding institutional change (Aoki 2001b). Complementarities between institutions may present substantial barriers to cross-national diffusion of business practices (Streeck 1996). But conversely, complementarities may entail that change in one institution create momentum for changes in other institutions, such that even if viability of a potential institution x is low, the presence of complementary institutions or policy in other domains may amplify the impact of change so that, once a momentum is initiated, x may gradually evolve as a viable institution (Milgrom et al. 1991). Institutional innovation is often an unintended consequence as institutions co-evolve and become rebundled into new combinations or undergo "conversion" to new purposes (Streeck and Thelen 2005; Aoki 2007). The historical evolution of corporate governance in Japan illustrates how institutions emerged in a piecemeal fashion, often fitting together in ways that were unintended rather than by design (Aoki 1997; Okazaki and Okuno-Fujiwara 1999; Jackson 2001).

In the last several years, a handful of works in English have begun to explore empirically various aspects of change in the Japanese firm (see, for example, Dore 2000; Hoshi and Kashyap 2001; Learmount 2002; Yamamura and Streeck 2003; Jacoby 2004; Inagami and Whittaker 2005; Vogel 2006). This book aims to take stock of these developments by bringing together scholars from different disciplines including economics, management, sociology, and law. The contributions reflect a common effort to integrate empirical analysis drawn from new or unique data sources, on one hand, with a comparative institutional analysis of the Japanese firm, on the other (Aoki 2001b). In doing so, the book collectively aims to address four inter-related questions:

- First, what sorts of changes can we observe empirically in the key features of Japanese corporate governance?
- Second, do these amount to a fundamental change in Japan's post-war corporate governance institutions or an adjustment of the past system to changed circumstances?
- Third, how are changes in the various aspects of corporate governance inter-related?
- Last, what is the relationship between corporate governance arrangements and firm performance?

---

[2] This perspective draws insights from the growing literature on the comparative institutional advantages of diverse varieties of capitalism (see Hall and Soskice 2001; Jackson and Deeg 2006), as well as comparative institutional analysis in economics or historical institutionalism in political economy (Thelen 1999; Aoki 2001b; Crouch 2005; Streeck and Thelen 2005).

In answering these questions, we argue that rather than a "lost decade," Japan has reached a major turning point in its post-war business history. As suggested by the title of the book, we see this process of institutional change as being tightly linked to a growing diversity of corporate governance practices across firms. In developing this answer, section 1.1 begins by briefly introducing the main characteristics of corporate governance in Japan. Section 1.2 sketches the economic and political forces promoting reform or change in corporate governance. Section 1.3 introduces the main empirical findings of the subsequent chapters in four areas: ownership and finance, financial distress and corporate restructuring, labor management, and the board of directors. Section 1.4 interprets the emerging patterns of diversity and institutional change in light of theories of the convergence or path dependence of national corporate governance systems, as well as developing an empirically grounded typology of emerging hybrid forms of corporate governance in Japan. The conclusion provides some brief conjectures about future issues and developments.

1.1 CORPORATE GOVERNANCE AND THE JAPANESE FIRM

Various labels have been used to describe the system of corporate governance in Japan, such as bank-based, relationship-oriented, network, insider, stakeholder, or coordinated model of corporate governance. While seemingly deviating from the shareholder-orientation and liberal market principles, a large body of research documented the economic logic and competitive advantages of the Japanese firm. The competitive strength of post-war Japan seemed not to rest on the allocative efficiency of the market, but the organizational efficiency of firms generated by the investment of stakeholders in developing and maintaining firm-specific capabilities. Corporate governance has played an important role in facilitating these long-term investments and promoting cooperation, representing an important alternative to the US model (Aoki 1988; Porter 1990).

Here we outline the main institutional features of corporate governance in Japan in three broad areas: corporate ownership and finance, employment and industrial relations, and the board of directors.[3] As we shall see, these three domains are also influenced by the role of the state. The salience of various institutions has varied throughout the post-war period and any description is inevitably stylized. The intention is to provide a picture of how the Japanese firm looked up to the collapse of the Bubble economy in the early 1990s as a baseline for understanding the subsequent trajectory of change.

Corporate ownership in Japan is characterized by "stable shareholders" with reciprocally held cross-shareholdings among corporations and banks. The largest

---

[3] Our description of the main institutional features of corporate governance in Japan is based loosely around the model of the J-firm develop by Masahiko Aoki in various writings (Aoki 1984, 1988, 1994).

single shareholder, which is often the main bank, does not typically exceed a 5% stake but the web of small reciprocal cross-shareholdings often account for 20% of shares and stable shareholders over 40%. These horizontal groupings form a dense and stable network of long-term relationships (Kester 1992; Osano 1996). These ownership ties often overlap with and underwrite various other cooperative business relationships within corporate groups. These groups include both the bank-centred horizontal *keiretsu* such as the Mitsubishi group (Gerlach 1992) or the vertically structured *keiretsu* such as the famous buyer–supplier relationships in the Japanese automobile industry (Sako 1992). Stable shareholders also protect firms from hostile takeovers and short-term stock market pressures. In return, stable shareholders received stable dividends and could expect modest growth of share prices. Meanwhile, more active institutional investors, such as private pension funds, were generally absent until the early 1990s (see Jackson and Vitols 2001).

The Japanese main bank plays a central role in monitoring management (Aoki and Patrick 1994; Miyajima 1999; Miyajima and Aoki 2002).[4] Bank lending was the main source of external corporate financing during Japan's period of high growth and was supported through the 1980s by regulatory policies that restricted markets for bonds and equity, segmented Japanese financial institutions, and limited the options for household savings. The main bank traditionally has long-term relationships with client firms that involve providing credit, maintaining equity stakes, offering financial services and advice, and, importantly, helping to overcome information asymmetries with client firms. The main bank monitors through a "contingent governance" mechanism (Aoki and Patrick 1994). In good times or where the demand for external bank finance remains low, management retains considerable autonomy. When performance declines below a certain threshold, the main bank intervenes as a delegated monitor on behalf of other banks and shareholders, often taking seats on corporate boards and being active in corporate rescues. Banks undertake these costly rescues, but recoup costs in the context of their long-term relationships. This mechanism avoids expensive formal bankruptcy procedures and safeguards against premature liquidations that disrupt long-term business relations with suppliers or employees.

Japan is also well known as a stakeholder model of corporate governance, where employee interests play a predominant role (Dore 2000). This idea of the firm as a community of people is manifest in a number of human resource management (HRM) practices geared to mobilize long-term commitment to the enterprise. "Lifetime employment" is a norm for regular and usually male employees in large firms, which became institutionalized in tandem with the emergence of cooperative enterprise-based unions in the early post-war period (Gordon 1998). While lifetime employment reflects strong legal constraints on dismissals, firms also

---

[4] The historical role of the main bank relationship has been recently debated (see exchanges in Milhaupt 2002; Ramseyer and Miwa 2005). While these arguments cannot be addressed here, we consider the conventional understanding of the main bank system as basically accurate.

invest in firm-specific skills and maintain internal flexibility of employees with regards to job functions within the firm or related firms. This system is supported by seniority-related wages, a rank-hierarchy system of promotion, training through job rotation, and a strong socialization into company culture (Koike 1988). Hence, mid-career hiring remains an exception and average job tenures in Japan are high. In addition, employee participation facilitates information sharing at the shop floor level (e.g. quality circles) and information and consultation at the corporate headquarters (e.g. joint labour–management consultation over major company decisions).

The board of directors is, in part, an extension of this internal promotion system: the president is perhaps more a "top employee" than representative of shareholders. These boards often grow to 20 or 30 members, consisting almost entirely of internally promoted managers who have risen through the ranks of the company as employees (Miyajima and Aoki 2002). Pay differentials between board members and ordinary employees are extremely low and stock options or incentive pay were almost non-existent until the late 1990s. Meanwhile, external recruitment of top managers and independent outside board members are uncommon. Any outsiders tend to come from banks, group companies, or government ministries (Kaplan and Minton 1994). Given this structure, Japanese boards reflect a low degree of formal separation between strategy and operations, as well as monitoring and management roles. Monitoring is a legal duty of the statutory auditor (*kansayaku*), who has the right to attend board meetings but no power to appoint or dismiss the CEO. Hence, the statutory auditor has evolved as a largely honorary position bestowed to former employees in their transition to retirement. Meanwhile, other mechanisms of internal governance may be important to explain managerial accountability in Japan (see Blair 2003; Hirota and Kawamura 2003) rooted more in bottom up consensus building, and the strong social norms and loyalty among life-long co-workers (Dore 2005).

Japanese corporate governance has co-evolved alongside its political institutions. Post-war economic policies were developed through strong but informal linkages between the Liberal Democratic Party, government ministries and industry (Aoki 2001b). The Ministry of Finance (MOF) and Ministry of International Trade and Industry (MITI) helped share the benefits of growth across different firms and sectors through subsidies, protections and credit allocation. While large firms benefited from support, these firms also internalized many social welfare functions. This pattern of "administrative guidance" promoted a cohesive and solidaristic model of national political economy. Although not without its critics or skeptics, the post-war Japan state achieved both high economic growth and social equality by actively organizing and placing constraints on the role of markets (Yamamura and Streeck 2003).

In sum, Japanese corporate governance involves a number of inter-related elements that are argued to display *institutional complementarity* (Aoki 1994). Complementarity may be defined as situations where the difference in utility difference between two alternative institutions $U(x')-U(x'')$ increases when an institution z′ rather than z″ prevails in domain Z, and vice-versa, such that x′ and z′ (as well as, x″ and z″) complement each other and constitute alternative equilibrium combinations (Milgrom and Roberts 1990; Milgrom et al. 1991; Aoki 2007). For example, insider-oriented boards serve to protect the firm-specific investments necessary to support commitment work practices, but are also complemented by contingent governance by the main bank. Many other examples can be cited. The complementary nature of these institutions also supported a set of distinct comparative institutional advantages of Japanese firms (Hall and Soskice 2001). After initially catching-up to the technological frontier of the US, distinct advantages emerged for incremental innovation in product quality and process in manufacturing sectors. The long-term nature of employment, high skills, and cooperation with suppliers allowed Japanese firms to build strong organizational efficiencies, in the sense of Leibenstein (1966).

Given the "coordinated" nature of Japanese business groups and strong complementarities between their different elements, Japanese firms also displayed a high degree of *institutional isomorphism*. Institutional isomorphism refers to the attempts to gain legitimacy, reduce uncertainty or adapt to social norms that lead firms in a population to resemble other firms facing the same institutional conditions (DiMaggio and Powell 1991; Aoki 1998). Particularly from the 1960s to the 1990s, Japanese firms reflected a rather homogeneous "national model" with relative low variation across firms relative to more liberal market economies like the US. Of course, some variation has always existed as to the extent of *keiretsu*-affiliation, reliance on main bank lending, or employment conditions between core or more peripheral firms. Some successful Japanese firms have remained relatively independent of traditional corporate groups, due to the legacies of charismatic owner/entrepreneurs (e.g. Sony) or family ownership (e.g. Suntory). However, on the whole, post-war Japanese firms came to follow a remarkably uniform pattern of organization.

1.2 THE FORCES AND POLITICS OF CHANGE

In hindsight, the early-1990s marked a peak in scholarship on the economic virtues of the post-war Japanese firm, but also expressed an impending sense of change (Aoki and Dore 1994). Growing international competition, it was suggested, may drive a convergence of corporate governance across countries—either by combining best practices across countries into a single model or through the imposition of one dominant system. Even if national differences were to be preserved, Masahiko Aoki argued that Japanese firms would adopt a "hybrid" model that involved at least partial adaptation to international constraints, but in ways conditioned by existing national constraints (Aoki 1988, 1994). Others predicted change due to shifts in social values and broader social change that may undermine social solidarity. As Ron Dore (1994: 390) noted, "Japan's competitors … can look forward to the erosion of togetherness, just as has occurred in Britain, as Japanese society becomes progressively internationalized."

Over the 1990s, corporate governance in Japan underwent substantial change, as well as reflecting a growing diversity and more varied fortunes (see Table 1.1). Ownership by foreign and institutional investors increased, while stable and cross-shareholding arrangements eroded. The importance of bank lending decreased in large firms, while increasing in smaller ones. After 1997, Japanese firms began to launch board reforms by introducing outsider directors, executive board systems and stock options. Many mature firms began to slowly reduce levels of diversification and consolidate their businesses, change their internal structures from a uniform functional structure to the decentralized in-house company system

Table 1.1 Changes in Corporate Governance Structure, 1990–2000

		The end of FY 1990		The end of FY 1995		The end of FY 2000	
		Average	Standard deviation	Average	Standard deviation	Average	Standard deviation
Ownership structure	Institutional investors:	9.28	6.87	11.79	8.52	12.89	11.76
	Foreign:	4.38	6.79	7.80	8.51	8.13	10.13
	Stable shareholders:	25.35	11.19	23.71	11.15	18.71	11.41
	Cross-shareholding:	14.63	8.52	14.07	8.41	10.99	8.55
	Individuals:	20.62	8.43	22.49	10.10	29.18	14.28
	Largest ten shareholders:	45.22	12.07	43.86	12.51	45.01	13.98
Debt	Debt/Asset Ratio:	51.57	17.77	50.00	19.49	49.60	23.55
	Borrowing from main bank/total asset:	4.61	4.92	5.29	5.77	–	–
Board composition	Number of directors:	18.72	7.84	17.73	7.66	12.88	6.18
	Number of auditors:	2.94	0.53	3.86	0.53	3.81	0.55
	Number of outside director:	3.69	3.56	3.93	3.65	3.36	3.39
	From Banks:	0.69	1.40	0.62	1.18	0.48	0.94
	From parent firms:	1.09	2.46	1.12	2.51	1.00	2.25
	Number of firms introducing the executive officer system:	476 firms/1333 firms(the end of FY 2002)					
	Stock option:	333 firms/1333 firms(the end of 2002)					
Organization structure	Diversification index:	.58		.56		.56	
	Percentage of firms adopting in-house company system:	4.5		5.5		17.1	
	Percentage of firms adopting pure holding company:	0.0		0.0		1.6	

(similar to a US multi-divisional pattern) or holding company structure. In this section, we review the forces behind these changes, and their emergence since the mid-1990s, namely: internationalization, the deregulation of the banking sector and banking crisis, changing technological paradigms, and the politics of corporate governance reform.

1.2.1 From Strengths to Weaknesses?

After riding high on the Bubble economy of the 1980s, Japanese corporations faced a serious performance crisis and new governance dilemmas during the 1990s. As recession turned into deflation and the banking crisis emerged, this crisis grew more severe through the mid- and late 1990s. Past economic strengths seemed to erode, and potential weaknesses that had remained latent during the period of high growth became more acute. Table 1.2 presents, in highly stylized terms, a set of theoretical arguments about how various strengths also came to imply potential weaknesses. The main bank system may play a significant role for reducing asymmetric information and mobilizing patient investment, but may be less effective under conditions of slowed growth and greater financial liberalization, thus leading to problems of adverse selection of clients and declining monitoring capabilities. Cross-shareholding may safeguard top management focus on long-term businesses strategy, but also act as a precondition for vesting insider control and preventing strategic change of Japanese firms. Lifetime

Table 1.2 Hypothesized Strengths and Weaknesses of *J*-type Firms

Golden age behaviour	Function during Golden Age	Characteristics	Function after Bubble	Early 1990s behaviour
	Risk sharing	**Horizontal corporate groups**	Moral hazard	
Growth oriented	Mitigating pressure from myopic stock market	**Stable shareholder schemes**	Less discipline on management	Excess investment
Long-term investment	Continuity of management	**One-tier insider-dominated board**	Less response to external changes Empire building	Delay in restructuring
Organizational efficiency	Increasing no. of positions	**Long-term employment**	Keeping a division or a subsidiary with low performance	Delay in entering new business areas
Preventing from excess liquidation Preserving firm-specific skills	Mitigating asymmetric information	**Main bank system**	Soft-budgeting	Delay in restructuring

employment and seniority wages contribute to investment in firm-specific skills, but potentially hinder or delay needed restructuring. The insider-dominated board structure and managerial career patterns assure the continuity of business policies and long-term view, but also favour business conservatism and empire building. Some studies even suggested corporate governance arrangements are one of the main reasons for the long run recession, and led to criticism of the past understandings of the *J*-firm (Hall and Weinstein 1996).

During the 1990s, the performance of listed firms, as measured by return on assets (ROA), declined and also became much more heterogeneous during the long recession especially in the period after 1998 (see Figure 1.1). The growing diversity in performance is not due simply to performance difference among industries. Rather, the variation in performance among firms in the same industry has also increased as shown by the standard deviation of ROA. Various studies have also suggested that certain governance patterns such as cross-shareholding or main bank ties may be associated with poor firm performance (Weinstein and Yafeh 1998; Morck et al. 2000) and such poor performance may, in theory, be an important driver of change. But through the late 1990s, poorly performing firms faced few mechanisms of competitive selection—such as bankruptcy, an active market for corporate control or the like. It also appeared uncertain as to whether adopting certain corporate governance reforms would actually improve performance. For example, piecemeal imitation of US corporate governance practices may not produce the desired effects in Japan, due to the absence of other complementary supporting institutions.

During this weak economic climate of the late-1990s, corporate governance reform emerged as a serious issue in Japan. Due to its upswing in performance, the

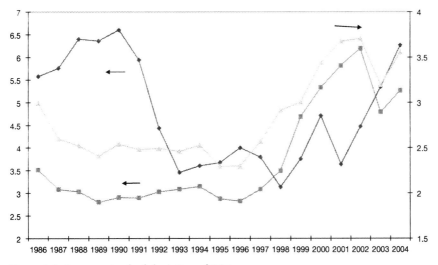

Figure 1.1 Average, standard deviation of ROA

Notes: Non-financial listed firms at Tokyo Stock Exchange first Section; ━■━ Standard deviation among firms; ━◆━ ROA; ⋯⋯ Standard deviation of normalized ROA (ROAi - ROAi).

US economy again became a benchmark for reform efforts. European countries also intensified financial market integration, which involved reforms in capital market regulation, disclosure, transparency, takeover regulation and (to a lesser extent) board practices and compensation. Critics argued that Japan lagged behind and this sentiment was fuelled further by various corporate scandals. The practice of paying Japanese corporate racketeers (*sokaiya*) became increasingly exposed in cases such as Nikko Securities and Daiwa Securities in 1997. Other scandals related to internal control issues, such as copper trading losses at Sumitomo Corporation in 1996, product defect cover-ups by Mitsubishi Motors in the 1990s, scandals surrounding food safety in 2000 and mislabeling of meat in 2002 at Snow Brand, or the empire building and collapse of Sogo Department store chain in 2000. Still, much ambivalence remains about whether US-style corporate governance practices are suitable for Japan. The idea that corporations should first and foremost serve the interests of their shareholders remains at odds with other elements of solidarity and equality within Japanese society. Shareholder value may also undermine past strengths of Japanese firms, and critics of the US model rightly cite the problems of excessive executive pay and short-termism. The scandal at Enron also reawakened many of these criticisms, which tended to be overlooked during the economic boom of the late 1990s. Before pursuing these political debates further, we next introduce three sets of specific pressures on Japanese corporate governance.

1.2.2 Internationalization

A first set of pressures on corporate governance stems from the changing international environment of Japan. In March 2005, foreign investors owned 23.7% of stocks listed on the Tokyo Stock exchange in terms of market value, compared to just 14.1% in 1999 and 6% in 1992 (TSE various years). Stock market turnover increased dramatically from 27% of market capitalization in the low year of 1992 to a historically high level of 108.8% in 2005 (TSE various years). Foreign investors accounted for just 9.8% of stock market transactions in 1990, but 34.3% in 2005. The perceptions of foreign investors thus play a key role in market movements, and hence the financial stability of stable shareholding patterns among firms and banks. The shift toward corporate bonds over bank loans among large Japanese firms also gives greater influence to international credit agencies.

Since the late 1990s, foreign direct investment emerged as a key policy priority in Japan aimed at revitalizing the economy. Here corporate governance reform was intended to promote international investment by facilitating M&A, privatizing government business, or liberalizing the use of stock options that foreign firms used as incentives to attract qualified staff. FDI into Japan did increase, and foreign companies made unprecedented acquisitions of large stakes in major companies. The results have been mixed as seen by the two contrasting examples of Renault Motors purchase of a stake in Nissan in 1999 or DaimlerChrysler stake purchase in Mitsubishi Motors during 2000. The Nissan case gained publicity as a successful rejuvenation of the firm under new leadership. Meanwhile, Mitsubishi Motors proved riddled with scandals, and Daimler eventually divested its stake in 2005. A further spectacular example concerns Ripplewood Holdings involvement in the formation of Shinsei Bank and subsequent IPO, which generated large profits for the US investor group. Alongside inward FDI, Japanese companies have become increasingly internationalized with overseas production facilities and operations. Multinational firms often want to increase internal transparency and use global standards familiar to stakeholders abroad. For example, Toyota cites its main motivation for introducing the executive officer system in 2003 as being to realize the global group management, although board members remain company insiders and are still required to have shop-floor experience.

These trends have increased the salience of international standards for Japanese firms. For example, the principles of corporate governance spelled out by the OECD in 1998 generated substantial debate in Japan. The Japan Corporate Governance Forum (JCGF), a private study group of academics and business leaders, issued a set of voluntary corporate governance principles that focused on introducing independent outside directors, as well as improved transparency and disclosure (JCGF 1998). The JCGF more recently developed its own index of corporate governance practices in order to rank the compliance of listed companies with its guidelines (JCGF 2005). Subsequently, the Tokyo Stock Exchange adopted corporate governance principles along the lines of the OECD guidelines in 2004. The content is notably broad and reflects a compromise of diverging viewpoints, such as by stressing shareholder interests but within a context of obligations to a wider set of stakeholders. Importantly, however, the TSE principles do not have the force of mandatory listing requirements or British "comply or explain" rules (TSE 2004).[5]

International accounting rules have also become more salient. Japanese accounting traditionally allowed asset valuation at cost rather than market value. Meanwhile, both US GAAP (Generally Accepted Accounting Practices) and IAS (International Accounting Standards) are significantly more shareholder-oriented by stressing market valuations and strict definitions of profits. Japan initiated accounting reforms in 1996 through the Ministry of Finance as part of the financial Big Bang called for by Prime Minister Ryotaro Hashimoto in 1996. The banking crisis helped mobilize political support for reform and opened a window to push changes in line with US pressure. Despite high adjustment costs, parliamentary opposition proved politically costly and led the influential business association, Keidanren, to eventually express support for the recognition of US Securities and Exchange Commission (SEC) standards under domestic law (Keidanren 2001).

---

[5] The TSE committee rejected these on the grounds that firms needed sufficient time to adjust recent legal changes and experiment with various new corporate governance practices, rather than being pushed toward a single model at the early stage of reform (TSE 2004).

Finally, international standards sometimes may also have direct extra-territorial application to Japanese companies, such as listing requirements on foreign stock exchanges (Coffee 1999; Gilson 2000). Japanese companies listing on the New York Stock Exchange (NYSE) is not a new phenomenon. Only ten of the 19 Japanese firms now listed on the NYSE obtained their listings since 1990, and companies such as Sony, Matsushita, or Honda have been listed since the 1970s. The impact of the Sarbanes-Oxley (SOX) again raised concerns about compatibility between US and Japanese practices, but the fallout appears to be relatively mild. The statutory auditor system was recognized as being acceptable under SOX, whereas Japan's new committee system ironically has greater difficulty since these firms must give much additional explanation of how their boards operate. SOX is unlikely to lead to radical reforms of Japanese practices. If anything, SOX seems to have led Japanese firms to withdraw from the US market.[6] For example, Daiwa Securities have delayed their listing on the NYSE and Ito-Yokado delisted from Nasdaq in May 2003 after 25 years.[7]

1.2.3 Financial Deregulation and the Banking Crisis

Despite their importance, international pressures alone are not sufficient to explain changes in Japanese corporate governance. One reason is that the proportion of firms exposed to foreign investors, listing requirements and international bond ratings remains fairly small. A second set of forces for change relate to domestic financial deregulation. Financial deregulation in Japan was a gradual process spanning the mid-1970s to mid-1990s, culminating in the so-called deregulatory Big Bang (Hoshi and Kashyap 2001; Toya 2006). Following the oil crisis and expanding public debt of the 1970s, Japan deregulated the secondary market for government bonds in 1977. From that time onward, the strict criteria for issuing corporate bonds were gradually lowered. The corporate bond market also benefited from the parallel development of new financial products, abolishment of controls on foreign exchange and removal of interest rate controls. Further deregulation allowed firms to issue equity at market prices. These factors led to a great increase in equity finance, particularly during the bubble years of 1987–90.

Growing choices in corporate finance also led to a very gradual erosion of bank–firm relationships. Whereas in 1970s bank debt represented some 36% of assets among listed manufacturing firms, this figure dropped to 12.7% in 1990 and has remained low (Hoshi and Kashyap 2001: 247). Slowing macroeconomic growth led corporations to cut investment and curtailed demand for external funds. By the mid-1990s, the Japanese corporate sector had a net surplus of funds and aggregate bank lending to large manufacturing firms slowed (EPA 1999).

---

[6] No Japanese firms have listed or de-listed from the NYSE following three Japanese firms listing in 2002, three listing in 2001, one listing and one delisting in 2000.

[7] We are indebted to Darrell Whitten for these observations.

Meanwhile, large corporations could increasingly raise external funds by directly issuing corporate bonds, and often used these funds to write off or refinance bank loans. Bonds became increasingly attractive in financing international expansion by raising funds in local currencies. Japanese corporate bonds also benefited from very low interest rates in Japan. The growing independence of larger firms from banks continues to be reflected in the more than doubling of outstanding corporate bonds between 1996 and 2004 to around ¥6.3 trillion (TSE various years).

Japan also experienced a Bubble Economy during the late 1980s, followed by a rapid collapse of the stock market in the years 1990–92 and subsequent macro-economic stagnation. By 1997, Japanese banks were left with a huge legacy of non-performing loans (NPLs) and losses on stock purchased at the height of the Bubble. During the Bubble, banks had compensated for the decline in borrowing by large lending by lending to new clients such as small and medium size enterprises—particularly, risky construction ventures during the land price asset boom. While large firms reduced their dependence of bank loans, smaller firms without good access to bond markets became even more dependent on banks as the economic situation deteriorated (Arikawa and Miyajima 2005). At their peak in March 2002, the resulting non-performing loans of major banks (city banks, trust banks, and long-term credit banks) were recorded to be ¥28.4 trillion or 9.6% of all outstanding loans. Following mounting criticisms of government inaction, the passage of the Financial Revitalization Program in October 2002 represented an important turning point that has allowed banks to address to the NPL issue, reducing the overall volume of bad loans to ¥7.6 trillion or 3.2% of outstanding loans by major banks in the end of FY 2004.

As the banking crisis unfolded, the corporate governance role of Japanese banks was greatly affected. Banks reduced outstanding loans to meet capital adequacy ratios despite the Bank of Japan's zero interest rate policy. Meanwhile, the introduction of market-based accounting further exposed balance sheet losses from shares. Given the banks' own financial stress, loans to bankrupt clients were rolled over and undermined the credible threat of bank intervention in client firms. Thus, banks had not only lost large firms as clients, but were less effective in governing relationships with remaining firms. Financial distress also led banks to sell and repurchase cross-shareholdings in order to book unrealized gains and improve balance sheets. But eventually the shift sparked a large divestment of banks from stable shareholdings. Whereas city banks and other banks accounted for 15.6% of share ownership in 1992, this figure was just 11.3% in 2000 and 5.3% in March 2005 (TSE various years). Meanwhile, banks have reorganized as new banking groups, with shares now held within separate subsidiaries under new holding company structures. The banking crisis sparked further pressure for deregulation and shift toward a more transparent and rule-based regime of financial regulation. A key element was the creation of the Financial Services Agency (FSA) independent from the MOF. Greater transparency and market-oriented accounting rules further reduced advantages of private information that underpinned relational contracting between firms and their main banks. The future of the main bank system and capacity of Japanese banks to act as effective corporate monitors represents a key issue to be explored in this book.

1.2.4 Shifts in Organizational Architecture

A final set of pressures for change relate to the organizational architecture of firms. The relative efficiency of different forms of corporate governance depends, in part, on market and technological conditions that shape patterns of innovation in particular economic sectors. As stressed by the resource-based theories of the firm (Barney 2001), the internal capacities for coordination and the processing of information within the firm should match or fit with environmental conditions. Depending on the relative importance of idiosyncratic local information or systemic environmental information, different organizational architectures may be more effective and require different sets of corporate governance arrangements (Aoki 2001b). For example, corporate governance may thus differ over the "life-cycle" of the firm through its birth, development, maturity, and decline (Filatotchev and Wright 2005).

Traditionally, Japanese firms had strengths in incremental innovation, which allowed gradual improvements in process and product quality, based on integrated organizational architectures and strong shop floor skills. When compared to the "short-termism" of the liberal US model, Japan's strength rested on it's superior ability to mobilize long-term investment through bank finance and long-term employment (Porter 1990). However, after the end of Japan's post-war period of high growth, main bank relationships and long-term employment were argued to be less well adapted to promoting corporate restructuring and consolidation of mature or declining industries. In addition, the rapid advancement of information technology (IT) and radical innovation in fields such as biotech gave renewed competitive advantages to the US. Its corporate governance institutions support radical breakthrough technology through more rapid entry and exit from business areas, as well as a large supply of risk capital for venture finance. Debates emerged about how to promote new models of innovation (see Yamamura and Streeck 2003), particularly by supporting stock markets, venture capital finance, and stronger external labor markets based on portable professional qualifications.

These changes led to a historically high level of "creative destruction" in Japan since the late-1990s. First, a high number of new firms were created, which was reflected by an average of 99 new firms being listed per year during the period 1997–2004, compared to just 36 per year during 1990–96 or only 26 per year between 1981–89. Similarly, 41 firms delisted from the stock exchange per year between 1997–2004 compared to just four or five firms per year during the 1980s and early 1990s. Second, firms have rapidly sought to restructure their business portfolios, as reflected in the high level of both entry and exits from lines of business. Third, mature firms in stagnant or declining industries have undergone major corporate restructuring and consolidation. Large and mature firms, such as Hitachi or Matsushita, have increasingly decentralized their business decisions by introducing so-called in-house company systems which made it possible for each business unit (in-house company) to enjoy independence in decision making with clear responsibility. It is also getting popular to introduce new group management through holding companies. These changes are closely linked to changes in corporate boards, such as the introduction of the executive officer system and greater separation of monitoring and management functions.

All of these changes draw increasingly on mergers and acquisitions (M&A).[8] The number of M&A transactions increased from 252 per year in 1991–97 to 1381 deals annually in 1998–2005. Their value increased from 0.4% to 2.5% of GDP during those same periods. While M&A in Japan remains behind other large OECD countries, this increase represents a massive change for Japanese firms. While many M&A transactions remain within traditional corporate groups, poorly performing firms have been targeted in M&A transactions at higher rates than US or UK firms. Still, only 15 cases emerged of meaningfully "contested" control through hostile stakebuilding or unsolicited offers during the period 1991–2005. Of these, the only successful hostile takeover was of International Digital Communication by Cable & Wireless PLC in 1999. Nonetheless these cases have attracted strong media attention, such as Livedoor's bid for Nippon Broadcasting System (NBS).[9] Thus, while hostile takeover attempts remain relatively rare, a growing threat of hostile bids is perceived and has prompted METI to issue guidelines with regard to defensive measures, such as poison pills.

1.2.5 Path Dependence and Politics of Corporate Governance Reform

While Japanese firms face many pressures to reform their corporate governance practices, these pressures affect different groups of firms to greater or lesser degrees. They also do not necessarily engender a unanimous or coordinated response. Policy makers and practitioners have lacked a clear consensus about the strengths and weaknesses of Japanese corporate governance and the merits of various solutions. Meanwhile, institutional pressures also promote rigidities that impede change or shape it in particular ways. It is thus important to examine potential pressures path dependence, including how pressures for change are constrained by power and politics.

---

[8] This section draws upon material in Jackson and Miyajima (2007).

[9] M&A Consulting Inc (MAC) was founded by Yoshiaki Murakami (an ex-MITI official) with financial backing of Softbank and made unsuccessful bids for Shoei Corporation in 2000 and Seibu Railway Co Ltd in 2005, as well as submitting a widely publicized shareholder proposal at Tokyo Style. Murakami was indicted for insider trading in June 2006. A US private equity firm (Steel Partners Japan Strategic Fund) made two failed bids for Sotoh and Yushiro in 2003. The targets of MAC and Steel Partners have been cash-rich and pay low dividends, have low degrees of bank dependence and high foreign ownership, but haven't performed systemically worse than listed companies as a whole (Maezawa 2005; Xu 2006).

Institutional theory stresses that corporate governance systems may exhibit path dependence due to lock-in through sunk costs (North 1990), the presence of private benefits accruing to particular groups (Bebchuk and Roe 1999), and powerful actors which may effectively block or shape change (Crouch 2005). Also, adopting a new practice may be effective or viable only in combination with other organizational practices and supported by a broader institutional framework outside the individual firm (Aoki 1994: 34). The diffusion or borrowing new corporate governance institutions may face serious barriers and isolated or incremental efforts to change past strategies may be ineffective within some coordinated effort to change.[10] However, complementarities also suggest dynamic potential for change, since initial changes in one direction may gain momentum through positive feedback with institutions in other domains (Milgrom et al. 1991).

Given such institutional rigidities, corporate governance reform in Japan has been carried out in an incremental fashion. A long series of amendments were made to the Commercial Code and other related laws throughout the 1990s (see Table 1.3). Various associations such as the Japan Corporate Directors Association, the Japan Corporate Governance Forum (JCGF), the Shareholders Ombudsman, or most recently the Pension Funds Association strongly advocated greater attention to shareholders and board reforms, such as outside directors. While these groups are effective in highlighting issues and galvanizing public opinion, but their political influence over the government ministries and political parties that shape policy is limited compared to major industry associations, such as Nippon Keidanren. Meanwhile, the major industry association (Keidanren), the employers' association (Nikkeiren), and the Japan Association of Corporate Executives (Keizai Doyukai) largely opposed reforms that would represent major inroads against managerial autonomy (Keizai Doyukai 1996; Keizai Doyukai 1998; Nikkeiren 1998).[11] For example, Keidanren remained opposed to introducing mandatory independent outside directors. Given their opposition, actual corporate governance reforms have focused largely on improving the independence of statutory auditors or giving firms the option to voluntarily adopt a new "company with committees" system modeled on US boards. Business associations have favored reforms that would facilitate corporate restructuring and give management greater flexibility in the use of corporate equity. Meanwhile, despite much talk about shareholder value, the basic notion of stakeholder-oriented corporate governance seems largely intact.

How substantial is the cumulative impact of these changes? In the next section, we review the main findings from the empirical chapters of this book in order to address the degree and direction of change in Japanese corporate governance.

---

[10] Complementarity may imply non-concavity whereby no change in one dimension, no matter how large, can improve performance (Roberts 2004). Nor will simultaneous but small changes in multiple dimensions improve performance. We are indebted to Hideshi Itoh suggesting these points.

[11] Nikkeiren and Keidanren subsequently merged to form Nippon Keidanren.

Table 1.3 Legal Changes in Corporate Governance since the mid-1990s

Year	Event	Changes
1993	Commercial Code:	Introduction of outside auditors and board of corporate auditors; Extended period appointment for auditors (from 2 to 3 years); Substantially lowered fee for shareholders' derivative action suit to a fixed price of ¥8200 per suit.
1994	Commercial Code:	Removed prohibition on the purchase of the company's own shares.
1997	Commercial Code:	Treasury stock options (up to 10% of shares) can be granted pending a general resolution of the AGM specifying the name, the number of shares, transfer price, exercise period, and conditions of exercise; Allows changes in company articles to empower board of directors to carry out share buy-backs.
	Anti-monopoly Act:	Lifted ban on holding companies.
	Tax Code:	Introduction of market value method for trading operation for financial institutions.
1998	Commercial Code:	Further relaxed conditions of share buy-backs; Relaxed restrictions on cancellation of shares; Creation of bank holding companies.
	Tax Code:	Exception to taxation concerning financial holding companies; Cancellation of own shares by capital reserve.
1999	Anti-monopoly Act:	Revisions concerning regulations for business combination through mergers and owning shares.
	Commercial Code:	Introduced share swap system allowing a parent firm (A) to buy subsidiary (B) through an exchange of shares.
	Tax Code:	Exception to taxation concerning share exchanges.
	Accounting Standards:	Fundamental review in the procedures for consolidated financial statement; The introduction in consolidated statement of cash flows and that of tax affect accounting (April 1999).
2000	Commercial Code:	Established stock-split system.
	Tax Code:	Introduction of current prices in financial instruments.
	Accounting Standards:	Introduction of current prices in financial instruments, accounting standards for retirement benefits, and interim consolidated financial statement (April 2000).
2001	Commercial Code:	Creation of law on corporate spin-offs; Lifting a ban on treasury stocks.
	Tax Code:	Improved tax rules regarding corporate reorganization, and purchase and sale of treasury stocks; Introduced consolidated taxation system.
	Accounting Standards:	Accounting rules for pension fund liabilities; Introduction of current value accounting for financial products.
2002	Commercial Code:	Introduction of optional committee system for major corporations.
	Accounting Standards:	Introduction of current value accounting for cross-shareholdings.
2003	Accounting Standards:	Introduction of asset-impairment accounting (April 2003); Full-scale introduction of asset-impairment accounting (April 2005).

1.3 PATTERNS OF INSTITUTIONAL CHANGE SINCE THE MID-1990S

A central message of this book is that several core features of Japanese corporate governance have changed substantially. Yet these changes are uneven across different elements of corporate governance, and fall considerably short of what we would regard as "convergence" on Anglo-American corporate governance. Moreover, changes are occurring to different degrees across different groups of firms, leading to greater heterogeneity among firms within Japan. While corporate governance retains a distinct "Japanese" profile compared to other countries, Japan has a less homogeneous "national model" and the degree of institutional isomorphism is decreasing (DiMaggio and Powell 1991), particularly due to the enabling nature of legal reforms that give greater choice to Japanese firms.

1.3.1 Changes in Corporate Ownership and Finance

The first part of the book explores the external changes of corporate governance related to corporate finance and ownership. Chapters 2 through 5 look at changes in the main bank relationship (Arikawa and Miyajima), the erosion of cross-shareholding arrangements (Miyajima and Kuroki), the impact of growing ownership by foreign investors (Ahmadjian), and the development of venture capital in Japan (Hata, Ando, and Ishii). Chapters 6 and 7 are concerned with the consequence of these changes for corporate governance under conditions of financial distress. Given the weakened role of main bank monitoring, legal reforms have attempted to strengthen bankruptcy procedures by introducing more flexible debtor-in-possession options (Xu) and private equity funds have begun to emerge as a new specialist for corporate restructuring (Yanagawa).

Bank–Firm Relationships

In Chapter 2, *Yasuhiro Arikawa* and *Hideaki Miyajima* examine the changes in the Japanese main bank system. The chapter begins with an overview of corporate finance among listed firms during the 1990s. In spite of the deregulation of the bond market in the mid-1990s, the overall dependence of firms on bank borrowing increased rather than decreased. Large firms lessened ties with banks and began financing through bonds, but smaller listed firms continued borrowing from banks. In particular, firms with already high levels of bank debt relied on their main bank for an increasing proportion of those loans. Meanwhile, Japanese banks entered into a period of serious financial distress that culminated in the banking crisis.

These facts raise questions as to the corporate governance role of banks during this period. On one hand, the authors find little evidence that the banking crisis led to a "credit crunch" among firms with strong growth opportunities. On the other hand, their empirical findings suggest that debt did play a disciplinary role in the 1990s, but that a high concentration of loans with the main bank tended to delay the corporate restructuring. This suggests that banks facing financial distress engaged in soft-budgeting and followed an "evergreen" policy of rolling over loans. This situation made the threat of bank intervention in poorly per-forming firms less credible. Thus, close ties with a main bank no longer performed the positive disciplinary role of "contingent governance" in Aoki's sense.

Relationship banking in Japan is not likely to disappear, but will play a more limited role. Roughly speaking, one-third of all listed firms now depend on capital markets for external finance, but these mostly large firms constitute approximately 70% of total firm value and over 50% of total employees among all firms on the First Section of the Tokyo Stock Exchange in 2002. For these firms, bank loans are now based on an explicit and arms-length contract (e.g. credit line or loan syndication). For these firms, market pressure through institutional investors and bond ratings are now playing a major role in corporate governance and banks are unlikely to regain their past monitoring role. Mean-while, the majority of smaller firms continue to depend on bank borrowing. Here banks have continued advantages through private information, which can help overcome difficulties in raising external finance. Whether banks can once again effectively monitor these firms depends very much on their financial health. Some recent developments look quite positive in this regard. A series of mergers among major banks have helped recapture economies of scale and their health has been recovering. The banks also brought together firms from competing *keiretsu* groups, which has helped promote M&A activities across these groups. The 2002 program of financial revitalization (*Kinyu-saisei*) is also underway, and non-performing loans are down from peak levels. Finally, banks have increasingly used private equity funds to strengthen their role in corporate restructuring (see Chapter 7 by Yanagawa). In sum, corporate finance in Japan is increasingly characterized by the co-existence of two different, and in ways competing logics—a pattern rather similar to Germany or Italy (Deeg 2005). While the main bank system has not disappeared, it has been institutionally displaced and its scope limited to a more specific niche segment of firms than in the past.

Cross-Shareholding

The weakening of main bank relationships is an important element in a wider trend of declining ownership by strategically oriented stable shareholders. Cross-shareholding is often associated with promoting growth due to a release from short-run market pressure or lowering risks by sharing them within groups (see Yafeh 2003). The proportion of cross-shareholding fell from 15% of all shares in 1990 to just 7.2 in 2002 (Kuroki 2003). Likewise, the proportion of stable shareholders, defined as cross-shareholdings plus shares held by long-term inves-tors such as financial institutions or related business firms, fell from 43.1% in 1990 to just 26% in 2002. Meanwhile, ownership by institutional investors and foreign investors has increased, and brought greater demands for share liquidity and financial returns (see also Aguilera and Jackson 2003).

Chapter 3 by *Hideaki Miyajima* and *Fumiaki Kuroki* explores why the ratio of cross-shareholding declined during the mid-1990s using the detailed data developed by Nissay Research Institute (NRI). As the mid-1990s banking crisis made it increasingly difficult for corporations to maintain cross-shareholding with banks and after 1997, major commercial banks also began selling corporate shares to raise funds for disposing of non-performing loans and meet regulations regarding their capital adequacy. However, the unwinding of cross-shareholding has not proceeded uniformly. Cross-shareholding dissolved among firms where bank finance declined, but was maintained among firms that continued borrowing from their main banks. The authors show that more profitable firms with easy to access capital markets and high foreign ownership at the beginning of the 1990s reduced their financial relationships with banks and sought to improve their market valuation by unwinding of cross-shareholdings. Meanwhile, cross-shareholding was maintained by less profitable firms, which faced difficulty accessing capital markets and remained dependent on bank finance.

The result of this process has been the growing diversity of ownership patterns among Japanese firms. Notably, while the percentage of shares held by business corporations dropped from 29% of total market value in 1992 to 21.8% in 2001, the level has remained stabile through 2005 (TSE various years). While institutional investors and private equity funds have further pressured firms to review their equity portfolios, the desire for protection from hostile takeovers remains a major reason why managers continue to retain some level of stable shareholding. The authors thus argue that the ownership structure of Japanese firms with cross-shareholding will remain a diverse mix of stable shareholding and ownership by institutional investors.

Foreign and Institutional Investors

As stable shareholding and bank–firm relations weaken, institutional investors are becoming more important. In Chapter 4, *Christine Ahmadjian* examines the impact of foreign institutional investors on various aspects of corporate governance and corporate restructuring. In addition to well-known cases of FDI by foreign corporations, foreign ownership by American and British mutual funds and pension funds has increased rapidly. Compared to Japanese "stable shareholders," these investors are much less tied to existing strategic alliances among Japanese business groups and tend to be motivated by more purely financial considerations and sense of fiduciary responsibility to promote "shareholder value." Foreign investors have concentrated on a relatively narrow segment of very large, export-oriented blue chip companies with high market capitalization, liquidity, and good performance. However, these investors have a strong impact on the corporate governance of these firms.

Drawing on detailed interview materials, Ahmadjian explores how foreign investors exert influence through both the threat of exit and the cultivation of voice. In terms of exit, foreign investors are much more active in portfolio management than domestic Japanese investors. In terms of voice, foreign investors often do not attend annual general meetings (AGMs) or intervene actively in particular firms with poor performance—their stakes remain too small and coordination costs too high. Rather, investors focus their voice to promote generic "best practices" such as accounting, board independence, etc. Foreign investors meet with companies informally and increasingly engage with top management and investor relation's officers. Ahmadjian stresses the combined role of informal voice and threat of exit, which exert pressure in less direct but nonetheless powerful ways. Japanese firms are improving disclosure in response to investors, and a two-way dialogue is emerging, wherein management must increasingly consider the types of issues raised by foreign investors. Using the Japan Corporate Governance Index for 2003 developed by the Japan Corporate Governance Forum for TSE First Section firms, the chapter shows that firms with higher levels of foreign ownership are more likely to adopt "Anglo-American" style corporate governance reforms, such as equity-based performance measures, changes in the structure and function of the board, and communication with shareholders. Moreover, foreign ownership is also strongly linked to the likelihood of corporate downsizing in terms of employment or divestment.

Taken together, foreign institutional investors have a powerful external influence, but are unlikely to actively monitor specific companies and directly intervene to turn around companies. Rather, institutional investors create a context of higher market discipline, particularly in terms of disclosure and business strategies.[12] Meanwhile, counter-veiling pressures arise from firms' embeddedness within the broader institutional context exposes firms to, depending on the industry, strength of unions, main bank ties or relational contracting within business groups (Ahmadjian and Robinson 2001). As a result, smaller firms or large firms within more stable business groups remain less exposed to these pressures, which suggest a growing heterogeneity among Japanese firms.

Venture Capital

Chapter 5 by *Nobuyuki Hata, Haruhiko Ando and Yoshiaki Ishii* examines corporate governance in the context of Japanese venture capital (VC) firms. VC represents a unique combination of network-based equity finance, expertise, and monitoring that differs greatly from traditional forms of industrial organization. The chapter cites a number of institutional factors which limited the development of early stage VC investment and independent VC firms in Japan, such as the strongly bank-based financial system, industrial organization based around *keiretsu* groups and predominance of firm-internal labor markets and career patterns. For example, strong firm-internal labor markets reduce the pool of potential entrepreneurs for new start-ups compared to the highly mobile professional labor markets found in the US. Culturally, Japanese entrepreneurs also remain highly committed to their firms as going ventures and less oriented to exit at the

---

[12] We remain agnostic as to whether market pressures will also lead to acute short-term pressures among Japanese firms.

IPO stage. The authors document the importance of so-called Second Generation venture capital funds in Japan, which were organized by banks and targeted only late-stage ventures. These VC funds have not typically adopted the hands on approach to start-up firms typical of Silicon Valley venture capitalists.

Still, the authors also note the more recent emergence of a new Third Generation of VC in Japan. Following the establishment of new IPO markets, such as MOTHERS or JASDAQ, and new legislation to enable corporate spin-offs or firm restructuring, a better legal and market infrastructure exists for new start-up firms in Japan. The number of newly listed firms in Japan increased dramatically since the late 1990s and includes a large proportion of firms in IT or new technology sectors. The authors also stress the role of a new generation of entrepreneurs. These younger entrepreneurs have been socialized outside the milieu of traditional Japanese salaried employees and take a different attitude towards risk and nature of the firm, reflected in greater willingness to disclose information and maintain their independence from established organizations. These developments have also influenced the attitude of the Second Generation venture capitalists to take a more open, equity-oriented approach. While serious challenges remain for venture capital business, the authors are optimistic for the future potential of VC in Japan.

Bankruptcy

In Chapter 6, *Peng Xu* turns to issues related to corporate governance in firms facing severe financial distress and on recent changes in the process of bankruptcy, in particular. In the past, contingent governance by Japanese main banks meant that banks had a wide scope for intervening to rescue firms prior to legal bankruptcy. As bank monitoring has weakened, however, the number of corporate bankruptcies has grown. In April 2000, bankruptcy procedures underwent substantial reform through the passage of the Civil Rehabilitation Law. One big difference between the new Civil Rehabilitation Law and Corporate Reorganization Law is that the debtor management operates the firm and works out a Rehabilitation plan or liquidation, unless the management is incompetent. This debtor in possession aspect of Civil Rehabilitation Law aims to provide incentives for managers of failing firms to file for bankruptcy at an earlier stage under Rehabilitation Law, by reducing their personal burdens. The Civil Rehabilitation Law also simplifies the bankruptcy reorganization, since secured creditors do not participate in the procedure.

Focusing on the differences between Corporate Reorganization Law and a new debtor-in-possession Civil Rehabilitation Law, Xu investigates corporate governance in financial distress and bankruptcy resolution in the late 1990s. Bank lenders are less likely to intervene than they used to be. Most bankrupt firms also experienced non-standard president turnover around bankruptcy filings, regardless the introduction of debtor-in-possession. Priority is less violated in bankruptcy resolution than in the United States. Moreover, Civil Rehabilitation firms spend in bankruptcy a substantially shorter time than Corporate Reorganization firms. Internationally, Japanese bankrupt firms exit faster from reorganization than do

US Chapter 11 firms. Thus, Xu concludes that the Civil Rehabilitation Law appears highly successful in providing an incentive to distressed firms to file for bankruptcy at an earlier stage and thereby ward off the accumulation of more severe problems.

Corporate Revival Funds

Chapter 7 by *Noboyuki Yanagawa* explores the dramatic growth of corporate revival funds in Japan. These funds are made up of private equity and represent another new alternative to main bank intervention in promoting corporate restructuring. Moreover, corporate revival funds have contributed to the reduction of non performing loans in the banking sector. These funds also play a very active role in promoting M&A activities, which also increase incentives for managers to engage in corporate restructuring. The author notes that many of these emerging funds specialized on corporate revival are, in fact, closely related to Japanese banks. While revival funds were nearly all managed by foreign companies before 2000, new government related funds have also emerged, such as the Industrial Revitalization Corporation.

   Following this government push, new, "bank related" funds emerged. However, important questions exist as to whether these funds act independently or simply as a division of Japanese banks. Yanagawa focuses on these bank related funds, showing how these funds' activities are distinct and may complement traditional forms of bank monitoring over client firms. In particular, a potential merit of bank related funds is to diminish moral hazard problems by separating rehabilitation activities from the banks. This separation involves selling NPLs to separate funds, thereby making the present value of the NPLs transparent. While observers were initially skeptical whether bank-related funds are simply a way to move non-performing loans off banks' balance sheets, Yanagawa argues that corporate revival funds will contribute to improving the banking sector and the Japanese financial system. However, the success of the funds remains dependent on finding appropriate management systems and incentive mechanisms to avoid adding more moral hazard problems into the financial system. In particular, the purchase of loans with improper prices by the funds just to decrease the non-performing of banks must be avoided.

1.3.2 Changes in Corporate Organization, Employment, and the Board of Directors

The next section of the book turns to the internal aspects of Japanese corporate governance, such as corporate organization, employment patterns, and importantly, the board of directors. Chapter 8 looks at the internal structure of Japanese business groups and their business portfolio (Kikutani, Itoh, and Hayashida). Chapters 9 and 10 look at the relation of corporate governance and human resource management in terms of their complementarities (Abe and Hoshi) and patterns of recent change (Jackson). Chapters 11 through 13 then turn to the role of the board of directors by looking at the impact of legal reforms on the board (Shishido), the patterns of adoption of corporate governance and board reform across firms (Miyajima) and the impact of those changes in relation to the insider-nature of the career patterns, incentives, and social norms of managers (Dore).

Business Portfolio

In Chapter 8, *Tatsuya Kikutani, Hideshi Itoh, and Osamu Hayashida* examine the restructuring of Japanese business groups during the 1990s. The authors use a unique database from the Basic Survey of Business Structure and Activity (*Kigyo Katsu Kihon Chosa*) to explore the business portfolio of Japanese firms, but taking account of the group structure of parent and affiliate firms. While previous studies have examined the net shift in diversification or specialization of business, the authors adopt an original approach by looking at the actual flow of entry and exit from business segments. Their results suggest that the degree and nature of corporate restructuring in Japan has been previously under-appreciated.

The chapter stresses that Japanese business groups engaged in a high level of restructuring through both entry and exit from business areas in the 1990s. Most activity occurs at the group level, reflecting the fact that Japanese firms prefer separating business into their subsidiaries rather than managing them in-house. The authors show that the business portfolio of Japanese firms has no strong overall trend toward greater diversification or greater focus on core businesses. Rather, Japanese firms have exited from existing business segments, but also actively entered new segments. In fact, many firms engaged in both entry and exit at the same time. The authors also explore the factors influencing firms' decisions of entry and exit, and show that entry and exit are less active for large firms, but more active when the debt ratio is higher and the initial number of segments is larger. Likewise, increases in the riskiness of core businesses cause more entry and exit. Finally, the authors showed that the firms' performance is likely to increase by engaging in both entry and exit, and hence entry and exit are likely to be complementary. While questions remain about the direct impact of corporate governance parameters on business portfolio restructuring, the overall picture suggests a dynamic development of Japanese business.

Human Resource Management

The substantial changes in bank–firm relations and corporate ownership in Japan have led to much speculation about how these changes have impacted other stakeholders, particularly regular employees. A large comparative literature now shows that recent shifts in corporate governance affect human resource management (HRM) and industrial relations in different countries (Gospel and Pendleton 2005). Strategies promoting "shareholder value" may provoke a number of conflicts with employees around the issues of corporate disclosure, business portfolios, equity-oriented performance targets, and the use of performance-oriented pay, such as stock options. Shareholder value creates pressure for more market responsiveness in employment through reducing excess employment, divesting from less profitable businesses and decentralizing bargaining to match wages to productivity. In Japan, a debate thus centres on how changes in corporate governance impact the specific institutions of lifetime employment, seniority wages, the rank-hierarchy system for promotion and cooperative industrial relations. As will be discussed below, a particular research challenge has been the scarcity of company-level data on HRM practices that can be linked to corporate governance outcomes.

Chapter 9 by *Masahiro Abe and Takeo Hoshi* presents a theoretical model that specifies the institutional complementarities between finance and HRM practices. Their model distinguishes two broad patterns—complementarity between bank finance and in-house training that characterized the traditional Japanese firm and between stock market financing and individual training as in the US. Their model has much in common with other work on diverse varieties of capitalism stressing the role of coordination in safeguarding relationship-specific investments (Hall and Soskice 2001). In particular, the long-term nature of bank finance is often seen as a necessary precondition for long-term employment and consequently shifts from bank finance to equity market finance are likely to threaten Japanese-style HRM. Given the strong complementarities posited between finance patterns and employment patterns, any changes in prevailing patterns of finance are likely to have a strong effect on employment outcomes.

In seeking empirical evidence regarding complementarities between finance and HRM, the chapter draws on a small but unique dataset on Japanese HRM practices in 1995 and 2000 collected by the Institute of Labor Administration. These data show the diffusion of various new HRM elements in Japan during the late 1990s, such as the so-called annual salary system (based on performance) and fast-track promotion patterns. The authors' empirical results are consistent with the expected relationships between finance and ownership, on one hand, and HRM, on the other. For example, levels of foreign ownership are associated with a lower likelihood of firms using seniority-based pay. But in many cases, the results proved statistically insignificant or small, given the constraints of the dataset. This result may suggest, contrary to conventional understanding, that the complementarities between finance and relationship-based employment may be weaker than expected. Thus, we cannot rule out the potential compatibility between market-based finance and relational aspects of long-term employment and high investment in firm-specific skills.

Employment Stability and Industrial Relations

In Chapter 10, *Gregory Jackson* explores this issue by further looking at HRM practices and employment adjustment drawing on both survey data and case study materials. Using data from the 2003 METI "Survey on the Corporate System and Employment," Jackson finds evidence for the continued commitment to lifetime employment in over 80% of firms. Nonetheless, few firms maintain the very traditional pattern of lifetime employment with seniority-based pay. Most firms have adopted merit-based payment systems based on individual performance evaluations (about 40%) or have moved to a more complex type of HRM scheme that integrates both seniority and merit elements (about 40%). Turning to the role of corporate governance, Jackson finds a positive relationship between the use of managerial stock options, equity-based performance measures, and more market-oriented employment patterns. Meanwhile, the percentage of in-house executives within the board had a negative impact on market employment patterns, and foreign ownership had no significant impact on employment outcomes. This suggests that external market pressures may be less important than the style of insider governance in determining employment patterns, which is one theme of Chapter 12 by Miyajima. Despite this continued commitment to lifetime employment, the core of employees covered under such arrangements is shrinking. For example, the largest 1% of firms employed nearly 23,000 people on average in 1993, but just 17,400 employees in 2002. Japanese firms have been actively restructuring by "benevolent" employment adjustment—early retirement measures, hiring freezes, transfers and so on. The chapter shows that between 2000 and 2003 surveyed firms reduced their workforce by 15% on average, but only 4% of total exits came through outright lay-offs. Thus, while lifetime employment is being preserved as a norm for corporate insiders, large firms are undergoing a degree of social closure that makes it difficult for outsiders to enter. In sum, changes in corporate governance have affected the role of employees but, in fact, some elements of Japanese-style HRM may be compatible with a wider range of corporate governance institutions than suggested by some theories of complementarity.

Corporate Law and Board Reform

In Chapter 11, *Zenichi Shishido* examines the impact of legal reforms on the scope of behavior of top management. Shishido identifies 1997 as a major turning point in reform process, distinguishing between demand–pull measures promoted by business associations such as Keidanren to facilitate the introduction of new practices in response to market pressures or other business interests, and policy–push reforms initiated by the ministries or the legislature in order to push change in existing corporate governance practices. Demand–pull measures included removing prohibitions of share buybacks, introduction of stock options, and introduction of share swaps and spin-offs to support corporate reorganization through M&A. Another major revision regards the 1947 Antimonopoly Law to lift the post-war ban on pure holding companies. The reform aims at allowing firms to centralize strategic management of multiple businesses, isolate risks, heighten flexibility during M&A, and differentiate employment conditions across business units (Aoki 2001a). Alongside these measures, Shishido also notes the importance of policy–push reforms, such as changes to accounting rules. Here new mark-to-the-market principles were introduced for valuing financial assets, which has resulted in major pressure on cross-shareholding and exposed unfunded pension liabilities. The introduction of consolidated accounting also promotes transparency by making it harder to hide losses in subsidiary firms.

Meanwhile, the most politicized reform concerns the board of directors. In 2001, the Ministry of Economy, Trade, and Industry (METI) was involved in other proposals to require independent outside directors, which were later dropped due to opposition by Keidanren. However, the epoch making 2002 amendment to the Company Law introduced the American style board of directors, termed "board with committees" (which entailed the formation of three committees responsible for appointments, compensation, and audits respectively, all with outsider majorities) as a second option alongside the traditional Japanese style board with statutory auditors. This "reform as choice" represents an important political compromise by using law to enable new practices, rather than impose strict mandatory requirements (Gilson and Milhaupt 2004). On the whole, Shishido argues that by facilitating these new practices, Japanese corporate law has undergone a formal convergence with the US model. However, he argues that the diversity of actual choices among firms will reflect continued functional divergence due to differences in the incentive patterns among corporate stakeholders. Thus, legal reform holds an ambiguous potential.

The Diffusion of Board Reforms

During much of the post-war period, the boards of Japanese firms had been composed primarily of insiders drawn from the ranks of employees who had been promoted from within; outsiders had been invited to join as directors only on rare occasions. These insider boards exhibited a low degree of separation between the management and monitoring functions, and compensated their members with salaries that were lower and less sensitive to corporate performance compared to those paid to their counterparts in the US and even compared to those paid to directors in pre-war Japan.

Chapter 12 by *Hideaki Miyajima* addresses how firms have changed the structure and composition of their corporate boards since 1997. A most common measure has been introducing the executive officer system (*shikkō-yakuin sei*), as an alternative to the traditional board structure. This system has been used to decrease board size by making a distinction between executive officers in charge of operating divisions and board members with monitoring responsibilities. This system was first introduced by Sony in 1997, and has been emulated by many other companies in many industries. Some firms have also introduced outside directors, and performance related compensation schemes, such as stock options. This raises a number of questions regarding what factors influence the decision to implement board reforms, and whether adoption of these measures has mattered for corporate performance?

In order to answer these questions, this chapter measures the extent of corporate governance reforms among Japanese firms using questionnaire results to construct a Corporate Governance Score (CGS) for each corporation The author shows that higher CGS scores are associated with better performance. Yet this result reflects a strong association of information disclosure with better performance, whereas investor protection and the separation of monitoring and management yield ambiguous results. This chapter looks at the firm-level determinants of reform in terms of whether increasing capital market pressures facilitate and employee power impede reforms, as is often assumed. The empirical result shows, as predicted, that board reforms are associated with a higher percentage of foreign (institutional) shareholders, and a lower percentage of stable shareholders. Likewise, the higher the firm's dependence on the capital market and the lower the firm's dependence on bank borrowing are associated with greater degrees of reform.

One interesting finding relates to the impact of employee participation and human resource management systems on corporate governance reform. A high degree of employee involvement in management and long-term employment have generally been perceived to be factors which impede board reforms that are meant to tilt the balance toward shareholders' interests. Miyajima shows that no clear negative relationship exists between employee involvement and corporate governance reform. On the contrary, among firms exposed to capital market pressures, the presence of employee participation has a significantly positive relationship on the degree of reform. Moreover, companies retaining long-term employment but who have shifted from seniority-based to merit-based wage systems have been very actively implementing corporate governance reforms to promote information disclosure. These results are consistent with the following observations: when employees are aware of current trends toward greater reliance on the capital market, they are more involved in the management of the company; and the greater a company's reliance on long-term employment, the more willing it is to implement corporate governance reform.

Management and Internal Governance

Given the traditional weakness of external control by outside directors, Japanese firms are well know for the strong internal mechanisms of corporate governance. Turning to the issue of internal mechanisms to promote accountability within Japanese firms, Chapter 13 by *Ronald Dore* approaches these debates by distinguishing between the shareholder vs. stakeholder dimension of corporate governance, on one hand, and the issue of accountability as a common underlying factor of good corporate governance, on the other. Dore argues that accountability can be achieved in both shareholder and stakeholder-oriented systems of corporate governance, but in different ways. Here one overlooked aspect of the Japanese system concerns the socialization and career paths of top managers. In Japan, managers enter the firm as ordinary employees, slowly work their way up through the ranks, and rise into the highest ranks ahead of their cohort peers only very late in their careers. This long-term socialization into a corporate culture during one's career path provides important motivational resources for Japanese managers that place many important checks on opportunistic behavior.

Dore explores how the institutions governing careers influence motivational resources that underlie different governance institutions across countries. For example, the importance of intrinsic motivations to establish a good reputation among company peers is greater in Japan relative to extrinsic motivations for monetary reward. These and other internal mechanisms of social control are often lost in US-dominated debates over external mechanisms of corporate governance that see outsiders as necessary and involve high powered incentives and punishments. Dore's analysis raises serious questions as to whether adopting US style corporate governance practices will improve corporate accountability in Japan. Rather, he interprets recent change as being primarily about the distributional outcomes—the question of who gets what. Here Japan faces a great challenge to its solidaristic and more egalitarian institutions that reduce inequality between top managers and employees.

1.3.3 Diversity and Institutional Change

Japan is often understood as a case of a coordinated market economy (CME) facing pressure for institutional change in the direction of becoming a more liberal market economy (LME) (Hall and Soskice 2001). The penultimate chapter by *Mari Sako* examines how such institutional change is related to organizational diversity, drawing on a wide range of evidence from both financial markets and labor markets. The chapter argues that as economies move from coordinated to more liberal types of institutions, organizational diversity will increase at the level of the national economy, sector, or even corporate group. While building CME types of institutions require high levels of mutual investment in relationship-specific assets, Sako argues that moves toward LME-type institutions allow greater scope for organizational diversity.

Drawing on a model of incremental institutional change (Streeck and Thelen 2005), the chapter shows that new market-oriented rules have been "layered" on top of older institutions in ways that facilitate new corporate strategies, while leaving old strategies intact. For example, new stock exchanges were created for venture capital, but these additions did not directly threaten or replace existing institutions of relational banking and stock exchanges for established public corporations. New forms of contingent employment have been similarly "layered" onto the norm of lifetime employment, reinforcing the dualism of Japanese labor markets but not undoing employment patterns of core employees. Likewise, institutions may undergo "conversion" or adaptation to new and diverse purposes. For example, the function of Shunto is changing from coordinated pay bargaining to a mechanism for legitimizing pay restraint and dispersion. Conversion and layering lead to greater organizational diversity because the change and adaptation of institutionalized practices involves local issues of power and contention among stakeholders at the level of individual companies. These conflictual elements of institutional change are shown nicely by Sako's comparison of the very different motives and effects of adopting new holding company structures for incumbent firms, such as NTT, or new firms, such as Softbank.

The concluding chapter by *Masahiko Aoki* revisits the issue of institutional change and Japanese corporate governance from a more theoretical angle. The chapter interprets the changes described in this volume in light of the economic models of corporate governance suggested by comparative institution analysis. The chapter outlines the basic features of the models: shareholder sovereignty model, the corporatism-codetermination model and the relational contingent governance model. These correspond in broad stylized fashion to the accentuated features of corporate governance in the US, Germany, and Japan. Aoki further introduces the notion of a fourth model based on the external monitoring of internal linkage (EMIL model), where capital markets play a stronger role in monitoring the internal links business models and investments in skills by stakeholders, such as employees.

In applying these models to Japan's changing situation, Aoki argues that no single clear pattern has emerged with regard to the future of Japanese corporate governance. Rather, firms have responded to pressures in diverse ways over the last years. The result has been an increasing diversity of corporate governance, since changes in the role of main banks and capital markets have lessened constraints on organizations with regard to choices in other domains, such as business strategy and structure, management and employment patterns. Aoki argues that a new hybrid EMIL model of corporate governance may be emerging in Japan that combines characteristics from the relational model, which characterized post-war Japan, and monitoring via the capital market. Meanwhile, Aoki sees a shift to a US-style shareholder sovereignty model of corporate governance as unlikely.

A key issue for this hybrid remains with regard to who will replace management under conditions of poor performance? The EMIL model suggests that stock market signals will play an increasing role, but these need to be translated into tangible mechanisms of corporate governance. Aoki's analysis suggests that diversity may remain a defining feature of Japanese corporate governance precisely because this may happen in different ways such as through banks, private owners, venture capitalists, boards with committees, and so on. For example, monitoring at venture capital firms involves strong involvement from venture capitalists, whereas independent board members might play a parallel role at larger mature firms. While Aoki notes that changes in politics away from Japan's model of bureau-pluralism and toward a more regulatory state, politics will continue to play an important role in shaping the ongoing evolution of corporate governance.

1.4 ORGANIZATIONAL DIVERSITY AND INSTITUTIONAL CHANGE

The chapters of this volume present a rich picture of corporate governance in Japan that contains elements of both continuity and change. The largest changes have been regarding external elements of corporate governance described in Part

1 of this book, such as finance and ownership patterns. Main bank lending has lessened and rates of cross-shareholding have declined. While these features have not disappeared, their scope and significance have changed. Meanwhile, the internal aspects of corporate governance described in Part 2 have adapted to these changes, but in a more incremental and selective fashion. Revisions to the Commercial Code facilitate the adoption of US-style board practices, but are designed around system choice that enable rather than mandate change. Japanese firms have increased corporate disclosure and become more transparent, but implemented more limited changes with regard to shareholder involvement and boards of directors. Stock options have spread, but their size and importance remains much less than in the US or UK. Likewise, lifetime employment has persisted, although sometimes adapted through a growing use of merit-based pay as a supplementary component alongside the more traditional system of seniority-oriented ranks.

Debates continue as to whether Japan is now converging on a US-model of corporate governance, or whether corporate governance will maintain distinctive national characteristics. No single way exists to resolve this issue. Theories of convergence point to growing international capital mobility and competitive pressures to generate higher shareholder returns. Shareholder primacy is also seen as a global norm (Hansmann and Kraakman 2001) or as being promoted by the hegemonic influence of the United States (Dore 2000). These pressures are argued to push corporate governance systems toward a single and arguably best way—either through formal convergence of rules or a functional convergence of practices (Gilson 2000). As noted in section 1.2, however, institutional theory has stressed path dependence and persistence of national diversity (Guillén 2000) due to several distinct mechanisms such as sunk costs, learning effects, coordination effects, or institutional complementarities. States may face strong political resistance to corporate governance reform, and corporate insiders may defend vested private benefits (Bebchuk and Roe 1999). Also, firms are unlikely to change if their corporate governance practices promote distinct comparative institutional advantages for different types of economic behavior (Hall and Soskice 2001).

The findings of this book suggest that the empirical case for convergence is relatively weak. Looking at change based on broad national averages (e.g. ownership, employment stability, number of outside directors, etc.), Japan has clearly moved toward a more market-oriented form of corporate governance. But comparing corporate governance in terms of levels, very large differences remain between Japan and liberal market economies like the US or UK. Might Japanese firms simply be undergoing a transition phase that will ultimately lead to convergence? Not all firms are equally exposed to pressures for change and existing institutions also constrain change along particular trajectories. For example, the norm of lifetime employment has remained remarkably robust, although the number of full time employees has gradually decreased. However, it would be erroneous to infer that because Japan has not "converged," that the past Japanese model has remained intact. We have stressed the importance of changes in the role and scope of the main bank as an institution, new pressures from foreign institutional investors, and the efforts of firms to increase transparency and adapt the structure of their corporate boards.

Our aim here is to summarize more precisely how corporate governance in Japan is changing, and how its various elements interact as an emerging "bundle" or system. Here we argue that the current period of change can usefully be understood in terms of two inter-related trends: the growing organizational diversity of corporate governance practices within Japan, and the recombination of corporate governance practices which result in new "hybrid" forms of corporate governance which are unlike either the past Japanese model or the US model of corporate governance. The following sections deal with each issue in turn.

1.4.1 The Emerging Diversity of Corporate Governance in Japan

In this section, we develop an inductively based typology of the corporate governance patterns among Japanese firms using survey data collected by the Policy Research Institute of the Ministry of Finance in 2003.[13] The sample is limited to non-financial firms, and some well known firms (Sony and Orix) are not included. The typology is based on a cluster analysis, which groups firms into distinct clusters that maximize the statistical differences between each group, while minimizing the variation within each group.[14] The cluster analysis thus highlights the most common configurations of variables within the sample of Japanese firms. Fourteen data items were included in the analysis that can be interpreted broadly along three theoretical dimensions:

- Finance and ownership characteristics: market-oriented (e.g. bond finance and institutional investors) or relational (e.g. bank finance and cross-shareholding).
- Board and management characteristics: outsider-oriented (e.g. outsider boards and high disclosure) or insider-oriented (e.g. insider boards and private information).
- Employment and incentive characteristics: market-oriented (e.g. no lifetime employment, merit pay, and use of stock options) or relational (e.g. lifetime employment, seniority pay, and no stock options).

---

[13] This data is described in detail in Chapter 12 of this volume by Miyajima.

[14] The analysis was performed using the two-step cluster routine in SPSS. The number of clusters was determined by the cubic clustering criterion, which measures within-cluster homogeneity relative to between-cluster heterogeneity and suggests an "optimum" number of clusters (Kretchen Jr. and Shook 1996). The two-step procedure is appropriate for using dichotomous or categorical data alongside other continuous measures, and the clustering algorithm proves robust even when the variables are not statistically independent. Continuous variables were standardized in order to eliminate biases from variables with large ranges (e.g. where elements are separated by greater distances), and the consistency of solutions was assessed by performing the analysis on a split sample. To reflect the validity of the clusters, only variables are highlighted in the analysis that are statistically significant different means across groups at a 95% confidence level.

(A)

	Outsider board	Insider board
RELATIONAL FINANCE	Inverse hybrid	*J* model
MARKET FINANCE	US model	EMIL or hybrid model

(B)

	Market employment	Relational employment
RELATIONAL FINANCE	Inverse hybrid	*J* model
MARKET FINANCE	US model	EMIL or hybrid model

Figure 1.2 Corporate governance: possible relationships between external and internal characteristics

These aspects are usually expected to co-vary between the financial characteristics, on one hand, and the two sets of internal characteristics related to boards and employment, on the other hand, as indicated by the grey shaded areas (see Figure 1.2). As will be discussed below, Aoki's EMIL pattern is represented by combinations of market finance with greater insider or relational orientation in terms of internal characteristics.

Table 1.4 shows the average values for each group identified in the cluster analysis (Table 1.5 also provides the correlation matrix among the underlying variables). The results suggest that Japanese firms fall into three broad groups: traditional Japanese (*J*-type) firms with strong relational elements on all dimensions (42% of sample firms accounting for 16% of total employment), "hybrid" firms that are similar to Aoki's EMIL model (24% of sample firms accounting for 67% of total employment), and an intermediate group has relational finance or insider boards with more market-oriented employment and incentive patterns (34% of sample firms accounting for 18% of total employment). This distribution suggests that while the "hybrid" pattern is small in terms of the number of firms, it is becoming the predominant pattern among large Japanese firms, as reflected in the high share of employment. These three groups can be further divided into two sub-clusters in order to highlight potential variation within each broad "type." For presentational purposes, Figure 1.3 plots these six groups in terms of the three theoretical dimensions discussed in terms of whether it was below average (zero), average (one), or above average (two) on each dimension. To reflect the concentration of large firms within the hybrid clusters, the size of the circle represents each group weighted by the share of total employees.

Table 1.4 Corporate Governance Indicators, By Cluster

Major cluster		J-firm			Hybrid			Inverse hybrid			Total
Sub-group		1	1a	1b	2	2a	2b	3	3a	3b	
Financial and Ownership Characteristics											
Bond Ratio	Mean	**0.02**	0.01	0.02	**0.09**	0.06	0.10	**0.02**	0.01	0.03	**0.03**
Bank Loan Ratio	Mean	**0.18**	0.20	0.14	**0.11**	0.06	0.14	**0.19**	0.21	0.17	**0.16**
Percentage shares owned by: *financial*											
institutions	Mean	**21.9**	23.1	19.9	**43.7**	45.6	42.5	**21.8**	21.5	22.1	**27.1**
other firms	Mean	**32.7**	34.6	29.5	**17.6**	16.2	18.5	**30.3**	34.1	28.0	**28.3**
foreigners	Mean	**2.6**	2.0	3.6	**14.5**	18.3	12.2	**4.0**	3.1	4.6	**6.0**
individuals	Mean	**42.0**	39.5	46.2	**23.3**	19.2	25.9	**43.1**	40.7	44.6	**37.9**
Board and Management Characteristics											
CGI-shareholders	Mean	**3.9**	3.4	4.7	**7.2**	7.8	6.8	**5.5**	5.1	5.7	**5.2**
CGI-board	Mean	**9.5**	9.4	9.6	**13.7**	13.9	13.6	**10.6**	10.5	10.6	**10.9**
CGI-transparency	Mean	**7.9**	7.1	9.2	**18.2**	19.7	17.1	**10.3**	9.3	11.0	**11.2**
Decentralization	Mean	**2.4**	2.4	2.3	**2.7**	2.6	2.7	**2.3**	2.4	2.2	**2.4**
Employment and Incentive Characteristics											
Lifetime Employment	% Firms	**100%**	100%	100%	**94%**	84%	100%	**56%**	100%	29%	**84%**
Merit-based Pay	% Firms	**0%**	0%	0%	**45%**	100%	10%	**100%**	100%	100%	**45%**
Stock Options	% Firms	**19%**	0%	46%	**39%**	45%	35%	**35%**	0%	56%	**28%**
Union	% Firms	**70%**	100%	19%	**99%**	100%	99%	**58%**	70%	51%	**73%**
Other Information											
Percentage of firms	% Firms	**42%**	26.2	15.8	**24%**	9.4	14.7	**34%**	13.0	21.0	
Employees	Mean	856	940	718	6293	7574	5493	1142	1325	1030	2065
Share of employees	% Firms	**16%**	11%	5%	**67%**	31%	36%	**18%**	8%	10%	
ROA	Mean	0.00	−0.72	1.22	0.96	1.74	.47	**0.71**	−0.44	1.45	0.49

Note: The diagram shows the results of a cluster analysis using log-likelihood method to compute linkages among 723 firms based on finance (ratio of bonds and bank borrowing to total assets) and ownership characteristics (ratios of foreign, personal and inter-firm holdings), board and management characteristics (based on a corporate governance index of shareholders rights, board reform and disclosure, as well as decentralization of decisions to business units) and employment and incentive characteristics (use of lifetime employment, merit-based pay, stock options and the presence of a labor union).

Sources: Ministry of Finance Survey (2003) and Nikkei, see Chapter 12 this volume (for detailed definitions).

Looking at Figure 1.3, three of the clusters are close to the upper right-hand corner, which represents *J*-style corporate governance with relational finance, insider boards, and relational employment. Meanwhile, no cluster of firms is found in the bottom left-hand corner, which approximates US-style corporate governance with market finance, outsider boards, and market employment patterns. The two "hybrid" clusters do have market-oriented finance and ownership, but retain relational elements along the employment dimension and to a lesser degree some characteristics of insider boards (e.g. high transparency but fewer independent outsiders). Finally, the "adversarial" cluster is an inverse hybrid pattern with market-oriented employment combined with relational finance and insider boards. Next, we describe these groups in detail.

Table 1.5 Correlation among Corporate Governance Variables

	Bond	Bank	Financial	Other firms	Foreign	Individual	CGI-share	CGI-board	CGI-trans	Decentral	LTE	Merit	Stock options	Union
Financial and Ownership Characteristics														
Bond Ratio	1													
Bank Loan Ratio	−.041	1												
Ownership: financial institutions	.344(**)	−.135(**)	1											
Ownership: other firms	−.212(**)	.102(**)	−.555(**)	1										
Ownership: foreigners	.166(**)	−.296(**)	.418(**)	−.395(**)	1									
Ownership: individuals	−.164(**)	.145(**)	−.494(**)	−.354(**)	−.434(**)	1								
Board and Management Characteristics														
CGI-shareholders	.211(**)	−.104(**)	.086(*)	−.123(**)	.228(**)	−.057	1							
CGI-board	.186(**)	.004	.182(**)	−.099(**)	.180(**)	−.143(**)	.182(**)	1						
CGI-transparency	.321(**)	−.261(**)	.413(**)	−.327(**)	.482(**)	−.251(**)	.407(**)	.256(**)	1					
Decentralization	.101(**)	.045	.159(**)	−.042	.060	−.128(**)	.038	.077(*)	.091(*)	1				
Employment and Incentive Characteristics														
Lifetime Employment	.054	−.029	.075(*)	.000	−.028	−.051	−.069	.000	.000	.068	1			
Merit-based Pay	.002	−.002	.029	−.078(*)	.112(**)	.004	.163(**)	.091(*)	.155(**)	−.029	−.491(**)	1		
Stock Options	.076(*)	−.155(**)	.050	−.169(**)	.147(**)	.060	.108(**)	.105(**)	.231(**)	−.101(**)	−.110(**)	.145(**)	1	
Union	.153(**)	.055	.292(**)	.047	.062	−.329(**)	−.037	.083(*)	.011	.162(**)	.133(**)	−.091(**)	−.179(**)	1

Notes: ** Correlation is significant at the 0.01 level (2-tailed); * Correlation is significant at the 0.05 level (2-tailed).

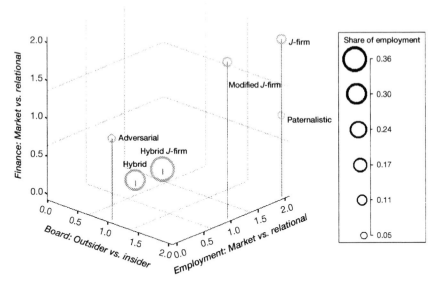

Figure 1.3 Corporate governance in Japan: Finance, board and employment characteristics

J-Firm Clusters

The first broad group in column 1 are traditional *J*-type firms, which have not undertaken large reforms of their corporate governance practices by 2002. In terms of finance and ownership, these firms use predominantly bank finance rather than bonds and have high levels of inter-firm shareholding, but low levels of ownership by foreigners or financial institutions. In terms of boards and management, these firms have low scores across all aspects of the corporate governance index, reflecting low shareholder influence, few outsiders on the board, and low levels of transparency. In terms of employment and incentives, these firms maintain lifetime employment norms and seniority-based pay systems. Only a small percentage adopted stock options as a form of managerial incentive and most of the firms have enterprise unions. As such, these characteristics are consistent with the traditional *J*-type firm, described in the outset of this chapter.

The *J*-firm cluster is also internally relatively homogeneous. Breaking the group into two smaller clusters shows a first sub-group (1A) with almost ideal-typical *J*-firm characteristics. This group contains a large number of firms from the construction, chemicals, apparel and textiles, machinery, and automotive sectors.[15] The second and smaller sub-group (1B) has significantly higher

---

[15] While many of them are small and lesser known firms, the group includes the Imperial Hotel or Sanyo Electric Railway, members of vertical keiretsu groups such as Daihatsu Diesel Manufacturing and Tosoh Corporation (a chemicals firm associated with the Mizuho Bank group).

levels of individual ownership, lower levels of bank finance, and somewhat greater transparency, shareholder rights, and likelihood of adopting stock options.[16] This group also have "paternalistic" labor relations where lifetime employment exists despite lower levels of unionization in sectors such as specialized trading companies (e.g. Japan Pulp and Paper) and lower-skilled business service firms (e.g. restaurant service provider Tokyo Kaikan), as well as the presence of family-controlled firms in electrical machinery (e.g. Icom Incorporated) or foods (e.g. Natori or Nagatanien).

Hybrid Clusters

The second broad cluster of firms display a "hybrid" pattern based on market-oriented finance and ownership characteristics, alongside relational employment and partially insider board structures. This group thus mixes market-oriented elements externally with non-market or relational internal characteristics. These firms make strong use of corporate bonds as a source of finance, and display high levels of ownership by foreigners and financial institutions. Meanwhile, the levels of bank loans and inter-firm ownership are much lower than the J-firm cluster. Turning to internal aspects of board and management, these firms have been the more likely to adopt shareholder rights and bring outsiders onto boards, but have changed most strongly with regard to greater corporate disclosure and transparency. Notably, however, these firms combine this strong capital market orientation with a relational employment pattern based on lifetime employment norms and very high levels of unionization. These firms have partially adapted relational employment patterns by implementing merit-based pay schemes (45% of these firms). This group includes a number of large internationally oriented firms. Electronics and communications are well represented, but wide ranging in terms of sectoral characteristics.

The "hybrid" cluster is also more internally heterogeneous than the J-firm cluster and suggests distinct patterns of change. The first sub-group (2a) is distinguished by very high levels of transparency and foreign ownership, as well as the strong use of merit-based pay systems. This sub-group includes prominent Japanese blue-chips such as Toyota, Canon, Kao, Yamaha Corporation, or Kikkoman. Toyota Motor Corporation is a good example, having changed its finance methods from bank borrowing to bonds, attained high levels of foreign shareholders and lower levels of inter-firm shareholding, and implementing changes toward greater transparency and stock options. Notably, Toyota has resisted placing outside members on the board and strongly upholds its lifetime employment pattern. The second sub-group (2b) has made more modest reforms to corporate governance in terms of boards and disclosure, and reflects a stronger use

---

[16] For example, the machine tools trading firm Yamazen Corporation has long-term owners such as two associations of business partners and Mizuho Bank, but has adopted greater transparency. Likewise, drinks maker Yakult Honsha was approached by the French firm Danone, resulting in a strategic alliance and increased transparency.

of corporate bonds but more modest levels of foreign ownership. This sub-group also retains some more traditional J-firm characteristics, such as modest use of bank borrowing and predominance of seniority-based pay. Well-known examples of this sub-group include Hitachi, NTT DoCoMo, Ajinomoto, and utilities firms such as Tokyo Electric Power, as well as Mitsubishi group firms such as Mitsubishi Chemicals, Mitsubishi Heavy Industry and Mitsubishi Motors. On the whole, the two hybrid groups also have stronger economic performance, in terms of return on assets, than the J-firm groups (see Table 1.4), which suggests the potential effectiveness of hybrid forms.

Inverse Hybrid Cluster

The final cluster occupies a somewhat intermediate position between the previous J-firm and hybrid cluster. The external elements are rather similar to the J-firm group, such as strong bank finance and an average level of inter-firm ownership. Turning to internal aspects of boards and management, the scores of the corporate governance index are average across the board, placing them slightly higher than the J-firm group but far lower than the hybrid group. Meanwhile, this group is most distinctive in terms of its pervasive use of merit-based pay systems and the lower percentage of firms with lifetime employment norms (56%). The first sub-group (3a) is actually very close to the classic J-firms, in having high inter-firm ownership and lifetime employment norms, but "modified" the J-type pattern by using merit-based pay among retail establishments (e.g. Kintetsu or Tokyu Department Stores) or automotive firms from the Toyota group (e.g. Hino Motors or Toyota Auto Body). However, the second sub-group (3b) are more market-oriented or "adversarial" in terms of employment patterns with very low levels of lifetime employment and unionization, as well as frequently using stock options. This group includes IT or other high-tech service firms (e.g. Fuji Soft Inc. or Sorun Corporation), retail establishments (e.g. Izumiya or the Livedoor subsidiary Internet-based retailer, Cecile Corporation), general trading companies (e.g. Suzuken or Ryoshoko) or family-owned companies (e.g. Itoham Foods). In these sectors, competitive advantage is either less strongly based on high employee skills or utilizes a more mobile external occupational labor market, such as in IT services. In sum, despite the relational pattern of finance and insider board structure, employment and incentive patterns are more market-oriented.

In sum, this analysis suggests the increasing *heterogeneity of corporate governance practices* among firms between those maintaining J-firm characteristics and those changing toward hybrid patterns over the last decade. The J-firm patterns remain the majority in Japan: 42% of firms fall clearly within this cluster and another 21% of firms belong to the intermediate cluster with modified J-type characteristics (3a). The major new phenomena in Japan are "hybrid" forms of corporate governance among roughly one-fourth of Japanese listed firms. These hybrid groups include many of the largest Japanese firms and thus account for 67% of total employment compared to 16% in the J-firm cluster, and 18% in the intermediate cluster. Meanwhile, only 13% of firms fall into the group with strongly market-oriented employment patterns (3b).

1.4.2 Hybrid Forms of Corporate Governance

The major new phenomenon revealed by the cluster analysis is the new "hybrid" pattern of corporate governance that involves a mix of elements from the "old" Japanese model and "new" more Anglo-American practices. The concept of hybridization refers to the *innovative recombination of elements* (Pieterse 1994) in ways that rejects both an economic determinism of a single best model, as well as societal determinism which suggests that practices can never be transferred across social contexts.[17] But a useful concept of hybridization requires further specification in terms of *what combinations* and how these relate to institutional complementarities. Not all combinations are viable or will achieve equal economic performance, and so hybrids may be unstable—resulting in further institutional change, inefficient outcomes, or abandonment of an initial change. Might a hybrid model represent only a transitional stage toward more fully market-oriented corporate governance along the lines of the US model?

Central to the emerging hybrid in Japan are the unexpectedly diverse ways in which both finance and ownership characteristics, as well as board characteristics combine with employment and incentive characteristics. For example, the *J*-firm (1A), paternalistic (1B), and modified *J*-firm (3A) groups are similar in terms of having inter-corporate holdings, bank finance, and low levels of board reform, but have diverse employment and incentive patterns. Likewise, the two hybrid groups have market-oriented finance and ownership, but have not abandoned lifetime employment norms. The hybrid patterns correspond rather closely to Aoki's discussion of the EMIL model of corporate governance (see Chapter 15) where the capital market evaluates the business models of each firm, rather than the main bank monitoring based on private information.

Given the strong complementarity often posited between external (finance and ownership) and internal (board and employment) elements, this pattern of hybridization has puzzling implications. In particular, how complementary is this emerging mix of market-orientated external governance and relationship-oriented internal governance? Here three points seem relevant. First, the market may have diverse and evolving opinions about how appropriate the linkage is between firms' business models and the choice of internal governance practices. For example, Moody's famously downgraded Toyota's bond rating in 1998 citing its continued commitment to lifetime employment, but later revised their view of

---

[17] The concept of hybrids has affinities with literatures on legal transplants (Kanda and Milhaupt 2003), production and assembly systems (Boyer et al. 1998), conversion and layering of institutions (Thelen 1999; Streeck and Thelen 2005), reconfiguration of the relationships between institutional domains (Aoki 2001b), or sociological theories of action stressing ambiguity and creativity in interpreting institutional rules (Jackson 2005).

Toyota's business model and upgraded Toyota again in 2003.[18] Second, extending the analysis to additional domains may suggest wider sets of complementarities (Crouch et al. 2005). The type of complementarities between finance and employment may be contingent upon the specific aspects of business strategy, organizational architecture, and related forms of human capital. Here organizational diversity may be a better solution than a single institutionalized pattern, since firms can better adapt to local and sectoral conditions (Aoki 1998). Third, some institutional forms can be adapted or "converted" to new strategic purposes over time (Streeck and Thelen 2005). For example, corporate transparency and disclosure may serve shareholder interests, but equally the interests of other stakeholders, such as employees. Likewise, merit-based systems of pay can be compatible with lifetime employment and even offer functional equivalents to seniority pay in terms of long-term career incentives.

Of course, it is an open empirical question under what local conditions market finance and relational employment patterns can coexist. Table 1.4 suggests that the hybrid groups have strong economic performance, and thus Aoki's EMIL model may quite possibly be a viable alternative to corporate governance based on "shareholder value" that is devoid of a stakeholder element. Ultimately, the EMIL model itself will be one characterized by diversity, in light of the diverse ways in which market perceptions get translated into actual mechanisms of corporate governance through M&A, buyout funds, boards of directors, venture capitalists or other actors. Market mechanisms may translate themselves into corporate governance in diverse ways, and their relative effectiveness in evaluating and monitoring the different types of business models among Japanese firms will be an important area for future research.

1.5 THE TRANSFORMATION OF CORPORATE GOVERNANCE IN JAPAN

This volume has shown a number of important changes in the corporate governance features of Japanese companies. The most noteworthy of these changes have involved external elements of corporate governance, such as shifts in the financing of corporations and subsequent ownership patterns. Here a significant proportion of the largest firms have become significantly more capital market-oriented as bank finance shifted to the use of the external bond market, and stable shareholding has declined in favor of foreign and institutional share ownership. The legal framework was also dramatically changed. Now Japanese firms can choose from a wide menu of market-based options, such as the holding company structure, the US type of board (committee system), stock options, and acquisitions through

---

[18] A very interesting ongoing case is the hostile takeover bid by Oji Paper Company for Hokuetsu Paper Mills in July 2006. This case is the first hostile bid by a traditional Japanese company for another one, prompting Mitsubishi Trading Company to acquire a 24% stake in defence of Hokuetsu.

share swaps. These changes have also prompted Japanese firms to change elements of their internal governance structure, such as their efforts at transparency, structure of their companies' boards, incentive schemes, and labor management practices. However, these changes are relatively modest in comparison. Perhaps more importantly, changes to the internal aspects of corporate governance have been more partial and more selective depending on their organizational architectures, leading to very diverse patterns of corporate governance in Japan.

The process of institutional change has been largely incremental or path dependent in nature, but clearly transformative.[19] This evolution has involved gradual exhaustion of some institutions, the layering of new institutions on top of old ones, and the conversion of existing institutions to fit new purposes and adjust to new circumstances. Following slow changes in corporate finance since the middle of the 1980s, corporate ownership also gradually changed through the influx of foreign institutional investors in Japan since 1990. The year 1997 represents a more dramatic turning point. It was in 1997 that a rapid decline of cross-shareholding began and a number of important legal changes in corporate law introduced more choice in terms of how companies use equity and structure their boards. Since then, Japanese firms began to gradually adjust aspects of their internal corporate governance structures by selectively introducing measures such as the executive officer system, stock options, or outside directors (e.g. the committee system). This process of change also occurred during a period of the banking crisis and macroeconomic slump. This slow adjustment process prompted further government intervention around 2002 to strengthen the process of corporate restructuring through the disposal of bad bank loans. Meanwhile, other elements of Japanese firms, such as lifetime employment, have been maintained, albeit slowly adjusted to these changes in external aspects of finance and ownership. The result of this process has been the emergence of diverse new "hybrid" forms of corporate governance in Japan.

Meanwhile firms that still maintain traditional J-firm patterns of corporate governance are also beginning to undergo a new process of creative destruction through mechanisms such as M&A, bankruptcy, and private equity investments. Despite macroeconomic recovery, these firms appear to perform less well on average and have been very slow to adopt corporate governance reform. However, due to their smaller size, it is unlikely that bond ratings or foreign institutional investors will develop a strong role in corporate governance. While these firms remain strongly embedded in bank–firm relationships and inter-firm networks, the nature of these relationships has also changed since major players, such as the banks, can increasingly use elements of the market to promote corporate restructuring. Thus, the traditional J-firm also faces gradual but increasing pressure to modernize itself even if corporate governance for these firms will remain different from larger hybrid firms.

---

[19] Streeck and Thelen (2005) offer a framework for theorizing incremental forms of institutional change, and Vogel (2006) offers an insightful analysis of the Japanese political economy along similar lines.

Now in 2006, this process of change in corporate governance would appear to be reaching a point of culmination. The number of firms introducing the committee system has slowed and the debate on reforming corporate boards has cooled down. Japan has also entered a period of macroeconomic recovery, and corporate restructuring has become routine. Japanese firms are less plagued with corporate restructuring and free cash flow problems, while being more concerned with guarding against over-investment and encouraging innovation. Thus, we anticipate that the changes in corporate governance described in this book are likely to be further consolidated. Here three developments are important. First, a planned modernization of Japanese corporate law is likely to result in greater freedom for Japanese corporations to adopt different governance structures as part of their articles of incorporation, thus reinforcing the approach of enabling reform by giving corporations greater choice. Second, some internal aspects of corporate governance remain to be addressed, such as a system for monitoring business divisions within multi-divisional firms or holding companies is still important. The existence of listed subsidiary companies has increasingly come under criticism from shareholder activists, who suggest a conflict of interests between parent company shareholders and other minority shareholders. After introducing the next company law amendment (the Japanese version of the Sarbanes-Oxley Act), firms are required to provide a report on the internal control and auditing procedures. Third, the decline in cross-share-holding among industrial firms seems to have halted and may even be on the increase. The immanent deregulation of M&A with foreign firms through share-to-share exchange has increased fears of hostile takeovers in Japan. While few Japanese banks are in a position to rebuild cross-shareholding patterns, firms have been forging new alliances for cross-shareholding as a form of takeover protection. Thus, the most important ongoing developments suggest the future stability of the "hybrid" model of corporate governance in Japan, which combines relationship-oriented aspects of corporate governance with a greater role of the external capital market in evaluating the growth prospects of firms—as suggested by Aoki's EMIL model.

In our view, the future viability and effectiveness of hybrid or EMIL-type corporate governance depends on a two-fold set of conditions. The greater role of the capital market may be compatible with relational elements of governance to the extent that the pressures for hostile takeovers remain limited. A dramatic increase in the number of hostile takeovers might be sufficient to generate "breaches of trust" and undermine long-term commitments to stakeholders, which are so important in Japan. Likewise, internal elements of corporate governance such as internal management systems and employee participation must play a greater role in promoting checks and balances, and thus the accountability of top managers. The market only provides broad signals as to the quality of firm strategies, but does not necessarily provide mechanisms for shareholder involvement in the selection of the top management team. Here the experience of the US or UK suggests that independent boards or management incentives are insufficient to assure managerial accountability on their own (Filatotchev et al.

2007). The mechanisms of internal governance outlined by Dore will remain of continued importance in Japan. As such, the evolution of corporate governance in Japan will remain a dynamic topic over the next decades.

BIBLIOGRAPHY

Aguilera, R. V. and G. Jackson (2003). 'The Cross-National Diversity of Corporate Governance: Dimensions and Determinants,' *Academy of Management Review*, 28(3): 447–65.

Ahmadjian, C. L. and P. Robinson (2001). 'Safety in Numbers: Downsizing and the Deinstitutionalization of Permanent Employment in Japan,' *Administrative Science Quarterly*, 46: 622–54.

Aoki, M. (1984). *The Economic Analysis of the Japanese Firm*. Amsterdam: North-Holland.

—— (1988). *Information, Incentives, and Bargaining in the Japanese Economy*. Cambridge: Cambridge University Press.

—— (1994). 'The Japanese Firm as a System of Attributes,' in M. Aoki and R. Dore (eds.), *The Japanese Firm: Sources of Competitive Strength*. Oxford: Oxford University Press, 11–40.

—— (1997). 'Unintended Fit: Organizational Evolution and Government Design of Institutions in Japan,' in M. Aoki et al. (eds.), *The Role of Government in East Asian Economic Development: Comparative Institutional Analysis*. Oxford: Clarendon Press, 233–53.

—— (1998). 'The Evolution of Organizational Conventions and Gains from Diversity,' *Industrial and Corporate Change*, 7(3): 399–431.

—— (2001a). *Information, Corporate Governance, and Institutional Diversity*. Oxford: Oxford University Press.

—— (2001b). *Toward a Comparative Institutional Analysis*. Cambridge, MA: MIT Press.

—— (2007). 'Endogenizing Institutions and Institutional Changes,' *Journal of Institutional Economics*, 3: 1–18.

—— R. P. Dore (1994). *The Japanese Firm: The Sources of Competitive Strength*. Oxford: Oxford University Press.

—— H. Patrick (eds.) (1994). *The Japanese Main Bank System: Its Relevance for Developing and Transforming Economies*. Oxford: Oxford University Press.

Arikawa, Y. and H. Miyajima (2005). 'Relationship Banking and Debt Choice: Evidence from Japan,' *Corporate Governance: An International Review*, 11: 408–18.

Barney, J. (2001). 'Is the Resource-Based View a Useful Perspective for Strategic Management Research? Yes,' *Academy of Management Review*, 26(1): 41–56.

Bebchuk, L. A. and M. J. Roe (1999). 'A Theory of Path Dependence in Corporate Governance and Ownership,' *Columbia Law School, Center for Law and Economic Studies, Working Papers*, No. 131.

Blair, M. M. (2003). 'Post-Enron Reflections on Comparative Corporate Governance,' *Journal of Interdisciplinary Economics*, 14: 113–24.

Boyer, R., E. Charron, U. Jürgens, and S. Tolliday (eds.) (1998). *Between Imitation and Innovation. The Transfer and Hybridization of Productive Models in the International Automobile Industry*. Oxford: Oxford University Press.

Coffee, J. C. (1999). 'The Future as History: The Prospects for Global Convergence in Corporate Governance and its Implications,' *Northwestern University Law Review*, 93(3): 641–708.

Crouch, C. (2005). *Capitalist Diversity and Change. Recombinant Governance and Institutional Entrepreneurs.* Oxford: Oxford University Press.

—— W. Streeck, R. Boyer, B. Amable, P. A. Hall, and G. Jackson (2005). 'Dialogue on "Institutional Complementarity and Political Economy",' *Socio-Economic Review*, 2(4): 359–82.

Deeg, R. (2005). 'Change from Within: German and Italian Finance in the 1990s,' in W. Streeck and K. Thelen (eds.), *Beyond Continuity: Institutional Change in Advanced Political Economies.* Oxford: Oxford University Press.

DiMaggio, P. J. and W. W. Powell (1991). 'The Iron Cage Revisited: Institutional Isomorphism and Collective Rationality in Organization Fields,' in W. W. Powell and P. J. Dimaggio (ed.), *The New Institutionalism in Organizational Analysis.* Chicago, IL: University of Chicago Press, 63–82.

Dore, R. (1994). 'Equity–Efficiency Trade-offs: Japanese Perceptions and Choices,' in M. Aoki and R. Dore (eds.), *The Japanese Firm: The Sources of Competitive Strength.* Oxford: Oxford University Press, 379–92.

—— (2000). *Stock Market Capitalism: Welfare Capitalism: Japan and Germany Versus the Anglo-Saxons.* Oxford: Oxford University Press.

—— (2005). 'Deviant or Different? Corporate Governance in Japan and Germany,' *Corporate Governance: An International Review*, 13(3): 437–46.

EPA (Economic Planning Agency) (1999). *Economic Survey of Japan.* Tokyo: EPA.

Filatotchev, I. and M. Wright (eds.) (2005). *Corporate Governance Life-Cycle.* London: Edward Elgar.

—— G. Jackson, H. Gospel and D. Allcock (2007). *Key Drivers of 'Good' Corporate Governance and the Appropriateness of UK Policy Responses.* London: Department of Trade and Industry.

Gerlach, M. L. (1992). *Alliance Capitalism: The Social Organization of Japanese Business.* Berkeley: University of California Press.

Gilson, R. J. (2000). 'The Globalization of Corporate Governance: Convergence of Form or Function,' *Columbia Law School, Center for Law and Economic Studies, Working Papers*, No. 192.

—— C. Milhaupt (2004). 'Choice as Regulatory Reform: The Case of Japanese Corporate Governance,' *ECGI—Law Working Paper*, No. 22/2004.

Gordon, A. (1998). *The Wages of Affluence: Labor and Management in Postwar Japan.* Cambridge, MA: Harvard University Press.

Gospel, H. and A. Pendleton (eds.) (2005). *Corporate Governance and Labour Management: An International Comparison.* Oxford: Oxford University Press.

Guillén, M. F. (2000). 'Corporate Governance and Globalization: Is There Convergence Across Countries?' *Advances in International Comparative Management*, 13: 175–204.

Hall, B. J. and D. E. Weinstein (1996). *The Myth of the Patient Japanese: Corporate Myopia and Financial Distress in Japan and the US.* Cambridge, MA: National Bureau of Economic Research.

Hall, P. A. and D. Soskice (eds.) (2001). *Varieties of Capitalism: The Institutional Foundations of Comparative Advantage.* Oxford: Oxford University Press.

Hansmann, H. and R. Kraakman (2001). 'The End of History for Corporate Law,' *Georgetown Law Journal*, 89: 439.

Hirota, S. and K. Kawamura (2003). 'Corporate Survival Without Governance: A Control Mechanism of Managers Inside the Firm,' *Waseda University, Institute of Finance Working Papers*, WIF-03-006.

Hoshi, T. and A. Kashyap (2001). *Corporate Financing and Governance in Japan: The Road to the Future*. Cambridge, MA: MIT Press.

Inagami, T. and D. H. Whittaker (2005). *The New Community Firm. Employment, Governance and Management Reform in Japan*. Cambridge: Cambridge University Press.

Jackson, G. (2001). 'The Origins of Nonliberal Corporate Governance in Germany and Japan,' in W. Streeck and K. Yamamura (eds.), *The Origins of Nonliberal Capitalism: Germany and Japan in Comparison*. Ithaca, NY: Cornell University Press, 121–70.

—— (2005). 'Contested Boundaries: Ambiguity and Creativity in the Evolution of German Codetermination,' in W. Streeck and K. Thelen (eds.), *Beyond Continuity: Explorations in the Dynamics of Advanced Political Economies*. Oxford: Oxford University Press, 229–54.

—— R. Deeg (2006). 'How Many Varieties of Capitalism? Comparing the Comparative Institutional Analyses of Capitalist Diversity,' *Max-Planck-Institut fuer Gesellschaftsforschung, Discussion Paper*, 06/2.

—— H. Miyajima (2007). 'Varieties of Takeover Markets: Comparing Mergers and Acquisitions in Japan with Europe and the USA,' *RIETI Discussion Paper*, forthcoming.

—— S. Vitols (2001). 'Between Financial Commitment, Market Liquidity and Corporate Governance: Occupational Pensions in Britain, Germany, Japan and the USA,' in B. Ebbinghaus and P. Manow (eds.), *Comparing Welfare Capitalism. Social Policy and Political Economy in Europe, Japan and the USA*. London: Routledge, 171–89.

Jacoby, S. M. (2004). *The Embedded Corporation: Corporate Governance and Employment Relations in Japan and the United States*. Princeton: Princeton University Press.

JCGF (Japan Corporate Governance Forum) (1998). *Corporate Governance Principles—A Japanese View (Final Report)*. Tokyo: Corporate Governance Forum of Japan.

—— (2005). *Japan Corporate Governance Index*. Tokyo: Corporate Governance Forum of Japan.

Kanda, H. and C. Milhaupt (2003). 'Re-examining Legal Transplants: The Director's Fiduciary Duty in Japanese Corporate Law,' *Columbia Law and Economics Working Paper*, no. 219.

Kaplan, S. N. and B. A Minton (1994). 'Appointments of Outsiders to Japanese Boards: Determinants and Implications for Managers,' *Journal of Financial Economics*, 36(2): 225.

Keidanren (2001). 'A Proposal for Better Corporate Accounting,' *Keidanren*, March 27. Available at: www.keidenren.or.jp

Keizai Doyukai (Japan Assocation of Corporate Executives) (1996). *Kigyo hakusho 12-kai: Nihon kigyo no keiei-kozo kaikaku* (Enterprise White Paper No.12: Reform of the Management Structures of Japanese Firms). Tokyo: Keizai Doyukai.

—— (1998). *Kigyo hakusho 13-kai: Shihon-koritsu-jushi keiei* (Enterprise White Paper No.13: Management Which Prioritizes the Efficient Use of Capital). Tokyo: Keizai Doyukai.

Kester, W. C. (1992). 'Industrial Groups as Systems of Contractual Governance,' *Oxford Review of Economic Policy*, 8(3): 24–44.

Koike, K. (1988). *Understanding Industrial Relations in Modern Japan*. London: Macmillan.

Kretchen Jr., D. J. and C. L. Shook (1996). 'The Application of Cluster Analysis in Strategic Management Research: An Analysis and Critique,' *Strategic Management Journal*, 17(6): 441–58.

Kuroki, F. (2003). 'The Relationship of Companies and Banks as Cross-Shareholdings Unwind—Fiscal 2002 Cross-Shareholding Survey,' *NLI Research*, 157.

Learmount, S. (2002). *Corporate Governance: What Can be Learned from Japan?* Oxford: Oxford University Press.

Leibenstein, H. (1966). 'Allocative Efficiency vs. X-Efficiency,' *American Economic Review*, June.

Maezawa, H. (2005). 'Investment Funds Target Cash Rich Firms—Foreign Share Ownership not to be Overlooked as a Factor,' *JCER Researcher Report*, 67.

Milgrom, P. R. and J. Roberts (1990). 'Rationalizability, Learning, and Equilibrium in Games with Strategic Complementarities,' *Econometrica*, 59(1255–77).

—— Y. Qian, and J. Roberts (1991). 'Complementarities, Momentum, and the Evolution of Modern Manufacturing,' *American Economic Review*, 81: 84–8.

Milhaupt, C. J. (2002). 'On the (Fleeting) Existence of the Main Bank System and other Japanese Economic Institutions,' *Law and Social Inquiry*, 27.

Miyajima, H. (1999). 'The Evolution and Change of Contingent Governance Structure in the J-Firm System: An Approach to Presidential Turnover and Firm Performance,' in D. Dirks, J. F Huchet, and T. Ribault (eds.), *Japanese Management in the Low Growth Era: Between External Shock and Internal Evolution*. Springer Verlag.

Miyajima, H. and H. Aoki (2002). 'Changes in the J-Type Firm: From Bank-Centered Governance to Internal Governance,' in J. Maswood et al. (eds.), *Japan—Change and Continuity*. London: RoutledgeCurzon, 72–105.

Morck, R., M. Nakamura, and A. Shivdasani (2000). 'Banks, Ownership, and Firm Value in Japan,' *The Journal of Business*, 73(4): 539–67.

Nikkeiren (Nikkeiren Kokusai Tokubetsu Iinkai: Japan Employers' Federation, Special International Committee) (1998). *Nihon-kigyo no kooporeeto gabanansu kaikaku no hoko: Shihon-shijo kara mo rodoshijo kara mo sentaku sareru kigyo o mezashite (Directions for Reforming the Governance of Japanese Corporations: Towards Corporations Favored by Both Capital and Labor Markets)*. Tokyo: Nikkeiren.

North, D. C. (1990). *Institutions, Institutional Change and Economic Performance*. Cambridge: Cambridge University Press.

Okazaki, T. and M. Okuno-Fujiwara (eds.) (1999). *The Japanese Economic System and its Historical Origins*. Oxford: Oxford University Press.

Osano, H. (1996). 'Intercorporate Shareholdings and Corporate Control in the Japanese Firm,' *Journal of Banking and Finance*, 20: 1047–68.

Pieterse, J. N. (1994). 'Globalization as Hybridization,' *International Sociology*, 9(2): 161–84.

Porter, M. E. (1990). *The Competitive Advantage of Nations*. New York: The Free Press.

Ramseyer, J. M. and Y. Miwa (2005). 'Does Relationship Banking Matter? The Myth of the Japanese Main Bank,' *Journal of Empirical Legal Studies*, 2: 261.

Roberts, J. (2004). *The Modern Firm*. Oxford: Oxford University Press.

Sako, M. (1992). *Prices, Quality, and Trust. Inter-Firm Relations in Britain and Japan*. Cambridge: Cambridge University Press.

Streeck, W. (1996). 'Lean Production in the German Automobile Industry: A Test Case for Convergence Theory,' in S. Berger and R. Dore (eds.), *National Diversity and Global Capitalism*. Ithaca, NY: Cornell University Press, 138–70.

Streeck, W. and K. Thelen (eds.) (2005). *Beyond Continuity: Explorations in the Dynamics of Advanced Political Economies*. Oxford: Oxford University Press.

Thelen, K. (1999). 'Historical Institutionalism in Comparative Politics,' *American Review of Political Science*, 2: 369–404.

Toya, T. (2006). *The Political Economy of the Japanese Financial Big Bang: Institutional Change in Finance and Public Policymaking*. Oxford: Oxford University Press.

TSE (Tokyo Stock Exchange) (2004). *Principles of Corporate Governance for Listed Companies*. Tokyo: Tokyo Stock Exchange.

—— (various years). *Tokyo Stock Exchange Fact Book*. Tokyo: TSE.

Vogel, S. K. (2006). *Japan Remodeled*. Ithaca, NY: Cornell University Press.

Weinstein, D. and Y. Yafeh (1998). 'On the Costs of a Bank-Centered Financial System: Evidence from the Changing Main Bank Relations in Japan,' *Journal of Finance*, 53(2): 635–72.

Xu, P. (2006). 'What are the Characteristics of Companies Prone to Become a Hostile Takeover Target?' (in Japanese), *RIETI Discussion Paper*, 06-J-008.

Yafeh, Y. (2003). 'An International Perspective of Japan's Corporate Groups and their Prospects,' in M. Blomström et al (ed.), *Structural Impediments to Growth in Japan*. Chicago, IL: University of Chicago Press, 259–84.

Yamamura, K. and W. Streeck (eds.) (2003). *The End of Diversity? Prospects of German and Japanese Capitalism*. Ithaca: Cornell University Press.

Part I

Changes in Ownership and Finance

2

Relationship Banking in Post-Bubble Japan: Coexistence of Soft- and Hard-Budget Constraints[1]

Yasuhiro Arikawa and Hideaki Miyajima

2.1 INTRODUCTION

The Japanese financial system, which gives banks a more prominent role than banks in other countries, has been categorized as relationship-based.[2] In the heyday of the relationship-based financial system, main banks in particular played an active role not only in supplying funds to client firms but also in ex-ante, interim, and ex-post monitoring to discipline top management (Aoki et al. 1994). Under this system of relational banking, main banks were expected to supply new money to fund the investment projects of clients, and to mitigate asymmetric information problems between lenders and borrowers through intensive monitoring. Main banks generally did not intervene in the management of well-performing borrowers, although in times of financial distress, they dispatched representatives to troubled clients, and on occasion took over their boards and assumed the initiative in restructuring efforts. Under this financial system, the disciplinary mechanism differed from that of the Anglo-American system, which has relied on takeovers and bankruptcy procedures.

In its heyday (1960s–1970s), the relationship-based financial system was supported by various types of regulations on new entry, interest rates on deposits, and market financing (bond issuance). These regulations guaranteed to banks monopolistic rents that gave them an incentive to adopt long-term strategies because, as Petersen and Rajan (1994) explain, banks in monopolistic markets can bail out distressed firms with the expectation that they will be able to impose higher interest rates in the future.

[1] The two authors wrote this paper with financial support from RIETI. The paper uses data constructed with the help of Keisuke Nitta, Nao Saito, and Fumiaki Kuroki. Yurie Otsu also provided excellent assistance. An early draft was presented at Hitotsubashi University, Waseda University, RIETI, and the College of William and Mary. Comments from Naoto Abe, Katsuyuki Kubo, Shinichi Hirota, Yupana Wiwattanakantang, and Juro Teranishi have been extremely helpful.

[2] Under a relational financing system, the financier is expected to extend additional funding in an uncontractible state in the expectation of future rents (Aoki and Dinc 2000: 20).

However, banking and securities regulations were liberalized beginning in the early 1980s. Financial restraint in the sense of Helman et al. (1997) disappeared with the deregulation of deposit interest rates, and the deregulation of bond issuance proceeded gradually, culminating with the removal of bond issuing criteria and other covenants in January 1996 that freed Japanese firms from regulatory restrictions on debt choice.[3] Moreover, new entry regulations have been relaxed since the Financial System Reform Act of 1993, and completely abolished with the financial "Big Bang" of 1996. These changes in the regulatory framework, together with the decline of demand for new money among firms, have affected the incentives that firms and banks have for maintaining the relational financing system.

Furthermore, the problems afflicting the banking sector over the past decade have rebounded on the bank–firm relationship. The dramatic decline of asset prices in the early 1990s exacerbated the non-performing loan problem in the banking sector. After the costly resolution of the *Jusen* problem caused by the insolvencies of housing loan companies, the Japanese banking sector faced serious crisis in November 1997. It became imperative for banks to write off non-performing loans, which reduced their ability to extend further loans to borrowers. The financial difficulties of banks also placed tremendous stress on bank–firm relationships.

In this context, the perceived flaws of the main bank system gradually began to overshadow its perceived merits. Recent works document that close ties with main banks induced firms to undertake "excessive" investment during the bubble period.[4] The banking crisis of the 1990s may have placed financial constraints on bank-dependent firms (Kang and Stultz 2000), but also gave banks an incentive to engage in the "evergreening" of old loans to nearly insolvent firms to improve their own balance sheets (Peek and Rosengren 2005).

This chapter provides an overview of relational banking in Japan in the 1990s, and addresses the following questions: Can the Japanese financial system still be described as relationship-based? If so (at least to some extent), does relational banking (or the main bank system) play a welfare-enhancing role (merit) or rather does it have a welfare-decreasing role (flaw)? If the negative aspects of the main bank system overwhelm its positive aspects, what are the reasons for this and what are the implications for the future?

To address these issues, we first summarize some proxies of the bank–firm relationship in the 1990s that suggest that there is a growing variance of capital and debt composition among firms, and that the relationship between Japanese firms and their banks is no longer a homogenous one. Then we highlight two previously untouched, but puzzling, facts. The first is the increase in dependence on bank borrowing in spite of the deregulation of the bond market in the mid-1990s. By

---

[3] In November 1990, all criteria except ratings were removed from the Bond Issue Guidelines. In April 1993, the lowest bound of the ratings criteria for issuing unsecured straight bonds was lowered to BBB. See details in Hoshi et al. (1993).

[4] For instance, see Horiuchi (1995); Morck et al. (2000); and Miyajima et al. (2002).

looking at the determinants of debt choice, we suggest that bank borrowing has become increasingly important especially for firms with higher risk. Second, although bank-dependent firms are likely to have higher risk, the degree of concentration of loans from main banks has actually increased among firms with higher levels of bank borrowing. We put forth two possible explanations for this increase in commitment: 1) it is a result of main banks' initiative in promoting necessary corporate restructuring by smoothing renegotiations on loans from other banks; or 2) it is a reflection of loan roll-overs (or evergreen policies) by main banks that led to delays in the restructuring of less profitable borrowers and allowed other banks to escape.

Although banks were hurt by the non-performing loan problems in the 1990s, it is also essential to understand the impact of the banking crisis on borrowers in order to assess the current state of bank–firm relationships. Referring to the growing literature on this topic, including Brewer et al. (2003) and Miyajima and Yafeh (2003), which focuses on the market response of borrowers to the events of the banking crisis (bank failure, bond down-grading), we also emphasize that the banking crisis has not affected Japanese firms equally. The banking crisis was especially detrimental not only to highly leveraged firms with high bank dependence, but also to firms with low profitability in low-tech industries. These results imply that the market promoted "creative destruction," and thus the banking crisis was not necessarily welfare-decreasing. The "creative destruction" interpretation based on the market model sheds some light on the short-term market response of firms to the banking crisis, but it remains necessary to examine whether the banking crisis substantially altered the behavior of borrowers.

Before assessing the effect of the banking crisis, however, we review the theories of Japanese main banking, and suggest the possibility of a double-edged commitment problem (Aoki 2001). Relational-contingent governance presupposes that banks wield a credible threat to terminate a loan, which is directly related to the bank's financial health. Without this condition, relational-contingent governance is reduced either to short-term-ism (under-investment) or the soft-budget constraint (over-investment).

Bearing these conjectures in mind, we examine whether firms with positive net present value (NPV) suffered from the credit crunch in the 1990s. By investigating the relationship between internal funds and investment, we show that there is little evidence that those with high growth opportunities faced a serious credit crunch among listed firms. We presume, however, that their experience differed from that of small and medium-sized firms with similar high growth opportunities.

Furthermore, we examine whether main banks encouraged corporate restructuring or discouraged profitable projects with slow pay-offs. By estimating the employment adjustment function, we show that contrary to the prevailing view, high bank dependence encouraged corporate restructuring; however, a high level of main bank commitment to client firms played a reverse role. Indeed, a high commitment by the main bank clearly served as an impediment to "creative destruction" in the late 1990s because it reduced the credibility of the threat to terminate loans. Thus, what is unique in the bank–firm relationship of late 1990s Japan is that bank lending in general tended to impose a hard-budget constraint on firms. but a high level of commitment by the main bank often led to a soft-budget constraint on firms with poor performance.

The chapter is organized as follows: the next section summarizes the changes in the debt composition of Japanese firms in the 1990s; section 2.3 explores the effect of the banking crisis on Japanese firms; section 2.4 contains a discussion of the theoretical framework of corporate governance by main banks; section 2.5 examines problems arising from the credit crunch; section 2.6 addresses the role of main banks in the restructuring of firms with declining profits. The last section provides some conclusions and perspectives.

2.2 PUZZLING FEATURES OF CORPORATE FINANCE

2.2.1 Changes in Corporate Finance

Against a backdrop of drastically changing macroeconomic circumstances and deregulation, to what extent did the corporate finance practices of Japanese listed firms shift away from the formerly bank-based pattern during the 1990s? Let us begin to answer this question by summarizing the corporate finance practices of non-financial listed firms in the First Section of the Tokyo Stock Exchange.

Our starting point is the end of FY 1989, when the bubble was about to collapse. After the vigorous use of equity-related financing during the late 1980s, the capital structure of Japanese firms underwent a dramatic transformation. Figure 2.1 provides the time-series changes of the financial status of listed firms from 1980 to 2002, following Aoki et al. (1994). It is clear that the weight of category E2 (exclusive dependence on bond issuance) increased from almost zero (0.2%) in 1980 to 7.8% in 1990, while category N (exclusive dependence on bank borrowing) decreased from 58% in 1980 to 28% in 1991.

Detailed information on capital composition is presented in Table 2.1. First, we see that the debt–asset ratio in 1990 decreased 4.5% points from 1986 with low standard deviation, while borrowing over total debt (the sum of bonds and borrowing) decreased from 69.5% in 1986 to 54.5% in 1990. The decrease in bank dependence was the result of rational choices between banks and firms under deregulation. According to Hoshi et al. (1993) and Miyajima et al. (2002) firms with higher profitability increasingly depended on bonds for their financial resources, while firms with lower profitability continued to depend on bank borrowing during the 1980s. On the other hand, facing the large shift from borrowing to bonds, banks increased loans to small and medium-sized firms, and to the non-manufacturing sector. Many of these loans were collateralized with land. Although such behavior is completely rational ex ante, it was inevitable ex post that the loan portfolios of banks would deteriorate at the end of the asset price bubble given that (1) firms with low profitability remained clients of the

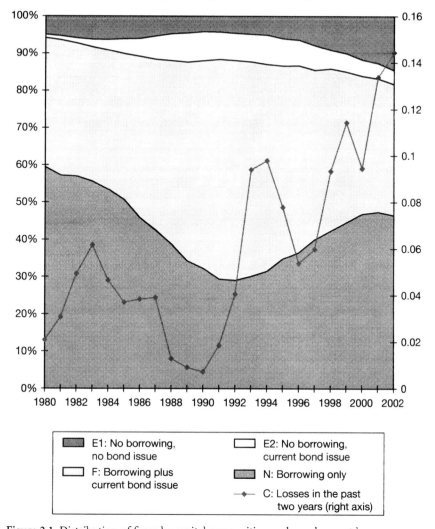

Figure 2.1 Distribution of firms by capital composition and numbers-net loss

banks; and (2) land-collateralized loans to the non-manufacturing sector, and to small and medium-sized firms, increased.

While starting from the initial structure, the listed firms have greatly diversified their capital composition during the 1990s.

Figure 2.1 shows that E1 (no longer dependent on external financial resource) increased from 4.2% in 1990 to 11.7% in 2000, while category N (exclusively dependent upon bank borrowing) increased from 29.4% in 1991 to 46.9% in 2000. Thus, category E2 (exclusively dependent on bond issuance) and F (mixture of bond issuance and bank borrowing) constantly decreased. The aggregate share of category E2 and F in 2000 is 41.4%, compared to 63.6% in 1990.

Table 2.1 Capital Composition, 1986–2000

Year	N	(Bonds +Borrowing)/Assets		Bank Borrowing		Bonds		Bank loans/Debt	
		Mean	Std.Dev.	Mean	Std.Dev.	Mean	Std.Dev.	Mean	Std.Dev.
1986	969	0.310	0.195	0.239	0.205	0.071	0.083	0.695	0.345
1987	992	0.303	0.187	0.219	0.200	0.084	0.089	0.637	0.361
1988	1012	0.293	0.177	0.199	0.191	0.094	0.092	0.601	0.368
1989	1036	0.276	0.168	0.172	0.175	0.104	0.098	0.551	0.370
1990	1059	0.275	0.172	0.169	0.172	0.106	0.097	0.545	0.363
1991	1086	0.291	0.174	0.173	0.172	0.118	0.103	0.541	0.360
1992	1090	0.301	0.182	0.184	0.179	0.117	0.105	0.554	0.355
1993	1092	0.305	0.185	0.192	0.184	0.113	0.105	0.570	0.358
1994	1098	0.299	0.186	0.190	0.187	0.109	0.106	0.571	0.365
1995	1122	0.288	0.194	0.191	0.193	0.097	0.103	0.598	0.368
1996	1154	0.281	0.191	0.187	0.187	0.094	0.103	0.611	0.370
1997	1184	0.275	0.197	0.190	0.192	0.085	0.098	0.635	0.368
1998	1191	0.288	0.208	0.207	0.202	0.081	0.099	0.666	0.354
1999	1261	0.276	0.259	0.203	0.252	0.073	0.096	0.685	0.350
2000	1341	0.251	0.251	0.188	0.242	0.063	0.090	0.707	0.347

Notes: Bank Borrowing = bank borrowing divided by total assets. Bonds = bonds outstanding divided by total assets.

The increasing diversity in the capital composition among firms is also clear from Table 2.1. Even though the debt–asset ratio of firms on average is almost constant, its variance has significantly increased during the past decade, especially since 1997. The standard deviation of the debt–asset ratio in 2000 is 25.1% compared to 17.2% in 1990. The differences in bank dependence between industries also widened in the 1990s. As is well documented, bank dependence on average among firms in manufacturing sectors has decreased since 1993, while firms in non-manufacturing sectors, particularly construction, real estate, and retail, increased bank borrowing. Stressing that the declining profitability of these sectors has been apparent to bankers since 1993, Hoshi (2000) and Peek and Rosengren (2005) suggested that there have been serious credit misallocations since the mid-1990s.

Another feature of corporate finance in the 1990s is the change in debt composition. It is remarkable that the ratio of borrowing to total debt consistently increased, especially from 1997 to 1999. This ratio in 2000 was 70.7%, which is higher than in 1986, when bond issuance was still heavily regulated. Why did the borrowing substitute for bond issuance in this period? Since the demand for new money stagnated during the 1990s, it is highly plausible that bonds issued in the late 1980s were amortized and replaced with bank borrowing. What types of firms continued to raise their funds through bond issuance? And what types of firms switched their financial resources from corporate bonds to bank borrowing?

2.2.2 Debt Choice after Complete Deregulation

One way to explain the determinants of the choice between bonds and borrowing is to stress the comparative advantage of a bank as a monitor. By emphasizing the ability of banks to mitigate the costs of asymmetric information, Diamond (1991) constructed a model that shows firms with less established reputations tended to borrow from banks, while firms that were more successful tended to issue bonds.[5] Thakor and Wilson (1995) discuss another benefit of bank borrowing. Because of its concentrated ownership, the banking sector decides efficiently whether to liquidate or bail out a firm in financial distress by renegotiating the terms of the debt contract with borrowers. Since the ownership of public bonds is dispersed among bondholders, they cannot rescue financially distressed firms as efficiently as banks do. Furthermore, as Chemmanur and Fulghieri (1994) show, a bank devotes more resources to renegotiating with client in financial distress than do bond holders because banks are concerned with their long-term reputation.

Although bank borrowing has benefits for borrowers, there exist offsetting costs that prevent firms from borrowing exclusively from banks. One approach for explaining the cost of bank borrowing suggested by Sharpe (1990) and Rajan (1992) is based on the observation that while a bank can reduce agency problems, the firm-specific information acquired by a bank may create a hold-up problem. Rajan (1992), for example, argues that the informational rents extracted by banks ex post distort the firm's investment by reducing the entrepreneur's returns from successful projects.[6]

Following this theoretical literature, we present the hypothesis that a firm does not use bank borrowing when default risks are sufficiently low or expected future profits are sufficiently high. To empirically test the validity of this hypothesis, we focus on debt choice after 1996, when regulations for bond issuance were completely lifted, and the reverse shift from bonds to borrowing became clear.[7] We use listed firms on the TSE First Section from 1996 to 2000 as our sample and exclude firms in finance and public utilities. The average total assets for our sample firms in 2000 is $24.1 billion and the average number of employees is about 2800, whereas the median of total assets and number of employees is $9 billion and 2000 respectively. Thus, our sample includes not only large firms but also medium-sized firms.

To test our hypothesis, we regress the debt structure on some explanatory variables at the previous year. The Tobit model is used for estimation,

---

[5] Petersen and Rajan (1994) find empirical evidence that close relationships with banks have made it possible for small US firms to borrow at lower costs.

[6] Houston and James (1996) find that large US firms with substantial growth opportunities tend to limit the use of bank debt because of the serious hold-up problem.

[7] Arikawa and Miyajima (2005) present empirical evidence on what determines the Japanese firm's choice between unsecured bonds and bank-borrowing in the 1980s and the early 1990s. They test the hypothesis that the firm does not use bank borrowing with implicit rescue-insurance when the default risk is low or future profitability is sufficiently high.

since dependent variables are truncated at both zero and one. We use the ratio of bank borrowing to total debt as a dependent variable. As an explanatory variable, debt divided by total assets is used as a proxy for likelihood of financial distress.[8] We predict that high values of this variable would encourage a firm to use bank borrowing, while lowly leveraged firms tend to issue more bonds in order to avoid strict monitoring by banks. The volatility of monthly stock returns over the last three years is also included as a proxy of risk. We also adopt Tobin's q to capture the firm's growth opportunity in the same way as Hoshi et al. (1993).[9] Following Wu et al. (2002), we further introduce the square of Tobin's q in the regression to capture the possibility that firms with high growth opportunities but facing large uncertainty demand bank borrowing. In addition, we add the logarithm of assets to the explanatory variables to control for the effect of firm size on debt choice. Lastly, the year dummy variable is included for controlling macroeconomic factors and other exogenous factors such as the banking crisis associated with the downgrading of government bonds, and so on.

The estimation results are shown in Table 2.2. The coefficient of the year dummy in 1997 is significant, and its magnitude is large. The ratio of bank borrowing to total debt in 1997 is roughly 5% to 7% higher than in other years, other variables being equal. Ironically, the banking crisis brought about increasing bank dependence. The coefficient of the log of assets as a proxy for firm size is significantly negative. This means that larger firms can issue bonds more easily by trading on their reputation. Firms' choice of bank borrowing is significantly and positively correlated with the debt–asset ratio. A higher possibility of financial distress implies larger demand for bank borrowing. Similarly, the coefficient of volatility is significantly positive.

On the other hand, the relation between the ratio of bank borrowing to total debt and q is significantly negative. The firm with better prospects tends to move away from bank borrowing. The coefficient of q^2 is significantly positive, and this result is consistent with the result of Wu et al. (2002). The threshold of q is approximately 1.9, although the value of the threshold slightly varies by the specification. Roughly speaking, approximately 5% to 10% of firms out of the entire sample locate to the right hand side of this threshold.

The estimation result that firms with high growth opportunities and low risk are dependent on bond issuance would be consistent with theoretical predictions, and could explain the drastic decrease of bond issuance in the 1990s. While firms that are relatively large with low default risk and high growth opportunities continue to depend on the capital market, other firms even in the First Section of TSE depend on bank borrowing due to decreasing profitability and increasing default risk. Consequently, the importance of bank borrowing has been revived again in the 1990s.

---

[8] Here, we use the market value of land and securities held, but other tangible assets are accounted by book value.

[9] Anderson and Makhija (1999) adopt growth opportunities for investigating the determinants of debt choice.

Table 2.2 Debt Choice after Complete Deregulation

Model	I	II	III	IV
Constant	1.987 ***	2.266 ***	2.225 ***	2.454 ***
	(0.086)	(0.150)	(0.094)	(0.155)
q	−0.137 ***	−0.115 ***	−0.577 ***	−0.477 ***
	(0.020)	(0.021)	(0.073)	(0.075)
q^2			0.150 ***	0.121 ***
			(0.024)	(0.024)
DAR	0.926 ***	0.802 ***	1.003 ***	0.872 ***
	(0.043)	(0.050)	(0.045)	(0.052)
Volatility	0.026 ***	0.028 ***	0.025 ***	0.027 ***
	(0.002)	(0.002)	(0.002)	(0.002)
Size	−0.159 ***	−0.165 ***	−0.157 ***	−0.162 ***
	(0.007)	(0.007)	(0.007)	(0.007)
Y97	0.066 ***	0.071 ***	0.051 **	0.058 ***
	(0.023)	(0.022)	(0.023)	(0.022)
Y98	0.023	0.025	−0.002	0.003
	(0.023)	(0.023)	(0.024)	(0.022)
Y99	0.023	0.023	−0.007	−0.003
	(0.024)	(0.023)	(0.023)	(0.024)
Y00	0.022	0.019	−0.015	−0.012
	(0.024)	(0.024)	(0.025)	(0.025)
Industrial dummy	No	Yes	No	Yes
Log Likelihood	−3937.57	−3837.646	−3917.589	−3825.09
Pseudo R^2	0.1664	0.1876	0.1706	0.1902
N	5309	5309	5309	5309

Notes: As our sample, we use listed companies on the TSE First Section from FY 1996 to 2000. We use a 2-limit Tobit model with dependent variable restricted within [0,1]. The dependent variable is the ratio of bank borrowing to total debt. q is the market-book ratio of the firm, calculated as the ratio of the market value of the firm (the market value of stock plus the book value of total debt) divided by the market value of the assets. DAR is total debt, divided by total assets. Volatility is stock returns volatility. Size is the log of total assets. Standard errors are reported in parentheses. ***, ** and * denote coefficients significant at the 1, 5, and 10% levels.

Second, the positive sign of q^2 suggests that bank borrowing is important for firms with quite high growth opportunities, although such firms are relatively limited in number. They tend to be relatively young, and thus have less of a reputation in the capital market. It implies that there were some firms with high growth opportunities that depended on bank borrowing even in the 1990s, and the banking sector kept lending to these firms even during the banking crisis.

2.2.3 Increasing Main Bank Loan Concentration

Along with increasing dependence on bank borrowing, another remarkable feature of corporate finance among Japanese firms in the 1990s is the increasing degree of concentration of loans from main banks. Is this the result of the strengthening of the bank–firm relationship among Japanese firms? We address this problem below.

We define the largest lender among lending banks as its main bank based on the "financial data base" of the Developmental Bank of Japan. Since main bank ties are characterized as long-term and stable, we check whether the main bank of each firm is the same as five years ago. If a firm has a main bank that has not changed for five years, then we consider it to be a firm with stable main bank ties. Using this definition, we have roughly identified about three-quarters of all firms as having a main bank.

According to Table 2.3, as long as we look at the number of firms with main banks, the stable relationship between banks and firms appears to have been sustained until 1997 and began to change afterward when the banking crisis became serious. From 1998 to 1999, the number of firms with (stable) main banks fell by 82. If we examine the causes of this unravelling of main-bank ties, we find that 14 of the firms had been delisted, 26 cases can be attributed to three bank failures, and the remaining 42 cases were the result of firms' switching of main banks. In this regard, the banking crisis may mark the beginning of the dissolution of the stable relationship between banks and firms.

The right side of Table 2.3 illustrates the overall change of main bank ties in the 1990s. First, the practice of dispatching bank members to client firms seems to be decreasing. This is consistent with the finding that bank intervention became less systematic in the 1990s than before (Hirota and Miyajima 2001). Second, the percentage share held by the main bank is stable, as far as the median and third quartile are concerned (not reported). This result is consistent with the fact that a bank tends to keep the equity holdings of firms when it is their main bank (see Chapter 3). Third, most remarkably, the ratio of borrowing from main banks to assets, *MBR,* has consistently increased with escalating standard deviation since 1991, especially after the financial crisis of 1997. Decomposing this ratio into the ratio of borrowing over assets and the ratio of borrowing from main banks over total borrowing, we find that not only the ratio of borrowing over assets, but also the ratio of borrowing from main banks over total borrowing increased constantly.

Since the non-performing loan problem is quite serious in the construction, real estate, and retail sectors, we compare the main bank relationship in these three sectors with that of relatively better performing sectors such as transportation, electricals, and industrial machinery. We find that the ratio of borrowing from main banks to assets increases in both sectors. However, in the poorer performing sectors, we find a higher percentage of firms with close main bank ties and a higher ratio of borrowing from main banks to assets with generally lower standard deviation, and a larger amount of borrowing compared to the three machinery industries. In fact, bank dependence and main bank commitment increased during the 1990s in these three poorly performing sectors.

How then should we interpret this increase in main bank loan concentration? According to estimated results that use the same model as the one for debt choice, we find that the determinants of main bank loan concentration are almost the same as those for debt choice (not reported). The ratio of borrowing from main banks to assets is negatively sensitive to Tobin's *q,* and positively associated with the debt–asset ratio and volatility of monthly stock returns over the last three years.

Table 2.3 Summary Statistics on the Main Bank Relationship

Panel 1: Entire sample

| | No. of sample firms | No. of firms that have MB | Percentage | Average number of outside directors from main bank | Firms that are identified as having main bank ties | | | | |
| | | | | | Percentage share held by a main bank | | Loans from main bank/total assets | | |
					Mean	Median	Mean	Median	Std.dev
1987	949	714	75.2	0.65	4.19	4.62	5.43	4.40	5.20
1988	977	696	71.2	0.65	4.20	4.63	5.12	4.00	5.44
1989	1002	674	67.3	0.62	4.19	4.56	4.57	3.37	4.95
1990	1024	665	64.9	0.63	4.27	4.65	4.48	3.40	4.28
1991	1021	705	69.0	0.63	4.28	4.69	4.63	3.42	4.84
1992	1016	732	72.0	0.61	4.27	4.69	4.87	3.68	5.21
1993	1008	744	73.8	0.62	4.28	4.68	5.14	3.82	5.20
1994	1002	762	76.0	0.62	4.28	4.69	5.23	3.85	5.53
1995	996	785	78.8	0.60	4.24	4.64	5.23	3.77	5.72
1996	986	798	80.9	0.57	4.26	4.67	5.52	3.93	6.16
1997	968	794	82.0	0.57	4.24	4.65	5.95	4.18	6.52
1998	945	769	81.4	0.53	4.21	4.64	6.73	4.70	7.27
1999	931	687	73.8	0.52	4.18	4.60	7.02	4.75	8.20

Panel 2

| | No. of sample firms | No. of firms that have MB | Percentage | Firms that are identified as having main bank ties | | | | | |
| | | | | Loans from main bank/total assets | | | Loans from MB/total | Loans /total assets | Borrowing |
				Mean	Median	Std.dev	Mean	Mean	Mean
Construction, real estate, and retail									
1989	161	123	76.40	3.92	2.75	6.00	22.75	17.26	56,111
1994	166	140	84.34	5.19	3.56	6.64	23.61	22.00	84,273
1999	158	122	77.22	7.86	4.62	8.80	27.14	28.97	90,525
Transportation, electricals and industrial machinery									
1989	180	112	62.22	3.91	2.46	6.41	25.92	15.08	29,077
1994	186	129	69.35	4.19	2.53	5.63	24.80	16.90	36,262
1999	183	121	66.12	5.62	2.88	11.07	26.51	21.21	34,726

Note: We identify a bank as a main bank (MB) if it is the largest lender at time t and was also the largest lender five years previously.

There are two possible ways of interpreting these results. First, since the concentrated debt holding by main banks helps mitigate free-rider behavior of debt holders when firms are in distress (Bulow and Shoven 1978; Hall and Weinstein 2000), the increase of the ratio of borrowing from main banks to assets could be the result of, and condition for, the main bank's coordination of other lenders, and assumption of the initiative in restructuring borrowers. Second, an increasing commitment to borrowers by main banks may also be possible if banks continued to roll over loans to less profitable borrowers at the expense of their loan portfolio diversification in the hope of recovering loans or to dress up their own balance sheets, while arms-length lenders refrain from lending to borrowers on the verge of bankruptcy.

Put differently, the increase in main bank lending concentration could be interpreted as either: (1) the result of banks taking the initiative in corporate restructuring of client firms by coordinating other banks' loans; or (2) the result of banks rolling over their loans to less profitable firms or adopting "evergreen polices" based on their perverse incentives, thus resulting in credit misallocation and the delay of corporate restructuring of borrowers. We ask later which type of behavior is more common.

2.3 THE IMPACT OF THE BANKING CRISIS ON THE BANK–FIRM RELATIONSHIP

The banking crisis was the most important influence on relational banking in the 1990s in Japan,[10] dealing a severe blow to the banks that had been expected to rescue borrowers in financial distress. What effect did the banking crisis have on the bank–firm relationship?

The poor performance of the banking sector has been a serious issue since the emergence of the *Jusen* (housing loan company insolvency) problem in 1995. Subsequently, the Euro market began to impose a "Japan premium" on Japanese banks (Ito and Harada 2000). Bank stock prices declined relative to other stock prices starting around the end of 1995 (see Chapter 11, Figure 11.2). The price/book value ratio of major banks and local banks on average decreased from 4.04 in the end of 1990 to 2.48 in the end of 1996. The credit rating of major banks was AA or higher in the early 1990s. However, following the *Jusen* crisis and some bank bailouts, many banks were downgraded to A or lower. It was in November 1997 when the financial crisis overwhelmed the Japanese financial system. On November 3, Sanyo Securities defaulted in the inter-bank loan market, and this news was followed by the failure of Hokkaido Takushoku Bank and Yamaichi Securities, one of the four large securities houses. Subsequently, two long-term loan banks, Long Term Credit Bank and Nihon Credit Bank teetered on the brink of bankruptcy and were nationalized in 1998. During this banking crisis, the Japan premium increased, and the stock price decline of banks accelerated. As a result, the price/book value ratio of banks declined further to 1.19 at the end of 1998. The downgrading of banks also continued, and the credit rating of almost all banks was BBB or lower at the end of 1998.[11]

---

[10] For details on the banking crisis and its overall impact, see Hoshi and Kashyap (2001); Nakaso (2001); Peek and Rosengren (2001).

[11] For downgrading of majar banks, see Miyajima and Yafeh (2003), appendix A.

There is a growing literature that focuses on the effect of the banking crisis on client firms. Yamori and Murakami (1999) and Brewer et al. (2003) examine the impact of the news of Japanese bank distress on the stock prices of non-financial institutions, and highlight the negative response of stock prices. Extending this literature, Miyajima and Yafeh (2003) investigate the effect of the banking crisis on Japanese firms using about 800 listed firms on the First Section of the Tokyo Stock Exchange. Their main question is, who has the most to lose?

The empirical analysis is based on the standard event study method; measurement of abnormal stock returns for the sample firms around the date of an event related to the banking crisis. As in all event studies, they begin by estimating the market model.[12] Considering existing intensive studies of the effect of bank failure on client firms, they focus on three different types of events—bank downgrading, government action, and bank mergers—from 1995 to 2000. In their empirical works, estimated cumulative abnormal returns are regressed on firm size, the leverage calculated by the debt over total assets, the bond rating of firm i (the proxy for access to the capital market), and Tobin's q as a proxy of firm quality. They also introduce a dummy variable that is given the value of one if a firm belongs to high R&D industries, following Carlin and Mayer (2003), which predicts that R&D activity rarely relies on bank finance. Finally, the ratio of borrowing from main banks to total assets is introduced to capture the effect of main bank dependence.

The essence of their empirical results is as follows. First, they show that government actions, which are supposed to improve the stability of the banking system, have been important. In particular, injections of capital have constituted "good news" for the typical bank dependent company operating in a low-tech sector (low R&D expenditure), with limited access to bond markets and a high degree of leverage. Similarly, the main beneficiaries of improved banking supervision were also small firms, which were less profitable, in low-tech sectors, with limited access to bond financing (low bond rating) and a high degree of leverage. They conclude that government actions matter, and firms characterized as bank-dependent were more responsive to such government actions.

Second, they show that downgrading announcements of banks' credit ratings appear to have been particularly harmful to highly leveraged companies, where the coefficient is statistically significant with substantial magnitude.[13] Also sensitive to downgrading were firms in low R&D industries with low credit ratings, although its effect was smaller than that of leverage. In addition, there is evidence that large and profitable firms seemed to suffer less from the downgrading of their banks.

---

[12] For each firm, stock returns are regressed on (a constant and) the market returns (Tokyo Stock Exchange Price Index, the TOPIX index), using 40 daily observations between dates −60 and −20 (where date zero is the date of the event in question). The estimated parameters of the regression are then used to generate the predicted return for each firm around the event date. Finally, abnormal returns are defined as the actual stock returns in excess of the model's prediction.

[13] For example, firms with leverage two standard deviations above the mean experienced 7% lower CAR.

Lastly, the stock price of firms with higher dependence on bank borrowing as well as main bank loans responded more negatively to downgrading and more positively to government action.

In sum, the negative stock price response of firms with high leverage and high main bank dependence to the troubles of main banks and the positive response to government action suggest that the bank–firm relationship does matter. More importantly, however, the banking crisis does not affect client firms equally. The banking crisis is especially harmful for low-tech, less profitable firms with difficulty accessing the capital market. The banking crisis might be a catalyst for "creative destruction." In other words, what occurred during the banking crisis is a slow "cleansing process."

The above research examined the short-term market response of borrowing firms to the banking crisis, but it is still unclear whether the banking crisis had a substantial effect on borrowing firm behavior.

2.4 DOUBLE-EDGED COMMITMENT PROBLEMS UNDER THE MAIN BANK SYSTEM

Prior to examining the effect of the banking crisis on the bank–firm relationship, we review the theoretical framework of corporate governance by main banks. Aoki (2001) characterizes the corporate governance by main banks as relational-contingent governance. When the main bank monitors a borrower, the output level determining to whom control rights belong can be divided into four regions: the borrower (insider)-control region, the bank-control region, the bailing-out region, and the termination region. What is unique in this relational-contingent governance is the existence of an output level where the main bank bails out a borrower under financial distress because the rents that banks can extract from the borrower in the future exceed the total costs of rescuing. The debt supplied by the main bank is *de facto* debt with implicit rescue insurance, and a borrowing firm's managers expect rescue by the bank when the firm faces financial distress.

When this relational-contingent governance works well, the effort level of insiders of the firm (managers or workers) increases because they have strong incentives to entrench themselves against bank intervention. On the other hand, the rescue of client firms in financial distress with the lending of additional money and interest reductions would be helpful to avoid the inefficiencies that occur when profitable projects with long time horizons that do not produce immediate returns are discouraged.[14]

However, there exist double-edged commitment problems in relational-contingent governance (Aoki 2001). One problem is the short-term-ism that

---

[14] However, Hanazaki and Horiuchi (2000) denied that main banks played a role in corporate governance, insisting that the efficiency of firms was basically sustained by market competition even in the high growth era.

arises when a firm which should be rescued by the main bank is liquidated due to insufficient expected rents resulting from rescue. Sufficient expected future rents from the rescue of a client firm under financial distress allows the main bank to refinance its client firm.[15] However, if the main bank cannot expect enough rents in the future in exchange for current losses from the rescue of a firm in financial distress, the main bank can terminate a firm that would be bailed out socially. There are several possible reasons that rescues of client firms may yield insufficient future rents: (1) high monitoring costs; (2) competition with other sources of funding; and (3) the presence of incentives to contract the volume of lending. In the context of 1990s Japan, the third reason was especially important. If the benefits from reducing the volume of loans outweigh the rents from rescuing a client firm under financial distress with further lending because of BIS regulations, the main bank might prefer to terminate a firm instead of rescuing it. This scenario occurs during a credit crunch. In this situation, borrowing firms are likely to refrain from investing in promising projects with long time horizons for fear of being terminated by the main bank unless they have sufficient internal funds. The financial constraint affects the behavior of the borrowing firm, and the result can be under-investment.

Another problem is the failure of the main bank to commit to terminating loans to a client firm in the bankruptcy region because the main bank expects extremely high rents (soft-budget problem). Under this scenario, the main bank steps in to rescue a firm that ought to be liquidated. If the threat of termination were not credible, it would be highly plausible that the borrower engage in over-investment, because it can depend on rescue by the main bank. One reason why the main bank might not be able to commit to liquidating a poorly performing borrower is that both main bank and borrower could be better off refinancing loans ex post when the initial lending is treated as a sunk cost (Dewatripont and Maskin 1995). Another reason is that the main bank may have an incentive to dress up its balance sheet. Suppose that a bank balance sheet is deteriorating, and the bank is highly committed to an unprofitable borrower. It may decide to supply additional lending to that borrower not on the basis of an evaluation of the borrower's reconstruction potential, but rather as a means of avoiding non-performing loans in order to meet the capital requirements under the Basel Accord. This perverse incentive to lend to the unprofitable borrower is even stronger when the bank is the main bank of that borrower because the loans from the main bank are subordinated to loans from other banks, and the loans are often substantial in size and thus critical to the main bank's balance sheet.

In light of these hypotheses and the market response to the banking crisis discussed in the previous section, we examine two empirical problems:

---

[15] The future rents come from various sources such as the bank's informational advantages that accrue from monitoring of a client firm's future profitability (Von Thadden 1995), market power over the client firm that provides future monopoly rents to a bank (Petersen and Rajan 1994), and the reputation rent that the main bank extracts by building a reputation for commitment to rescue a firm in financial distress (Sharp 1990; Boot et al. 1993; Aoki 1994; Dinc 2000).

1.   If most firms that were sensitive to the banking crisis were less profitable and had less growth potential, reducing bank lending to them was not detrimental to the Japanese economy. However, if that were not the case, then the welfare implications were quite serious. Thus, the question to ask is whether firms with positive NPV were free from the financial constraint problem or not.

2.   If the market response encouraged "creative destruction," then did high bank dependence actually drive corporate restructuring, and did the main bank assume the initiative in that process? Or, did the high bank dependence undermine incentives for firms to take necessary corporate restructuring measures?

2.5 SHORT-TERM-ISM AND UNDER-INVESTMENT

The first problem is addressed in the large volume of literature that treats the issue of under-investment from various perspectives (particularly during Japan's credit crunch in the 1990s). One popular approach focuses on the supply side, examining whether the non-performing loan problem or risk-based capital ratios really brought about the contraction of bank lending. If that were the case, then we could conclude that the under-investment problem was caused by the credit crunch in the banking sector. For instance, Itoh and Sasaki (2002) show that banks with lower capital ratios tended to issue more subordinated debt and to reduce lending. Honda (2002) and Montgomery (2005) examine the differential effects of the Basel Accords on domestic and international banks, and show that international banks with relatively low capital ratios tended to contract their overall assets and shift their asset portfolios out of loans and into safe assets such as government bonds. These studies show that there was a contraction of lending in Japan in the 1990s because the banking sector sought to keep risk-based capital ratios at a high level. However, one study argues that the contraction in lending was of short duration, and limited to the few years immediately following the bankruptcies of large banks (Woo 1999).

The second approach is to look at the demand side of loans by addressing whether the credit crunch affects the real economy or not. Motonishi and Yoshikawa (1999) estimate investment functions for large and small firms using the Bank of Japan Diffusion Indices (DIs) of real profitability and bank's willingness to lend as the explanatory variables. Employing the latter variables as an indicator of possible financing constraints, they find that the financing constraints significantly affect investments of small firms but not those of large firms. Thus, they conclude that the credit crunch does not explain the long stagnation of investment throughout the 1990s, but it had a negative impact on investment during 1997–98.

To further investigate the credit crunch problem in the 1990s, we estimate the standard investment function with cash flow developed by Fazzari et al. (1988). To avoid heterogeneity among samples, we use manufacturing firms listed on the TSE First Section from 1993 to 2000 as the sample. The estimation formula is as follows:

(2) $$I_t = f(q_{t-1}, CF_t, SUB, CF^*H(L)Q, YD)$$

Here, I is the investment level, which is calculated as depreciation plus the difference of fixed assets from period $t-1$ to period t divided by fixed assets. q is Tobin's q. CF is cash flow calculated as the depreciation plus after-tax profit minus dividends and bonuses paid to directors divided by total assets. CF is introduced to capture the cash flow constraint. For controlling the effect of parent companies on the investment of related firms, we introduce the SUB dummy if more than 15% of the firm's issued stock is held by other single non-financial institutions.

Using this model, we perform the credit crunch test. If firms with positive NPV face liquidity constraint, their investment is seriously constrained by their internal funds. In order to test this hypothesis, we divide sample firms into three sub-groups based on a three-year average of a firm's Tobin's q prior to selected firm year. Firms are defined as those with high growth opportunities (hereafter HQ firms) if their Tobin's q is higher than the third quartile of the whole sample, while firms are defined as those with low growth opportunities (hereafter LQ firms) if their Tobin's q is lower than the first quartile of the whole sample. Then, we introduce the interaction term between the HQ and LQ dummy and CF in regression. The estimation results of manufacturing firms from 1993–2000 are reported in Table 2.4.

The coefficient of CF is significantly positive in columns 1 and 2. When we examine the interaction term of CF with HQ and LQ dummy (columns 3 and 4), there is no evidence that the investment of HQ firms is more sensitive to their cash flow than that of LQ firms. Rather, the sensitivity of investment in LQ firms is much higher than that of high growth opportunities. These results imply that firms with low growth opportunities presumably face the free cash flow problems in the sense of Jensen (1986), whereas firms with high growth opportunities could invest regardless of their cash flow, and consequently they are free from the constraint of internal funds. This is also consistent with the result of Miyajima et al. (2002), which shows that physical investment of firms with high growth opportunities were relatively free from financial constraints, being different from R&D investment.

The investment in HQ firms is less constrained by their internal funds if we limit sample firms to the shorter sub-period (1993–95, 1995–97, and 1997–2000). By 1997, there is no evidence that investment of HQ firms faced cash flow constraints (columns 5 and 6). It is true that the HQ firm is financially constrained during the banking crisis period (1997–2000). However, the coefficient of CF in HQ firms is much lower than that of LQ firms.[16]

This result is consistent with the market response estimation in section three where profitable firms suffered less from the banking crisis (downgrading). Furthermore, the result is also consistent with the debt choice estimation in section 2.2, where bank borrowing is important for firms with quite high growth opportunities, which implies that banks supplied money to firms with high

---

[16] Ogawa (2003) points out that small firms faced the debt overhang problem in the 1990s. Since non-listed firms with high growth opportunities have no financial options except bank borrowing, they may face such problems to a more serious degree, given a less developed capital market.

Table 2.4 Internal Funds and Investment

Model	1	2	3	4	5 93–95	6 95–97	7 97–2000
q	0.052 ***	0.047 ***	0.053 ***	0.049 ***	0.072 *	0.092 **	0.047 ***
	(0.011)	(0.011)	(0.011)	(0.011)	(0.042)	(0.036)	(0.016)
CF	0.014 ***	0.009 ***	0.012	0.009	0.154 ***	−0.041	−0.008
	(0.004)	(0.004)	(0.009)	(0.009)	(0.053)	(0.027)	(0.01)
dY		0.300 **		0.297 ***			
		(0.027)		(0.027)			
SUB	−0.032	−0.033	−0.035	−0.035	0.073	0.050	−0.021
	(0.023)	(0.023)	(0.023)	(0.023)	(0.07)	(0.054)	(0.042)
HQ*CF			−0.001	−0.003	−0.142 ***	0.049	0.028 **
			(0.01)	(0.01)	(0.052)	(0.033)	(0.012)
LQ*CF			0.070 ***	0.061 ***	0.073	0.117 ***	0.064 **
			(0.02)	(0.02)	(0.096)	(0.045)	(0.024)
SIZE	−0.082 ***	−0.048 ***	−0.087 ***	−0.054 **	−0.347 ***	−0.102	−0.305 ***
	(0.023)	(0.023)	(0.023)	(0.023)	(0.071)	(0.075)	(0.042)
Year Dummy	Yes	Yes	Yes	Yes	Yes	Yes	Yes
Adj.R^2	0.0245	0.0486	0.0273	0.0508	0.0427	0.0193	0.0633
N	5744	5744	5744	5744	2113	2142	2917

Notes: The table presents results of fixed-effect regressions for the sample of all listed firms in manufacturing industries in the First Section of TSE. Column 5 uses sample from 1993 to 1995. Column 6 uses sample from 1995 to 1997. Column 7 uses sample from 1997 to 2000. Firms are defined as firms with high growth opportunities (*HQ*), if their q is higher than the third quartile of the entiresample, while firms are defined as those with low growth opportunities (*LQ*), if q is lower than the first quartile. Independent variables: *I* is the investment level, which is calculated as depreciation plus the difference of fixed assets from period t − 1 to period t divided by fixed assets. q is Tobin's q. *CF* is cash flow calculated as the depreciation plus after-tax profits minus dividends and bonuses paid to directors divided by total assets. *SUB* is a dummy variable, which is one if over 15% of a firm's issued stock were held by another non-financial institution, and otherwise zero. *SIZE* is log of total asset. Standard errors, asymptopically robust to heteroskedasticity, are reported in parentheses. ***, ** and * denote coefficients significant at the 1%, 5%, and 10% levels.

growth opportunities even during the banking crisis. Thus, all the results support Hoshi and Kashyap's (2004) prediction that firms with high q could raise money through various measures, and were basically free from the credit crunch. There is no doubt that small and medium-sized firms may have faced a credit crunch, which was most serious during 1997–98. However, large firms (firms listed on the TSE) generally did not.

2.6 CORPORATE RESTRUCTURING

There are several approaches to examining relational-contingent governance in Japanese firms in terms of the threat of termination to the borrowing firm. The first approach is to focus on the relation between profitability of the borrowing firms and the loan increase, which suggests the existence of a soft-budget problem or credit misallocation by banks. For example, Peek and Rosengren (2005) find that banks increased credit to poorly performing firms between 1993 and 1999, and main banks were more likely to lend to these firms than other banks. Furthermore, they show that this credit misallocation was more frequent when the bank's balance sheet was weak.[17]

The second approach is to examine corporate restructuring when a firm faces a serious earnings decline. Hoshi et al. (1990) have pioneered this field by documenting that firms with close main bank ties maintain investment levels comparable to independent firms even when the firms faced financial distress in the structural adjustment period (1978–82). On the other hand, Kang and Shivdasani (1997) show that firms with closer main bank ties reduced their assets even more during the business upturn of the late 1980s. Although the role of main banks that they reported seems to be diametrically opposed, they stress the positive side of main banks based on private information: the avoidance of inefficient early liquidation (Hoshi et al. 1990) and exertion of appropriate discipline on client firms (Kang and Shivdasani 1997).

However, since both works did not go beyond the late 1980s, it is still an open question whether the main bank system played such a significant role in the late 1990s. To answer this question, we estimate the employment adjustment function and investigate whether firms with close main bank ties implemented necessary corporate restructuring when they faced serious performance declines. In the estimation equation, the dependent variable is the percentage change of employment. For independent variables, we use the following: log of the percentage change of employment, and change of real sales growth rate to control the effect of firm performance. To test the effect of the bank–firm relationship on corporate restructuring, we introduce the ratio of debt to assets, the ratio of bank borrowing to debt, and the ratio of borrowing from main banks to assets.

---

[17] Another approach is to test whether presidential turnover or banks' dispatching of managers to client firms is systematically related to corporate performance (see Introduction, this volume).

Furthermore, following Kang and Shivdasani (1997), we produce the dummy variable, *NAD*, as a proxy of the necessity of corporate restructuring. This dummy variable equals one if the three-year average of operational profits from 1993–95 of sample firms is 50% lower than that of 1988–90, and otherwise it is zero. We define a firm as facing the need to restructure if this dummy variable equals one. Hereafter, we consider the firm with this dummy variable equaling one an *NAD* firm.

By focusing on the interaction term between *NAD* and debt composition variables, we can test whether the (main) bank urges these firms to take the necessary restructuring measures or merely helps them to put off solving the problem. Table 2.5 presents the distribution and descriptive statistics of sample firms. Being different from Kang and Shivdasani (1997), which addresses the business upturns (the late 1980s), our study finds that the number of firms that faced significant declines in operational profits is larger in the late 1990s. Roughly speaking, two-thirds of sample firms are identified as firms that needed to reconstruct their businesses. Looking at industry distribution, as expected, we found that a large number of these firms were in the construction and retail industries. However, it should be noted that textiles, iron and steel, and even the machine sector (electrical and transportation) included large numbers of firms with performance declines. In Panel 2, we can find that the ratio of employment reduction is much larger for *NAD* firms, and leverage, bank dependence and main bank loan concentration are also much higher in the *NAD* firms. Estimation results are summarized in Table 2.6.

The coefficient of the change of real sale growth is positive and highly significant for all estimations. A one percent decrease in this variable is associated with approximately 0.13–0.2% employment reduction. On the other hand, the coefficient of the debt–asset ratio is negative and significant. The leverage has a negative effect on employment as is normally expected. However, there is no difference between firms with restructuring need and other firms in this effect, judging from the interaction term between the debt–asset ratio and *NAD* in column 2.[18] The coefficient of the ratio of bank borrowing to debt is significantly negative in general (column 3), but no difference between *NAD* firms and others firms was found in column 4. Thus, we cannot determine whether high leverage and high bank dependence promote "creative destruction" in client firms.

However, once we add the ratio of borrowing from main banks over assets to the regression, the coefficient of the interaction term between the ratio of bank borrowing over debt and *NAD* is significantly negative and the coefficient of the ratio of borrowing from main banks over assets and *NAD* is positive in column 6. This result contrasts with column 5, where the coefficient of the ratio of borrowing from main banks over assets is not significant. That is, among firms facing a serious need to restructure, bank dependence was associated with rapid employment adjustment,

---

[18] This result is supported by the comparison of the *DAR* of *NAD* firms with that of other firms in columns 7 and 8.

Table 2.5 Summary Statistics on Employment Adjustment

Industry	No. of firms NAD=1 & NAD=0	No. of firms NAD=1	Percentage=A	No of firms NAD=0	Percentage=B	A/B
Construction	94	75	11.33%	19	4.97%	2.28
Electric equipment	116	75	11.33%	41	10.73%	1.06
Machinery manufacturing	92	70	10.57%	22	5.76%	1.84
Chemical manufacturing	97	50	7.55%	47	12.30%	0.61
Retail trade	56	43	6.50%	13	3.40%	1.91
Textile	48	40	6.04%	8	2.09%	2.89
Wholesale trade	65	40	6.04%	25	6.54%	0.92
Transportation equipment	55	39	5.89%	16	4.19%	1.41
Iron and steel	35	31	4.68%	4	1.05%	4.47
Food	56	24	3.63%	32	8.38%	0.43
Stone, clay, glass, and concrete products	27	19	2.87%	8	2.09%	1.37
Metal products	26	19	2.87%	7	1.83%	1.57
Miscellaneous manufacturing industries	26	17	2.57%	9	2.36%	1.09
Service	26	16	2.42%	10	2.62%	0.92
Non-ferrous metal	24	15	2.27%	9	2.36%	0.96
Computer and electronic product manufacturing	17	13	1.96%	4	1.05%	1.88
Paper manufacturing	17	11	1.66%	6	1.57%	1.06
Rail and truck	27	11	1.66%	16	4.19%	0.40
Real estate	18	10	1.51%	8	2.09%	0.72
Warehousing	12	8	1.21%	4	1.05%	1.15
Pharmaceuticals	32	7	1.06%	25	6.54%	0.16
Total	966	633		333		

Notes: **Panel 1. Industry distribution of firms facing serious earnings declines**
The sample firms are all listed firms in the First Section of TSE except finance and public utilities. Firms are identified as NAD firms if their three-year average of operational profits from 1993–95 was 50% lower than the average for 1988–1990, and otherwise zero.

	Total		NAD=1		NAD=0	
	Mean	Std.dev	Mean	Std.dev	Mean	Std.dev
ΔL	−0.030	0.145	−0.043	0.101	−0.020	0.077
ΔS	0.002	0.125	−0.014	0.117	0.020	0.108
SUB	0.318	0.466	0.290	0.454	0.268	0.443
DAR	0.282	0.197	0.312	0.186	0.268	0.211
LDR	0.627	0.365	0.673	0.345	0.548	0.379
MBR	0.046	0.061	0.053	0.063	0.040	0.063
NMBR	0.146	0.151	0.172	0.153	0.127	0.151

Notes: **Panel 2. Descriptive statistics**
ΔL is the percentage change of employment, ΔS is the change of real sales growth. SUB is a dummy variable, which is one if over 15% of a firm's issued stock were held by another non-financial institution, and otherwise zero. DAR is bonds and borrowing, divided by the market value of the assets. LDR is the ratio of borrowing to the sum of borrowing and bonds. MBR is the ratio of loans from main bank to total assets. NMBR is the ratio of non-main bank debt (bank borrowing plus bonds) to total asset.

Table 2.6 Estimation Results of Employment Adjustment Function in Firms

Model	Discipline by debt		Bank dependence		Main bank loan concentration		NAD=0	NAD=1	Main bank loan vs. arm's length debt
	1	2	3	4	5	6	7	8	9
ΔL_{t-1}	0.093 *** (0.023)	0.101 *** (0.025)	0.092 *** (0.027)	0.093 *** (0.027)	0.091 *** (0.027)	0.090 *** (0.028)	0.090 *** (0.034)	0.078 ** (0.036)	0.100 *** (0.025)
ΔS_{t-1}	0.171 *** (0.063)	0.147 *** (0.032)	0.123 ** (0.061)	0.139 *** (0.032)	0.123 ** (0.061)	0.139 *** (0.032)	0.201 *** (0.059)	0.115 *** (0.038)	0.147 *** (0.032)
SUB	−0.026 (0.034)	0.012 (0.027)	−0.015 (0.035)	0.012 (0.030)	−0.016 (0.035)	0.014 (0.031)	−0.012 (0.048)	0.027 (0.037)	0.013 (0.028)
DAR_{t-1}	−0.182 ** (0.072)	−0.223 ** (0.103)	−0.161 ** (0.073)	−0.228 ** (0.105)	−0.192 *** (0.065)	−0.174 ** (0.087)	−0.184 ** (0.079)	−0.163 *** (0.073)	
$DAR \times NAD$		0.168 (0.121)		0.180 (0.124)		0.019 (0.110)			
LDR_{t-1}			−0.029 ** (0.014)	0.001 (0.016)	−0.036 ** (0.016)	0.012 (0.016)	0.008 (0.016)	−0.038 ** (0.017)	
$LDR \times NAD$				−0.013 (0.019)		−0.052 ** (0.023)			
MBR_{t-1}					0.134 (0.173)	−0.233 (0.161)	−0.192 (0.155)	0.457 ** (0.227)	−0.389 ** (0.180)
$MBR \times NAD$						0.711 ** (0.280)			0.651 ** (0.264)
$NMBR_{t-1}$									−0.178 ** (0.085)
$NMBR \times NAD$									0.043 (0.105)
Year Dummy	Yes	Yes	Yes	Yes	Yes	Yes	Yes	Yes	Yes
AR(2)	1.80	1.56	1.54	1.07	1.53	1.10	0.00	1.28	1.60
Sargan test(d.f.)	76.03(56)	153.44(56)	82.84(56)	164.3(56)	82.97(56)	164.19(56)	108(56)	194.84(56)	153.08(56)
Wald test(d.f.)	112.03(9)	117.26(10)	93.6(10)	108.59(12)	94.25(11)	114.81(14)	54.62(11)	76.55(11)	123.45(12)
N	6586	6100	6221	5802	6221	5802	2037	3765	6100

Notes: Sample is composed of all listed firms in the First Section of TSE except financial institutions and public utilities. ΔL is the percentage changes of employment, ΔL_{t-1} is the lag of ΔL, ΔS is the change of real sales growth. SUB is a dummy variable, which is one if over 15% of a firm's issued stock were held by another non-financial institution, and otherwise zero. NAD is a dummy variable which is equal to one if the three-year average of operational profits from 1993–95 of sample firms was 50% lower than the average for 1988–90, and otherwise zero. DAR is the sum of bonds and borrowings divided by the market value of the assets. LDR is the ratio of borrowings to the sum of borrowing and bond. MBR is the ratio of loans from the main bank to total assets. $NMBR$ is the ratio of non-main bank debt (bank borrowing plus bonds) to total assets. All regressions include year dummy. Arellano–Bond dynamic panel estimation is used. Standard errors, asymptotically robust-to-heteroskedasticity, are reported in parentheses. AR(2) are the results of the test for second-order autocorrelation. Sargan tests are only valid in the case of i.i.d. errors. ***, **, and * denote coefficients significant at the 1%, 5%, and 10% levels.

while the high concentration of borrowing from main banks was associated with slow employment adjustment.

This contrast between the results for bank dependence and main bank loan concentration is also clear in columns 7 and 8, where we divide sample firms into firms that need restructuring and other firms, and estimate the same model separately. The coefficient of the ratio of bank borrowing to debt is significantly negative and that of the ratio of borrowing from main banks to assets is positive in *NAD* firms.

In order to disentangle the effect of the loans from main banks and other debt more clearly, we introduce the ratio of non-main bank debt to total borrowing. Here non-main bank debt includes borrowing from banks except main banks and bonds; we could regard this as arm's length debt. In column 9, we find the ratio of non-main bank debt to total borrowing is significantly negative, which suggests that firms are more likely to downsize their employment when they depend more on non-main bank borrowing, or arm's length debt. On the other hand, the interaction term between the ratio of borrowing from main banks to assets and *NAD* dummy is significantly positive, while the ratio of borrowing from main banks to assets itself is negative.[19] This result suggests that the high main bank loan concentration in non-*NAD* firms might be associated with "excessive" reduction of employment,[20] whereas that of *NAD* firms is definitely associated with a relatively higher growth rate of employment.

The estimation result reported above still awaits further robustness checks by using assets instead of employment, or consolidated data instead of the current unconsolidated data. But we can suggest the following implications in view of the existing literature.

First, recent studies such as Peek and Rosengren (2005) argue that Japanese banks tend to bail out nearly bankrupt firms by evergreening old loans and keeping their ties with unprofitable firms. Caballero et al. (2004) called these artificially surviving firms "zombies". Our estimation result suggests that the evergreen policy taken by banks and the resulting "zombies" might not be so prevalent among Japanese firms because high bank dependence tends to reduce the growth rate of employment in *NAD* firms. The high bank dependent firms, whose stock prices are sensitive to the troubles of the banking sector, also reduce their employment levels when they face serious performance declines. In the midst of the banking crisis, bank loans actually imposed hard-budget constraints on client firms. In this regard, banks played a disciplinary role, although it was not the result of conscious discipline imposed by the banks. Thus, what has occurred after the banking crisis is a slow "cleansing" process as Miyajima and Yafeh (2003) have emphasized.

Second however, what the current literature insists upon is certainly on the mark if we limit bank-dependent firms to firms whose main bank loan

---

[19] When we used the fixed effect model, the result was unchanged.

[20] This interpretation is not so plausible, because the negative sign of MBR in columns 6 and 7 is not significant. Even if this were the case, the reduction of employment would not necessarily be efficiency reducing.

concentrations are high. The higher concentration of bank loans to firms with poor performance gives stronger incentives to the main bank not to push the necessary restructuring measures onto the client to avoid a serious capital shortage. To put it differently, a delay in corporate restructuring is likely to occur if and only if the main bank loan concentration (commitment) is sufficiently high by undermining the credibility of the threat to terminate. Returning to two interpretations of the increase in main loan concentration in the late 1990s, the result of the employment adjustment function suggests that it is more likely to be associated with main banks' evergreen policies on old loans, and not with their taking the initiative in the restructuring of borrowers.

In sum, our results imply that the main bank has undergone a transition of its role. Under state-contingent governance, the main bank is expected to help firms avoid inefficient corporate restructuring, and by doing so, to maintain firm-specific skills, while fostering appropriate discipline for firms facing serious earnings declines. However, our results show that the main bank urges some firms to reduce employment, while allowing firms facing larger performance declines to delay necessary restructuring if its commitment to these firms is high.

2.7 CONCLUDING REMARKS

After financial deregulation and the drastic changes in the macroeconomic situation since the late 1990s, the financial system in Japan has grown more heterogeneous compared to the high-growth era when the main bank system dominated.

Among listed firms in the First Section of the TSE, a certain percentage of firms with high growth opportunities continued to depend on capital markets. Firms with easy access to capital markets in high-tech sectors were relatively free from the banking crisis of 1997. Roughly speaking, one-third of all listed firms (with bond ratings of A or higher) now depend on capital markets for their financing. They occupied approximately 70% of the total firm value, 60% of the total book assets, and over 50% of total employees out of all firms on the First Section of the TSE. For those firms, short-term loans are currently supplied by banks based on an explicit contract (credit line). Although bank subsidiaries engaged in bond-related services (Hamao and Hoshi 2000) and the credit lines were normally supplied by former main banks, it is safe to conclude that main banks became less important to those firms with bond ratings of A or higher. Looking at the corporate governance side, these firms have increasingly been under market pressure. Among these firms, approximately 20% of the issued shares are now held by foreign institutional investors, and they are actively carrying out corporate board reforms as well as information disclosure measures (see Chapter 11). Thus, market pressure by institutional investors and bond ratings are now playing a major role in corporate governance for those firms.

On the other hand however, the rest of the firms continued to depend, or rather increased their dependence, on bank borrowing in the 1990s. These firms fell into two different categories. In the first category were firms with low growth opportunities for whom the main bank was potentially expected to serve a disciplinary role to prevent them from over-investment or to encourage corporate restructuring. In the second category were firms that faced high growth opportunities, but found it difficult to access capital markets. For these firms, the main bank was supposed to play a facilitating role in corporate finance by mitigating asymmetric information problems.

The banking troubles of the 1990s possibly impacted on the role that main banks played for both types of firms. Firms with high growth opportunities were basically free from any financial constraints. On the other hand, as long as the market responded to the events related to the banking crisis, firms in low-tech sectors with low profitability and difficulty accessing the capital markets were harmed more than the large firms in high-tech sectors with high q and easy access to capital markets. In this sense, the banking crisis may not necessarily have had a welfare-reducing effect, and may have encouraged "creative destruction."

Under the inexorable process of "creative destruction," however, the extent of the corporate restructuring was highly dependent on the debt composition and the main bank loan concentration. Differing from the interpretations of recent studies, we suggest that high bank dependence has encouraged corporate restructuring. However, the main bank commitment to client firms played a reverse role. Rolling over its loans to client firms, the main bank tended to depress employment reduction in firms that needed to reconstruct their businesses. To put it differently, the high commitment of the main bank clearly became an impediment to "creative destruction" in the late 1990s by reducing the credibility of the threat to terminate loans. Thus, what is unique in the bank–firm relationship of late 1990s Japan is that bank lending imposed a hard-budget constraint on firms while main bank commitment imposed a soft-budget constraint on firms with poor performance.

In this sense, relational banking in Japan is not necessarily on the way out. Given increasing bank dependence even among listed firms, it is still highly important that, based on their private information, banks supply money to firms with high growth opportunities but with difficulty accessing capital markets, and take the initiative in restructuring firms with low growth opportunities. Since one of the reasons for the functional change in the main bank system is the declining soundness of the banking sector, it is clear that, as many observers have insisted, the restructuring of this sector is highly urgent.

There is some good news on this front. First, after the banking crisis was partially eased with capital infusions from the government, a series of mergers among major banks occurred and their health has begun to recover. Second, the program of financial revitalization (*Kinyu-saisei*) in 2002 is now underway, and non-performing loans are down from peak levels.[21] Third, private equity plays an

---

[21] The number of non-performing loans (major banks base) declined from ¥27.6 trillion (9.4% of total loans) at the peak in March 2002 to ¥13.6 trillion (5.5%) in March 2004.

increasingly important role in the corporate restructuring process, complementary to the main bank bail-out mechanism, and bankruptcy procedures are well established under recent regulatory reforms. All these current changes may contribute to restoring the health of banks and their monitoring capabilities, which, in turn, will make their ability to threaten client firms with termination credible.

Thus, the optimistic scenario is that the bank–firm relationship in Japan is now in transition toward a healthier and more competitive one that is sustainable over the long term. An increasing commitment by banks to client firms could help them to promote corporate restructuring by mitigating free-rider problems. And once their health and monitoring capabilities are restored, banks will be in a stronger position to extend funds to encourage restructuring while also supplying new money to firms with high growth opportunities. Of course, nobody knows how long the transition will take.

REFERENCES

Anderson, C. W. and Makhija, A. K. (1999). 'Deregulation, Disintermediation, and Agency Costs of Debt: Evidence from Japan,' *Journal of Financial Economics*, 51: 309–39.

Aoki, M. (1994). 'Monitoring Characteristics of the Main Bank System,' in M. Aoki and H. Patrick (eds.), *The Japanese Main Bank System: Its Relevancy for Developing and Transforming Economies*. Oxford: Oxford University Press, 109–41.

—— (2001). *Toward a Comparative Institutional Analysis*. Cambridge, MA: MIT Press.

—— Dinc, S. (2000). 'Relational Financing as an Institution and Its Viability under Competition,' in M. Aoki and G. R. Saxonhouse (eds.), *Finance, Governance, and Competitiveness in Japan*. Oxford: Oxford University Press, 19–42.

—— H. Patrick, and P. Sheard (1994). 'The Japanese Main Bank System: An Introductory Overview,' in M. Aoki and H. Patrick (eds.), *The Japanese Main Bank System: Its Relevancy for Developing and Transforming Economies*. Oxford: Oxford University Press, 1–50.

Arikawa, Y. and H. Miyajima (2005). 'Relationship Banking and Debt Choice: Evidence from Japan,' *Corporate Governance: An International Review*, 13: 408–18.

Boot, A. and V. A. Thakor (2000). 'Can Relationship Banking Survive Competition?' *Journal of Finance*, 55: 679–713.

—— S. Greenbaum, and V. A. Thakor (1993). 'Reputation and Discretion in Financial Contracting,' *American Economic Review*, 83: 1165–63.

Brewer, E., H. Genay, W. Hunter, and G. Kaufman (2003). 'The Value of Banking Relationships during a Financial Crisis: Evidence from Failures of Japanese Banks,' *Journal of the Japanese and International Economies*, 17: 233–62.

Bulow, J. and J. Shoven (1978). 'The Bankruptcy Decision,' *Bell Journal of Economics*, 9: 437–56.

Caballero, R., T. Hoshi, and A. Kashyap (2004). 'Zombie Lending and Depressed Restructuring in Japan.' Unpublished manuscript. University of Chicago, Chicago, IL.

Carlin, W. and C. Mayer (2003). 'Finance, Investment, and Growth,' *Journal of Financial Economics*, 69: 191–226.

Chemmanur, T. and P. Fulghieri (1994). 'Reputation, Renegotiation, and Publicly Held Traded Debt,' *Review of Financial Studies*, 7: 475–506.

Diamond, D. (1991). 'Monitoring and Reputation: The Choice between Bank Loans and Directly Placed Debt,' *Journal of Political Economy*, 99: 689–721.

Dinc, S. (2000). 'Bank Reputation, Bank Commitment and the Effects of the Competition in Credit Markets,' *Review of Financial Studies*, 13: 781–812.

Dewatripont, M. and E. Maskin (1995). 'Credit and Efficiency in Centralized and Decentralized Economies,' *Review of Economic Studies*, 62: 541–55.

Fazzari, S. M., R. G. Hubbard, and B. C. Petersen (1988). 'Financing Constraints and Corporate Investment,' *Brookings Papers on Economic Activity*, 1: 141–95.

Hall, B. and D. Weinstein (2000). 'Main Banks, Creditor Concentration, and the Resolution of Financial Distress in Japan,' in M. Aoki and G. R. Saxonhouse (eds.), *Finance, Governance, and Competitiveness in Japan*. Oxford: Oxford University Press, 64–80.

Hamao, Y. and T. Hoshi (2000). *Bank Underwriting of Corporate Bonds: Evidence from Post-1994 Japan*. California: University of California at San Diego.

Hanazaki, M. and A. Horiuchi (2000). 'Is Japan's Financial System Efficient?' *Oxford Review of Economic Policy*, 16: 61–73.

Hellmann, T., K. Murdock, and J. Stiglitz (1997). 'Financial Restraint: Toward a New Paradigm,' in M. Aoki., K. Murdock, and M. Okuno-Fujiwara (eds.), *The Role of Government in East Asian Economic Development: Comparative Institutional Analysis*. Oxford: Oxford University Press, 163–207.

Hirota, S. and Miyajima, H. (2001). 'Ginko kainyu gata Gabanansu wa Henka shitaka (Is Bank-based Governance Really Changing? Empirical Test for 1970s to 1990s),' *Gendai Fainansu* (in Japanese).

Honda, Y. (2002). 'The Effects of Basle Accord on Bank Credit: The Case of Japan,' *Applied Econometrics*, 34: 1233–9.

Horiuchi, A. (1995). 'Financial Structure and Managerial Discretion in the Japanese Firm: An Implication of the Surge of Equity-Related Bond,' in: M. Okabe (ed.), *The Structure of the Japanese Economy*. London: Macmillan.

Hoshi, T. (2000). 'Naze Nihon wa Ryudo-sei no wana kara nogarerarenainoka? (Why is the Japanese Economy unable to get out of a liquidity trap?)' in M. Fukao and H. Yoshikawa (eds.), *Zero Kinri to Nihon Keizai* (Zero Interest Rate and the Japanese Economy). Tokyo: Nihon Keizai Shimbunsha, 233–66.

—— A. Kashyap (2001). *Corporate Finance and Governance in Japan*. Cambridge, MA: MIT Press.

—— —— (2004). 'Japan's Economic and Financial Crisis: An Overview,' *Journal of Economic Perspectives*, 18: 3–26.

—— —— D. Sharfstein (1990). 'The Role of Banks in Reducing the Costs of Financial Distress in Japan,' *Journal of Financial Economics*, 27: 67–88.

—— —— —— (1993). 'The Choice between Public and Private Debt: An Analysis of Post Deregulation Corporate Financing in Japan,' *NBER Working Paper*, 4421.

Houston, J. and C. James (1996). 'Bank Information Monopolies and the Mix of Public and Private Debt Claims,' *Journal of Finance*, 51: 1863–89.

Ito, T. and K. Harada (2000). 'Japan Premium and Stock Prices: Two Mirrors of Japanese Banking Crises,' *NBER Working Paper*, 7997.

—— Y. N. Sasaki, (2002). 'Impacts of the Basle Capital Standard on Japanese Banks' Behavior,' *Journal of the Japanese and International Economies*, 16: 372–97.

Jensen, M. C. (1986). 'Agency Costs of Free Cash Flow, Corporate Finance, and Takeovers,' *American Economic Review*, 76: 323–39.

Kang, J. and A. Shivdasani (1997). 'Corporate Restructuring During Performance Declines in Japan,' *Journal of Financial Economics*, 46: 29–65.

—— R. Stulz (2000). 'Do Banking Shocks Affect Firm Performance? An Analysis of the Japanese Experience,' *Journal of Business*, 73: 1–23.

Miyajima, H. and Y. Yafeh (2003). 'Japan's Banking Crisis: Who has the Most to Lose?' Discussion Paper, No. 4403, Center for Economic Policy Research.

—— Y. Arikawa, and A. Kato (2002). 'Corporate Governance, Relational Banking and R&D Investment: Evidence from Japanese Large Firms in the 1980s and 1990s,' *International Journal of Technology Management*, 23: 769–87.

Morck, R., M. Nakamura, and A. Shivdasani (2000). 'Banks, Ownership Structure, and Firm Value in Japan,' *The Journal of Business*, 73: 539–67.

Montgomery, H. (2005). 'The Effect of the Basel Accord on Bank Portfolios in Japan,' *Journal of the Japanese and International Economies*, 19: 24–36.

Motonishi, T. and Yoshikawa, H. (1999). 'Causes of the Long Stagnation of Japan during the 1990s: Financial or Real?' *Journal of the Japanese and International Economies*, 13: 181–200.

Nakaso, H. (2001). 'The Financial Crisis in Japan during the 1990s,' *BIS Discussion Paper*, No. 6.

Ogawa, K. (2003). *Dai Fukyo no Keizai Bunseki* (Economic Analysis of the Great Recession). Tokyo: Nihon Keizai Shimbun-sha.

Peek, J. and E. Rosengren (2001). 'Determinants of the Japan Premium: Actions Speak Louder than Words,' *Journal of International Economics*, 53: 283–305.

—— —— (2005). 'Unnatural Selection: Perverse Incentives and the Misallocation of Credit in Japan,' *NBER Working Paper*, 9643.

Petersen, M. A. and R. G. Rajan (1994). 'Benefits from Lending Relationships: Evidence from Small Business Data,' *Journal of Finance*, 49: 3–37.

Rajan, R. (1992). 'Insiders and Outsiders: The Choice between Informed and Arm's-Length Debt,' *Journal of Finance*, 47: 1367–400.

Sekine, T., K. Kobayashi, and Y. Saita (2003). 'Forbearance Lending: The Case of Japanese Firms,' *Monetary and Economics Studies*, 21: 69–92.

Sharpe, S. A. (1990). 'Asymmetric Information, Bank Lending, and Implicit Contracts: A Stylized Model of Customer Relationships,' *Journal of Finance*, 45: 1069–87.

Thakor, V. A. and F. Wilson (1995). 'Capital Requirements, Loan Renegotiations and the Borrower's Choice of Financing Source,' *J. Banking Finance*, 19: 693–711.

Woo, D. (1999). 'In Search of Capital Crunch: Supply Factors behind the Credit Slowdown in Japan,' *IMF Working Paper*.

Wu, X., P. Sercu, and J. Yao (2002). 'Reexamining the Relation between Corporate Debt Mix and Growth in Japan.' Unpublished paper.

Von Thadden, E. (1995). 'Long-Term Contracts, Short-Term Investment and Monitoring,' *Review of Economic Studies*, 62: 557–75.

Yamori, N. and A. Murakami (1999). 'Does Bank Relationship Have an Economics Value? The Effect of Main Bank Failure on Client Firms,' *Economics Letters*, 65: 115–20.

3

The Unwinding of Cross-Shareholding in Japan: Causes, Effects, and Implications[1]

Hideaki Miyajima and Fumiaki Kuroki

3.1 INTRODUCTION

The ownership structure of Japanese firms used to have the following character-istics: shares were highly dispersed, managers and foreigners owned only limited stakes in companies, and substantial blocks of shares were held by corporations and financial institutions. Cross-shareholding, or intercorporate shareholding between banks and corporations, and among corporations, was extensive, and played an important role in distinguishing, at least until the early 1990s, Japan's ownership structure from that of other countries. Evolving from the post-war economic reforms, Japan's unique ownership structure had become well estab-lished by the late 1960s, mainly because top managers considered it to be effective in warding off hostile takeover threats. This ownership structure was remarkably stable, lasting for almost three decades.

Cross-shareholding has also played a key role in supporting Japanese manage-ment and growth-oriented firm behavior in the post-war period (Abegglen and Stalk 1985; Porter 1992, 1994). It encouraged the patterns of stable shareholding that have allowed managers to choose growth rates that deviated from the stock price maximization path (Odagiri 1992) and to adopt steady dividend policies that were insensitive to profit (with important implications for governance). Furthermore, the joint ownership of debt and equity by banks purportedly enhanced corporate performance by improving their monitoring of client firms and helping to mitigate asset substitution problems. The high level of ownership by non-financial institutions has also had a significant influence on the monitor-ing of Japanese companies (Sheard 1994; Yafeh and Yosha 2003).

The ownership structure that took root during the post-war period has under-gone dramatic changes over the past decade, however. Foreign investors began to increase their stakes in Japanese companies in the early 1990s, especially in larger

[1] Keisuke Nitta and Nao Saito helped us to construct the data on which this study is based. Yurie Otsu provided us with excellent assistance. An early draft was presented at RIETI, Hitotsubashi University, the Japan Association for Financial Studies, and Tōkei-kenkyū-kai. Comments from Naohito Abe, Katsuyuki Kubo, Takeo Hoshi, Noriyuki Yanagawa, Kazumi Asako, and Hiroshi Osano were extremely helpful.

firms. And more recently, the ratio of shares held by stable shareholders (*antei kabunushi*) began to plummet from previous heights. Table 3.1 shows the stable shareholder ratio for the period from 1987 to 2002 (estimated by Nippon Life Insurance Research Institute (NLIR)). The stable shareholder ratio is defined as the ratio of shares held by commercial banks, insurance companies, and non-financial firms (business partners and the parent company) to total shares issued by listed firms, calculated on a value basis (market valuation on the reference date). Until the 1990s stable shareholders were assumed to be friendly insiders. The stable shareholder ratio has been declining since the mid-1990s, and the rate of decline has accelerated since 1999. The ratio was 45% in the early 1990s but plunged to only 27.1% in 2002. The last three columns of Table 3.1 show the shares owned by the three categories of investors categorized as stable share-holders—banks, insurance companies, and non-financial firms. While cross-shareholding between corporations decreased only slightly, ownership of corporate shares by financial institutions, and banks in particular, dropped significantly.

It is important to note that the changes to the ownership structure of Japanese firms that occurred in the 1990s were accompanied by growing diversity of ownership. According to Table 3.2, the degree of dispersion of ownership rose as foreigners and individuals boosted their stake in Japanese corporations. Although the average ratio of shares held by financial institutions decreased 5% points during this decade, the standard deviation of this ratio increased. As the ownership structure of Japanese companies has become increasingly differen-tiated and diversified, stable shareholdings have unwound.

The dramatic changes mentioned above naturally give rise to a series of ques-tions: Why is foreign shareholding in Japanese firms on an increasing trend? Why did cross-shareholding, which had been fairly constant for more than 30 years, begin to dissolve in the mid-1990s? If cross-shareholding had been a response to a rising takeover threat, then why did this practice begin to decline just as the takeover threat grew much more serious than it had been in the 1980s? Given the increasing variance in the cross-shareholding ratio among firms, what attri-butes of firms determine the extent of their cross-shareholding? And lastly, what are the welfare implications of the changing ownership structure for firm per-formance? The task of this chapter is to answer these questions, using detailed and comprehensive data on ownership structure and individual cross-shareholding relationships developed by NLIR and Waseda University.

To determine why foreigners are increasing their stakes in Japanese firms, we conduct a brief test of the home bias hypothesis, which predicts that such investors tend to purchase large and well-established stocks (Kang and Stultz 1997; Murase 2001). Using simple estimation, we present evidence that foreigners increased investments not only in large firms with high bond dependency, but also in growing firms with low default risk.

Next, to shed light on the primary concern of this chapter—the causes of the unwinding of cross-shareholding, we approach the choice to sell from two sides, looking at the choice made by corporations to sell their bank shares, and by banks to sell their corporation shares. For the former, we estimate a Logit model in

Table 3.1 Stable Shareholder Ratio

The end of FY	No. of firms	Total firm value (Trillion yen)	Stable shareholder ratio (% of Total)	(Change)	Banks (% of Total)	(Change)	Insurance firms (% of Total)	(Change)	Non-financial firms (% of Total)	(Change)
1987	1,924	433	45.8		14.9		16.4		14.4	
1988	1,975	517	45.7	▲ 0.10	15.6	0.70	16.6	0.20	13.3	▲ 1.10
1989	2,031	500	44.9	▲ 0.80	15.6	0.00	15.7	▲ 0.90	13.4	0.10
1990	2,078	450	45.6	0.70	15.7	0.10	15.8	0.10	14.0	0.60
1991	2,107	326	45.6	0.00	15.6	▲ 0.10	16.2	0.40	13.7	▲ 0.30
1992	2,120	328	45.7	0.10	15.6	0.00	16.2	0.00	13.8	0.10
1993	2,161	367	45.2	▲ 0.50	15.4	▲ 0.20	15.8	▲ 0.40	14.0	0.20
1994	2,214	311	44.9	▲ 0.30	15.4	0.00	15.7	▲ 0.10	13.7	▲ 0.30
1995	2,279	393	43.4	▲ 1.50	15.0	▲ 0.40	14.7	▲ 1.00	13.5	▲ 0.20
1996	2,341	335	42.1	▲ 1.30	15.1	0.10	14.7	0.00	12.2	▲ 1.30
1997	2,389	308	40.5	▲ 1.60	14.8	▲ 0.30	14.1	▲ 0.60	11.6	▲ 0.60
1998	2,433	331	39.9	▲ 0.60	13.7	▲ 1.10	13.0	▲ 1.10	13.2	1.60
1999	2,487	463	37.9	▲ 2.00	11.3	▲ 2.40	10.6	▲ 2.40	15.9	2.70
2000	2,602	368	33.0	▲ 4.90	9.8	▲ 1.50	10.9	0.30	12.3	▲ 3.60
2001	2,668	313	30.2	▲ 2.80	8.7	▲ 1.10	10.1	▲ 0.80	11.4	▲ 0.90
2002	2,674	237	27.1	▲ 3.10	7.7	▲ 1.00	9.3	▲ 0.80	10.0	▲ 1.40

Notes: Stable shareholder ratio is the percentage of market value of listed firms owned by stable shareholders (value of shares owned by stable shareholders/total firm market value). Stable shareholders are defined as banks, insurance firms, and non-financial firms.

Source: NLI Research Institute.

Table 3.2 The Ratio of Shareholding by Type of Shareholder

Year	Percentage of shares held by foreigners			Percentage of shares held by individuals			Percentage of shares held by corporations and banks		
	1990	1995	2000	1990	1995	2000	1990	1995	2000
Mean	4.3	7.8	7.9	20.8	22.6	30.6	37.5	34.9	32.6
Std. dev.	5.8	8.0	10.1	8.1	9.7	14.3	13.2	13.0	14.4
Coef. of variance	1.37	1.02	1.27	0.39	0.43	0.47	0.35	0.37	0.44
Median	2.4	5.7	3.3	19.6	21.5	30.3	35.8	32.9	30.6
First quartile	1.1	1.8	1.2	14.9	15.2	18.9	27.7	25.0	21.7
Third quartile	5.2	11.4	11.3	25.9	28.6	40.2	46.7	43.6	41.4
3Q–1Q	4.0	9.6	10.1	11.0	13.4	21.3	18.9	18.6	19.7

Notes: Sample consists of 931 non-financial firms listed on the First Section of the Tokyo Stock Exchange for the entire period from the end of 1990 to the end of 2000. The percentage of shares held by individuals excludes shares held by board members.

Source: Based on financial statements of each firm, major shareholder data (Tōyō Keizai Shinpōsha), etc.

which a corporation's decision to sell off bank shares is regressed on its need to sell, the financial health of the bank, pressure from capital markets on the corporation, the takeover threat, and the corporation's relationship to the bank. From this estimation, we found that profitable firms with easy access to capital markets and high levels of foreign ownership prior to the banking crisis tended to wind down cross-shareholding, while low-profitability firms with difficulty accessing capital markets and low levels of foreign ownership in the early 1990s tended to maintain cross-shareholding arrangements with their banks.

Our second Logit model regresses the bank's choice to sell corporate shares on the bank's portfolio factors, the bank's need to sell, market pressure on the bank, growth potential, the risk level of the corporate investment, and the strength of the bank's relationships with those corporations. Consequently, we found that a bank's decision to sell off a stock is determined not only by portfolio factors, but also by its long-term relationships with firms. After the banking crisis, and particularly after 1999, banks reduced shareholding mainly by selling shares with higher liquidity and higher expected rates of return (i.e. shares which were easy to sell), while holding onto shares of firms with which they had long-term relationships. This was especially true when a main-bank relationship existed. Thus, the investment behavior of banks was shaped by a perverse incentive that not only undermined corporate governance but also led to the degrading of their own portfolios.

Lastly, we estimate a standard model to measure the effects of firms' cross-shareholding and other shareholding patterns on corporate performance. The conjectures that are tested in this estimation support the view that stresses the costs rather than the benefits of the Japanese ownership structure. Cross-shareholding may reduce the pressure from stock markets but also may encourage managerial entrenchment and diminish rather than enhance performance by allowing managers to stay put for long periods of time. Banks that played a dual role as debt-holders and shareholders have at times used their ownership stakes to encourage client firms to take on projects with low profitability instead of preventing asset substitution. Parent firms that controlled a high percentage of the shares in their (listed) subsidiaries were prone to transfer funds from minority shareholders to controlling shareholders (parent firms) instead of encouraging better performance. Institutional investors, on the other hand, played a significant positive role in monitoring firms instead of inducing managerial myopia.

Indeed, this study provides evidence that high levels of institutional shareholding (either foreign or domestic) and, somewhat surprisingly, block shareholding by corporations have a positive effect on firm performance. In contrast, bank ownership has had a consistently negative effect on firm performance since the mid-1980s. These results imply the following: (1) institutional shareholders are now playing a significant monitoring role in Japanese firms by taking over some of the tasks previously performed by the (main) banks; (2) the unwinding of cross-shareholding between banks and corporations clearly produces efficiency gains; and (3) although the reasons offered up in the past to justify bank ownership of both equity and loans no longer seem to hold, the economic rationale for high levels of block holding by corporations and cross-shareholding among firms remains valid.

The remainder of this chapter is organized as follows. In the next section, we briefly summarize the evolution of the ownership structure of Japanese listed firms since the post-war reforms. In the third section, we address the causes of this evolutionary change, and examine the determinants of the choice between holding and selling shares by both banks and non-financial institutions. The fourth section highlights the effect of changing ownership structure on performance. The fifth section provides a conclusion and some perspectives on future trends.

3.2 APPROACHING THE STABLE SHAREHOLDER PROBLEM

3.2.1 The Puzzle

Stable shareholders have usually been considered insiders friendly to share issuers. Or to put it differently, they are shareholders who make implicit contracts with issuers, promising not to sell their shares to unfriendly third parties such as green-mailers or parties who may attempt hostile takeovers, unless the issuers face a severe financial crisis that triggers suspension of dividend payments (Sheard 1994; Okabe 2002).

Defining stable shareholders as corporations and financial institutions that own shares for the long term, we found that the percentage of shares held by them clearly increased in two steps (Figure 3.1): the first increase occurred from 1950 to 1955, and the second from 1965 to 1974. The post-World War II reforms included compulsory redistribution of corporate ownership centering on the dissolution of the *zaibatsu*. Consequently, block shareholders (*zaibatsu* family and holding

(%)

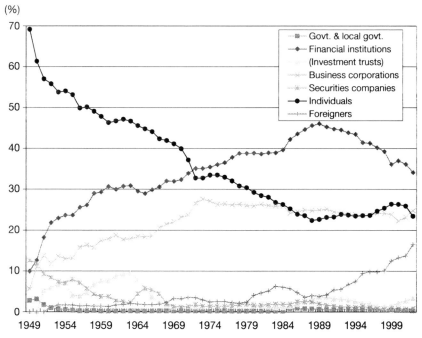

Figure 3.1 Long-term trends in ownership structure of Japanese listed firms

Source: 2002 Shareownership Survey. All domestic stock exchanges.

companies) were eliminated, and individual shareholding increased. The Occupation era reforms produced the dispersed ownership structure with the low level
of managerial ownership that has characterized post-war Japanese firms. The new
managers who emerged to run Japanese corporations were free from effective
control by large shareholders but were exposed to the myopic pressures of the
stock market. Their response was to seek to stabilize the stock issued by their
firms through existing networks. The adage that "shareholders don't choose
managers, managers choose friendly shareholders" aptly sums up what happened. Indeed, the fundamental principles of joint stock corporations appear to
have been violated. In particular, ex-*zaibatsu* firms whose stock had been dispersed pressed same-line firms to purchase their stocks. The government also
promoted corporate shareholding and encouraged life insurance companies to
acquire stock. The movement toward stable shareholding accelerated in the wake
of revisions to the Antitrust Law that deregulated shareholding (Miyajima 1995).
Consequently, due to sharp increases in shareholding by financial institutions and
corporations (friendly insiders), the ratio of stable shareholders increased from
23.6% in 1950 to 36.8% in 1955.

After a period characterized by a relatively stable ownership structure (1956–
64), ownership of shares by financial institutions and corporations increased
sharply once again, with the stable shareholder ratio climbing from 47.4% in

1965 to 62.2% in 1974. During the period of capital liberalization that followed the stock price decline of 1962, corporate managers feared hostile takeovers by foreign competitors. Consequently, friendly corporations and large banks boosted their ownership stakes in firms, boosting the stable shareholder ratio. In addition, the cooperative stockholding institutions that were originally established to maintain stock prices also promoted shareholder stabilization because they sold their holdings to the affiliates or main banks of the issuers after stock prices recovered. Miyajima et al. (2003) showed that the changing ratio of shares held by banks or main banks from 1964–69 was positively sensitive not only to existing relationships (measured by the level of (main) bank dependence at the beginning of the estimation), but also to corporate performance (rate of return on assets, ROA) and growth opportunities (Tobin's q). As delegated monitors, main banks carefully reviewed the credit risks and growth opportunities of corporations that offered shares.[2]

On the other hand, non-financial corporations that held onto bank shares were rational actors because the market return on bank shares was stable and usually outperformed the Tokyo Stock Exchange Stock Price Index (TOPIX).[3] To further encourage stable shareholding, the regulatory framework under the Commercial Code was revised to allow top managers (corporate insiders) to issue new shares by allotting them to friendly third parties without approval from the general shareholders' meeting. To use the terminology of the law and finance literature (La Porta et al. 1998), we could say that protections for minority shareholders were weakened during this phase.

From the early 1970s to the early 1990s, the ownership structure of Japanese firms was remarkably stable, as many observers have emphasized.[4] Even after the mid-1980s when the Antitrust Law was revised to lower the ceiling on shareholding by a financial institution to 5% from 10%, financial institutions increased their total share in Japanese corporations. The stylized portrait of the ownership structure of Japanese firms familiar to most of us is based on this period of stable shareholding. In the 1990s, however, the stable ownership structure was undergoing quiet but important changes. We can observe from Figure 3.1 that these changes were of significant degree when placed in the context of the post-war evolution of Japanese corporate ownership, and in fact comparable in scale to the transformation of the late 1960s.

To get a grasp of these changes, we will focus on the following questions: Why did shareholding by foreigners begin to increase and stable shareholding decrease in the 1990s? Why did the cross-shareholdings that had been extremely stable

---

[2] Miyajima et al. (2003) also reported that (main) bank ownership of manufacturing firms was negatively sensitive to credit risk as measured by the interest coverage ratio. But it should be noted that the positive relationship to ROA and Q is only observed for 1964–69, and not significant in the period from 1969–74. This positive correlation between bank ownership of shares and performance is consistent with Prowse (1990) and Flath (1993), which stress the role of the main bank as delegated monitor, and provide supportive results for the 1980s.

[3] See Miyajima et al. (2003) for details.

[4] See Prowse 1990; Flath 1993; Sheard 1994; Weinstein and Yafeh 1998; and Yafeh and Yosha 2003.

begin to unwind from 1995? If the primary motivation for shareholder stabilization was to mitigate the threat of takeover, why did stable shareholding begin to decline just as the takeover threat began to increase following the plunge in stock prices and the rise in foreign ownership of shares? In the following section, we solve this puzzle by taking a close look at the factors that characterized the ownership structure in the 1990s.

3.2.2 Increase in Foreign Shareholding

Table 3.3 summarizes the value and volume of net selling and buying of shares by category of shareholder. We find that the rise in the fraction of shares owned by foreign investors preceded changes in the Japanese ownership structure. Foreign investors have increased their presence in the Japanese market since 1991, becoming important net buyers, while securities investment trusts turned into net sellers due to the drop in stock prices. One reason for the rise in purchases by foreign investors was the growth in pension funds in the US (see Chapter 4). Ironically, falling stock prices have supported this trend since 1990. As stock prices soared during the asset bubble period, foreign institutional investors representing internationally diversified investment funds considered Japanese stocks to be overpriced. After stock prices fell, however, foreign investors could buy larger volumes of shares with a given pool of money, and began to incorporate Japanese stocks into their portfolios.

The investment behavior of foreign investors is believed to be affected by a so-called home bias, i.e. the preference for large and well-established stocks (Kang and Stultz 1997; Murase 2001). To confirm this hypothesis, we tested the following simple model:

$$(1) \qquad \Delta FOR_t = F(FOR_{t-1}, AVQ_t, SIZE_{t-1}, BON_{t-1}, DAR_{t-1}, DIST_t, IND)$$

where *FOR* is the percentage share held by foreign institutional investors,[5] *AVQ* is the period average of Tobin's *q*, *SIZE* is the logarithm of total assets, and *BON* is the degree of dependence on bonds (i.e. the ratio of bonds to the sum of borrowing and bonds). In addition, we included leverage, *DAR*, a dummy variable for financial distress, *DIST*, which is 1 if net profit is negative at least one time in the estimated period, and otherwise 0, and an industry dummy, *IND*. The results are presented in Table 3.4.

Even with this simple estimation, we can observe that firm size, growth opportunity (Tobin's *q*), and degree of dependence on bonds have significant positive effects on foreign ownership while leverage and financial distress have negative effects. Foreign investors increased investment in both large firms and growing firms with low default risk and high bond dependency. Moreover,

---

[5] *FOR* excludes the share held by foreign companies such as Ford in Mazda, Renault in Nissan, and GM in Fuji Heavy Ind.Co.

Table 3.3 Trading Volume of Stocks by Investor Category

Year	Total			Net purchases							
	Sales	Purchases	Net purchases	Securities companies	Individuals	Investment trusts	Foreigners	Business companies	Insurance companies	LTCB, city and regional banks	Trust banks
1990	125,253	125,362	109	94	1,467	852	▲ 1,806	780	118	▲ 1,223	
1991	94,030	94,983	952	▲ 164	▲ 2,159	▲ 1,324	4,146	▲ 1,593	370	1,429	
1992	71,913	72,467	554	▲ 103	160	366	229	▲ 1,002	▲ 172	1,307	
1993	89,154	89,860	706	▲ 109	▲ 1,025	▲ 581	1,298	▲ 1,961	▲ 45	3,060	
1994	92,894	93,726	831	▲ 149	▲ 1,843	▲ 1,727	4,969	▲ 2,062	▲ 634	1,739	
1995	103,521	103,933	412	116	615	▲ 1,252	3,357	▲ 1,303	▲ 2,020	▲ 313	
1996	108,919	109,517	599	▲ 91	▲ 1,101	▲ 1,021	2,473	▲ 1,314	▲ 520	1,017	1,664
1997	112,241	112,102	▲ 139	410	4,398	▲ 1,580	▲ 1,154	▲ 152	▲ 1,498	▲ 1,382	2,451
1998	118,067	117,792	▲ 275	323	4,098	▲ 518	2,092	▲ 1,251	▲ 1,849	▲ 1,856	2,854
1999	150,259	149,877	▲ 382	374	2,626	▲ 390	7,229	▲ 2,280	▲ 2,468	▲ 2,415	▲ 1,491
2000	167,397	167,370	▲ 27	396	943	1,030	▲ 729	▲ 1,828	▲ 722	▲ 1,507	933
2001	184,767	185,179	412	198	1,338	607	▲ 976	▲ 605	▲ 1,432	▲ 1,496	2,122
2002	194,690	194,878	188	10	1,064	▲ 46	▲ 223	328	▲ 840	▲ 1,376	1,530

Note: Unit is One Million Shares.

Source: Tokyo Stock Exchange, *Annual Report on Stock Statistics* (Based on three markets—Tokyo, Osaka, Nagoya).

Table 3.4 Determinants of Foreign Shareholding in Ownership Structure (Cross Section)

Variable	1989–94		1994–99	
	Est. Coef. (t-stat.)	Est. Coef. (t-stat.)	Est. Coef. (t-stat.)	Est. Coef. (t-stat.)
C	−22.388 ***	−22.446 ***	−39.053 ***	−38.991 ***
	(−7.13)	(−7.16)	(−9.60)	(−9.60)
$FOR(−5)$	−0.005	−0.014	−0.062	−0.072 *
	(−0.17)	(−0.46)	(−1.60)	(−1.85)
AVQ	2.181 **	2.369 **	6.082 ***	6.202 ***
	(2.20)	(2.38)	(5.86)	(5.97)
$SIZE(−5)$	1.786 ***	1.881 ***	2.051 ***	2.145 ***
	(9.96)	(10.04)	(8.40)	(8.57)
$DAR(−5)$		−0.028 *		−0.031 *
		(−1.72)		(−1.66)
$BON(−5)$	1.971 ***	1.618 **	0.729	0.260
	(3.26)	(2.54)	(0.93)	(0.31)
$DIST$	−0.839 *	−0.664	−2.178 ***	−1.980 ***
	(−1.96)	(−1.51)	(−4.10)	(−3.65)
Industry Dummy	YES	YES	YES	YES
Adjusted R^2	0.23	0.23	0.30	0.31
Number of Observations	588	588	564	564

Notes: *** denotes significance at the 1% level, ** denotes significance at the 5% level, and * denotes significance at the 10% level. Sample firms are large listed firms in the First Section of Tokyo Stock Exchange, which have over 50 billion yen turnover. Financial institutions and public utilities are excluded. Dependent variable ΔFOR: difference in the shareholding ratio by foreigners in each five-year period. FOR is the share held by foreign shareholders, which excludes the share held by foreign corporations. AVQ is the five-year average of Tobin's q. SIZE is the logarithm of total assets (market value). DAR is the leverage: the sum of borrowing and bonds divided by the total assets. BON is the degree of dependence on bonds: bonds divided by the total assets. DIST is a dummy variable that is given the value of 1 if net profit (after-tax profit) becomes non-positive at any time in the estimation period. This table first appeared in Miyajima et al. (2003).

comparing the two half-periods (1989–94, and 1994–99), we can see that *SIZE* and *BON* had a larger effect in the former half-period. This implies that investors targeted large and established firms. On the other hand, after 1995, the estimated effect of *AVQ* and *DIST* improved, implying that investors increasingly took corporate performance into account in the late 1990s.

3.2.3 The Sale of Financial Institution Shares by Corporations

The increase in foreign investors forced incumbent managers to act in the interests of general shareholders and thus to reconsider cross-shareholding arrangements. At the same time, the need to keep firms in sound financial health in order to earn high credit ratings played an important part in encouraging managers to review their securities portfolios. Moreover, with the drop in stock prices after 1995, the rate of decline of bank share prices started to exceed TOPIX's decline, reflecting the failures of several local banks and *jusen* housing loan companies, and the price correction triggered by the Daiwa Bank incident in the fall of 1995 (Itoh and Harada 2000).

The timing of this change in bank share prices, which had previously been synchronized with TOPIX, corresponded to the appearance of a Japan premium in the inter-bank market (Peek and Rosengren 2001).

Figure 3.2 not only shows that the gap between the performance of bank shares and TOPIX widened since 1995 but also that the bank share price trend began to deviate from that which prevailed during the formative period of stable shareholding (1965–74), when bank shares had a higher return on investment than TOPIX (Miyajima et al. 2003). We can infer that because of both the decline in market returns of bank shares and the increased risk associated with holding onto them, firms for the first time in the post-war period had to confront the problem of whether or not to sell bank shares. According to Figure 3.3, however, which summarizes the ratio of bank shares sold during the fiscal year to shares held by corporations at the beginning of the period (henceforth, the rate of selling by corporations; see Figure 3.3, note),[6] the rate of selling by corporations in 1995 and 1996 did not grow significantly when compared with previous periods. Indeed, only a limited number of firms sold their bank shares.

However, the importance of the corporate choice to sell off bank shares or not increased significantly from the end of 1997 to the beginning of 1999. This period saw the bankruptcies of Hokkaido Takushoku Bank (November 1997), Yamaichi

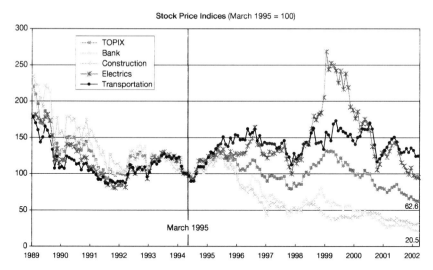

Figure 3.2 Co-movement of industry-specific stock price indexes and bank stock prices, 1995–2002

Note: Based on the Tokyo Stock Exchange industry-specific indices.

---

[6] We consider a reduction in the number of shares during the period to be a sell-off. We arrived at a figure for sell-offs by comparing the number of shares held by corporations (after adjusting for capital transfers) at the beginning and end of the firm year. The rate of selling is computed by dividing the number of sell-offs by the total number of recognized cross-shareholding relationships.

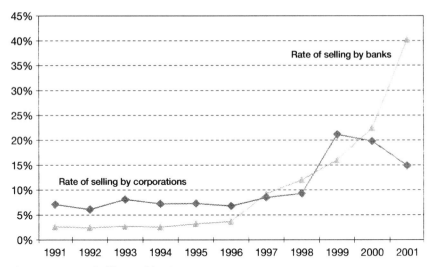

Figure 3.3 Rate of selling and buying

Notes: Rate of selling by banks = number of corporate stocks sold by banks during a firm year/number of corporate stocks held at the beginning of the firm year. Rate of selling by corporations = number of bank stocks sold during a firm year/number of bank stocks held at the beginning of the firm year. When it was not possible to determine the number of shares held at the end of period and whether the shares were sold or the shares were not disclosed, we did not count the case as an instance of selling.

Securities Co. (November 1997), Long-Term Credit Bank of Japan (October 1998), and Nippon Credit Bank (December 1998). As the gap between bank share returns and TOPIX widened, the Japan premium rose and the credit ratings of the major commercial banks dropped. By February 1999, the index for bank shares was 53.8 (compared to 100 in March 1995), which was far below the 85.6 for TOPIX. It became apparent that bank shares not only offered low rates of return but also carried high levels of risk. Furthermore, the introduction of consolidated accounting (implemented in 1999) and current value accounting put even more pressure on corporations to sell their bank shares. Consequently, the rate of corporate selling of bank shares has been increasing since 1997 and exceeded 20% in 1999.

3.2.4 Banking Crisis and Its Impact

As corporations sold their financial institution shares, banks and other financial institutions began to unload their corporate shares. Insurance companies led the way, turning into major net sellers, especially after the banking crisis worsened in 1997 (Table 3.3). It is said that domestic institutional investors, including life insurance companies, changed their behavior in response to the increased emphasis that was placed on fiduciary duty in the late 1990s.

Moreover, banks, which had been net buyers from 1991–96, turned into large net sellers. The rate of selling rose to over 10% by 1997 (Figure 3.3). Factors influencing this trend included both the need to dispose of non-performing loans and to satisfy BIS rules as well as the introduction of current value accounting. Also important was that bankers had begun to recognize that their holdings of corporate shares had become lightning rods for criticism. Under BIS rules that required banks to calculate Tier 1 capital by including unrealized capital gains and losses from shareholdings, shares held by banks (estimated to be almost twice Tier 1 capital in 1999) were expected to have a tremendous impact on their lending behavior as stock prices declined, triggering a credit crunch. The banking crisis in late 1997 marked an important turning point for Japan's corporate ownership structure, as public and policy attitudes toward cross-shareholding clearly changed from supportive, or at least neutral, to critical and unsupportive.

3.2.5 Banks' Shareholding Restriction Law

Although a second injection of public funds in March 1999 was supposed to help banks put their non-performing loan problem behind them, the loans still posed serious challenges into 2001. The government's response to the lingering problem was to enact policies to dissolve cross-shareholding. In April 2001, new regulations on banks' Tier 1 capital shareholdings were implemented as part of an emergency economic package. In addition, the Banks' Shareholding Restriction Law was enacted in September, with a targeted implementation date of September 2004. Major banks' shareholdings were 1.5 times Tier 1 capital in March 2001, so they were required to reduce their shareholdings by ¥10 trillion. Because a bridge bank would be needed to handle the sale of shares by major banks, the Banks' Shareholdings Purchase Corporation (BSPC) was established and started purchasing shares in February 2002. Also, revisions to the Commercial Code abolished restrictions on share buy-backs and treasury stock, allowing firms to hold onto their shares after acquiring them. While banks and corporations continued to sell off their mutually held shares at a brisk pace, the banks' selling rate increased rapidly. Although the corporate selling rate had been at least as high as that of the banks for most of this period, banks began selling off shares at a higher rate than corporations in 2000, with their selling rate reaching 40% in 2001.

3.3 DETERMINANTS OF THE UNWINDING OF CROSS-SHAREHOLDING

3.3.1 The Data

As described above, there was a general decline in cross-shareholding but the changes in the shareholding structure did affect firms uniformly. What are the firm characteristics that encouraged a firm to either unwind cross-shareholding relationships, or to maintain them at current levels? Given that corporations were relatively more likely to maintain cross-shareholding relationships with other corporations in the 1990s than with banks, as is shown in Table 3.1, we focus our analysis below on cross-shareholding relationships between corporations and banks. Our data set is based on the *Survey of Cross-Shareholding* conducted by the NLIR since 1987. The data allows for rigorous analysis of individual cross-shareholding relationships between corporations and banks.[7]

This analysis is concerned with yearly changes in cross-shareholding from FY 1995 (March 1995) to FY 2001 (March 2002). Recall that the banking crisis of 1997 increased both banks' and corporations' tendencies to sell off mutually held shares and that the Banks' Shareholding Restriction Law that was under discussion from 1999 provided banks with further incentive to unwind cross-shareholdings. In the following analysis, in addition to making estimates for the entire period from FY 1991 to FY 2001, we conduct separate analyses for three sub-periods: period I (FY 1995–96); period II (FY 1997–98); and period III (FY 1999 and after).

Our data set has two parts: non-financial corporations that are listed in the First Section of the Tokyo Stock Exchange,[8] and commercial banks. The latter includes major commercial banks and long-term credit banks that went public by the end of each year of observation. We exclude trust banks since it is not possible to separate shares that they hold as assets and shares held in trust for customers. We also exclude banks that have been de-listed from the stock exchange due to bankruptcy and nationalization, e.g. Hokkaido Takushoku Bank in 1997 and Long-Term Credit Bank of Japan in 1998, because it was not clear who owned the shares held by these institutions.

Because we focus on the choices made by corporations (to sell bank shares) and banks (to sell corporation shares), we limit our analysis to matters related to a corporation's holding of bank shares at the beginning of each period, and to a bank's holding of corporate shares at the beginning of each period.[9] Thus, the sample size decreases each year.

For the beginning point (March 1995), the data include 14 banks and 1087 corporations. Within this sample, there are 1065 corporations that issued shares held by banks and 1067 corporations that held bank shares. The data reveals that

[7] Refer to http://www.nli-research.co.jp/eng/resea/econo/eco031118.pdf for more detailed information on the cross-shareholding data.

[8] Firms that merge with the other listed firms during an observation period are excluded from the sample for the year of the merger since it is difficult to capture the change in shareholdings.

[9] During the time period of this analysis, large banks were being integrated into bank groups (centered on holding companies), making it more difficult to trace the bank-holding company shares held by corporations at the end of the period to the bank shares they had owned at the beginning of the period. Therefore, we analyze the relationships between corporations and bank groups by using the total amount of loans and total shares held by group banks as proxies for the relationship between corporations and the bank group. For instance, in the case of Mizuho Holdings, established in September 2000, firms which held shares in any of the following banks—Industrial Bank of Japan, Fuji Bank, and Dai-Ichi Kangyo Bank—as of March 2000 are considered to own Mizuho Holdings' shares as of March 2001, and are treated as having owned Mizuho Holdings' shares from the beginning of the period.

cross-shareholding relationships were widespread: 1039 corporations, or 95% of the sample, had cross-shareholding relationships. Furthermore, the cross-shareholding relationship for each corporation was not limited to one bank. On average, corporations held shares in 5.4 banks at the beginning of this period. There were 5879 instances of bank share ownership by corporations. If we limit our focus to mutual shareholding cases, corporations held shares in an average of 3.2 banks in 3545 instances. Henceforth, the unit of analysis will be the shareholder's decision to sell or hold shares.

3.3.2 Corporate Decision on Holding Bank Shares

We begin our analysis by examining the non-financial corporation's decision to sell off bank shareholdings at a time when holding onto these shares is increasingly associated with higher risk and lower market returns, as described above. In general, a firm's current portfolio, liquidity constraints, and banks' creditworthiness ratings all affect the decision to sell. Additionally, other factors might also come into play. The first is capital market pressure as represented by the credit ratings on corporate bonds. The importance of bond financing has increased since the late 1980s such that maintaining at least a BBB rating became critical for corporate financing in the 1990s. Given capital market pressures, selling bank shares signaled a rational management style that put an emphasis on ROE and transparency. However, firms that sought to unwind cross-shareholding relationships also faced retaliation from banks that could sell off massive blocks of corporate shares. Thus, corporations may have decided to hold onto their bank shares and accept the higher financial risk. Additionally, managers whose firms were likely takeover targets might have been reluctant to sell as well.

To test the above hypotheses, we estimate the Logit model below that explains a corporation's decision to sell off bank shares based on the following variables: (1) the need to sell, X_1; (2) the financial health of the bank, X_2; (3) pressure from capital markets, X_3; (4) potential threat of takeover, X_4; and (5) the relationship to the bank, X_5.

(1) $$CSL_{ij} = F(X_1, X_2, X_3, X_4, X_5)$$

The dependent variable CSL_{ij} represents the decision of corporation i on holding bank j's shares. It takes the value 1 if in the current period we observe the selling of shares which were held at the beginning of the period (reduction of shares held), and 0 otherwise. The definitions of explanatory variables $X_1 - X_5$ are in Appendix 1.[10] Table 3.5 presents the estimation results.[11] To show the

[10] In our following analysis, when treating outliers for all explanatory variables except dummy variables, we replace all the values deviating more than three standard deviations from sample means with sample means plus three standard deviations.

[11] In addition to them, we introduce a variable D_BM, a dummy variable which takes the value of 1 if several banks which are separate entities in the beginning of period are integrated by the end of period, to control for the effect of bank mergers. We also add year dummy, D_YY, which controls for the year effect.

Table 3.5 Corporation's Decision to Sell Bank Shares

		Model 1								Model 2		Model 3	
		Entire Period FY95–FY2001		Period I FY95–96		Period II FY97–98		Period III FY99–2001		Entire Period FY95–FY2001		Entire Period FY95–FY2001	
Variable	Definition	Est. Coef. (t-stat)	σ_x*dP/dX	Est. Coef. (t-stat)	σ_x*dP/dX	Est. Coef. (t-stat)	σ_x*dP/dX	Est. Coef. (t-stat)	σ_x*dP/dX	Est. Coef. (t-stat)	σ_x*dP/dX	Est. Coef. (t-stat)	σ_x*dP/dX
C	Constant	-3.641 *** (-20.20)		-6.314 *** (-14.29)		-4.910 *** (-14.26)		-2.925 *** (-12.50)		-4.681 *** (-19.38)		-3.637 *** (-20.16)	
X_1 D_ICR	1 if ICR < 1.5	0.311 *** (6.44)	0.012	0.573 *** (5.88)	0.015	0.396 *** (4.30)	0.012	0.152 ** (2.11)	0.008	0.428 *** (6.80)	0.013	0.260 *** (4.93)	0.010
D/E	D/E ratio (interest-bearing debt/owned capital)	0.214 *** (17.97)	0.030	0.184 *** (8.82)	0.019	0.133 *** (5.82)	0.016	0.142 *** (13.01)	0.044	0.249 *** (14.81)	0.027	0.215 *** (18.00)	0.030
BSV/A	Bank shares at market value divided by total assets	37.622 *** (21.73)	0.045	19.658 *** (9.57)	0.023	37.455 *** (11.27)	0.036	35.384 *** (14.55)	0.062	30.150 *** (18.87)	0.039	37.080 *** (21.23)	0.044
X_2 D/FRD	Dummy variable is 1 if bank finance rating is less than D (dummy is 1 if less than E since 1999)	0.387 *** (9.80)	0.018	0.210 *** (2.59)	0.007	0.421 *** (5.58)	0.016	0.443 *** (7.69)	0.030	0.273 *** (5.04)	0.011	0.446 *** (10.44)	0.021
X_3 D_CRB	Dummy for rating (worst among four rating companies) is BB-BBB	0.333 *** (7.28)	0.014	0.415 *** (4.19)	0.011	0.324 *** (3.44)	0.011	0.331 *** (5.32)	0.022	0.371 *** (6.09)	0.013	0.334 *** (7.29)	0.014
D_CRA	Dummy for rating (worst among four rating companies) is A-AAA	0.101 * (1.76)	0.004	0.043 (0.34)	0.001	0.184 * (1.69)	0.006	0.016 (0.20)	0.001	0.083 (1.05)	0.003	0.103 * (1.79)	0.004

			Model 1		Model 2		Model 3		Model 4		Model 5		Model 6	
X_4	LEMV	Logarithm of a corporation's aggregate market value of shares	0.143 *** (9.39)	0.019	0.249 *** (6.55)	0.019	0.209 *** (6.88)	0.022	0.087 *** (4.38)	0.020	0.151 *** (7.33)	0.017	0.142 *** (9.33)	0.019
	NOST	Ratio of shareholding by non-stabilized shareholders if the corporation has cross-shareholding relationship with banks	−0.007 *** (−4.22)	0.010	−0.008 ** (−2.13)	−0.007	0.004 (1.04)	0.004	−0.010 *** (−4.64)	−0.023			−0.007 *** (−4.27)	−0.010
X_5	BBR	A corporation's borrowing from the bank divided by total borrowing from private financial institutions	−0.014 *** (−5.80)	−0.014	−0.005 (−0.95)	−0.003	0.025 *** (4.30)	0.019	−0.012 *** (−4.16)	−0.022	−0.006 ** (−2.36)	−0.006	−0.014 *** (5.89)	−0.014
	BHR	The bank's shareholding ratio	−0.192 *** (−11.06)	−0.034	−0.057 (−1.51)	0.006	0.343 *** (−8.42)	0.047	0.167 *** (7.60)	0.049	0.168 *** (8.15)	0.020	−0.191 *** (−10.96)	−0.034
	D_MB	Dummy for main bank relationship	0.111 * (1.81)	0.004	0.186 (1.37)	0.004	0.347 ** (2.47)	0.010	−0.008 (−0.10)	0.001	0.158 ** (2.38)	0.006	0.234 *** (2.82)	0.009
X_6	BSL	Dummy for a bank's selling of corporate shares in the same year									1.277 *** (20.65)	0.034		
	PBSL	Dummy for a bank's selling of corporate shares in the previous year									0.203 ** (2.48)	0.004		

(Continued)

Table 3.5 (Continued)

Variable	Definition	Model 1								Model 2		Model 3	
		Entire Period FY95–FY2001		Period I FY95–96		Period II FY97–98		Period III FY99–2001		Entire Period FY95–FY2001		Entire Period FY95–FY2001	
		Est. Coef. (t-stat)	$\sigma_x * dP/dX$	Est. Coef. (t-stat)	$\sigma_x * dP/dX$	Est. Coef. (t-stat)	$\sigma_x * dP/dX$	Est. Coef. (t-stat)	$\sigma_x * dP/dX$	Est. Coef. (t-stat)	$\sigma_x * dP/dX$	Est. Coef. (t-stat)	$\sigma_x * dP/dX$
MB MBICR	Main bank interaction term (D_ICR)											0.284** (2.54)	0.005
MBFRD	Main bank interaction term (D_MDD)											−0.342*** (−3.57)	0.009
D_BM	Dummy for multiple bank merger	0.398*** (4.11)	0.006	0.621*** (2.98)	0.006			0.322*** (2.91)	0.011	0.246** (2.19)	0.004	0.426*** (4.38)	0.007
D_YY	Year dummy	YES		YES		YES		YES		YES		YES	
Number of Observations		31,700		11,163		10,029		10,508		20,947		31,700	
Number of Selling Cases		3,657		785		877		1,995		2,074		3,657	
Rate of Selling		11.5%		7.0%		8.7%		19.0%		9.9%		11.5%	
Log Likelihood		−10,269		−2,658		−2,777		−4,794		−5,886		−10,260	

Notes: *** denotes significance at the 1% level, ** denotes significance at the 5% level, and * denotes significance at the 10% level. Estimated with Logit model in which the dependent variable is given a value of 1 when corporate shares held by banks decrease compared to the beginning of the period and 0 otherwise. σ_x denotes the explanatory variable's standard deviation; dP/dX denotes the marginal effect. Model 2 is limited to samples identifiable as instances of cross-shareholding between banks and corporations.

magnitude of each explanatory variable on the sell-off rate, we provide the estimated marginal effect multiplied by one standard deviation in Table 3.5 (column $\sigma_X{}^*dP/dX$). For instance, 0.030 for X_1, D/E, means that when this variable increases by one standard deviation above its mean, the probability of sell-off increases approximately 3% points.

First, we found that each corporation's choice to hold bank shares is determined by perceived need to sell. The coefficients on the variable D_ICR, a proxy for the degree of need to sell off bank shares for liquidity reasons, and the variable D/E, the ratio of debt to equity, are both positive and significant at the 1% level. Firms facing a liquidity crisis or excess debt risk are more likely to sell their bank shares. The coefficient on BSV/A, which was included to capture the skewness of an equity portfolio for specific bank shares, is also positive and significant. This indicates that firms are more likely to sell off bank shares when those shares are their main assets. The magnitude of the coefficient of BSV/A, 4.5%, is larger than that for other variables. When observed over our three periods, it increases from 2.3% to 3.6% to 6.2%. This implies that bank shares are increasingly being viewed as risky assets. This result is consistent with our conjecture that high risk is one factor that increases a corporation's tendency to sell off bank shares.

A corporation's choice to sell its bank shares is also determined by the financial health of the bank in which it holds shares. The positive and significant coefficient on X_2, D_FRD, implies that less financially healthy banks tend to be candidates for a sell-off. The reduction of holding risk appears to be one of the main factors in this choice. Also, the effect becomes larger as time passes within the period of observation. The banking crisis apparently triggered a rising awareness of the risk of holding bank shares.

Now let us focus on X_3 through X_5. The coefficient on X_3 supports the view that firm managers that issued bonds in the beginning of each period needed to sell bank shares in order to send signals to the market to maintain or raise their credit ratings. Notice that firms with at least a BBB rating, generally considered the prerequisite for issuing bonds, had a 1.4% higher probability of selling. This implies that maintaining and improving a good credit rating is a vital concern for those firms. Also, D_CRB has a greater effect in period III. The results support the conjecture that it became increasingly critical for firms to keep or improve their credit ratings after 1999, when foreign rating agencies imposed stricter requirements for BBB ratings and the probability of default among listed firms increased.

On the other hand, estimation results for X_4 indicate that the threat of a hostile takeover restrained the unwinding of cross-shareholding. The coefficient for the total market capitalization, $LEMV$, is positive and significant at a magnitude of 1.9%. Firms with a small current value of total shares appear to accept the increasing risk of holding bank shares to avoid retaliatory sell-offs. In addition, the coefficient on the ratio of non-stable shareholders, $NOST$, is significantly negative, implying that firms susceptible to hostile takeovers tend to keep their cross-shareholding relationships with banks.

Last, the estimation results for variable X_5, which captures relationships with banks, mostly support the conjecture that firms with strong relationships with banks are less likely to liquidate bank shares regardless of holding risk. For example, the coefficient on *BBR*, a proxy of dependency on bank loans, is significantly negative. This suggests that firms avoid selling off shares of banks on which they depend for financing. Note that the magnitude of this effect grows larger after the banking crisis. Firms could not sell bank shares in spite of the higher holding risk, given the possibility that funding could be withdrawn.

The coefficient on *BHR*, a proxy for a firm's dependence on a bank (on the equity side), is also significantly negative and large at 3.4%. Thus, if the bank is a block holder, then the firm tends to avoid selling off the bank's shares. This effect is significantly negative in period II, after the banking crisis occurred. It implies that firms chose to hold shares from banks that were their important stable shareholders, fearing retaliatory sell-offs by banks.

In sum, corporations considered not only equity portfolios or their liquidity needs, but also the risk of holding bank shares, the threat of takeover, and their long-term relationship with banks when choosing to sell off bank shares. The fact that high dependence on banks (for both equity and loans) has a negative effect on the decision to sell is especially important. Even as selling bank shares became an increasingly rational choice, some firms chose to maintain cross-shareholding if capital market pressure was weak, the possibility for hostile takeovers was relatively high, or if there was a strong pre-existing relationship with a bank. However, one variable of X_5, *D_MB*, which represents main-bank relationships, has a positive and significant coefficient in period II. This does not support the hypothesis that firms avoided unwinding cross-shareholding with banks with which they had strong relationships. Why then did firms choose to unwind cross-shareholding with main banks, which were considered to have the closest relationships to firms? We return to this question in a later section.

3.3.3 Bank Decision on Selling of Corporate Shares

As noted above, the selling off of corporate shares by banks began after 1997. In this section, we will address why banks chose to sell.

Although identifying the determinants of the investment behavior of banks in general terms is not a simple exercise, we can assume that banks do not sell shares based merely on the fact that they may have determined that their holdings of a certain stock are excessive compared to their overall market portfolios or that the stock has low liquidity. But banks will prefer to sell risky shares, since they rely on deposits as a source of investment funds. Furthermore, following Flath (1993) and Prowse (1990), we predict that banks tend to hold shares of firms with high growth opportunities because banks feel a need to monitor managers of firms that have afforded them a considerable degree of discretion.

On the other hand, it is highly plausible that a bank's decision to sell is strongly influenced by its financing and shareholding relationship with a given firm. This is particularly reasonable if the bank is the firm's main bank. Additionally, if there is an urgent need to secure funds in order to eliminate a non-performing loan, banks may skew their selling toward shares of firms with high share prices. Bank behavior based on such (perverse) incentives leads to negative influences on corporate governance for corporations as well as the deterioration of their portfolios.

To test our conjectures, we estimate the following simple Logit model that measures a bank's choice to sell corporate shares with the following variables: (1) the bank's portfolio factor and its need to sell, Z_1; (2) market pressure on the bank, Z_2; (3) the growth potential and risk level of given firms, Z_3; and (4) the strength of the relationship with the given firms, Z_4.

(2) $$BSL_{ij} = F(Z_1, Z_2, Z_3, Z_4)$$

The dependent variable BSL_{ij} shows whether bank j sells or holds shares of corporation i. It is 1 if in the current period we observe the selling of shares held at the beginning of the period (reduction of shares held), and 0 otherwise. The definitions of explanatory variables $Z_1 - Z_4$ are in Appendix 3.2. Table 3.6 presents the estimation results.

The variables of Z_1 explain a bank's need to sell shares. Both $BHR/T1$, a proxy of the bank's portfolio factor, and $LEMV$, a proxy for liquidity, have positive coefficients as expected. The magnitude of $LEMV$ is large at 2.7%. Banks selected both over-invested company stocks and those that are easier to sell due to high liquidity as targets for sell-off. Also, in time-series, these trends are stronger in period III. Until the banking crisis, banks refrained from selling shares of corporations for which they were the main shareholders. This implies that the banks' level of awareness of holding risks was low. However, in period III, when public policy promoted the unwinding of cross-shareholding relationships, the need to reduce holdings became an important determinant in explaining a bank's selling behavior.

On the other hand, Z_2, which tests the market's evaluation of banks' financial health, has a strongly positive and significant coefficient in period II.[12] When we divided sample firms into two groups by financial health and compared the probability of sell-off between them, we found that the probability of sell-off for a less healthy bank was 15.6%, whereas that of a healthy bank was much smaller at 9.3%. Thus, it appears that those banks that took market and rating agency evaluations of firms seriously believed that it was important to send strong signals by reducing shareholding risk.

---

[12] In period III, this variable has a significantly negative coefficient, which seems to represent the effect from in-kind contributions of diverse stocks to ETF (Exchange Traded Fund) in 2001 by Tokyo Mitsubishi Bank, which has a high financial rating. In fact, if we exclude it from the sample, the coefficient becomes significantly positive.

Table 3.6 Model of Banks' Decision to Sell Corporate Shares

| | | Model 1 | | | | | | | | Model 2 | | Model 3 | |
| | | Entire Period FY95–FY2001 | | Period I FY95–96 | | Period II FY97–98 | | Period III FY99–2001 | | Entire Period FY95–FY2001 | | Entire Period FY95–FY2001 | |
Variable	Definition	Est. Coef. (t-stat)	$\sigma_x * dP/dX$	Est. Coef. (t-stat)	$\sigma_x * dP/dX$	Est. Coef. (t-stat)	$\sigma_x * dP/dX$	Est. Coef. (t-stat)	$\sigma_x * dP/dX$	Est. Coef. (t-stat)	$\sigma_x * dP/dX$	Est. Coef. (t-stat)	$\sigma_x * dP/dX$
C	Constant	−2.785 *** (−12.27)		−8.148 *** (−8.97)		−4.039 *** (−7.76)		−2.593 *** (−9.98)		−2.881 *** (−11.74)		−2.892 *** (−12.67)	
Z_1 BHR/T1	Shareholding ratio divided by Tier 1 owned capital	0.643 *** (2.61)	0.007	1.382 ** (2.38)	0.005	−1.196 *** (−3.20)	−0.013	1.981 *** (5.27)	0.027	0.472 * (1.83)	0.005	0.569 ** (2.28)	0.006
LEMV	Logarithm of a corporation's aggregate market value of shares	0.181 *** (11.24)	0.026	0.350 *** (5.86)	0.014	0.158 *** (4.38)	0.019	0.181 *** (9.44)	0.047	0.156 *** (8.69)	0.020	0.183 *** (11.34)	0.026
Z_2 D_FRD	Dummy variable is one if bank finance rating is less than D (dummy is one if less than E since 1999)	0.075 (1.65)	0.004	−0.102 (−0.68)	−0.002	0.593 *** (6.89)	0.026	−0.136 ** (−2.33)	−0.011	0.062 (1.22)	0.003	0.179 *** (3.42)	0.009
Z_3 D_ICR	One if ICR < 1.5	0.187 *** (3.34)	0.008	0.500 *** (3.03)	0.007	0.135 (1.27)	0.005	0.111 (1.53)	0.007	0.085 (1.35)	0.003	0.346 *** (5.57)	0.014
D_AVQ	One if Tobin's q > 2	0.145 (1.34)	0.002	0.112 (0.28)	0.000	−0.284 (−0.97)	−0.004	0.219 * (1.75)	0.008	0.278 ** (2.29)	0.004	0.136 (1.25)	0.002
D/E	D/E ratio (interest-bearing debt/owned capital)	−0.005 (−0.37)	−0.001	0.042 (1.17)	0.002	−0.003 (−0.13)	0.000	−0.025 * (−1.93)	−0.010	−0.045 ** (−2.52)	−0.006	−0.006 (−0.38)	−0.001
SDRTN	Standard deviation of monthly return from a corporation's share in the past 36 months	0.046 *** (7.77)	0.018	0.117 *** (4.51)	0.010	0.090 *** (6.69)	0.030	0.028 *** (4.39)	0.022	0.047 *** (6.77)	0.016	0.047 *** (7.84)	0.018
Z_4 BBR	A corporation's borrowing from the bank divided by total borrowing from private financial institutions	−0.017 *** (−8.38)	−0.021	−0.034 *** (−3.77)	−0.011	−0.034 *** (−6.74)	−0.034	−0.010 *** (−4.44)	−0.023	−0.018 *** (−8.01)	−0.020	−0.017 *** (−8.14)	−0.020

		dP/dX	Coef.	dP/dX	Coef.	dP/dX	Coef.	dP/dX	Coef.	dP/dX	Coef.	dP/dX	Coef.
D_CSH	Dummy for cross-shareholding relationship	−0.007	−0.224*** (−3.51)	−0.007	−0.473** (−2.18)	−0.004	−0.466*** (−3.69)	−0.011	−0.152** (−1.97)	−0.009	−0.317*** (−5.50)	−0.007	−0.229*** (−3.57)
D_MB	Dummy for main bank relationship	−0.013	−0.286*** (−5.39)	−0.013	−0.399** (−1.99)	−0.006	−0.238** (−2.01)	−0.009	−0.281*** (−4.44)	−0.023		0.004	0.086 (1.07)
Z_5 CSL	Dummy for a corporation's selling of bank shares in the same year									0.035	1.260*** (21.20)		
PCSL	Dummy for a corporation's selling of bank shares in the previous year									0.018	0.762*** (10.46)		
MB MBICR	Main bank interaction term (D_ICR×D_MB)											−0.016	−0.692*** (−5.48)
MBFRD	Main bank interaction term (D_MDD×D_MB)											−0.014	−0.416*** (−4.27)
D_BM	Dummy for multiple banks merger	0.021	1.080*** (12.62)	0.004	1.897*** (4.13)			0.048	0.963*** (10.97)	0.019	1.091*** (11.62)	0.021	1.107*** (12.80)
D_YY	Year dummy		YES		YES		YES		YES		YES		YES
Number of Observations			22,982		7,328		6,981		8,673		20,881		22,982
Number of Selling Cases			3,186		250		732		2,204		2,728		3,186
Rate of Selling			13.9%		3.4%		10.5%		25.4%		13.1%		13.9%
Log Likelihood			−7,866		−1,031		−2,209		−4,527		−6,552		−7,840

Notes: *** denotes significance at the 1% level, ** denotes significance at the 5% level, and * denotes significance at the 10% level. Estimated with a Logit model in which the dependent variable takes the value of 1 when corporate shares held by banks decrease compared to the beginning of the period and 0 otherwise. Model 2 is limited to samples identified as cases of cross-shareholding between banks and corporations. σ_X denotes the explanatory variable's standard deviation; dP/dX denotes marginal effects.

Having made the above observations, we turned our focus to how banks evaluated a firm's risk or quality in choosing corporate shares to sell off. From the results for Z_3, we found that banks' risk consideration declined following the banking crisis. The coefficient of the variable DICR, which represents a firm's credit risk, is positive in the estimation for both the whole period and in period I. However, in period III, when disposal became widespread, the coefficient is statistically insignificant. More importantly, the coefficient of the variable D/E, another proxy for a firm's credit risk, is positive in period I, but becomes negative in period II and significantly negative in the last period. Thus we can infer that banks that sold high-risk shares until period I became less concerned about the risks of holding shares in periods II and III, when disposal was highly imperative.[13]

On the other hand, the coefficient of D_AVQ, a proxy for the expected return or growth opportunity of a stock, is insignificant until period II. However, rather surprisingly, it becomes significantly positive in period III. As explained above, according to standard agency theory, D_AVQ should have a negative sign. However, banks sold high value shares systematically. To put it differently, as banks were required to reduce their holding shares, they sold firms with high market valuations rather than riskier firms. We can conjecture that, since 1999, when financial health became their primary concern, banks started to give priority to securing funds to eliminate non-performing loans. This resulted in a systematic deterioration of banks' equity portfolios.

Last, the result for Z_4 in Table 3.6 strongly supports the hypothesis that a long-term relationship with a firm influences a bank's decision to sell off shares. The coefficient on BBR, a proxy for the closeness of financing relationships, and the coefficient on D_CSH, which represents cross-shareholding relationships, and the coefficient on D_MB, which represents main-bank relationships, are all significantly negative at the 1% level. As far as BBR is concerned, its coefficient is significantly negative at the 1% level in all periods, although the effect is stronger in period II when the banking crisis occurred. If a firm's degree of dependence on bank loans is one standard deviation (10.9%) higher than the mean (12.5%), then the bank's probability of selling declines by 3.4% points. This is more than 30% of the 10.5% probability of selling in period II. Based on these results, we conclude that banks chose to maintain cross-shareholding with firms with which they had formed strong relationships.

As shown above, a bank's decision to sell off a stock is determined not only by its concern for adjusting its portfolio, but also by its long-term relationships with firms. Especially after the banking crisis, banks that received poor market valuations began to sell shares actively, and their decision to sell was based more on the nature of their financial relationships with firms than on the credit risks of those firms. Moreover, after 1999, while banks reduced shareholding mainly by selling shares with higher liquidity and higher expected rates of return

---

[13] We observe that the effect of SDRTN, which represents stock price fluctuation risk, has strengthened after period II. This result is likely to mean that the reduction of stock holding risk is an important factor in recent decision-making on sell-offs.

(those which were easy to sell), they held onto shares of firms with which they had long-term relationships. This was especially true in cases where main-bank relationships existed. In this sense, banks' investment behavior was based on a perverse incentive which not only undermined corporate governance but also degraded their own portfolios.

3.3.4 Cooperative and Non-Cooperative Unwinding

As described in the preceding sections, even as shareholding risk has come to be clearly recognized since 1997, banks have tended to refrain from selling corporate shares of firms with which they have formed long-term relationships. In particular, when cross-shareholding relationships existed, the threat that one side's sell-off of shares would invite a retaliatory sell-off by the other was one factor that helped to maintain cross-shareholdings. We now shed light on the question of whether cross-shareholding was terminated under an implicit contract between both parties (cooperative unwinding) or under circumstances in which one party's actions invited a retaliatory sell-off by the other (non-cooperative unwinding).

To determine whether the unwinding of cross-shareholding happened cooperatively or not, we need to deepen our analysis and take the actual negotiation process into account. Given that the mutual shareholding as such is a form of implicit contract, in cases where shares were sold simultaneously it is likely that the termination of the relationship is determined by an implicit agreement by both sides to do so. When there was a lag in the timing of the choice, however, we will assume that one side made a choice to sell off independently of the other, and was subjected to retaliatory action. Under these assumptions, we introduce a dummy variable X_6 to represent bank j selling corporation i's shares in the current or previous year into equation (1) in section 3.3.2.

We also introduce the dummy variable Z_5 to represent corporation i's selling bank j's shares in the current or previous year into the bank's shareholding choice model (equation (2) in section 3.3.3). Of the 2,074 instances of shares sold by corporations in the entire period, there were 718 instances in which the partner bank sold off in the same year (*BSL*), and 304 instances in which the partner bank sold off in the previous year (*PBSL*). On the other hand, of the 2,728 instances of shares sold by banks for the entire period, there were 718 instances in which the partner corporation sold off in the same year (*CSL*), and 440 instances in which the partner corporation sold off in the previous year (*PCSL*). The estimation results for the entire period are shown in Model 2 in Table 3.5 and Table 3.6. The estimation results by period are shown in Table 3.7 (only results for the dummy variables are reported). Although this estimation cannot identify sell-off behavior stretching over multiple years, we can make two observations from these results.[14]

---

[14] Since banks have a large shareholding ratio in each firm, they presumably sold parts of their shares in multiple periods.

Table 3.7 Cooperative and Non-Cooperative Unwinding

Panel 1: The impact of bank selling on corporate selling

	Variable	Definition	Period I (FY95–96) Est. Coef. (t-stat)	$\sigma_x * dP/dX$	Period II (FY97–98) Est. Coef. (t-stat)	$\sigma_x * dP/dX$	Period III (FY99–2001) Est. Coef. (t-stat)	$\sigma_x * dP/dX$
X_6	BSL	Dummy for Bank Selling (Same Year)	1.676 *** (9.07)	0.017	2.011 *** (15.77)	0.032	0.976 *** (12.98)	0.051
	PBSL	Dummy for Bank Selling (Previous Year)	0.044 (0.15)	0.000	−0.097 (−0.47)	−0.001	0.254 *** (2.72)	0.010

Panel 2: The impact of corporate selling on bank selling

	Variable	Definition	Period I (FY95–96) Est. Coef. (t-stat)	$\sigma_x * dP/dX$	Period II (FY97–98) Est. Coef. (t-stat)	$\sigma_x * dP/dX$	Period III (FY99–2001) Est. Coef. (t-stat)	$\sigma_x * dP/dX$
Z_5	CSL	Dummy for Corporate Selling (Same Year)	1.580 *** (8.55)	0.012	1.874 *** (15.37)	0.037	1.028 *** (14.11)	0.060
	PCSL	Dummy for Corporate Selling (Previous Year)	0.289 (1.29)	0.002	0.987*** (6.27)	0.017	0.748 *** (8.31)	0.035

Notes: *** denotes significance at the 1% level, ** denotes significance at the 5% level, and * denotes significance at the 10% level. Estimated with a Logit model in which the dependent variable takes the value of 1 when corporate shares held by banks decrease compared to the beginning of period and 0 otherwise. σ_x denotes the explanatory variable's standard deviation; dP/dX denotes marginal effects. X1–X5 in panel 1 and Z1–Z4 in panel 2 are not reported.

First, both a bank's and a corporation's choice of stocks to sell responds to the variable which represents the choice to sell by the other party in the same year. For instance, the marginal effect on *BSL*, a bank's sell-off in the same year, is 5.1%. On the other hand, the marginal effect on *CSL*, a corporation's sell-off in the same year, is 6%. Recent instances of cross-shareholding termination appear to have proceeded cooperatively, seemingly under implicit contracts agreed to by both parties.

Second, there is evidence, however, that cross-shareholding relationships also end non-cooperatively. The variables representing sell-offs by the other party in the previous year have significantly positive coefficients in the entire period sample. The lag effect is in general much smaller than same-year effects, and the lag effect of a bank's sell-off (*PBSL*) on corporate choice is quite small and insignificant until period II. On the other hand, a bank's choice to sell in response to the disposal of corporate shares in the previous year (*PCSL*) is significantly positive but only after period II. This implies that a corporation's choice to sell, considering the rise of holding risk, strongly influences a bank's choice. In summary, the results show that there was both a cooperative effect and a non-cooperative effect, whereby corporations sold their bank shares first and banks retaliated. This supplementary factor led to a rapid disintegration of many cross-shareholding relationships.

3.3.5 Influence of the Main-Bank Relationship on Choice

The relationship between a corporation and a bank is generally stronger when the bank is the corporation's main bank. In fact, banks tended to refrain from selling shares of firms with which they have had a main-bank relationship. However, estimation results for corporations show that they were more likely to sell shares of their main bank. This counter-intuitive result is a puzzle. How did main-bank relationships affect sell-off behaviors? Why did corporations liquidate main-banks' shares and why was that possible?

To shed light on this puzzle, we estimate models that include the interaction term of the main bank dummy D_MB with the interest coverage ratio, D_ICR, and the bank's financial rating, D_FRD. Here, D_ICR represents the necessity to sell for corporations and the holding risk for banks, respectively. In contrast, D_FRD represents the necessity to sell for banks and the holding risk for corporations. This estimation allows us to test the conjecture that even though the choice to sell a bank stock is financially rational, a sell-off is avoided when the main bank relationship is strong. The results for corporation choices are presented in Model 3 of Table 3.5.

First, we find that the estimate for the interaction term between D_FRD and D_MB has a significantly negative coefficient. This result shows that, although the financial condition of banks in which corporations invested got worse and their holding risk increased, corporations tended to avoid selling a bank's shares if they had a main-bank relationship with that bank.

Second, we should note that the coefficient of the interaction term between D_MB and D_ICR, a proxy for the financial degradation of shareholding corporations themselves, is significantly positive. Corporations facing liquidity crises tend to selectively liquidate shares of their main banks. When we divide the sample into two sets, one with cross-shareholding with main-bank relationships and the other without, and estimate equations (1) in two sets respectively, we achieve mostly the same results as above. Therefore, under main-bank relationships, corporations liquidated shares of their main bank (in other words, in cases in which the main bank did not stop the sell-off) only when the corporations experienced a financial crisis, which produced the puzzling outcome mentioned above.

On the other hand, estimation results for banks (Model 3 in Table 3.6) show that the main-bank relationship restrains a bank's sell-off of shares of partner corporations. The coefficient of the interaction term between the firm partner's financial condition and the *D_MB* dummy (*D_MBXD_FRD*) is significantly negative. This implies that even though a bank's unhealthy financial condition may cause increasing market pressure to reduce shareholding, the bank tends to selectively hold shares of corporations with which it has a main-bank relationship. Also, the coefficient of the interaction term between a corporation's credit risk and the *D_MB* dummy (*D_MBXD_ICR*) is significantly negative. This is especially so in period III (not reported). This result suggests that the bank tends to avoid selling off shares of corporations with high credit risk if the bank has long-term relationships with those corporations.[15]

The puzzling asymmetrical response between banks and corporations in selling their partners' shares can be explained by the bail-out efforts of the main bank. Since banks deeply value a main-bank relationship, they permit these corporations to liquidate their bank shares in a crisis. In contrast, they hold onto their shares of a corporation in crisis since selling would send a clear signal to the market that the corporation is in bad financial shape.

Consequently, the asymmetric effect of the main-bank relationship further accelerated the degradation of a bank's equity portfolio. As discussed above, banks mainly liquidated shares of corporations with high expected rates of return, regardless of the level to which credit risk skewed their equity portfolio to firms with low rates of return. Moreover, the above results show that banks held shares of the corporations with which they were the main bank in order to maintain a long-term relationship, even when corporations presumably face a financial crisis.

3.4 EFFECT OF OWNERSHIP ON CORPORATE PERFORMANCE

3.4.1 The Costs and Benefits of Cross-Shareholding

So far, we have examined the causes of the recent rapid unwinding of cross-shareholding. What then are its welfare implications? In this section, we address this issue by examining the relationship between ownership structure and corporate performance.

The growth of Japanese firms up to the 1990s has been credited in part to the existence of stable shareholders. These stable shareholders, according to this theory, freed managers from both the threat of hostile takeovers and myopic shareholder pressures, allowing them to focus on long-run decision-making (Abegglen and Stalk 1985; Odagiri 1992; Porter 1992). Moreover, many corporate activities are supposed to run efficiently under a high level of cross-shareholding. It provided incentives to employees with firm-specific human capital by protecting

---

[15] The same result can be observed from the estimation in which the sample is divided into main-bank firms (firms with main banks) and non-main-bank firms.

them against adverse shocks, and therefore reducing risk (Aoki 1988; Aoki and Patrick 1994; Sheard 1994; Okabe 2002).

Bank ownership of borrowing firms could also help banks to monitor and mitigate asset substitution problems, thereby improving firm performance. Prowse (1990) and Flath (1993) examine patterns of bank shareholding in Japan as a proxy of bank monitoring. Some previous studies addressing the effect of financial ownership on corporate performance showed that shareholdings by financial institutions improved management efficiency (Lichtenberg and Pushner 1994) and attributed this improved efficiency to effective monitoring.

The role of large shareholders (parent firms) is also supposed to play a significant monitoring role in the corporate governance of Japanese firms. Sheard (1994) addresses the significant role of large shareholders (parent firms) and main banks in Japanese firms. Kang and Shivdasani (1995), and more recently Morck et al. (2000) confirmed this understanding. Focusing on entertainment expenses, Yafeh and Yosha (2003) show that concentrated shareholding is associated with lower expenditures on activities with a potential to generate private benefits for managers.[16]

In the mid-1990s, however, when it became evident that the Japanese economy faced prolonged stagnation, the costs of Japan's unique ownership structure came under scrutiny. Because stable shareholders faithfully held shares over long periods, cross-shareholding almost by definition could potentially foster a moral hazard among incumbent managers (insider control). As management became entrenched, this resulted in low performance due either to over-investment or low effort levels in relation to capital and labor input.[17] The agency cost associated with cross-shareholding may become even more acute than in cases of high managerial ownership with managers wielding controlling interests in their companies.[18]

It is also plausible that bank ownership could play a negative role in corporate governance when banks use their stakes to encourage client firms to take on projects that deviate from value maximization rather than taking steps to reduce asset substitution.[19] Weinstein and Yafeh (1998) first suggested that banks both

---

[16] They conclude that large shareholders are probably more important than banks for monitoring.

[17] For instance, the sensitivity of dividends to profit among Japanese firms has declined to almost zero since the late 1960s when stabilization progressed. It is true that adopting a dividend policy less sensitive to profit may promote firms' investment when firms have high growth opportunities. However, if firms' growth opportunities are low, then adopting such a dividend policy generates free cash flow in Jensen's (1986) sense. In the late 1980s, during the so-called bubble period, low dividends may have emerged as a source of the excessive investment problem.

[18] When managers have a high degree of ownership, they suffer losses when there is empire-building or effort aversion, while in cases in which there is a high level of cross-shareholding, incumbent managers have not been held responsible for any losses associated with such morally hazardous behaviors.

[19] The concern with ownership's effect on corporate efficiency is relatively new, while many previous studies have shown that firms belonging to bank-centered corporate groups performed significantly worse than independent firms (Nakatani 1984; Weinstein and Yafeh 1998). In these analyses, the main instrument by which groups influenced corporate performance was the rent extracted by banks with strong bargaining power.

induced clients to borrow more than profit maximization warranted and encouraged them to adopt low-risk and low-return investment strategies. Subsequently, Morck et al. (2000) stressed that assigning the task of corporate governance to banks does not always lead to maximization of firm value because banks as creditors have different objectives from banks as shareholders. Focusing on FY 1986, the year before the ceiling on a bank's ownership was reduced from 10% to 5%, they found that equity ownership by the main bank and firm value are inversely related. They suggested that higher bank ownership is associated with relaxed financial constraints, allowing firms to undertake more marginally acceptable investment opportunities. In the same vein, Miyajima et al. (2001) report that corporate investment was sensitive to internal funds only among firms with low growth opportunities in the late 1980s, and that this relationship was stronger among the firms with high ratios of shares held by main banks.

Another possible cost to Japanese firms belonging to vertically integrated corporate groups (*keiretsu*) is the conflict of interest between large shareholders (parent firms) and minority shareholders. A growing literature has blamed corporate groups for the expropriation of minority shareholders. Classens et al. (1999) and Johnson et al. (2000) argue that corporate groups are associated with minority shareholder exploitation in Asia. If this argument were applicable to the vertical corporate groups in Japan, it is likely that parent firms with a high ownership stake in subsidiaries (listed subsidiaries) could transfer funds from minority shareholders to controlling shareholders, lowering performance.[20]

The consensus view has seemingly moved from highlighting the benefits of the ownership structure of Japanese firms to stressing its costs. However, so far there has been little empirical research on whether ownership structure affects corporate performance. The limited studies that have been carried out only cover the late 1980s. Furthermore, there is no research that directly addresses the effect of cross-shareholding on performance.

3.4.2 The Data

To fill this gap, we focus on the relationship between ownership structure and performance after the bubble period, using the comprehensive database developed by NLIR and Waseda. This database has a wide range of advantages over the data sets used in previous studies, which often depend on information disclosed in financial reports (*Yūkashōken-hōkokusho*). For instance, previous research used "shares held by financial institutions" as a measure of the ownership stake of banks or "stabilized" shareholders. However, needless to say, "shares held by financial institutions" in financial reports includes various types of financial institutions: city banks that are characterized by their joint ownership of debt

---

[20] Low performance is also plausible if the monitoring of a listed subsidiary by a parent firm were so strict as to deprive managers and employees of incentives (Burkart et al. 1997).

and equity, trust banks whose shareholdings were mainly comprised of pension and investment trust funds, and the insurance companies that hold shares in both their general account (where they assume the risk) and special accounts (where risk is delegated). Additionally, "shares held by non-financial institutions" in the reports also includes both those shares held by business partners (group firms) and block holders such as parent companies.

By contrast, the NLIR-Waseda database, which is constructed on the basis of lists of the 20 largest shareholders for individual firms, provides the accurate shareholding ratio of each stakeholder in line with standard economic theory. Thus, it provides the ratio of stable shareholders by aggregating the shares held by banks (excluding trust banks), shares held by insurance companies and the shares held by non-financial institutions. Consequently, we can disentangle the overall effect of the stabilization of shareholders and that of bank ownership on corporate performance.

Second, the NLIR-Waseda database also provides the accurate ratio held by institutional shareholders, both foreign and domestic. It presents the exact ratio of shareholding by foreign institutional investors by distinguishing shares held by foreign financial and non-financial corporations.[21] It also estimates the shareholding ratio of domestic institutional investors by aggregating the increasingly large number of pension and mutual funds entrusted to domestic financial institutions (mainly trust banks and insurance companies).

Last, this data provides the shares held by main banks and large shareholders among non-financial institutions. The main bank is defined as the largest lender to client firms, while the threshold of the ownership stake of the large shareholder is set at 15%. This data made it possible for us to identify which effects, costs, and benefits dominated in cases of ownership by main banks and large corporate shareholders.

3.4.3 Results and Discussion

Our sample firms are the non-financial firms in the First Section of the Tokyo Stock Exchange.[22] We conducted estimates for the firm years from 1985 to 2002. This period is further divided into three sub-periods: the bubble (1985–92), post-bubble (1990–97), and the banking crisis period (1995–2002). We use the standard model that regresses corporate performance on fundamental variables as well as governance variables including ownership structure, following studies by Lichtenberg and Pushner (1994), Yafeh (2000), and Horiuchi and Hanazaki (2000). Given that our data has a panel structure, we employ a fixed effect

---

[21] Previous research used the foreign ownership ratios in financial reports, which include both the shares held by foreign institutional investors as well as foreign non-financial companies (for example, Renault and Ford)

[22] We also conducted estimates for all 2600 listed firms with the same sample period. The results are basically the same.

model to control for time-invariant unobserved individual (firm specific) effects.[23] The estimated model is:

$$(3) \qquad P_{i,t} - P_{j,t} = a_i + \Sigma\beta Gov_{i,t-1} + \chi SIZE_{i,t-1} + \delta DAR_{i,t-1} + Year_t + \epsilon_{i,t}$$

where $P_{i,t}$ is the performance in year t, and $P_{j,t}$ is the performance of industry j (based on the 33 industry classifications of the Tokyo Stock Exchange) which firm i belongs to in year t. Thus the dependent variable is the standardized perform-ance.[24] It is highly relevant to use the standardized performance because the issue here is corporate efficiency which is independent of industry common factors. It could also reduce the reverse causality problem: the estimation might capture a stakeholder that bought or held onto a high performer's shares rather than signifying the large shareholder's promotion of firm efficiency. Because consoli-dated accounting data is available in our NLIR-Waseda database, the current value ROA on a consolidated basis and Tobin's q are used for the index of performance.[25]

The explanatory variable $SIZE_{i,t}$ is the logarithm of total assets, $DAR_{i,t}$ is the leverage (interest-bearing debt / total assets) of firm i in year t, and $Year_t$ is a dummy variable which takes the value 1 in year t. These are included to control for factors affecting performance other than ownership structure.

$Gov_{i,t-1}$ is the governance structure of firm i in year $t-1$. It includes the various shareholding ratios for domestic and foreign institutional investors and for the ratio of stable shareholders. To obtain a variable that represents foreign institutional investors more precisely, we calculate the share of foreign institutional investors, *FRGN*. This is done by eliminating foreign corporations and domestic pension funds via foreign countries from the shares held by foreign shareholders. *STAB* is the ratio of stable shareholders, which is then decomposed into the ratio of bank ownership *BKSH* and that of non-bank ownership, *NBKSH*. Notice that the correlation between *FRGN* and *STAB* (*BKSH*, *NBSKH*) is not very high. For instance, the correlation coefficient between *FRGN* and *BKSH* is -0.17. We also include the share of the main bank, *D_MBS*, which takes the value 1 if the main bank shareholding is nearly 5% (we take 4.9% as its threshold). We found that 26% of the entire sample of firms met this requirement.

Further, we added the dummy variable, *D_PAR*, which is given the value of 1 when a corporation holds more than 15% of shares. This variable enables us to test the possibility that minority shareholders are exploited by controlling

---

[23] Considering the effect of outliers on the estimation results for explanatory variables except dummy variables, all values deviating more than three standard deviations from sample means are replaced by sample means plus three standard deviations.

[24] We also estimated the regression using (1) each of the row figures of the performance index, and (2) the yearly changes of the industry-standardized performance as dependent variables. The results are unchanged.

[25] Tobin's q is strictly constructed in the NLIR and Waseda database by estimating current value of tangible assets, land, and securities, following the standard literature. See Miyajima et al. (2001).

shareholders (parent companies). The ratio of such firms in our sample, namely, the ratio of "listed subsidiaries," is 26%. Last, to capture the effect of managerial ownership, we introduced the dummy variable, D_DIR, which is 1 if managerial ownership is higher than 5%.[26] The ratio of firms with the D_DIR equal to 1 is 13.1% in our sample.

In addition to the above variables for ownership structure, following Yermack (1996), we also added variables on the size of the board of directors, BRN, and the ratio of outsider directors, ODR, to the model. The expected sign of BRN is negative because poor communication and decision-making are associated with large boards. All the explanatory variables are lagged by one period from the dependent variable to clarify the causality with corporate performance. Detailed definitions of the variables are in Appendix 3.3. The estimation results are presented in Table 3.8 on the full sample period and Table 3.9 on sub-periods.

First, we observe that leverage has a positive effect on corporate performance. The result is consistent with the standard theoretical understanding of the disciplinary role of debt since Jensen (1986) and also coincides with recent studies by Horiuchi and Hanazaki (2000). According to Table 3.9, the effect of leverage is larger in the post-bubble and banking crisis periods than during the bubble period. This supports the notion that debt in general played an increasingly significant role for corporate governance in the 1990s.

Second, the ratio of outside directors, ODR, and the board size, BRN, have the expected signs but are not necessarily stable. While the sign of outside directors is positive and significant in both ROA and Q for the whole period, the results for sub-periods are not sufficiently significant in either ROA or Q (results are not shown). On the other hand, the size of boards is an insignificant factor in ROA over the whole period, whereas it shows high significance in sub-periods. From these results we see that the relationship between small boards and high performance that Yermack (1996) observed in US firms is also the case for Japanese firms, particularly during the post-bubble period.

Third, managerial ownership levels exceeding a certain threshold may have negative effects on corporate performance.[27] Although the significance level is not sufficiently high, there is a possibility that managerial entrenchment is associated with high managerial ownership. The effect is clear in the bubble period and to a lesser extent in the post-bubble period. These results are consistent with the understanding that some family-owned firms tend to be over-invested.

Changing our focus to ownership structure, we observe that the ownership level of particular categories of stakeholders has strongly influenced corporate performance. First, shareholding by both domestic and foreign institutional

---

[26] We set this threshold following Morck et al. (1988).

[27] Morck et al. (2000) reported a monotonous positive relationship between managerial ownership and Tobin's q, interpreting it to be the result of the alignment effect between managers' concerns and shareholders' interests. But we did not find such a relationship.

Table **3.8** Estimation Results of the Effect of Cross-shareholding on Firm Performance (1985–2002)

Variable	Definition	Consolidated basis		Consolidated basis	
		ROA	Tobin's q (Q)	ROA	Tobin's q (Q)
		Est. Coef. (t-stat.)	Est. Coef. (t-stat.)	Est. Coef. (t-stat.)	Est. Coef. (t-stat.)
SIZE	Logarithm of total assets (replacement value of assets)	−1.332*** (−16.21)	−0.148*** (−14.65)	−1.318*** (−16.05)	−0.147*** (−14.50)
DAR	Leverage (interest-bearing debt / total assets)	2.173*** (9.21)	0.477*** (16.38)	2.181*** (9.24)	0.478*** (16.41)
FRGN	Shareholding ratio of foreign institutional investors	0.071*** (15.15)	0.013*** (22.69)	0.069*** (14.73)	0.013*** (22.29)
DINS	Shareholding ratio of domestic institutional investors	0.093*** (13.83)	0.008*** (10.24)	0.090*** (13.39)	0.008*** (9.86)
STAB	Shareholding ratio of stable shareholders	−0.007*** (−2.74)	−0.001*** (−2.98)		
BKSH	Ratio of bank stable ownership			−0.044*** (−4.60)	−0.005*** (−4.15)
NBKSH	Ratio of non-bank stable ownership			−0.004 (−1.48)	−0.001* (−1.84)
ODR	Ratio of outside board members	0.634*** (2.80)	0.116*** (4.15)	0.616*** (2.72)	0.114*** (4.08)
BRN	Relative number of board members	−0.033*** (−0.72)	−0.025*** (−4.35)	−0.027 (−0.59)	−0.024*** (−4.24)
D_DIR	Board member share-holding dummy	−0.149* (−1.77)	−0.023** (−2.25)	−0.145* (−1.72)	−0.023** (−2.20)
D_PAR	Parent company dummy	0.859*** (7.04)	0.080*** (5.34)	0.792*** (6.43)	0.073*** (4.82)
D_MBS	Main bank shareholding dummy	−0.191*** (−3.64)	−0.026*** (−3.99)	−0.156*** (−2.94)	−0.022*** (−3.37)
D_YY	Year dummy	YES	YES	YES	YES
Number of Observations		18,196	18,196	18,196	18,196
Number of Firms		1,305	1,305	1,305	1,305
Adjusted R²		0.55	0.50	0.55	0.50

Notes: *** denotes significance at the 1% level, ** denotes significance at the 5% level, and * denotes significance at the 10% level. Sample firms are non-financial firms listed in the three markets (excluding firms with less than one billion yen in owned capital or firms which have been listed less than three years). The estimation period is FY 1985 to 2002. *ROA* (return on assets on a consolidated basis) is the operating profit divided by current total assets (average at the beginning and end of the period), where total assets is the sum of book value total assets, unrealized capital gain (loss) from tangible fixed assets, and unrealized capital gain (loss) from securities. Tobin's q (Q) on a consolidated basis the value of the firm/total assets (end of period), where the value of the firm is the sum of market value of equity, book value debt and minority equity. For more detail on definitions and methods of calculation, see Appendix 3.3

investors has significantly positive effects. We generally expect that monitoring pressure for management increases if institutional investors hold shares above a certain level (Shleifer and Vishny 1986). Also, several authors have pointed out that since institutional investors have high monitoring abilities, they are effective at mitigating agency problems (McConnell and Servaes 1995). Consistent with these predictions, institutional investors likely contributed to performance enhancements by disciplining managers in the late 1990s. This effect is observed among not only foreign institutional investors but also domestic institutional investors.

Second, firms that have parent companies perform significantly better. This is consistent with Kang and Shivdasani (1995) and Morck et al. (2000). In spite of the perceived conflict of interest between parent companies and minority shareholders, as far as the listed firms are concerned, serious problems regarding corporate governance are less likely in vertical corporate groups (*keiretsu*). In contrast, it appears that parent firms as block holders monitored their listed subsidiaries (related firms) effectively and improved their efficiencies.

Finally, as for stabilized shareholders, we find an inverse relationship between the shares held by stable shareholders and performance in both *ROA* and Tobin's *q*.[28] In sub-sample estimation, the inverse relationship is clear in the bubble and post-bubble period. This is consistent with the idea that high stabilized shareholding can insulate managers from external pressures. On the other hand, the sign of main bank shareholding is negative and highly significant for the whole sample as well as both the post-bubble and banking crisis sub-periods. This result is also consistent with the entrenchment rather than monitoring view of the role of the main bank.

As we mentioned, both banks and non-banks were stable shareholders. Thus, the interesting task is to identify which of the two has a stronger effect on insulating managers from external pressures. Panel 2 of Table 3.9 decompose the stabilized shareholding ratio into the shares held by banks, *BKSH*, and the shares held by non-banks, *NBKSH*. Shares held by non-banks include shares held by non-financial institutions and insurance companies. Interestingly, in both ROA and Tobin's *q* estimation, the coefficient of *BKSH* is highly significant, while that of the *NBKSH* is negative but less significant. This suggests that the negative effect on performance came not from the shareholding among firms, but mainly from the shareholding by banks.

Furthermore, we observe in Table 3.9 that the coefficient of *BKSH* is consistently negative and highly significant in all sub-sample periods. The magnitude of the effect is determined by multiplying the coefficient by one standard deviation of *BKSH*: −0.269 percent in the bubble period, −0.467 percent in the post-bubble period, and −0.317 percent in the banking crisis period respectively. This magnitude is almost the same as, or even higher than, that of foreign ownership.[29] The

---

[28] The result holds if the independent variable is replaced with TFP (Miyajima et al. 2004).

[29] The magnitude of *FOR* is 0.355 in the bubble period, 0.258 in the post-bubble period, and 0.310 in the banking crisis period.

Table 3.9 Performance (*ROA*) and Corporate Governance
Panel 1: Estimation by Sub-periods

Variable	Definition	The Bubble Period FY 1985–92 Est. Coef. (t-stat.)	Post-Bubble Period FY 1990–97 Est. Coef. (t-stat.)	Banking Crisis FY1995–2002 Est. Coef. (t-stat.)
SIZE	Logarithm of total assets	−1.826 ***	−1.302 ***	−2.884 ***
	(replacement value of assets)	(−13.77)	(−7.31)	(−15.90)
DAR	Leverage (interest-bearing	1.898 ***	4.957 ***	3.876 ***
	debt / total assets)	(5.18)	(10.92)	(8.29)
FRGN	Shareholding ratio of for-	0.081 ***	0.052 ***	0.049 ***
	eign institutional investors	(11.48)	(6.39)	(6.10)
DINS	Shareholding ratio	0.054 ***	0.071 ***	0.065 ***
	of domestic institutional	(5.82)	(5.85)	(6.15)
	investors			
STAB	Shareholding ratio of stable	−0.009 **	−0.022 **	−0.006
	shareholders	(−2.48)	(−2.68)	(−1.59)
ODR	Ratio of outside board	0.473	0.588	0.265
	members	(1.26)	(1.53)	(0.71)
BRN	Relative number of board	−0.249 ***	−0.289 ***	−0.124 **
	members	(−2.69)	(−3.04)	(−2.05)
D_DIR	Board member shareholding	−0.375 ***	−0.270 ***	−0.002
	dummy	(−3.23)	(−1.79)	(−0.01)
D_PAR	Parent company	0.885 ***	0.568 ***	0.894 ***
	dummy	(5.24)	(2.50)	(4.41)
D_MBS	Main bank shareholding	0.087	−0.167 **	−0.154 *
	dummy	(1.26)	(−1.98)	(−1.72)
D_YY	Year dummy	YES	YES	YES
Number of Observations		7,483	8,217	8,646
Number of Firms		1,030	1,103	1,273
Adjusted R²		0.69	0.64	0.66

Panel 2: Decomposing the stabilized shareholder

Variable	Definition	The Bubble Period FY 1985–92 Est. Coef. (t-stat.)	Post-Bubble Period FY 1990–97 Est. Coef. (t-stat.)	Banking Crisis FY1995–2002 Est. Coef. (t-stat.)
SIZE	Logarithm of total assets	−1.826 ***	−1.314 ***	−2.836 ***
	(replacement value of assets)	(−13.77)	(−7.39)	(−15.61)
DAR	The leverage (interest-bear-	1.940 ***	4.994 ***	3.914 ***
	ing debt / total assets)	(5.29)	(11.01)	(8.38)
FRGN	Shareholding ratio of foreign	0.081 ***	0.051 ***	0.045 ***
	institutional investors	(11.45)	(6.19)	(5.60)
DINS	Shareholding ratio of do-	0.052 ***	0.069 ***	0.060 ***
	mestic institutional investors	(5.58)	(5.69)	(5.62)
BKSH	Ratio of bank stable owner-	−0.049 ***	−0.089 ***	−0.062 ***
	ship	(−3.34)	(−3.73)	(−4.01)
NBKSH	Ratio of non-bank stable	−0.006	−0.013	−0.002
	ownership	(−1.55)	(−1.39)	(−0.52)
ODR	Ratio of outside board	0.517	0.525	0.225
	members	(1.38)	(1.36)	(0.61)
BRN	Relative number of board	−0.241 ***	−0.294 ***	−0.120 **
	members	(−2.60)	(−3.09)	(−1.97)

D_DIR	Board member shareholding	−0.378 ***	−0.266 *	−0.003 *
	dummy	(−3.26)	(−1.77)	(−0.02)
D_PAR	Parent company dummy	0.858 ***	0.507 **	0.797 ***
		(5.08)	(2.22)	(3.90)
D_YY	Year dummy	YES	YES	YES
Number of Observations		7,483	8,217	8,646
Number of Firms		1,030	1,103	1,273
Adjusted R^2		0.69	0.64	0.66

Notes: *** denotes significance at the 1% level, ** denotes significance at the 5% level, and * denotes significance at the 10% level. Sample firms are non-financial firms listed in the three markets (excluding firms with less than ¥1 billion in owned capital or firms which have been listed less than three years). The estimation period is FY 1985–2002. The dependent variable is *ROA* (return on assets on a consolidated basis) which is the operating profit divided by current total assets (average at the beginning and end of period), where total assets is the sum of book value of total assets, unrealized capital gain (loss) from tangible fixed assets, and unrealized capital gain (loss) from securities. For more details on definitions and methods of calculation, see Appendix 3.3

largest negative effect was during the post-bubble period. Thus, it is unlikely that mutual shareholding among non-financial institutions promoted managerial discretion by shielding top management from market pressure. It is highly plausible that significant bank ownership or main bank shareholding negatively affected corporate governance, although we cannot disentangle whether this result came from the entrenchment effect or propping-up effect.

The above estimations are not completely free from endogeneity problems. Even with standardized performance as a dependent variable and the appropriate lag and firm specific effects as independent variables, we cannot rule out that the estimation captures the reverse relationship (i.e. a stakeholder invested in high performers' shares rather than trying to keep firms efficient). Thus, further tests are necessary and the result is still tentative. These points notwithstanding, however, these results have several important implications.

First, the fact that institutional shareholding is consistently associated with high performance implies that it helps raise efficiency and is economically rational. There is no doubt that institutional shareholders played a significant monitoring role in Japanese firms by partly substituting for the (main) bank.

Second, the inverse relation between bank ownership and performance suggests that unwinding the cross-shareholding between banks and corporations clearly allows for efficiency gains. It is often pointed out that unwinding cross-shareholding may increase unnecessary pressures on management to think myopically (i.e. in terms of short-term fluctuations in the price of their stock). However, as far as the cross-shareholding between banks and firms is concerned, the long-run positive effect of its unwinding on corporate governance in Japan is larger than any possible myopia effect in the 1990s.

Third, given that stable shareholding and high bank ownership stakes have had a consistently negative effect on corporate efficiency since the bubble period, the inefficiency associated with bank ownership per se was not necessary to cause the unwinding of cross-shareholding. The notion that less efficient institutions could not survive is not the case by the mid-1990s. There was inertia among firms and banks in their decision to hold stocks. As we explained in the previous section, it took an external shock such as the banking crisis to disrupt this inertia.

Last, in contrast with previous research, mutual shareholding among non-financial institutions may not have a strong negative effect on corporate performance. Similarly, in contrast with a conflict of interest view of corporate shareholding, block shareholding of other non-financial institutions constantly played a significant role in corporate governance in Japanese firms. It is also unlikely that large numbers of block holders enabled the transfer of funds from minority shareholders to the controlling shareholders as part of a "tunneling" scheme. While bank ownership of equity and loans, one of the salient features of the ownership structure in Japanese firms, has lost its raison d'être, other features such as the high share of block holding by corporations and cross-shareholding among firms have retained their economic rationale.

3.5 CONCLUSION AND PERSPECTIVES

3.5.1 The Uneven Unwinding of Cross-Shareholding

This chapter investigated the causes and implications of the unwinding of cross-shareholding, which has been a major feature of the ownership structure of Japanese firms for the past few decades.

Why did the stable ownership structure begin to unwind in the late 1990s? The banking crisis was a crucial factor that directly led to the termination of many cross-shareholding arrangements between financial institutions and firms. After 1995, and especially since 1997, when the banking crisis came to the surface and grew acute, it became increasingly irrational for corporations to hold bank (financial institution) shares due to the high holding risk. Major commercial banks also began to sell off shares after the crisis mainly because of the need to secure funds to dispose of non-performing loans and to respond to BIS regulations. Because cross-shareholding is a mutual relationship, once one side decides to sell its partner's share, it is natural that the partner will respond and the unwinding will begin to accelerate.

However, it is worth noting that crucial changes were occurring prior to the banking crisis. First, large, highly profitable firms with outstanding credit ratings already depended on bonds and equities for their external financing. This eroded the simultaneous ownership of both debt and equity claims by Japanese banks. Second, foreign investors increased their stakes in these firms in the early 1990s. Subsequently, the share held by domestic institutional investors also rose. Institutional investors encouraged top managers to consider shareholders value such as *ROE* and stock price. Third, it became evident that bank ownership was associated with low performance. This is possibly because higher bank ownership was associated with relaxed financial constraints, allowing firms to undertake more marginally accept-able investment opportunities.

These facts are extremely important because they explain the unevenness of the unwinding of cross-shareholding. As we emphasized in this chapter, the unwinding of cross-shareholding did not proceed uniformly among Japanese firms. The growing differentiation in the post-banking crisis period between firms that rapidly unwound cross-shareholding and firms that con-tinued cross-shareholding was the result of rational choices by both corpor-ations and banks.

Managers of profitable firms with easy access to capital markets and high foreign ownership prior to the banking crisis found little need to maintain financial relationships with banks. This made the unwinding of cross-sharehold-ings a rational way to earn a high market valuation. As Chapter 12 will explain, firms that actively reformed their boards of directors maintained high perform-ance through capital market discipline. For low-profit firms with difficulty accessing capital markets and low foreign ownership in the early 1990s—cross-shareholding, in particular between banks and firms, was maintained since managers needed strong relationships with banks for both financing and to stabilize ownership. As a result, management discipline was sacrificed and this led to poor performance. These are the firms that are both reluctant to reform their boards of directors and still maintain main-bank relationships as we saw in Chapter 2. They have fallen into a vicious circle of cross-shareholding and lax governance.

A key point is that firms that maintain cross-shareholding have little incentive to dissolve it. Managers of the firms with low profitability and strong bank relationships (in terms of both financing and shareholding) prior to the banking crisis do not have incentives to sell shares of banks whose profitability declined and holding risk went up. For banks, it is rational to continue holding onto corporate shares since selling the shares of firms with which they are connected sends negative signals to the market and can expose bad debts. If this circumstance continues, then the low market evaluations of these corporations are sustained and pressure from institutional investors or credit rating agencies has no effect. This mechanism explains how conventional *J*-type firms locked in to their trad-itional pattern of cross-shareholding in the late 1990s.

Against this backdrop, the simultaneous ownership of debt and equity became a systemic problem for Japanese firms in the late 1990s, and constituted an impediment to corporate reform. Locked-in firms have emerged as the most important targets of reform in Japan.

Moreover, the continuation of the above situation implies a degradation of banks' equity portfolios. The fact that the composition of borrowers deteriorated through the process of deregulation in the late 1980s has been pointed out by other studies (Miyajima and Arikawa 2000). The key result that has emerged from this chapter is that after 1997, when the banking crisis occurred, banks sold shares of firms with high growth opportunities (large Tobin's q) and held shares of firms with which they had main-bank relationships even as their holding risks rose.

3.5.2 Perspectives on the Future

By examining the causes and effects of the unwinding of cross-shareholding, we can extract some perspectives on the future.

We emphasized the vicious circle between bank ownership and low levels of governance, and the organizational lock-in of conventional J-type firms. However, this does not necessarily imply the existence of a stable equilibrium. Policy-makers have gradually recognized the vicious circle described above and taken various measures that have started to show some effect. The Banks' Shareholding Restriction Law, promulgated in September 2001, required banks to reduce their stock holdings up to the same amount of their equity (originally by September 2004, and with recent revisions, by September 2006). This provided a substantial impetus to sell off corporate shares. Both the Banks' Shareholdings Purchase Corporation (BSPC) and the Bank of Japan began to buy stock directly from city banks at market price with certain conditions in 2002. However, since the law only required a reduction in the total volume of shares held, and the Bank of Japan's purchases were limited to stock with credit ratings of BBB and higher, it is likely that banks may have held onto shares of firms with low profitability and high risk, and sold only equity with high liquidity.

In this context, the bank mergers may have a substantial effect on further steps to encourage the severing of the vicious circle. Given the current Antitrust Law that sets a ceiling on the holding of stock by financial institutions of up to 5%, the merged banks were required to sell holding shares. Furthermore, the changing ownership structure among major city banks themselves may give them an incentive to sell shares of firms with low profitability. In the process of reconstructing banks, the shares held by institutional shareholders increased as cross-shareholding with corporations dissolved. This would make it difficult for them to hold onto low-profit, high-risk firms. Thus, one possible (and optimistic) scenario has the locked-in relationship between major banks and firms gradually dissolving.

What then can we expect to happen to the ownership structure in the future? Cross-shareholding between banks and firms will without a doubt decrease from previous levels, while institutional shareholders will increase their stakes. In particular, domestic institutional investors will increase their presence. However, the cross-shareholding among firms will not be dissolved on a large scale, since corporate ownership of shares has its own economic rationale. For instance, cross-shareholding arrangements help reduce moral hazard risks (opportunistic behaviors) among trading partners, thus facilitating transaction-specific invest-ment (Flath 1993). In addition, there is no indication that it has played a negative role in corporate governance (corporate block holding has in fact played a positive role). Japanese firms now have the option of forming a holding company, which will also encourage corporate ownership of shares. Thus, the ownership structure of Japanese firms that was characterized by cross-shareholding among corporations and financial institutions will gradually change to a more market-based system but still retain some of the features of cross-shareholding arrangements, perhaps by combining cross-ownership by corporations and shareholding by institutional investors.

In this process, a decrease in stable shareholding is likely to increase the likelihood of hostile takeovers. In fact, some have already occurred in the 2000s. The amendment to the Company Law slated for 2007 will make it possible for foreign firms to buy Japanese firms through exchanges of stock. This will certainly open the door wider to mergers and acquisitions. Accordingly, the real challenge that Japanese firms will face (or have been facing) is how to manage the hostile takeover threat. The key for policymakers is to design an institutional framework that utilizes the emerging market for corporate control on the one hand while providing firms with appropriate means to fend off unwanted suitors.

APPENDICES: DEFINITION OF VARIABLES

Appendix 3.1: Corporation's Choice of Bank Shareholding

X_1 Variables Representing the Need to Sell off Shares

D_ICR: Dummy variable is 1 if corporation i's interest coverage ratio [(operating profit + interest and dividends income)/interest cost] is 1.5 or less.
D/E: Corporation i's D/E ratio (interest-bearing debt/equity capital).
BSV/A: The ratio of bank j's shares held by corporation i at market value in its total assets.

X_2 Financial Health

D_FRD: Dummy variable is 1 if Moody's bank financial rating is D or below (all banks have received D or below since 1999, thus the dummy is 1 if E or below for this period), otherwise 0. Seven out of 14 banks received C or above ratings in 1995, six banks received C or above in 1997, and no banks received C and only three received D or above in 1999.

X_3 Variables Representing Pressure from Capital Market

D_CRB: Dummy variable takes value of 1 if corporation i's credit rating for long-term bonds is BB-BBB (if the corporation received ratings from multiple rating agencies, we choose the most conservative rating).
D_CRA: Dummy variable takes value of 1 if corporation i's credit rating for long-term bonds is A-AAA (if the corporation received ratings from multiple rating agencies, we choose the most conservative rating).

X_4 *Variable Representing Managerial Entrenchment Against the Threat of Takeover*

LEMV: Logarithm of corporation i's total market capitalization.

NOST: Ratio of shareholding by non-stable shareholders (the sum of shares held by individuals excluding board members, foreign and domestic institutional investors) if the corporation has cross-shareholding relationship with banks, and 0 otherwise.

X_5 *Variables Representing the Relationship Between Corporations and Banks*

BBR: Corporation i's borrowing from bank j divided by total borrowing from private financial institutions.

BHR: Bank j's shareholding of corporation i divided by total issued shares of corporation i.

D_MB: Dummy variable is 1 if bank j is a main bank of some corporation (this represents closeness to corporations in total financial transactions). The main bank is defined as a bank that is the top listed bank in the "business partner banks" column in Tōyō Keizai's *Japan Company Handbook.*

The distribution of *BBR* (mean, standard deviation) is (8.7%, 9.5%) in period I, (9.4%, 10.1%) in period II, and (12.3%, 12.8%) in period III. The distribution of *BHR* is (1.7%, 1.8%) in period I, (1.9%, 1.8%) in period II, and (2.4%, 2.0%) in period III. The mean values of both variables are increasing due to the effect of bank restructurings.

X_6 *Dummy Variables Representing Bank j's Sell Off of Corporation i's Shares*

BSL: Dummy variable representing that bank j sold off corporation i's shares in the same year.

PBSL: Dummy variable representing that bank j sold off corporation i's shares in the previous year.

D_BM: Dummy variable to control for the effects of a bank merger, which is 1 if shares of separate banks in the beginning of the period become shares of the same bank by the end of the period.

D_YY: Dummy variable for year effects.

Appendix 3.2: Bank's Choice of Shareholding

Z_1 *Variables to Control for Bank j's Investment Behavior*

BHR/T1: Bank j's shareholding ratio of corporation i's shares divided by Tier 1 capital.

LEMV: Logarithm of corporation i's total market capitalization (This represents liquidity and ease of selling off).

Z_2 *A Variable Representing Pressure from Capital Market to Banks*

D_FRD: Dummy variable is 1 if Moody's bank financial rating is D or below (all banks have received D or below since 1999, thus dummy is 1 if E or below for this period).

Z_3 Variables Representing Corporation I's (Investment Target Firm) Risk (Credit Risk and Volatility) and Growth Opportunities

D_ICR: Dummy variable is 1 if corporation i's interest coverage ratio [(operating profit + interest and dividends income)/ interest cost] is 1.5 or less.
D_AVQ: Dummy variable is 1 if corporation *i*'s Tobin's *q* is 2 or more.
D/E: Corporation i's D/E ratio (interest-bearing debt/equity capital).
SDRTN: Standard deviation of monthly return from corporation *i*'s share in the past 36 months.

Z_4 Variables Representing the Long-Term Relationship Between Banks and Corporations

BBR: Corporation *i*'s borrowing from bank *j* divided by total borrowing from private financial institutions (this represents the degree of dependency on the liabilities side).
D_CSH: Dummy variable is 1 if corporation *i* holds bank *j*'s shares (cross-shareholding) at the beginning of the period.
D_MB: Dummy variable is 1 if bank *j* is a main bank of some corporation.

Z_5 Variables Representing Corporation I's Sale of Bank J's Shares

CSL: Dummy variable indicating that corporation *i* sold off bank *j*'s shares in the same year.
PCSL: Dummy variable indicating that corporation *i* sold off bank *j*'s shares in the previous year.

Appendix 3.3: Effect of Ownership on Corporate Performance

Dependent Variables

ROA: (return on assets) business profit/total assets (average at the beginning and end of period).
Business profit = operating profit + interest and dividend income.
Total assets = book value of total assets + unrealized capital gain (loss) from tangible fixed assets + unrealized capital gain (loss) from securities
AVQ: Tobin's *q* value of the firm (end of period)/total assets (end of period).
Value of the firm = market value of shareholder's equity + book value debt + minority equity
Total assets = book value of total assets + unrealized capital gain (loss) from tangible fixed assets + unrealized capital gain (loss) from securities

Independent Variables

FRGN: Shareholding ratio of foreign institutional investors: shareholding ratio of foreigners − shareholding ratio of foreign corporate block shareholders.

DINS: Shareholding ratio of domestic institutional investors: annuity trust + investment trust + total shareholding ratio of life insurance companies' special accounting.

STAB: Ratio of stable shareholders: ratio of cross-shareholding + total shareholding ratio of banks and life insurance companies.

ODR: Ratio of outside board members: number of outside board members/number of board members.

BRN: Relative number of board members: number of board members/logarithm of the number of employees.

D_DIR: Board member shareholding dummy: Dummy variable is 1 if shareholding ratio of board members is more than 5%.

D_PAR: Domestic and foreign parent company dummy: Dummy variable is 1 if there is a related parent company (domestic or foreign non-financial corporation which has more than 15% shareholding ratio).

D_MBS: Main bank shareholding dummy. Dummy variable is 1 if main bank shareholding ratio is nearly 5% (we take 4.9% as its threshold).

REFERENCES

Abegglen, J. C. and G. Stalk Jr. (1985). *Kaisha: The Japanese Corporation.* Boston, MA: Charles E. Tuttle.

Allen, F. and D. Gale (2000). *Comparing Financial Systems.* Cambridge, MA: MIT Press.

Aoki, M. (1988). *Information, Incentives, and Bargaining in the Japanese Economy.* Cambridge: Cambridge University Press.

—— H. Patrick (eds.) (1994). *The Japanese Main-bank System: Its Relevancy for Developing and Transforming Economies.* Oxford: Oxford University Press.

Burkart, M., D. Gromb, and F. Panunzi (1997). 'Large Shareholders, Monitoring, and the Value of the Firm,' *The Quarterly Journal of Economics*, 112(3): 693–728.

Classens, S., S. Djankow, J. Fan, and L. Lang (1999). 'The Rationale for Groups: Evidence from East Asia,' Unpublished manuscript, The World Bank.

Flath, D. (1993). 'Shareholding in the *Keiretsu*: Japan's Financial Groups,' *The Review of Economics and Statistics*, 75(2): 249–57.

Horiuchi, A. and M. Hanazaki (2000). 'Did the Main-bank Relationship Help Make Corporate Management Efficient? Empirical Analysis of the Manufacturing Industry,' *Keizai Keiei Kenkyu* (Research Institute of Capital Formation, Development Bank of Japan), 21(1): 1–89 (in Japanese).

Itoh, T. and K. Harada (2000). 'Japan Premium and Stock Prices: Two Mirrors of Japanese Banking Crises,' *NBER Working Paper*, 7997.

Jensen, M. C. (1986). 'Agency Costs of Free Cash Flow, Corporate Finance, and Takeover,' *American Economic Review*, 76: 323–9.

Johnson, S., P. Boone, A. Breach, and E. Friedman (2000). 'Corporate Governance in the Asian Financial Crisis,' *Journal of Financial Economics*, 58(1): 141–86.

Kang, J. and A. Shivdasani (1995). 'Firm Performance, Corporate Governance, and Top Executive Turnover in Japan,' *Journal of Financial Economics*, 38(1): 29–58.

—— R. Stultz, (1997), 'Why is There a Home Bias? An Analysis of Foreign Portfolio Equity Ownership in Japan,' *Journal of Financial Economics*, 46(1): 3–28.

La Porta, R., F. Lopez-de-Silanes, A. Shleifer, and R. Vishny (1998). 'Law and Finance,' *Journal of Political Economy*, 106(6): 1113–55.

Lichtenberg, F. R. and G. M. Pushner (1994). 'Ownership Structure and Corporate Performance in Japan,' *Japan and World Economy*, 6: 239–61.

McConnell, J. J. and H. Servaes (1995). 'Equity Ownership and the Two Faces of Debt,' *Journal of Financial Economics*, 39(1): 131–57.

Miyajima, H. (1995). 'The Privatization of Ex-zaibatsu Holding Stocks and the Emergence of Bank-centered Corporate Groups,' in M. Aoki (ed.), *Corporate Governance in Transitional Economy*, The World Bank, 361–403.

—— (2004). Economic History on Industrial Policy and Corporate Governance. *Tokyo: Yūhikaku (in Japanese)*.

—— Y. Arikawa (2000). 'Relational Banking and Debt Choice: Evidence from the Liberalization in Japan,' *IFMP Discussion Paper Series*, A00–07.

—— F. Kuroki (2002). 'Quantitative Analysis of the Unwinding of Cross-shareholding by Japanese Firms,' *Security Analysts Journal*, 40(12): 30–46 (in Japanese).

—— Y. Arikawa, and T. Saito (2001). 'Japanese Corporate Governance and "Excess" Investment: Comparative Analysis of Oil Shocks and Bubble Years,' *Financial Review* (Policy Research Institute of MOF), 60: 139–68 (in Japanese).

—— K. Haramura, and Y. Enami (2003). 'Evolution of Ownership Structure in Postwar Japan: Formulation and Unwinding of Stable Shareholders,' *Financial Review* (Policy Research Institute of MOF), 68: 156–93 (in Japanese).

—— K. Nitta, T. Saito, and Y. Omi (2002). 'Governance Structure and Productivity of Japanese Firms in the 1990s: Did Transformation of Governance Structure Contribute to the Improvement of Managerial Efficiency?' *Working Paper*, WFIS-02-001, Waseda University Institute of Financial Studies (in Japanese).

Morck, R. and B. Yeung (2001). 'Japanese Economic Success and the Curious Characteristics of the Japanese Stock Market,' Paper presented at IMF-Hitotsubashi Conference, September.

—— A. Shleifer, and R. Vishny (1988). 'Management Ownership and Market Valuation: An Empirical Analysis,' *Journal of Financial Economics*, 20: 293–315.

—— M. Nakamura, and A. Shivdasani (2000). 'Banks, Ownership Structure, and Firm Value in Japan,' *The Journal of Business*, 73(4): 539–67.

Murase, A. (2001). 'Stock Investment Performance of Japanese Financial Institutions, Corporations, Individuals, and Foreign Investors,' *Review of Monetary and Financial Studies*, 17 (in Japanese).

Nakatani, I. (1984). 'The Economic Role of Financial Corporate Groupings,' in Masahiko Aoki (ed.), *The Economic Analysis of the Japanese Firm*. Amsterdam: North-Holland.

Odagiri, H. (1992). *Growth through Competition, Competition through Growth: Strategic Management and the Economy in Japan*. Oxford: Oxford University Press.

Okabe, M. (2002). *Cross Shareholding in Japan: A New Unified Perspective of the Economic System*. Cheltenham: Edward Elgar Publishing.

Peek, J. and E. Rosengren (2001). 'Determinants of the Japan Premium: Actions Speak Louder than Words,' *Journal of International Economics*, 53: 283–305.

Porter, M. E. (1992). 'Capital Disadvantage: America's Failing Capital Investment System,' *Harvard Business Review*, 70: 65–82.

—— (1994). *Capital Choices*. Cambridge, MA: Harvard University Press.

Prowse, S. (1990). 'Institutional Investment Patterns and Corporate Financial Behaviors in the United States and Japan,' *Journal of Financial Economics*, 27(1): 43–66.

Sheard, P. (1994). 'Interlocking Shareholdings and Corporate Governance in Japan,' in M. Aoki and R. Dore (eds.), *The Japanese Firm: Sources of Competitive Strength*. Oxford: Oxford University Press.

Shleifer, A. and R. W. Vishny (1986). 'Large Shareholders and Corporate Control,' *Journal of Political Economy*, 94(3): 461–88.

Weinstein, D. and Y. Yafeh (1998). 'On the Costs of a Bank-centered Financial System: Evidence from the Changing Main-bank Relations in Japan,' *Journal of Finance*, 53: 635–72.

Yermack, D. (1996). 'Higher Market Valuation of Companies with a Small Board of Directors,' *Journal of Financial Economics*, 40(2): 185–211.

Yafeh Y. (2000). 'Corporate Governance in Japan: Past Performance and Future Prospects,' *Oxford Review of Economic Policy*, 16(2): 74–84.

—— O. Yosha. (2003). 'Large Shareholders and Banks: Who Monitors and How?' *Economic Journal*, 113(484): 128–46.

4

Foreign Investors and Corporate Governance in Japan[1]

Christina Ahmadjian

4.1 INTRODUCTION

Corporate governance systems vary around the world. These differences result from differing legal systems, systems of corporate finance and corporate ownership, as well as divergent norms around a firm's responsibilities to its various stakeholders (Charkham 1994; Shleifer and Vishny 1997; Dore 2000). While much research has considered how these differences originated and why they persist (see, for example, Roe 1994; Hall and Soskice 2001; Jackson 2002), far less research has considered what happens when different systems of corporate governance come into direct contact.

Different systems of corporate governance came into direct contact in the 1990s in Japan. Foreign ownership of shares of Japanese firms increased from about 4.2% in 1990 to 16.5% in 2002 (TSE 2003). This increase in foreign ownership came as the core, stable shareholders of the past—primarily banks and insurance companies—sold their shares at an increasing rate in response to financial crisis and changing accounting standards. While financial institutions held 45.2% of all shares in 1990, by 2002, their share ownership had dropped to 34.1% (TSE 2003).

This change in ownership brought two very different notions of corporate governance into direct conflict. In Japan, shareholders tended to be stakeholders with long-term interests in the firm in addition to return on their equity investment. Banks, for example, held shares as part of a broader relationship of managing financial transactions and supplying loans. Corporations held shares of their suppliers and buyers. These interconnected and complementary sets of relationships supported the fundamental attributes of the Japanese system of capitalism—stable purchase–supply transactions, long-term employment relationships, and patient capital (Aoki 1990). Foreign portfolio investors, on the other hand, had very different interests. They stood apart from the Japanese

[1] I am grateful to Gregory Jackson, Hideaki Miyajima, and members of RIETI's workshop on corporate governance for their helpful comments on this chapter, and to Tomoko Furukawa, Pekka Latiinen, and Masamoto Lee for their research assistance. I am also grateful to the center for Global Partnership for research support through an Abe fellowship.

system of relational capitalism, and had no interest in on-going business relationships with Japanese firms. They were beholden to their own investors, who were looking for a return on their investment through global diversification. These foreign portfolio investors were familiar with, and often active in, the shareholder movements that had transformed corporate governance in the USA, and increasingly, Europe (Davis and Thompson 1994; Useem 1996).

What was the result of this encounter between systems of corporate governance? To what extent did foreign investors attempt to impose their own notions of corporate governance on Japanese firms? What means of influence did they have? How successful were they in transforming corporate governance practices in Japan? This chapter explores these questions, and provides an overview on the identities and the interests of foreign investors in Japan. For this chapter, I define corporate governance as a set of laws, practices, and norms that concern the relationship between a firm and its various stakeholders. I present analyses of the relationship between foreign investors and boards of directors as well as disclosure and transparency. I also consider the effect of foreign ownership on downsizing and divestiture of assets—practices that represent very different norms around the relationship between a firm and its shareholders and employees, and reflect one of the main points of divergence between Anglo-American and Japanese conceptions of corporate governance.

The empirical materials are drawn from a number of sources and research methods. I present results from my own analyses of foreign ownership and downsizing, based on publicly available firm-level data. Analyses of the relationship between board structure and other corporate governance practices and foreign ownership come from surveys carried out by the Japan Corporate Governance Research Institute in 2002 and 2003. I also use material collected in approximately 50 interviews with leading corporate executives, investors, and government officials on Japanese corporate governance, carried out between 2001 and 2003.[2]

4.2 TRENDS IN FOREIGN INVESTMENT IN JAPAN, 1990–2002

From 1990 to 2002, the percentage of publicly listed Japanese shares held by foreigners increased from 4.2% to 16.5% (Figure 4.1). When measured by value, foreign holdings increased from 4.7% in 1990 to a peak of 18.8% in 2000, and down to 17.7% in 2002 (TSE 2003). The increase in foreign share ownership in Japan in the 1990s reflected a larger worldwide trend. Foreign ownership of listed French firms increased from approximately 10% to 40%, while ownership of shares in the UK by foreigners increased from about 7% in the 1960s to 32% in

---

[2] In order to encourage free and open discussion of sensitive issues, I assured confidentiality to the interview subjects.

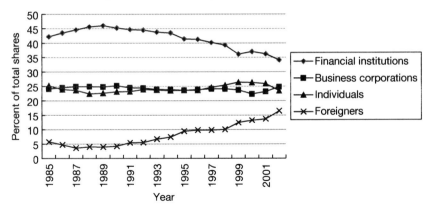

Figure 4.1 Trends in ownership of Japanese shares (unit share base)

Source: Tokyo Stock Exchange Fact Book 2003.

2000 (Anonymous 2002). Foreign ownership of US shares increased as well, from 6.9% in 1990 to 8.9% in 2000 (NYSE 2001).

These numbers indicate that this increase in foreign investment was not limited to Japan, but rather was a worldwide phenomenon, traceable to the rise of institutional investors, especially pension funds. Peter Drucker (1976) was one of the first to note the transformation of US capitalism, as pension funds increasingly owned firm shares and workers, through their participation in pensions became owners. This trend accelerated in the 1980s as the money managed by institutions increased, and as pensions became more willing to invest their funds in equity. In the US, the percentage of shares in large firms held by institutional investors increased from about 43% in 1985 to 57% in 1994 (measured by institutional ownership of the largest 1000 firms). This change in corporate ownership and influence of institutional investors led to the upsurge in shareholder activism in the US in the 1980s and 1990s (Useem 1996).

In 1989, US investors invested 94% of their assets domestically, while British investors kept 82% of their assets in the UK (Useem 1996). Beginning in the 1990s, however, institutional investors began to move their money abroad, as investors sought to diversify their portfolios across currencies and economies and investment managers gave them the opportunity to do so. US investors were an important driver of this trend. US residents increased their holdings of foreign equities from $6.6 billion in 1970, to $197.6 billion in 1990, to $776.8 billion in 1995, to $1830.4 billion in 2000 (NYSE 2001). Notes Useem (1996: 25):

Prior to the 1990s, one-fifth or less on average of new net investments in equity funds was allocated to international and global funds. By 1993, nearly 30 percent of new equity investments were going into international and global funds; during the first half of 1994, nearly 40 percent.

4.2.1 Who Were the Foreign Investors in Japan?

The leading foreign investors in Japan were American and European, especially British, funds (Shirota 2002). In the late 1990s, the size and influence of American investors became especially significant. Figure 4.2 shows net purchases of shares between 1998 and 2002 on all Japanese stock exchanges, and indicates that compared to investors from other regions, Americans were net purchasers of shares (TSE 2003). Most foreigners were institutional investors: in 2002, only .4% of foreign investors in Japanese publicly listed equities were individual investors (TSE 2003).

Foreign direct investment, where foreign investors take a large and strategic stake in a Japanese firm or set up their own operations, received much publicity during this period. Among the most dramatic and highly publicized cases were Renault's purchase of a controlling stake in Nissan and the acquisition and turnaround by the private equity fund Ripplewood of Long Term Credit Bank. Yet, the volume of portfolio investment by foreign funds dwarfed these investments, and arguably, had a greater effect on corporate governance and other economic and financial reforms (see Tiberghien 2002).

A study commissioned by the American Chamber of Commerce in Japan indicated that foreign direct investment in Japan, defined as strategic investment with the intention of transferring management resources and know-how, was quite low in an international comparison. In 2000, foreign direct investment in Japan was 1.1% of GDP, while that in the UK was 32.4%, Germany was 22.4% and the US 27.9% (ACCJ 2003: 2). In contrast, the portfolio investment by foreigners was broadly comparable to other developed countries.

4.2.2 Composition of Foreign Ownership

To further explore the identities and objectives of foreign stockholders, I examined ownership of 1376 Tokyo Stock Exchange First Section non-financial firms

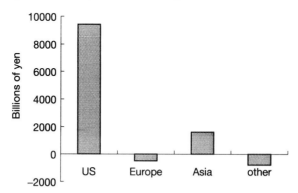

Figure 4.2 Net purchases of shares by region, 1998–2002

Source: Tokyo Stock Exchange Fact Book 2003.

Table 4.1 Distribution of Foreign Ownership, 1376 Non-Financial TSE First Section Firms, 2000

Foreign stake	Number of firms
> 50%	9
33%–50%	30
20%–33%	91
10%–20%	270
5%–10%	228
0–5%	719

Source: Calculated from Yuka Shoken Hokokusho (via QUICK).

in 2000. Table 4.1 shows the distribution of firms by level of foreign ownership. In nine firms, foreigners had controlling stakes of over 50%, while foreigners owned over 33.3% of an additional 30 firms (this is a level that allows for veto rights over board decisions). In a substantial number of firms, foreign ownership was over 10%.

Appendix 4.1 lists the 50 firms (of this group of 1376 TSE First Section firms) with the highest levels of foreign ownership. I identified cases in which the purpose of the foreign shareholder could be classified as "strategic." These were cases in which a foreign corporation (not a bank or investment fund) was one of the top 10 shareholders and the investment was for strategic, rather than portfolio purposes. In about 19 cases, largely in autos and pharmaceuticals, foreign investors could be considered strategic. This leaves a substantial number of large and well-known firms of whose shares 30% or more were in the hands of foreign portfolio investors, including Sony, Canon, and Kao.

For a more detailed look at these foreign portfolio investors, I identified the foreign investors that appeared in the list of the ten top shareholders for each of the largest 200 firms (by assets) in 2000 (list available separately from the author). Chase Manhattan appeared in the top ten for 59 firms, State Street for 49 firms, JP Morgan for seven, Morgan Stanley for six, and Boston Safe Deposit for five.

With the exception of Morgan Stanley, these firms were global custodians, holding shares for a range of funds. While these global custodians hold large numbers of shares, they cannot be considered as single shareholders. While Chase may be the registered shareholder for a variety of funds, individual funds give the directions on how to vote their proxies (I describe the voting process later in the chapter). Similarly, even if Chase is registered as holding 10% of a firm's shares, this does not mean that Chase will sell all of the shares at the same time, since this is a decision of the individual funds.

While the analysis suggests that in 2000 firms with high foreign ownership tended to have relatively diffuse foreign ownership, there was an increasing tendency for single funds to take large stakes. For example, in 2001, Capital Research held 20.7% in Shionogi & Co. and 20% in Chugai, Goldman Sachs had a 14.1% stake in Mycal, Fidelity Investment and Trust held 13.8% of Tokyo

Seimitsu, and 13.5% of Japan Medical Dynamic Marketing (*Nikkei Weekly* 2001).
In 2003, Goldman Sachs purchased $1.27 billion of preferred shares, convertible
into regular shares in a number of years, in Sumitomo Mitsui Bank. These more
concentrated stakes by single funds suggested that foreign ownership would
become increasingly influential over time.

4.2.3 What Kinds of Japanese Firms did Foreign Investors Prefer?

The ample media coverage of strategic investments by private equity firms such as
Ripplewood would suggest that investors tended to focus on troubled firms—
distressed automakers, failed banks, and spun off suppliers and affiliates. However, the quieter, and more influential trend of increasing foreign portfolio
investment targeted another type of firm. My analyses, and those of other
researchers, suggest that foreign portfolio investors tended to purchase stakes in
larger, export-oriented, and higher-performing firms.

I examined the relationship of foreign ownership to different types of firm
characteristics, using the group of TSE First Section non-financial firms in 2000
mentioned above. First, I compared the percentage of foreign ownership in larger
and smaller firms. Figure 4.3 compares the percentage of foreign ownership in
firms one standard deviation above and one standard deviation below the mean
of logged assets, and indicates that foreigners tended to invest in larger firms.
Figure 4.4 indicates that foreigners tended to own shares in firms with higher
ratio of exports to sales. Although these comparisons did not include the controls
of a regression analysis, they are consistent with other research that has found that
foreign investment in Japan was biased towards large, export-oriented firms
(Hiraki et al. 2003). Research by Miyajima and colleagues (cited elsewhere in

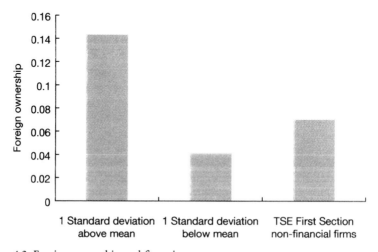

Figure 4.3 Foreign ownership and firm size

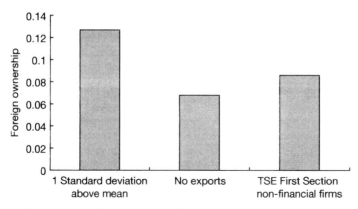

Figure 4.4 Foreign ownership and export/sales ratio

Source: Calculated from Yuka Shoken Hokokusho (via QUICK).

this volume) further indicates that foreigners are more likely to invest in companies that are high performers, and that have a high reputation in the debt markets, as measured by high levels of borrowing through bonds.

4.2.4 Interests of Foreign Investors

Foreign investors had very different interests from the majority of Japanese investors. Foreign investors had a very different set of obligations to their beneficiaries than Japanese funds. The concept of fiduciary duty was one that differentiated local and foreign investors. US pensions had clear obligations of fiduciary duty mandated by ERISA, the Employee Retirement Income Security Act of 1974, and could be the object of a civil suit for not fulfilling these duties. The UK Pensions Act of 1995 clarified fiduciary duties for UK funds. During the 1990s, the concept of fiduciary duty was increasingly discussed with respect to Japanese pension funds, but remained vague and under-enforced.

Furthermore, in most cases foreign investors were investing purely for return on investment, whereas Japanese investors were often wrapped in a web of other ties and obligations with the firms whose shares they held, and their own affiliated banks and other corporations. Japanese institutional investors tended to be closely linked to banks or to corporations that had other interests in the firms in which they were investing (Hiraki et al. 2003). Institutional investors—such as trust banks—tended to have close equity relationships with banks, and would vote according to the interests of its affiliated bank, which was likely to have a close lending relationship with the firm. A corporate pension fund might hold shares in an important business partner of the corporation and would not dare to press too hard as a shareholder. Thus, Japanese domestic institutional investors were part of a system of close relationships that went beyond shareholding stakes and thus were unlikely to demand the same level of returns as an investor that sought only a return on investment.

The difference in voting patterns between foreign and domestic shareholders was apparent in the case of Tokyo Style. In 2001, M&A Consulting, a domestic activist fund, purchased an 11.9% stake in a medium-sized clothing firm, Tokyo Style, and demanded it pay investors a ¥500 dividend, buy back its shares, and appoint two independent directors. The proposal was defeated, as friendly banks and affiliated companies came to Tokyo Style's aid (Singer 2002). Foreign investors, who held about 30% of Tokyo Style, largely voted with M&A Consulting. Domestic shareholders, in contrast, tended to support management. Isetan, a shareholder, and an important retailer of Tokyo Style's products voted with management, as did affiliated banks. Nippon Life also voted with management. Nippon Life's interest in Tokyo Style went beyond its 3.3% stake, since it also managed its tax-qualified pension program (*Nikkei Weekly* 2002). Yano Tomomi, the head of the Japanese Pension Fund Association, and one of the very few activists among Japanese domestic investors, criticized the local institutional investors: "[Institutional investors] claim they are ready to act, but in fact many of them are bound by conventional thinking" (*Nikkei Weekly* 2002).

Foreign investors, in particular those from Anglo-American economies, were also likely to be strong proponents of the ideology of shareholder capitalism, and to have little patience for Japan's existing system of balancing various stakeholders. Foreigners were particularly focused on issues of board independence and transparency. For example, in its corporate governance guidelines for Japan, the California state employees retirement fund, CalPERS, highlighted the importance of independent boards, using the language of shareholder value that characterized US-style corporate governance: "The board's focus should be on safeguarding the interests of shareholders and providing them with the highest possible long-term returns on their investment." According to a McKinsey survey, institutional investors claimed that they would pay a premium of 20% for a Japanese company that adhered to Anglo-American standards of best corporate governance practices (Coombs and Watson 2000).[3]

It is, perhaps, not surprising that US and British investors would promote Anglo-American corporate governance. Yet, even investors from other systems promoted Anglo-American corporate governance. For example, during the 1990s, French asset management firms changed their orientation, promoting "American" investment practices and management (Kleiner 2003). German banks, led by Deutsche Bank, had become far more Anglo-American in outlook, particularly in their investment businesses. Even more important than their ideological orientation, however, was the fact that foreign investors had very different objectives than domestic investors. They were investing in Japan to make money through a return on their investment, unlike Japanese shareholders, which often had a set of other interests besides the investment itself.

---

[3] The same investors said that they would pay a premium of 18% for a well-governed US firm, acknowledging the gap between theory and practice in the Anglo-American model.

4.3 MECHANISMS OF INFLUENCE BY FOREIGN INVESTORS

Foreign investors in Japan could influence firms to adopt their desired corporate governance practices through exit—the threat of selling their shares—and through formal and informal exercise of voice—exercising voting rights and making their opinions known through less formal channels. The threat of exit, as well as more informal channels exercise of voice, provided the more effective channels of influence. Foreigners were less likely to wield influence through exercising voting rights, though this had begun to change in the 2000s.

4.3.1 Influence Through Exit

In the 1990s, foreign investors had an influence over Japanese share prices far in excess of their actual stakes. As Tiberghien (2002) notes, the large percentage of Japanese shares that were held in cross-holdings and were not liquid, meant that the real impact of foreign buying and selling was even higher than percentages suggested: after taking into account the illiquidity of cross-held shares, a 10% stake by foreigners was equivalent in influence to a 30% stake. Foreign investors were more likely to buy—and sell—shares than Japanese investors, and Japanese institutional investors tended to observe and follow the moves of foreigners in and out of stocks. Foreign investors were net buyers of Japanese shares for eight years between 1990 and 2003 (TSE 2003), and Japanese firms that desired to maintain attractive share prices strove to attract and retain foreign investors. Retaining foreign investors was a challenge, since foreigners were more likely to sell than Japanese investors. In 2003, for example, when foreigners were actually net purchasers of stock, they were responsible for about 30% of all share sales, down only slightly from 2002, when foreigners were responsible for about 32% of all share sales (as measured by value) (TSE 2003). During these same years, foreigners were responsible for 33% and 32% of all share purchases.

To Japanese firms, foreign investors propped up share prices at a time when banks and other long-term shareholders were selling their holdings, and were therefore attractive investors. On the other hand, they injected a new sense of instability, and firms realized that if they did not satisfy their foreign investors, their share price could drop drastically. This buying and selling of stock could have strong effects on individual firms. In his book on foreign ownership in the Japanese stock market, Shirota Jun (2002: 6) documents the effect of foreigners on the shares of Yamanouchi pharmaceuticals. Until March 2001 foreigners were strong buyers of Yamanouchi shares, but became strong sellers after March. The share price, 4840 in January fell to 3160 by May, a loss of 37.4% of its value. The Nikkei average as a whole lost 5.5% during this period.

Research on Japanese companies in the 1980s suggested that Japanese managers did not care much about share price, and emphasized measures such as market share and growth instead (Abegglen and Stalk 1985). Even in the early

2000s, relatively few Japanese managers were willing to accept the notion that maximizing shareholder value was the primary objective of the firm. Yet, my interviews with corporate executives suggested that there was concern about keeping share price at a reasonable level (compared to historical levels and those of their competitors) and preventing drastic declines.

Share prices were also a macroeconomic issue. Government bureaucrats followed the level of the stock market to monitor the health of the Japanese economy, and lower stock prices were an impetus for reform (Tiberghien 2002). Lowered stock prices also had an impact on banks' shareholdings—and if share prices went too low, they threatened to affect their capital adequacy ratios (Okabe 2002). Thus, general levels of share prices, highly influenced by foreign investors, could be seen as a driver of reform on a more macro-economic level, in areas such as reform of the Commercial Code (Tiberghien 2002).

Among executives of US firms, one source of anxiety around share price was the threat of hostile takeover. The evidence that Japanese executives took a takeover threat seriously is weak, but not non-existent. A Sony official stated that one of the reasons that it adopted new corporate governance practices in the mid-1990's was a fear that a foreign firm would take advantage of its depressed share price to launch a hostile takeover (interview with former Sony executive). And, older Japanese executives were likely to have a memory of the threat of hostile takeover during the early post-war period, before firms were able to develop mutual protection through cross-holdings.

The Japanese and foreign business press were on the lookout for the emergence of hostile takeovers in Japan, but except for a few well-publicized examples, such cases were rare. In 2004, a US investment fund, Steel Partners, made a hostile tender offer for a textile company, Sotoh. Sotoh finally warded Steel Partners off by increasing its dividend by 30%, increasing its stock price and making it impossible for Steel Partners to get the necessary number of shares (*Japan Times* 2004). Steel Partners made a similar bid for Yushiro Chemical, and was rebuffed through a similar increase in dividends.

Other reasons that Japanese executives paid attention to their share price included the use of stocks as a currency for takeover and means of corporate finance. In the 1990s, stock swaps were legalized as a means for merger between Japanese companies, though they remained banned for mergers between foreign and Japanese firms. Furthermore, since the mid-1980s, Japanese firms became increasingly dependent on the capital markets for funding. There was an increased use of equity-linked instruments, though this dropped in the mid-1990s as the economy stagnated (Hoshi and Kashyap 2001). Even as the importance of equity-linked finance increased, dependence on the capital markets made firms sensitive to bond ratings, which were increasingly tied to corporate governance.

While it is important not to over-estimate the importance of share price in Japan in the 1990s and early 2000s, it was definitely a topic of interest for managers. While the objective may not have been to maximize shareholder value, keeping stock price healthy was very important—and an increasing challenge to firms as foreigners replaced stable shareholders.

4.3.2 Foreigners and Voice

In addition to exit, foreign shareholders could exercise influence through voice: both through formal means such as exercising voting rights and through more informal means of influence.

While foreign investors paid little attention to exercising their voting rights in the 1990s, this changed significantly in the early 2000s. According to one survey, foreign and other institutional investors exercised their voting rights against management proposals in 19% of the companies surveyed in 1999. By 2003, this had gone up to 43.7% of the companies surveyed (Shouji Houmu 1998–2003).[4]

A number of barriers made it difficult for foreigners to exercise their voting rights. According to Tamura Yoshiaki, a Tokyo Stock Exchange official, it was estimated that almost 100% of shares held by Japanese banks and 95% held by domestic investment trusts and insurance companies were being voted. Among foreigners, however, only about 25% of the shares were voted, although this was growing (*Global Custodian* 2004).

One of the problems in executing voting rights by foreigners was in how shares were held, and the mechanisms of voting. The Commercial Code mandated that firms issue the agenda for the annual shareholder meeting a minimum of 14 days before the meeting. This agenda, with proposals to be voted on, was sent to the sub-custodian in Japan, then to the global custodian, such as J.P. Morgan Chase, then to the actual shareholders, who then had to return their votes via the same process. (The Tokyo Stock Exchange was moving to promote electronic voting to simply this complicated process, to be implemented by fall 2004.)

In 2001, Institutional Shareholders established an office in Japan, greatly facilitating voting by both foreigners and domestic funds. ISS provides recommendations on exercising voting rights, and has been a highly influential voice in US corporate governance. Its recommendations, consistent with Anglo-American corporate governance practices, have made it easier for investors to know how to vote, without an expensive and time-consuming process of research.

Beginning in 2003, foreigners also found a strong domestic ally in exercising voting rights. The Pension Fund Association, a public group that manages $45.2 billion of corporate pension money, issued a set of guidelines for exercising its voting rights. During the June shareholders' meeting season in 2003, it opposed about 60% of management proposals, voting against re-election of directors in 635 out of 1101 cases, against retirement payments in 689 of 1071 cases, and against dividend policy at 466 companies (Jopson and Rahman 2004). The PFA's move toward shareholder activism was largely due to the efforts of its chairman,

---

[4] Shouji Houmu does not separate foreign and other domestic institutional investors in its survey—it is rather interesting that it titles its findings as "foreign and other"—it is not clear if this means that it is mostly foreigners that have exercised their voting rights—or if it is simply the expectation that foreigners are likely to be noisier and more aggressive than domestic investors.

Yano Tomomi, an outspoken advocate of Anglo-American style corporate governance, and was an important boost to foreign investors: Mark Goldstein, the director of research at Institutional Shareholder Services in Tokyo told the Financial Times "The decision increases the likelihood that many of the issues raised by foreign shareholders will actually be adopted" (Nakamoto 2003: 29).

4.3.3 Informal Use of Voice

While foreign investors increasingly exercised their voting rights against management, their greatest influence was through more informal means, such as asking questions at analysts meetings and shareholders meetings and through private meetings with CEOs. Between 2001 and 2003, I interviewed a number of Japanese CEOs and other senior executives as well as foreign investors and asked about these means of influence. Most Japanese executives interviewed were highly aware of the presence of foreigners on their ownership rosters, but most admitted that foreigners limited their influence to more informal means.

The head of IR for a major corporation said: "We've had foreign pressure. For example, a well-known fund is a 5% shareholder. We can't turn them down when this fund asks our president to breakfast." The CEO from another company said: "We visit the US and Europe twice a year. This is because we have a bit more than 30% foreign investors. We've been doing this for about 10 years now." Another CEO said: "I wish I could go back in time and be a company president in the old days. One big part of the job today is investor relations. In the old days, no one wanted to say anything that rocked the boat—but now, we need to address questions from fund managers."

Not all executives had felt direct pressure from foreign shareholders. One said: "There is no direct influence of foreign investors, though we have to expect that this will increase in the future." Another: "25 or 26% of our shares are owned by foreigners, and I'm sure that CalPERS is in there. The foreigners have not applied direct pressure, at the annual shareholders meeting, for example. They approve of what we are doing. If they didn't, I'm sure they would start pressuring us."

A number of the executives interviewed suggested that the influence of foreigners was less a result of overt pressure, and more through learning, and through the exercise of having to be transparent and explain policies and results. The head of IR at the firm mentioned previously said:

From my point of view, I particularly like to meet with foreign investors, since they are always raising new questions and waking me up. I am excited to see foreign investors and get new ideas. Yesterday, I got a call from someone at Fund A with a small question. A few days ago, I visited Fund B. Such communication is important...Japanese investors often seem to be trying to get us to reveal insider information. We would like to teach them ethics.

A senior executive at another firm said:

We can learn from our investors. Japanese investors are becoming more vocal, but are hesitant to speak out. CalPERS is vocal generally, but they have never written us a letter.

But their publicity is a very good thing—it prepares us. We are ready for what investors ask. We listen to investors.

A cynic might argue that senior Japanese executives have become skilled at telling foreign investors what they want to hear. But, that is the point. In the last decade or so, the role of the CEO or company president, in particular, has come to include talking to foreign investors, and many companies have set up investor relations departments to deal with these foreigners, listen to their concerns, and explain themselves.

While the executives that I interviewed suggested that Japanese institutional investors were becoming more active, they maintained that most of their investor relations activities were directed towards foreigners. A senior official at a US investment bank said that foreigners got more attention because they were simply more vocal:

Japanese investors are not able to ask the sorts of questions that we do. They are unwilling to speak up to senior people at companies. They are happy to see the IR department, but the IR department is weak and knows little about strategy—you might as well just read the newspaper. Japanese investors are also not as respected by companies as the foreigners, and thus are unable to get in to senior management.

Another investment strategist with a foreign firm said: "One of our competitive advantages is that we get in to see senior management." Another:

We are trying to do what we can to improve corporate governance among Japanese firms. For example, we are going to senior management and asking them about shareholder value, and they are at least paying lip service to it. Top managers now talk about increasing return on equity, and give us targets for improvements on ROE. But, when we press them harder, they are lost about how, exactly, to do it.

One official at a foreign bank argued that Japanese managers used foreign investors as bearers of bad news:

Sometimes, I go talk to a CEO. And the CEO talks about a 3–5 year plan that is very ambitious and not terribly realistic. After the CEO leaves, the IR guy admits that the plan has lots of problems. I agree and the response of the IR guy is "Next time you meet the CEO, please tell him what you just told me."

This is a part of a time-honored tradition of gai-atsu, or pressure from the outside, in which Japanese government officials or firms have used foreign pressure to excuse painful decisions.

Foreign investors that I interviewed seemed to strive to present themselves as constructive and helpful, rather than as aggressive. There has been little evidence of open campaigns by foreign shareholders to target poorly governed firms (in contrast, for example, to CalPERS in the US which publishes a corporate governance watch list, or, more recently, Hermes in the UK that has taken a more aggressive stance on matters related to corporate governance). There is no evidence that foreign investors have used the legal recourse to sue firms for negligence towards shareholders.

The propensity of foreigners to take a gentle approach to governance, and not to rely on legal recourse or aggressive shareholder activism, seems more a case of social norms than to institutional and legal barriers to action. Shareholder derivative suits were available for use, but though numbers of these suits had increased after a decrease in the filing fee in the early 1990s, foreign shareholders did not use them. There was no reason that a fund such as CalPERS could not have publicized a watch list of poorly governed firms, as it has done in the US. However, foreign investors that I interviewed suggested that they were concerned about not appearing too aggressive and demanding, especially when it concerned such sensitive issues as downsizing. They noted that many foreigners were concerned about not being perceived as closely linked to M&A Consulting, the domestic shareholder activist fund that attracted much publicity (much of it negative) for campaigns against management of Tokyo Style and other companies.

There was also, among foreign investors, especially the investment banks, a concern that over-aggressive behavior would be punished. During the 1990s and 2000s, foreign investment banks had had numerous penalties slapped on them for various trading irregularities. In 2002, the FSA put a sudden ban on short-selling that hurt foreign firms, which were more active in short sales, in particular. It was by no means clear that the government was scapegoating foreign firms, and punishing them for what they saw as anti-social behavior, but this was a common belief among the foreign investment community during this period. A fear of government reprisal was likely one of the reasons that foreign investors remained low-key in their activism.

Just because foreign investors took a rather muted approach to activism does not mean that they were not successful—and their approach may say less about the Japanese market than about how institutional investors in general effectively exercise influence. Research on institutional investor activism in the US has found that besides high profile campaigns by investors such as CalPERS aside, institutional investors have been relatively quiet (Black 1998; Gillian and Starks 2003). Even much of CalPERS influence seems to be through more informal routes, of behind the scenes persuasion. For example, a study by Carleton et al. (1998) found that among 45 firms that TIAA-CREF targeted for corporate governance changes, 71% reached a negotiated settlement without a vote. Thus, influence by foreign investors in Japan may simply work in much the same way it works in other places—through informal influence and relationships.

4.3.4 Corporate Governance Funds

The year 2003 saw the emergence of a new source of influence, in the form of two corporate governance funds, both funded by CalPERS. CalPERS joined with the Sparx Asset Management in Japan and Relational Investors LLC in California to set up a $200 million corporate governance fund in Japan. It also invested $200 million in the Taiyo Fund, a venture of W.L. Ross and Co. and Taiyo Pacific

Partners LLC to invest in medium-sized cash rich Japanese firms and work with management to improve management. In 2004, the Pension Fund Association announced that it would initiate a corporate governance fund, targeting large listed firms that had outstanding (Anglo-American) corporate governance.

4.3.5 Foreign Influence and the State

Foreigners also exerted influence through trying to change the legal framework for corporate governance. A key actor was the American Chamber of Commerce in Japan (ACCJ), an association of American and other foreign businesses. The ACCJ formed committees on the reform of the Commercial Code and on Foreign Direct Investment, dedicated to studying issues related to foreign investment and influencing policy makers to make changes congenial to foreign investors. The ACCJ advocated a number of changes to commercial law—including legal reforms to facilitate cross-boarder M&A transactions as well as changes in board structure, and requirements for independent directors. The ACCJ's record was mixed—the reformed Commercial Code allowed firms to choose between an existing Japanese style board and a new American style board with independent directors, and thus, did not mandate independent directors for any firms. Yet, the ACCJ was a vocal and consistent advocate of US style reforms, and was a catalyst for change.

4.3.6 Listing on Foreign Stock Exchanges

Listing on US stock exchanges pushed a handful of firms to adopt US corporate governance practices, but this influence was very limited. As of 2004, 19 Japanese firms were listed on the New York Stock Exchange and 13 on NASDAQ (compared to over 3000 firms listed in Japan). This was an increase from 12 on the NYSE and 13 on NASDAQ in 1999.

Firms listed in the US adopted US standards for disclosure and transparency, but the record of adopting American-style board practices was mixed. Some of the firms most vocal about corporate governance reform, such as Orix, were listed in the US, while some of the most vocal against US style boards, such as Canon and Toyota also had US listings. Sarbanes-Oxley had little impact on the board practices of these firms: after strong lobbying by Keidanren, Japan's big business lobbying association, Japanese firms (along with Italian firms) were allowed to skip the requirement to set up an independent director-dominated auditing committee, with the rationale that statutory corporate auditors (kansayaku) served a similar purpose. While Japanese firms complained about the burden of fulfilling other aspects of Sarbanes-Oxley (as did American firms), as of 2004, there was no evidence of Japanese firms de-listing because of these requirements.

4.4 FOREIGN OWNERSHIP AND CORPORATE GOVERNANCE PRACTICES

Above, I argued that foreign investors had the means to influence Japanese firms through both exit and voice. To what extent were foreign investors effective in influencing corporate governance practices? As I noted earlier, corporate governance refers to a broad range of laws, corporate practices, and norms that define the relationship of a firm to its stakeholders. In this section, I focus on the relationship between foreign investors and a set of corporate governance practices, including the function and structure of boards of directors and disclosure. Analyses are based on a 2003 survey of TSE First Section firms by the Japan Corporate Governance Research Institute (JCGR 2003).

In 2002 and 2003, the Japan Corporate Governance Index Research Institute surveyed Tokyo Stock Exchange First Section firms on their corporate governance practices. Based on these surveys, the JCGIndex measures how close a firm's governance adheres to Anglo-American standards. Practices evaluated include how a firm sets it performance objectives, accountability of the CEO, structure of the board of directors (size, independence, responsibilities), compensation system, management of subsidiaries, internal audit and control, and disclosure and transparency (more details can be found at www.jcgr.org).

Though the response rates in both 2003 and 2002 were relatively low, the distributions of the JCGIndex and correlations with performance and firm characteristics were quite similar across the two years, suggesting robust findings. There is also considerable overlap with the findings in the Ministry of Finance survey that Miyajima discusses in Chapter 12, both in the relationship between corporate governance and firm characteristics as well as between corporate governance and performance.

The JCGIndex ranges from 0 to 100: a hypothetical firm that receives 100 points would have a significant number of independent directors on its board, and a board that had adopted a committee structure (of audit, compensation, and nominating committees dominated by independent directors). The firm would set its performance goals based on metrics valued by shareholder (return on invested capital), and the CEO would be accountable for achieving these goals.

Firms that scored higher on the JCGIndex tended to have larger percentages of foreign ownership. Figure 4.5 compares the levels of foreign ownership in firms whose JCGIndex was one standard deviation above the mean, those one standard deviation below the mean, and all respondents (201 of 1523 TSE First Section firms in 2003). Higher JCGIndex firms had a significantly (at the 1% level) higher level of foreign ownership than the low scorers.

The JCGIndex is based on questions that address four different aspects of corporate governance: performance objectives and CEO accountability, structure and function of boards of directors, internal management and control, and transparency and disclosure. High JCGIndex scores in each of these components

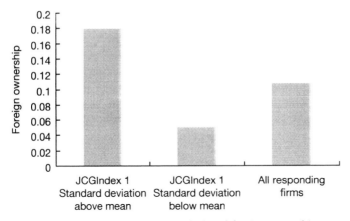

Figure 4.5 JCGIndex (corporate governance index) and foreign ownership

were associated with higher levels of foreign ownership, indicating that foreign investors are influential in all of these areas.

Figure 4.6 shows that firms that scored high in board structure and function had higher levels of foreign ownership than low scoring firms (significant at the 5% level). Firms that received high scores on this component had relatively high levels of board independence as measured by presence of independent directors, criteria for board appointments, and ability and authority of the board to monitor the CEO. Firms adopting the board with committee structure, legalized in the revised Commercial Code in 2003, received extra points for board structure and independence.

A number of companies typify this relationship between foreign ownership and board structure. For example, Hoya, one of the highest JCGIndex firms, introduced its first independent director, Takeo Shiina, CEO of Japan IBM, in 1995, and by 2003 had five independent directors and only three insiders. In 2004, foreigners held 50.4% of Hoya's shares. When Sony initiated its board reforms, which included appointment of independent directors and reduction in its board size, foreigners held about 50% of its shares. Orix, another firm with high foreign ownership (50.6% in 2004) had four outside and eight inside directors.[5] This relationship between board independence and foreign ownership, however, was not perfect. Canon, with foreign ownership of 49.8%, loudly protested against independent boards, though its continued high performance made it a favorite of foreign investors.

As Figure 4.7 shows, firms with high JCGIndex scores for disclosure and transparency also had higher levels of foreign ownership (significant at the 1% level). This subcomponent was based on questions concerning investor relations

---

[5] This made Orix's board one of the most independent among Japanese firms. If Orix had been a US firm, however, having "only" four outside directors on a board of 12 would probably draw criticism for lack of independence.

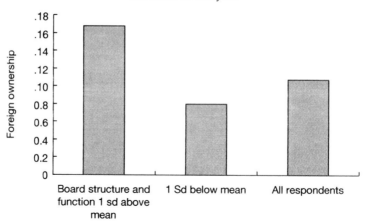

Figure 4.6 Foreign ownership and board structure and function (JCGIndex)

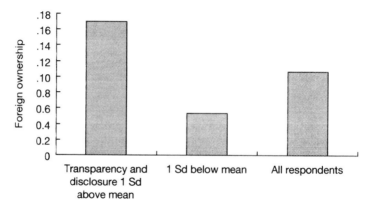

Figure 4.7 Foreign ownership and disclosure and transparency (JCGIndex)

activities, posting of shareholder-information on the web, meetings between CEO and domestic and foreign analysts, as well as management of shareholder meetings.

Foreign investors have led to an increase in shareholder relations activities. For example, the Ministry of Finance survey cited by Miyajima in Chapter 11 found that nearly 45% of surveyed firms had investor relations offices, up from a rate that was probably nearly zero before the 1990s.

These correlations between the JCGIndex and its various subcomponents and foreign ownership demonstrate an association, but not causation. In other words, it is not clear from these results whether foreign investors pressured firms to revise their corporate governance, or foreign investors gravitated to firms that were closer to an Anglo-American ideal of governance. Corporate executives that I interviewed indicated that corporate governance issues—especially surrounding boards of directors—were a key focus of questions by foreign investors, suggesting that at least some of the causation was due to foreign investors pressuring firms to change.

4.5 FOREIGN INVESTORS AND RESTRUCTURING

One of the major points of divergence between the post-war Japanese and the Anglo-American systems of governance has been the different priorities on employees versus shareholders. In the US, downsizing has become prevalent, with firms downsizing to "maximize shareholder value," even in the absence of a dire need for restructuring (Budros 1997; Davis and Robbins 2002). In Japan, in contrast, firms have been hesitant to downsize, and downsizing has, in general, been considered an unpalatable tradeoff of employee interests for those of shareholders (Ahmadjian and Robinson 2001).

In a study of downsizing and asset divestiture among 1626 TSE first and second section non-financial firms between 1991 and 1997 (excluding firms with foreign strategic investors), Ahmadjian and Robbins (2005) found that foreign ownership was significantly related to propensity to downsize in firms with low levels of financial ownership. Firms that were not highly embedded in the existing Japanese system through close banking relationships were particularly susceptible to foreign influence in downsizing and asset divestiture.[6]

Figure 4.8 shows this relationship for downsizing. As the proportion of foreign investors went up, a firm without close ownership ties to Japanese financial institutions and corporations experienced an increased likelihood of downsizing (here, downsizing is measured as reductions of employees of 5% or more). In firms in which domestic financial ownership is over 30%, foreign ownership did not increase the propensity to downsize.

There is a similar relationship between foreign ownership and divestiture of assets (measure by a decrease in tangible fixed assets by 5% or more). (The relationship is nearly identical to the relationship between foreign ownership and downsizing shown in Figure 4.8.) These findings suggest that foreign investors are particularly influential in firms that are not as closely linked to powerful financial institutions. Such firms are less likely to have a cushion of protection from banks if they encounter financial distress, and such firms do not have the luxury of a cushion of stable shareholders who will not sell their shares even if they encounter hard times.

As in the case of the JCGIndex, we cannot prove the direction of causality. However, there was no evidence that an increase in downsizing led to an increase in foreign investment among firms in the sample, which would be expected if downsizing firms attracted foreign investors. Note that we defined downsizing as a decrease in number of employees, which could have occurred by redeployment

---

[6] See also Ahmadjian and Robinson (2001) for similar results.

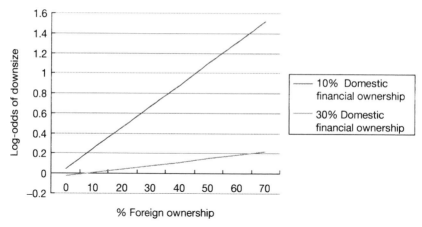

Figure 4.8 Relationship between foreign ownership and 5% downsizing, different levels of financial ownership

of employees to related companies as well as through layoffs. In Japan, outright layoffs are far less frequent than in the US, and tend to be couched as early retirements or, less and less frequently, assignment to related firms. Nevertheless, these downsizings increased at a rapid rate over the 1990s, and represented a relatively large proportion of firms. In 2000, for example, over about 35% of the firms had shrunk from the previous year in 5% or more of the number of employees, while about 15% made cuts of 10% or more. Foreign investors were not the only factor that led to downsizing (see Ahmadjian and Robinson 2001), but they were a significant one, and we can see that these labor reductions were an important force in the decade and more after 1990.

4.6 DISCUSSION AND CONCLUSION

In this chapter, I examined foreign portfolio investors and their effect on corporate governance in Japanese firms. I highlighted several points:

1. Foreign portfolio ownership of Japanese equity increased significantly from the 1990s.
2. Foreign investors were advocates of Anglo-American style corporate governance.
3. Foreign investors influenced Japanese firms both through exit and voice. Their propensity to buy and sell shares gave them strong influence over share price in general, and made exit a particular threat to firms. Their influence through voice was largely informal—through meeting with CEOs and senior executives, and making their wishes known.

4. There has been a clear relationship between foreign investors and practices related to corporate governance—including board independence, transparency and disclosure, and propensity to downsize and divest assets.

Though it is impossible to establish a definitive direction of causation between foreign ownership and corporate governance practices, it is clear that the increase in foreign ownership was inextricably linked to the transformation of corporate governance practices in Japan since the early 1990s. Whether foreigners actually influenced firms to change their governance practices or firms changed their governance practices to attract more foreign investors, increased board independence, disclosure and transparency, downsizing and asset divestiture occurred in response to an increase in foreign portfolio investment in Japan.

While the research presented in this chapter suggests that foreign investors are associated with a shift towards Anglo-American governance practices in Japan, this does not mean that there is likely to be wholesale convergence, and that Japan is on course to be exactly like the US. How much is Japanese corporate governance likely to change? How far will this shift to Anglo-American style corporate governance proceed? There are several possible scenarios, based on different theoretical presumptions of how institutional change occurs.

One possible scenario is based on the assumption that changes in corporate governance are a direct response to pressure by foreign investors. If this is the case, Anglo-American style corporate governance will remain limited to firms with high levels of foreign ownership. This will result in a bifurcated economy—with a set of firms that have adopted US style board practices, and have moved away from Japanese style permanent employment, and a perhaps larger set of firms that retain a version of the existing Japanese system (it is difficult, however, to imagine that Japanese firms will ever fully adopt the cavalier attitude towards employees that has become part of US-style shareholder capitalism). There is some evidence of this, in the patterns of adoptions of the new "American style" board with committees, after a reform of the Commercial Code in 2003 allowed firms to choose between this and the existing board structure. As of mid-2004, only 45 firms of about 3000 listed firms had adopted this new structure, among them, firms with some of the highest level of foreign ownership, while the vast majority of other firms maintained their existing system, with no board committees and statutory corporate auditors (Gilson and Milhaupt 2004).

Another possibility is that foreign investors have opened a floodgate, and allowed other firms to adopt practices that have heretofore been seen as illegitimate. This scenario is based on the assumption that Anglo-American corporate governance practices are considered illegitimate, yet desirable and effective—and many firms hesitate to adopt them. As Milhaupt (2001) notes, corporate governance is not only determined by law and institutional structures, but also is a product of norms. Many domestic firms may be unwilling to defy these norms, at least until others go first. In their study of downsizing, Ahmadjian and Robinson (2001) found evidence consistent with this proposition. Downsizing in Japan in the 1990s followed a pattern of "safety in numbers," in which less prestigious, smaller firms went first, and larger firms, with greater visibility and more to lose waited until some of the stigma of illegitimacy declined. This pattern is likely to follow if companies decide that Anglo-American corporate governance is beneficial in ways other than pleasing foreign shareholders—if, for example, US board structure brings real benefits in decision-making, speed and corporate performance, or if downsizing really does result in increased corporate vitality. Companies may simply be waiting until a few other companies go first, and then will jump on the bandwagon. In this scenario, foreign-owned firms are the first movers, and as the illegitimacy of their behavior recedes, other firms follow.

Another possibility is that Japanese corporate governance will begin to converge with Anglo-American practices as local institutions are transformed and local actors demand change. Research highlights how an institutional and legal framework that defines the rights and obligations of shareholders and managers shapes corporate governance practices around the world (Shleifer and Vishny 1997; Coffee 2000; Gilson and Milhaupt 2004). In this scenario, changing corporate law and disclosure regulations in Japan drive greater convergence with Anglo-American practice. While the revision in the Commercial Code to allow "American-style" boards with committees has not led to widespread change, changing regulations in financial reporting and disclosure may have a more substantial effect. For example, fair market value accounting requires firms to report cross-held shares at market value, and means that even domestic, stable shareholders will have to consider their equity stakes in other firms as investments, and sources of risk (Okabe 2002). This has already led to an increased unwinding of cross-shareholding, and in theory at least, should lead to more similar behavior between domestic and foreign investors.

Corporate governance reform may also proceed as local institutional investors become more committed to an activist stance. There is some evidence of this with the Pension Fund Association's adoption of guidelines for exercising voting rights. In 2004, the PFA linked with Nomura to initiate a corporate governance fund that would invest in firms that had the highest levels (in other words, the most Anglo-Saxon) corporate governance. It was not clear, however, the degree to which this shareholder activism went beyond the PFA, and, even within the PFA, how widely the dedication to corporate governance was shared, beyond its chief, Mr. Yano.

Yet another possibility for the future of corporate governance in Japan is a backlash against Anglo-American practices. The corporate governance debate in Japan has often been framed as "US-style" versus "Japanese-style" corporate governance, and a number of influential business leaders, in particular, Okuda Hiroshi of Toyota and Mitarai Fujio of Canon have been strongly critical of "US-style" corporate governance, saying that it threatens the management practices that have served Japanese companies well.

It is not clear yet which of these scenarios will prevail, but there are several factors that are likely to determine the outcome. The first is whether firms, and not only those with high levels of foreign ownership, come to believe that Anglo-American style corporate governance practices are more effective than Japanese practices. The second is whether local investors will decide that corporate governance activism will bring them greater returns. The third is the degree to which local actors, particularly labor, will resist change. Up until the early 2000s, it was not yet clear which positions local managers, investors, and labor would assume. In 2004, however, the union of Kanebo rejected a merger of its cosmetics division with Kao, showing the power of unions in forestalling actions in the clear interest of shareholders. It is not clear if this is an isolated act, or evidence of a resurgence of labor power in defining the course of restructuring and reform.

While this future state is not certain, it is clear that an increase in foreign portfolio investment in Japan is associated with a range of new practices consistent with the Anglo-American model of corporate governance. The research presented in this chapter has implications not only for Japan, but, for the bigger question of globalization. While there has been an extensive debate on the role of globalization on change in business practices and economic systems (see Berger and Dore 1996; Guillen 1999; Guillen 2001; Streeck 2001), researchers, to date, have paid relatively little attention to the global spread of institutional investors, and how they have influenced local systems of corporate governance (see, however, Useem 1998). This chapter demonstrates that foreign investors have made profound changes in the Japanese economy. But, Japan is not an isolated case. Foreign portfolio investment has been associated with changes in corporate governance around the world—including South Korea, France, and Germany. This chapter suggests the need for detailed research on foreign capital and local business systems around the world.

APPENDIX 4.1

Fifty TSE First Section Non-Bank Firms with Greatest Foreign Ownership, 2000

Foreign ownership	
0.77	Banyu Seiyaku (strategic)
0.77	Japan Oracle (strategic)
0.70	Densei Ramada (strategic)
0.68	Nihon Air Liquide (strategic)
0.68	Trend Micro (strategic)
0.64	Showa Shell Sekiyu (strategic)
0.61	Nissan (strategic)
0.52	Isuzu (strategic)
0.52	Bosch (strategic)
0.48	Mitsubishi Motors (strategic)
0.48	Yamatake (strategic)
0.46	Tokai Kanko (strategic)
0.45	Mazda (strategic)

(*Continued*)

APPENDIX 4.1 (*Continued*)

Foreign ownership	
0.44	Suzuki (strategic)
0.43	Yamanouchi Seiyaku
0.42	Asatsu DK (strategic)
0.42	Chugai Seiyaku
0.41	Shohkoh Fund
0.40	Canon
0.40	Sony
0.39	Yamada Denki
0.39	Orix
0.39	Rohm
0.38	Fuji Heavy Industries (strategic)
0.38	Shionogi Seiyaku
0.37	Fuji Photo Film
0.36	Nihon Unisys (strategic)
0.36	TDK
0.36	Tokyo Electron
0.35	Komatsu
0.35	Minebea
0.35	Sankyo
0.35	Konami
0.34	Kurita Kogyo
0.34	Chiyoda
0.34	Hirose Denki
0.34	Shimura Kako
0.34	Nichicon
0.33	Hakuto
0.33	Yorozu (strategic)
0.32	Pioneer
0.32	Kao
0.32	Meitec
0.32	NOK (strategic)
0.32	Hoya
0.31	Muji Co.
0.31	Murata
0.31	Nintendo
0.30	Hoshiden

REFERENCES

Abegglen, J. C. and G. Stalk, Jr. (1985). *Kaisha: The Japanese Corporation.* New York: Basic Books.

Ahmadjian, C. L. and G. Robbins (2005). 'A Clash of Capitalisms: Foreign Ownership and Restructuring in 1990s Japan,' *American Sociological Review*, 70(2): 451–71

Ahmadjian, C. L. and P. Robinson (2001). 'Safety in Numbers: Downsizing and the Deinstitutionalization of Permanent Employment in Japan,' *Administrative Science Quarterly*, 46(4): 622–54.

ACCJ (American Chamber of Commerce in Japan) (2003). *From Goals to Reality: FDI Policy in Japan*. Tokyo: American Chamber of Commerce in Japan.

Anonymous (2002). 'Editorial: Institutional Investors and the Growth of Global Influence,' *Corporate Governance: An International Review*, 10(2): 67–8.

Aoki, M. (1990). 'Toward an Economic Model of the Japanese Firm,' *Journal of Economic Literature*, 28: 1–27.

Berger, S. and R. Dore (1996). *National Diversity and Global Capitalism*. Ithaca, NY: Cornell University Press.

Black, B. S. (1998). 'Shareholder Activism and Corporate Governance in the United States,' in P. Newman (ed.), *The New Palgrave Dictionary of Economics and the Law*. London: Palgrave.

Budros, A. (1997). 'The New Capitalism and Organizational Rationality: The Adoption of Downsizing Programs, 1979–1994,' *Social Forces*, 76(1): 229–50.

CalPERS. Corporate governance principles for Japan. Available at: www.calpers-governance. org/principles/international/japan (viewed 3/8/2004).

Carleton, W., J. Nelson, et al. (1998). 'The Influence of Institutions on Corporate Governance Through Private Negotiations: Evidence from TIAA-CREF,' *Journal of Finance*, 53(4): 1335–62.

Charkham, J. (1994). *Keeping Good Company: A Study of Corporate Governance in Five Countries*. Oxford: Oxford University Press.

Coffee, Jr., J. C. (2000). 'The Future as History: The Prospects for Global Convergence in Corporate Governance and its Implications,' *Northwestern University Law Review*, 93: 641–708.

Coombs, P. and M. Watson (2000). 'Three Surveys on Corporate Governance,' *The McKinsey Quarterly*, 74–7

Davis, G. F. and T. A. Thompson (1994). 'A Social Movement Perspective on Corporate Control,' *Administrative Science Quarterly*, 36: 141–73

—— G. E. Robbins (2002). 'The Fate of the Conglomerate Firm in the United States,' in W. W. Powell (ed.), *Bending the Bars of the Iron Cage: Institutional Dynamics and Processes*. Chicago: University of Chicago Press.

Dore, R. (2000). *Stock Market Capitalism. Welfare Capitalism: Japan and Germany versus the Anglo-Saxons*. New York, Oxford University Press.

Drucker, P. F. (1976). *The Unseen Revolution: How Penson Fund Socialism Came to America*. New York: Harper and Row.

Gillian, S. L. and L. T. Starks (2003). *Corporate Governance, Corporate Ownership, and the Role of Institutional Investors: A Global Perspective*. Delaware: John L. Weinberg Center for Corporate Governance, University of Delaware.

Gilson, R. J. and C. J. Milhaupt (2004). *Choice as Regulatory Reform: The Case of Japanese Corporate Governance*. Columbia: Columbia Law School.

Global Custodian (2004). Interview with Yoshiaki Tamura. Available at: globalcustodian. com/main.jsp?type=rndtbln&page=81

Gordon, P. (2000). *While the World Watches Jose Bove, France Adapts to Globalization. July 10th 2000*. Washington, DC: Brookings Institution.

Guillen, M. F. (1999). 'Is Globalization Civilizing, Destructive or Feeble? A Critique of Six Key Debates in the Social-Science Literature,' *Annual Review of Sociology*.

Guillen, M. (2001). *The Limits of Convergence: Globalization and Organizational Change in Argentina, South Korea, and Spain.* Princeton, NJ: Princeton University Press.

Hall, P. A. and D. Soskice (2001). 'An Introduction to Varieties of Capitalism,' *Varieties of Capitalism: The Institutional Foundations of Comparative Advantage.* New York: Oxford University Press, 1–70.

Hiraki, T., H. Inoue, A, Itoh, F. Kuroki, and H. Masuda. (2003). 'Investor Biases in Japan,' *Working Paper.* Niigata: International University of Japan.

Hoshi, T. and A. Kashyap (2001). *Corporate Financing and Governance in Japan: The Road to the Future.* Cambridge, MA: MIT Press.

Jackson, G. (2002). 'Corporate Governance in Germany and Japan: Liberalization Pressures and Responses during the 1990's,' in W. Streeck and K. Yamamura (eds.), *The Future of Nationally Embedded Capitalism in a Global Economy.* Ithaca, NY: Cornell University Press.

JCGR (Japan Corporate Governance Research Institute) (2003). Report on the 2003 Japan Corporate Governance Survey. Available at: www.jcgr.org

Japan Times (2004). 'U.S. Fund's Hostile Sotoh Bid Fails,' February 25.

Jopson, B. and B. Rahman (2004). 'Pensions Body Targets Directors,' *Financial Times,* London Edition, June 27: 29.

Kleiner, T. (2003). 'Building Up an Asset Management Industry: Forays of an Anglo-Saxon Logic into the French Business System,' M.-L. Djelic and S. Quack (eds.), *Globalization and Institutions: Redefining the Rules of the Economic Game.* Cheltenham: Edward Elgar.

Milhaupt, C. (2001). 'Creative Norm Destruction: Evolution of Non-legal Rules in Japanese Corporate Governance,' *University of Pennsylvania Law Review,* 149: 2083.

Miyajima, H., K. Haramura, and Y. Konan (2002). 'Sengo Nihon kigyo no kabushiki shoyu kozo' (The Structure of Shareholding in Japanese Companies in the Post-war Period). Presented at the Japan Finance Association Meetings, Autumn.

Nakamoto, M. (2003). 'Japanese Pension Funds Act,' *Financial Times,* London Edition, February 27: 29.

NYSE (New York Stock Exchange) (2001). *Fact Book.* New York: New York Stock Exchange.

Nikkei Weekly (2001). 'Foreign Institutions Snap up Greater Share of Japan Firms,' July 16.

—— (2002). 'Institutions Threaten Corporate Governance,' July 22.

Okabe, M. (2002). *Cross Shareholdings in Japan: A New Unified Perspective of the Economic System.* Cheltenham: Edward Elgar.

Roe, M. J. (1994). *Strong Managers, Weak Owners.* Princeton: Princeton University Press.

Shirota, J. (2002). *Foreign Investors in the Japanese Stock Market.* Tokyo: Toyo Keizai (in Japanese).

Shleifer, A. and R. Vishny (1997). 'A Survey of Corporate Governance,' *Journal of Finance,* LII(2).

Streeck, W. (2001). 'Introduction: Explorations into the Origins of Nonliberal Capitalism in Germany and Japan,' in W. Streeck and K. Yamamura (eds.), *The Origins of Nonliberal Capitalism.* Ithaca, NY: Cornell University Press, 1–38.

Tiberghien, Y. (2002). 'State Mediation of Global Financial Forces: Different Paths of Structural Reforms in Japan and South Korea,' *Journal of East Asian Studies,* 4(August).

TSE (Tokyo Stock Exchange) (2003). *Fact Book.* Tokyo: Tokyo Stock Exchange.

Useem, M. (1996). *Investor Capitalism: How Money Managers are Changing the Face of Corporate America.* New York: Basic Books/HarperCollins.

—— (1998). 'Corporate Leadership in a Globalizing Equity Market,' *Academy of Management Executive,* 12(4): 43–59.

5

Venture Capital and its Governance: The Emergence of Equity Financing Conduits in Japan

Nobuyuki Hata, Haruhiko Ando, and Yoshiaki Ishii

5.1 INTRODUCTION

After the drastic evolution of ICT (Information and Communication Technology) in the 1990s, new industries emerged where modular organizational architecture became dominant. ICT related sectors, healthcare and other related fields became a driving force behind economic growth. And here new venture capital-backed companies became the central players of this "new economy." Venture businesses seemed to operate under very different rules than conventional industries based on integrated architectures, such as the automobile industry. They rapidly attained huge market value relative to the very industries which had been the driving force of Japan's economy during the 1980s. Stimulated by the powerful structural changes forced by the "Power of Modularity," venture capital (VC) in Japan has also been drastically re-inventing itself since the late 1990s.

The current situation of venture capital in Japan is provided by data from Venture Enterprise Center, a METI sponsored foundation. By 2005, the accumulated venture capital investment reached 16,406 investment projects worth a total of ¥859 billion.

In FY 2004 itself, 2,759 cases of new investments were recorded totaling ¥197 billion—increased 24% by number and 34% by amount from the previous year. Regionally, the Tokyo area received a dominant share (41.4%) of investment, followed by Osaka (10.8%). ICT related sectors were the top recipients with a 33.74% share of total investment, followed by the rapidly growing biotechnology/health care sector's 23.5%. The sources of new VC funds came largely from corporations (20.1%), banks (17.6%), individuals (14.4%), and insurance companies (8.8%).

Although, Japan's VC sector is decisively underdeveloped compared with the US and Europe counterparts. At the end of 2002, an influential equity strategy analyst launched a rigorous critique[1] of the Japanese equity market and the image

---

[1] Alexander Kinmont "Equity strategy—the irrelevance of Japan" (12/19/2002), Report by Nikko Salomon Smith Barney.

of being "an intellectually sterile market" has spread. Some international private equity financing entities decided to withdraw from the Japanese market and others reduced their operations. Unfortunately, international comparison may support this image (see Figures 5.1 and 5.2). During 1998–2001, Japan's VC investment amounted to just 0.05% of GDP, the lowest of the OECD countries. At the end of FY 2004 the cumulative VC investment in Japan of ¥834 billion is just 1/34 of the US (¥27 trillion) and 1/26 of the European level (¥21 trillion).

These comparisons raise several key issues: Why does Japan have such a low level of venture capital development compared to other OECD countries? Will this gap continue in the medium-term, or will the impact of recent reforms mean that we can expect more rapid development? And what is the significance for the Japanese economy?

This chapter argues that the slow development of VC in Japan can be explained by three macroeconomic factors. First, Japan's catch-up development process led to the dominance of debt finance, as opposed to equity markets. Second, the dualistic structure of Japanese industry (big enterprises and SMEs) and pyramid-like *keiretsu* Under dominating integral architecture posed substantial barriers to entrepreneurial activities. Third, institutional structure of the Japanese economy had been obstructing newly emerging venture activities in as far as it tends to favor proven insiders within established economic groups and disadvantages new comers or outsiders. Given this situation, Japan's VCs developed in a unique, but limited way.

Recent reforms supporting VC have nonetheless started to promote change, as witnessed by the growth of equity finance and early stage investment. More

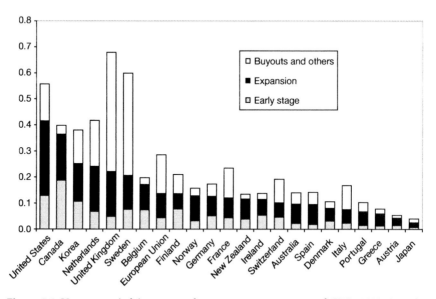

Figure 5.1 Venture capital investment by stage as a percentage of GDP, 1998–2001 in selected OECD countries

(¥10 billion)

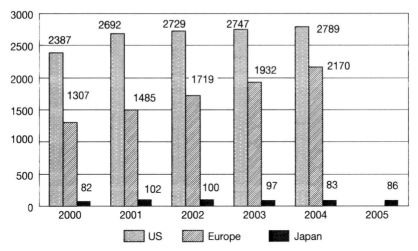

Figure 5.2 Comparison of accumulated venture investment in Japan, US, and Europe
Source: Venture Enterprise Center.

importantly, we observe a qualitative transformation in the nature of a new generation of venture capitalists. Hence, we argue that these reforms in VC will have a significant effect on Japan's economy, because VC is likely to promote new types of innovation and high value technologies which consequently stimulate the economy.

The rest of the chapter explores the development and organization of VC in Japan, as well as related public policy measures. Section 5.2 outlines the broad characteristics of VC entities and the related issues of governance. Section 5.3 examines the historical development of VC entities in Japan. Section 5.4 presents a detailed typology of three "generations" of VC entities in Japan, and discusses the particular forms of corporate governance found in each of them. Section 5.5 discusses the institutional factors that have influenced the historical trajectory of VC in Japan. Section 5.6 concludes with a reflection on future challenges and perspectives.

5.2 VC ENTITIES AND CORPORATE GOVERNANCE

"Classic VC firms"[2] are entities, whose principle activities are to make multi-round equity investments and to take an active role in value creation from start-up to "exit" (e.g. by an initial public offering (IPO) of shares to outside investors

---

[2] In the US, new VC firms emerged in the 1980s, which shifted their focus from value creation to financial techniques specialized around later stage companies. To distinguish these from orthodox VC firms, which invest in start-up or early stage companies and provide hands-on support to entrepreneurs, the former are called "classic VC"(Bygrave and Timmons 1992).

or liquidation through mergers and acquisitions (M&A)) in order to acquire a relatively high rate of return mainly in the form of capital gain through portfolio investments with a VC fund. The typical investment process includes raising a fund, finding investors for the fund, searching for promising venture projects or companies, conducting due diligence and evaluating possible investments, negotiating a term sheet, finalizing a contract, creating value through hands-on involvement, and payback of return.

VC firms finance new enterprises through an interesting mix of equity investment, and hands-on involvement in the management of new ventures. Debt finance is generally not appropriate until a company has eliminated precedent debt and achieved a stable cash flow. By establishing a fund, VC firms can invest in a diverse, but carefully selected portfolio of projects. VCs contribute to helping new high risk firms overcome the threshold of start-up investment, but can expect a relatively high rate of return on their portfolio as a whole. Meanwhile, VC firms increase the value of their investments through "hands-on involvement." Many start-up companies face high business risks related to both their management and technology, their research is costly and often remote from commercial applications, and therefore the firms lack stability. Through hands-on involvement and their own reputations, venture capitalists mitigate such risks, use their social networks to bring together various important forms of social capital around these ventures, and guide the companies towards stable growth (Podolny 2001). Gorman and Sahlman (1989) state that almost all VC firms in the US spend time actively involved with the management of the companies they invest in. Around one quarter of VC firms spend more than three quarters of their time on value creation after investment.[3] As such, VC represents a hybrid form of capital investment that is simultaneously both high-risk and patient.

The growth of an enterprise can be usefully divided into four stages: seed (start-up), early stage (soon after start-up), expansion or middle stage (growing) and later or mezzanine stage (just before IPO or M&A). Venture capitalists use their expertise, skills and contacts to actively support the company at each of these stages in a variety of ways, including:

- *Seed stage*: conduct of a feasibility study; development of the business plan; recruitment of the CEO and the rest of the management team; procurement of offices and equipment.
- *Early stage*: assistance in forming the company and starting operations; a first round equity investment.
- *Expansion stage*: involvement with management as a part-time Board member (to monitor, check and review the business plan, to activate the Board and to secure objective and reasonable decision-making); assistance in building up basic strategy; supporting management in areas such as research and development, marketing, finance and accounting, intellectual property strategy,

---

[3] Higashide and Birley (1999) argue that the allocation of time for after care in the UK was very low compared with US in the mid-90s.

legal affairs, human resource management, and policy making up to "exit"; brokerage of strategic alliances for marketing or technology break-through, follow-up investments that may include co-investments with other VC firms.
- *Later stage*: brokerage of strategic alliances leading to M&A, preparation for IPO, assistance with the IPO procedure.

Corporate governance in the context of venture capital funds involves two sets of agency problems: first, between the VC entities and the entrepreneurs receiving the equity investment, and second, between the VC entities and the investors in the VC funds. At the first level, complications may arise when more than one VC entity invests in the same company. Sometimes a lead investor invites other equity investors to share the burden of heavy investments during the growth of the company. Sometimes a third party VC entity, which has no relation or *ex ante* coordination with the existing lead investor, also invests and results in a washing out the existing investors. In these cases, a very complicated adjustment of rights and re-establishment of the governance structure may be required among the existing VC entities, the new VC entities and other stock holders.[4] At the second level, complications may occur when the VC entity operates more than one VC fund or invests money from its own account as well as from a number of other funds. These practices are rather unique to Japan, and may create a conflict of interests between the VC entity and the investors of each fund.

Aoki (2001) uses a game theoretic model of the "tournament mechanism" to analyze the competition for innovation and governance among a cluster of VC firms in Silicon Valley. The model describes the practice of milestone equity investment, whereby a sequence of expanding investments is made during the growth of the venture companies. In cases of co-investment, which often occur during the expansion stage, Aoki suggests that the "rule of reputation" in repeated rounds of investments builds up a common standard or norm for compliance. Here the venture capitalist plays a key role as an intermediary or a judge of the tournament.

The work of Aoki (2001) complements the extensive works on the economics of modularity in the design of products and processes. Baldwin and Clark (2000) suggest that modularity, whereby independent modules are linked by pre-established interfaces (i.e. design rules), may create value through independent experimentation and testing of new technologies, which are later combined in new ways. However, the organization of module processes may require new types of governance structures, such as VC investment and adequate incentive mechanisms, are required to enable venture companies to compete in each module. Baldwin and Clark (2000) also point out that each module task should be nested in a single organization, which is involved in "joint investment" in order to avoid transaction or agency costs. However they do not deal directly with the relationship between VC entities and the venture companies competing in a specific module.

---

[4] The relationship between entrepreneurs and employees is not discussed here.

In terms of governance, VC entities and entrepreneurs can agree a set of overall goals by jointly investing in their own venture project. However, in many cases joint investment is not sufficiently effective to overcome complicated conflicts of interest which can easily lead to *ex post* "hold-up" problems. Although the "rule of reputation" (Aoki 2001) may provide some degree of discipline or order, additional institutionalized enforcement is required. Kaplan and Strömberg (2000) analyze this issue in greater detail using a wealth of empirical data. For example, VC entities in the US normally purchase "preferred stocks" as a legal means of avoiding "hold-up" problems. Furthermore, certain terms and conditions are written in "term sheets of preferred stocks."

Among these VC related governance mechanisms, the most important contractual terms, inter alia,[5] are the right to select and fire members of the board and anti-dilution. The former gives the VC entities the "legal" right to nominate or fire some executives, including themselves, and to secure significant decision-making seats on the Board of the company. This right ensures that the venture capitalists can involve themselves in management activities. The VC entities may reserve the right to fire the CEO who is often the entrepreneur. This legal measure acts as a control over the entrepreneur and deters *ex post* opportunistic behavior to a certain extent. The latter term protects the VC entities' decision-making right from being diluted by the participation of a third party. VC entities can reserve the right to allocate or issue new stock, undertake new joint investments to maintain the share or request to purchase the share of a third party.

Given their voluntary nature, the terms of VC investments vary significantly from contract to contract. Hence, the term sheet and the valuation of shares are key elements of negotiation over VC investments. Unfortunately in Japan, neither the government nor the private sector recognized the importance of developing a legal framework supporting these modes of governance until the end of the 1990s. Since then various amendments have been made to Commercial Code.

The lack of legal framework was consistent with early development of VC style investment in Japan. As will be discussed below, VC entities in Japan were often affiliated to financial *keiretsu* companies, such as banks, security companies and insurance companies. Consequently, the need for special monitoring measures between the VC entities and the investors in the funds, which were often parent institutions, was rarely recognized—essentially funds were being raised within the *keiretsu* group and the general discipline of the group was considered sufficient. Moreover, between the VC entities and entrepreneurs, joint equity investment was rarely coordinated because VC entities provided almost no "hands-on involvement." However, severe corporate governance problems (e.g. dilution of shares by a third party) tended not to occur because investments were generally made at the later stage in the growth of the company and did not result in huge

---

[5] Kaplan and Strömberg (2000) cite other rights such as residual cash-flow rights, liquidation rights, automatic conversion provisions and so on. This analysis treats co-investments as one comprehensive investment and does not distinguish between complicated cases of multiple governance and other cases.

capital gains. Such problems were also prevented by the traditional Japanese business practice of establishing a structure of cross shareholding, which applies to both the public stock market and private equity market.

5.3 THE EVOLUTION OF VC IN JAPAN

At every stage, the growth of venture capital entities in Japan has been stimulated by the evolution of venture capital in the US. Broadly, Japan has experienced three generations of VC entities, each with its own investment style: the first generation public VC Corporations established in 1963; the second generation private financial keiretsu VC companies, established around 1972–73 and again in the early 1980s; and the third generation of independent VC firms which emerged from the late 1990s. The second generation still account for the main body of Japanese VCs, although we argue here that the development of the third generation is having a significant impact on the overall prospects of VC in Japan.

The first VC firm in the world was American Research and Development (ARD), established in Boston in 1946 by Professor Doriot of Harvard Business School and his colleagues.[6] The proposal to provide risk capital to commercialize technologies created during World War II had originally been tabled at a meeting of the US security companies association, but was then supported by the chairman of the Boston Reserve Board. Given the lack of understanding of risk capital and equity finance at the time, the ARD got off to a bumpy start. Initially, it attracted only 70% of the targeted fund of US$5 million, and in 1949 57% of a new offering issued to boost the fund size attracted no buyers. Gradually, consensus developed around the idea that the federal government should support the provision of risk capital to improve the financial viability of small businesses especially in the start-up period. Thus, the Small Business Investment Act was introduced in 1958 and venture investments were promoted through Small Business Investment Companies (SBICs) supported with leveraged fundraising by the US Small Business Agency. This development inspired the Japanese government to create a similar legal scheme. Three Japanese SBICs were established respectively in Tokyo, Osaka,

---

[6] Hands-on support by Georges Doriot in the early period of ARD mainly aimed at avoiding risks, rather than positive value creation. For example, in 1957 ARD invested US$70,000 to take a 77% stake in the establishment of DEC (Digital Equipment Corporation). In 1971 the market value of DEC had grown to 5000 times the initial investment. This marvelous "big deal" became a huge benchmark for entrepreneurs, venture capitalists, and business angels. But at the outset, Professor Doriot gave very cautious advice: first, the firm should start not a whole computer but only "printed circuit modules" so as not to get attention from big competitors like IBM and, second, he insisted on changing the name of the company from "Digital Computer Corporation" to "Digital Equipment Corporation" for the same reason. Next year DEC begun to sell its first product, "Digital Laboratory Module" and "Digital System Module" with transistors which were very precious at that time. After the start-up investment was made, the company announced a plan to make computers with transistors, which Doriot considered reckless conduct and considered withdrawing from the project (Ono 1997: 135).

and Nagoya in 1963 as special public corporations affiliated to the Ministry of International Trade and Industry (MITI) becoming the first generation of venture capital in Japan.

In the US, success stories such as Fairchild Semiconductor, DEC, and Intel encouraged venture investment and fueled developments in fields where modularity and digital technology were dominant, such as in semiconductors, computer hardware, software, telecommunications, and life sciences. By 1969, the number of IPOs peaked at 1298. However, the huge fiscal deficit caused by the cost of the war in Vietnam compelled the government to raise capital gains tax from a rate of 25% to a prohibitive 49% thereby causing the "death of VC," and precipitating the eventual sale of the symbolic and heroic ARD.

During this period Japan experienced the take-off of a second generation of VCs, which were private VC firms, often affiliated with established financial firms from Japan's well-known financial *keiretsu* groups. In 1971, senior executive members of Kyoto *Keizai Doyukai* (the Kyoto Association of Corporate Executives) visited Boston to observe US high-tech industries and particularly the ARD, which they envisioned should serve as the model for a new VC entity in Japan. As a result, Kyoto Enterprise Development Co Ltd (KED) was established with investments from local firms including Tateishi Denki (known as Omron), Kyoto Exchange Market, and Kyoto Bank. Some financial keiretsu groups followed suit and established their own VC companies. For example, the Nippon Enterprise Development Corporation (NED) was formed by 39 companies led by Long Term Credit Bank (now Shinsei Bank), Fuji Bank (now Tokyo-Mitsubishi UFJ Bank), Daiwa Securities, Itochu Corporation. Nippon Venture Capital Co Ltd (NVCC) was formed by 16 companies, including the Sumitomo Group. Likewise, the Japan Associated Finance Co Ltd (now JAFCO) was created under leadership of Nomura Securities, Sanwa Bank (now Tokyo-Mitsubishi UFJ Bank), and Nippon Life Insurance Company. These entities were set up as normal limited stock companies since, at the time, a legal framework for limited liability partnerships did not exist. The first Oil Shock hit Japan's economy severely, triggering a steep and unprecedented recession, which marked the end of the expansionary phase of second generation VCs. The number of IPOs declined sharply from 66 in 1973 to an average of 20–30 in the late 1970s, as investment activity weakened. The KED was finally liquidated in 1980.

Over the 1970s, the environment for venture investment in the US improved steadily through measures such as cuts in capital gains tax in 1978 and 1981, and the issuing of new regulations in 1979 and 1980 that eased restrictions of pension fund investment under the 1974 Employee Retirement Income Security Act. Brisk business in the NASDAQ and robust venture investment had a knock-on effect in Japan, too. Initial listing requirements for the over-the-counter market were deregulated and from 1982–85 more Japanese VC companies were established. Again, these new VC firms are part of the second Generation firms, which are largely affiliated to established banks and security companies. In 1982, JAFCO set up the first VC Fund in Japan, the "JAFCO No.1 Fund," which was structured as a limited liability partnership investment fund under the Civil Code. This new vehicle for venture investment was able to attract investors from outside, and allowed funds to be set up that went beyond the VC companies' own internal funds. Unfortunately, this second venture capital boom was curtailed by the appreciation of the yen and the deep recession following the Plaza Accord in 1985. Many venture companies were forced into bankruptcy and venture investment again went into decline.

In the US, on the other hand, the number of VC firms multiplied and competition became fiercer. Venture investment took off in earnest with the emergence of the Internet big-bang expansion after 1993. The Netscape IPO became an influential role model for venture investment and inspired a small group of skilful Japanese venture capitalists to establish their own "independent VC firms," the third generation of VC firms in Japan, which are organized as partnerships around a core of skilful venture capitalists.

Over the last decade, the Japanese government has developed a raft of policies to support new firms funded by venture capital and adopted legal and regulatory measures to remove certain obstacles to progress. The Ministry of International Trade and Industry (MITI) established a new division in 1994 to support the venture industries. A legal framework was created with the aim of assuring effective governance of invested venture companies. In the same year, the guidelines of the Act on Prohibition of Private Monopolization and Maintenance of Fair Trade were amended. These guidelines lifted the ban on the dispatching of executives by VC firms to invested companies, thereby allowing VC firms to provide hands-on support to such companies. In 1995, the Law on Temporary Measures to Facilitate Specific New Business was revised introducing a limited stock options scheme. In 1997, the Commercial Code was revised to liberalize the use of stock options scheme and, after a further revision in 2001, allowed stock options to be issued up to a numerical limit. In addition, new and full-scale preferred stock was introduced, as a measure to prevent the kind of "hold-ups" common in VC investment by maintaining key rights to appoint and fire board members, as well as provisions to combat dilution.

In 1997, another key change was introduced by the Limited Partnership Act for Venture Capital Investment. This measure established a scheme for limited partnership funds (LPS) with an explicit limited liability for fund investors through the legal status of limited partner, as in the US. This LPS soon became an effective vehicle for VC funds. In 1999, the MITI-affiliated Japan Small Business Corporation (now the Japan Small and Medium Enterprise Corporation) introduced a new scheme to support independent and hands-on LPS schemes with a growing budget of public co-investment.

In parallel supportive measures were introduced for investing in venture companies, including: the SME Creative Business Promotion Law[7] aimed at supporting technology-oriented SMEs, Venture Support Foundations (set up by local governments in virtually every prefecture), the "Venture Plaza" which

[7] Temporary law Concerning Measures for the Promotion of the Creative Business Activities of Small and Medium Enterprises.

Table 5.1 Major Improvements in the Environment for Venture Capital in Japan

1963	Establishment of three SBICs
1983	Deregulation of initial listing requirements for the over-the-counter market
1994	Creation of division for new industries to support venture industries established in MITI
	Permission for detachment of executives by VC firms to invested companies
1995	SME Creative Business Promotion Law
	Set up of Venture Support Foundations by many local governments; Venture Plaza; Special treatment in the over-the-counter market; Introduction of stock options on an approval basis
1997	Generalization of stock options by Commercial Code
1998	Limited Partnership Act for Venture Capital Investment
1999	Establishment of Mothers by Tokyo Stock Exchange
	Support for hands-on type of equity investment; support for start-ups; Venture Fair; Amendment of Small and Medium Enterprise Basic Law
2000	Establishment of NASDAQ Japan
2001	Expansion of stock option and other revision of Commercial Code
2002	Introduction of a substantial preferred stock scheme by Commercial Code

promotes the matching of venture companies with potential investors, mentors and partners, subsidies for promising start-ups (a kind of substitute for the angels' role in the US), and the "Venture Fair." The latter is a national exhibition providing an opportunity for start-ups, which have developed pilot products to seek potential investors, mentors and partners. In addition, the Small and Medium Enterprise Basic Law was revised in 1999 and the promotion of start-ups and venture enterprises became a pillar of national policy. Furthermore, the exit process for VC firms and investors was supported by the establishment of new IPO markets such as NASDAQ Japan, and Mothers (market of the high-growth and emerging stocks of the Tokyo Stock Exchange). Moreover, firms were now permitted to undertake IPOs even during financial deficit.

These various measures are summarized in Table 5.1, and, taken together, helped to substantially boost Japanese venture investment. Nonetheless, the burst of the IT bubble in the spring of 2000 damaged Japan's venture markets, the volume of venture investment dropped drastically and the high growth rate of IPOs could not be maintained. Nevertheless, some skilful independent venture capitalists were still able to achieve satisfactory results.

5.4 CORPORATE GOVERNANCE ACROSS THREE GENERATIONS OF VC IN JAPAN

The previous section showed the sporadic development of VC entities in Japan, and outlined some changes in the basic approach to VC alongside the various innovations in public policy. This section turns to the specific forms and problems of corporate governance in each of the three "generations" of VC entities, as well as recent developments in the second generation entities as they borrow certain governance devices from the third generation.

5.4.1 The First Generation: Public VC Corporation (from 1963)

The three Small and Medium Enterprises Investment Corporations (hereinafter called "Japanese SBICs") were established in 1963. The government directly controlled the three Japanese SBICs as special public corporations, providing capital and retaining the controlling right to nominate their executives. These SBICs were modeled on the Small Business Investment Companies (SBICs) in the US, but their investment style was, in fact, almost totally different. By providing government insurance and other support, the US scheme enabled skilled private sector talent who met certain criteria to raise sufficient funds and start venture capital investment. In contrast, the publicly controlled Japanese SBICs mainly invested in SMEs which could guarantee a stable 6% annual dividend. Taking 20–30% of the SME's stock and remaining a very long-term shareholder, Japanese SBICs contributed to the stable management of the invested SMEs. In accordance with the very strict initial listing requirements at that time, an IPO was not the ultimate goal of Japanese SBIC's investment. Rather, the primary goal was to augment the SME's capital in order to stabilize the SME structure and return a flow of income to the Japanese SBICs.

This system had a number of advantages. First, after receiving initial investments, SMEs could improve their debt–equity ratio by increasing their own equity capital with public money, as well as acquire a reputation as a sound business meriting official investment. SMEs could use this good reputation to build relationships with financial institutions and commercial partners. Second, the existence of long-term and outside shareholders with impartial position, who did not get involved in company management, could prevent *ex ante* opportunistic behavior on the part of the CEO, especially in family companies where competing factions could make decision-making very difficult. Third, the SBIC could achieve advantages regarding the complex inheritance tax valuation of non-publicly traded stocks and thereby smooth inheritance of family business ventures.[8] The tax authority would issue an official instruction confirming that the invested price by Japanese SBICs may be applied to the base of calculation of inheritance tax. In this way, Japanese SBICs can easily achieve a good rate of return by investing at a relatively low price compared to the substantial value of the shares, and then realize a larger potential capital gain in the future from the sale of those shares to the SME's owner, rather than from an IPO. As far as the owner of the SME is concerned, this official instruction from the tax authority

---

[8] Three different formulas are used in inheritance tax as follows: the net asset value formula, the comparison formula to a similar company in the same or similar sector, and the last transaction price formula.

allows them to calculate the price of their stock on a lower basis than would be the case if other formulas were used.

This type of long-term investment without involvement by Japanese SBICs was consistent with the role of SMEs within the stable pyramidal structures of Japanese *keiretsu*-type industrial groups under dominating integral architecture. However, after the recent deregulation of the initial listing requirements, some IPOs managed to achieve large capital gains and a good rate of return despite the fact that they were publicly-sponsored institutions. Meanwhile, SBICs did not get actively involved in management of the SMEs and invested only when both sides derived advantage from their participation as stable long-term investors. In other words, investment in sound SMEs could secure a stable cash flow at relatively low risk investment. But if the performance of the invested SME declined, SBICs had little capacity to get involved in management and effectively rectifying the situation. In this sense, Japanese SBICs' governance role in their venture SMEs was very limited and marginal.

5.4.2 The Second Generation: Financial Keiretsu VC Companies (from 1972)

Private VCs emerged in Japan from the early 1970s. With the exception of KED (Kyoto Enterprise Development Co Ltd), almost all VCs were affiliated to banks, securities and insurance companies of the major established financial *keiretsu* groups.[9] VC finance was provided primarily through group companies, rather than wealthy individuals or pension funds as in the US. These arrangements were criticized on the grounds that they simply mirrored existing *mochiai* structures (cross share holdings in the group) among pre-IPO group companies (we can call this a "minor league") in parallel to *mochiai* structures in large publicly-traded companies ("major league"). The VC entities themselves were normal share-issuing limited companies, not partnerships as in the US. However, they often established their investment schemes with highly complex structures, and no clear distinction existed between the VC companies' own resources and the finance provided by corporate investors, thereby risking potential conflicts of interest. The group companies investing in the VC entity basically acted as banks or security companies act toward other companies within their *keiretsu* groups, and remained unenthusiastic about disclosure regarding VC companies and their funds and investments.

Furthermore, a single VC company might raise multiple funds for the same investment objects, which could also cause moral hazard and conflicts of interest between the different funds. Even with the introduction of investment funds raising capital from outside investors, these VC companies continued to invest their own money in a separate fund—an arrangement called "body investment." Since the 1980s, some VC companies also made IPOs themselves. This raised an important question in the worldwide VC industry: was it preferable to invest in a VC company's shares or in their funds?

---

[9] We call these "VC companies" to distinguish them from VC firms.

The investment strategies of these VC companies were not focused on investing in premature start-ups. VC companies' main investment style was to seek out potential IPO candidates from among sound and expanding medium-sized companies which could safely be predicted to undertake an IPO within several years. As the main investment target was "later-stage" firms on the threshold of an IPO, VC's revenue source could not be derived solely from capital gains. Given the strict initial listing requirements which prevailed at that time, VC companies also counted on income from IPO consulting fees and charges for pre-IPO services. In order to determine the market valuation of the company to be invested in, a net asset value formula was normally utilized and investments were made in the face amount, which helped to keep the investment price relatively low. However, the amount of investment often failed to match the financing required and was determined mainly with reference to the *ex post* VC's share. If there was a gap between the investment offered and amount required, debt financing through loans or insurance bonds were often arranged as well. In addition, financing with a discrete type of warrant bond was also typical such that the invested company often issued a separate type of warrant bond to the VC company, which in turn sold most of the warrant back to the owner at a nominal price, and as soon as possible, in order to minimize its own risks. This instrument was essentially a kind of mezzanine investment useful in adjusting the share between the owner and the VC company in order to reimburse the bond, and avoid risks to the VC company.

The types of business targeted by second generation VC investment were essentially late-stage ventures, which were anticipated as being near to the IPO stage. Businesses regarded as IPO candidates were not technology-based ventures, but emerging companies in established industries. These industries included retail, distribution and restaurants, which operated through franchise chain networks and were supported by the market or consumers. Other businesses were created as a result of deregulation, such as employment agencies involved in manpower placement. Here VC companies would give advice to these businesses on the detailed procedures necessary to meet the strict initial listing requirements for the IPO. As a result, the VC companies did become involved with certain aspects of the invested company's internal organization in a manner termed "*ni no bu*," (Part 2 of IPO Application Form which contains detailed templates) whereby VC companies keep checks and "guided" the IPO candidates to fulfill the certain detailed organizational templates.

The second generation VC companies viewed R&D-oriented ventures as being too uncertain and high risk, and extended this view more generally toward new start-ups. For this reason, the skills and knowledge about technology roadmaps and technology marketing, which are critical tools for innovation management in any decentralized modular-based industries, were simply not necessary in Japanese VC companies. Thus, self-styled capitalists with little knowledge of cutting-edge technologies continued to play a role for many years.

Despite this rather detached or passive style of investment, some VC companies managed to perform very well in the 1980s, and Japanese VC was regarded as successful. (This was at a time when US VC firms were experiencing very harsh conditions.) However, this success was more to do with the fact that VC companies could invest at relatively low prices initially, and capture gains from a market that was brisk, with buoyant stock prices (including newly listed ones for which demand was high) and a high number of good potential IPO candidates.

As noted above, VC companies did not need to get deeply involved in the corporate governance of these enterprises. They remained distant from the entrepreneurs and from issues such as risk management, value creation, marketing, or technological developments. The role of VC companies was largely confined to guiding the development of the company's internal organization and ensuring an adequate checks and balances system had been set up. Up until the late 1990s, VC companies did not dispatch executives to invested companies to lend hands-on support, owing to the effect of anti-trust legislation.

This approach to VC reflected the broader regulatory environment at the time. Legislation to combat opportunistic behavior by the entrepreneurs' side had not yet been developed. VC companies had no legal means at their disposal to deal with entrepreneurs or managers who decided against an IPO half way through the process owing to stock market conditions or for other internal reasons. Preferred stock schemes were limited to preference dividends and therefore, the only way for a VC company to maintain the right to nominate executives was to contract with all stock holders, a method which proved somewhat ineffective. Moreover, given the focus on later stage investments, the use of milestone investments do not provide a powerful means to maintain influence within corporate governance. Thus, some firms became so-called living-dead, having given up on an IPO and persisting without effective governance mechanisms.

In sum, the dominant investment style in Japan was characterized by co-investments with relatively low amount of investment each (below US$1 million), but these investments delivered modest capital gains and other income from consulting fees, charges for services, interest on bonds etc. Pooling of smaller investment to numerous smaller investors allowed risks to be managed in a portfolio fashion. However, VC companies often neglected the poorly-performing invested companies to which they provided no assistance to improve their management, regarding it as "a waste of time." Indeed, VC companies lacked both the will and organizational skills to offer such support. This approach stands in marked contrast to the US style, which involved investing huge and significant amounts of money, as well as providing hands-on support.

5.4.3 The Third Generation: Emergence of Independent VC Firms (From Late 90s)

Related to Japan's catching-up process of economic development and dominance of debt finance and integral architecture, the first and second generation VC companies in Japan developed a unique investment style, which did not take on the "orthodox" characteristics of VC equity finance, such as high-risk early stage investment and hands on involvement rapidly growing ventures. Towards the end of the 1990s, VC companies began to shift their focus toward early-stage investments. This change arose from a combination of factors. Economically, new potential IPO candidates grew scarce, and VC companies faced both stock market turmoil and the shrinking of capital gains as entrepreneurs and investors gained a growing knowledge of valuation. However, a shift towards early stage investment required certain changes in VC companies such as more rapid decision-making, higher amounts of equity investment, value creation through a hands-on style, and a potential for VC firms to establish spin-offs. The lack of management expertise meant that few second generation VC companies were able to take advantage of this climate.

In the late 1990s, new independent VC "firms" emerged which did adopt the "orthodox" style of VC investment and established themselves as a third generation of venture capitalists in Japan. Although few in number, the third generation VC entities have a remarkable track record. Talented venture capitalists now take advantage of partnership-style funds, which resemble those of classic VC firms in Silicon Valley. One pull factor behind the emergence of the third generation VC firms was the successful performance of classic VC firms in Silicon Valley in the 1990s and the key role they played in transforming industrial structures around the world. A push factor was the aforementioned deadlock of second generation VCs in Japan. Meanwhile, improvements in the regulatory structure served to strengthen the basis of independent VC firms in Japan. For example, new legislation supported spin-offs by allowing funds to be raised on the basis of limited partnerships. Preferred stock was introduced to assure control rights to invested companies. And new stock market segments were opened to allow more openness and competition in IPO markets.

A specific feature of the third generation are talented venture capitalists who become involved in the business venture during start up and assist in the development of technology-oriented ventures or novel business models. After start up, venture capitalists participate directly in the company's management as part-time executives, in order to engage the Board in discussions over the quality of management, create value through hands-on support, and ultimately allow invested technology-based ventures to move toward the goal of an IPO. Their involvement and hands-on support are at least equal to that in Silicon Valley. Unlike second generation VC companies linked to *keiretsu* groups, anecdotal evidence suggests that these new firms are "real" capitalists with substantial entrepreneurial spirit. For example, some Japanese VCs have made very rapid decisions to commit up to several million US dollars of seed investment to very promising projects after just fifteen minutes' consideration. A boutique size Japanese venture fund was able to achieve a very high performance reflected in a ratio of IPOs exceeding 60% and a triple digit internal rate of return (IRR); this compares with performance of around 30% of IPO ratio and 20–30% of IRR for a typical US first class venture capital firm. Although managers who develop into skillful and highly experienced venture capitalists remain very rare in Japan compared to the US, some skillful venture capitalists can now be found with experience in VC companies and making good investments in fields related to cutting-edge technology roadmaps used for module-based innovation.[10]

The new type of entrepreneurs invest in the "orthodox" manner by using a simple structure and the current price valuation formula, replacing other complicated investment structures such as warrant bonds, as found in second generation VCs. Starting up with sufficient equity helps entrepreneurs to avoid over-burdensome self-financing and follows the US model, where the founders of venture projects are normally required to commit their own money up to 30% in cash or liquidity up front, rather than offer their personal property and cars as collateral. The third generation VCs are likewise moving toward "zero gravity" start-up's where entrepreneurs are required to commit some money (to avoid opportunistic behavior). Under the new arrangements, even if the venture fails and becomes bankrupt, entrepreneurs can move onto fresh challenges or find new employment. They no longer face the destruction and loss of their personal wealth and livelihood—which is a completely new phenomenon in Japan. As an alternative to bankruptcy, a VC may also arrange an M&A deal which may have sufficient synergy with the venture project, and managers in the failed firms are "sent to the showers"—again, which constitutes a sea change in attitudes. Previously in Japan, it has been widely held that failure in starting up and managing an SME led directly to both social and even physical death. Some opinion polls have shown that the fear of starting up in Japan is three times as high as in the US.

Although empirical research is needed on this issue, it seems clear that the mind-set of entrepreneurs in Japan has also shifted dramatically in recent years. Many of the new third generation venture capitalists and invested entrepreneurs are people with talent, experience and high social status with profiles similar to those in the US—such as Harvard Business School MBAs, PhDs from prestigious US universities, engineers from large, high profile Japanese companies, university professors, and CEOs of foreign-affiliated multinationals. In contrast to the dominance of big business and lifetime employment patterns, a growing number of exceptional individuals not only have skills but also enthusiasm and ethical values to become entrepreneurs and create start-ups with equity from independent VC firms.

Likewise, attitudes towards IPOs are also changing. IPOs remained exceptional in Japan due to strict listing requirements and low supply of capital oriented toward high-risk equity investment. VC companies tended to invest in late-stage companies, which were at least 15 years old. Many Japanese founding owners (entrepreneurs) of pre-IPO companies treated the companies as their own inseparable pieces of flesh and blood calling them "my company," not "your company" nor even "our company." They were often highly reluctant to cede any equity to other persons and investors, except in special circumstances like

---

[10] The most famous technology road map is "International Technology Roadmap for Semiconductors" (ITRS). Technology Roadmap shares information among all participants of a "modular cluster" and provides rough guidance in a set of decentralized innovations without a central planner. For venture companies working toward a specific module, the roadmap becomes an important point of reference (Ando and Motohashi 2002).

inheritance. If the company grew steadily, finance could be provided indirectly by the banking system and IPOs did not seem to be a financial necessity. Furthermore, requirements for regular audits, disclosure and investor relationships worked as a disincentive for IPOs. Despite the negative incentives toward IPOs, entrepreneurs who accomplished successful IPOs earned great respect and acquired substantial personal wealth through capital gains. Although only few IPOs can serve as role models, an IPO has now become one of the key goals for entrepreneurs starting out.[11]

While the collapse of the IT bubble in 2000 put a break on emerging developments, independent VC firms felt it provided a kind of a "cooling off" period during which excellent players could be identified and resources placed at their disposal. Sooner or later the negative stereotype of start-ups in Japan is likely to dissipate. Meanwhile, the third generation of venture capitalists has substantially changed the approach to corporate governance in Japan, becoming directly involved in the management as part-time executives and providing hands-on support in various ways:

- *Pre-consultation:* consultation with entrepreneurial candidates before spin off and the establishment of venture companies, and the clearing of any outstanding obstacles. One key element is getting full acceptance and support of the candidate's family, and especially their spouse.
- *Daily meetings:* Just after start up, daily meetings take place to check and review managerial strategy and the business plan.
- *Plan-Do-Check-Act (PDCA) cycle:* If the venture project underperforms, a detailed analysis is conducted and agreement is reached on the best way forward.
- *Periodic checks:* After taking-off, VC firms reduce their involvement but still require regular "health" check-ups. They participate in monthly Board meetings at which entrepreneurs are required to present management progress reports and respond to members' questions. In this way, entrepreneurial managers deepen their understanding of business processes, sharpen their problem solving faculties and prioritize the issues on which the managerial team has to act. In turn this improves the quality of Board meetings which become a critical element in the management of the company.
- *Value creation through social networks:* Making best use of capitalists' personal networks and reputation is also an essential element in hands-on support. In this way, they arrange alliances with large multinationals to cooperate as marketing channels or technology R&D, and make arrangements for sharing information or seeking potential new partnerships among invested companies, establishing horizontal alliances and synergy effects as the most famous venture capital firm, KPCB, does in the manner called "Keiretsu"

---

[11] Recently a young entrepreneur of a successful IT venture announced his engagement to a famous TV star, and another bought professional soccer and baseball teams. These signs of success serve to accelerate this trend.

(that is a horizontal alliance in this turn.)[12]. As for an intellectual property strategy, capitalists daily visit a first class patent office which has know-how and knowledge of cutting-edge business model patents so they can help the company put in place an effective strategy. The same goes for the new company's legal strategy; capitalists introduce experienced and reliable lawyers who are accustomed to venture dealings.

- *Daily care and contingent action:* VC firms pay attention to the mental health of chief executives and the management team. They take advantage of Japanese-style communications and entertain stressed entrepreneurs by going to a sauna or for a drink in order to improve their mood and refresh them. In urgent cases such as illness, the venture capitalists may temporarily stand-in for a top manager of an invested company.

By means of these daily low-key efforts, independent Japanese VC firms create value by being involved directly in the management of the invested venture companies and encourage chief executives to exercise more entrepreneurial management. It is said that classic US venture capital firms invest within a 50-mile radius or an hour's drive of their office. This also occurs in Japan. Independent VC firms have their offices very close to metro stations—in the Tokyo metropolitan area, there is a safe and well developed efficient metro network (instead of daily traffic jams in California), which allows them to pay frequent visits to invested venture companies and guide the management directly. A leading independent VC firm, which focuses on early stage investments, encourages start-ups to cluster inside a several kilometer square radius from its office.

The governance style of independent Japanese VC firms was reinforced and benefited from various legal reforms. For example, the introduction of legislation on preferred stock allows them to keep adequate control rights with less fear of dilution. This key moral hazard issue, which was typical for VC investments by second generation VC companies, has been substantially reduced. Moreover, the limited partnership status allows independent VC firms to attract outside investors and establish funds based mainly on the personal assets of wealthy persons, as in the US VC firms place considerable stress on their independence and attempt to raise funds without relying on established corporate investors from the traditional financial *keiretsu* groups which may cause severe conflicts during the expansion of invested companies.[13]

---

[12] KPCB (Kleiner Perkins Caufield and Byers) was formed "with the goal of providing operating advice and resources to entrepreneurs in addition to capital investment" by *Eugene Kleiner* who was a founder of Fairchild Semiconductor and others in 1972. KPCB introduced a so-called *keiretsu*-style concept, which involved an informal business network consisting of invested companies in the same field. (The website states "We pioneered the idea 20 years ago of bringing the businesses we work with into an informal network, which we call a *Keiretsu.*") KPCB is a first class VC firm and invested in more than 350 companies including many eminent venture companies such as America Online, Amazon, Sun, Genentech, Compaq, and Netscape. This network provides a valuable and useful platform for entrepreneurs starting new venture projects.

[13] New ventures often raise competitive challenges to established large companies, and so independent VCs avoid fund raising from corporate investors, who may be biased against certain promising venture projects.

However, independent outside investors demand a high degree of accountability within the fund that invests their individual assets. The third generation VC firms have thus adopted a very different style of investor relationships and are positive toward disclosure. The Japanese social custom of good faith between individuals works positively here and exerts pressure on capitalists to maintain high ethical standards, and consequently leads to high performance. According to the opinion of a top capitalist, "Independence is a key for venture projects as the deep nature of venture implies overwhelming the establishments," and he noted that:

[the] mental pressure from individual investors is now very strong compared with when I worked in a VC company before. At an investors meeting, one well-known investor, who is himself an entrepreneur of a very successful company, asked me "You are without hesitation or anxiety in this decision, aren't you? If you are sure and confident, that is enough to satisfy me." This short question had a sobering effect and made me realize the deep personal trust that had been placed in me.

This episode indicates that some top capitalists in Japan respect ethical norms and fair play. In the field of private equity, moral hazard occurs often and thus personal reputation and ethical codes of conduct plays an important role. Elitzur and Gavious (2003) stress the importance of good relationships between entrepreneurs, business angels and entrepreneurs from venture capital who received angels' investment in order to reduce moral hazard and promote the development of viable companies.

5.4.4 Learning and Imitation: The Emergence of a Neo Second Generation

Some of the talented third generation venture capitalists previously worked in core positions for second generation VC companies, and later spun off and formed their own independent VC firms. This competitive challenge prompted a change in second generation VC companies, which lost core human capital. Over a number of years, some of the biggest VC companies introduced teams to monitor venture projects, transforming a vertically segmented internal organization and aiming to shift to hands-on investment in early stage investments, including starting up. Equity investments with current price valuation also became the main investment vehicle, rather than a mezzanine type loan through warrant bonds. These changes are only slowly emerging and the second generation VC companies haven't yet transformed themselves completely. Thus, the traditional type of investment continues to represent the main bulk of investments. Although the third generation venture capital is emerging, good start-ups still cannot necessarily attract equity investments at the early stages of their business. Many VC companies still do not possess the necessary skills for hands-on support and cannot invest in significant volume. Consequently, VC companies can only invest in small amounts, such as less than US$1 million per project and tend to follow the crowd.

Still, from the end of the 1990s, ICT-related companies and major trading houses began to establish their own VC funds. These resemble second generation as their finance and corporate governance are essentially controlled by a parent company, and hence we label them as a neo-second-generation. Generally speaking, these companies have abundant financial capacity but lack the skills and organization for hands-on support. They tend to control invested companies with output quotas or numerical targets, but aim to build up synergy effects by offering managerial resources such as technology or know-how in specific business fields such as ICT-related sector or franchise chain, as well as valuable networking opportunities with customers, distributors and business partners. Some funds invest in a diversified portfolio-style manner using a large number of projects, but rather focused on a specific industrial sector.

A number of foreign VC firms also entered into the Japanese market at the end of the 1990s, although some have already withdrawn. Furthermore, a portion of VC firms has begun to shift to buyout dealings in the response to Japan's economy and efforts for revitalization (see the chapter by Yanagawa in this volume). Table 5.2 summarizes the investment style and the feature of governance of each VC generation following the above discussion.

Table 5.2 Features of VC Investment Style and Corporate Governance, by Generation

Generations	Circumstance	Investment style	Governance	
			VC→ Invested Companies	Investors→ VC
1st gen.: Public VCs	Strict initial listing requirement, Restricted capital market	Improvement of equity of core SMEs (small amount of equity, contract on fixed rate of return, Tax incentive, official admission effect)	*Ex ante* selection, No involvement (long term stable tacit share holder)	Governmental guidance for affiliated special Corporation
2nd gen.: Financial *keiretsu* VC companies	Strict requirement→ Deregulation	Later stage just before IPO laissez-faire portfolio (forming "mochiai" cross-share holding structure)	Nominal. Internal organizational shifts for later stage(vertical division)	Control for keiretsu affiliated company ("Mochiai" cross-share holding, Conflict of interest, Poor disclosure)
3rd gen.: independent VC firms	Establishment of New IPO markets	Zero-stage, start-up, early stage Technology-oriented Silicon Valley way	Direct involvement (hands-on) Contribution for value creation through participation to management as part time executive and mentor to entrepreneurs	Trusted relation based on "reliance between individuals" Fundraise keeping independence Transparency, disclosure

Neo 2nd gen.: Trading house /Corporate Owned VC	Establishment of New IPO markets	Focus on specific fields such as distributors, franchise, ICT related sectors Forming a portfolio in specific fields based on abundant financing capacity	Indirect (hands-off) Control by setting only output quota etc, Supply managerial resources and network as customers, etc,	Control as keiretsu affiliated companies Cross shareholding, Conflict of interest Insufficient disclosure

5.4.5 A Brief Statistical Comparison

Table 5.3 shows the situation of investments and loans for each generation in 2002 using data from the Venture Enterprise Center and Japan Small and Medium Enterprise Corporation.[14] From the viewpoint of accumulated finance, the second generation represents 51.7% of total investment, the neo-second-generation accounts for 27.7%. The third generation accounts for just 13.2% and the first generation has 7.5%. The average amount of accumulated financing per VC entity is as follows: ¥29.3 billion for the first generation, ¥21.7 billion for the neo-second-generation, ¥12.6 billion for the second generation, and ¥6.2 billion for the third generation. Within second generation VC companies, security company-related investment is ¥49.4 billion, insurance company-related investment is ¥8.9 billion and bank-related is ¥5.7 billion. In terms of the utilization of VC sources of finance (e.g. the VC fund size divided by total accumulated financing including other financing measures), some differences between the generations are readily apparent. The level VC utilization in the neo-second-generation corporate-related is 87.0%, third independent is 85.2%, second generation security company related is 67.8%, second insurance company related 65.8%. Meanwhile, the utilization level among the first generation is 4.6%, neo-second trade house related is 12.2% and second bank related is 27.4% (these do not actively use and invest in the manner of "body investment"

---

[14] This data was gathered from 103 VC entities which responded to the Venture Enterprise Center (2003) and the Japan Small and Medium Enterprise Corporation (2003). And the total accumulated financing surpasses the data of the Venture Enterprise Center (2003). Other publications such as the "Nikkei venture business annual report" (*Nikkeishinnbunsha*) show that there seem to be about 200 VC entities in Japan, including some 50 independent entities. However, it is hard to get exact information about the smaller ones and some are not very active. We estimate that around 103 VC entities are active in Japan.

Table 5.3 VC Financing in 2002, by Generation

Generation	Sample	Accumulated finance (JPY)	Share of total VC investment	Average accumulated investment per entity (JPY)	Share of usage of funds
1st: Public VC Corporation	3	88.0	7.5%	29.3	4.6%
2nd: financial keiretsu VC Company	49	606.2	51.7%	12.6	55.0%
Bank related	33	189.5	16.1%	5.7	27.4%
Security company related	8	345.8	29.5%	49.4	67.8%
Insurance company related	8	70.9	6.0%	8.9	65.8%
3rd: independent VC Firms	36	154.4	13.2%	6.2	85.2%
Neo 2nd: corporate/trade house related VC Company	15	324.9	27.7%	21.7	53.2%
Corporate related	8	177.3	15.1%	22.2	87.0%
Trade house related	7	147.7	12.6%	21.1	12.2%
Total	103	1173.6	100.0%	12.9	54.6%

from their own account). Hata and Kamijo (1996) also analyze the number of establishments for each generation by vintage year.

5.5 THE INSTITUTIONAL FRAMEWORK FOR VC DEVELOPMENT IN JAPAN

Turning back to the arguments in section 5.1, the unique and limited development of Japan's VCs can be broadly explained by three macroeconomic factors, as well as a number of other related institutional factors (see Table 5.4).

First, the bank-based financial system that emerged in Japan as part of catch-up economic development after World War II made long-term debt financing the dominant mode of corporate finance in Japan. Financial targets were often very clear and followed proven models, business risks were very limited, and the overall amount of money was regarded as the key issue because industries were being urged to invest in new, large factories and equipment to acquire economies of scale. Under these conditions, debt financing was highly appropriate. Therefore large commercial banks, long-term credit banks and governmental institutions using *yucho-zaito* mechanisms (postal savings and public financing with low interest rates) became the main players in the financial sector. Meanwhile, the lack of an IPO market, the lack of private pension funds which might include venture funds in their portfolios, and the lack of business angels have also contributed to the poor development of equity investment.

Second, the dualistic structure of Japanese industry, divided between big companies and SMEs, and the pyramid-like *keiretsu* long posed a formidable barrier to independent entrepreneurial activities. This structure helped to establish Japan's strong competitiveness in integrated assembly industries, such as the automobile industry, domestic electronics and industrial machines. However, the social and economic status of SMEs, especially start-ups, remained low. Most employees of large companies were not prepared to give up their social and economic status as members of a large organization, as well as the protections of lifetime employment. The norm was to stay within the long-term company community, rather than spinning off to start a new independent venture. Likewise, students tended to seek out jobs within large companies in order to take advantage of their career incentives and relative security.

Consequently, Japan's entrepreneurs had few role models to inspire them—unlike the situation in the US, where entrepreneurs had abundant role models such as Intel and Fairchild for engineers; DEC, DELL, Microsoft, Netscape, Yahoo for students; or Amgen and Genentech for chemical scientists. Meanwhile, legal support for entrepreneurs were inadequate and the risk of bankruptcy very high. Bankruptcy was regarded not only as a business failure, but also a social "death" (sometimes leading to real death). In some sense, accepting the challenge to create a new start-up literally meant being prepared to die. This inevitably reduced the number of entrepreneurial challengers in Japan.

Third, venture activities have been obstructed by the socio-economic structure segmenting Japanese industry into durable "enterprise communities" characterized by long-term relationships and stakeholder-oriented corporate governance. Large Japanese companies cultivated a "*takotsubo*-type," insider-only method of sharing information, whereby decisions are negotiated within the organization or *keiretsu* group using an informal consensus-building mechanism called "*nemawasi*." This mechanism is eminently suited to an integral manufacturing system with many interdependent tasks like the automobile industry (Aoki 2001). The focus on incremental innovation within these stable structures (Hall and Soskice 2001) has, however, also limited the demand for outside technological development and arguably stunted entrepreneurial activity. The custom of keeping information within the organization has made it difficult to establish common goals such as technology roadmaps with third party companies. Since board members are largely insiders promoted within the company, managers have tended to focus on developing internal organizational capacities, rather than looking outside the firm for solutions on the cutting edge of innovation. Risky start-up ventures and technological roadmaps have been outside their line of vision.

Furthermore, big companies and consumers in Japan (unlike in the US) have been resistant to buying from unknown ventures with a limited business record. Newcomers have few opportunities to penetrate the strongly united *keiretsu* groups, which prevent opportunistic behavior through mutual reliance. The same applies to governmental procurement as government officials are normally very conservative and look for a proven business record. In the US, on the other hand, the government has taken a very positive approach to purchasing from ventures without previous records, to the extent that it promotes procurement through, for example, the SBIR (Small Business Innovation Research) program.

Against this background, Japan's VC players in the public and private sectors have repeatedly attempted to import US-style venture capitalism. The two early attempts resulted in a significant transformation of Japanese business organization, but basically ended in failure. As argued in the previous sections, VC development in Japan tried to emulate developments in the US, but lacked a deep understanding of the VC system and its macroeconomic and institutional prerequisites. Whether intentionally or unconsciously, the players modified and fine-tuned the US system to accommodate the powerful macroeconomic and institutional factors unique to Japan.

In the 1960s the Japanese government established SBICs based on the US model. SBICs formed the basis of the hugely successful venture economy in the US and continue to support the supply of a significant amount of risk money for innovations. However, the imported system was completely altered to suit an environment with many family owned companies and a stable SME structure. Later in the 1970s, the private sector established private VC companies following the success of ARD, the world's first VC. However, these VC companies acted in a completely different manner and used mezzanine-style financing within the context of Japan's bank-based financial system complementary group company structure. Moreover, Japan's pyramid-like *keiretsu* groups under dominating integral architecture strongly affected corporate governance between VC entities and entrepreneurs, as well as VC entities and investors. VC governance, which by its very nature should be based on trust between individuals and ethical business

Table 5.4 Institutional Factors Restricting the Development of a Venture Economy in Japan

Legal/Institutions	Lack of or insufficient IPO market, bankruptcy law, limited partnership law, limited liability company law, preferred stock, fair benchmark for performance
Historical	Lack of business angels and capitalists with skill or experience of a CEO
	Lack of knowledge for rational valuation
	Lack of innovation management with technology road-mapping and marketing
	Lack of "heroes" or role models such as Intel, Fairchild for engineers, DEC, DELL, Microsoft, Netscape, Yahoo for students, Amgen and Genentech for chemists
Social system	Fear of failure, especially starting up own business
	Poor status of new entrepreneurs
	Higher status of employees of a bigger company

norms to ensure the efficiency and fairness of the business activities, consisted only of monitoring within bank-centered *keiretsu* groups.

We have argued that the third generation of VC represents a significant break with the past efforts to create VC, and is beginning to overcome the major institutional barriers to VC for the first time. The essential difference lies in the classic hands-on type VC firm, and the fact that the third generation VC entities, whose corporate governance is strongly tied to individual reputation and business ethics, are able to create huge value through hands-on involvement. Thus, VC in Japan has already begun to change.

5.6 FUTURE PERSPECTIVES

This chapter has examined the historical trajectory of VC entities and their governance in Japan. Just as the main financial institutions in Japan developed in a unique way, VC entities headed in a very different direction from their US counterparts and built their own risk-averse equity investment style. This style is characterized by late-stage investment and rather passive corporate governance with minimal "hands on involvement."

When the catch-up economic development process involving "*kaizen*" activities almost reached a saturation point in the late 1980s, Japan's economic growth ceased and coincided with the collapse of the bubble economy. Since then, Japan faced the difficult question of how to remain a front-runner in innovation and encourage new entrepreneurial activities. The developments of the 1990s also revealed limitations of Japanese style VC companies, and the wide gap between the Japanese and US venture scene created a sense of crisis. Japan undertook drastic institutional improvements such as the establishment of two new IPO markets, Mothers and NASDAQ Japan, a revision of JASDAQ and a move to introduce a legal framework for limited partnerships. The long recession also altered the mind-sets of students and engineers in big companies. Against this background the third generation VC entities emerged with greater focus on high-risk start-up firms and hands-on involvement. The corporate governance aspects of VC were also much improved and regulatory reforms have put the Japanese legal framework arguably on a par with the US. Central government and local governments are focusing on support for start-ups.

While skilled third generation venture capitalists are making a strong impact on the whole VC industry, a number of institutional issues have yet to be resolved in order for there to be substantial future progress.

Concerning governance for VC entities, a legal scheme of LLCs (Limited Liability Companies) is crucial. The LLC scheme which was established in 1977 in Wyoming has become widespread in the US. The LLC scheme has provided effective organizational options for VC firms, VC funds, and expert-based enterprises such as law firms and accounting firms. An LLC has persona *sui juris* (i.e. status as a legal entity), limited liability, internal autonomy, and a choice of taxation on constituents as a feature of partnership organization. An LLC is an intermediate organization and provides a number of organizational options for fundraising. Using the LLC scheme, capitalists can be confident of achieving a return which corresponds to the effort of developing invested companies, while keeping limited responsibility and establishing a balanced governance structure between investors and invested companies. It is an indispensable legal scheme especially for third generation capitalists. In 2005 new legal frameworks of modified LLC and LLP (Limited Liability Partnership) have been enforced in Japan so that VC firms could choose from these options as their legal entity for their activities.[15]

Another issue is the continued use of providing personal insurance for equity investment. This practice is incompatible by nature with risk capital investment, and takes advantage of the ignorance and vulnerable position of the entrepreneur. The second generation VC companies often request this personal insurance, which shows that they haven't entirely outgrown the dependence on collateral, which has been common practice in the bank-based financial system of Japan. While disagreement exists as to whether the matter should be left to competition or subject to regulation, the issue of personal insurance needs to be adequately addressed in some manner.

More broadly, Japan's VC investment is still the lowest among OECD countries. Although the quality of VC investment is improving, its effect on the macro economy as a whole is still limited. Increasing the supply of risk capital available remains a key challenge. Here a comprehensive policy package including tax incentives for personal investment is likely to be required, such as the introduction of an SBIC scheme and providing tax incentives for both angel investors and start-ups. At the same time, role models are important for the development of an entrepreneurial culture. An SBIR scheme which successfully screened new venture projects and provided support from the public sector, such as through government procurement, might also encourage entrepreneurs. Moreover,

---

[15] All three authors have contributed directly to this new legislation. In 1998, Ando was working as an official of Ministry of International Trade and Industry (MITI) and recognized through his discussions with entrepreneur, Mr. Kazutaka Muraguchi. However, given the possible conflicts of interests among Limited Partners (Investors) and General Partners (Venture capitalists) discussed in this article, it was premature to put the item on the policy agenda at that time. About two years later Mr. Akihito ("Aki") Nakamachi commented that LLC as General Partner of Limited Partnership of VC funds had become dominant practice in Silicon Valley. In the meantime, Ando had become a director of the Economic and Fiscal Management of Cabinet Office and brought this policy item into Prime Minister Koizumi's Structural Reform in 2002, although a certain ministry objected to bringing the issue further. The following year, at Ando's urging, Mr. Satoshi Kusakabe, Director of Industrial Organization Division of METI (transformed from MITI) bravely took it up. Next, Ishii got involved in a devoted effort to formulate and pass this new legislation. Ishii and his team drafted the major legal articles and framework, following review by Cabinet Law Bureau, tough negotiations with the Ministry of Finance and Ministry of Justice, and "nemawashi" (consensus building communications) among Diet members involved in passing the draft law. During these efforts, Hata used his influence as a Chair or a member of Governmental Committee, Official Research Groups and a Chair of VC Committee of Venture Society of Japan, to support, advise, and guided other co-authors on these issues.

university reform may support new start-ups via spin-off from top level universities, and affect the mind-sets of students towards venture projects.

A final element relates to the importance of good corporate governance practices. The establishment of new IPO markets also led to evidence of unethical behavior among new companies. The "rule of reputation" remains underdeveloped as a governance mechanism within the industry. To protect the integrity of the IPO markets the industry needs gatekeepers,[16] who judge fairly and provide positive incentives for disclosure. Moreover, a mature VC industry association[17] is needed to provide guidance on adequate disclosure and other self-regulatory measures within the industry. Developing the mechanism of reputation is very important so that venture capitalists can exercise their full potential and increase in number. Indeed, corporate governance should be the touchstone for the development of the VC industry in Japan and the revitalization of Japan's economy in the age of modularity.

In 2003, Mothers, the new IPO market on the Tokyo Stock Exchange, achieved an historical record with 31 IPOs and expanded its share in the new IPO markets from 6.5% (2002) to 25.6 % (2003). The total number of IPOs in 2003 was 121 in spite of a very low level of IPOs in NASDAQ after the collapse of the IT bubble in 2000. These figures may be a good portent for the new era of venture financing in Japan.

BIBLIOGRAPHY

Ando, H. and K. Motohashi (2002). *Nihon keizai kyōsōryoku no kōsō* (Vision for the Competitiveness of Japan's Economy). Tokyo: Nihon Keizai Shinbunsha.
Aoki, M. (2001). *Towards a Comparative Institutional Analysis.* Cambridge, MA: MIT Press.
Baldwin, C. Y. and K. B. Clark (2000). *Design Rules.* Cambridge, MA: MIT Press.
Bygrave, W. D. and Timmons, J.A. (1992). *Venture Capital at the Crossroads.* Boston: Harvard Business School Press.
Elitzur, R. and A. Gavious (2003). 'Contracting, Signaling, and Moral Hazard: A Model of Entrepreneurs, "Angels", and Venture Capitalists,' *Journal of Business Venturing,* 18(6): 709–25.
Gorman, M. and W. A. Sahlman (1989). 'What Do Venture Capitalists Do?' *Journal of Business Venturing,* 4(4): 231–48.
Harmon, S. and J. Doerr (1999). *Zero Gravity: Riding Venture Capital from High-tech Start-up to Breakout IPO.* London: Bloomberg Press.

---

[16] Gatekeepers are expert consultants and choose promising VC funds for institutional investors and pension funds. Their tasks range from advice on fund operation to research and valuation of fund managers (Korver 1999). However, very few gatekeepers or experts in these activities exist in Japan.

[17] In 2002, the Japan Venture Capital Association (JVCA) was established with two goals: "to bring the venture capital world together and to help venture capital to better support venture businesses." However, its activities are limited compared with the National Venture Capital Association (NVCA) and the National Association of Small Business Investment companies (NASBIC) in the US.

Hata, N. and M. Kamijo (1996). *Bencha fainansu no Tayōka* (Variegation of Venture Financing). Tokyo: Nihon Keizai Shinbunsha.

Hall, P. A. and D. Soskice (2001). *Varieties of Capitalism*. Oxford: Oxford University Press.

Higashide, H. and S. Birley (1999). 'Eikoku bencha kyapitarisuto no katudō: Tōshi anken tono kakawarikata' (Activities of English Venture Capitalists), *Nihon Bencha Gakkai shi*, 1: 197–204.

Japan Small and Medium Enterprise Corporation (2003). 'Shuyō Bencha Kyapitaru no Tōshijūtenbunya to shien no jissai' (The Real Practice of a Focusing on a Field for Investment and Support by Major Venture Capital Companies), Mimeo.

Kaplan, S. and P. J. Strömberg (2000). 'Financial Contracting Theory Meets the Real World: An Empirical Analysis of Venture Capital Contracts,' *CEPR Discussion Papers*, 2421.

Korver, M. J. (1999). *Puraibeto ekuiti kachisōzō no tōshishuhō* (Private Equity—Investment Measure for Value Creation). Tokyo: Tōyōkeizai shimpōsha.

Ono, M. (1997) *Bencha kigyō to tōshi no jissaichishiki* (Practical Knowledge for Venture Start-up and Investment). Tokyo: Tōyōkeizai shimpōsha.

Podolny, J. M. (2001). 'Networks As the Pipes and Prisms of the Market,' *American Journal of Sociology*, 107(1): 33–60.

Reynolds, P. D, W. D. Bygrave, E. Autio, and M. Hay (2002). *GEM Global 2002 Executive Report*. GEM.

Venture Enterprise Center (2003). *Heisei 14 Nendo Bencha Kyapitaru Tōshijōkyō Chōsa Hōkoku* (Report on venture capital investment in FY2002). Available at: http://www.meti.go.jp/policy/newbusiness/houkokusyo/capital.pdf

6

Corporate Governance in Financial Distress: The New Role of Bankruptcy[1]

Peng Xu

6.1 INTRODUCTION

To date, a striking aspect of the Japanese main bank system has been that it provides a flexible, more effective private alternative to bankruptcy reorganization, and for dealing with financial distress and debt restructurings. Until the early 1990s, bankruptcy resolutions were rarely employed for large Japanese firms. Most financially distressed large firms in Japan successfully restructured troubled debt privately with main bank intervention, rather than through formal bankruptcy. Three main reasons are considered regarding the main bank system. First, banks used to represent interests of various classes of claimholders, usually holding both equities and loans. Second, the debt and equities of Japanese firms were concentrated with a small number of banks, and usually banks held the largest blocks of Japanese firms. Third, Japanese firms traditionally rely heavily on bank loans (Sheard 1994).

However, Japan's debt restructuring practice after the mid-1990s suggests that bank lenders are less likely to rescue failing borrowers than they were before the early 1990s (Hirota and Miyajima 2001; Xu 2003a, b, 2004). The recent Japanese firm's choices between bankruptcy and private workouts are similar to the American firm's reaction during the recession of the 1980s. Empirical results demonstrate a significant change in Japan–US comparative corporate governance: similarities dominate over differences in comparing the US bankruptcy wave of the 1980s and the Japanese bankruptcy wave of the late 1990s. To date, earlier studies have found many differences in comparing a downturn of the US economy and an upturn of the Japanese economy in the 1980s.

[1] This chapter is based on work undertaken as a project of REITI and collaborative research with KDI. A grant-in-aid from the Zengin Foundation for Studies on Economics and Finance is gratefully acknowledged. The author would like to thank Franklin Allen, Masahiko Aoki, Yoshihiro Arikawa, Keiichi Ohmura, Kaori Hatanaka, Takeo Hoshi, Gregory Jackson, Sung-In Jun, Hiroshi Maruyama, Colin Mayer, Curtis Millhaupt, Hideki Miyajima, Hirohiko Nakahara, Soogeun Oh, Hiroshi Osano, Zenichi Shishido, Oren Sussman, Hiroshi Teruyama, Noriyuki Yanagawa, Tsung-ming Yeh, Masako Furusawa, and Yoshie Ozaku for their helpful comments and assistance.

The importance of bankruptcy is increasing in Japan, reforms are emerging such as new legal procedures for bankruptcy that are designed to encourage failing firms to file for bankruptcy sooner, thus facilitating faster bankruptcy conclusions. Until 1999, mostly Corporate Reorganization or Liquidation filings were available to corporations in Japan. A significant difference between Japanese Reorganization Law and chapter 11 of US law is that a court-appointed receiver operates the firm and works out a reorganization plan rather than the debtor's management. In principle incumbent managers depart the firm, once Corporate Reorganization proceeding commences. In other words, incumbent managers experience large personal costs under Corporate Reorganization Law. This aspect is rather similar to chapter 7 of the US bankruptcy code as well as the Liquidation Law of Japan. Because the managers are displaced, in almost all cases equity becomes worthless; managers therefore have a strong incentive to resist Liquidation or Reorganization. This demonstrates that both Liquidation and Reorganization can be inefficient procedures, as argued in White (1983).

As a response to this issue, an updated Civil Rehabilitation Law was passed that took effect April 1, 2000. The passage of the Civil Rehabilitation Law has substantially revised bankruptcy administration in Japan. One positive change of the Civil Rehabilitation Law is that debtor management continues to operate the firm and works out a Rehabilitation plan or liquidation, unless management is incompetent. This debtor in possession aspect of Civil Rehabilitation Law aims to provide incentives for managers of failing firms to file for bankruptcy at an earlier stage under Rehabilitation Law, by reducing their personal burdens. Another important feature of Civil Rehabilitation Law is that secured creditors do not participate in the procedure, which simplifies the bankruptcy reorganization procedure.

In this chapter, I aim to evaluate bankruptcy reform empirically in Japan. My key questions are the following: What is the experience of incumbent management of bankrupt firms under the debtor-in-possession Civil Rehabilitation Law? How does the passage of the Civil Rehabilitation Law affect bankruptcy resolution? And how long does it take for Reorganization firms and Rehabilitation firms to work out a resolution? More importantly, do the bankruptcy reforms improve the efficiency of bankruptcy procedures? Furthermore, a comparative corporate governance analysis of bankruptcy is attempted.

To empirically evaluate the bankruptcy reform of 2000, I use a sample of bankrupt firms, which try to restructure their debt by filing for Corporate Reorganization or Civil Rehabilitation in the late 1990s. Only a small fraction of the firms were firstly rescued by their bank lenders but finally ended in bankruptcies regardless of the bank lenders' rescue operations. At the same time, most of the financially distressed firms immediately filed for bankruptcy, while bank lenders rejected any financial rescues until the firm filed for bankruptcy. With or without bank lender intervention, most firms experienced president turnover and asset restructuring prior to bankruptcy filings. In a reorganization bankruptcy, in principle the incumbent management departs and instead a court appointed receiver operates the firm and works out a reorganization plan. By comparison, in a Civil Rehabilitation bankruptcy, it is possible for the incumbent debtor's management to remain and operate the firm to work out a rehabilitation plan. In about half of Civil Rehabilitation firms, presidents remain after proceedings commence. However, most of the presidents seem less likely to be responsible for the management failures: they are either newly appointed or appointed by large shareholders, bank lenders.

Priority of secured claims is less likely to be violated, as it is in the US. Also, priority violation is rare for unsecured claims. In contrast, priority violation for unsecured creditors is more likely to occur in the US. The average time from filing of the bankruptcy petition under Corporate Reorganization Law to resolution is 2.2 years, and on average it takes 0.57 years for Civil Rehabilitation firms to reach resolution from petition filing, 1.6 years less than that of Corporate Reorganization Law. Bankrupt firms emerged substantially faster after the 2000 bankruptcy reform. The average time from bankruptcy petition to resolution in Japan is 1.2 years, about 1.3 years shorter than the average time of US firms in Weiss (1990). Hence, internationally Japan has quite an effective bankruptcy legal system, with respect to bankruptcy duration.

More importantly, the analysis on the duration of bankruptcy shows that leverage has no significant effect on duration in Corporate Reorganization but highly leveraged Civil Rehabilitation firms are less likely to quickly emerge from the process. This suggests that before the bankruptcy legal reform in 2000 financially distressed firms seem to have no incentives to file for Corporate Reorganization earlier, because they would lose anything regardless of the speed of the bankruptcy legal process. If more and more managers of firms in economic difficulties realize that it is more likely to quickly emerge from Civil Rehabilitation they would file for Rehabilitation sooner, Civil Rehabilitation Law would then provide an incentive for firms in economic difficulties to file for Civil Rehabilitation more expeditiously.

Despite the short Civil Rehabilitation duration, the practice during the first three years after the passage of Civil Rehabilitation law provides no evidence to support the claim that financially distressed firms file for bankruptcy earlier than before passage of the Civil Rehabilitation law. Rather, Civil Rehabilitation firms have higher leverage ratios than Corporate Reorganization firms. Also, recovery rates for unsecured creditors are as low as before. However, this can be partially attributed to the hesitancy of many firms which were waiting for the passage of Civil Rehabilitation law, rather than filing for Corporate Reorganization. This is emerging as an important theme in the future.

The study is organized as follows. In section 6.2, I provide new evidence on private restructurings in the late 1990s. Section 6.3 provides descriptions on bankruptcy procedures in Japan, in particular, the procedures of Civil Rehabilitation Law, which took effect in April 2000 as a response to increasing bankruptcies, as well as data descriptions on bankruptcy filings. In section 6.4, I investigate top management turnover around bankruptcy, priority violation and the duration of bankruptcy. Section 6.5 concludes.

6.2 OUT-OF-COURT DEBT RESTRUCTURINGS VERSUS BANKRUPTCIES

A firm that must restructure its debt contracts to avoid default has two choices; it can attempt to renegotiate with its creditors privately, as a means to work itself out of bankruptcy (workout) or file for bankruptcy. The alternatives are similar in that the firm is reorganized when creditors consent to rewrite the terms of debt contracts. If private renegotiation is an alternative to bankruptcy reorganization, then firms' incentives to settle with creditors out of court will reflect transaction costs of private renegotiation and bankruptcy costs. This section briefly identifies economic factors that affect the choice between bankruptcy and private workouts.

6.2.1 Review of the Previous Literature

Many attempts have been made to measure bankruptcy costs for reorganization (Warner 1977; Weiss 1990). Bankruptcy costs are direct and indirect. Direct costs encompass the cost of legal and other professional services. Indirect costs include a wide range of opportunity costs, such as lost investment opportunities and lost sales. And it is frequently cited that indirect costs are significantly higher for bankruptcy reorganization than private renegotiation. For example, Aghion et al. (1991) argue that chapter 11 of the US bankruptcy code creates serious theoretical and practical problems. Jensen (1989) argues that deviations of priority arising from provisions of the formal reorganization process in the US violates debt contracts and that the costs of formal reorganization are high enough to explain the high incidence of private workouts.

Two factors are important for financial distress to be resolved through out of court private workouts or bankruptcy (Gilson et al. 1990). First, claimholders will collectively benefit from settling out of court when private renegotiation generates lower costs than bankruptcy. For example, secured creditors benefit more than unsecured creditors, because secured creditors are fully repaid while unsecured creditors incur bankruptcy costs. Second, claimholders can consent how to share the cost savings. Private workouts are more likely to fail when diffused public bondholders have stronger incentives to hold out for favorable treatment under the debt-restructuring plan. It is widely believed that a benefit from borrowing from commercial banks and other private sources is that private debt is much easier to renegotiate and restructure than public bonds.

Consistent with this view, Gilson et al. (1990) find that bank debt ratio increases the probability of successful private restructuring. Also, US banks sometimes place their representatives on the board of firms in financial distress directly and gain additional control over the firms' investment and financing policies (Gilson 1990). In addition, the findings of James (1995, 1996) suggest that the debt structure significantly affects the firm's ability to restructure its debt privately. These findings support the view that bank lenders' monitoring can avoid the redundancy of monitoring from a small set of creditors such as bondholders. Banks have an information advantage and thus can intervene into troubled borrowing firms' affairs more efficiently than small creditors.

However, several papers raise new questions regarding the role of a bank in private workouts. For example, Diamond (1993) and Gertner and Scharfstein (1991) argue that because the bank lenders' claims are generally secured they have few incentives to make concessions when a firm also has subordinated public debt outstanding. In support of this view, Asquith et al. (1994) find that the fraction of bank and private debt impedes out of court restructurings and increase the probability of a chapter 11 filing. On the other hand, there are several reasons why transaction costs are more important in private restructurings than formal reorganization. For example, private lenders have less discretion to time loan writedowns in chapter 11; and the tax penalty for reducing debt is more severe in out of court debt restructurings (Gilson 1997). Also, prohibition on US banks holding common stock limit the ability of US banks to forgive their debt claims in distressed firms (Gilson 1994). However, there is an important exception to this prohibition, which is the authority for banks to hold corporate common stock in loan workouts in the US (James 1995).

In international comparative corporate governance, three main differences in lending methods between Japan and the US are considered. First, Japanese banks represent interests of various classes of claimholders, usually holding both equities and loans. Second, both debt and equities of Japanese firms are concentrated with a small number of banks, and usually banks hold the largest blocks of Japanese firms. Third, Japanese firms have traditionally relied heavily on bank loans (Sheard 1994). Most importantly, Japanese banks were able to extract regulatory rents from a continuing main bank relationship (Aoki 1994).

In comparing the US and Japanese legal regimes, however, Ramseyer (1994) suggests the following hypotheses, even though he asserts that we know only that both Japanese and US banks rescue a few large troubled firms and jettison most. First, Japanese firms rely more heavily on bank loans than US firms, in part because of regulatory restrictions on bond issuance. Second, traditionally US judges have looked skeptically at creditors who intervene in a debtor's business and sometimes US judges subordinate their claims, if a bank intervenes. It is called, "the doctrine of equitable subordination." US banks tend to rescue their borrowers less frequently, perhaps, because rescues tend to be unprofitable. Under lender liability law in the US, creditors intervening in a debtor's affairs can be sued to pay various debtor liabilities.

As a result, until the early 1990s, bankruptcy resolution was rarely employed for large Japanese firms. On occasion a publicly traded firm filed for bankruptcy under Corporate Reorganization Law, but it usually followed "a period of close involvement by the main bank in its restructuring effort" and was "triggered by the main bank's decision to curtail its activist role and risking financial exposure," as noted in Sheard (1994). Most financially distressed large firms in Japan successfully restructure troubled debt privately with main bank intervention, rather than through formal bankruptcy. Consequently, there are few studies on the choice between private workouts and bankruptcy in Japan, as well as bankruptcy resolution.

Recent empirical work, however, suggests that Japanese banks were less likely to intervene if a firm was in financial distress in the 1990s than they were after the oil shocks of the 1970s, considering that even bank lenders were involved; the timing of top management turnover and the recovery of profit were slower in the 1990s than in the 1970s (Hirota and Miyajima 2001). Shikano (1995) points out that the successes of rescue operations of the 1980s were mainly due to the industrial recovery rather than the improvement of relative performance of rescued firms. In the late 1990s, many Japanese firms were being forced to exit. Consequently, the delay of industrial recoveries diminished the likelihood of successful bank interventions in the late 1990s. Meanwhile, it also increased the bad loans of Japanese banks.

6.2.2 The Choice Between Private Debt Restructurings and Bankruptcy in the Late 1990s' Japan

In this chapter, I first focus on the choice between private debt restructurings and bankruptcy. A private restructuring is defined as one of the following consequences (1) required interest or principal payments on loans are reduced; (2) the maturities of loans are extended; or (3) loans are swapped with equities. Xu (2004) documents loan forgiveness in the late 1990s demonstrating that Japan's banks forgave failing borrowing firms debt in unsecured loans only. It is helpful for understanding determinants of the choice between a private restructuring and bankruptcy,[2] starting with a typical case—the Sogo Shock.

In April 2000, the Industrial Bank of Japan (IBJ) was orchestrating a restructuring plan of Sogo, one of the highest-rated department stores in Japan with a 170-year history. Like many retailers in Japan, Sogo had expanded its operations both domestically and abroad during the 1980s bubble. After 1990, it became financially distressed. Both IBJ and LTCB continued to rescue Sogo. The plan had seventy-three banks forgiving ¥630 billion (about $6.3 billion, at an approximate exchange rate of ¥100 to $1) of outstanding unsecured loans to the Sogo Group. As is traditional in Japan's practice, the main bank—IBJ and the second largest bank lender Shinsei were requested to forgive ¥180 billion ($1.8 billion), ¥98 billion ($980 million), or 94% and 86% of their unsecured loans respectively. All other banks needed to give debt forgiveness of ¥362 billion ($3.6 billion) or 49% of their unsecured loans.

However, Shinsei's unsecured loans to Sogo had become secured! Japan's government guaranteed them. Shinsei used to be Long Term Credit Bank (LTCB), which collapsed in 1998. It was sold to Ripplewood Holdings, an American private equity group in March 2000, soon after being nationalized. The bank was renamed Shinsei or "new birth" after its sale. Japan's government

---

[2] I thank Professor Miyajima for suggesting documenting the Sogo Shock.

had promised that during the first three years the purchaser could hand any bad loans back to the government if they lost more than 20% of their value. This "cancellation right" or *kashi-tampo* in Japan is equivalent to a put option. Even stranger was that the sales contract also ruled that Shinsei could not return loans to the government once Shinsei had given debt forgiveness.[3] In short, according to the sales contract between the government and Ripplewood, all Shinsei's loans were secured by "cancellation right" in the first three years.[4]

To convince Shinsei to accept the restructuring plan, in June 2000 IBJ revised the plan that it agreed to swap more ¥9.2 billion ($92 million) of its unsecured loans to equity. Notice that IBJ had planned to extend debt forgiveness of 94% in unsecured loans. Indeed, IBJ agreed to extend debt forgiveness of 100% of its unsecured loans after further revision of the plan. Consequently, there was nothing more that could be done to rescue Sogo, short of forgiving Sogo debt in its secured loans. However, forgiving a borrower's secured debt is viewed as taboo in Japan. Even worse, it is akin to a crime or a breach of trust. Japan's banks are afraid not only that their shareholders will sue them but also that executives will go to jail if they extend debt forgiveness to include secured loans.

Not surprisingly, on June 27 Shinsei's president Yashiro decided to refuse to extend debt forgiveness to Sogo and informed Sogo that it would return its ¥200 billion ($20 billion) Sogo's loans to the government. After that, Japan's government tried to work out a plan to rescue Sogo that was by then effectively bankrupt. But parliament was unwilling to let the government bail out Sogo, because there was a strong social pressure against rescuing troubled companies such as Sogo. In the end, the refusal of Shinsei to forgive Sogo's debt triggered Sogo's collapse. On July 12, Sogo declared that it would file for Civil Rehabilitation.

The Sogo Shock epitomizes bank lenders' incentives for extending debt forgiveness. Japan's banks forgive borrowing firms' debt only in unsecured loans, because of the following reasons. First, as described above, Japan's banks are afraid not only that their shareholders will sue them but also that executives will be guilty for a breach of trust if they extend debt forgiveness in secured loans. Another reason is that the percentage of claims paid to secured creditors is as high as 90% and also priority is less likely to be violated for secured creditors in bankruptcy, as shown in the next section. In summary, the fraction of bank debt secured increases the likelihood of bankruptcy and impedes the probability of out-of-court restructuring initiated by bank lenders.

Table 6.1 shows selected financial characteristics for financially distressed firms during the period January 1997–December 2003. This consist of a sample of 84 publicly traded firms that filed for bankruptcy under Corporate Reorganization Law, Civil Rehabilitation Law, Composition Law and Liquidation, as well as 38

---

[3] For details, see Tett (2003) which tells the history of one specific bank that epitomizes recent Japan's economic problems—the Long Term Credit Bank, as well as the Sogo Shock.

[4] Like LTCB, another collapsed Japan's bank—Nippon Credit Bank was sold with "cancellation right." It was renamed Aozora or "blue sky." Similarly, all Aozora's loans were secured during the "cancellation right" period.

Table 6.1 Selected Financial Characteristics for 122 Financially Distressed Firms During the Period January 1997–December 2003

	Bankruptcy			Out-of-court debt restructuring		
	Mean	Std.Dev.	Median	Mean	Std.Dev.	Median
Assets (hundred million yen)	936 ***	1920	231 ***	4640	3940	3410
Fraction of bank debt unsecured	0.365 ***	0.318	0.300 ***	0.593	0.338	0.632
Fraction of bank debt unsecured > 90%	0.083 ***	0.278	0 ***	0.316	0.471	0
Bonds/total liability	0.025 *	0.057	0	0.011	0.024	0
Shinsei's lending fraction	0.048 *	0.125	0	0.016	0.037	0
Shinsei and Aozora's lending fraction	0.058 *	0.127	0.002	0.027	0.044	0
Fraction of Main bank's loans	0.365	0.184	0.336	0.361	0.166	0.348
Main bank's shareholding	0.034 ***	0.018	0.042 **	0.044	0.015	0.048
EBITDA/assets	−0.329	1.403	−0.023	−0.073	0.150	−0.017
Leverage (total liability/assets)	1.017	0.659	0.927 **	0.998	0.176	0.955
N (sample size)	84			38		

Notes: Fraction of bank debt unsecured is the ratio of short-term and long-term bank loans unsecured to short-term and long-term bank debt. Bonds/liability is the ratio of book value of corporate bonds outstanding to total liability. Shinsei's lending fraction is the ratio of short-term and long-term loans borrowed from Shinsei Bank to short-term and long-term bank debt. Shinsei and Aozora's lending fraction is the ratio of short-term and long-term loans borrowed from Shinsei bank and Aozora bank to short-term and long-term bank debt. Shinsei Bank and Aozora Bank loan assets of nationalized Long-Term Credit Bank, Bond default which are guaranteed by the Japanese government. EBITDA/assets is the ratio of earnings before interests, taxes and depreciation to total assets. Leverage is the ratio of total liability to assets. Earnings or loss carry-forwards is the ratio of earnings or loss carry-forwards to assets.

out-of-court restructuring publicly traded firms. A sample firm is identified by the reference to a bankruptcy filing under Corporate Reorganization Law, Liquidation Law, Composition Law before April 2000, or Civil Rehabilitation Law after *Nikkei Shinbun, Nikkei Kaisha Jyoho (Nikkei Japan Company Handbook)*. Banks, housing loan companies, insurance companies and security companies are excluded, because the government will strongly intervene in those cases. Information and relevant data are obtained from Nikkei Financial Quest and the latest fiscal company annual report before bankruptcy filings or out of court restructurings. Firms without bank loans and firms without available data are excluded.

One striking difference consistently has been that the fraction of secured bank debt is higher for bankrupt firms than that for out-of-court restructuring firms. The bankruptcy firms' mean (median) fraction of unsecured bank debt is 36.5% (30.0%), while the out-of-court debt restructuring firms' mean (median) fraction of unsecured bank debt is 59.3% (63.2%). Also, among out-of-court debt restructuring 31.6% of firms have fractions of unsecured bank debt higher than 90%. In contrast, there are only 8.3% of bankruptcy firms with a fraction of unsecured bank debt more than 90%. The differences are statistically significant at the 1% level. Additionally, Table 6.1 also suggests that Shinsei has managed to purge most of the old LTCB's bad loans. It is consistent with Tett (2003) that Shinsei has been sending its troubled borrowers into bankruptcy.[5] The analysis supports the view point of Diamond (1993) and Gertner and Scharfstein (1991) that a bank is less likely to extend debt forgiveness if most of its claims are secured. Also, Table 6.1 indicates that large firms, firms with fewer bonds outstanding are more likely to restructure their debt out of court. However, profitability is not substantially different between the two groups.

Recently, Hoshi and Kashyap (2004) point out that Japan's banks continue to extend credits to zombie firms without any prospects of being repaid. In most cases, the only choice for banks is to extend credits to zombie firms when most banks' claims are unsecured. Banks' unsecured claims are less likely to be repaid when a borrowing firm's bargaining power is extremely strong (Diamond and Rajan 2000, 2001). In other words, the only means to force the entrepreneur to repay its debt is that banks can commit to foreclose on their collateral for secured loans. Moreover, unsecured creditors get almost nothing even when they send troubled firms into bankruptcy. The case of Haseko, a huge construction company vividly tells this story. At the end of March 1990, the fraction of unsecured loans to Haseko was as high as 95%. After the 1980s bubble collapsed, lending banks extended debt forgiveness to Haseko two times including a debt equity swap. In May 1999, 32 banks extended ¥350 billion ($3.5 billion) of debt forgiveness. Three years later, Haseko's three main banks, Daiwa Bank, Chuo Mitsui Trust Bank, and IBJ agreed to swap ¥150 billion ($1.5 billion) debt to

---

[5] After Sogo, Dai-ichi Hotel, a hotel group, Life, a consumer finance group with loans from Shinsei filed for bankruptcy. And DKB and Sumitomo bought out Shinsei of its loans and extended debt forgiveness to Hazama and Kumagai Gumi, two giant construction companies.

equity. The cause of keeping zombies in business is that Japan's banks were extending too many unsecured credits in the late 1980s bubble. Now, however, it is still a question whether Haseko can really revamp. Will Haseko ask for debt forgiveness again in the future? I believe that there will be debt forgiveness for a third time if the construction industry fails to recover.

My study is the first to focus on the association between Japanese banks' unsecured loans and banks' rescue decisions. Also worth noting is that the debt restructuring practice of Japanese firms in the late 1990s is similar to that of American firms in the 1980s. Gilson (1997) identifies 51 publicly traded firms that recontracted with their creditors by restructuring their debt out of court, and 57 publicly traded firms under chapter 11. Similarly, Franks and Torouts (1993) identify a sample of 45 private restructurings and 37 chapter 11 reorganizations. Out of 122 firms, only 38 firms restructured their debt privately, with help initiated by their bank lenders. This suggests a big change in Japan's corporate governance in financial distress—Japanese banks are less willing to rescue their corporate borrowers in financial distress than they used to be.

While this period of Japan represents an upturn in the Japanese economy it has been compared with that of a downturn in the US economy. Earlier studies have found many differences when comparing a downturn of the US economy with an upturn of the Japanese economy during the 1980s. This paper demonstrates a significant change in Japan–US comparative corporate governance: similarities dominate differences in comparing the US bankruptcy wave in the 1980s and this bankruptcy wave in Japan. It is worthwhile to point out that private debt restructurings initiated by banks are alternatives to formal bankruptcy, while formal bankruptcy is increasing in importance during this downturn of the Japanese economy. The two systems are complementary, not only in the US but also in Japan when the economy confronts a wave of bankruptcies. I believe my study complements the comparison studies done on Japan and US corporate governance for the 1980s.

6.3 THE INSOLVENCY LEGAL SYSTEM REFORM IN JAPAN

The number of business failures in Japan skyrocketed from 6468 in 1990 to 18,988 in 1998; 18,769 in 2000; 19,164 in 2001; and 19,087 in 2002 (Tokyo Shoko Research Ltd). Similarly, most of the bankruptcy filings of publicly traded firms are clustered in the years 1997–2002, as shown in Table 6.2. Here a bankrupt firm before 1997 is identified by the same way described in section 6.2. Financial firms such as banks, housing loan companies, insurance companies, and security companies are excluded. This is consistent with the timing of the 1990s recession in Japan, which continues today.

In response to the skyrocketing increase of bankruptcy filings, Japan is reforming its bankruptcy legal system. Hereafter, I focus on the legal mechanism of bankruptcy for large firms, because only data of large bankrupt firms is available.

Table 6.2 Time Series of Filings for Bankruptcy Under Corporate Reorganization Law, Civil Rehabilitation Law and Liquidation Law of Japan in the Years of 1987–2002

Year	Number of Corporate Reorganization filings	Number of Civil Rehabilitation filings	Number of Liquidation filings	Total
1987–96	10	–	0	10
1997	6	–	0	6
1998	4	–	3	7
1999	2	–	0	2
2000	3	7	1	11
2001	3	12	1	15
2002	8	14	5	27

Notes: Banks, security companies, housing loan companies and insurance companies are excluded.

Before April 1, 2000, mainly two types of bankruptcy filings were available to large firms in Japan: Corporate Reorganization Law[6] and Liquidation Law. Liquidation Law, equivalent to chapter 7 of the US bankruptcy code, provides for the orderly liquidation of a firm's assets by a court-appointed trustee. Corporate Reorganization Law is roughly equivalent to chapter 11 of the US bankruptcy code, and it provides for reorganization of a bankrupt firm, which is expected to continue as a going concern.

6.3.1 Reorganization Law

In this chapter, I mainly focus on Corporate Reorganization Law rather than Liquidation Law. Like chapter 11 of the US bankruptcy code, the court may order a stay that prevents creditors from collecting their debt, or, foreclosing on their collateral from the date of the ruling to the date of approval of the reorganization plan, or, until the termination of the proceeding, or for the period of a year from the date of the ruling. Even before the ruling of commencement, the court may order a stay, if the court feels it is necessary; however there is no automatic stay.

A reorganization plan should be approved by each class of claimholders: at least two-thirds of the votes from reorganization creditors, at least three-fourths of the votes from the reorganization secured creditors, and a majority of the shareholders. With regard to a draft which provides for the reduction or exemption of reorganization security rights, or contains other provisions affecting the security rights, the consent shall be obtained from those who possess the right to vote corresponding to at least four-fifths of the reorganization secured creditors. Moreover, consent should be obtained from all the reorganization secured creditors, with regard to a draft whose contents are liquidation when it is clear

---

[6] Composition Law also provided for reorganization without a court-appointed receiver. In practice, however, Composition Law filings are extremely rare for large companies. Hereafter, I focus on Reorganization Law and Liquidation Law in Japan rather than Composition Law.

that it is difficult to prepare a draft plan of reorganization whose contents are to continue the business as a going concern or through amalgamation, formation of a new company, or transfer of business. Obviously, secured creditors are endowed with strong powers under Corporate Reorganization Law. On the other hand, the shareholder shall not have the right to vote; in the scenario by which the company cannot fully satisfy its obligations with its assets.

The court may also confirm a reorganization plan, even if the draft plan of reorganization is voted on, but there are groups that failed to consent, or it is evident that it is impossible to obtain the consent from persons whose voting rights exceed the amount prescribed by laws, through modification of the plan and stipulating the terms to protect the rights of dissenting persons. This is similar to "cram-down" under US chapter 11 discussed in White (1990), the "fair and equitable" standard closely mirrors the absolute priority rule in liquidation. If the contents of the plan are to continue the business as a going concern or through amalgamation, form a new company, transfer to a new company, assign to others, or to preserve as it is, then it is required that the secured creditors retain their pre-bankruptcy lien rights on the assets and thus get payments equal to the value of their claims. If the firm is sold piecemeal, the proceeds of the sale of the properties are to be appropriated to pay the claims with respect to secured creditors, unsecured creditors, and shareholders in the aforementioned order. Also the trustee may pay a fair price equal to the claims of a dissenting group according to its priority. If no plan is submitted or adopted, the confirmed plan is insolvent, the court may rule for the discontinuance of reorganization proceedings. In that case, the court may order a shift of the firm's bankruptcy filing to Liquidation.[7]

A big difference between Japanese Reorganization practice and the practice of US chapter 11 is that a court-appointed receiver operates the firm and works out a reorganization plan,[8] not the debtor's management. In principle incumbent managers depart the firm, once the Corporate Reorganization proceeding commences. In other words, incumbent managers experience large personal costs under Corporate Reorganization Law. This aspect is rather similar to chapter 7 of the US bankruptcy code as well as the Liquidation Law of Japan. When managers are displaced, in almost all cases equity becomes worthless, therefore managers have strong incentives to resist Liquidation or Reorganization as long as possible. This means both Liquidation and Reorganization can be inefficient procedures in terms of ex ante bankruptcy costs in White (1983). *Ex ante* bankruptcy costs arise because of bankruptcy-induced distortions in managerial incentives. Typically, management is more likely to choose continuation rather than bankruptcy or liquidation, even though continuation is inefficient.

---

[7] Also a shift to Civil Rehabilitation is possible after April 2000.

[8] Under Corporate Reorganization Law, it is possible that a director or an executive of bankrupt firms be appointed as a receiver. In practice, however, in most cases only lawyers are appointed. The amended Corporate Reorganization Law explicitly states the condition for a debtor's director or executive to be capable as receiver.

6.3.2 Civil Rehabilitation Law

As a response to this issue, Civil Rehabilitation Law was passed and it took effect after April 1, 2000.[9] The passage of Civil Rehabilitation Law has substantially revised bankruptcy administration in Japan. One aspect that is equivalent to chapter 11 of the US bankruptcy code is the following: the debtor's management operates the firm and works out a Rehabilitation plan or Liquidation, unless an interested party can prove management is incompetent. In a case where the debtor's management is incompetent, Civil Rehabilitation Law provides the appointment of a trustee. This debtor in possession aspect of Civil Rehabilitation Law aims to provide incentives for managers of failing firms to file for bankruptcy under Rehabilitation Law by reducing their personal burdens.

The passage of a rehabilitation draft plan requires affirmative votes by only the rehabilitation creditors who have attended the assembly and who constitute a majority of the attending persons entitled to vote, one further constraint is that they must constitute a simple majority of those entitled to vote. Generally, secured creditors may exercise their rights outside the rehabilitation proceedings. The court may also give an approval for a person to file a rehabilitation plan that includes terms for reduction of capital, in cases where a rehabilitation debtor company fails to meet its payment obligations with its properties. Compared with the passage of a reorganization draft plan, the approval seems simple. Different from chapter 11 of the US bankruptcy code, Civil Rehabilitation Law does not impose an automatic stay to protect the firm from creditors' harassment. Based on the application of an interested party, the court may, in cases where an application for commencement of rehabilitation has been filed, order a discontinuance of exercise of a security right existing on properties of the rehabilitation debtor. Moreover, the rehabilitation debtor, may, in a case where collateral properties are indispensable for the continuation of the business of the debtor, make an application to the court for an approval of extinguishing all the security rights to the properties, by paying money equivalent to the market value of the properties to the court. Main differences between Corporate Reorganization Law and Civil Rehabilitation Law are summarized in Table 6.3.

As shown above, to continue as a going concern, a large Japanese firm could file for bankruptcy under Corporate Reorganization Law before April 2000. As Civil Rehabilitation Law took effect on April 1, 2000, a bankrupt firm can file for either Reorganization or Rehabilitation. In practice, corporate debtors seem to prefer Civil Rehabilitation filings to Corporate Reorganization filings, as suggested by a

---

[9] At the same time, Composition Law was abolished. Small and middle firms sometimes used it. A firm was able to file for Composition only if the firm failed to meet its debt payment obligations. Typically, a firm is viewed to be unable to meet it debt payment obligations if banks refuse to honor its bills. This condition is equivalent to Liquidation filings. Also, a Composition filing should be prepackaged, in other words, the firm would have to submit a Composition plan when they filed for Composition. The court was not authorized to order a stay in any circumstance. For the above reasons, Composition filings were extremely rare for large firms.

Table 6.3 Main Differences Between Corporate Reorganization Law and Civil Rehabilitation Law

Corporate Reorganization	Civil Rehabilitation
The firm continues as a going concern.	The firm continues as a going concern.
A court-appointed receiver in reorganization takes control, while the debtor management departs the firm.	The debtor management continues to take control (debtor in possession), unless the debtor management is incompetent, for instance, management fraud. The court may appoint receivers in case of incompetence by the debtor management based on an application of an interested party.
The court may order a stay if necessary to protect the firm from creditor harassment after the filing. The stay is in effect upon the ruling of the commencement of Corporate Reorganization.	The court may order a discontinuance of exercise of a security right existing on properties. And in a case where collateral are indispensable for continuation of business, the rehabilitation debtor may make an application to the court for an approval of extinguishing all the security rights on the properties, by paying money equivalent to the market value.
Secured creditors, unsecured creditors and shareholders approve a reorganization plan. But shareholders cannot have the right to vote in a case where the company fails to fully satisfy its obligations with its properties.	Unsecured creditors approve a rehabilitation plan. Generally, secured creditors may exercise their rights without following the rehabilitation proceedings. And capital may be reduced without shareholders' approval in cases where the rehabilitation company fails to fully satisfy its obligations with its properties.

rush of Civil Rehabilitation filings soon after Civil Rehabilitation Law came into force on April 1, 2000. Table 6.2 shows Civil Rehabilitation filings increased sharply from 2000. Incumbent managers that could expect to remain with their bankrupt firms are probably more in favor of filing for bankruptcy under Civil Rehabilitation Law rather than Corporate Reorganization Law, or Liquidation Law. Indeed, there are four Corporate Reorganization filings but no bankruptcy filings, when comparing nineteen firms filing for bankruptcy under Civil Rehabilitation Law, from April 2000 through September 2001.

There are possible problems arising from the passage and practice of the Civil Rehabilitation Law. One problem is the prioritization of the two procedures. For example, if two different interested parties file for Reorganization and Rehabilitation respectively, which is the priority? The Reorganization procedure has the highest priority, including consideration of the Liquidation procedure. One possible scenario that may occur when two interested parties are filing for Rehabilitation and Reorganization respectively; the court may order the suspension of Rehabilitation procedure upon the application of the interested party filing Reorganization.[10] The incumbent management virtually always has to convert to Reorganization from Rehabilitation when large creditors are against

---

[10] Liquidation has the lowest priority. The court may order suspension of Liquidation procedure upon the application of interested parties.

the Rehabilitation filing. The most well known case is Mycal's conversion into Corporate Reorganization. Mycal was a big retailer in Japan. During the 1980s bubble, it had expanded its operations, borrowing ¥1.2 trillion ($12 billion) to build huge supermarkets and hotels until the late 1990s. In January 2001, the top manager was replaced; this was initiated by the top lender Dai-Ichi Kango Bank (DKB),[11] to force Mycal to speed asset restructuring. In the summer, however, the new president realized that Mycal was effectively bankrupt and had to make a decision to file for bankruptcy.

For the choice of bankruptcy procedures, the top bank lender DKB preferred Corporate Reorganization to Civil Rehabilitation, because all creditors equally share the loss and it is less burdensome for the top bank lender under Corporate Reorganization Law. At the same time, quite a few directors were attempting to file for Civil Rehabilitation, dreaming that they might remain under the debtor in possession (DIP) procedure. At a meeting of the board of directors, the president and the executive director, who were former bank officers were dismissed, the firm then declared its intention to file for Civil Rehabilitation. As soon as DKB was informed, they stopped financing operating capital for Mycal. Finally, Mycal ended up in Corporate Reorganization filing and the dream of debtor in possession did not come true. After Mycal's conversion into Corporate Reorganization, Corporate Reorganization filings increased again and a few firms filed for bankruptcy under the Liquidation Law, probably because their creditors opposed Civil Rehabilitation filings initiated by debtors' managers, who of course attempted to avoid taking responsibility for bankruptcies.

6.4 BANKRUPTCY RESOLUTION IN JAPAN: CORPORATE REORGANIZATION VERSUS CIVIL REHABILITATION

The remainder of this chapter describes bankruptcy resolutions in Japan. The main concern is the impact of the passage of the Civil Rehabilitation Law. Thus I focus on cases where bankrupt firms were expected to continue as going concerns, in the years 1997–2002, when formal bankruptcy was common. This study consists of a sample of 52 publicly traded firms that filed for bankruptcy under Corporate Reorganization Law and Civil Rehabilitation Law from 1997 to 2002, after deleting three Civil Rehabilitation firms for which data was not available. I investigated the following issues: What is the experience of the incumbent management of bankrupt firms? What is bankruptcy resolution like in Japan? How does the passage of Civil Rehabilitation Law affect bankruptcy resolution? And how long does it take for Reorganization firms and Rehabilitation firms to work out a resolution?

---

[11] After M&A with Fuji Bank and IBJ (Nihon Kogyo Bank), the three banks were renamed as Mizuho Financial Group.

6.4.1 Management Turnover Around Bankruptcy

The treatment of incumbent management during the process of Rehabilitation has become an important theme. Since all incumbent managers depart once a receiver in reorganization is appointed by the court, I first looked into presidential turnover prior to Corporate Reorganization filings, when I compared management turnover in Reorganization and that in Rehabilitation. Starting four years before the year of Corporate Reorganization filing, I tracked presidential changes. As reported in Kaplan (1994), standard top management succession is referred to a case when a retired president remains on the board of directors as Chairman and non-standard presidential turnover is strongly correlated to poor firm performance. Table 6.4 shows positions/occupations of the top executive after turnover, from date −4 to the date of Corporate Reorganization filing, measured in years. After turnover, most former presidents remain on the board of directors such as advisory directors, part-time directors, directors without other titles, or advisory only. Two of the replaced presidents were demoted to vice president. Three replaced presidents held no intended positions/occupations after turnover—probably they left their companies. In two firms former directors of a bank lender were appointed, and in one case a former director of the top shareholder was appointed.

Using the same methods, I tracked the presidential changes for Rehabilitation firms. Panel B in Table 6.4 documents 29 non-standard presidential changes experienced by 27 firms around Civil Rehabilitation filing. This study excluded

Table 6.4 Intended Positions/Occupations Reported in Nikkei of Replaced Presidents Tracked for Four Years, Starting Four Years Before the Year of Bankruptcy Filing

Panel A: Corporation Reorganization Filings

	Number of managers holding specified positions/occupations
Chairman	3
Vice president	2
Advisory with directorship	2
Part-time director	1
Advisory	5
No positions/occupations	3

Panel B: Civil Rehabilitation Filings

	Number of managers holding specified positions/occupations
Chairman	3
Advisory with directorship	1
Director but no other titles	5
Advisory	3
Managing director of other group firm	2
No positions/occupations	15

two bankrupt firms, due to management fraud. Firms that experienced non-standard presidential turnover account for 89% of all cases. Probably being forced to depart, half of the presidents after replacement held no specified positions or occupations. Including one president who intended to resign, about 90% of all firms experienced president change once around Rehabilitation filings. I also kept track of presidents who remained after rehabilitation commences. Out of 13 cases, four presidents were appointed through actions initiated by bank lenders and large shareholders prior to rehabilitation; and therefore it seems less problematic for them to continue to control the firms. Another five insider presidents had careers as a president for less than two years. In all, there are only four insider presidents who seemed to be responsible for their firm's bankruptcy but still remained with the firm after rehabilitation. This strongly suggests that, whatever legal procedures a bankrupt firm chooses, the president is both less likely to remain and accept the responsibility of poor performance, which caused the bankruptcy.

On the other hand, this finding also suggests that Civil Rehabilitation Law probably reduces the personal burdens for incumbent managers. Under Corporate Reorganization, all incumbent directors and officers have to incur heavy personal costs because all of them must usually depart. After Rehabilitation filings, however, at least thirteen presidents continued to hold office. While this turnover rate is higher than that in other countries, it is much lower than the 100% turnover rate under Corporate Reorganization law.[12] The rush of rehabilitation filings of large firms soon after the passage of law supports this viewpoint. There is only a three-year history of DIP bankruptcy practice; more evidence in the future will be needed to examine what roles DIP plays.

6.4.2 Priority Violation

Deviations from absolute priority can be regarded as indirect costs of formal reorganization. Jensen (1989) argues that deviations of priority arising from the provisions of the formal reorganization process in the US violate debt contracts. In this section, I identify 24 Rehabilitation plans, and 22 Reorganization plans. Tables 6.5 and 6.6 summarize violation of priority for the firms. Participants in a Reorganization bankruptcy approve a Reorganization plan, leaving room for negotiations among the various classes of claimholders and for violation of priority of claims. Priority of claims can be violated for both secured creditors and unsecured creditors. Priority of secured claims is violated in 14% (3/22) of the cases. But the percentage of claims paid to secured creditors is still as high as 90% in each case. Shareholders received nothing and thus the low priority afforded to unsecured creditors holds in all cases of Reorganization. Under Rehabilitation Law, secured creditors may exercise their rights outside the

---

[12] Professor Soogeun Oh points out that high turnover rate of presidents might be evidence that DIP is not the incentive in Japan as much as in other countries.

Rehabilitation proceedings. The Rehabilitation debtor may, however, in a case where collateral properties are indispensable for the continuation of the business of the debtor, make an application to the court for an approval of extinguishing all the security rights on the properties, by paying money equivalent to market value. I have not found any cases of extinguishing security rights in practice. Thus we can conclude that there is no violation of priority for secured claims in Rehabilitation. However, priority of claims for unsecured creditors is violated for 17% (4/24) of the cases in Rehabilitation.

In all, the priority of claims for secured creditors is less likely to be violated in Japan. It only counts for 6% (3/46). This is also true in the US, where priority is less likely to be violated for secured firms. Priority of claims for the secured creditors is virtually always maintained at 92% (34/37) in the resolution for the 37 exchange-listed firms filing for bankruptcy between 1980 and 1986 reported in Weiss (1990). On the other hand, however, the priority violation for unsecured creditors is more likely to occur in the US than in Japan. The percentage of

Table 6.5 Summary of Claims Resolution for 22 Publicly Trading Firms Filing Bankruptcy Under Corporate Reorganization Law in January 1997–August 2002

	Percentage or description of claim paid		
Firm name	Secured creditors	Unsecured creditors	Shareholders
	Priority violated for secured creditors only		
YAOHAN JAPAN	90%	3%	0
DAI-ICHI HOTEL	90%	4%	0
SASAKI GLASS	90%–100%	3%–8%	0
	Priority held		
KYOTARU	100%	20%	0
TOKAI KOGYO	100%	2%–8%	0
TADA	100%	13%	0
DAITO KOGYO	100%	8%	0
TOSHOKU	100%	8%	0
MITSUI WHARF	100%	36.9%–100%	0
ASAKAWAGUMI	100%	5%–10%	0
LONGCHAMP	100%	9%	0
JDC	100%	9%–10%	0
NIKKO ELECTRIC INDUSTRY	100%	10%	0
KOKOKU STEEL WIRE	100%	6.50%	0
NAGASAKIYA	100%	0.50%	0
LIFE	100%	47.72%–	0
JAPAN METALS & CHEMICALS	100%	?	0
SATO KOGYO	100%	4%	0
NISSAN CONSTRUCTION	100%	7%–100%	0
KEISHIN WAREHOUSE	100%	8%	0
HOKO FISHING	100%	23%–100%	0
HOKUBU	100%	25%	0

Table 6.6 Summary of Claims Resolution for 24 Publidy Trading Firms Filing Bankruptcy Under Civil Rehabilitation Law in April 2000–August 2002

	Percentage or description of claim paid	
Firm name	Unsecured creditors	Shareholders
Priority held		
TOYO STEEL	NA	0
AKAI ELECTRIC	NA	0
SOGO	5%	0
FUJII	50%	0
MARUTOMI GROUP	15%	0
FUJI CAR MFG.	8%–10%	0
IKEGAI	1.59%	0
FOOTWORK INTERNATIONAL	NA	0
BETTER LIFE	10%	0
OHKURA ELECTRIC	1.50%	0
ERGOTECH	NA	0
AOKI CORPORATION	2%	0
KOTOBUKIYA	0.70%	0
SHOKUSAN JUTAKU SOGO	NA	0
KITANOKAZOKU	6%	0
SOGO DENKI	NA	0
NAKAMICHI	NA	0
IZUMI INDUSTRIES	NA	0
ISEKI POLY-TECH	NA	0
DAI NIPPON CONSTRUCTION	2%	0
Priority violated for unsecured creditors only		
NICHIBOSHIN	4.14%	1%
KAWADEN	22.43%	21%
HAKUSUI TECH	NA	10%
FUJIKI KOMUTEN	5%–100%	100%

violation of priority of claims for unsecured creditors can be as high as 70% (26/ 37). In total, strict priority of claims in 39 cases (85%) held among a sample of 46 publicly traded firms that filed for Corporate Reorganization or Civil Rehabilitation, when comparing that with eight (22%) cases of maintenance of priority among the 37 cases in Weiss (1990).

It is not surprising that priority of claims is less violated for secured creditors, since secured creditors are protected even if there is a stay under Reorganization Law, or if secured creditors are outside the procedure under Rehabilitation Law. One reason for the high percentage for maintenance of priority of claims for unsecured creditors is that typically financial institutions such as bank lenders and insurance company lenders hold proportional equity of a borrowing firm. This mitigates the conflict between shareholders and unsecured creditors. In practice shareholders usually do not have the right to vote, because most Reorganization companies fail to fully pay the claims of unsecured creditors. More importantly, the bargaining power of shareholders is much weaker in

Reorganization where court-appointed trustees are in control than that of the debtor-in-possession reorganization workout process, in particular for owner or family controlled firms. Consequently, there are no priority violations of claims for unsecured creditors in Reorganization.

Deviations in favor of equity holders seem more likely to occur in Rehabilitation, since the incumbent management is potentially allowed to remain. However, unsecured creditors can vote against a rehabilitation plan in which priority is violated for unsecured creditors. Notice that only unsecured creditors are exclusively entitled the right of vote. Consistently there are only four (17%) cases of priority violation for unsecured creditors in the 24 cases of Rehabilitation. The percentage of priority violation for unsecured creditors in Rehabilitation is higher than that in Reorganization, but still much lower than that in US bankruptcy resolution.

6.4.3 The Duration in Bankruptcy

Finally, I address the following questions empirically: How are firm characteristics related to the speed of bankruptcy resolution in Japan? Does bankruptcy reform in Japan facilitate a faster conclusion of bankruptcy? What incentives does Civil Rehabilitation Law provide to a distressed firm? The length of the bankruptcy legal process is important because it can affect the eventual outcome as well as the value of the firm's assets. Some indirect bankruptcy costs, such as lost sales, lost investment opportunities may rise as time in bankruptcy increases, as suggested in Giammarino (1989); Gertner and Scharfstein (1991); Mooradian (1994); and Roe (1987). In detail, bargaining and coordination problems may delay both Reorganization and Rehabilitation processes. Empirical studies of Helwege (1999); Li (1999); and Orbe et al. (2001) show that firm size affects the duration of bankruptcy for US firms. Recently, Dahiya et al. (2003) found that DIP financed bankrupt firms are quicker to emerge and quicker to liquidate.

Individual duration data for 25 Reorganization firms and 27 Rehabilitation firms is shown in Figure 6.1. In this dataset, only one Corporate Reorganization observation is censored; that is, by the time this study is completed this firm will still be in Corporate Reorganization. As shown, the shortest stay in Corporate Reorganization is 0.84 years. And the longest time a Corporate Reorganization firm takes to exit is 3.5 years. For Civil Rehabilitation, the shortest stay is 0.35 years and the longest duration is 0.91 years. Out of 27 Civil Rehabilitation firms, 26 firms exit from bankruptcy faster than the fastest Corporate Reorganization firm. As Table 6.8 shows, the average time from filing of the bankruptcy petition under Corporate Reorganization Law to resolution is 1.9 years for the sample of 24 firms. On average it takes 0.6 years for 27 firms to reach resolution from Civil Rehabilitation petition filing. It is 1.3 years shorter than that of Corporate Reorganization Law. This fact suggests that the passage of Civil Rehabilitation Law facilitates a faster exit from bankruptcy. Thus the main purpose of Civil Rehabilitation Law is achieved.

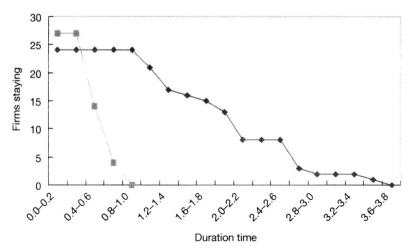

Figure 6.1 Stay time: Civil Rehabilitation versus Corporate Reorganization

Notes. ──◆── Corporate Reorganization ──■── Civil Rehabilitation.

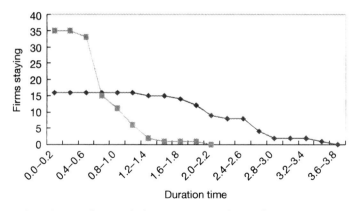

Figure 6.2 Stay time: Bankruptcy before 2000 versus afterward

Notes. ──◆── Bankruptcy before 2000 ──■── Bankruptcy afterward.

The recent bankruptcy reform in Japan has been highly influenced by the US bankruptcy code, in particular, chapter 11. The bankruptcy duration in the US also provides an important benchmark to evaluate the bankruptcy duration in Japan. Franks and Torouts (1989) report an average of 4.5 years for 16 firms filing before the revision of the US bankruptcy code in 1979, and 2.7 years for 14 firms filing afterward. Similarly, Weiss (1990) reports that on average a firm spends 2.5 years in bankruptcy, with this study using 37 New York and American

Stock Exchange firms filing for bankruptcy during a large downturn of the American economy between November 1979 and December 1986. The average time from the filing of the bankruptcy petition to the resolution in Japan is 1.2 years, taking Corporate Reorganization and Civil Rehabilitation as a whole. It is about 1.3 years less than the US average bankruptcy duration. After the 2000 bankruptcy reform, it is even faster. The result is summarized at Table 6.8. Limited to bankruptcy duration, Japan has quite an effective legal system.

Xu (2003a) investigates how firm characteristics are related to the speed of bankruptcy resolution in Japan by a log-logistic survival model. That is, the period from a firm filing for reorganization or rehabilitation, until the approval of a plan by the court. The first concern is whether the bankruptcy legal system provides an incentive for financially troubled firms to file for bankruptcy. As

Table 6.7 Descriptive Statistics for 25 Publicly Traded Firms Filing for Corporate Reorganization in 1997–August 2002 and 27 Publicly Traded Firms Filing for Civil Rehabilitation in April 2000–August 2002.

	Reorganization firms			
	Mean	Med.	Std.Dev.	Cases
Asset (millions of yen)	204.60	114.90	309.08	25
Public bonds/liability	0.0370377	0	0.08173	25
Leverage	0.891696	0.924708	0.112048	25
	Rehabilitation firms			
	Mean	Med.	Std.Dev.	Cases
Asset (millions of yen)	54.54	22.71	90.47	27
Public bonds/liability	0.0124753	0	0.027838	27
Leverage	1.29515	0.933156	1.08802	27

Notes: Asset is the book value of total assets as reported for the last fiscal year before the bankruptcy filing. *Leverage* is the ratio of the total liability to the total assets. *Public bonds/liability* is the fraction of public bonds outstanding in the total liability.

Table 6.8 Mean Time from Bankruptcy Petition to Resolution: US Versus Japan

JAPAN (current volume)		
Corporate Reorganization	2.2 years	24 firms
Civil Rehabilitation	.57 years	27 firms
Whole	1.2 years	51 firms
Before 2000	2.2	16 firms
Afterward	.71	35 firms
USA (Franks and Torouts 1989)		
Before 1979	4.5 years	16 firms
Afterward	2.7 years	14 firms
USA (Weiss 1990)		
After 1979	2.5 years	37 firms

shown in Table 6.7, bankrupt firms are typically highly leveraged. This implies that the managers of a financially distressed firm have a strong incentive to hope for a miraculous reverse of fortune rather than to file for bankruptcy expeditiously. The greater the loss a bankrupt firm suffers, the higher the leverage. Consequentially, leverage can be a good proxy for how late a firm files for bankruptcy. As Baird (2001) points out, a firm in desperate straits will not bode well for the bargaining process in bankruptcy. Therefore, highly leveraged firms could take a longer time to exit from bankruptcy.

It has been found that leverage has no significant effect on duration in Corporate Reorganization but highly leveraged Civil Rehabilitation firms are less likely to quickly emerge from the process. This empirical finding in Xu (2003a) can be interpreted as such; before the bankruptcy legal reform in 2000 financially distressed firms seemed to have no incentives to file for Corporate Reorganization earlier, because they would lose anything regardless of the speed of the bankruptcy legal process. In addition, Civil Rehabilitation is a debtor-in-possession procedure. Once managers of firms in economic difficulties realize that it is more likely to quickly emerge from Civil Rehabilitation if they file for Rehabilitation in a timely fashion, Civil Rehabilitation Law may then provide an incentive for firms in economic difficulties to file for Civil Rehabilitation earlier. Further data is needed to test this hypothesis more conclusively. Also, it is important to examine whether the debtor's managers are more likely to remain if they file for Rehabilitation quickly.

Despite short Civil Rehabilitation duration, the practice during the first three years after the passage of Civil Rehabilitation law provides no more hard evidence in support that financially distressed firms file for bankruptcy earlier than before. Rather, Civil Rehabilitation firms have higher leverage ratios than Corporate Reorganization firms, as Table 6.7 indicates. However, these are partially due to the fact that many firms were waiting for the passage of Civil Rehabilitation law rather than filing for Corporate Reorganization. This is an emerging theme of great importance in the future. It is also worth mentioning that recovery rates for unsecured creditors are as low as before.[13]

6.5 CONCLUSIONS

In the late 1990s, Japanese banks were less likely to rescue troubled borrowing firms than they were at any prior time. This practice of debt restructuring is quite similar to that of the recession of the 1980s in the US economy. In response to the skyrocketing increase of bankruptcies, Japan reformed its bankruptcy legal

---

[13] The passage of the Civil Rehabilitation Law is a little helpful at encouraging banks to send zombie firms into bankruptcy. As discussed above, the main reason for keeping zombie firms is that banks had extended large unsecured loans during the 1980s bubble so that the banks could neither withdraw their loans or charge high interest rates, unless their unsecured loans were to become secured loans as was the case of Shinsei.

system. Their actions facilitated faster bankruptcy conclusions by implementing Civil Rehabilitation Law, an explicit debtor-in-possession procedure, which was passed in 2000. Civil Rehabilitation firms spend substantially shorter in bankruptcy than Corporate Reorganization firms. When compared internationally, a bankrupt firm exits faster than a US firm filing for chapter 11, which has strongly influenced bankruptcy reform in Japan. Most importantly, Civil Rehabilitation Law may provide an incentive to failing firms to file for bankruptcy quickly, although future evidence is needed. I believe this study complements previous studies that investigate private debt restructurings initiated by bank lenders until the 1980s.

REFERENCES

Aghion, P. and P. Bolton (1992). 'An Incomplete Contract Approach to Financial Contracting,' *Review of Economic Studies*, 59: 473–94.
Aoki, M. (1994). 'Monitoring Characteristics of the Main Bank System: An Analysis and Development View,' in M. Aoki and H. Patric (eds.), *The Japanese Main Bank System— Its Relevance for Developing and Transforming Economics*. Oxford: Oxford University Press, 109–41.
—— H. Patrick (eds.) (1994). *The Japanese Main Bank System—Its Relevance for Developing and Transforming Economics*. Oxford: Oxford University Press.
Asquith, P., R. Gertner, and D. Scharfstein (1994). 'Anatomy of Financial Distress: An Examination of Junk-bond Issue,' *The Quarter Journal of Economics 1994*, 109: 625–58.
Baird, D. G. (2001). *Elements of Bankruptcy*. London: Foundation Press.
Dahiya, S., K. John, M. Puri, and G. Ramirez (2003). 'Debtor-in-Possession Financing and Bankruptcy Resolution: Empirical Evidence,' *Journal of Financial Economics*, 69: 259–80.
Diamond, D. W. (1993). 'Seniority and Maturity of Debt Contracts,' *Journal of Financial Economics*, 33: 341–68.
Franks, J. R. and W. N. Torous (1989). 'An Empirical Investigation of U.S. Firms in Reorganization,' *Journal of Finance*, 44: 747–69.
—— —— (1994). 'A Comparison of Financial Recontracting in Distressed Exchanges and Chapter 11 Reorganizations,' *Journal of Financial Economics*, 35: 349–70.
Gertner, R. and D. Scharfstein (1991). 'A Theory of Workouts and the Effects of Reorganization Law,' *Journal of Finance*, 46: 1189–222.
Giammarino, R. M. (1989). 'The Resolution of Financial Distress,' *Review of Financial Studies*, 2: 25–47.
Gilson, S. C. (1989). 'Management Turnover and Financial Distress,' *Journal of Financial Economics*, 25: 241–62.
—— (1990). 'Bankruptcy, Boards, Banks, and Block Holders,' *Journal of Financial Economics*, 27: 355–87.
—— (1997). 'Transactions Costs and Capital Structure Choice: Evidence from Financially Distressed Firms,' *Journal of Finance*, 52: 161–96.

—— K. John, and L. H. P. Lang (1990). 'Troubled Debt Restructurings,' *Journal of Financial Economics*, 27: 315–53.

Hart, O. and J. Moore (1995). 'Debt and Seniority: An Analysis of the Role of Hard Claims in Constraining Management,' *American Economic Review*, 85: 567–85.

Helwege, J. (1999). 'How Long Do Junk Bonds Spend in Default?' *Journal of Finance*, 54: 341–67.

Hirota, S. and H. Miyajima (2001). 'Mein banku kainyugata koporeito gabanansu ha hennka shitaka? 1990 nenndai to sekiyu shokku tono hikaku' (Did Bank Intervention Based Corporate Governance in Japan Change? A Comparison Between the 1990s and Oil Crises Era), *Gendai Fainansu*, 10: 35–61

Hoshi, T. and A. K. Kashyap (2004). 'Japan's Financial Crisis and Economic Stagnation,' *Journal of Economic Perspectives*, 18: 3–26.

James, C. (1995). 'When Do Banks Take Equity? An Analysis of Bank Loan Restructuring and the Role of Public Debt,' *Review of Financial Studies*, 85: 567–85.

—— (1996). 'Bank Debt Restructuring and Composition of Exchange Offers in Financial Distress,' *Journal of Finance*, 51: 711–27.

Jensen, M. (1989). 'Active Investors, LBOs, and the Privatization of Bankruptcy,' *Journal of Applied Corporate Finance*, 2: 35–44.

Kaplan, S. N. (1994). 'Top Executive Rewards and Firm Performance: A Comparison of Japan and the United States,' *Journal of Political Economy*, 102: 510–46.

Li, K. (1999). 'Baysian Analysis of Duration Models: An Application to Chapter 11 Bankruptcy,' *Economic Letters*, 63: 305–12.

Mooradian, R. M. (1994). 'The Effect of Bankruptcy Protection on Investment,' *Journal of Finance*, 49: 1403–30.

Orbe, J., E. Ferreira, and N.-A. Vincente (2001). 'Modelling the Duration of Firms in Chapter 11 Bankruptcy Using a Flexible Model,' *Economic Letters*, 71: 35–42.

Ramseyer, J. M. (1994). 'Explicit Reasons for Implicit Contracts,' in M. Aoki and H. Patrick (eds.), *The Japanese Main Bank System—Its Relevance for Developing and Transforming Economics*. Oxford: Oxford University Press.

Roe, M. J. (1987). 'The Voting Prohibition in Bond Workouts,' *The Yale Law Review*, 97: 232–79.

Sheard, P. (1994). 'Main Banks and the Governance of Financial Distress,' in M. Aoki and H. Patrick (eds.), *The Japanese Main Bank System—Its Relevance for Developing and Transforming Economics*. Oxford: Oxford University Press.

Shikano, Y. (1995). *Nihon no ginko to kinyu soshiki* (The financial and banking systems in Japan). Tokyo: Toyo Keizai Shinposha.

Shleifer, A. and R. W. Vishny (1997). 'A Survey of Corporate Governance,' *Journal of Finance*, 54: 737–83.

Tett, G. (2003). *Saving the Sun: A Wall Street Gamble to Rescue Japan from its Trillion-Dollar Melt-Down*. New York: Harper-Collins Business.

Warner, J. (1997). 'Bankruptcy Costs: Some Evidence,' *Journal of Finance*, 32: 337–47.

Weiss, L. A. (1990). 'Bankruptcy Resolution,' *Journal of Financial Economics*, 27: 285–314.

White, M. (1983). 'Bankruptcy Costs and the New Bankruptcy Code,' *Journal of Finance*, 38: 477–88.

—— (1990). 'The Corporate Bankruptcy Decision,' *Journal of Economic Perspectives*, 3: 129–51.

Xu, P. (2003a). 'Bankruptcy Resolution in Japan: Corporate Reorganization vs. Civil Rehabilitation,' *REITI Discussion Paper*.

—— (2003b). 'Increasing Bankruptcy Filings and the Bankruptcy Reform in Japan,' in S. Claessens and D.-S. Kang (eds.), *Empirical Evaluation of Corporate Restructuring*. Seoul: Korean Development Institute, 245–72.

—— (2004). 'Kigyo Saimu Risutora ni okeru Shiteki seiri to hoteiki seiri' (Private Workouts Versus Formal Bankruptcies in Japan), presented at the Joint 9th Decentralization Conference; 2003 TECR Microeconomics Conference; 2004 Nippon Finance Association Annual Conference; and 2004 Japan Economic Association Autumn Conference.

7

The Rise of Bank-Related Corporate Revival Funds

Noriyuki Yanagawa

7.1 INTRODUCTION

Over the past few years, "corporate revival funds" have emerged as key players in the corporate rehabilitation process. Corporate revival funds should be considered crucial catalysts for change because they help banks to dispose of non-performing loans on their balance sheets that have been a drag on the Japanese macro-economy, and in doing so rehabilitate businesses suffering from excessive debt and rejuvenate the financial sector. This chapter takes a look at the role that corporate revival funds have played in the restructuring process in Japan, paying particular attention to the rapid growth of the funds closely related to Japanese banks and their impact on the structure of corporate governance. Of course, the funds are so new that many of their effects may still not be apparent.

The rehabilitation of financially distressed corporations is playing an important role in pulling the Japanese economy out of its prolonged recession. As the macro-economy sputtered, businesses struggled and bankruptcies surged. The need for mechanisms to facilitate corporate turnarounds increased. Since the Japanese economy has been in the doldrums for so long, however, achieving a self-sustaining recovery will require not only improvement in the general business environment but also structural reform. Efforts to rehabilitate ailing firms, therefore, will not simply improve the outlook of individual firms, but also contribute to the health of the overall economy insofar as they propel reform.

For most of the post-war period, Japanese main banks assumed the lead role in rehabilitating distressed businesses. Typically, the main bank of a troubled firm stepped in to provide guidance and governance, saving the firm from collapse. Sheard (1994) provides a detailed explanation of the rescue role of the main banks. In recent years, as pointed out by Hoshi and Kashyap (2004),[1] main banks have not been able to fulfill their traditional role. The mountains of non-performing loans on their books have prevented banks assuming greater

---

[1] Arikawa and Miyajima also examine the changing role of banks in Chapter 2.

responsibility for rehabilitating firms. As bad loans mounted, banks became more reluctant to become active participants in the restructuring process because they wanted to avoid higher risk and greater losses. Instead of taking the lead in workouts, banks preferred to roll over loans. The diminished role of banks can also be blamed on the declining effectiveness of their traditional methods of doing business. As the banks' capacity to analyze risk and assist in corporate revivals atrophied during the 1980s boom, they became more bureaucratic in their decision-making and began to shy away from making the bold decisions needed to turn companies around.[2] As the banks began to pull back from financial rescues, corporate revival funds have stepped in to fill the vacuum.

These trends form the backdrop to the growth of corporate revival funds, which are taking on the role in corporate rehabilitation as banks relinquish it. These funds are better suited to tackling high-risk investments than banks, and increasingly serve as a source of financing for inherently risky corporate rehabilitation ventures. Unlike banks, the funds permit investors to participate in the corporate rehabilitation process as shareholders who have a strong say over the future course of the restructuring firm. Rescuers who own shares in the corporations undergoing rehabilitation are thought to be better positioned to push drastic reorganization plans and major reform initiatives. The growth of corporate revival funds has also been fostered by new laws governing their operation and the government's policies to encourage the disposal of non-performing loans. In particular, the government announced a "Program for Financial Revival" in 2002 to reduce the non-performing loans held by major banks. Thus, the demand for corporate revival funds is expected to increase.[3]

Major banks responded to the government initiative by selling loans to the corporate revival funds, and many banks set up fund-management companies to invest in these funds. In fact, most funds currently have close ties with Japanese banks and many fund managers used to work for major Japanese banks. Even the foreign-owned funds are staffed with former employees of Japanese banks.

The rest of this chapter is organized as follows. Section 7.2 provides a general overview of the "corporate revival" process and section 7.3 focuses on the rapid growth of corporate revival funds. Section 7.4 examines the relationship between the revival funds and the major banks. Section 7.5 presents a simple model to help conceptualize the role of bank-related funds, and section 6 offers a brief case study of a bank-related revival fund. Section 7.7 takes a look at the Japanese government's active role in expanding the growth of these funds through the Development Bank of Japan and the Industrial Revitalization Corporation Japan. Section 7.8 presents concluding arguments.

---

[2] See, for example, the arguments in Hoshi and Patrick (2000).

[3] It should also be noted that Japanese banks are now prevented from becoming shareholders in firms by numerous regulations (see Chapter 4).

7.2 NON-PERFORMING LOANS AND THE CORPORATE REVIVAL PROCESS

The objectives of the "corporate revival" process are determined by the stage or degree of financial distress of the ailing firms. If the firm acknowledges its problems at the earliest signs of financial distress, it may even be able to rein in its operations on its own without help from outsiders. If the firm is struggling with excessive debt, banks in some cases may be able to offer advice on restructuring. But if the firm fails to take effective corrective action or experiences a major adverse shock, it may be forced to seek financial assistance from its creditors, and to overhaul its business structure to boost profitability. All of the procedures implemented to revive a firm are considered to be part of the "corporate revival" or "corporate rehabilitation" process. Since the early attempts at restructuring in the 1990s were often unsuccessful, the amount of non-performing loans surged, debt burdens ballooned, and many firms were driven to bankruptcy.

There are two basic approaches to rescuing a firm with excessive debts. Under a "private resolution," the firm and its creditors reach an agreement on debt forgiveness and business restructuring without turning to the legal system. On the other hand, a "legal disposition" involves legal procedures and court supervision.[4] Both "private resolutions" and "legal dispositions" can be structured to either revive (reconstruct) or liquidate the firm. Even though revival may be the objective at the outset, the firm will have to be liquidated if its assets or profits are insufficient to sustain its business. A legal disposition for the purpose of reconstruction must follow the provisions of the Civil Rehabilitation Law (Minji Saisei Hō) and the Corporate Rehabilitation Law (Kaisha Kōsei Hō), while cases involving liquidation must invoke the Bankruptcy Law (Hasan Hō). It should be noted, however, that even under a legal disposition that aims at liquidation, the business of a firm does not necessarily have to be terminated. If an entity that wishes to purchase a firm's assets surfaces during the revival process, (parts of) the business of the firm may continue to operate even after liquidation.

There are several differences between a private resolution and legal disposition. A private resolution requires an agreement by all concerned parties. Consequently, working out a consensus on an efficient corporate rehabilitation plan may be difficult. Indeed, in practice, a private resolution is implemented only after a consensus among the major creditors is formed. On the other hand, a legal disposition requires an agreement on a rehabilitation plan hammered out under the supervision of the court and in accordance with legal procedures. Reaching an agreement may require considerable time because the process is governed by formal legal procedures, but the concerned parties are more likely to line

---

[4] Xu examined the effects of legal dispositions in more detail in Chapter 6.

up behind the agreement in the end. In Japanese society, however, the term "legal disposition" conjures up negative images of failure and collapse among business partners, creditors, and employees, so resorting to one can undermine the future viability of the business. The stigma attached to legal dispositions helps to explain why concerned parties usually try to avoid them in Japan.

7.3 CORPORATE REVIVAL FUNDS AND THE JAPANESE GOVERNMENT'S "BIG PUSH"

The legal rules for the corporate revival process have undergone dramatic changes in recent years. The Civil Rehabilitation Law (Minji Saisei Hō), enacted in 2000, and the Corporate Rehabilitation Law (Kaisha Kōsei Hō), revised in 2002, stipulate rules for legal dispositions that aim to reconstruct a firm. The Guidelines on Private Liquidation (Shiteki Seiri Guidelines) adopted in 2001 govern private resolutions. In addition, the Japanese government established public entities to dispose of non-performing loans and promote corporate revivals: the Resolution and Collection Corporation (RCC) in 2001, and the Industrial Rehabilitation Organization in 2003. Moreover, the Japanese government unveiled its "Program for Financial Revival" in 2002, calling for a reduction in the NPL (non-performing loan/total loan) ratio by about half by the end of March 2004.[5] This announcement provided major banks with a strong incentive to reduce the amount of non-performing loans on their books. Indeed, the NPL ratio fell drastically from 8.4% in March 2002 to 2.9% in March 2005.[6]

After the Japanese government changed the legal rules and embarked on its "Big Push" to dispose of non-performing loans, corporate revival funds which target ailing firms sprouted up (see Figure 7.1). Prior to 2000, the funds were managed mainly by foreign companies. But after the "Big Push," the number of Japanese bank-related funds surged.

The investment capital of these corporate revival funds also increased to surpass 1.3 trillion yen (Figure 7.2) as the funds acquired more than 200 companies with total assets of more than ¥1.2 trillion in 2004.[7]

Corporate revival funds purchased not only non-performing loans from banks but also a significant share of the equity of firms under duress (usually but not necessarily firms with excessive debt burdens) to assert control rights over them.[8] The control rights enabled the funds to implement drastic and effective rehabilitation plans. The new laws governing reconstruction also made it easier to resort to legal procedures to facilitate turnarounds. Moreover, in some cases, the corporate revival funds acquired equity from debt–equity swaps (DES).

---

[5] See: http://www.kantei.go.jp/jp/singi/keizai/tousin/021030program.pdf

[6] See: http://www.jijigaho.or.jp/index_cabi.html

[7] *Nikkei Business*, November 29, 2004.

[8] See Hellmann (1988) for the allocation of control rights in venture capital firms.

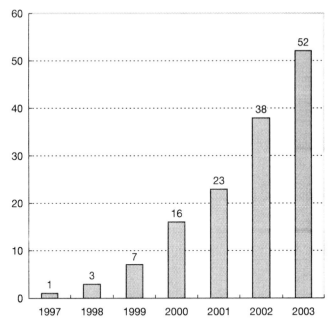

Figure 7.1 Number of Japanese buyout funds

Source: Chikusei Partners (2004).

If a firm earns an excess profit from a successful rehabilitation, the corporate revival funds recover their investment by selling their equity in the firm. Since the corporate revival funds take on the risk of failure of rehabilitation projects, they have a strong incentive to improve the profitability of the rehabilitated firms.

The rapid growth of corporate revival funds, many of which were formed to help banks dispose of non-performing loans, has transformed the corporate revival process. The corporate revival funds do not hesitate to resort to the legal dispositions mentioned above, and other types of rescuers are also beginning to turn to them. The behavior of these rescuers is very different from that of Japanese main banks as depicted by Sheard (1994). It should be noted, however, that Japanese banks too are beginning to turn to legal dispositions, though not as frequently as the corporate revival funds.

Another important development in the corporate rehabilitation field is the growth in mergers and acquisitions (M&A). It is widely recognized that M&A can play a vital role in rationalizing and restructuring businesses. Corporate revival funds and foreign investment banks have been very active in pursuing M&A deals. The lack of bank expertise in M&A is another reason that funds have assumed a prominent role in the rehabilitation process. The growing threat of M&A may provide managers with additional incentives to improve the conditions of their distressed firms and implementation of restructuring measures.

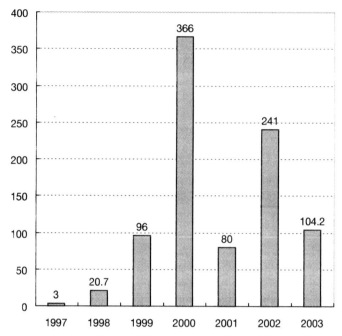

Figure 7.2 Amount raised by buyout funds in fiscal year (billion yen)

So far, companies that manage corporate revival funds have tended to appoint two types of fund managers: (1) managers who are deeply committed to the firms that receive their investments; or (2) specialist managers dispatched from a third party. After Shroeder Ventures (currently MKS Partners) acquired BENEX Corporation (formerly Benkan), a pipe (butt-welding) fitting manufacturer, it installed its own representative director and managing partner, Takaaki Kawashima, as president of BENEX. The investment fund Ripplewood Holdings, on the other hand, prefers to hire third-party specialists. After acquiring SEAGAIA, a comprehensive leisure facility in Miyazaki Prefecture, Ripplewood hired a professional executive from the outside to design a new business structure for the facility. Ripplewood has become one of the most famous acquisition funds in Japan. It captured considerable market attention in 1999 after taking over the Long-Term Credit Bank of Japan (now Shinsei Bank), which was temporarily nationalized after falling into insolvency. Subsequently, Ripplewood acquired Niles Co. Ltd., a Nissan-related auto parts manufacturer, and Nippon Columbia. In 2004, Ripplewood sold the equity of Shinsei Bank for a large profit.

There is no evidence that the ownership of fund management companies has influenced the behavior of corporate revival funds. Whether a fund management company is owned by a foreign company or not does not appear to influence the type of strategy chosen in the corporate revival process (see Rachlin 2005). It should be noted, however, that bank-related funds may have a special impact on the Japanese financial system even though their behavior and strategies are indistinguishable from those of other funds. This point will be explored further in later sections.

7.4 BANK-RELATED FUNDS

Japanese city (commercial) banks have played an important role in fostering the growth of corporate revival funds. Although the behavior of bank-related funds does not appear to be different from that of other types of funds, the bank-related funds are particularly significant due to their potential to change the behavior of Japanese banks and thus influence the future development of the Japanese financial system. As discussed above, the disposal of non-performing loans had become a major issue for the banks. In addition to sales to offshore funds and financial institutions, the banks turned increasingly to new mechanisms to remove non-performing loans from their balance sheets. They set up companies to manage and invest in corporate revival funds, and established companies that specialize in corporate rehabilitation.

A large number of banks formed fund management companies to invest in corporate revival funds. Although most city banks invested in such funds, their level of commitment varied according to their strategy. Mizuho Corporate Bank, for example, put up 50% of the capital of Mizuho Capital Partners. By contrast, Tokyo-Mitsubishi Bank's close relationship with Phoenix Capital (a fund management company that will be examined below) did not involve a direct investment of capital in the company as such, although Tokyo-Mitsubishi did invest in Phoenix Capital's funds. Domestic bank-related funds generally have the following characteristics. First, they are managed by people who used to work at banks and who maintain close ties with their former employers. Many of their deals are referred to them by banks. Second, they have strong formal affiliations with banks, and should be considered "keiretsu" funds. The banks established fund management companies or invested in funds to reap benefits from close association—smooth sales of non-performing loans, and the possibility of earning returns from the funds. In short, the banks are trying to move non-performing loans off their balance sheets by selling them to funds while at the same time earning an upside from the returns generated by the funds.[9]

The August 27, 2003 issue of *Nihon Keizai Shimbun* reported that banks have established companies specializing in corporate revival to manage non-performing loans as separate organizations in order to achieve the following three objectives:

1. *To dispose of the bank's non-performing loans:* It should be noted that if a company specializing in corporate revival is a subsidiary of a bank, its results would be consolidated with those of the parent bank and therefore selling the

---

[9] *Weekly Diamond,* December 6, 2003.

company loans would not necessarily remove them from the bank's balance sheet.

2. *To acquire corporate rehabilitation and debt collection know-how from companies already specializing in these areas.*
3. *To acquire expertise in and experience with the latest financial technologies* (from specialty companies or by forming business alliances with foreign securities firms).

Unfortunately, no formal data exists on the activities of Japanese corporate revival funds. The scant information that is available suggests that the bank-related funds have been growing steadily. Figure 7.3 identifies the types of investors in Japanese corporate revival funds from October 2002 to September 2003. Surprisingly, Japanese banks have put up more than 60% of their capital. According to Mitsubishi Research Institute, 32 corporate revival funds were started in 2002 and 2003, 18 of which were funded by Japanese banks. *Nikkei Business* reported that bank-related funds have more than ¥1.25 trillion in capital, while independent funds and foreign funds have ¥0.5 trillion in capital. Clearly, bank-related funds have come to occupy a prominent place in this sector.[10]

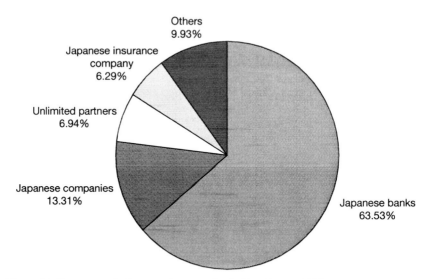

Figure 7.3 Investment in Japanese buy-out funds (2002/10–2003/9)

Source: Venture Enterprise Center (2004).

[10] *Nikkei Business*, November 29, 2004.

7.5 SIMPLE MODEL

In this section, I will examine the effects of bank-related funds on bank behavior and the implications for the financial system. The bank-related funds raise a number of interesting questions. Do they function as de facto divisions of the banks that invest in them? Does their existence affect the incentives and lending activities of major banks? Do they have a positive effect on the Japanese economy? To help answer these questions, I present a simple theoretical model of the rehabilitation activities of banks and bank-related funds. I focus on how the bank-related funds affect bank incentives, and how the monitoring incentives of banks are affected by the presence of these funds. One of the merits of bank-related funds is that they may mitigate incentive problems simply by providing the opportunity to separate rehabilitation activities from the banks.

To highlight the rehabilitation process, I formalize the relationship between the monitoring activities of a banker/loan officer and a bank's lending performance, putting a new twist on the simple principal–agent model. Here, the top management of the bank ("principal") hires a banker/loan officer ("agent") to make and monitor lending decisions. Since there is an asymmetric information problem between top management and the banker/loan officer, top management cannot control the behavior of the banker/loan officer perfectly. Let us assume that the banker/loan officer chooses to monitor at either a high effort (e^H) or low effort (e^L) level, which in turn affects the outcome of the lending decision. The banker/loan officer has to bear a private cost (C) for choosing a high effort level (e^H). Furthermore, let us assume that the monitoring of the lending activity produces either a good outcome (V^H) or a bad outcome (V^L), i.e. default. Since the bank has to obtain a repayment of D for the loan, we assume here that $V^H > D > V^L$. The monitoring level of the bank will improve the probability of a good outcome. Choosing to monitor at a high level (e^H) increases the probability of a good outcome to p^H; if the banker/loan officer chooses to monitor at a low level (e^L), the probability of a good outcome is reduced to p^L. Since a higher level of monitoring improves the probability of a good outcome, $p^H > p^L$.

I assume here that

$$(1) \qquad p^H V^H + (1 - p^H) V^L - C \geq p^L V^H + (1 - p^L) V^L.$$

The left hand side of this inequality is the net social benefit for choosing e^H and the right hand is that for choosing e^L. Clearly, it is efficient to choose a high effort level. Moreover, I also assume that

$$(2) \qquad p^H D + (1 - p^H) V^L - C \geq p^L D + (1 - p^L) V^L.$$

This inequality shows that the choice of a high level of effort improves bank profits. By setting an appropriate wage function (explained in footnote 14), the bank realizes a high effort level and the following profit,

(3) $\pi^H = p^H D + (1 - p^H)V^L - C = D - (1 - p^H)F - C.$[11]

To further develop the model, I will assume that the bank has the option of engaging in "rehabilitation activity."[12] The cost of this activity is F. It is assumed that by paying F, the outcome of the lending decision is greatly improved, and V^L becomes V^H with a probability of 1. Of course, this model oversimplifies by omitting the possibility that banks can choose to postpone decisions to classify loans as non-performing, but nevertheless clarifies the incentive problems faced by banks as they monitor loans. Let us assume here that

(3) $D - V^L > F.$

In other words, engaging in rehabilitation activity to rescue a firm from default (V^L) is always beneficial to the bank.

   If the top managers of the bank can observe the effort choice of the banker/loan officer, they will write a contract to extract a high level of effort. The compensation for high effort will be a wage payment of C. No wage payment is made for a low effort level. Under the contract, if the banker/loan officer chooses a high effort level (e^H), the bank receives a profit of π^*.

(4) $\pi^* = D - (1 - p^H)F - C > \pi^H$

Since it is assumed that the effort choice of a banker/loan officer and rehabilitation activities are unobservable and wage functions are contingent only upon the outcome, an incentive problem arises. If rehabilitation activity is undertaken, V^H is always realized and the bank will obtain repayment of D. Hence, if the top management of the bank is only able to observe the outcome of a lending decision (i.e. V^H or V^L), the payoff to the banker/loan officer will not be reduced even if he/she chooses to exert low effort. Thus, as long as the wage function of the banker/loan officer is linked to the outcome of the loan decision, he/she will be tempted to choose a low effort level. With the input of low level of effort, the profit of the bank becomes

(5) $\pi^L = D - (1 - p^L)F$

In other words, since the banker/loan officer exerts low effort, the probability that rehabilitation activity will be required increases and the expected cost of the

---

[11] The optimal wage function should satisfy the following incentive compatibility and the individual rationality constraints:

$$p^H W^H + (1 - p^H)W^L - C \geq p^L W^H + (1 - p^L)W^L$$

$$p^H W^H + (1 - p^H)W^L - C \geq 0$$

where $W^H(W^L)$ is the wage rate when the outcome is $V^H(V^L)$. Hence, by setting $W^H = (1 - p^L)C/(p^H - p^L)$ and $W^L = -p^L C/(p^H - p^L)$, the bank realizes π^H.

[12] See Aoki (2001) for more on the rehabilitation activities and contingent governance of banks.

rehabilitation activity rises to $(1 - p^L)F$. The moral hazard problem faced by the banker/loan officer reduces bank profits. Obviously, π^L is lower than π^* and even lower than π^H (the profit without the rehabilitation activity) as long as p^L is sufficiently low.

In sum, rehabilitation activities worsen the incentive problem for the banker/loan officer. Even though rehabilitation may have a positive effect on the lending outcome, it distorts the signal sent by the lending activity and magnifies the moral hazard problem for the banker/loan officer.

7.5.1 Effects of Bank-Related Funds

By setting up related funds and selling loans to them, banks can change this situation and solve the incentive problem. For simplicity's sake, let us assume here that the condition of a loan is observable to a fund. In other words, whether the outcome of a loan will be V^H or V^L is known to the fund as well as the bank. The fund pays a rehabilitation cost of F^* and the price of the loan is q. Here, it is not necessary to specify whether F^* is higher or lower than F, but it can be shown that even if F^* is higher than F, if the bank is more efficient than the fund at rehabilitating, selling the loan to the fund is effective.

It can be assumed that the loan will be classified as non-performing, i.e. the outcome will be bad (V^L), and rehabilitation activity is necessary. The bank will sell the loan to a fund at a price q that satisfies the following conditions.

$$(6) \qquad\qquad V^L \leq q \leq D - F^*.$$

Here, I will assume for simplicity's sake that the bank can exercise sufficient bargaining power over the selling price to extract a price of $q = D - F^*$; but even if I were to assume that $q = V^L$, the following results would not be qualitatively affected.[13] If the bank sells the non-performing loan, the selling price q becomes a verifiable parameter. Hence, the wage rate now becomes contingent upon the selling price. For example, if the selling price q is lower than D, the wage rate for the banker becomes negative. As long as such a penalty mechanism is possible and effective, the banker/loan officer will choose to exert a high effort and the profit of the bank becomes π^*:

$$(4) \qquad\qquad \pi^* = D - (1 - p^H)F - C$$

Hence, even though the fund may be related to the bank and function as nothing more than a separate division of the bank, the performance of the bank is improved by selling loans to the fund.

---

[13] In this simple model, I assume there is no asymmetric information problem between a bank and a fund. For more on the asymmetric information problem between buyers and sellers of securities, see Demarzo and Duffie (1999) or Boot and Thakor (1993).

It is remarkable that even if the outside fund engages in rehabilitation activity at a lower level of efficiency than the bank does, selling loans to the fund serves a useful purpose. For example, let us suppose that the cost of the rehabilitation activity for the fund (F^*) is higher than the cost of the rehabilitation activity for the bank (F). Even so, as long as

(7) $$D - (1 - p^H)F^* - C > D - (1 - p^L)F,$$

it is useful for the bank to sell NPLs to a fund. An intuitive explanation is that incentives are important to the banker/loan officer, and the selling price of the loan allows the top management of the bank to observe the outcome of the banker/loan officer's effort choice. Hence, as long as the fund's ability to rehabilitate is not markedly worse than that of the bank, selling NPLs to the funds benefits the bank.

If a bank sells NPLs to a bank-related fund, the transactions make the present value of the NPLs apparent and verifiable. This means that the level of the bank's monitoring activities becomes apparent and the moral hazard problem that arises when the wage payment is linked to outcome can be mitigated. Hence, even if the funds' rehabilitation capacities do not surpass those of the banks, their mere existence will benefit banks.

7.5.2 More Options

There is another benefit that arises from using funds to rehabilitate borrowers. As many banks shed divisions that handle rehabilitation activities, numerous bank-related funds are being established in their place. Consequently, banks are given a wider range of choices of funds. As Figure 7.4 shows, each bank has multiple choices of funds, and thus many options for rehabilitating defaulting firms. The increase in freedom and options should provide banks with more opportunities to do business with more appealing funds and thereby improve efficiency.

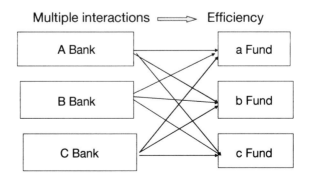

Figure 7.4 Merits of division of labor

To understand how banks benefit, let us suppose that the rehabilitation technology of Bank A is geared to small companies and that of Bank B to large companies. The rehabilitation cost for Bank A is low (F^L) for small companies and high $(F^H(> F^L))$ for large companies. On the other hand, the cost for Bank B is high (F^H) for small companies and low (F^L) for large companies. If a bank does not specialize and chooses to invest in and engage in rehabilitation activities for both small and large companies, the bank (A or B) has to use its own rehabilitation technology for both small and large companies. If a bank chooses to limit its rehabilitation activities to a certain segment of the market, however, it has the option of electing to employ better rehabilitation technologies for other segments of the market (for example, by selling loans to a corporate revival fund). Bank A may choose to use its own technology for small companies but use Bank B's technology (perhaps via a bank-related fund) for large companies. Hence, the cost of the rehabilitation activity converges on F^L for all companies. An increase in the number of bank-related funds should increase the benefit to banks because they will be given a wider range of choices.

7.5.3 Drawbacks of Bank-Related Funds

While corporate revival funds offer the benefit of a wider range of choices for banks, there are scenarios that would prevent banks from actually benefiting. First, the setting of an appropriate price by the bank and fund is a necessary condition. If the price q is manipulated to a high level, the banker/loan officer has an incentive to choose to exert a low effort level of effort (e^L) and the profit of the bank will decrease accordingly. Of course, inappropriate price setting will generate losses to funds that purchase loans over the long run. Hence, funds must adopt a proper governance and management system to ensure their independence from banks.

Second, if banks are reluctant to sell their NPLs to the funds, the funds will not be effective. If $F^* > F$, in particular, the *ex post* decision (that is, the decision after the choice of effort) of the bank would not be to sell the loan since the selling price would be too low. In this case, the incentive for the banker/loan officer is not improved, and the bank's profit becomes

(5) $$\pi^L = D - (1 - p^L)F.$$

Moreover, even if $F^* \leq F$, a bank might have an incentive to conceal its NPLs and hesitate to sell them. Thus, other commitment mechanisms (government regulations or policies) for selling the NPLs may be needed to make selling loans more attractive to banks.

Of course, it goes without saying that if the separation of lending from rehabilitation activities decreases efficiency substantially, i.e. the cost of the rehabilitation activities of funds is very high compared to that of banks $(F^* \gg F)$, the funds will not function well.

7.6 A CASE STUDY: PHOENIX CAPITAL

In the previous section, I laid out the positive and negative aspects of bank-related funds. In this section, I will examine the pros and cons more closely through a case study of a leading Japanese bank-related corporate revival fund—Phoenix Capital Co. Ltd. Phoenix Capital was established in 2002 to run the Japan Recovery Fund. Subsequently, Phoenix Capital has set up additional funds, and as of December 2004 runs four funds with a total investment of about ¥174 billion.

Phoenix Capital has a close connection to Tokyo-Mitsubishi Bank, a major Japanese city (commercial) bank. Its representative director (chief executive officer) is Yasushi Ando, who joined Mitsubishi Bank (now Tokyo-Mitsubishi Bank) after graduating from Tokyo University, serving in important positions until the founding of Phoenix Capital. While Tokyo-Mitsubishi Bank has not publicized details on the size of its investment in Phoenix Capital, its investment in the various funds that it runs is substantial, and regional banks with close ties to Tokyo-Mitsubishi Bank have also invested in Phoenix Capital. Furthermore, Phoenix Capital's investment targets include many firms that have borrowed money from Tokyo-Mitsubishi Bank. All of this evidence suggests that Phoenix Capital has a close connection to Tokyo-Mitsubishi Bank.

Among the famous corporate revivals attempted by Phoenix Capital is Ichida, a kimono manufacturer with a 130-year history but whose performance had deteriorated in recent years. In March 2002, Phoenix Capital purchased Ichida's debt from Tokyo-Mitsubishi Bank, Ichida's main bank, and invested ¥360 million in the firm as part of a debt–equity swap. Phoenix Capital then attempted to reconstruct the firm as a major shareholder. In addition to dispatching directors to Ichida, Phoenix Capital also prepared an "Ichida revival plan" in March 2003 to improve its management, and attempted to reform its operations. Consequently, its performance improved, turnover bottomed out in March 2003, and operating profits increased in March 2003 and March 2004.

Another prominent corporate revival target of Phoenix Capital is Mitsubishi Motor Co. (MMC), which also had a main-bank relationship with Tokyo-Mitsubishi Bank. After MMC's sales results deteriorated due to a string of scandals including an attempt to cover up recalls of defective cars, Tokyo-Mitsubishi Bank, Mitsubishi Heavy Industries, and other members of the Mitsubishi Group intervened to prop up MMC. In 2004, Phoenix Capital handled a ¥74 billion capital issue by MMC, surpassing DaimlerChrysler to become MMC's largest shareholder with 30 percent of its shares. And Phoenix Capital CEO Ando was appointed an external director of MMC to oversee its restructuring effort. MMC unveiled a new restructuring plan in 2005. After the automaker's corporate restructuring plan was hammered out, Ando stepped down as external director at the end of June 2005. At the same time, Phoenix Capital also announced that it would begin to sell off its shares in MMC. Some observers believe that Phoenix Capital's decision to sell its stake in MMC is not a sign that MMC's rehabilitation is going well but an indication of its differences of opinion with other backers of MMC and desire for an early exit.

Given the existence of strong ties between Phoenix Capital and Tokyo-Mitsubishi Bank, some skeptics have questioned whether Phoenix Capital has a reason to exist apart from Tokyo-Mitsubishi Bank. The simple model presented in the previous section, however, suggests that Phoenix Capital may benefit Tokyo-Mitsubishi Bank by allowing it to mitigate its moral hazard problem. Moreover, the above cases indicate that Phoenix Capital may possess rehabilitation expertise that is superior to Tokyo-Mitsubishi Bank's. Finally, benefits exist to being able to act as a shareholder rather than as a creditor. As noted above, Phoenix Capital places an emphasis on carrying out corporate rehabilitation as a shareholder.

Another important point is that Phoenix Capital has received investments from financial institutions other than Tokyo-Mitsubishi Bank. Mitsui-Sumitomo Bank, a major Japanese city bank that ranks with Tokyo-Mitsubishi Bank, also invests in Phoenix Capital, and has also sold it non-performing loans. Therefore, Phoenix Capital conducts not only business deals tied to Tokyo-Mitsubishi Bank but also transactions with other banks. As explained in the previous section and Figure 7.4, funds that carry out rehabilitations independently from related banks and with non-related financial institutions have a wider range of options.

Furthermore, Phoenix Capital has taken numerous steps to increase its independence from Tokyo-Mitsubishi Bank. First, although Tokyo-Mitsubishi Bank does invest in Phoenix Capital's recovery funds, it does not invest directly in Phoenix Capital, the entity that operates these funds. A number of mechanisms have been put in place to prevent investors from influencing investment decisions and the setting of purchase prices, and to prevent the fund from purchasing instruments at unjustifiably high prices. Actually, the mechanisms for maintaining independence help to decrease or prevent the drawbacks of bank-related funds alluded to in the previous section.

However, as the MMC case demonstrates, doubts linger over whether Phoenix Capital's decisions are heavily influenced by the Mitsubishi Group and Tokyo-Mitsubishi Bank. In this regard, Phoenix Capital's announcement that it was making an early withdrawal from the effort to rehabilitate MMC suggests that Phoenix Capital is not simply acting in accordance with wishes of Tokyo-Mitsubishi Bank, which would have preferred that Phoenix Capital continue to invest in MMC, given that the restructuring effort has not been completed. The raison d'être of corporate revival funds such as Phoenix Capital, which are under the influence of banks, is tied to their ability to maintain their independence. At this stage, the funds seem to have preserved a modicum of independence but do face potential pitfalls and must exercise considerable caution when conducting their deals.

7.7 GOVERNMENT ACTIVITY

The Japanese government has played a prominent role in promoting corporate rehabilitation by changing the legal rules and forcing Japanese banks to decrease their NPL ratios. In addition to these direct measures, the Japanese government has taken other, less direct actions to promote the disposal of non-performing loans and the growth of bank-related funds, including the establishment of the Development Bank of Japan and the Industrial Revitalization Corporation Japan.

7.7.1 Development Bank of Japan

The Development Bank of Japan, which is wholly owned by the Japanese government, actively invests in corporate revival funds. DBJ has invested in the "Daiei Restructuring Fund" and Nihon Mirai Capital, the first Japanese fund to specialize in corporate rehabilitation. Between May 2001 and June 2003, the aggregate investments made by DBJ in restructuring funds and bankrupt companies amounted to ¥100 billion (*Nikkei Financial Daily,* July 10, 2003), an indication that the Japanese government has played an important role in supporting Japanese corporate revival funds. Without the investments from the DBJ, many funds might not have been formed. Even the bank-related funds are affected by DBJ's investments.

In addition to investing in funds, DBJ provides debtor in possession (DIP) financing for insolvent companies.[14] Under the DIP process of the Civil Rehabilitation Law, a troubled business may continue to operate during rehabilitation proceedings. In Japan, DIP financing refers to the loans provided between the filing for and approval of corporate rehabilitation under the Civil Rehabilitation and Corporate Reorganization Laws, which regulate restructuring-oriented bankruptcy proceedings. DBJ extends DIP financing to help bankrupt companies that file for corporate rehabilitation under the Civil Rehabilitation Law if they lack operating funds and the operation of their businesses may suffer between the time of application and approval. DIP financing generally enables such companies to obtain immediate operating funds to maintain the value of their enterprises. DBJ has been extending DIP financing to ailing firms even before private financial institutions began to provide this service. Companies that have received DIP financing from DBJ include Footwork Express, Niigata Engineering, Mycal, and Hirota, a confection manufacturer. Following in the footsteps of DBJ, private banks such as Aozora Bank and Shinsei Bank have also launched DIP services.

7.7.2 Industrial Revitalization Corporation Japan

After announcing its "Program for Financial Revival," the Japanese government provided the financing to establish the Industrial Revitalization Corporation Japan (IRCJ) as a joint stock company. The purpose of this corporation is to purchase the non-performing loans of Japanese banks. As private funds grew

---

[14] This section is based on the DIP financing section of the Development Bank of Japan's homepage.

rapidly in recent years, most non-performing loans were purchased by those funds and not by IRCJ. While IRCJ has been criticized for duplicating the role of private revival funds, IRCJ maintains that in corporate rehabilitation cases where financial creditors have difficulty resolving issues, it seeks to act as a "neutral and fair third party in order to generate a solution that is equitable to all concerned parties."[15]

In general, IRCJ only invests in a firm when it expects to turn a profit from the investment and cannot easily funnel money into unprofitable projects and firms even if they are politically important. IRCJ's emphasis on profit might be one reason why it has not became a major purchaser of NPLs. But the size of its footprint in the rehabilitation field is gradually increasing. It purchased the debt of Kanebo, a famous cosmetic company, and that of Daiei, one of the largest supermarket chains. The rehabilitation of these firms is important to the Japanese economy and Japanese government. For example, the Kanebo group had total sales in excess of ¥0.5 trillion in 2004, and employed more than 14,000. Daiei had total sales of ¥1.3 trillion and employed 10,000.[16] The Japanese government thought that the bankruptcy of these firms would deal a severe blow to the Japanese economy. Even so, such fears may not have been the primary reason for IRCJ's decision to support these companies. Since IRCJ must earn a profit from its investments, it is expected to pursue the proper revival of these companies.

Although IRCJ was potentially a major competitor to the bank-related funds, it initially refrained from purchasing NPLs. While IRCJ is now devoting its rehabilitation efforts to Kanebo, Daiei and other troubled firms, it is required to obtain a return on its investments in the near term. Hence, IRCJ will have to sell its loans or equity within a few years, perhaps to bank-related funds. The relationship between IRCJ and revival funds is quite complex. IRCJ does not simply duplicate their functions; it sometimes complements them.

7.8 CONCLUSION

Corporate revival funds are growing rapidly and transforming the corporate revival process in Japan. The Japanese government has played a positive role by laying the groundwork for rehabilitation activities, and the government-financed DBJ and the IRCJ have actively promoted the growth of private funds.

One interesting feature of the corporate revival market is the strong relationship between the revival funds and Japanese banks. Whether the behavior of bank-related funds is significantly different from that of foreign-owned funds is an interesting, but still unanswered question. One might surmise that bank-related funds serve only to purchase non-performing loans from banks and thus

---

[15] See: http://www.ircj.co.jp/english/background/role.html
[16] See: http://www.daiei.jp/corporate/ir/jigyou_houkoku/pdf/54.pdf

exist solely for the purpose of keeping "zombie" firms afloat. This possibility cannot be denied and indeed some funds may act in this manner. On the other hand, I have also shown that the funds improve the incentive mechanisms of Japanese banks. When banks sell NPLs to bank-related funds, the results of their monitoring activities become more transparent and verifiable. This transparency makes it possible to more rigorously check on the monitoring of loans by bankers/loan officers, and enables banks to mitigate the moral hazard problem.

The growth of corporate revival funds may usher in improvements to the banking sector and the financial system in Japan, as suggested by my simple theoretical model. However, appropriate management systems and incentive mechanisms will still have to be adopted to allow the funds to continue to make a positive contribution. Although I have stressed the agency problem that exists within banks, a similar problem may exist inside the funds. Hence, it is necessary to construct good incentive or (investor-led) monitoring mechanisms to keep an eye on the behavior or decisions of fund managers. Good information on these funds will also be needed. Without good incentive mechanisms, these funds may generate another moral hazard problem in the financial system. In particular, if the funds purchase loans at improper prices simply to decrease the amount of non-performing loans on the books of banks, they will be part of the problem and not the solution.

REFERENCES

Allen, F. and D. Gale (2000). *Comparing Financial Systems.* Cambridge, MA: MIT Press.

Aoki, M. (2001). *Toward a Comparative Institutional Analysis.* Cambridge, MA: MIT Press.

Boot, A. and A. Thakor (1992). 'Security Design,' *Journal of Finance*, 48: 1349–78.

Caballero, R., T. Hoshi and A. K. Kashyap (2004). 'Zombie Lending and Depressed Restructuring in Japan,' Mimeo.

Chikusei Partners (2004). *Japanese Buyout Fund Boom.* Tokyo: Mitsubishi Research Institute.

Demarzo, P. and D. Duffie (1999). 'A Liquidity-Based Model of Security Design,' *Econometrica*, 67: 65–99.

Hellmann, T. (1988). 'The Allocation of Control Rights in Venture Capital Contracts,' *Rand Journal of Economics*, 29: 57–76.

Hoshi, T. and A. K. Kashyap (2004). 'Japan's Financial Crisis and Economic Stagnation,' *Journal of Economic Perspectives*, Winter, 18(1): 3–26.

Hoshi, T. and H. Patrick (eds.) (2000). *Crisis and Change in the Japanese Financial System.* London: Kluwer Academic Publishers.

Koshi, J. (2000). *Puraibe-to ·ekuiti—kyūkakudai suru mikōkai kabushiki tōshi no sekai.* Tokyo: Nihon keizai shinbunsha.

—— (2001). *Nihon no puraibe-to ·ekuiti.* Tokyo: Nihon keizai shinbunsha (Nikkei Business).

Rachlin, M. (2005). 'Private Equity in Japan: A Comparison of Foreign and Domestic Funds,' MSc Dissertation, Department of Management, King's College, London.

Sheard, P. (1994). 'Main Banks and the Governance of Financial Distress,' in M. Aoki and H. Patrick (eds.), *The Japanese Main Bank System—Its Relevance for Developing and Transforming Economies*. Oxford: Oxford University Press.

Tett, G. (2003). *Saving the Sun: How Wall Street Mavericks Shook Up Japan's Financial World and Made Billions*. New York: Harper Business.

Venture Enterprise Center (2004). *Heisei 15 Nendo Venture Capital to Tōshi Dōko Chōsa*. Available at: http://www.vec.or.jp/vc/survey-15j.pdf

Wada, T. (2002). *Baishū fando—hagetaka ka keiei kakumeika*. Tokyo: Kōbunsha.

—— (2003). *Kigyōsaisei Fanndo—furyōsaiken bijinesu no kyo to jitsu*. Tokyo: Kōbunsha.

Part II

Changes in Organization, Employment, and Corporate Boards

8

Business Portfolio Restructuring of Japanese
Firms in the 1990s: Entry and Exit Analysis*

Tatsuya Kikutani, Hideshi Itoh, and Osamu Hayashida

8.1 INTRODUCTION

What restructuring efforts did Japanese firms make in the 1990s, ten years that
were characterized by long-term recession as well as a rapid development of
information technology? Restructuring encompasses a broad range of issues
including (i) corporate governance, (ii) internal organization, and (iii) the
firm's configuration of lines of business. In this chapter we will focus on the
last issue, which we call *portfolio restructuring*.

Most existing studies of business portfolio restructuring began with an evaluation
of diversification behavior of the firm, pioneered by Wernerfelt and Montgomery
(1988). Lang and Stulz (1994) show empirically that diversification can impair firm
values, and Berger and Ofek (1995) find, using the excess value approach, that
unrelated diversification has negative effects on the value of the firm.

A series of empirical studies including those cited above have set a negative
tone for diversification.[1] Under this trend, restructuring means focusing on a few
core lines of businesses. Comment and Jarrell (1995) argue that a focusing

*We are grateful to Gregory Jackson, Hideaki Miyajima, Masayuki Morikawa, two anonymous
referees, and the seminar participants at the Conference on Corporate Reform and Performance held
at Hitotsubashi University on September 26–27, 2003, for helpful comments and suggestions. This
study is partly based on the second author's work in the project on "Changing Corporate Governance
and Its Effects on Productivity in Japan" in collaboration with the Research and Statistics Department
of the METI (Ministry of Economy, Trade and Industry). We would like to thank the METI and the
Ministry of Public Management, Home Affairs, Posts and Telecommunications, for making the firm-
level data of the Basic Survey of Business Structure and Activity available for our research. However,
only the second author has kept access to the data during the current research. Special thanks go to
Sadao Nagaoka, head of the project, who gave the second author the opportunity to participate in the
project. The second author is also grateful to Yoichiro Nishimura for his superb research assistance.
Financial support from the 21st Century COE program "Dynamics of Knowledge, Corporate System
and Innovation" at Graduate School of Commerce and Management, Hitotsubashi University, is
gratefully acknowledged.
[1] Recent studies such as Compa and Kedia (2002) and Graham et al. (2002) argue that
diversificationdoes not always destroy the firm value. Mansi and Reeb (2002) point out that not
only shareholder values but bond holder values should be taken into consideration.

strategy is consistent with the maximization of shareholder value, and Daley et al. (1997) find that the firm can increase its value through spinning off of the unrelated lines of business. Denis et al. (1997) and Berger and Ofek (1999) suggest that focusing is caused by outside governance pressure.

Literature on portfolio restructuring in Japan during the 1990s is scarce. However, Hiramoto (2002), Miyajima and Inagaki (2003), and Funaoka (2003) find negative relationships between diversification and the firm value, and Morikawa (1998a, b) and Miyajima and Inagaki (2003) discover a trend of focusing.[2]

Our purpose in this chapter is not to join the previously cited literature in evaluating diversification strategies of Japanese firms, but to shed new light on portfolio restructuring in Japan from the aspects of entry into new business segments and exit from existing segments. In contrast to most of the previous research that analyzes portfolio restructuring within the framework of "diversifying or focusing," we will highlight entry and exit activities as more fundamental elements of restructuring than diversifying or focusing. If a firm's degree of diversification could be measured by the number of business segments within the firm, entry into new segments increases the degree of diversification, while exit from the existing segments decreases it. Diversifying thus corresponds to the case where more entry is undertaken than exit, while focusing corresponds to the opposite case. Diversifying and focusing thus represent only net effects.

We argue that the "diversifying or focusing" approach to portfolio restructuring may be misleading. Even when neither diversifying nor focusing was observed, the firm may have actively engaged in entry and exit. Since both activities offset each other, the "diversifying or focusing" approach cannot distinguish between one firm with no entry and exit, and another with the same number of entry and exit segments. Obviously the latter firm is far more likely to engage in restructuring behavior. Through analysis of entry and exit separately, we can detect firms that shift their business configuration drastically or relocate their business domains.

Another distinctive feature of our analysis is that we add the viewpoint of a "business group" to the analysis of business restructuring. It is well known that Japanese firms typically form networks of affiliated companies which we refer to as business groups throughout this chapter.[3] It is often argued that the existence of business groups explains the comparatively lower adoption ratio of multidivisional form among Japanese firms than their American counterparts.[4] In fact,

---

[2] On the contrary, the empirical analysis of the high economic growth era (Yoshihara et al., 1981; Goto, 1981), and that of the post-growth era until the end of the bubble economy (Japan Fair Trade Commission, 1992; Yasuki, 1995) finds that Japanese firms were diversifying during these periods.

[3] There are other types of business groups in Japan, that are not analyzed in this chapter. The first type is the well known *zaibatsu*-originated or bank-oriented group such as Mitsubishi, Mitsui, and Sumitomo. This type of business group, often called financial *keiretsu*, is a loose horizontal association of large firms across industries, including general trading companies, banks, insurance companies, as well as manufacturers. The second type is often called the vertical *keiretsu* group which has become internationally renowned since the Japan–U.S. Structural Impediments Initiatives held between 1989 and 1990. It is a network based on long-term and continuous business relationships.

[4] See Itoh (2003) for more on multi-divisional form in Japan and the U.S.

the average ratio of investment in affiliated companies to total assets is higher for Japanese firms. It suggests that Japanese firms prefer separating businesses into their subsidiaries and affiliates to managing them in-house.

Portfolio restructuring of business groups therefore must be taken into consideration. For example, the core firm of a business group may move into a new business not by themselves but by establishing an affiliate. The core firm may transfer one of their business segments to an affiliate (and hence no exit from the group's standpoint), or divest it to a firm outside the group (and hence the group exits from the business). The viewpoint of business groups is thus indispensable for the analysis of portfolio restructuring. Nevertheless, either theoretical or empirical study of business groups in our sense is scarce, in contrast to a large body of literature on the other types of business groups.[5]

Incorporating these two features into analysis requires business portfolio data based on a standardized industrial classification both at the firm level and the group level. These requirements are in part satisfied by the compulsory survey performed by the Ministry of Economy, Trade and Industry (METI) called the Basic Survey of Business Structure and Activity (Kigyo Katsudo Kihon Chosa). For 1991FY, 1994FY, and every year thereafter (data up to 2000FY are available), it covers all firms with more than 50 engaged employees and with capital more than 30 million yen. Each sample reports its sales as well as the number of affiliated companies for each standardized segment of business.[6] We can thus construct measures of diversification, entry, and exit at the parent firm level as well as the group level. However, we cannot obtain financial data of the affiliated companies of the sample parent firms, and hence our regression analyses are limited to parent firms.

We find that during the 1990s Japanese parent firms not only exited from the existing business segments but also actively entered new segments. Moreover, many firms engaged in both entry and exit at the same time. This finding supports our argument that the simple diversifying or focusing approach is misleading, and it is necessary to study restructuring as a rearrangement of the business portfolio of the firm from the standpoint of entry and exit: while there were both active entry and exit, we find a weak trend of focusing during the 1990s. Although the Japanese economy during the 1990s is often referred to as a "lost decade" because of the delay in disposing of nonperforming loans in the financial sectors, the manufacturing sectors are likely to rearrange their businesses actively. We in fact find that firm performance is likely to improve only when both entry and exit take place simultaneously, which implies that portfolio restructuring with the combination of entry and exit is likely to lead to better performance at the end of the 1990s.

We next estimate what factors affect the parent firm's decision of entry and exit, and obtain the following results: entry and exit are less likely for larger firms, controlling the number of business segments; conversely, entry and exit are more

---

[5] See footnote 3. Important exceptions are Morikawa(1998a, b) and Miyajima and Inagaki(2003).

[6] Morikawa (1998a, b) also use the Basic Survey for the analysis of entry and exit activities as well as that of business groups. Our study also owes much to his pioneering work, while he does not relate entry and exit with diversification, and he only compares between 1991FY and 1994FY.

likely as the debt ratio is higher and the initial number of segments is larger; if the core business of a firm steadily grows, entry and exit activities are restrained; and an increase in riskiness of the core business causes more entry and exit. Of particular interest is that larger firm size makes both entry and exit less likely, and hence the number of business segments can be affected simultaneously in opposite directions. Therefore, the net effect of firm size on diversifying is ambiguous. We however find that a larger firm is more likely to engage in diversifying. A standard explanation for this is that the larger firm has more organizational capabilities or unused resources to diversify its business lines. However, since firm size has negative effects both on entry and exit, increasing firm size reduces the possibility of exit more than that of entry, which is in sharp contrast to the standard explanation based on a positive effect of firm size on entry.

Our finding that entry and exit occur simultaneously in combination is important since it suggests that entry and exit activities be interdependent with one another. Since we show that the parent firm's performance is likely to increase by engaging in both entry and exit, entry and exit are likely to be complementary.

The rest of the chapter is organized as follows. We explain our data set and variables in section 8.2. Sections 8.3 and 8.4 are the main parts of the chapter. In section 8.3 we report summary statistics and trends of the 1990s. In section 8.4 we report estimation results concerning determinants of entry and exit, diversifying and focusing, and relationships between portfolio restructuring and performance, all at the parent firm level. Section 8.5 gives our concluding remarks.

8.2 DATA

8.2.1 Data Source

The Basic Survey of Business Structures and Activities (hereafter called the Basic Survey) is a compulsory survey by the Ministry of Economy, Trade and Industry ("METI"), conducted for fiscal years (FY) 1991 and 1994, and every year thereafter. The data available to us are up to fiscal year 2000. The Survey covers all firms having more than 50 employees and with a capital of more than 30 million yen.

Two features of the Basic Survey are noteworthy: (i) non-listed middle and small sized firms are included; and (ii) it is a firm-level survey in contrast to many other statistical data including Census, that are made on an establishment basis. The Basic Survey is of value for the purpose of our research because each sample reports its sales as well as the number of subsidiaries, for each business segment based on the standardized three-digit industry classification. Although the annual financial report also includes sales by business segment and the number of subsidiaries, the business classifications are based on subjective standards and hence hard to compare across firms. Furthermore, only the total number of subsidiaries is reported, and no information concerning the subsidiaries' business segments is contained in the annual report.

8.2.2 Definitions of Main Variables

The Basic Survey provides not only detailed financial data including sales, total assets, and debts for each sample firm, but also indicates whether each sample firm has a parent firm (defined as owning more than half of the shares). Accordingly we define a sample firm as a *parent firm* if it does not have any parent firm.

Diversification Index of the Parent Firm

The Basic Survey contains data on sales per business segment defined by the three-digit industry classification. We can thus calculate the Herfindahl index which is often used as a measure for the degree of diversification of a firm. We however do not employ this index for the following reasons. First, the index is affected not only by the firm's corporate strategies but by market conditions in each segment. Second, the corresponding index for the group cannot be obtained because the affiliates' sales per segment are not available. We thus use only the number of business segments (with positive sales) as an index representing the degree of diversification.

Diversification Index of the parent firm: the number of business segments in which the parent firm reports positive sales.

Since our concern is corporate decision making of business portfolio configurations, it is better to use only the number of segments that the firm can decide. We call a firm *single-segment* if its number of segments is one, and *multi-segment* (or diversified) if it has more than one segment.

Since we are only able to access sales data from mining and manufacturing, we only count the number of mining and manufacturing segments, and do not cover diversification into non-manufacturing segments such as financial, service, or real estate segments.

Entry and Exit of the Parent Firm

Using the segment sales data explained above, we define entry into a new segment and exit from an existing segment for each parent firm during a given phase[7] as follows:

Entry into a segment by a parent firm: the sales of the segment are not reported at the beginning of the phase but are reported at the end of the

Exit phase. from a segment by a parent firm: the sales of the segment are reported at the beginning of the phase but are not reported at the end of the phase.

Restructuring by the Business Group

The Basic Survey also reports the number of subsidiaries and related firms for each business segment defined by the same three-digit industry classification as

---

[7] Time phases will be explained in the next subsection 8.2.3.

well as for each ownership category (wholly owned, more than 50% owned, or 20–50% owned by the parent firm). Note that the affiliates' sales per segment are not reported. Using this information concerning the number of affiliates (subsidiaries or related companies), we measure the degree of diversification of each *business group* as follows. First, we define a business group as a group consisting of a parent firm and its subsidiaries and related companies. We restrict samples to those parent firms who report at least one subsidiary or related company. Next, for each sample parent firm, we measure the degree of diversification of its affiliates by the number of segments where at least one affiliated company exists. In other words, we assume as if each sample had one large pseudo-affiliated firm, and measure its degree of diversification. Finally, for each parent firm, we combine information on the parent's segments and the affiliates' segments. The measure for the group's degree of diversification is calculated by adding the number of segments for the parent and that for the affiliates, and subtracting the number of segments existing both at the parent level and the affiliate level (and hence doubly counted).

Diversification Index of the business group: the number of business segments in which the parent firm reports positive sales, plus the number of segments where the parent firm's affiliates exist, minus the number of segments existing both at the parent level and the affiliate level

We also define the *overlapping ratio* of the business group, by the ratio of the number of overlapping business segments between the parent firm and its affiliates, to the total number of segments of the group.

Note that although we can obtain data on the number of affiliates for non-manufacturing segments, we focus on manufacturing segments for most of the analysis because many affiliates are engaged only in selling the products manufactured by their parent firm, and such cases can hardly be considered as diversification of the business group.

Similarly to the parent firm, entry to new business segments and exit from the existing segments by the business group are defined as follows:

Entry into a segment by a business group: in the segment no sales is reported by the parent and no affiliate exists at the beginning of the period, but the parent firm reports positive sales or at least one affiliate exists at the end of the period.

Exit from a segment by a business group: in the segment the parent firm reports positive sales or at least one affiliate exists at the beginning of the period, but no sales is reported by the parent and no affiliate exists at the end of the period.

8.2.3 Time Periods

The data available to us covers fiscal years 1991, 1994, and every year from 1995 up to 2000. We divide the period into the following three phases, examining portfolio restructuring in the 1990s by comparing among changes observed in the respective time phases.

1991–94: Phase I (beginning)
1994–97: Phase II (intermediate)
1997–2000: Phase III (end)

Before examining the changes of business configuration in the next section, we outline Japanese economic conditions in the respective phases. In the first phase, the Japanese economy was experiencing the immediate aftermath of the bubble burst in 1990. Business was rapidly declining along with declining land prices, and non-performing loans at financial institutions were rapidly increasing. In the second phase, business recovered slightly despite the delayed disposal of bad loans. However, in early 1997, the boundary year between Phase II and Phase III, the Japanese government raised the consumption tax rate from 3% to 5%, which caused another economic downturn. On November 1997 Yamaichi Securities went bankrupt (called the Yamaichi-shock), and since then, we have seen many cases of temporary nationalization as well as bank mergers during Phase III.

8.3 SUMMARY STATISTICS AND TRENDS IN THE 1990S

In this section we present summary statistics in order to understand the trend in business portfolio restructuring during the 1990s. Our main findings are as follows: (a) there is a weak tendency for the parent firm to focus their businesses; (b) there is active restructuring in terms of entry and exit, and parent firms are likely to undertake entry and exit simultaneously; (c) restructuring is more active at the beginning than the end of the 1990s; (d) although the major part of restructuring activities occurs inside the business group (between the parent firm and its affiliates), there are more changes in business configuration of the group than observation of only diversification measures suggests.

8.3.1 Diversification Strategy of the Parent Firm

The most basic indicator of diversification is whether the firm is single-segment (specialized firm) or multi-segment (diversified firm). In Figure 8.1 we plot the mean ratio of single-segment firms year by year.[8] Single-segment firms account for around 65% of manufacturing parent companies, and the ratio is almost flat throughout the 1990s. We have also conducted t tests that the ratios of single-segment firms between the beginning and the end of each time phase have the same mean, there was no significant difference.

We next look at the diversification index measured by the number of segments for sample parent firms. To eliminate the effects from the change in the ratio of single-segment parents, we plot the average number of segments of the multi-segment

---

[8] In each of Figures 8.1 and 8.2, two trends, one for parent firms and the other for business groups, are shown. The latter trend will be discussed in subsection 8.3.3.

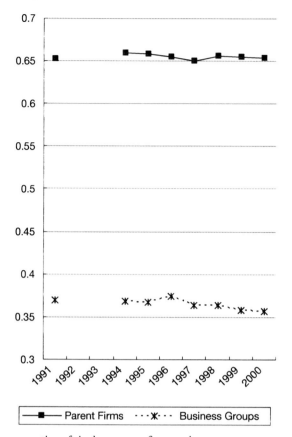

Figure 8.1. Average ratios of single-segment firms and groups

Note: Samples are restricted to multi-segment parent firms, and business groups whose core parent firms are multi-segment.

parent firm in Figure 8.2. The multi-segment parent firm sold on average for 2.64 segments in 1991 and 2.58 in 1999, and the number was gradually declining. And we find the mean difference between 1991 and 2000 is significant at the 10% level. In this sense there was a slight trend toward focusing. However, we could not confirm such a significant trend from the Herfindahl Index calculated from segment sales (not reported); we only find a weak trend toward focusing in Phases I and II.

8.3.2 Restructuring: Entry and Exit of the Parent Firm

Specializing versus Diversifying

By comparing business configuration between the beginning and the end of each phase we can analyze how the firm undertakes business restructuring during a

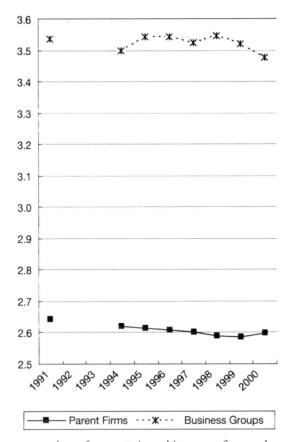

Figure 8.2. Average numbers of segments in multi-segment firms and groups

particular phase. One of the most fundamental restructuring strategies of a firm is whether or not the single-segment firm maintains specialization, and whether or not the multi-segment firm abandons diversification and specializes in one segment. Hence we first address the case where a single-segment parent firm diversifies (called *diversifying*) and the case in which a multi-segment parent specializes (*specializing*). As described in the previous subsection, single-segment parent firms account for approximately 65% throughout the 1990s. This stability, however, does not necessarily imply that these firms remained single-segment from the beginning to the end: It can result from the net changes of some previously multi-segment parents specializing and some previously single-segment parents diversifying. It is thus important to examine specializing and diversifying moves.

Table 8.1 (a) shows the average ratio of the parent firms which changed from single-segment to multi-segment, and the ratio of the parents which changed

Table 8.1. Changing Business Portfolio of Parent Firms

		Phase I	Phase II	Phase III
(a)	Ratio of Specializing Parent Firms (%)	12.11	9.76	9.91
	Ratio of Diversifying Parent Firms (%)	11.43	9.62	9.53
(b)	Average Number of Entry	0.5916	0.4420	0.3936
	Average Number of Exit	0.6329	0.4673	0.3949
(c)	Ratio of Neither Entry nor Exit (%)	48.17	57.13	61.92
	Ratio of Both Entry and Exit (%)	33.18	23.91	20.90
	Ratio of Entry Only (%)	8.66	9.45	8.46
	Ratio of Exit Only (%)	9.99	9.51	8.72

Notes: The numbers of sample parent firms are different across phases, and given as follows: (a) 3,609–56; (b) and (c) 1,501–77. For each phase, samples in (b) and (c) are restricted to those parent firms which are multi-segment at both the beginning and the phase.

from multi-segment to single-segment. Surprisingly, around 10% of the parent firms change between single-segment and multi-segment in each phase. Although these changes cancel out so that the ratio of single-segment firms looked relatively stable, behind the illusion of stability there was significant transformation in their business portfolio. Both ratios were high in Phase I, and tended to gradually decline. This trend appears to be different from the general view that business restructuring was accelerated more in the latter half of the 1990s.

Entry and Exit

We next examine changes in business configuration in more detail, by analyzing entry into new manufacturing segments and exit from the current segments. To this purpose, we restrict our attention to the multi-segment parent firms. As defined in section 8.2, the number of entry during each phase represents the number of the segments the sales of which had not been reported at the beginning of the phase but were reported at the end of the phase. And the number of exit represents the number of the segments the sales of which were reported at the beginning of the phase but were not reported at the end of the phase.

Table 8.1 (b) shows that both average numbers of entry and exit by the parent firm were the highest in Phase I and then continued a downward trend as the phase progressed. For example, the average number of entry was 0.59 per parent firm in Phase I. Since the average parent firm had 2.64 business segments in 1991 (Figure 8.2), quite a few segments (22% of 2.64 segments) were entered for three years. The number of exit was even larger (0.63 segments) in Phase I. The difference between the number of entry and that of exit results in the decrease of segments in the parent firm. Although the differences were gradually decreasing, the number of exit remained larger than that of entry. It confirms the trend toward focusing by the parent firm we observed in Figure 8.2.

These observations are important because they show that portfolio restructuring by the parent firm is far more dynamic than the net change reveals. In other words, although the number of exit was high throughout the 1990s, exit was accompanied by considerable entry activities at the same time. It thus may be misleading to look only at the net change in the number of segments to understand portfolio restructuring.[9] Note that the numbers of entry and exit were in a downward trend throughout the 1990s (though they were still high in Phase III). This trend is consistent with the decreasing trend in both specializing and diversifying in Table 8.1 (a). The regression analysis in the next section indicates that the nature of such business restructuring is somewhat different between Phases II and III.

Table 8.2 reports the average numbers of entry and exit by multi-segment parent firms in various manufacturing industries. Compared with the numbers reported in Table 8.1 (b), the average numbers of entry and exit by firms in mature industries such as Food, Paper, and Printing are lower while those in competitive industries such as Machinery, Electric, Transport, and Precision are

Table 8.2. Average Numbers of Entry and Exit of Parents by Industry

Industry	Entry			Exit		
	Phase I	Phase II	Phase III	Phase I	Phase II	Phase III
Food	0.2653	0.1165	0.1111	0.2449	0.1942	0.1222
	(98)	(113)	(90)	(98)	(113)	(90)
Textile	0.5091	0.4717	0.2292	0.3273	0.4906	0.1667
	(55)	(53)	(48)	(55)	(53)	(48)
Paper	0.3438	0.2000	0.1800	0.4688	0.2600	0.2000
	(32)	(50)	(50)	(32)	(50)	(50)
Printing	0.2609	0.1250	0.0909	0.2391	0.1250	0.0682
	(46)	(48)	(44)	(46)	(48)	(44)
Chemical	0.5946	0.3219	0.2925	0.5270	0.3973	0.2789
	(148)	(146)	(147)	(148)	(146)	(147)
Plastic	0.6275	0.2558	0.3393	0.6667	0.4651	0.3929
	(51)	(43)	(56)	(51)	(43)	(56)
Ceramic	0.4043	0.4600	0.3409	0.3404	0.2800	0.4545
	(47)	(50)	(44)	(47)	(50)	(44)
Steel	0.5738	0.3770	0.3922	0.5574	0.5082	0.3725
	(61)	(61)	(51)	(61)	(61)	(51)
Metal Product	0.4742	0.4828	0.3971	0.5567	0.5517	0.4118
	(97)	(116)	(136)	(97)	(116)	(136)
Machinery	0.6507	0.4918	0.4397	0.7860	0.5943	0.5129
	(229)	(244)	(232)	(229)	(244)	(232)
Electric	0.7939	0.6721	0.5678	0.9474	0.6189	0.4449
	(228)	(244)	(236)	(228)	(244)	(236)
Transport	0.6697	0.5046	0.4760	0.6787	0.4954	0.5371
	(221)	(218)	(229)	(221)	(218)	(229)
Precision	0.7059	0.6809	0.4500	0.6176	0.4681	0.6750
	(34)	(47)	(40)	(34)	(47)	(40)

Notes: The average numbers of entry and exit by multi-segment parent firms in each industry are reported. Figures in parentheses are the numbers of samples. The industries with 30 or less sample firms are omitted.

⁹ This point was already made by Morikawa (1998a) for the period from 1991 to 1994.

higher. Firms in the Ceramic and Metal Product have less entry and exit than the industry-wide average in Phase I, while they have more entry and exit in Phases II and III. Similar to our finding in Table 8.1 (b), the average numbers are the highest in Phase I and then decline in most industries. Interestingly, there are more entry than exit in Phases II and III for firms in the Electric industry, which may be counterintuitive.

Combination of Entry and Exit

When both entry and exit are actively undertaken, there are two possibilities: (P1) within each industry, some firms engage in exit only while others engage only in entry; or (P2) the same firms undertake both entry and exit at once. Which is more likely to hold?

In Table 8.1 (c) we classify multi-segment parent firms into four possible combinations of entry and exit. Firms which entered at least one new segment are classified into "entry" and those which exited from at least one segment are classified into "exit." Table 8.1 (c) shows the following: (Q1) The ratio of the parent firms which undertook neither entry nor exit is always the largest, followed by the ratio of those which undertook both entry and exit. The latter category accounted for one third in Phase I and then decreased to one fifth in Phase III, whereas the former ratio was increasing. (Q2) The ratio of the parent firms which undertook only exit and that of the parent firms with only entry were similar at around 9%, and the percentages remained more or less stable.

Observation (Q1) means that case (P2) is far more applicable. This finding, that many firms were likely to both scrap and build their segments is important because they attempted to overcome the post-bubble business crisis not by a simple exit strategy but by a more proactive strategy of shifting business configurations through the combination of entry and exit. Although it is often argued that Japanese companies were slow in changing business configurations in contrast with their U.S. counterparts during the 1990s, our finding suggests that this common belief be reexamined more carefully. Furthermore, it shows that the standard question of whether to diversify or focus is misleading since both of these occur simultaneously.

In Japan, many large diversified firms prefer using the key word, "selection and focusing" in restructuring. Focusing here does not necessarily mean only exit from existing segments but capital investment in promising new business segments related to the core segments with competitive advantage. For examples, Asahi Kasei, whose core business is in chemical industry, and Hitachi Zosen in shipbuilding industry both have aimed at developing a wide range of businesses around promising segments such as health care (for Asahi Kasei) and environment (Hitachi Zosen). Many companies shifted from mature core businesses (fabrics, chemicals, sewing machines, cameras, etc.) to information technology ("IT") related businesses, because the IT related businesses have a wide range of supporting industries. For example, they can enter the IT related businesses

through a variety of channels including research and development of new products, application of the existing processing techniques, and development of new
material. When entering such segments, they actively pursue alliances, joint
ventures, and acquisitions. Even small and medium firms have to engage in
restructuring for survival, and regional banks have been playing important
roles of offering financing and know-how. Recently, both national and local
governments attempted to enrich menus of various policies supporting business
portfolio restructuring of small and medium firms.

On the other hand, observation (Q2) implies that case (P1) appears to be true
as well, although the difference between the two ratios is small and stable. The fact
that these ratios cancel out, again provide more evidence that examining only
average diversification measures is likely to be misleading.

8.3.3 Business Groups

We have so far examined the parent firms' trends in business portfolio restructuring.
However, as we argue in section 8.1, to understand portfolio restructuring of the
Japanese firm, it is important to extend the scope from the firm level to the level of
the business group in the sense of a network of a parent (core) company and its
affiliated companies. The affiliates are classified into more than 50% owned subsidiaries that are included in consolidated statements, and 20% to 50% owned related
companies to which the equity method is applied. According to the Basic Survey used
in this study, the average number of affiliates per parent firm is around 15.[10]

Although available data is more restricted at the group level than the firm level,
in this subsection we examine the business group's business portfolio restructuring, using the variables defined in section 8.2.

Diversification Strategy at the Group Level

Back to Figure 8.1, we first examine whether the group is single-segment or multi-
segment. A sample group is single-segment if both the parent firm and its affiliates as
a whole are single-segment, *and* they specialize in the same segment. As shown in
Figure 8.1, the average ratio of single-segment groups is obviously smaller than that
of parent firms, while it is interesting to find that more than one–third of our sample
groups are single-segment.[11] As for time trend, the ratio of single-segment groups
is decreasing, compared with that of single-segment firms, although mean ratios
are not significantly different across periods: there is a weak trend toward diversification at the group level. This is due to a gradual trend toward diversification by
affiliated companies, as well as a decreasing trend in overlap of business segments
between the parent firm and its affiliates, as we will see shortly in Figure 8.4.

---

[10] In Japan pure holding companies had been prohibited by the antitrust law till 1997, and hence
the parent firms had their own in-house businesses during most periods to be studied in this chapter.

[11] Note that we restrict samples to those parent firms who report at least one subsidiary or related
company.

The mean diversification index of the business group (the average number of segments for the group) is plotted in Figure 8.2. The mean number of segments is around 3.5 for the group, which is higher than that of the parent firm. The difference is less than one, however, because of overlap of segments between the parent firm and its affiliates. Although we find a slight trend toward focusing for the parent firm, we do not observe such a monotonic trend for the group: there is some trend toward diversification during Phase II, and then toward focusing during Phase III. We also find relatively large variation at the group level, compared with the firm level. This implies that changes in the number of segments of affiliated companies be larger than that of the parent firm.

In order to shed more light on structural changes of the business group, we further present trends in a few additional variables characterizing the group. In Figure 8.3 we plot year by year the average number of affiliated companies and wholly owned subsidiaries, all reported by our sample parent firms. The number of affiliates (including subsidiaries and related companies) is decreasing after 1994. An important finding is that while there is a clear downward trend in the total number of affiliates, the mean number of wholly owned subsidiaries does not decrease as fast as that of all affiliates and the trend is, if any, upward during Phase III. It is likely that the Japanese firm does not simply reduce the number of affiliates, but shift toward more concentrated ownership. This is consistent with the recent trend that the parent company transforms some of its affiliates to wholly owned subsidiaries, and pursues group strategies under the parent's strong managerial control.

We next examine how the business portfolio of a parent firm is related to that of its affiliated firms as a whole. In Japan, the parent company and its affiliates often engage in the same business segments. To examine the level of overlap, we use the overlapping ratio, the ratio of the number of overlapping business segments to the total number of segments of the business group. According to Figure 8.4, over 40% of the total business segments of the business group overlap, and the ratio is decreasing after 1996. Figure 8.4 also includes a graph of the ratio of affiliates belonging to the same business segment as the parent firm's core business (the manufacturing segment with the highest sales). Nearly a half of manufacturing affiliates engage in the same business segment as the core business of the parent. This ratio is also in a downward trend, especially after 1996.

Note that in spite of the clear downward trend of overlap after 1996, no increasing trend was observed in terms of the number of segments of the business group in Figure 8.2. These observations are more compatible with the case that the parent firm or the affiliated companies (or both) were reducing the number of overlapping segments rather than the case that the number of non-overlapping segments was increasing. Taking into account the decrease in the number of the parent's segments in Figure 8.2, we can conjecture that those businesses that the parent firm ceased to operate contained many overlapping segments.

One of the following two cases applies to the typical relationship between the parent firm and its affiliates in the overlapping segments. The first case is horizontal specialization within the same business segment. For example, a parent company

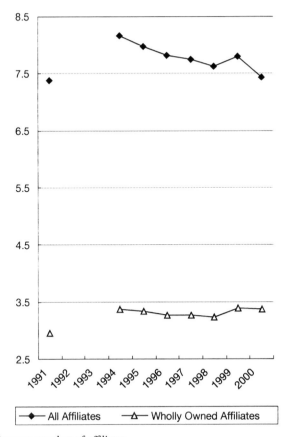

Figure 8.3. Average number of affiliates

manufactures television sets while its affiliates manufacture refrigerators. The second case is vertical specialization within the same segment. For example, the parent company manufactures cathode-ray tubes while its affiliates assemble them into television sets. If we restrict attention to listed companies and use consolidated financial data, we find that there is a significant positive correlation between the overlapping ratio and the ratio of vertical specialization to the total sales of the group. This suggests that vertical specialization is likely to be dominant.

Entry and Exit at the Group Level

Table 8.3 summarizes restructuring measures at the group level, which correspond to those at the parent firm level in Table 8.1. Table 8.3 (a) shows that changes from multi-segment to single-segment groups and from single-segment to multi-segment groups are twice as high as the corresponding changes by parent firms. These changes can occur even if the parent firm stays single-segment

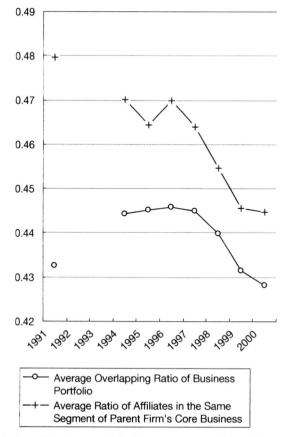

Figure 8.4. Relation of business portfolio between parent and its affiliates

or multi-segment, because its affiliates may change from single-segment to multi-segment (or vice versa), and/or a single-segment parent and its single-segment affiliates may specialize in the same segment or in different segments. Although the ratio of specializing groups and that of diversifying groups are both decreasing, the former decreases relatively faster, and as a result the change from multi-segment to single-segment is more frequent during Phase I while the opposite direction from single to multi-segment is more frequent during Phases II and III. This observation is consistent with the trend toward diversification shown in Figure 8.1.

Table 8.3 (b) shows that similar to the parent firm level, the average number of entry at the group level is in a decreasing trend. The average number of exit also decreases from Phase I (0.795) to Phase II (0.544), but from Phase II to Phase III (0.550) there is little change at the group level, compared with a clear decreasing trend at the parent firm level (0.467 to 0.395). Both at the group level and the parent firm level, exit is more active than entry during each phase. However, the

Table 8.3. Changing Business Portfolio of Business Groups

		Phase I	Phase II	Phase III
(a)	Ratio of Specializing Groups (%)	25.45	17.02	16.94
	Ratio of Diversifying Groups (%)	22.91	20.00	20.44
(b)	Average Number of Entry	0.4082	0.3040	0.2829
	Average Number of Exit	0.7954	0.5441	0.5499
(c)	Ratio of Neither Entry nor Exit (%)	59.15	71.15	69.23
	Ratio of Both Entry and Exit (%)	18.54	11.80	11.60
	Ratio of Entry Only (%)	7.91	7.32	5.86
	Ratio of Exit Only (%)	14.40	9.73	13.32

Notes: The numbers of sample groups are different across phases, and given as follows: (a) 585–641; (b) 904–87; and (c) 847–915. For each phase, samples in (b) and (c) are restricted to those business groups whose core (parent) firms are multi-segment at both the beginning and the end of the phase.

average number of entry is always larger at the firm level than at the group level.[12] This implies that there be substantial portfolio changes *within* groups, that is, segments formerly conducted by the affiliated firms move to their parent firm, and hence counted as entry events at the parent firm level. Although there may be new entries at the affiliate level, the number does not seem to contribute enough to increase the average number of entry at the group level more than that at the parent firm level.

On the other hand, the average number of exit is always larger at the group level than at the firm level, implying that transferring segments from the affiliated firms to the outside of the group have more effects than within-group changes (exit by the parent firm resulting in entry by its affiliates). From these observations we can conjecture that an average business group enters a new segment mainly at the parent firm while it exits from a segment mainly at the affiliated companies.

Table 8.3 (c) shows that the ratio of neither entry nor exit is higher while that of both entry and exit is smaller at the group level than at the parent firm level. This observation implies that a substantial part of restructuring activities are within groups, that is, between parent firms and their affiliates. However, we still find that more than 10% engage in both entry and exit during each phase. The ratio of entry only is lower while that of exit only is higher at the group level than at the firm level. And there is the biggest difference between these two ratios at the group level during Phase III (5.86 and 13.32), while the difference is far smaller at the parent firm level (8.46 and 8.72). This observation is consistent with the clearer trend toward focusing at the group level than at the firm level during Phase III, as shown in Figure 8.2.

In summary, our assertion that portfolio restructuring by the Japanese firm during the 1990s was more active than mere diversification measures indicate seems to still hold at the group level as well, taking into account within-group changes of business configuration.

[12] These comparisons are not affected if we restrict sample parent firms in Table 8.1 (b) to the same samples as those in Table 8.3 (b).

8.4 CAUSES AND EFFECTS OF PORTFOLIO RESTRUCTURING

What determines entry and exit behavior of the firm? How do those determinants affect the firm's portfolio restructuring? Our finding that the firm tends to engage simultaneously in entry and exit suggests that (E1) a factor leading to entry into a new business also encourages exit from existing businesses, and conversely, (E2) a factor discouraging entry also reduces the likelihood of exit. From the viewpoint of diversifying and focusing, these possibilities imply that the common factor affect both diversifying and focusing in the same direction.

However, our finding does not necessarily preclude (F1), a factor leading to entry decreases the likelihood of exit, and hence leads to diversifying, or conversely (F2), a factor discouraging entry increases the likelihood of exit, and hence leads to focusing. The standard analysis of diversification strategy presupposes (F1) and (F2), because observing only the resulting diversifying and focusing in the standard analysis cannot identify cases such as (E1) and (E2). In contrast, we can analyze effects of the factors typically studied as determinants of diversifying and focusing on entry and exit, identify factors characterized as each of (E1), (E2), (F1), and (F2), and then examine how they lead to diversifying or focusing. This procedure enables us to analyze the factors characterizing portfolio restructuring in more detail than the standard analysis.

Since we measure the degree of diversification by the number of segments, whether restructuring leads to diversifying or focusing depends on which of entry and exit dominates. As we have observed in the previous section, there were frequent entry and exit throughout the 1990s. It is thus important to estimate the effects of various possible determinants for entry and exit (the first step), before we estimate how these determinants lead to diversifying or focusing (the second step).

It is also important to study how business portfolio restructuring affects the performance of the firm. We thus briefly examine which combination of entry and exit exhibits better performance after we analyze determinants of entry, exit, diversifying, and focusing.

Some remarks are worth emphasizing here: first, we only analyze entry, exit, diversifying, and focusing of parent firms (not business groups) due to limitation on data at the group level. Second, we study only Phases II and III because no data for 1992 and 1993 is available in Phase I, even at the parent firm level. Third, since single-segment firms cannot focus, in the analysis in subsections 8.4.1 and 8.4.2 we restrict the samples to those parent firms that are multi-segment at the beginning of each phase.

8.4.1 Determinants of Entry and Exit

In this subsection we first analyze what factors determine entry and exit of parent firms in Phases II and III of the 1990s. Although it is possible to estimate what factors lead single-segment firms to diversify, or multi-segment firms to specialize, we restrict our attention to multi-segment parent firms and concentrate on the analysis of entry and exit.

Based on the existing research on diversification (Yoshihara et al., 1981; Berger and Ofek, 1999; Miyajima and Inagaki, 2003), we first discuss explanatory variables for entry and exit. Generally, factors leading to entry and those to exit can be different, but we presuppose that the factors themselves are the same, while the direction of their effects (positive or negative) on entry and exit can be different. It may be useful to classify these factors into two groups, firm specific factors and external environmental factors directly susceptible to the influences of economic environments.

The first firm specific factor is the size of the firm. Large organizations tend to accumulate abundant managerial resources, which represent a high organizational capability. A larger firm is thus more likely to enter new business segments or to diversify. The positive relationship between size and entry can alternatively be derived from the manager's empire building preferences, the larger the firm is, the easier the manager can build empires or the more difficult it is to discipline the manager's activities. On the other hand, large firms rarely choose to exit because their capacity is strong enough to hold out their lines of business using accumulated resources. Furthermore, as is often said, large organizations tend to be slow in decision making, in particular, when they must reverse their previous decisions. The negative effect of large size on exit may apply more to large Japanese firms which emphasize the shakeholders' interests such as employment or long-term relationships with suppliers.

The next firm specific factor is the scope of business portfolio which is measured by the number of segments. For example, if a firm has already managed many segments, adding new segments may harm its efficiency, and hence the firm is less likely to enter new segments further. On the other hand, if the wide scope of businesses means plenty of managerial resources accumulated or high organization capacity, a more diversified firm can enter new segments more easily. In addition, the more segments a firm has, the more likely the firm is to enjoy synergy among them. As for exit, the effects mentioned above will work in the opposite direction. That is, if a firm has enough or excessive segments, it is more likely to exit, and if such a firm possesses plenty of resources, it is less likely to exit.

Portfolio restructuring in the core firm may also be influenced by the business relation with its affiliates. As discussed in subsection 8.3.3, it is a feature of the Japanese business group that business configuration of the parent firm and that of its affiliates frequently overlap. If the overlapping ratio represents the degree of a vertical transaction relationship between the core firm and its affiliates, we expect that it is less costly for the parent firm with a higher overlapping ratio (hence better developed division of labor) to enter new segments. At the same time exit from some segments may be more likely for such a core firm because it can more easily transfer those segments to its affiliates. Note however that if a firm develops more close-knit vertical relationships with the affiliates, it may be more costly for both the core firm and the affiliates to exit.

Performance is a firm specific factor that is also influenced by market conditions. We use return on capital (ROA) as a performance measure. As a firm's performance is lower at the beginning of the phase, it is more likely to exit from its unprofitable segments and enter new ones. Bad performance can serve as a discipline device. For example, Berger and Ofek (1999) point out that the lower the initial ROA is, the more likely the firm is to undertake focusing. The initial ROA is thus likely to be negatively correlated with exit and entry. However, the low ROA also means that the firm has little cash flow. The existing research including Fazzari et al. (1988), Hoshi et al. (1991), and Miyajima et al. (2001) confirms that under certain conditions, investment levels are reactive to volume of internal funds. There is thus a possibility that when the initial performance is low, entry into new segments may be constrained by the shortage of necessary funds, and hence the initial ROA and entry may be positively correlated.

The proposition that the shortage of internal funds constrains new investment is based on the premise that the financial market is incomplete due to information asymmetry hence it may be difficult for the firm to raise funds. To incorporate this possibility we use fixed debt ratio as a variable representing how easy it is for the firm to access banks for raising funds.[13] Controlling cash flow, we expect that the higher the fixed debt ratio is, the less severe the problem due to information asymmetry, and hence the firm is more likely to engage in entry and less likely to exit. Note however that if large debt intensifies the governance by banks, exit may become more active.

We next consider two external environmental factors. The first factor is the growth of the core business. A firm with a faster growing core business faces less demand to enter new segments as well as to stay at segments other than the core business. We thus expect that the growth of the core business is negatively correlated with entry while it is positively correlated with exit. We measure the growth prospect by the mean sales growth rate of the core business within each time phase.

The second external factor is riskiness of the core business. If the core business faces higher market uncertainty, the firm will attempt to enter other segments or diversify its lines of business, and refrain from exit in order to avoid business risk. However, there is also a possibility that exit from segments other than the core business may enable the firm to concentrate their resources on the core business. We measure risk by the standard deviation of the sales growth rate of the core business within each time phase.

We use the following dependent variables to represent portfolio restructuring. The first variable is an entry dummy variable which takes the value of one if a parent firm enters at least one new manufacturing segment during each phase, and zero if there is no entry. The second variable is an exit dummy variable which takes the value of one if a parent firm exits from at least one segment during each phase, and zero if there is no exit. We use bivariate probit models in estimation, because sample firms do not decide entry and exit independently. The results to

---

[13] Though fixed debt includes firm bonds, they account for only a small part of the total fixed debt because our data set includes many small and middle sized firms. The fixed debt ratio is preferable to total debt ratio because the latter generally includes huge amounts of inter-business credits.

follow actually show that they should not be estimated separately. Because there is no data for1992 and 1993 in Phase I, we conduct the cross sectional analysis of Phases II and III, and then compare the results between these phases in order to discuss changes in portfolio restructuring of the late 1990s. For $t = 1997, 2000$, the variables are defined as follows:

ENTRY$_t$: dummy variable indicating whether a firm enters at least one segment or not between year $t - 3$ and t.
EXIT$_t$: dummy variable indicating whether a firm exits from at least one segment or not between year $t - 3$ and t.
ASSET$_{t-3}$: natural logarithm of initial total assets.
SEG$_{t-3}$: number of initial business segments.
OVERLAP$_{t-3}$: initial ratio of overlapping segments to total group segments.
ROA$_{t-3}$: initial ROI (operating income divided by total capital).
LEVERAGE$_{t-3}$: initial leverage (book value of fixed debt divided by total assets).
GROWTH$_t$: mean sales growth rate in core business in each phase.[14]
RISK$_t$: standard deviation of sales growth rates in core business in each phase.[15]

Summary statistics are given in Table 8.4.

Table 8.5 (a) presents the estimation results concerning entry and exit dummy variables of the parent firm. Controlling the number of segments, we do not find a positive effect of the firm size (ASSET$_{t-3}$) on entry. The effects are in fact negative in both phases (the coefficient is almost significant in Phase II), which means that the smaller the firm is, the more actively entry is pursued. One possible interpretation is that a smaller firm can more easily enter niche markets. Another explanation is that large Japanese firms do not suffer from the managers' empire building preferences. The effects of firm size on exit are negative and significant in both phases. This result can be interpreted in various ways as mentioned above: a larger firm has more managerial resources for sustaining loss-making business; it is more costly for a larger firm to exit from the existing segments; and larger organization is slower in decision making. It is also consistent with the hypothesis that large Japanese firms care about various shareholders' interests. Summarizing these results, we find that both entry and exit are less likely to occur as the size becomes larger. It is thus ambiguous whether the net number of segments increases or decreases in size. This question will be answered in the next subsection where we conduct estimation on diversification.

The initial number of segments (SEG$_{t-3}$) has positive and significant effects on both entry and exit in Phases II and III. A firm with more segments actively engages in portfolio restructuring. Although Berger and Ofek (1999) find in their U.S. data that a firm with more segments has a greater chance to pursue focusing, things are not so simple for the Japanese firm. Because more segments facilitate not only exit but also entry, whether restructuring leads to either focusing or diversifying

---

[14] GROWTH$_t$ = $(1/3) \sum_{i=t-3}^{t-1} g_i$ where g_i is the growth rate from year i to year $i + 1$.

[15] RISK$_t$ = $\sqrt{(1/3) \sum_{i=t-3}^{t-1} (gi - \text{GROWTH}_t)^2}$.

Table 8.4. Basic Statistics of Variables

	Phase II ($t = 1997$)				
Variable	Obs	Mean	Std. Dev.	Min	Max
ENTRY$_t$	1926	0.3029	0.4593	0	1
EXIT$_t$	1926	0.4569	0.4983	0	1
ASSET$_{t-3}$	1926	8.9024	1.6768	5.4467	15.6614
ASSET$_t$	1926	8.9685	1.6691	5.4806	15.7650
SEG$_{t-3}$	1926	2.6210	1.0428	2	11
SEG$_t$	1926	2.3744	1.1638	1	11
OVERLAP$_{t-3}$	1125	0.3198	0.2758	0	1
ROA$_{t-3}$	1926	−0.0035	0.0475	−0.5193	0.3941
ROA$_t$	1926	−0.0011	0.0446	−0.3270	0.6206
LEVERAGE$_{t-3}$	1926	0.2689	0.1646	0	0.9255
GROWTH$_t$	1799	0.0351	0.1125	−0.2681	2.4630
RISK$_t$	1799	0.1260	0.1898	0.0009	4.8442
OnlyEXIT$_t$	1926	0.2321	0.4223	0	1
OnlyENTRY$_t$	1926	0.0774	0.2672	0	1
BOTH$_t$	1926	0.2248	0.4176	0	1
	Phase III ($t = 2000$)				
Variable	Obs	Mean	Std. Dev.	Min	Max
ENTRY$_t$	1894	0.2555	0.4363	0	1
EXIT$_t$	1894	0.4256	0.4946	0	1
ASSET$_{t-3}$	1894	8.9772	1.6673	5.4806	15.7650
ASSET$_t$	1894	8.9845	1.6981	5.3936	15.9310
SEG$_{t-3}$	1894	2.6014	1.0160	2	11
SEG$_t$	1894	2.3664	1.1454	1	10
OVERLAP$_{t-3}$	1142	0.3206	0.2720	0	1
ROA$_{t-3}$	1894	−0.0002	0.0403	−0.1701	0.2732
ROA$_t$	1894	0.0002	0.0437	−0.2067	0.2703
LEVERAGE$_{t-3}$	1894	0.2446	0.1663	0	0.9445
GROWTH$_t$	1782	0.0077	0.1106	−0.4860	2.9144
RISK$_t$	1782	0.1324	0.1779	0.0024	5.3037
OnlyEXIT$_t$	1894	0.2381	0.4260	0	1
OnlyENTRY$_t$	1894	0.0681	0.2520	0	1
BOTH$_t$	1894	0.1874	0.3904	0	1

depends on which of exit and entry is more active. This finding is consistent with the observation discussed in subsection 8.3.2 that firms often undertake entry and exit simultaneously. It suggests that entry into new segments may not result in too many segments because it is offset by exit. The finding also suggests that the costs associated with exit from the existing businesses, such as dealing with excess workforce, be reduced by new entry. Note that a firm with more segments tends to be larger, while our estimation shows that the number of segments and firm size have negative effects on entry and exit. It is not clear which of large firms or medium and small sized firms engage in portfolio restructuring more actively.

Table 8.5. Estimations of Entry, Exit, and Diversification

| | (a) ENTRY and EXIT | | | | (b) DIVERSIFICATION | |
| | Phase II ($t = 1997$) | | Phase III ($t = 2000$) | | | |
Variables	ENTRY	EXIT	ENTRY	EXIT	Phase II	Phase III
ASSET$_{t-3}$	-0.0432	-0.1349***	-0.0200	-0.0506**	0.0624***	0.0498***
	(-1.60)	(-5.17)	(-0.73)	(-1.94)	(3.92)	(3.37)
SEG$_{t-3}$	0.1495***	0.2332***	0.1483***	0.2140***	0.7956***	0.8212***
	(4.07)	(6.25)	(4.03)	(5.85)	(34.94)	(39.03)
OVERLAP$_{t-3}$	-0.0527	-0.2299	-0.1290	-0.0834	0.1189	-0.0154
	(-0.33)	(-1.52)	(-0.79)	(-0.55)	(1.25)	(-0.18)
ROA$_{t-3}$	-0.1590	-0.7311	0.4678	0.4651	0.0044	-0.0013
	(-0.15)	(-0.71)	(0.41)	(0.43)	(0.95)	(-1.01)
LEVERAGE$_{t-3}$	0.5054*	0.3626	0.3914	0.3967	0.1044	-0.1443
	(1.71)	(1.27)	(1.35)	(1.44)	(0.58)	(-1.01)
GROWTH$_t$	-1.8049***	1.2072**	-2.3046***	1.3065**	-1.9429***	-2.2176***
	(-3.07)	(2.10)	(-4.02)	(2.35)	(-5.39)	(-6.75)
RISK$_t$	0.8492**	-0.1731	1.6895***	1.8395***	0.5761***	-0.5233**
	(2.19)	(-0.55)	(4.06)	(4.44)	(2.82)	(-2.20)
const	-0.7337***	0.4130	-1.1528***	-0.6739**	-0.3296**	-0.0891
	(-2.63)	(1.59)	(-4.00)	(-2.48)	(-2.02)	(-0.57)
Number	1054		1074		1055	1082
Log Likelihood	-1212.0853		-1185.5717			
rho	15.12		13.84			
adj. R^2					0.5878	0.5879

Notes: The dependent variable in (b) is SEG$_t$. Figures in parentheses are t values. The asterisks denote levels of significance. ***: 1%; **: 5%; and *: 10%. Samples are restricted to those parent firms that are multi-segment at the beginning of each phase.

The coefficients of OVERLAP$_{t-3}$ are all negative but not significant. The coefficient is almost significant for exit in Phase II, which weakly suggests that a firm whose segments are more overlapping with those of its affiliates is less likely to undertake exit.

LEVERAGE$_{t-3}$ has positive effects on both entry and exit, and the coefficient is significant in entry in Phase II. The result implies that a firm with easier access to external funds engage in both entry and exit more actively. In other words, we can conjecture that such a firm raised funds necessary for entry and exit through borrowing. Alternatively, if high leverage intensifies the governance by main banks, the result suggests that bank governance may force the firm to undertake not only exit but also entry, and hence to rearrange or relocate its business configuration, rather than to simply engage in focusing.[16]

The coefficients of GROWTH$_t$ are negative for entry and positive for exit in both Phases II and III. Moreover, they are all significant. When the core business steadily grows, entry is restrained on one hand, and on the other hand exit is promoted. We thus find that the steady growth of the core business causes the firm to move toward focusing in both time phases.

The effects of RISK$_t$ are somewhat complicated. The effect on entry is positive and significant in either of the phases, while both the absolute value of the coefficient and the t value are larger for Phase III than Phase II. It suggests that risk in the core business should encourage the firm to enter new business segments at the end of the 1990s. However, the effect on exit is also positive and significant in Phase III. This means that an increase in risk in the core business leads to more entry and exit, and hence more active portfolio shifting. Whether the increase in RISK$_t$ leads to diversifying or focusing in Phase III will be answered in the next subsection.

8.4.2 Determinants of Diversification

If an explanatory variable affects entry and exit in the same direction, which effect is stronger? To answer this question, we must estimate diversification as the net effect of entry and exit.

Table 8.6. Causal Relationships in Diversifying and Focusing

Entry	Exit	Diversifying/Focusing
+	−	?
+	−	Diversifying
−	+	Focusing
−	−	?

---

[16] Lang et al. (1996) find a negative correlation between the debt ratio and the growth of the firm.

Table 8.6 summarizes the relationships of entry and exit with diversifying and focusing. Factors (explanatory variables) have either positive or negative effects on entry and exit. When a factor brings a positive effect on entry and a negative effect on exit, it drives the firm to diversifying. In contrast, when a factor has a positive effect on exit and a negative effect on entry, it leads the firm to focusing. When a factor has positive effects both on entry and exit or negative effects on both, whether the factor leads to diversifying or focusing is ambiguous. In these cases, estimation on diversification can find on which of entry or exit the factor has a larger effect. The combination of these three estimations concerning entry, exit, and diversification will clarify how individual explanatory variables result in diversifying or focusing through their effects on entry and exit.

We estimate diversification using the following partial adjustment model. A firm makes an effort to adjust its business configuration by increasing or decreasing the number of segments to realize the desirable number of segments (the degree of diversification). The firm, however, can adjust only part of the business configuration during a given period. That is, it is assumed that the difference between the desirable number of segments and the actual number can be fulfilled only by the rate λ $(0 < \lambda < 1)$.

[number of segments to be increased or decreased during the phase]
  $= \lambda \cdot$ ([desirable number of segments] $-$ [initial number of segments])

This is rewritten as follows:

[number of segments at the end of the phase]
  $= \lambda \cdot$ [desirable number of segments] $+ (1 - \lambda) \cdot$ [initial number of segments]

We estimate this equation by changing the dependent variable in the previous estimation of entry and exit in subsection 8.4.1 to the number of segments at the end of the phase. The OLS estimation results are reported in Table 8.5 (b). A noteworthy result is that some coefficients that are not significant in the separate estimation of exit and entry can become significant in this estimation on diversification.

The adjustment parameter can be obtained from subtracting from one the estimated coefficient of the number of initial segments. It is 0.204 ($= 1 - 0.796$) in Phase II and 0.179 ($= 1 - 0.821$) in Phase III, and hence the adjustment speed (toward focusing) slightly decelerated from Phase II to III.[17]

The effects of firm size on diversification are positive and significant. We want to emphasize that this effect does not come from the advantage of large firms in entering new businesses. Since firm size restrains both entry and exit simultaneously (Table 8.5 (a) discussed in subsection 8.4.1), the positive effect of firm size on diversification implies that size negatively affects exit more than entry. This observation is in contrast to the standard interpretation that larger firm size leads

---

[17] Although the result of this model itself does not show us whether there is diversifying or focusing, the analysis in section 8.3 tells us that the firms were likely to be focusing.

to accumulation of more managerial resources as in Yoshihara et al. (1981) and Miyajima and Inagaki (2003). It is crucial to analyze entry and exit before estimating diversification; otherwise, the interpretation of the firm's diversifying behavior would be drastically different and possibly misleading.

Although the signs of the coefficients of ROA, the initial leverage, and the overlapping ratio change from Phase II to Phase III, neither of them are significant. In particular, the coefficient of initial leverage is not significant, probably because higher leverage encourages both entry and exit, and hence these effects cancel out.

The effects of sales growth rate in the core business are significant and negative in both phases. This is a natural consequence from the finding in subsection 8.4.1 that high sales growth rate has a negative effect on entry while it has a positive effect on exit. This finding is also consistent with the result by Berger and Ofek (1999) that the firm with more segments is more likely to perform business refocusing.[18]

Of particular interest is the effect of instability in the core business on diversification: It is positive and significant in Phase II, while it is negative and significant in Phase III. This suggests that the reason for diversification might have changed from Phase II to Phase III. Although the estimation result for Phase II is consistent with the standard hypothesis of diversification for spreading risk, the result for Phase III is in contrast, and is different from the empirical results by Miyajima and Inagaki (2003) which confirm the risk spreading hypothesis in this phase. We find in subsection 8.4.1 that the more risky the core business is, the more active both entry and exit are in Phase III. Taking this into account, we can infer that focusing in Phase III was caused by the positive effect of exit dominating over entry. One interpretation of the result is that responding to the increasing risk in the core business, the firm intensively used its resources on the core business as well as new segments related to the core business, while exiting from many other segments. This tendency corresponds to "selection and focusing," often used as a catch phrase by many Japanese firms in these phases.[19]

8.4.3 Portfolio Restructuring and Performance

In this subsection, we analyze how portfolio restructuring affects performance of the parent firm. As briefly summarized in section 8.1, there is a plethora of existing literature concerning the diversification discount in the U.S., and a further examination of whether diversification may destroy the firm's value, causing the firm to pursue focusing. Research on Japanese firms also follows this literature for the most part. However, as we mentioned above, portfolio restructuring as observed during the 1990s is not a simple focusing strategy.

One prominent feature of business portfolio restructuring by Japanese firms found in our analysis is that many firms simultaneously pursued entry into new

---

[18] Note that Berger and Ofek (1999) use the sales growth rate of the whole businesses rather than the core business.

[19] See the discussion at the end of subsection 8.3.2.

segments and exit from some existing segments. In this respect, it is crucial to examine entry and exit not only individually but also their combination and the resultant affect on performance.[20]

We define the explanatory variables representing the combination of entry and exit as follows. Taking the case in which "a firm neither enters nor exits between years $t - 3$ and t" as a base, let OnlyEXIT$_t$ be the dummy variable indicating whether "a firm exited, but did not enter," OnlyENTRY$_t$ the dummy variable indicating whether "the firm only entered, but did not exit between years $t - 3$ and t," and BOTH$_t$ the dummy variable indicating whether "a firm both entered and exited between years $t - 3$ and t." We also include the firm size (ASSET$_{t-3}$), and the fixed debt ratio (LEVERAGE$_{t-3}$) as explanatory variables.

The performance of the parent firm is measured by ROA (operating income divided by total assets). Although all our sample parent firms belong to the manufacturing sector, ROA can still be affected by industry specific characteristics. To cope with this problem, we use the "standardized" ROA which is obtained by taking the difference from the average ROA over the firms with the same core business, denoted by adjROA$_t$. The model to be tested is as follows.

$$\text{adjROA}_t = f(\text{OnlyEXIT}_t, \text{OnlyENTRY}_t, \text{BOTH}_t, \text{ASSET}_{t-3}, \text{LEVERAGE}_{t-3})$$

where t is either 1997 or 2000, and the variables are defined as follows:

adjROA$_t$: standardized ROA at the end of year t.
OnlyEXIT$_t$: dummy variable indicating whether a firm only exited or not between year $t - 3$ and t.
OnlyENTRY$_t$: dummy variable indicating whether a firm only entered or not between year $t - 3$ and t.
BOTH$_t$: dummy variable indicating whether a firm simultaneously entered and exited between year $t - 3$ and t.
ASSET$_{t-3}$: natural logarithm of initial total assets.
LEVERAGE$_{t-3}$: initial leverage (book value of fixed debt divided by total assets).

Table 8.7 presents the results of the cross-section OLS estimation of these equations for Phases II and III. It is worth noting that the results are very different between Phase II and Phase III. It suggests that economic conditions for performance may have drastically changed. As observed in section 8.3, portfolio restructuring was likely to be performed more actively in Phase II than in Phase III. However, the estimation results imply that these efforts did not bring about improvement in performance in Phase II.

On the other hand, in Phase III, the coefficient of BOTH$_t$ is positive and significant, while the coefficients of the other types of restructuring are not significant. The performance is likely to improve only when both entry and exit take place simultaneously. Along with the estimation result in the previous subsection that the lower the initial performance in Phase III, the more actively the firm engages in entry and exit, this result implies that portfolio restructuring

---

[20] Note again that due to [a] restriction of financial data concerning affiliated companies, we will study only the relationship between the parent firm's restructuring and its performance.

Table 8.7. Estimations of Restructuring Effect on Performance

Variables	adjROA	
	Phase II	Phase III
OnlyEXIT$_t$	−0.00322	−0.00003
	(−1.23)	(−0.01)
OnlyENTRY$_t$	−0.00028	−0.00151
	(−0.07)	(−0.35)
BOTH$_t$	−0.00078	0.00622**
	(−0.29)	(2.18)
ASSET$_{t-3}$	0.00059	0.00195***
	(0.93)	(3.05)
LEVERAGE$_{t-3}$	−0.01298**	−0.02727***
	(−2.19)	(−4.58)
const	−0.00207	−0.01191*
	(−0.32)	(−1.84)
Number	1932	1918
adj.R^2	0.0020	0.0196

Notes: Figures in parentheses are t values. The asterisks denote levels of significance.***: 1%; **: 5%; and *: 10%. Samples are restricted to those parent firms that are multi-segment at the beginning of each phase.

with the combination of entry and exit is likely to improve the end performance in this phase.

While the existing research for the U.S. firms only studies the relationship between diversifying/focusing and performance, our estimation results show that restructuring only with entry or exit does not lead to improvement in performance unless both entry and exit are pursued simultaneously. In this sense there is a complementarity between entry and exit. We believe this finding has extremely important implications for Japanese business restructuring at the end of the 1990s, because this feature highlights a difference in restructuring between Japan and the U.S. Why this complementary effect was not observed in Phase II is an open question. However, it can be said that this is consistent with the estimation result of RISK$_t$ in subsection 8.4.2 in that in Phase II the risk spreading hypothesis is valid and the profit itself may be lowered. Note that the estimation results do not change if we estimate the performance at the end of Phase III using explanatory variables of business restructuring in Phase II.

Finally, we briefly review the effects of other variables. Firm size does not affect performance in Phase II, while it has a positive and significant effect in Phase III. This suggests that Phase II is an unusual period. The coefficient of the leverage is significantly negative in both Phases II and III. Controlling the types of portfolio restructuring, we find that the debt ratio negatively affects performance. This implies that the firm with a higher debt ratio is likely to suffer from low performance, given a particular type of portfolio restructuring. And this negative effect is stronger in Phase III.

8.5 CONCLUDING REMARKS

The main objective of this chapter is to argue that it is necessary to extend research on business portfolio restructuring by Japanese firms in the 1990s in the following two directions. One is to examine the firm's business diversifying and/or focusing behavior as a combination between entry into new segments and exit from existing segments. The other is to expand the scope from the firm level to the group level including the core firm and its affiliates. In particular, we demonstrate that firms and groups actively performed entry and exit simultaneously during the 1990s, often viewed negatively as a lost decade. The finding that entry into new segments was actively pursued has also an important implication for industrial policies, since it suggests the importance of policies to finance funds and provide valuable information for middle and small sized firms to transform their business configurations effectively.

Last, let us summarize some future research issues. First, because of data limitation, our regression analyses have been restricted to the parent firm level. It is a promising future research topic, to analyze the relationship between the parent firm and its affiliated companies as well as to extend the analyses to the business group. Second, we highlight the strategy pursuing entry and exit simultaneously, while some firms engaged in only entry or exit, or neither of them. It is also important to examine the decision making process of these strategies.

REFERENCES

Berger, P. G. and E. Ofek (1995), "Diversification's Effect on Firm Value," *Journal of Financial Economics* 37: 39–65.

—— —— (1999), "Causes and Effects of Corporate Refocusing Programs," *Review of Financial Studies* 12(2): 311–45.

Campa, J. M. and S. Kedia (2002), "Explaining the Diversification Discount," *Journal of Finance,* LVII(4): 1731–62.

Comment, R. and G. A. Jarrell (1995), "Corporate Focus and Stock Returns," *Journal of Financial Economics* 37: 67–87.

Daley, L., V. Mehrotra, and R. Sivakumar (1997), "Corporate Focus and Value Creation: Evidence from Spinoffs," *Journal of Financial Economics* 45: 257–81.

Denis, D. J., D. K. Denis, and A. Sarin (1997), "Agency Problems, Equity Ownership, and Corporate Diversification," *Journal of Finance* LII(1): 135–60.

Fazzari, S., G. Hubbard, and B. Petersen (1988), "Financing Constraints and Corporate Investment," *Brooking Papers on Economic Activity* 1: 141–206.

Funaoka, F. (2003), "Corporate Diversification and Performance [in Japanese]," Y. Matsuta and M. Shimizu (eds.), *Series Micro Statistical Analysis Vol. 4,* Nippon Hyoron sha.

Graham, J. R., M. L. Lemmon, and J. G. Wolf (2002), "Does Corporate Diversification Destroy Value?" *Journal of Finance* LVII(2): 695–720.

Goto, A. (1981), "Statistical Evidence on the Diversification of Japanese Large Firms," *Journal of Industrial Economics* 29.

Hiramoto, T. (2002), "Business Diversification and Firm Value [in Japanese]," *Gendai Finance* 12.

Hoshi, T., A. Kashyap, and D. Scharfstein (1991), "The Choice between Public and Private Debt: An Analysis of Post Deregulation Corporate Financing in Japan," *NBER Working Paper*, 4421.

Itoh, H. (2003), "Corporate Restructuring in Japan Part I: Can M-Form Organization Manage Diverse Businesses?" *Japanese Economic Review* 54: 49–73.

Japan Fair Trade Commission (1992), *Changing Economic Structures and Industrial Organization*.

Lang, L. H. P. and R. M. Stulz(1994), "Tobin's *q*, Corporate Diversification and Firm Performance," *Journal of Political Economy* 102: 1248–80.

—— E. Ofek, and R. M. Stulz (1996), "Leverage, Investment and Firm Growth," *Journal of Financial Economics* 40: 3–29.

Mansi, S. A. and D. M. Reeb (2002), "Corporate Diversification: What Gets Discounted?" *Journal of Finance* LVII(5): 2167–83.

Miyajima, H., Y. Arikawa, and S. Saito (2001), "Japanese Corporate Governance and Overinvestment: The Comparative Analysis of the Periods Before and After the Oil Shock and Those of the Bubble Economy in Japan [in Japanese]," *Financial Review* 60.

—— K. Inagaki (2003), "Report of the Research Committee on the Diversification of Japanese Companies and Corporate Governance: Analysis of Business Strategy, Group Management, and Decentralized Organizations [in Japanese]," Policy Research Institute, Ministry of Finance.

Morikawa, M. (1998a), "Entry into New Businesses and Exit from Existing Businesses: An Empirical Analysis of the Japanese Firm [in Japanese]," Discussion Paper #98-DOJ-87, Research Institute of MITI.

—— (1998b), "Business Activities of Parent Companies and Subsidiaries: An Empirical Analysis on the Causes and Consequences of Diversification and Concentration by Japanese Companies [in Japanese]," *Tsusan Kenkyu Review* 11.

Wernerfelt, B. and C. A. Montgomery (1988), "Tobin's *q* and the Importance of Focus in Firm Performance," *American Economic Review* 78: 246–50.

Yasuki, H. (1995), "Issues and Current Status on Corporate Diversification [in Japanese]," *Kansai Daigaku Keizai Ronshu* 44(5).

Yoshihara, H., A. Sakuma, H. Itami, and T. Kagono (1981), *The Diversification Strategy of the Japanese Firm* [in Japanese], Nihon Keizai Shinbun Sha.

9

Corporate Finance and Human Resource Management in Japan[1]

Masahiro Abe and Takeo Hoshi

9.1 INTRODUCTION

In the narrowest definition, corporate governance is "the ways in which the suppliers of finance to corporations assure themselves of getting a return on their investment" (Shleifer and Vishny 1997: 737). Most studies on corporate governance in economics have traditionally used this narrow definition when they examined the corporate governance of individual companies or the systems of corporate governance in different countries. Some recent research, however, started to stress the importance of understanding corporate governance more broadly as an institutional arrangement that involves not only managers and financiers but also other stakeholders such as workers, suppliers, and others. For example, Tirole (2001: 4) defines corporate governance as "design of institutions that induce or force management to internalize the welfare of stakeholders." Similarly Aoki (2001: 281) defines corporate governance as "a set of self-enforceable rules (formal or informal) that regulates the contingent action choices of the stakeholders (investors, workers, and managers)."

When one takes these broader views of corporate governance, it becomes clear that a system of corporate governance consists of various sub-systems. For example, corporate governance certainly includes the institution that governs the relation between managers and financiers (including both shareholders and creditors). In addition, corporate governance also includes the system of human resource management, which controls the relation between management and labor. Other institutions that regulate the relation between managers and other stakeholders, such as customers, suppliers, and sometimes local community in general, are also parts of corporate governance.

As Aoki (2001) points out, the various aspects of corporate governance are not combined randomly. Corporate governance is a system in the sense that

[1] A preliminary version of this paper was presented at "Corporate Governance from an International Perspective: Diversity or Convergence" held on January 8 and 9, 2002. We thank Masahiko Aoki, Gregory Jackson, and Mari Sako for useful comments. We thank Tatsuyoshi Okimoto and Kazuyuki Sakamoto for research assistance.

these various sub-systems are integrated to reinforce each other. For example, financial arrangement that heavily relies on the market for corporate control in disciplining the managers may work better with human resource management that puts less emphasis on firm-specific skills and on the job training than an alternative that stresses firm-specific skills that are acquired on the job.

This chapter examines such link between the financial aspect and the human resource management aspect of corporate governance. There is an increasing body of literature that considers the linkages between the sub-systems of (broadly defined) corporate governance. Many studies look at cross-country correlations of various aspects of the corporate governance. For example, Jackson (2004) finds close correlation between the corporate finance and labor management practices at country level.

Some studies examine the linkage by comparing different firms within a country. For Japan, for example, Ahmadjian and Robinson (2001) find that the firms with high foreign ownership and low bank ownership are more likely to downsize their workforce. Also using the firm level data from Japan, Abe (2002) finds that the firms with close main bank ties adjust their employment only slowly. We follow a similar approach and study the linkage by looking at data from individual Japanese corporations. Japanese firms used to have a well known system of corporate governance with seemingly complementary sub-systems. Recently, some corporations started to show substantial deviations from the traditional characteristics in the corporate finance and in human resource management. We study if the recent changes in both aspects of corporate governance are related. We examine if the firms that have non-traditional corporate financing also tend to have non-traditional employment practices.

The rest of the chapter is organized as follows. The next section briefly describes the stylized characteristics of the Japanese corporate governance to set the background. We especially focus on the complimentarity that seems to exist between the financial arrangement and human resource management. Section 9.3 discusses the recent changes that some Japanese corporations started to show in the corporate finance aspect and the human resource management aspect respectively of the corporate governance. Section 9.4 presents a simple theoretical model that helps us understand the potential complimentarity between the two aspects of the corporate governance. Section 9.5 reports the results of empirical investigation. Section 9.6 concludes by pointing out the agenda for future research on the link between corporate finance and human resource management.

9.2 JAPANESE CORPORATE GOVERNANCE

Many researchers have pointed out that the corporate governance of Japanese firms fits the stakeholder view of the corporate governance very well. Shareholders seem to play rather a limited role in monitoring and disciplining corporate management. Corporations seem to be operated in the interests of many types of stakeholders, including employees and customers.

The "Japanese" corporate governance is characterized by long-term relationships between the corporation and its many stakeholders.[2] A Japanese corporation has a long-term relationship with a bank, which is typically the largest lender, holds substantial amount of shares, and sometimes sends its (former) employees as board members of the corporation. In addition to this main bank relationship, the corporation also typically has a long-term relationship with other shareholders, who are most likely other corporations, and the corporation often holds shares of those corporations through "cross-shareholding" arrangement.

There exists a long-term relationship between the corporation and its employees as well. In the practice of "lifetime employment," regular employees are expected to continue working for the same company until the mandatory retirement age. The "seniority wage" that increases as long as a worker works for the same country gives a strong incentive for workers to stay. In return, the corporation provides various trainings for the workers to improve their skills. The corporation does not have to worry about losing the skilled workers to other companies. The workers do not mind acquiring skills that are only useful in the current company. Thus, the lifetime employment system encourages the development of human resource management that stresses the importance of firm-specific skills.

Long-term relationships are also observed between a Japanese firm and other types of stakeholders, such as customers and suppliers. Long-term relationships between a manufacturer and its core suppliers, most prominently observed in the auto industry, are a canonical example.

The various aspects of Japanese corporate governance are related and reinforce each other. In this sense, the Japanese corporate governance is considered to form a system of mutually complementary elements. For example, dependence on concentrated bank loans (rather than diffusedly held bonds or stocks) makes it easier for financially distressed firms to renegotiate its obligations. This reduces the chance of (premature) corporate failures and protects other long-term commitment, such as lifetime employment.

9.3 CHANGES IN THE JAPANESE CORPORATE GOVERNANCE

The Japanese corporate governance that we briefly described in the last section started to change in various ways around the late 1970s. This section reviews major changes in the two aspects that this paper focuses on: corporate finance and human resource management.

---

[2] Surveys of Japanese corporate governance include Fukao (1995); Hoshi (1998); Kojima (1997); and Aoki (2001, chap. 13).

Deregulation in corporate financing that started in the late 1970s allowed many large Japanese firms to use capital markets (rather than banks) for their financing.[3] Many corporations increased the bond issues (including convertibles and warrants) in domestic as well as foreign markets, and reduced their dependence on bank loans, a hallmark of Japanese corporate financing.

Cross-shareholding, another characteristic of Japanese corporate governance, also started to change. The change started later than the decline in the bank dependence. The magnitude of the change, however, has been equally dramatic. Kuroki (2003) develops a measure of cross-shareholding by first calculating the proportion of shares in a company held by the other companies whose shares are also held by the company and then taking the average for all listed firms in the Tokyo Stock Exchange. According to this measure, the cross-shareholding declined from 18% in the early 1990s to less than 8% by March 2003.

As the Japanese corporations and banks shed the shares that they traditionally held in each other, foreign investors gradually increased the ownership in the Tokyo Stock Exchange.[4] This is another notable change in Japanese corporate governance. The share of foreign ownership in the Tokyo Stock Exchange increased from about 4% in the early 1990s to more than 18% in 2002.

The human resource management aspect of corporate governance also started to show some remarkable changes after the 1990s. The changes have been observed in many areas of the human resource management practices, including employment practice, workers training, and promotion system.

The lifetime employment that characterized Japanese human resource management seems to have started to change in the 1990s. Some observers even claim that the lifetime employment system no longer exists (see Ono 2000 and Takahashi 2001). Although it is too soon to declare the death of the lifetime employment system, there is some evidence that suggests the popularity of the practice is indeed declining. Table 9.1 shows the response to a couple of questions posed in a 1998 survey by the Japan Institute of Labor (*Survey on Human Resource Management and Job Consciousness under Structural Adjustment*). When corporations are asked about the typical tenure of employees, about 80% of them answered that employees typically work at the same company till the retirement age and that some continue to work or are reemployed for a certain period thereafter. This tendency does not seem to depend on the type of jobs (management, specialist, clerical, or blue-collar). When the same corporations are asked about what they expect to happen in the future, only 60% of them answered that the tendency to work till the retirement age and possibly beyond will continue; 20–30% of respondents believe that it will become more likely for workers to be sent to work for other related companies or voluntarily quit before the retirement age. The expected change is clearest for management and white-collar jobs. Thus, many corporations are expecting that it will become increasingly difficult to preserve the lifetime employment system.

---

[3] For more detailed discussions, see, for example, Hoshi and Kashyap (2001, chap. 7).

[4] See Ahmadjian in this volume (Chapter 4) for more details of this process.

Table 9.1 Retirement Practice by Job Category (%)

	Managers		Specialists		Clerical workers		Blue-collar workers	
	Current practice	Expected in future	Current practice	Expected in future	Current practice	Expected in future	Current practice	Expected in future
No mandatory retirement	1.8	1.4	2	2	1.2	1.2	1.5	1.5
Mandatory retirement at a certain age but many re-employed after that	79	60.9	79.6	63.8	78	61.6	78.9	63.6
Mandatory retirement but many transferred to related companies before that	10.7	27.8	7.8	22.4	7.8	21.3	6.5	17.4
Many retires voluntarily before the mandatory retirement	2.7	2	1.7	4.6	2.6	6.3	4.7	8.9
Others	7.7	7.8	8	7.3	10.4	9.6	8.4	8.5

Note: The question asks each firm to choose a statement that best fits the current retirement practice and one that fits the future expected retirement practice for each job category.

Source: Japan Institute of Labor (1998).

In addition to changes in the lifetime employment practice, the practice in recruiting new workers also seems to be changing. Japanese corporations have traditionally given a preference to new (university) graduates when they hire new workers. However, the practice seems to be changing. Figure 9.1 shows the proportion of companies implementing mid-career hiring for each year from 1994 to 2002. Despite the worsening recession and increasing unemployment rate after 1998, the ratio of companies conducting mid-career hiring has been increasing. This suggests that mid-career hiring, which was not a usual practice for Japanese corporations, is becoming more standard.

The practice in termination of employment is also going through a change. Figure 9.2 shows the percentage of companies implementing employment adjustment. The figure also plots the proportion of companies that adjusted the labor force through dismissal or early retirement. Employment adjustment has previously been characterized by firms first implementing restrictions on overtime, then suspending the hiring of part-time workers and new graduates if necessary, and finally, only when unavoidable, encouraging early retirement and/or imposing outright dismissal. It is clear from Figure 9.2, however, that employment adjustment by means of voluntary retirement and dismissal has been increasing after 1998.

The increase in the adjustments of labor force through dismissal or early retirement is consistent with the finding on the increase in the speed of employment

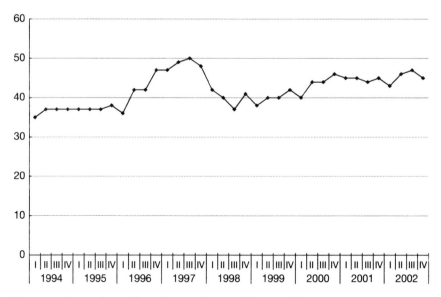

Figure 9.1 Proportion of firms that conducted mid-career hiring

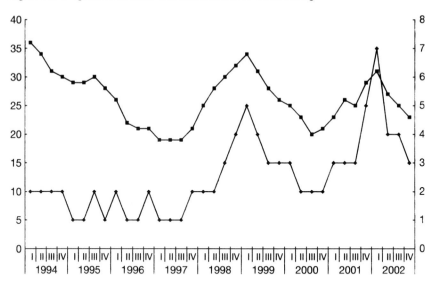

Figure 9.2 Proportion of firms that adjusted the labor force through dismissal or early retirement

Notes: ▬■▬ carried out the employment adjustment (left axis) ▬◆▬ dismissal/encouraging voluntary (right axis).

Table 9.2 Speed of Employment Adjustment

Period	Speed of adjustment	Implied number of quarters for full adjustment
1977.II–85.II	0.199	5
85.III–91.I	0.197	5.1
91.II–2001.IV	0.213	4.7

Source: White Paper on Welfare and Labor (Ministry of Health, Labor, and Welfare 2002).

adjustment estimated from the aggregate data. Table 9.2 reports the result of such a study. The table shows that the estimated speed of adjustment in the 1990s is greater than in the 1980s. Abe (2002) examines the relation between corporate governance structure and the speed of employment adjustment, and finds that the speed of adjustment is higher for the firms with smaller shareholding by financial institutions. Thus, Abe's result suggests that the changes in employment practice may be related to the changes in corporate financing that we discussed in the last section.

The education and training of workers have also been changing. Table 9.3 reports results from a survey conducted by the Sanwa Research Institute (2000). In 2000, 46.2% of the firms had education and training programs for all regular white-collar workers, and 51.6% of them provided such programs for selected workers only. When asked the plans for the future, only 26.6% answered that they will provide training programs for all regular white-collar workers while 71.3% of them plan to restrict the programs only for selected workers. The methods of training are also changing. In 2000, 80.8% of the firms trained workers primarily through on-the-job training (OJT). The proportion of the firms that plan to provide training primarily through OJT in the future drops to 72.3%. On the other hand, the proportion of the firms that primarily use off-the-job training (OffJT) is expected to increase from current 14.1–22.5%. Finally, the content of education is also expected to change. In 2000, 33.6% of firms allowed the workers to choose the content of their training. The proportion is expected to increase to 42.8%. In summary, many firms are planning to change their training

Table 9.3 Education and Training of White-Collar Workers

	Current policy		Future policy	
	A	B	A	B
Training provided for: (A) all workers or (B) selected workers	46.2	51.6	26.6	71.3
Method of Training: (A) OJT or (B) Off-JT	80.8	14.1	76.3	22.5
Training content selected by (A) employees or (B) company	33.6	64.3	42.8	54.8

Note: Table shows % of firms in each category.

Source: Investigation Report About IT Revolution Effect on Labour (Sanwa Research Institute 2000).

programs to be more individualized, primarily based on off-the-job training, and given only to selected workers.

Changes are observed in the system of promotion, too. The Japanese system of promotion has been traditionally characterized by "delayed promotion" and the "seniority wages." The delayed promotion was considered useful to keep the workers motivated (for career concerns) for a long time. The seniority wages discouraged the workers from leaving companies after short tenures and hence reinforced the lifetime employment.

Both delayed promotion and seniority wages started to change in many corporations. For example, Sanwa Research Institute (2000) reports that 39.5% of the respondent firms had brought forward the period when workers are put on different career tracks, suggesting a change in the delayed promotion. 61.6% are planning to move the period (yet) earlier in the near future. The use of seniority wages is also declining. In determining wages, many companies are starting to consider the factors other than seniority, which include workers' ability, performance and achievements. As shown in Table 9.4, firms that took into account the performance and achievements of management level employees in wage determination rose from 55.1% in 1998 to 64.2% in 2000. The firms that reflected the ability of management level staff to execute their tasks in their salaries increased from 69.9% to 79.7%. The trend is not limited to management personnel but more widely spread.

Another evidence of weakening seniority wages can be found in Table 9.5. The table shows that individual performance is reflected in wage levels in 65% of firms for management personnel and 66.1% for non-management jobs. Among these, 41.3% (39.5%) of firms have increased wage differentials over the past five years for management (non-management) jobs. In the next three years, 51.2% of them plan to increase the wage differentials among management personnel and 49.2% plan to do so for non-management employees. Sanwa Research Institute (2000) survey also obtains a similar result. In 2000, 42.3% of the firms that responded to the survey had increased wage differentials, while 65.2% intended to do so (again) in the future.

Table 9.4 Factors that Determine the Wages (Multiple Answers)

	Survey year	Factor for wage determination			
		Job or duty	Job performance	Achievement	Age/length of service, educational background
Administrative	1988	70.1	69.6	55.1	72.6
position	2000	72.8	79.7	64.2	73.9
Other than	1998	68.8	69.2	55.3	78.5
administrative position	2000	70.6	77.3	62.3	80.6

Source: 'Survey on Working Condition' (Ministry of Health, Labor, and Welfare 2000).

Table 9.5 Proportion of Firms that have Changed or Plan to Change the Wage System (%)

		Last five years				Next three years			
	Reflect an individual's performance	Changed the wage system	Expanded wage range	Reduced wage range	No change	Plan to change the wage system	Expand wage range	Reduce wage range	No plan to change
Administrative positions	[65.0]	100.0	49.7	41.3	8.4	50.3	54.4	51.2	3.2
Other positions	[66.1]	100.0	49.3	39.5	9.8	50.7	53.2	49.2	4.0

Note: A value in [ ] is % of firm whose wage system reflects on individual's performance.

Source: 'Survey on Working Condition' (Ministry of Health, Labor, and Welfare 2000).

9.4 COMPLEMENTARITY: A SIMPLE MODEL

The last section described the changes in both financing and human resource management practices of Japanese corporations. Are those two changes related? Because corporate finance and human resource management are two important aspects of corporate governance, it is likely that these changes are related. As one element of a system of corporate governance changes drastically, other elements may also be transformed to be consistent with the new system. This section presents a simple model by Hoshi (2002) that implies such a complementarity between corporate financing and human resource management. We use this model to motivate the empirical analysis in the next section.

The model augments the simplest version of the model in Tirole (2001), which focuses on potential agency problem between a financier and a manager, by adding potential moral hazard of workers. Thus, the model describes the corporate governance as an institution that has two distinct aspects (corporate financing and human resource management) that deal with two moral hazard problems (one by the managers and the other by the workers).

First, we start by modeling the financial aspect. Following Tirole (2001), consider an entrepreneur/manager who can choose between two types of projects. Both types require the initial investment of I and yield R ($>I$) if successful. If the project fails, the return is zero. The projects differ, however, in the probabilities of success. Let $p_H(p_L)$ be the probabilities that the "good" ("bad") project succeeds. We assume $p_H > p_L$. Thus, the "good" project has a greater expected return. The "bad" project is assumed to bring private (non-monetary) benefits of B to the manager. The manager is endowed with her own fund of A ($<I$). Since the own fund is not enough to cover the necessary investment, the manager must raise I–A from an investor. The investor's required rate of return is assumed to be zero. The choice of project is private information of the manager, which creates a potential moral hazard problem.

We assume the "good" project has a positive net expected value but the "bad" project has a negative net expected value, in the sense $p_H R - I > 0$ and $p_L R - I + B < 0$. It is easy to see that the investor rewards the manager only when the project succeeds so that the manager's incentive to take the "good" project is maximized. Let w_m be the manager's income (or equivalently net revenue minus the debt payment) when the project succeeds. The manager decides to choose the "good" project if and only if:

$$(1) \qquad (p_H - p_L)w_m \geq B$$

In words, the higher income that can be expected from taking the "good" project must be large enough to compensate for the lost private benefits. The equation (1) implies that the manager must receive no less than $B/(p_H - p_L)$ when the project succeeds in order for him to choose the "good" project. Thus, the maximum amount of income that the investor can expect is:

$$(2) \qquad p_H \left(R - \frac{B}{p_H - p_L} \right).$$

Tirole (2001) calls this the manager's "pledgeable income." Since we assume zero required rate of return, the manager can raise funds to finance the project if and only if the pledgeable income exceeds the amount of funds that need to be raised $(I{-}A)$, that is:

$$(3) \qquad p_H \left(R - \frac{B}{p_H - p_L} \right) \geq I - A$$

Note that a project with positive net value ($p_H R - I > 0$) may not be financed if the private benefit of the bad project is large (large B) or if the manager's own fund is small (small A).

Bank monitoring can alleviate the problem of the moral hazard here. Following Tirole (2001) again, assume the bank can reduce the private benefit of the manager (when he chooses the bad project) from B to b ($<B$) by paying the monitoring cost of c_b. Thus, under the bank monitoring, the pledgeable income increases to $p_H[R - b/(p_H - p_L)]$. When this is greater than the amount of bank loan plus the monitoring cost, the bank loans fund to the manager, who invests in the good project. The condition is given by:

$$(4) \qquad p_H \left(R - \frac{b}{p_H - p_L} \right) \geq I - A + c_b$$

Comparing (3) and (4), we see, for not too large c_b, the bank monitoring expands the set of good projects that will be financed.

Alternatively, takeover threat in the stock market may discipline the manager and make him choose the good project. First, suppose the manager finances the project by issuing shares (with control rights) to investors. The amount of shares held by the investors $(I-A)$ is assumed to be large enough so that the investors collectively can control the firm. Following Tirole (2001) again, assume the stock market participants observe a signal after the manager chooses the project. The signal can be "good" or "bad," and the probability that a "good" signal is observed depends on the manager's choice of the project. Let q_H be the probability that the signal is "good" when the manager chooses the good project, and let q_L be the probability that a "bad" signal is observed when the manager chooses the bad project. Assume $q_H > p_H$ and $q_L < p_L$. In other words, the signal is assumed to be more informative than the result of the project about the manager's choice. Let ν_G be the conditional probability that the project succeeds when a "good" signal is observed, and ν_B the conditional probability that the project succeeds when a "bad" signal is observed.[5]

Suppose there are investors in the market who have the ability to increase the conditional success probability of the project when the signal is "bad" from ν_B to $\nu_B + \delta$.[6] We call these investors "turnaround specialists." Since turnaround specialists can expect to earn more from the projects with bad signals than the current owners, they are willing to buy out those projects/firms. Assume the sales price of such a project to be $\nu_B R$.[7]

As Holmström (1979) showed, the optimal incentive pay can be contingent only on the signal, not the result of the project. Letting w_s be the payment to the manager when a good signal is observed, the manager chooses the good project if and only if:

$$(5) \qquad\qquad (q_H - q_L)w_s \geq B$$

Thus, the amount of pledgeable income is given by:[8]

$$(6) \qquad\qquad p_H R - q_H \frac{B}{q_H - q_L}$$

---

[5] Obviously, $p_H = q_H \nu_G + (1 - q_H)\nu_B$ and $p_L = q_L \nu_G + (1 - q_L)\nu_B$.

[6] We do not model where this special skill comes from. The new owners may be able to benefit from renegotiating various implicit commitments with the workers and the suppliers as argued by Shleifer and Summers (1988).

[7] In general, the sales price will be somewhere between $\nu_B R$ and $(\nu_B + \delta)R$ depending on the bargaining powers of the current and new owners. Here the assumption is that the current owner does not have any bargaining power. Giving some bargaining power to the current owner does not change the results of the model substantially.

[8] With probability q_H, a good signal is observed. The manager receives $B/(q_H - q_L)$ and the shareholder expects to get $\nu_G R$. With probability $(1 - q_H)$, a bad signal is observed. The manager gets nothing, and the shareholder sells the project to a turnaround specialist at $_B R$. Thus, the expected payoffs for the shareholder is given by $q_H \nu_G R - q_H [B/(q_H - q_L)] + (1 - q_H)\nu_B R = p_H R - q_H [B/(q_H - q_L)]$.

The manager can raise funds in the stock market and invests in the good project if:

$$(7) \qquad p_H R - q_H \frac{B}{q_H - q_L} \geq I - A.$$

Let us now turn to the human resource management aspect of the model. We assume that the manager needs to hire one worker to complete a project. A good project needs a skilled worker. If an unskilled worker is assigned to a good project, the probability of success falls from p_H to p_M (we assume $p_H > p_M > p_L$). The worker's skill is not important for a bad project.

Workers can acquire the skill only by making efforts, which cost them E, which is non-monetary. A worker's skill and the efforts to acquire the skill are assumed to be private information, which creates a potential moral hazard problem. We assume that it is socially desirable for a worker who is assigned to a good project to make an effort to acquire the skill, that is $p_H R - E > p_M R$.

We consider two alternative ways to alleviate this moral hazard problem. First, suppose a firm can pay e to train a worker to be skilled. Assume, in this case, the worker does not have to exert any efforts to acquire the skill.[9] We assume $e \leq E$, i.e., the training cost for the firm does not exceed the cost of individual efforts to acquire the skill. Let w^* be the market wage for an unskilled worker. The total cost for the firm to hire an unskilled worker and provide training is given by $w^* + e$.

Alternatively, we assume the firm can try to find a skilled worker in the labor market, which provides a signal that is correlated with the skill of the worker. Let r_H be the probability that a good signal is observed when the worker has made efforts and acquired the skill. We assume that the probability of a good signal when the worker has not made the efforts is zero. Thus, a firm can secure a skilled worker by hiring a worker with a good signal. Let w be the wage paid for such a skilled worker. Then, workers have incentive to invest in the skill if and only if:

$$(8) \qquad r_H w - E \geq w^*.$$

If we assume that the firm has all the bargaining power, the equilibrium wage for high skilled workers is given by:

$$(9) \qquad w = \frac{w^* + E}{r_H}$$

This model includes two alternative ways to alleviate the agency problem between the manager and the investor and two alternative ways to mitigate the agency problem between the worker and the manager. To deal with the agency problem between the manager and the investor, one can rely on bank monitoring or one can use the signal from the stock market. To deal with the agency problem

---

[9] The result does not change if we assume that the worker's effort is reduced compared with the self-training case.

between the manager and the worker, the manager can provide the in-house training to the (unskilled) worker or can go to the labor market with high enough wages to motivate the workers to invest in their own skills. Two sets of two alternative practices give us four combinations of these practices: (1) bank financing and in-house training; (2) stock market financing and in-house training; (3) bank financing and self-training (by the worker); and (4) stock market financing and self-training. In the rest of this section, we compare these four alternative arrangements of corporate governance, focusing on how successfully each arrangement can address the moral hazard problems.

Although the model includes two moral hazard problems, the one for the worker is completely solved by either of the mechanism. In equilibrium, the workers acquire the skills in either case. The difference is just the cost to achieve the efficient outcome. The cost difference influences the amount of the income that the manager can "pledge" to get financing, which determines, together with the financial arrangement, the extent that the agency problem between the manager and the investor is reduced. Thus, the comparison between different corporate governance arrangements comes down to the comparison of the amount of pledgeable income in each case.

First, let us consider the combination of bank financing and in-house training. The manager hires an unskilled worker by paying w^* and spends e to make him skilled. This reduces the pledgeable income by $w^* + e$. Subtracting $w^* + e$ from the left hand side of the inequality (4), we get:

$$(10) \qquad p_H \left(R - \frac{b}{p_H - p_L} \right) - w^* - e - c_b \geq I - A$$

as the condition for the manager to choose the good project under bank monitoring.

Next, consider the combination of stock market financing and in-house training. A major difference from the bank monitoring case is that the firm is sold to a new investor when the stock market signal is not good. We assume that the worker is fired and receives nothing in this event. Then, the manager has to promise a higher wage *ex ante* to compensate for the possibility of firing. Since the worker will be employed after the training with probability q_H, the firm has to promise to pay $\frac{w^*}{q_H}$. Adding the cost for in-house training, the pledgeable income of the firm is reduced by:

$$(11) \qquad \frac{w^*}{q_H} + e$$

Subtracting this from the left hand side of the inequality (7), the condition for the manager to choose the good project is given by:

$$(12) \qquad p_H R - q_H \frac{B}{q_H - q_L} - \frac{w^*}{q_H} - e \geq I - A$$

The third combination is bank financing and self-training. Each worker invests the effort of E to acquire the skill, and gets a job if the labor market produces the good signal. The wage that the firm pays to the worker is given by (9). Subtracting this from the left hand side of (4), we get the following condition for the manager to choose the good project.

$$(13) \qquad p_H \left(R - \frac{b}{p_H - p_L} \right) - \frac{w^* + E}{r_H} - c_b \geq I - A$$

Finally, let us consider the combination of stock market financing and self-training. We assume the stock market signal is observed before the labor market signal. Then, the firm gets to hire a worker and pays out the wage given by (9) only when it survives (with probability q_H). Thus, the condition for the manager to choose the good project is given by:

$$(14) \qquad p_H R - q_H \frac{B}{q_H - q_L} - q_H \frac{w^* + E}{r_H} \geq I - A$$

Note that (10), (12), (13), and (14) have the same right hand side. Let T_{10}, T_{12}, T_{13}, and T_{14} denote the left hand side of (10), (12), (13), and (14) respectively. Each one of these can be considered as a measure of the extent that each combination reduces the agency problems. A larger T implies that the condition for the manager to choose the good project holds for a wider set of parameters. A simple calculation yields:

$$(15) \qquad T_{10} - T_{12} = q_H \frac{B}{q_H - q_L} - p_H \frac{b}{p_H - p_L} - c_b + \frac{(1 - q_H)w^*}{q_H}$$

$$(16) \qquad T_{13} - T_{14} = q_H \frac{B}{q_H - q_L} - p_H \frac{b}{p_H - p_L} - c_b - (1 - q_H)\frac{w^* + E}{r_H}$$

$$(17) \qquad T_{10} - T_{13} = \frac{(1 - r_H)w^*}{r_H} + \frac{E}{r_H} - e$$

$$(18) \qquad T_{12} - T_{14} = \frac{q_H(w^* + E)}{r_H} - e - \frac{w^*}{q_H}$$

The equation (15) compares the combination of bank financing and in-house training to the combination of stock market financing and in-house combination. If this is positive, the combination of bank financing and in-house training dominates the combination of stock market financing and in-house training in the sense that there exists a set of parameters where the good project is chosen under bank financing and in-house training but not chosen under stock market financing and in-house training. Similarly, the equation (16) compares the combination of bank financing and self-training to the combination of stock market financing and self-training.

The first three terms in each equation shows the difference between the cost of disciplining the manager through the stock market (higher pay for a manager with the good signal) and the cost of disciplining the manager through bank monitoring. The lower is the cost of bank monitoring (c_b), the higher is the reduction of private benefit achieved by bank monitoring $(B-b)$, and the lower is the quality of the stock market signal (q_H/q_L), the more likely is the bank financing to dominate the stock market financing.

The last term of (15) shows the difference in the cost of in-house training under bank financing and under stock market financing. Under the stock market financing, workers demand higher wages to compensate for the possibility of being fired, which makes the wage payment higher compared with the bank financing case. Thus, the last term of (15) is positive. Similarly, the last term of (16) shows the difference in the cost of self-training under bank financing and under stock market financing. Since the firm does not have to hire a worker at all if the stock market signal turns out to be bad, the expected wage payment is smaller under stock market financing. Thus, the last term of (16) is negative.

Since the equations (15) and (16) have the same first three terms, (15) is always larger than (16). Thus, there exists a set of parameters that make (15) positive but (16) negative. In this case, bank monitoring dominates stock market financing if the workers acquire the skill through in-house training, but stock market financing dominates bank monitoring if the workers acquire the skill through self-training. In this sense, we find complementarity between the corporate financing and the human resource management: bank financing is complementary to in-house training while stock market financing is complementary to self-training.

The equations (17) and (18) compare the two alternative labor practices by holding the financial arrangement constant. If (17) is positive, in-house training dominates self-training under bank monitoring. If (18) is positive, in-house training dominates under stock market financing. The higher is the cost advantage of in-house training $(E-e)$ and the lower is the quality of the labor market signal (r_H), the more likely is in-house training to dominate self-training.

It is straightforward to show that (17) is always greater than (18).[10] Thus, there exists a set of parameters that makes (17) positive and (18) negative. For this set of parameters, in-house training dominates self-training under bank monitoring, but self-training dominates in-house training under stock market financing. Again we find the complementarity between the financial arrangement and human resource management in this sense.

---

10 $\frac{(1-r_H)w^*}{r_H} + \frac{E}{r_H} - e - \left(\frac{q_H(w^*+E)}{r_H} - e - \frac{w^*}{q_H} \right) = \frac{(1-q_H)(r_H+q_H)}{r_H q_H} w^* + \frac{(1-q_H)E}{r_H} > 0.$

In the next section, we examine the data for Japanese firms to see if we find the complementarity between the corporate financing and the human resource management practices suggested by this model. One approach would try to study how each combination of corporate governance practices influences the extent that the moral hazard problems are mitigated. With this approach, if we found one particular labor practice (for example, in-house training) is more effective in reducing the moral hazard problem under a particular financial arrangement (for example, bank financing) than the others, we would say the particular labor practice and the particular financial arrangement are complementary. It is difficult, however, to measure the extent that the moral hazard problem is reduced. Even in our simple model, where the extent of the remaining agency problem is perfectly captured by the amount of pledgeable income, it is difficult to find an empirical proxy for the pledgeable income.

In this paper, we take an alternative approach that examines whether a particular human resource management practice is more likely to be adopted by the firms with a particular corporate financial structure. Our model shows that bank financing and in-house training, which are consistent with the traditional Japanese corporate governance, are complementary to each other. The model also shows that stock market financing and self-training are complementary to each other. If these complementary relations exist, it is likely to find that most firms adopt either the combination of bank financing and in-house training or the combination of stock market financing and self-training. Since the other combinations are not optimal, one would expect the firms with non-complementary combination would eventually change one practice to make it complementary to the other practice.

9.5 EMPIRICAL ANALYSIS

We employ the three datasets for the examination. The data on human resource management practice come from the "Human Resource Management Systems Survey" ("Systems Survey" hereafter) conducted by the Institute of Labor Administration. This survey, which was most recently conducted in 1995, 1997, and 2001, asks a corporation to identify the presence or absence of each of approximately 180 human resource management practices. Firms surveyed include listed companies, major non-listed companies with capital exceeding ¥500 million and more than 500 employees, and small to medium-sized companies with capital exceeding ¥300 million and more than 100 employees. We examined only those firms that responded in both 1995 and 2001 surveys. We chose and analyzed the responses to the questions that we believed most relevant to corporate governance and are available in both 1995 and 2001 surveys. Table 9.6 lists those practices.

Table 9.6 Summary Statistics

Panel A

	Mean	
	1995	2000
Annual salary system	0.103	0.307
Bonus linked to achievement	0.172	0.138
Irregular working hours system	0.741	0.810
Length-of-service awards	0.879	0.759
Training for evaluators	0.741	0.690
Company sponsored education program (domestic)	0.293	0.293
Education abroad program	0.259	0.328
Female managers	0.586	0.466
In-house venture system	0.052	0.052
Permanent *shukko*	0.466	0.448
Financial assistance for self training	0.638	0.638
Exam to advance to a higher rank	0.103	0.086
Exam to advance to a higher job grade	0.362	0.448
Fast tracking	0.052	0.103
Small loan program	0.741	0.569

Panel B

	Mean (Std. Dev.)	
	1995	2000
Proportion of shares held by	0.374	0.328
financial institutions	(0.126)	(0.139)
Proportion of shares held by	0.082	0.086
foreign entities	(0.085)	(0.103)
Proportion of shares held by	0.460	0.438
the 10 largest shareholders	(0.120)	(0.110)
Ordinary profit (Ten Thou-	9,188,983	7,522,878
sand Yen)	(25,100,000)	(17,300,000)
Numbers of employees	3,147	2,667
	(5,922)	(5,413)
Proportion of (ex-)bankers in	7.7	7.2
the board	(7.9)	(7.4)
Bank debt to total debt ratio	0.247	0.277
	(0.193)	(0.209)

Most financial data are taken from the *Corporate Financial Databank* compiled by the Development Bank of Japan. The database contains information on the financial statements that listed companies file with stock exchanges.

Finally, we use the *Directors Handbook* (*Yakuin Shikihō*, Tōyō Keizai Shinpō-sha), a quarterly publication of information regarding executive personnel of listed companies. Using the data, we calculate the dependence on outside direct-ors (measured by dividing the number of directors sent by the financial institu-tions and related firms in total number of directors) for each company.

For 58 firms, we have been able to collect all the information that we use for our empirical analysis. The summary statistics for these 58 firms are reported in Table 9.6. Panel A of Table 9.6 lists the human resource management variables that we use in the analysis. A human resource management variable for each firm is a dummy variable that takes one when such a practice exists in the company and takes zero when such a practice is absent. For example, "annual salary system" takes one when the company uses annual salary system for some of its employees (typically in management positions) and zero otherwise. The first two columns of Panel A show the sample means of the variables in the 1995 survey and the 2000 survey respectively. The sample mean shows how much proportion of the sample had a particular human resource management practice. For example, the table shows 10.3% of the firms had annual salary system in 1995. The proportion increased to 30.7% in 2000.

The other (mostly financial) variables that we use for our analysis are listed in Panel B of Table 9.6. The table reports the sample means and standard deviations for the variables in 1995 and 2000. The ordinary profit is measured in million yen, and the number of employees is the raw number. All the other variables are measured in percentage term. The figures clearly suggest the declining importance of bank involvement in corporate governance of the firms in this sample. Although the bank debt to total debt ratio did not decline, both the shareholding by financial institutions and the proportion of bankers on the board declined substantially from 1995 to 2000.

For these 58 firms, Table 9.7 compares the ownership structure of the firms that adopt a certain employment practice to that of the firms that do not adopt such practice. The table shows the comparison for 1995 and 2000. For example, the upper number in the cell (annual salary system, bank ownership: 1995) shows the average proportion of shares, of the firms that had annual salary system in 1995, held by the financial institutions in 1995. The lower number in the cell shows the average proportion of shares, of the firms that did not have annual salary system as of 1995, held by the financial institutions in 1995.

We examine two measures of the ownership structure: the proportion of shares held by banks and the proportion of shares held by foreigners. The bank ownership is considered to be high for the firms that still maintain the traditional main bank relationship. Abe (2002) finds that these firms also tend to have slow speed of labor adjustment. We look at whether these firms also share the same tendency in other labor practices.

The foreign ownership is considered to be high for the firms that have substantially moved away from the traditional Japanese corporate financing. Ahmadjian, Chapter 4, this volume, indeed finds that the corporate governance at firms with high foreign ownership seems different from that at traditional Japanese firms. She finds that the firms with high foreign ownership tend to have higher levels of board independence, more disclosure, and exhibit other governance practices often associated with the "Anglo-American" standard. She also finds that the firms with high foreign ownership and low bank ownership are less reluctant to downsize when they are in distress.

Table 9.7 Human Resource Management Practices and Ownership Structure (Average % of Shareholding)

Practice	Adopted?	Bank ownership		Foreign ownership	
		1995	2000	1995	2000
(1) Annual salary system	Yes	0.3474	0.3368	0.0808	0.1082
	No	0.3774	0.3243	0.0819	0.0746
(2) Bonus linked to achievement	Yes	0.3651	0.3349	0.1031	0.0898
	No	0.3762	0.3274	0.0774	0.0850
(3) Irregular working hour system	Yes	0.3931 *	0.3434 *	0.0906	0.0908
	No	0.3204 *	0.2645 *	0.0567	0.0634
(4) Length-of-service awards	Yes	0.3801	0.3228	0.0787	0.0704 **
	No	0.3323	0.3459	0.1042	0.1336 **
(5) Training for evaluators	Yes	0.3843	0.3500 *	0.0823	0.0599
	No	0.3457	0.2804 *	0.0803	0.0972
(6) Company sponsored education program	Yes	0.3891	0.3820 *	0.1038	0.1414 ***
	No	0.3682	0.3062 *	0.0727	0.0625 ***
(7) Education abroad program	Yes	0.4436 **	0.4063 ***	0.1267 **	0.1421 ***
	No	0.3501 **	0.2905 ***	0.0662 **	0.0581 ***
(8) Female managers	Yes	0.3746	0.3695 **	0.0959	0.1259 ***
	No	0.3738	0.2926 **	0.0618	0.0506 ***
(9) In-house venture system	Yes	0.3697	0.5388 ***	0.1015	0.1685
	No	0.3745	0.3169 ***	0.0807	0.0811
(10) Permanent *shukko*	Yes	0.4060 *	0.3460	0.0869	0.0871
	No	0.3467 *	0.3141	0.0773	0.0845
(11) Financial assistance for self-training	Yes	0.3895	0.3320	0.0941	0.0842
	No	0.3474	0.3220	0.0601	0.0882
(12) Exam to advance to a higher rank	Yes	0.3309	0.2884	0.0522	0.0248
	No	0.3793	0.3322	0.0852	0.0914
(13) Exam to advance to a higher job grade	Yes	0.4139 *	0.3433	0.0744	0.0769
	No	0.3518 *	0.3163	0.0860	0.0928
(14) Fast tracking	Yes	0.4684	0.3351	0.0557	0.1677 **
	No	0.3692	0.3276	0.0832	0.0762 **

Note: *, **, and *** denote the difference in the means of the column variable between adopters and non-adopters is significant at 10%, 5%, and 1% level respectively.

The results in the table suggest several interesting differences in the ownership structure between the firms that have a certain employment practice and those that do not, and confirm our hypothesis that the two recent changes in the human resource management may be (at least partially) related to the changes in the corporate financing. The first row compares the ownership structure of the firms that have adopted the annual salary system to those that have not. The annual salary system literally means that the salaries are determined at annual rate, not monthly or weekly, but in Japan the annual salary system means that the annual salary is determined by achievements and performance during the previous year. Thus, the annual salary system is a clear deviation from the traditional practice of seniority wages where the level of salary is heavily influenced by the age of the employee regardless of the performance. The table shows that the foreign ownership of the firms that have annual salary system tend to be a little bit higher in 2000, but the difference is not statistically significant.

Linking the amount of bonus to a measure of achievement (rather than the amount of regular salary) is another deviation from the traditional practice. The table shows that the firms that link the bonuses to achievement tend to have high foreign ownership in 1995, but the difference is again insignificant.

The third row compares the firms that use irregular working hour system and those that do not. The advantage of introducing irregular working hours is that working hours can be kept flexible to match fluctuations in the intensity of business activity, or that, as in flextime, working hours can be left to the discretion of the employees. Either way, firms introduce irregular working hours to execute business more efficiently. In Japan, most firms with irregular working hours changes the working hours seasonally over a year, rather than introducing a flextime. Thus, the use of irregular working hours can be a deviation from the traditional pattern, but may just be a compromise move to increase the flexibility of working hours without moving all the way to flextime. The result in the table suggests that the firms that have irregular working hours tend to have marginally significantly higher bank ownership. They also tend to have high foreign ownership, but this result is not statistically significant. Thus, the firms with traditional ownership structure seem to use irregular working hours. This is consistent with the idea that the irregular working hour system is an attempt to introduce flexibility to the traditional labor management without drastically changing the traditional practice.

Length-of-service awards encourage employees to remain in a firm over a long time. Thus, the practice fits very well with traditional Japanese human resource management that promotes long-term employment. Table 9.7 suggests that the firms that have length-of-services awards tend to have low foreign ownership, suggesting they are indeed more likely to have the traditional ownership structure. The result is statistically significant for 2000.

To maintain fairness of personnel evaluation by minimizing discrepancies in evaluation standards between evaluators, some corporations have a systematic program to train the evaluators. As the wages and promotion come to depend more on merits and performances, the importance of personnel evaluation increases and hence the importance of training evaluators. Table 9.7 shows that the firms that provide such training for evaluators tend to have higher bank ownership in 2000, suggesting that the firms with traditional ownership structure are more likely to adopt this practice. The difference is statistically significant at 10% level.

A company sponsored education program and education abroad program are important components of off-the-job training (OffJT). Japanese companies traditionally relied more heavily on on-the-job training (OJT), although some major companies had OffJT programs such as education abroad programs as well. The table shows that the firms that have these OffJT programs tend to have higher bank ownership. The difference is statistically significant for the education abroad program in both 1995 and 2000. Interestingly, the firms that have high foreign ownership also tend to have these education programs. Another way to encourage OffJT is to provide financial assistance for self-training. Here we do not find any correlation with the ownership structure.

In traditional Japanese companies, it was rare to find female managers. In many companies, career tracks for female workers are different from their male counterpart. Women are expected to quit the firm when they get married, and training programs for them were often more limited than those for men. As some companies started to change their employment practices toward more merit-based ones, we have started to see the number of female managers to increase. The figures in Table 9.7 show that the firms that have female managers tend to have higher foreign ownership compared with those firms that do not have female managers. The result is statistically significant for 2000. In 2000, the firms with high bank ownership also seem to be more likely to have female managers.

The firms that had in-house venture system in 2000 seem to have higher bank ownership. The number of firms that had in-house venture system, however, was very small both in 1995 and 2000 (Table 9.6). Thus, the result may not be reliable.

Shukko is a system of inter-company employee transfer, which has been used by many Japanese companies. Under *shukko*, an employee is transferred (often temporarily) to work in a different company. *Shukko* is used, for example, in a group of related firms to move employees from a firm that is experiencing excess labor force to another firm in the group that is experiencing labor shortage. In many cases, *shukko* is an integral part of the employee training program, where an employee is temporarily sent to a different company to develop new skills. In some cases, *shukko* can be permanent in the sense the transferred employee is not expected to be called back to the original company. Permanent *shukko* is considered to be a method of employment adjustment more than anything. Many firms are reported to increase the use of permanent *shukko* to reduce the labor force without firing workers. An increased use of permanent *shukko* can be seen as an early stage of movement away from lifetime employment. In many cases, however, a tacit agreement to preserve the transferee's employment (at the new company) often exists. In this sense, permanent *shukko* may be viewed as an attempt to maintain the lifetime employment system in the increasingly volatile economy. Table 9.7 suggests that the firms that have permanent *shukko* had higher bank ownership than the others in 1995, but the difference is statistically insignificant in 2000.

In many Japanese companies, promotion to a higher job (from section chief to department manager, for example) is strictly separate from promotion to a higher rank (from rank 5 to rank 6, for example). Some companies use examinations to judge if an employee satisfies the standards for one or both types of promotion. The exams to advance to a higher rank are observed more often in a traditional Japanese human resource management, where the pay scale is more closely associated with ranks rather than jobs. Thus, it is interesting to find that the firms that do not have such exams tend to have higher foreign ownership, although the difference is not statistically significant. The companies that use exams to advance to higher job grades, however, do not have higher foreign ownership. Instead they tend to have higher bank ownership.

Finally, the firms that have a fast track system tend to have higher foreign ownership in both 1995 and 2000. Thus, the use of a fast track system, which is relatively new to many Japanese firms, tends to be associated with high foreign ownership in 2000.

Comparison of means of ownership variables suggests that certain human resource management practices may be indeed associated with a certain ownership structure. If we believe that a substantial part of the recent changes in the labor practices of large Japanese firms has been motivated by the changes in the ownership structure, the result suggests complementarity between ownership structure and human resource management practices.

The results in Table 9.7, however, are limited for several reasons. First, the number of observations is very small, which limits the power of statistical analysis. Second, simple comparison of means fails to control for other firm characteristics that are related to both financial structure and human resource management of the firms.

We have tried to address the second issue at least partially by estimating Probit regressions that relate the various human resource management practices to the corporate financial variables with some other control variables, such as the size of the firm.

Table 9.8 reports four of the 15 Probit models that we estimated for 2000 (each model regresses a human resource management variable listed in Panel A of Table 9.6 on the seven variables in Panel B of Table 9.6). We only report the regressions which show statistically significant relations between human resource management practice and at least one of the ownership variables. For the other specifications, we failed to find any statistically significant relations between human resource management and ownership structure. The small number of observations seems to impose a serious limit.

Column (4) (to match the numbers with Table 9.7) shows the result of regressing the length-of-service award (takes 1 if the firm has length-of-service awards) on the financial variables. The estimation result suggests that a firm with high foreign ownership is less likely to have length-of-service awards. Thus, firms with high foreign ownership do not seem to encourage many years of services as traditionally Japanese companies do.

The next two columns (6 and 7) show the regression analysis for the company sponsored education programs (domestic and abroad). For the domestic program, a larger company (measured with the number of employees) is more likely to have one. After controlling for the size, the high foreign ownership still increases the probability that the firm has the company sponsored education program within Japan. The bank ownership, however, is not significant. For the education abroad program, both bank ownership and foreign ownership increase the probability that the firm has a program. These results confirm the pattern found in Table 9.7 holds even after controlling for additional factors.

Table 9.8 Probit Estimation: 2000

	(4) Length-of-service award	(6) Company sponsored education program	(7) Education abroad program	(8) Female managers
c_bank	−0.3944	0.6039	1.5574 ***	0.1023
	(0.4936)	(0.5425)	(0.5382)	(0.6621)
c_foreign	−1.3199 **	1.2760 *	1.8133 **	1.7713 **
	(0.6095)	(0.7268)	(0.8275)	(0.8847)
c_big shareholder	−0.6084	−0.1616	0.8117	−2.1471 **
	(0.6124)	(0.7679)	(0.7386)	(0.8742)
ordinary profit/loss	0.0039	−0.0095	−0.0003	−0.0031
	(0.0084)	(0.0071)	(0.0053)	(0.0124)
employee	0.0015	0.0073 *	0.0015	0.0051
	(0.0032)	(0.0044)	(0.0021)	(0.0051)
executive ratio(from bank)	0.7338	0.0396	−1.5662	−0.9695
	(0.9455)	(1.0306)	(1.2961)	(1.1220)
borrowings ratio	−0.2182	0.1272	0.7140 *	0.0741
	(0.2903)	(0.3481)	(0.3716)	(0.3961)
Number of obs	58	58	58	58
LR chi^2(8)	9.16	13.81	21.98	19.49
Prob > chi^2	0.2415	0.0546	0.0026	0.0068
Pseudo R^2	0.1428	0.1968	0.2997	0.2432
Log likelihood	−27.475814	−28.179003	−25.690336	−30.321653

The last column shows the regression result for the existence of female managers. As we found in Table 9.7, a firm with high foreign ownership is more likely to have female managers. A company with more concentrated ownership (measured by the proportion of shares held by the ten largest shareholders), which presumably mean that a company is closely held by other Japanese companies, is less likely to have any female managers.

9.6 CONCLUSION AND FUTURE AGENDA

This paper has provided a brief overview on recent changes in two important aspects of the governance of Japanese corporations: financial arrangement and human resource management, and an examination of the complementarity between the two aspects. The availability of data on human resource management at individual firm level limits the scope and depth of our analysis, but the preliminary investigation seems to reveal a set of interesting findings concerning the effects of foreign ownership. The companies that show high level of foreign ownership were more likely to have human resource management practices that deviate from the traditional Japanese practice. For example, those companies were less likely to have the awards for longtime employees.

The foreign ownership, however, cannot explain all the changes in the human resource management practices that took place in Japan in the late 1990s. For example, many companies adjusted their wage system to reflect merits and performances of employees. These changes, however, do not seem to be related to the changes in foreign ownership.

There are several shortcomings in the current analysis, which make our conclusion tentative. First, the current analysis just examines the presence or absence of an employment management practice without asking more detailed questions about the ways the practice is implemented. This may be a serious problem. For example, even when a firm introduces a bonus system based on performance, the difficulty of measuring performance may make it impossible for bonus levels to reflect the achievements of employees correctly.[11] It may be important to go beyond the mere presence or absence of employment management systems and examine the actual implementations.

Second, the interpretations of the same practice can differ so widely between firms that it is hard to make sure that the practices of the same name indeed mean the same practice for two different firms. For instance, a contract employee system in one firm may mean the system to recruit and secure workers with certain expertise. A system of the same name, however, may be used just to recruit low skill labor for routine works in another firm. Thus, our results should be qualified, taking into account the possibility that a practice of the same name may mean totally different things in two firms.

Finally, the small sample size is a serious constraint for this study. This is especially clear in an unsatisfactory attempt to estimate Probit models of the choice of each human resource management practice. It may take a series of systematic surveys to collect the data that would better illuminate the relation between corporate finance and human resource management. This task is left for future research.

REFERENCES

Abe, M. (2002). 'Corporate Governance Structure and Employment Adjustment in Japan: An Empirical Analysis using Corporate Finance Data,' *Industrial Relations*, 41(4): 683–702.

Ahmadjian, C. and P. Robinson (2001). 'Safety in Numbers: Downsizing and the Deinstitutionalization of Permanent Employment in Japan,' *Administrative Science Quarterly*, 46: 622–54.

Aoki, M. (2001). *Towards a Comparative Institutional Analysis*. Cambridge, MA: MIT Press.

---

[11] For more on the relationships between measurement of performance, wage determination, and incentives, see Prendergast (1999), which discusses the incentive problem that arises in cases when it is difficult to objectively measure performance.

Fukao, M. (1995). *Financial Integration, Corporate Governance, and the Performance of Multinational Companies.* Washington, DC: The Brookings Institution.

Holmström, B. (1979). 'Moral Hazard and Observability,' *The Bell Journal of Economics*, 10: 74–91.

Hoshi, T. (1998). 'Japanese Corporate Governance as a System,' in K. J. Hopt, H. Kanda, M. J. Roe, E. Wymeersch, and S. Prigge (eds.), *Comparative Corporate Governance: The State of the Art and Emerging Research.* Oxford: Oxford University Press, 847–75.

—— (2002). 'Nihon-gata Corporate Governance' (Japanese Corporate Governance), *Keizai Kenkyu*, 53: 289–304 (in Japanese).

—— A. Kashyap (2001). *Corporate Financing and Governance in Japan: The Road to the Future.* Cambridge, MA: MIT Press.

Jackson, G. (2004). 'Toward a Comparative Perspective on Corporate Governance and Labour Management: Enterprise Coalitions and National Trajectories,' in H. Gospel and A. Pendleton (eds.), *Corporate Governance and Labour Management in Comparison.* Oxford: Oxford University Press.

Japan Institute of Labor (1998). *Survey of Human Resource Management and Job Consciousness under Structural Adjustment* (in Japanese).

Kojima, K. (1997). *Japanese Corporate Governance: An International Perspective.* Kobe: Kobe University.

Kuroki, F. (2003). 'The Relationship of Companies and Banks as Cross-Shareholdings Unwind: Fiscal 2002 Cross-Shareholding Survey,' *NLI Research Working Paper.*

Ono, A. (2000). 'Rōdō Shijō no Ryūdō-ka to Koyō Hendō' (Labor Fluctuations and Mobilization in Japanese Labor Market), *Eco-Forum*, 19–1: 20–4 (in Japanese).

Prendergast, C. (1999). 'The Provision of Incentives in Firms,' *Journal of Economic Literature*, 37: 7–63

Sanwa Research Institute (2000). *Questionnaire Survey on the Effects of the "IT Revolution" on Labour* (in Japanese). Tokyo: Sanwa Research Institute.

Shleifer, A. and R. W. Vishny (1997). 'A Survey of Corporate Governance,' *Journal of Finance*, 52: 737–87.

Takahashi, S. (2001). 'Chiteki Shihon Keiei no Jinzai Management' (Human Management as an Investor of Intellectual Capital), *Hitotsubashi Business Review*, 49-1: 68–80 (in Japanese).

Tirole, J. (2001). 'Corporate Governance,' *Econometrica*, 69: 1–35.

Tsuru, T., M. Abe, and K. Kubo (2003). 'Pay Structures and the Transformation of Japanese Firms: An Empirical Analysis of Performance and Pay Using Personnel Data,' *The Economic Review*, 54(3): 264–85 (in Japanese).

10

Employment Adjustment and Distributional Conflict in Japanese Firms[1]

Gregory Jackson

10.1 INTRODUCTION

Corporate governance in Japan is often described as a stakeholder-oriented system wherein employees play a central role. Japanese firms provide "lifetime employment" in the sense of long-term employment of regular, usually male employees in large firms. This social norm of employment security does not entail a secure entitlement to specific jobs, nor do employees necessarily remain at the same firm until retirement. But the idea of the firm as a community of people is manifest in a number of human resource management (HRM) practices geared to mobilize long-term commitment to the enterprise (Dore 1973). Firms make investments in firm-specific skills of their employees that develop through internal job rotation and are functionally flexible to allow people to be easily redeployed within the firm or among a group of related firms. These investments are rewarded through seniority-related wages, a rank-hierarchy system of promotion, and a strong socialization into the culture of the company (Koike 1988). Firms invest a good deal of effort in recruiting their young employees, who usually enter the firm directly from school or university and are expected to stay with the firm. Mid-career hiring remains an exception and average job tenures are longer than in other industrialized economies.

Lifetime employment has historical origins in the intense conflict between unions and management in the early post-war period and became widely institutionalized as a political compromise in tandem with cooperative enterprise-based unions (Gordon 1998). Enterprise unions in Japan have made employment security of their members their highest priority. A variety of employee participation practices exist that enhance information sharing at the level of the shop floor (e.g. quality circles) and allow for union consultation with the corporate headquarters

[1] My thanks go to RIETI for sponsoring this research and to Yukiko Yamazaki for providing excellent research assistance. My gratitude also goes to officials at METI, who kindly provided me with access to the survey data. Special thanks also to Ronald Dore, who provided me with the data on value added and engaged in very constructive debate with regard to the results, and to Robert Boyer for comments.

(e.g. joint labor–management consultation over major company decisions). These have become increasingly common over the post-war era. Finally, strong legal constraints on involuntary dismissals make it extremely difficult for firms to lay-off employees (Hanami 1985).

Long-term employment practices are argued to have complementarities with finance and corporate governance institutions, such as main bank monitoring and protection from stock market pressures (see Aoki 1988, but also Chapter 9 of this volume for a formal model). Numerous reforms since the mid-1990s have changed these corporate governance institutions, such as the weakening of the main bank relationship (see Chapter 2 of this volume), the partial unwinding of cross-shareholding arrangements (see Chapter 3) and the rise of foreign institutional investors (see Chapter 4). As capital market pressures have increased, debates emerged over the concept of "shareholder value" and the future of stakeholder-oriented corporate governance in Japan. Critics argued that lifetime employment was impeding corporate restructuring, whereas others proclaimed the "end of lifetime employment" as a growing number of blue chip corporations have announced large-scale job cuts at home and overseas, including Nissan Motor Co., Hitachi, Sony, and NEC (all in 1999), or Matsushita Electronic Corporation, Fujitsu, and Toshiba (all in 2001). After remarkably low levels of 1–2% the Japanese unemployment rate increased during the prolonged recession from 2.1% in 1990 to 4.1% in 1997 and peaked at a historically high rate of 5.4% in 2002 (Japan Institute for Labor Policy and Training 2006). Part-time employment also increased from 15.1% of employees in 1990 to 23.6% in 2002, soaring to levels substantially higher than in the US or Europe. Increasing media attention surrounded the term "Freeter," which describes a growing number of young atypical workers, who face fewer opportunities as regular employees, often have disrupted school-to-work transitions, and pursue part-time, temporary or other irregular work patterns (Honda 2005).

In this context, several studies re-examined the notion of the Japanese corporation as community and the challenges resulting from the economic and social changes since the 1990s, including changes in the finance and governance of large corporations (Jacoby 2004; Inagami and Whittaker 2005). These studies build on a growing amount of evidence showing important linkages between employment patterns, corporate finance, and corporate governance in different countries (for example, see Gospel and Pendleton 2005). As corporate governance reforms have been initiated throughout OECD countries since the mid-1990s, these changes have influenced labor management, particularly in countries with stakeholder-oriented corporate governance (Dore 2000; Ahmadjian and Robinson 2001; Höpner 2001; O'Sullivan 2003; Jackson 2003; Miyamoto 2006). Will corporate governance reform cause the convergence of employment and industrial relations on a market-based system?

This chapter examines these issues by examining various employment outcomes in Japan, such as employment adjustment patterns, payment systems, the distribution of value-added, and patterns of employee participation. The empirical evidence is drawn, in part, on the "Survey on the Corporate System and Employment" conducted on behalf of the Ministry of Economy, Trade and Industry in 2003. This survey was sent to 2000 large listed firms in Japan, and received 252 responses (a rate of 12.6%). Section 10.2 begins by reviewing recent changes in corporate governance and their potential impact on labor management in large Japanese firms. Section 10.3 presents the main empirical data on employment patterns based on the METI Survey and other statistical evidence. Section 10.4 revisits these themes through a detailed case study of a large manufacturing firm in order to examine how processes of change in corporate governance and labor are interrelated at the firm-level and have resulted in incremental changes to the Japanese model. Finally, the conclusion argues that while the Japanese system of long-term employment has not disappeared, important changes have occurred with regard to the content of lifetime employment practices—greater levels of adjustment, changes in the way employees are paid, a changing distribution of value-added among stakeholders and new challenges for employee participation.

10.2 LABOR MANAGEMENT IN JAPAN AND THE CHALLENGE OF SHAREHOLDER VALUE

Since the mid-1990s, Japanese firms have undergone substantial changes in their corporate governance practices that place new pressures on employees (Jackson 2003). Ownership by foreign and domestic institutional investors increased and the capacity of banks to monitor large firms has eroded, exposing firms to greater financial pressures to produce returns for shareholders. These capital market pressures are reinforced by more recent growth in mergers and acquisitions, and the small but growing threat of hostile takeover bids. Corporate restructuring has also been facilitated by the liberalization of corporate equity to facilitate spin-offs, acquisitions through share swaps, and share buy-backs. Other regulatory changes support greater transparency and disclosure of information, such as through market-based accounting rules and consolidation of accounts on a group-wide basis. Finally, corporate boards have changed to become smaller, more focused on overall corporate strategy, and outside directors are being encouraged through the new company-with-committees system. A growing number of managers have also received stock options as an element of executive compensation, although these schemes remain quite modest relative to the US or UK.

Such moves toward more shareholder-oriented corporate governance may provoke conflicts with employees (Vitols 2004). First, investors may demand a business portfolio focused on *core competence* that leads to conflicts with employees over the definition of core business units, divestment or closure of non-core units, and strategies of growth by diversification used to stabilize employment. Second, *equity-oriented performance* targets create conflicts over performance criteria, time horizons, and disciplining poorly performing units. Third, *performance-oriented pay* may be used to link employee incentives with business unit performance, raising issues of the equity and risks of contingent pay. Managerial stock options may also provoke controversy over income inequality and short-termism. Finally, financially oriented institutional investors may demand a greater share of *value-added* to maintain returns through higher dividends. In sum, all these factors create pressure to match employment to market conditions by reducing excess employees, divesting from less profitable businesses and decentralizing wage bargaining to match wages to productivity.

Table 10.1 presents a simple classification of employment systems among Japanese firms during 2003 using data from the METI Survey. A large proportion of firms report traditional patterns of lifetime employment based on age-related pay without any merit elements (8%) or limited merit elements (34%). The other common pattern is a hybrid combination of lifetime employment, but introduction of merit based pay systems (43%). Only a minority of firms report having merit pay with limited lifetime employment (2%) or merit pay with no lifetime employment policy (12%). These data are broadly consistent with a Ministry of Finance survey in 2002, which identifies three types of pay systems—50% of firms maintain traditional lifetime-employment and seniority pay, 29% utilize performance-based pay with lifetime employment and 16% utilize performance pay without lifetime employment (see Chapter 12 in this volume). Likewise, a Japan Institute of Labor survey conducted by Miyamoto (2006) finds four patterns— 22% of firms maintain lifetime employment with no merit pay elements and 50% retain lifetime employment but have introduced merit pay, whereas 20% have no lifetime employment and strong merit pay elements and only 9% of firms had no lifetime employment but also no merit pay. Thus, these three major surveys agree that lifetime employment remains a norm for 70–85% of listed companies, but also find a trend away from seniority or age-based remuneration and toward pay systems based on merit. In particular, the combination of lifetime employment and merit-based pay is characteristic of "hybrid" patterns of corporate governance, as discussed in the Introduction.

Table 10.1 Type of Employment System among Japanese Corporations

	Percentage of firms
No merit pay, lifetime employment	8%
Limited merit pay, lifetime employment	34%
Merit pay, lifetime employment	43%
Merit pay, limited lifetime employment	2%
Merit pay, no lifetime employment	12%
Other	1%

Source: METI Survey on the Corporate System and Employment 2003.

10.3 SOME RECENT EVIDENCE ON EMPLOYMENT OUTCOMES

This section looks at these developments in greater detail. It remains an open empirical question as to how Japanese firms adapt lifetime employment norms and implement merit based pay, and whether these patterns are influenced by corporate governance parameters of those firms. First, lifetime employment will be examined by examining the degree of employment stability and methods of employment adjustment at Japanese firms in recent years. Second, merit pay is explored by looking at more specific criteria used in determining pay at Japanese firms and how these are influenced by corporate governance parameters of those firms. Third, distributional conflicts are explored by looking at trends in the distribution of value-added of Japanese corporations, and the relative shares of employees and investors, such as the interest payments to banks and dividends paid to shareholders. Finally, trends in employee participation will be examined.

10.3.1 Employment Stability and Adjustment

Lifetime employment in Japan has been underpinned by highly developed firm-internal labor markets and low use of the external labor market, as well as a very high level of job security even during economic recession. While Japanese firms continue to support lifetime employment in principle, what changes have occurred in the degree of employment stability since the mid-1990s? Moreover, are any changes related to corporate governance? In order to assess these questions, Figure 10.1 reports the proportion of listed firms with over 2000 employees making aggregate annual employment reductions of 10% or more during the years 1991, 2001, and the period 2002–05 in Japan, France, Germany, the UK, and the US (see also Jackson 2005). This figure represents only aggregate net shifts in employment, and does not measure the number of individual employee exits in a particular year. The figure also does not distinguish between changes in employment due to outright lay-offs, or other shifts due to mergers and acquisitions or spin-offs. This indicator shows that only 2% of Japanese firms undertook downsizing in 1991, compared to 8% in France, 9% in the US, 10% in Germany, and 16% in the UK. However, the percentage of Japanese firms downsizing increased three-fold to 6% in 2001 and peaked at nearly 11% in 2002. This peak level is similar to average levels in the other four countries and far below the peak rates of 20% in Germany, 20% in the UK, and nearly 21% in the US.[2] Moreover, the downsizing rate in Japan fell back down to 6% in 2004 and under 4% in 2005, suggesting a return to more stable employment as the economy recovered.

---

[2] The comparison with Germany is particularly interesting, since both German and Japanese firms are viewed as having similar stakeholder oriented corporate governance. The higher downsizing rate in Germany may reflect the greater importance of the welfare state in sharing the costs of employment adjustment and the strength of occupational labor markets in Germany.

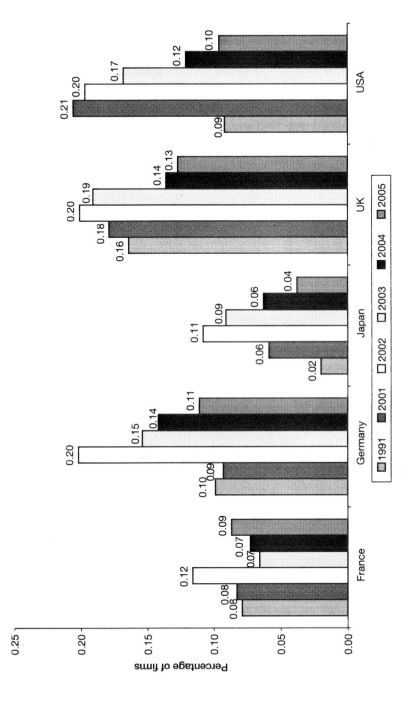

Figure 10.1 Rates of employment reduction for selected countries, 1991–2005

Notes: Sample covers listed corporations with over 2,000 employees. Employment Reduction is counted as a negative shift in total employment of 10% over a one year period. The sample size was an average of 207 firms per year in France, 237 in Germany, 865 in Japan, 373 in the UK and 1895 in the USA.

Table 10.2 Log Likelihood of Reducing Employment by 10% or more, 2002–05

	2005	2004	2003	2002
Log of assets	−0.09 *	−0.11 ***	−0.06	−0.16 ***
	0.05	*0.04*	*0.04*	*0.04*
Change in sales	−0.08 ***	−0.08 ***	−0.08 ***	−0.07 ***
	0.01	*0.01*	*0.00*	*0.00*
ROA (t−1)	−0.04 **	−0.01 *	−0.01 **	−0.04 ***
	0.01	*0.00*	*0.00*	*0.00*
Germany	−0.31	−0.29	−0.65 ***	0.13
	0.29	*0.24*	*0.23*	*0.19*
Japan	−1.29 ***	−1.20 ***	−1.02 ***	−0.75 ***
	0.22	*0.18*	*0.15*	*0.14*
France	−0.68 **	−0.86 ***	−1.54 ***	−0.35
	0.33	*0.31*	*0.32*	*0.25*
UK	−0.13 *	−0.20	−0.02	0.40 **
	0.22	*0.20*	*0.17*	*0.17*
Industry control variables	YES	YES	YES	YES
Constant	−19.50 ***	−17.80	−3.03 *	−0.30
	0.54	12.00	1.47	0.70
N	3053	3241	3388	3514
Pseudo-R-sq	0.22	0.19	0.19	0.23

Notes: Sample covers listed corporations with over 2,000 employees. Reduction is counted as a negative shift in total employment of 10% over a one year period. Standard errors are shown in italics. * Significant at 0.10; ** Significant at 0.05; ***Significant at 0.01.

Source: Own calculations from Thomson/Worldscope.

Table 10.2 further compares the likelihood of making employment adjustments in the years 2002–05 after controlling for firm size, changes in sales, return on assets (ROA) and industrial sector. These results confirm that Japanese firms were much less likely to downsize than their counterparts in the US for all years in the sample, even controlling for relative economic performance. Looking at the recent period of 2001–05, Japanese firms also adjusted employment levels less dramatically than their US counterparts. Among this sample of large Japanese firms, employment increased by an average of 7.5% over these four years, whereby firms in the bottom decile cut employment by 22.5% and firms in the top decile increased employment by 39.3%. US firms followed a more dynamic pattern, growing by an average of 18.9% during the same period, while firms in the bottom decile cut employment by 36.5% and firms in the top decile increased employment by 74%. In sum, these data suggest that Japanese firms remain more committed to stable employment relative to other advanced industrialized economies and undertake employment adjustment more gradually.

Several studies show that corporate governance characteristics have an impact on the propensity for employment adjustment. Ahmadjian and Robinson (2001) found that foreign ownership strongly increased the likelihood of downsizing in the early 1990s. Interestingly, this effect declined by the late-1990s as social norms became more supportive of reducing employment levels in Japan. Meanwhile, several studies demonstrate that strong ties to banks slowed or lessened the likelihood of reducing employment (Matsuura 2001; Abe 2002). Abe and Shimizutani (2005) demonstrate the influence of board composition on the likelihood to downsize, showing that firms with more outside directors are more likely to cut wages or reduce employees by layoffs or voluntary retirements, whereas firms with insider directors are more inclined to reduce employment by hiring freezes. The same study also suggests that foreign ownership had no significant impact on adjustment behavior in recent years. Finally, layoffs have been studied in the context of corporate finance. Tanisaka and Ohtake (2003) show that announcements of employment cuts had a small but positive influence on share prices in Japan, which has encouraged firms to become more proactive in restructuring. However, Japanese firms remain unlikely to resort to cutting employment in order to maintain shareholder returns. For example, Matsuura (2001) estimates that among financially distressed firms during the 1990s, 44% cut dividends only, 53% cut employment and dividends, and only 2% cut employment while maintaining dividends.

The employment adjustment patterns of Japanese firms have thus become more heterogeneous over the last decade, and differ according to the financial and corporate governance characteristics of those firms (see also Hurlin and Lechevalier 2003). This pattern presents a puzzle in that Japanese firms have increased efforts to adjust employment levels, but also claim to uphold the norm of lifetime employment. How have Japanese firms attempted to reconcile growing financial market pressures and restructuring with their commitments to core employees? Historically, Japanese firms have used flexibility to adjust wages or hours before resorting to adjustment of employment levels (Tachibanaki and Morikawa 2000). The stagnation or even decline of real wages may be a factor contributing to maintaining employment levels. Furthermore, when Japanese firms do adjust employment, they have relied largely on "benevolent" methods of adjustment that largely avoid outright dismissals of regular employees.

The METI survey contains data showing the percentage of firms that implemented different methods of adjustment in the period 2000–03. Table 10.3 divides this sample according to different levels of employment adjustment during this period. Among the whole sample, only 5% of firms resorted to outright layoffs of regular employees. Looking at those firms cutting 10% or more, the most common methods were a freeze in hiring new graduates (61%), voluntary early retirement (49%), transfers to other firms (37%), and internal reallocation (36%). Only 8% of these firms resorted to lay-offs. A very similar pattern applies to firms cutting more than 25% of their employees. Thus, Japanese firms have aimed to preserve their core workforce largely by reducing intake and giving incentives for exit to older employees. Further adjustment has relied on group-wide internal labor markets, shifting employment to related firms. Outright dismissals of domestic employees are almost always

Table 10.3 Methods of Employment Adjustment, 2000–03

	All firms	of which: No adjustment	Cutting 10%+	Cutting 25%+
Restricting overtime	14%	13%	16%	11%
Shorter hours	3%	1%	6%	0%
Cut in mid-year hiring	16%	16%	16%	21%
Reduction in outsourcing	9%	8%	9%	5%
Reallocation	28%	23%	36%	26%
Transfer to other companies	26%	20%	37%	37%
Cut in hiring new graduates	44%	34%	61%	63%
Reducing of non-regular employees	14%	14%	13%	11%
Layoff	5%	3%	8%	5%
Voluntary early retirement	28%	16%	49%	58%
Other	2%	1%	6%	11%
No adjustment method	33%	46%	10%	11%
Percentage change in employees	13%	33%	−20%	−37%
N	246	159	87	19
Percent of sample	100%	65%	35%	8%

Source: METI Survey 2003.

avoided.[3] Further analysis of this data suggests that corporate governance characteristics, such as the level of foreign ownership or presence of outside directors, had no influence on the choice of adjustment methods. This adjustment pattern is consistent with other econometric studies based on labor market data, which show that job retention rights display no major decline since the 1980s (Kato 2001).

Benevolent employment adjustment used by Japanese firms continues to have strong legal underpinnings, despite some recent changes in Japanese labor law (Yamakawa 2002; Araki 2005). Employment protection has historically developed through case law doctrines of the "abuse of the right to dismiss," based on four requirements: (1) a business-based need must exist to reduce personnel; (2) dismissals must be a last resort to cope with economic difficulties and employers must take every possible measure to avoid dismissals; (3) workers must be selected for dismissal in an objective and reasonable manner; and (4) the employer must consult with the representative labor union or employees regarding the dismissals. Recent court cases suggest important loosening of the standards being applied to judge abuse, suggesting that the four requirements should be seen as four factors in the courts' determination of whether or not a

---

[3] Another recent survey of listed firms conducted by RIETI in 2004 produced very similar results: 36% of companies reported carrying out employment adjustment measures between 2000 and 2003, cutting their workforce by 15% on average. The survey gives more exact data on employment adjustment in terms of numbers of employees, but shows again that the method was overwhelmingly "benevolent": 54% of reductions were by early retirement, 29% by hiring freeze, 5% by transfer, another 5% by spin-off, and only 4% through layoffs (see Jackson 2005).

dismissal is abusive or not.[4] However, the 2003 revision of the Labor Standards Law importantly reaffirmed the case law doctrine on abusive dismissals as part of statutory law for the first time. This revision is often seen as counterbalancing the loosing of the court interpretations, although its affect remains debated among labor lawyers. A number of other recent legal changes have also supported the participation of labor in restructuring, such as the Labor Contract Succession Law of 2000 to guarantee the transfer of employment conditions and collective agreements during mergers or spin-offs.

Despite continued institutional support for benevolent employment adjustment, this pattern also has costs and limits. The Japanese welfare state does not easily allow firms to externalize the costs of adjustment, such as sharing the costs of early retirement with the state. Transfers within corporate groups have also become less attractive since the introduction of consolidated accounting in 2000 (Nakata and Takehiro 2001). With unconsolidated accounting, firms had greater leeway to transact with related firms to smooth accounting results or transfer redundant workers from parent firms to subsidiaries either on a temporary basis involving a sharing of wage payments (*zaiseki shukko*) or permanent basis (*tenseki shukko*), thereby reducing labor cost pressures at the parent firm. Most transfers are among subsidiary or related firms, and often related to workforce reductions and lack of opportunities in the parent firm. However, consolidated accounting makes these transfers less attractive and thus limits the effectiveness of transfer as a means to reconcile benevolent employment adjustment with investors' expectations. An important case is the NTT group, where transfers among group companies were an important adjustment strategy that proved unsustainable without corresponding wage reductions for employees transferred to newly created outsourcing companies (Sako and Jackson 2006). Thus, corporate groups in Japan are developing more heterogeneous internal labor markets in response to growing market pressure.

While the evidence on employee adjustment suggests a high degree of continuity, the slow adjustment process has substantial cumulative impacts on the position of employees. Specifically, the last decade of employment adjustment has very substantially reduced the core of lifetime jobs available. For example, the largest firms (based on the 99th percentile) had over 22,974 employees in 1993, but just 17,417 at the end of 2001 based on unconsolidated accounting data (own calculations, DBJ database). Likewise, the METI Survey data show that 68% of the listed firms in the sample had zero or negative employment growth, and the gains among the top third did not offset the aggregate losses in the bottom two thirds—resulting in an average loss of 388 employees during the period 2000–03 or equivalent to 6% of those employed in these firms. The survey also shows that net reductions in regular employees were most likely among general office workers

---

[4] The National Westminster Bank case (3rd Provisional Disposition), 78 Rōdō Hanrei 32 (Tokyo District Court, January 21, 2000). For details of the case, which involved closing a department and dismissing a specialist employee, see Yamakawa 2002.

(53% of firms). Other establishment-level data on employee turnover also suggest a trend toward net job losses. Table 10.4 shows that both accessions and separations have remained stable in manufacturing sectors, but were greater in the period 2001–05 than during 1994–2000 for the economy as a whole. Looking at accessions minus separations for each year, net job attrition occurred in nearly all years, peaking in 2001 and 2002, but declining rapidly in 2004 and 2005. Job losses have been strongest in manufacturing, where total employment decreased from over 13 million regular employees in 1990 to 10.7 million in 2004, as jobs shift increasingly toward services (Japan Institute for Labor Policy and Training 2006). Japanese firms have thus attempted to uphold norms of lifetime employment in ways consistent with the notion of stakeholder oriented corporate governance, but the core of community firms has grown smaller as firms have adjusted to new market pressures, including those of the capital market.

10.3.2 Payment Systems

Lifetime employment is usually seen as being closely related to the use of seniority-based pay, which rewards employees based on years of service and thereby encourages long-term commitment. Moreover, linking salary to age or rank rather than particular job activities assures that firm-internal labor markets retain a high degree of functional flexibility. Often age-based payments occur

Table 10.4 Accessions and Separations in Manufacturing

Year	Accession rate All industries (%)	Accession rate Manufacturing (%)	Separation rate All industries (%)	Separation rate Manufacturing (%)	Accessions minus Separations All industries (%)	Accessions minus Separations Manufacturing (%)
1994	1.92	1.32	1.92	1.45	0.00	−0.13
1995	1.88	1.28	1.93	1.45	−0.05	−0.17
1996	1.93	1.29	1.92	1.40	0.01	−0.11
1997	1.99	1.43	2.00	1.47	−0.01	−0.04
1998	1.88	1.28	1.96	1.47	−0.08	−0.19
1999	1.99	1.29	2.04	1.47	−0.05	−0.18
2000	2.03	1.39	2.09	1.48	−0.06	−0.09
2001	2.06	1.28	2.15	1.59	−0.09	−0.31
2002	2.11	1.30	2.23	1.60	−0.12	−0.30
2003	2.09	1.33	2.17	1.48	−0.08	−0.15
2004	2.14	1.36	2.14	1.39	0.00	−0.03
2005	2.15	1.37	2.18	1.35	−0.03	0.02
Averages:						
1994–2000	1.95	1.33	1.98	1.46	−0.03	−0.13
2001–05	2.11	1.33	2.17	1.48	−0.06	−0.15

Note: Establishments with 5 or more employees.

Source: Final Report of the Monthly Labor Survey (Ministry of Health, Labor and Welfare, Japan, various years).

indirectly through ability-based grades or ranks, which are based on an orderly schedule of promotion through established career ladders. However, as shown in Table 10.1, the importance of such age-based salary elements has begun to decline in favor of salary schemes based on merit. For example, the Nissay Business Conditions Survey of 2004 reports that 21% of large firms have eliminated seniority-based pay for regular employees and another 41% of those firms plan to reduce its importance in determining salary (Komoto 2004). The term "merit" can have a variety of different meanings. Variation in pay may be related to individual performance, company or business unit performance, or other elements such as qualification or job activity. This section looks at this shift from seniority to merit-based payment systems, and examines the relationship with corporate governance.

Table 10.5 gives details from the METI survey on the payment systems used by Japanese firms. Most Japanese firms use ability-based grades (77%), individual performance (77%) and qualification (67%) in determining an employee's salary. Age, job, and company performance were also used in over 40% of companies. The Chi-square analysis compares firms adopting or not adopting merit pay systems, and whether they are more likely to actually utilize particular elements of setting pay. The results show that companies with merit pay systems had a lesser propensity to base salaries on age or tenure. These firms also had a greater

Table 10.5 Elements Used to Determine Employee Salary, by Type of Employment System

	All firms	Merit-based employment system				Lifetime employment system			
		Yes	No	Pearson Chi-2	P	Yes	No	Pearson Chi-2	P
Age	48%	38%	61%	13.16	0.000 **	52%	21%	8.01	0.005 **
Tenure	33%	24%	47%	14.01	0.000 **	35%	21%	2.43	0.119
Qualification	67%	64%	71%	1.26	0.261	70%	45%	8.01	0.005 **
Ability	77%	80%	73%	1.78	0.182	75%	85%	1.43	0.232
Position or job	44%	49%	38%	3.09	0.079	43%	52%	0.77	0.381
Company performance	42%	45%	39%	0.87	0.351	43%	39%	0.18	0.670
Business unit performance	19%	23%	15%	2.55	0.110	18%	30%	2.86	0.091
Individual performance	77%	82%	70%	4.48	0.034 *	76%	85%	1.30	0.254
Expected individual performance	19%	21%	17%	0.88	0.349	18%	27%	1.48	0.224
Long-term individual performance	22%	22%	21%	0.02	0.897	23%	18%	0.33	0.565
Competitors' wages	28%	25%	32%	1.44	0.230	28%	30%	0.07	0.793
Merit-based employment system	57%					50%	100%	28.51	0.000 **
Lifetime employment system	86%								

Source: 'Survey on the Corporate System and Employment,' METI Survey 2003.

propensity to use individual performance, although individual performance was used by the majority of firms in both merit and non-merit categories. Unexpectedly, merit pay systems had no significant relationship with any other *particular elements* of merit-pay. This result suggests that the notion of merit-pay is associated with less frequent use of "traditional" seniority-based salaries, but that merit-based pay systems lead to quite heterogeneous sets of practices and little in the way of a common pattern. The Chi-square analysis also shows that firms maintaining lifetime employment norms were more likely to utilize both age and qualification in determining salary. However, lifetime employment had no significant relationship with the adoption or non-adoption of any specific elements of merit-pay. This finding is surprising given the strong relationship between firms having lifetime employment and those answering they have merit pay systems (Pearsons Chi-square: 28.5052 $P = 0.000$).[5]

The introduction of merit-based pay systems in Japan is often associated with changes in ownership, such as increases in foreign ownership and corporate governance reform (see Introduction). Studies in Germany also show that the introduction of performance-based pay was associated with changes in corporate governance (Jackson et al. 2005). Again using data from the METI survey, Table 10.6 uses a logit estimation of the likelihood of adopting various pay elements depending on selected aspects of corporate governance. The METI survey only provides a few indicators related to corporate governance. Here we examine the level of foreign ownership as an indicator of external market pressure, as well as two indicators that reflect changes in the internal structure and incentives of the board, namely the ratio of directors that are insiders promoted from within the firm and the adoption of stock options as an incentive pay scheme for board members. All estimations controlled for the total number of employees, return on assets, the age of the firm, and average age of employees. Control variables for industrial sector were also included, but these are not reported in the table.

In terms of seniority-based pay, Table 10.6 shows that firms with greater foreign ownership were less likely to adopt age-based salaries and firms using managerial stock options were less likely to have salaries linked to tenure. Meanwhile, corporate governance factors had no significant impact on the likelihood of linking pay to qualification, ability, or job activity. Likewise, corporate governance factors had no significant influence on adopting merit pay elements based on individual performance, firm performance, business unit performance, or competitors' wages. Pay based on long-term performance of the individual was more likely in younger firms, but less likely in firms using managerial stock options. In terms of overall employment systems overall, firms using managerial stock options were more likely to report having merit-based pay systems and less likely to report having lifetime employment. Board composition

---

[5] One further point that deserves mention is that further analysis of the METI survey demonstrates that the pay patterns of managerial employees were largely the same as regular employees, and a strong correlation exists between the use of pay elements at both levels.

Table 10.6 Log Likelihood of Adopting Pay Elements

	Age		Tenure		Qualification		Ability		Job	
	Coef.	P > z	Coef.	P > z	Coef.	P > z	Coef.	P > z	Coef.	P > z
Employees	0.000	0.974	0.000	0.930	0.000	0.696	0.000	0.788	0.000	0.936
	0.000		*0.000*		*0.000*		*0.000*		*0.000*	
Average age	0.081	0.138	−0.017	0.773	−0.016	0.776	−0.049	0.448	0.027	0.620
	0.054		*0.058*		*0.056*		*0.065*		*0.054*	
Year founded	−0.004	0.481	0.006	0.499	−0.021	0.028**	0.012	0.134	0.003	0.664
	0.005		*0.008*		*0.009*		*0.008*		*0.007*	
ROA	−0.024	0.243	0.040	0.114	0.003	0.811	−0.022	0.196	−0.030	0.176
	0.021		*0.026*		*0.013*		*0.017*		*0.022*	
Foreign ownership ratio	−0.041	0.027**	−0.044	0.055	0.001	0.958	−0.001	0.940	0.003	0.789
	0.019		*0.023*		*0.012*		*0.016*		*0.012*	
Stock options	−0.083	0.822	−1.025	0.017**	−0.317	0.391	−0.289	0.522	−0.244	0.501
	0.367		*0.429*		*0.369*		*0.452*		*0.363*	
Majority insider board	0.571	0.151	0.290	0.494	0.436	0.262	−0.798	0.130	−0.587	0.138
	0.398		*0.423*		*0.389*		*0.527*		*0.395*	
Industry control variables	YES		YES		YES		YES		YES	
Constant	3.254	0.760	−11.528	0.509	42.907	0.028	−19.011	0.259	−8.465	0.582
	10.647		*17.445*		*19.515*		*16.849*		*15.394*	
Log likelihood	−125.346		−117.465		−122.037		−92.576		−131.090	
N	206		206		206		192		206	
LR chi2(15) =	34.860		27.770		15.800		23.940		20.590	
Prob > chi2 =	0.003		0.023		0.396		0.032		0.150	
Pseudo R² =	0.122		0.106		0.061		0.115		0.073	

(*Continued*)

Table 10.6 (*Continued*)

	Firm performance		Business unit performance		Individual performance		Long-term performance		Competitors' wages	
	Coef.	P > z	Coef.	P > z	Coef.	P > z	Coef.	P > z	Coef.	P > z
Employees	0.000	0.256	0.000	0.427	0.000	0.224	0.000	0.862	0.000	0.139
	0.000		*0.000*		*0.000*		*0.000*		*0.000*	
Average age	0.044	0.405	0.015	0.823	-0.082	0.175	0.039	0.561	-0.058	0.312
	0.053		*0.068*		*0.061*		*0.067*		*0.057*	
Year Founded	-0.009	0.223	-0.025	0.029**	0.001	0.880	0.032	0.004***	-0.003	0.556
	0.007		*0.011*		*0.007*		*0.011*		*0.005*	
ROA	-0.027	0.188	-0.009	0.610	0.000	0.981	-0.015	0.428	-0.004	0.771
	0.021		*0.017*		*0.013*		*0.019*		*0.014*	
Foreign ownership ratio	0.011	0.354	0.002	0.926	0.015	0.393	-0.021	0.309	0.009	0.496
	0.012		*0.017*		*0.018*		*0.021*		*0.013*	
Stock options	0.055	0.879	0.792	0.085	0.170	0.694	-1.042	0.032**	0.132	0.730
	0.361		*0.460*		*0.431*		*0.485*		*0.382*	
Majority insider board	-0.490	0.210	-0.512	0.321	-0.594	0.198	0.119	0.799	0.026	0.952
	0.391		*0.517*		*0.461*		*0.469*		*0.429*	
Industry control variables	YES		YES		YES		YES		YES	
Constant	15.716	0.292	45.798	0.048	3.682	0.797	-65.592	0.005	-111.095	
	14.920		*23.117*		*14.334*		*23.102*			
Log likelihood	-129.926		-82.951		-104.411		-94.753			
N	206		177		206		201		195	
LR chi²(15) =	23.370		20.770		19.500		24.270		18.530	
Prob > chi² =	0.077		0.078		0.192		0.043		0.138	
Pseudo R² =	0.083		0.111		0.085		0.114		0.077	

	Employee stock option plan		Merit pay system		Lifetime employment system	
	Coef.	P > z	Coef.	P > z	Coef.	P > z
Employees	0.000	0.192	0.000	0.124	0.000	0.280
	0.000		*0.000*		*0.000*	
Average age	−0.136	0.055*	0.004	0.935	0.048	0.573
	0.071		*0.054*		*0.085*	
Year founded	−0.029	0.026**	0.007	0.177	−0.007	0.645
	0.013		*0.005*		*0.015*	
ROA	0.009	0.636	−0.053	0.079	0.076	0.106
	0.018		*0.030*		*0.047*	
Foreign ownership ratio	−0.032	0.010***	0.008	0.495	−0.016	0.219
	0.012		*0.012*		*0.013*	
Stock options	1.028	0.064	0.823	0.027**	−1.485	0.006***
	0.556		*0.372*		*0.538*	
Majority insider board	0.189	0.713	−0.244	0.532	1.386	0.010***
	0.515		*0.390*		*0.538*	
Industry control variables	YES		YES		YES	
Constant	63.789	0.017	−12.282	0.258	13.891	0.642
	26.694		*10.861*		*29.921*	
Log likelihood	−79.043		−128.255		−58.946	
N	191		208		200	
LR chi²(15) =	26.810		30.610		36.660	
Prob > chi² =	0.013		0.010		0.001	
Pseudo R² =	0.145		0.107		0.237	

Notes: Standard errors are shown in italics. * Significant at 0.10; ** Significant at 0.05; ***Significant at 0.01.

Source: 'Survey on the Corporate System and Employment' (METI Survey 2003).

had no influence on the likelihood of having merit-based pay systems, but having insider dominated boards where a majority of executives were internally promoted to the board did positively influence the likelihood of maintaining lifetime employment. Finally, foreign ownership had no significant impact on the odds of using either merit pay or lifetime employment.

Taken together, this evidence confirms that Japanese firms are continuing to move away from traditional, seniority-based methods of remuneration and are now experimenting with new forms of pay that consider individual performance and ability alongside a host of other factors. However, the lack of a homogeneous new pattern of merit pay suggests the trend involves an *incremental modification* of pay systems, rather than a radical departure from past practices. Firms are experimenting with various new elements of pay based on individual and company performance, and creating more heterogeneity in human resource management of Japanese firms. These results are consistent with other studies, which show a growing trend toward merit pay elements since the mid-1990s (Morishima 2002). This study suggests further that corporate governance has a relatively small, but significant influence on these decisions. However, no strong one-to-one relationship exists between particular corporate governance elements and pay elements. Foreign ownership and stock options influence firms to depart from age- or tenure-based pay, but do not strictly determine what new pay elements firms adopt. Most firms have implemented merit pay based on performance in a context of stable lifetime employment and internal career patterns, not as an alternative but an adaptation of existing evaluation systems.

The resulting distribution of earnings in Japan reflects this mix of old and new elements, such that age–wage curves are flattening but not disappearing. Figure 10.2 shows an index of average wages for regular employees by age category. Comparing the year 1975 and 2004 shows a flattening of these curves across all education groups, including university graduates. However, the layering of new merit pay elements has also led to a greater dispersion of wages within age cohorts at the same firm. Other studies suggest that the impact of individual performance differentials on employee salary are quite small and constitute less than 5% of total wages in a majority of firms (Morishima 2002). As such, Japanese HRM involves a very complex set of factors, which smooth salaries by pooling merit and non-merit elements. Finally, firms remain cautious toward using overly strong financial rewards and punishments due to the potentially subjective nature of performance assessments by managers.

The reduction of seniority-based pay elements does raise questions as to whether performance-based pay elements are compatible with lifetime employment in the long run. On one hand, larger pay differentials within the firm may undermine solidarity and cooperation among employees within the firm. On the other hand, merit pay may be legitimate as necessary flexibility in exchange for lifetime employment guarantees. These questions are empirical and should inform future research. However, the existing evidence seems to suggest that lifetime employment is compatible with the incremental and adaptive manner in which Japanese firms have implemented merit pay thus far.

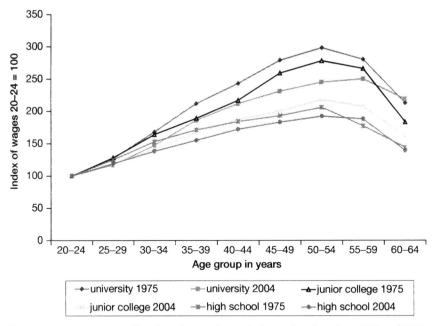

Figure 10.2 Age–wage profile of regular employees in Japan, by education, 1975 and 2004
Source: Japan Institute of Labour 2004.

10.3.3 The Distribution of Value-Added

Changes in the distribution of value-added between employees and investors are an imperfect, but potentially very interesting proxy of distribution of wealth among stakeholders (De Jong 1996). In Germany, Beyer and Hassel (2002) found that high ownership dispersion positively influenced the share of dividends, but had no direct impact on the labor share of value added. However, the same study shows that the adoption of shareholder-value oriented practices were associated with increasing share of dividends and a lower share for labor. The decline in labor share was largely due to a decrease in total employment through corporate restructuring, although remaining employees had higher wages on average.

In Japan, the Ministry of Finance compiles aggregate data on the value-added produced by corporations. Table 10.7 shows an adjusted calculation of gross value added from 1980 to 2005 based on the sum of payments to employees (salaries and benefits), directors (salary and bonuses), capital (interest payments, rent, and dividends), the state (corporate and other taxes), and the firm itself (depreciation, changes in reserves, and the net total of extraordinary and special profits/losses).[6] In terms of the relative factor shares of value-added, the labor share

[6] The Ministry of Finance calculates value-added by excluding depreciation, extraordinary profits and losses, and special profits and losses. The calculations in Table 10.7 use a broader adjusted definition of value added that is less affected by firms' accounting choices in terms of building internal reserves and the impact on non-operating income.

remained around 40% during the 1980s, but increased to a peak of 65% during
the recession year of 2001 due to the economic slowdown and low profitability.
During the recovery of 2001 to 2005, the labor share shrank rapidly back to 40%
of value-added. Meanwhile, directors slowly increased their share from 0.5% in
1980 to 1.3% in 2005. The capital share of value-added has shifted from interest
to dividends and rent. Interest payments have undergone a steady and dramatic
decline from 16% in 1980s to just 4% in 2005, as large firms reduced borrowing
from main banks. Rent payments increased moderately during this period. But
after dividends remained very stable between 2.5% and 3.5% through 2001, the
volume of dividends increased rapidly to 7% in 2005. Turning to the state, tax

Table 10.7 The Distribution of Adjusted Gross Value Added

Adjusted Gross Value Added in million Yen

	of which:	Labor	Directors	Capital			State	Firm
		Salary, benefits	Salary, bonus	Interest	Rent	Dividends	Tax	Depreciation, reserves
1980	53684527	38.4%	0.5%	16.4%	4.5%	2.6%	13.0%	24.6%
1981	55288897	40.5%	0.5%	16.4%	4.7%	2.7%	12.7%	22.5%
1982	57774405	41.3%	0.5%	15.3%	4.8%	2.7%	11.7%	23.6%
1983	61670617	41.0%	0.6%	14.2%	4.7%	2.7%	12.3%	24.6%
1984	66292859	40.7%	0.6%	13.1%	4.5%	2.6%	13.5%	25.0%
1985	75049674	40.9%	0.6%	12.1%	4.1%	2.6%	12.8%	27.0%
1986	74313873	42.1%	0.6%	11.0%	4.5%	2.7%	12.4%	26.7%
1987	77757507	41.8%	0.6%	9.8%	4.7%	2.7%	13.7%	26.8%
1988	89560125	40.2%	0.6%	9.6%	5.5%	2.7%	14.0%	27.4%
1989	101055722	39.6%	0.6%	10.0%	5.4%	2.7%	13.3%	28.5%
1990	114326156	38.5%	0.6%	11.9%	5.2%	2.5%	12.1%	29.2%
1991	116818018	40.6%	0.7%	11.8%	5.9%	2.6%	10.6%	27.8%
1992	112772518	43.7%	0.7%	11.1%	6.6%	2.5%	10.0%	25.4%
1993	109101890	45.9%	0.8%	9.9%	7.1%	2.4%	9.6%	24.3%
1994	108059326	47.0%	0.9%	9.3%	7.4%	2.5%	10.0%	22.9%
1995	109139910	47.6%	0.8%	7.7%	7.5%	2.6%	10.9%	22.9%
1996	110546052	48.1%	0.9%	6.5%	7.5%	2.7%	11.2%	23.0%
1997	107612057	50.2%	0.9%	6.4%	8.1%	2.8%	11.2%	20.3%
1998	98357823	54.0%	0.9%	6.6%	8.9%	3.1%	9.7%	16.9%
1999	89058910	58.0%	1.0%	6.6%	9.5%	3.5%	8.6%	12.8%
2000	93788003	55.2%	1.0%	5.8%	9.2%	3.7%	9.2%	15.9%
2001	79463430	65.4%	1.0%	6.1%	11.3%	3.9%	6.7%	5.5%
2002	95658720	52.5%	1.0%	4.5%	9.2%	4.3%	10.6%	17.8%
2003	105795185	47.1%	0.9%	3.9%	8.6%	4.8%	10.9%	23.8%
2004	106969002	45.9%	1.2%	3.4%	8.7%	5.0%	11.7%	24.1%
2005	120774104	40.1%	1.3%	4.1%	7.7%	7.1%	11.6%	28.1%

Source: Yearly Statistical Survey of Business Corporations, Policy Research institute, Ministry of Finance. The data
relate to all corporations with paid in capital of over ¥1 billion.

payments have fluctuated between 7% and 14% of value-added over the business cycle. Meanwhile, payments made "to the firm itself" remained around 25% during the 1980s, but were squeezed dramatically during the period 1997–2001 as firms booked extraordinary losses on bad debt and stock market losses post-bubble. During the period 2001–05, firms have once again increased these payments to 28%.

To put these changes into perspective, the percentage change in the value-added going to each group can be tabulated according to periods of economic growth or recession, as shown in Table 10.8. In the period 1980–86, the strong growth in value added and the benefits of declining interest were shared in remarkably equal proportions among labor, directors, rentiers, shareholders, the state and the firm. In the period 1986–97, Japan underwent a recession in 1986 following Plaza Accord, with slowed growth before the economy then entered the Bubble with large asset price inflation. During this period, growth in value added was shared by labor, directors, and shareholders in somewhat less equal proportions, while rentiers gained enormously from higher payments during the Bubble economy. However, payments to the firm contracted greatly, and interest payments maintained a gradual decline. In the period 1997–2001, value added contracted by roughly 5% per year. This burden was shouldered by a large contraction in tax payments and payments into the firms' internal reserves, as well as a more rapid decline in interest payments. Meanwhile, payments to labor remained nearly stable. During the period 2001–2005, however, a very different pattern emerges. Value added grew at a very rapid rate and these gains were reflected in a large increase in firms' internal reserves and taxes, as well as gains in dividends to shareholders and salaries and bonuses to directors. Meanwhile, payments to labor declined in absolute terms despite the overall growth in value added.

In sum, compared to the period of growth during the 1980s, a very different distributional pattern existed among stakeholder groups during the period 2001–2005. This distribution reflects a growing importance of shareholders and cleavage between directors and regular employees. During the 1990s, Japanese firms reducing employment tended to also cut dividends and very few firms redistributed wealth by reducing employment while raising dividends (Matsuura 2001). Since 1997, however, the cumulative volume of dividends paid increased by 180%, compared to a 10% decline in total salaries paid. This change may signal a shift from treating dividends as a quasi-fixed charge toward having a more variable relation with profits and negative relation to employment. Likewise,

Table 10.8 Average Annual Percentage Changes in Value Added

	Value added	Labor	Directors	Interest	Rent	Dividends	Tax	Firm
1980 to 1986	5.49	7.38	8.56	−1.01	5.62	6.18	4.61	7.18
1986 to 1997	3.73	6.06	11.10	−1.30	13.28	4.39	2.58	0.85
1997 to 2001	−5.23	−0.75	−3.31	−5.97	0.74	0.30	−11.14	−16.02
2001 to 2005	10.40	−1.35	17.51	0.22	0.71	35.52	32.15	136.09

payments to labor have declined by 10% in absolute terms since 1997, whereas payments to directors' share increased by 56%. Calculated on a per person basis, the average salary per director was just 1.9–2.2 times the salary of average employees 1980–2001, which demonstrates a remarkable correlation of salaries across both groups. However, this ratio increased to 3.1 in 2004 and 3.4 in 2005, reflecting some potential divergence in patterns of employee and executive pay.

10.3.4 Employee Participation and Negotiated Shareholder Value

Enterprise unions in Japan have played an important role in influencing the patterns of corporate restructuring. Japanese unions lack legally mandated forms of participation, such as codetermination rights of works councils and employee representatives on the Supervisory Board of German companies. However, joint labor management committees (JLMCs) became widespread among large corporations over the postwar era and could be found at roughly 80% of large firms by the 1990s—particularly among unionized manufacturing sector firms. Information sharing by JMLCs has significant positive effects on productivity (Kato and Morishima 2002; Kato 2003).

Today, the continued effectiveness of employee participation faces a number of challenges. First, the unionization rate has continuously declined from near 30% in the 1980s to just 19.6% in 2003 (Araki 2005). Second, the 2002 revision of the Labor Standards Law did establish a legally based system of representation called *roshi iinkai* (labor–management committee), but its scope of consultation is limited to working hours. For now, survey evidence suggests that the majority of directors think employee consultation does not hinder management decision-making, and a majority of HRM directors think unions should be involved in management decision making, suggesting that employee participation remains a legitimate element of corporate governance in the eyes of managers (Araki 2005). However, employees' position may be weakened if union density continues to decline and no legal rights to participation are created to strengthen labor's position. Finally, corporate restructuring has also led to increasingly complex corporate groups with various subsidiary firms. The strength of enterprise unions often depends upon defending the boundary of the firm or corporate group in order to internalize employment adjustment processes across various business units. Also since collective bargaining agreements are usually single employer agreements, unions may become dependent on accepting direct or indirect forms of pay cuts in order to assure job security. Major firms such as Mitsubishi Materials and Kobe Steel implemented flat-rate cuts, while other firms such as NTT and Keio Electric Railway created new regional subsidiaries with lower wages.

Unions have also been involved in the process of corporate governance reform. At the national level, the union federation Rengo Soken has supported the government's efforts to strengthen corporate monitoring through the use of statutory auditors, as well as for employees to become more involved in promoting corporate social responsibility—partly in response to scandals presenting dangers to customers and employees due to lapses in safety. However, a number of Rengo debates during the period 1999–2000 suggest that union-elected board members or auditors was not favored by a majority of union delegates, since such practices would blur the boundaries of unions and management, thereby sacrificing union independence.

An interesting aspect of union representation has been that the strong "voice" of employees in Japan has not prevented corporate governance reform. Rather, Japanese unions have cautiously and selectively supported reforms. For example, Miyajima (see Chapter 12 in this volume) finds that in firms exposed to capital market pressure, strong employee participation via labor-management councils had no positive or negative impact on information disclosure and shareholder rights, and had a positive effect on reforms to the board of directors. Likewise, Miyamoto (2006) shows that employees are likely to support or tolerate increased emphasis on shareholder value if firms' also maintain strong commitments to lifetime employment and retain modest salaries for board members. The peek Japanese union federation, Rengo, has supported greater disclosure on issues such as executive pay and pension liabilities. Greater checks and balances and better information may enhance the prospects for voice by both investors and employees, and hence be the source of stakeholder coalitions promoting greater corporate accountability (for a coalitional model of corporate governance see Aguilera and Jackson 2003). This pattern is rather similar to the stance of German works councils, who favor greater information disclosure and involvement of the Supervisory Board (Höpner 2001).

10.4 INCREMENTAL INSTITUTIONAL CHANGE: THE CASE OF COMPANY A

In order to illustrate the parallel processes of change in corporate governance and labor management, this section presents a brief case study drawn from company documents and interviews with the legal department, personnel department and enterprise union in both 1999 and 2004. Company A is a successful company in the foods sector, achieving strong sales growth and having only one loss making year in 2001. Their main business is domestic, but foreign sales grew from 16% in 1999 to 23% in 2003, with the highest proportion in Asia and Europe. Although Company A is not a member of a formal keiretsu group, the corporate governance pattern was broadly traditional in 1999. Three main banks provided lending, assistance with bond issues and consulting services. These relations have become more "business like" in recent years, and the last major investment to expand in East Asia was funded by a series of bond issues, rather than bank loans. Cross-shareholdings were also held with other insurance firms and industrial companies, and these ties were often linked to ongoing business relations, such as with a construction company. As banks underwent mergers and reduced their cross-shareholdings stakes from 5% to around 2–3% in the late 1990s, the overall level of stable shareholding has declined. However, new stable shareholding arrangements were also formed. Company A agreed to purchase a large stake from its main bank and form a new stable shareholding link to a company with which it had no prior relationship. Company A consciously aims to maintain a certain level of stable shareholders in order to fend off hostile takeover bids. Meanwhile, foreign ownership has increased rather dramatically from 7% in the mid-1990s to nearly 18% in 2003. Initially, communications with shareholders were a relatively small activity handled within the legal department, but the company later appointed an investor relations person in its public relations department and eventually established a separate investor relations department to answer a growing number of questions from large investors, analysts, and securities companies. While the company has not been targeted by activist investors or attracted large numbers of no votes at its shareholders' meeting, the level of transparency and communication with investors has improved very strongly.

A number of important but incremental changes have also occurred in the board of directors of Company A during this period. The board was reduced from 30 to 12 members, who all retain management positions in running company operations. In 1999, the company had no outside board members and expressed skepticism about outsiders' knowledge of company operations. Thus, all board members were recruited through the internal promotion system, and more than one-third come from science backgrounds, reflecting the fact that over 50% of regular employees are in science or production jobs. This insider board changed when the Chairman from a prominent securities think tank took a position as the only outside board member. Likewise, the company has not introduced stock options with one manager noting, "If managers stay a lifetime with the company, they have no chance to sell their shares." But by 2004, the company had introduced a more formalized performance based system making up 20–30% of total salary. Under this system, the CEO evaluates the company, departmental, and individual performance of the board members according to four grades (A, B, C, and D). The shareholders approve the overall salary of the board, but no individual salaries are disclosed.

In terms of employees, the company has reduced domestic employment at the parent firm from a peak of 6000 in the early 1990s to 4500 in 2004. No written guarantees for employment security have been made, but the union notes that, "Although we don't use the word 'lifetime employment,' the managers believe in it of course." Employment adjustment has thus been quite gradual and used "benevolent" methods. Some employees were transferred to other group companies, but a major reduction came through a hiring freeze with a resulting "gap in generations" with older and younger employees, but very few currently in their 40s. This demographic trend has also led union density at the parent firm to decline from around 75% in 1999 to 62% in 2004, as older union members retire and a growing proportion of employees are university educated and hold managerial positions.

A long-term shift in human resource management at Company A has been the growing importance of merit pay. Salaries are now determined by a combination of seniority and merit according to a complex system. The basic wage is still determined by age, but the increments have been adjusted in 2001 so that the peak salary is no longer at age 55 and followed by a decline, but at age 50 followed by a flat stable salary. Younger people also rise more quickly in the early years. Merit pay elements were introduced in 2002 according to four grades (A, B, C, and Special Merit). Employees are evaluated every six months by setting a number of goals with their supervisor, and assessed by a self-evaluation and interview with their supervisor to allocate points. Based on these points, the bottom 25% of employees are given grade C, 50% grade B, and 25% grade A. Special merit is given to a handful of employees for special achievements. The resulting salary differentials are small: Grade C employees then receive ¥2000 on their monthly salary, Grade B employees ¥5500, and Grade C employees ¥9000. Commenting on these differentials of roughly 5% of monthly salary, the union official noted, "The C rank makes people feel uncomfortable, but actually the wage difference is not so huge." Meanwhile, the larger variable pay factor remains the company bonus, which is calculated as 3.5 months salary multiplied by the ratio of achieved profits relative to target profits. The consequence of these changes has been a lowering of the total wage bill, as older employees retire, and some redistribution to younger employees—resulting in a flattening of age–wage curves. Due to the competitive environment of the company, basic wages have remained stable but collective bargaining has focused on reductions in total working hours and increases in vacation days.

Despite the relative stability of employment patterns at the parent Company A, other changes have occurred across the wider corporate group. A new group management plan was introduced in 1999 in order to consolidate management structures, and increase control over subsidiaries. The other domestic group companies employ 10,500 people, which are covered by nine different enterprise unions and coordinated through a union group council with monthly meetings and a yearly group wide consultation with the parent firm management. Since none of the group companies was established as a spin-off from the parent firm, each of them has very different HRM practices. Moreover, one group company is no longer covered by a union representation following a series of mergers. A partially owned subsidiary Company B was established within a joint venture with a major European company in the mid-1990s, but underwent consolidation and plant closures under direction of the European parent. Later, Company A repurchased this business unit and re-established it as a wholly owned subsidiary, but not without undermining the confidence of the subsidiaries' enterprise union.

In sum, the changes at Company A over the period of five years were largely incremental. Changes in ownership and finance have brought about greater pressures for transparency and disclosure, as well as stronger group level management of subsidiaries. However, the character of top management remains insider-dominated and avoided introducing high-power incentive contracts. Alongside these changes, employment levels have been slowly adjusted in line with business conditions and merit pay elements have been introduced alongside past seniority elements. The influence of the enterprise union has diminished somewhat as a result of these changes, but the union does play an active role in promoting issues around corporate ethics, corporate social responsibility and modest executive remuneration vis-à-vis top management. As such, Company A would appear to be quite representative of the main trends found in the statistical analysis. The case further suggests that this pattern of change involves an incremental adjustment of old practices through adaptation and layering of new practices, resulting in a new "hybrid" pattern or constellation of corporate governance practices.

10.5 CONCLUSION: THE END OF LIFETIME EMPLOYMENT?

Japanese firms have undergone large changes in their ownership, finance, and corporate governance. This chapter has examined the parallel changes in employment institutions and explored their interdependence with corporate governance. The main conclusion is that lifetime employment practices have not been abandoned, but their content has been slowly modified by gradual adjustment of employment levels, the introduction of merit based pay systems and changes in the distribution of value-added in favor of shareholders and directors. These changes have culminated in a shrinking core of lifetime employment and potential for growing social closure to these jobs for young Japanese.

Corporate governance has been an important driver of these changes, but has not resulted in a "convergence" of Japanese employment practices with those of more liberal market economies, such as the US or UK. Moreover, the impact of corporate governance on labor management is complex, and must be understood in relation to the more specific linkages between particular aspects of each. For example, the impact of foreign shareholders on lifetime employment or pay systems appears to be weaker than that of other corporate governance parameters such as inside directors or management pay, such as stock options. In this sense, the domains of finance and employment may be more loosely related empirically than often assumed in theoretical models based on complementarities between these domains.

Ultimately, the long-term and cumulative consequences of such changes remain unknown. In the medium-term, the existing evidence suggests that Japanese firms have sought to adapt and modify their stakeholder model of employment and employee participation to changing circumstances. However, a major factor underlying the commitment to lifetime employment remains the insider character of Japanese management—the internal career ladders leading to becoming a board member, the relatively egalitarian distribution of rewards between regular employees and top managers, and the social norms associated with these (see Chapter 13 by Dore, this volume). For the moment, corporate governance reform in Japan has not led to a radical shift toward having outside board members or US-style stock options, but has stressed other elements such as increasing transparency. Likewise, the market for corporate control has grown in importance but hostile takeovers remain relatively rare. Thus, it may be possible for firms to maintain long-term employment patterns even in a more market-oriented corporate governance environment to the extent that the strong internal linkage between managers, employees and business strategy remains intact.

Yet surely a key challenge for the future success of stakeholder-oriented corporate governance relates to finding ways to strengthen employees "voice" in the firm in ways that are complementary to investor pressure with regard to promoting greater corporate accountability. Effective employee participation may help constrain management from reacting to the excesses and short-term failures of capital markets. This internal aspect of corporate governance is also likely to benefit long-term institutional shareholders as well. It thus seems an open question whether organized labor can play a role in promoting an enlightened version of shareholder-value that can stress the positive-sum aspects of corporate governance and re-establish more egalitarian distributional outcomes. While the future cannot be predicted, what we can say is that the prospects for such a model will have a very real impact on the welfare of employees.

BIBLIOGRAPHY

Abe, M. (2002). 'Corporate Governance Structure and Employment Adjustment in Japan: An Empirical Analysis Using Corporate Finance Data,' *Industrial Relations*, 41: 683–702.

Abe, N. and S. Shimizutani (2005). 'Employment Policy and Corporate Governance: An Empirical Analysis on the Stakeholder Model in Japan,' *ESRI Discussion Paper Series* No.136. Economic and Social Research Institute, Cabinet Office, Tokyo.

Aguilera, R. V. and G. Jackson (2003). 'The Cross-National Diversity of Corporate Governance: Dimensions and Determinants,' *Academy of Management Review*, 28(3): 447–65.

Ahmadjian, C. L. and P. Robinson (2001). 'Safety in Numbers: Downsizing and the Deinstitutionalization of Permanent Employment in Japan,' *Administrative Science Quarterly*, 46, 622–54.

Aoki, M. (1988). *Information, Incentives, and Bargaining in the Japanese Economy*. Cambridge: Cambridge University Press.

Araki, T. (2005) 'Corporate Governance Reforms, Labor Law Developments, and the Future of Japan's Practice-Dependent Stakeholder Model,' *Japan Labor Review*, 2(1): 26–57.

Beyer, J. and A. Hassel (2002). 'The Effects of Convergence: Internationalisation and the Changing Distribution of Net Value Added in Large German Firms,' *Economy and Society*, 31(3): 309–32.

De Jong, H. W. (1996). 'European Capitalism Between Freedom and Social Justice,' in W. Bratton, J. McCahery, S. Picciotto, and C. Scott (eds.), *International Regulatory Competition and Coordination: Perspectives on Economic Regulation in Europe and the United States*. Oxford: Clarendon Press, 185–206.

Dore, R. (1973). *British Factory, Japanese Factory. The Origins of National Diversity in Industrial Relations*. Berkeley, CA: University of California Press.

Dore, R. (2000). *Stock Market Capitalism: Welfare Capitalism. Japan and Germany Versus the Anglo-Saxons.* Oxford: Oxford University Press.

Gordon, A. (1998). *The Wages of Affluence: Labor and Management in Postwar Japan.* Cambridge, MA: Harvard University Press.

Gospel, H. and A. Pendleton (eds.) (2005). *Corporate Governance and Labor Management: An International Comparison.* Oxford: Oxford University Press.

Hanami, T. A. (1985). *Labour Law and Industrial Relations in Japan.* Amsterdam: Kluwer Law International.

Honda, Y. (2005). '"Freeters:" Young Atypical Workers in Japan,' *Japan Labour Review*, 2(3): 1–21.

Höpner, M. (2001). 'Corporate Governance in Transition: Ten Empirical Findings on Shareholder Value and Industrial Relations in Germany,' *MPIfG Discussion Paper 01/5.* Köln: Max-Planck-Institut für Gesellschaftsforschung.

Hurlin, C. and S. Lechevalier (2003). 'The Heterogeneity of Employment Adjustment Across Japanese Firms: A Study Using Panel Data,' *Working paper* No.2003-10, CEPRE-MAP, Paris.

Inagami, T. and D. H. Whittaker (2005). *The New Community Firm. Employment, Governance and Management Reform in Japan.* Cambridge: Cambridge University Press.

Jackson, G. (2003). 'Corporate Governance in Germany and Japan: Liberalization Pressures and Responses,' in K. Yamamura, and W. Streeck (eds.), *The End of Diversity? Prospects for German and Japanese Capitalism.* Ithaca, NY: Cornell University Press, 261–305.

—— (2005a). 'Stakeholders under Pressure: Corporate Governance and Labor Management in Germany and Japan,' *Corporate Governance: An International Review*, 13(3): 419–28.

—— (2005b). 'Toward a Comparative Perspective on Corporate and Labour Management: Enterprise Coalitions and National Trajectories,' in H. Gospel and A. Pendleton (eds.), *Corporate Governance and Labour Management: An International Comparison.* Oxford: Oxford University Press, 284–309.

—— M. Hoepner and A. Kurdelbusch (2005). 'Corporate Governance and Employees in Germany: Changing Linkages, Complementarities, and Tensions,' in H. Gospel and A. Pendleton (eds.), *Corporate Governance and Labour Management: An International Comparison.* Oxford: Oxford University Press, 84–121.

Jacoby, S. M. (2004). *The Embedded Corporation: Corporate Governance and Employment Relations in Japan and the United States.* Princeton: Princeton University Press.

Japan Institute for Labor Policy and Training (ed.) (2006). *Japanese Working Life Profile 2005/2006—Labour Statistics.* Tokyo: Japan Institute for Labour Policy and Training.

Kato, T. (2001). 'The End of Lifetime Employment in Japan? Evidence from National Surveys and Field Research,' *Journal of the Japanese and International Economies*, 15: 489–514.

—— (2003) 'The Nature, Scope and Effects of Joint Labor–Management Committees in Japan,' *Working Paper 103–09*, Department of Economics, Colgate University.

—— M. Morishima (2002). 'The Productivity Effects of Participatory Employment Practices: Evidence from New Japanese Panel Data,' *Industrial Relations* 41(4): 487–520.

Koike, K. (1988). *Understanding Industrial Relations in Modern Japan.* London: Macmillan.

Komoto, K. (2004). 'Companies Make Progress in Reforming Employment and Wage Systems—February 2004 Nissay Business Conditions Survey,' *NLI Research*, May, 1–12.

Matsuura, K. (2001). 'Layoff and Dividend Policies of Japanese Firms—Evidence from Profitability Ratio, Capital Structures, Corporate Governance,' *Financial Review* (Ministry of Finance, Policy Research Institute), 60: 106–38.

Miyamoto, M. (2006). 'Human Resource Management of the Contemporary Japanese Firms (Gendai Nihonkigyo no Jinzai Management),' *JILPT Research report*, No.61.

Morishima, M. (2002). 'Pay Practices in Japanese Organizations: Changes and Nonchanges,' *Japan Labour Bulletin*, April, 8–13.

Nakata, Y. and R. Takehiro (2001). 'Joint Accounting System and Human Resource Management by Company Group,' *JIL Bulletin*, 40(10): 1–8.

O'Sullivan, M. (2003). 'The Political Economy of Comparative Corporate Governance,' *Review of International Political Economy*, 10: 23–72.

Sako, M. and G. Jackson (2006). 'Strategy Meets Institutions: The Transformation of Management–Labor Relations at Deutsche Telekom and NTT,' *Industrial and Labor Relations Review*, April, 59(3): 347–66.

Tachibanaki, T. and M. Morikawa (2000). 'Employment Adjustment, Wage Cut and Shutdown: An Empirical Analysis Based on the Micro-data of Manufacturing Industry,' *MITI/RI Discussion Paper*, #00-DOF-34.

Tanisaka, N. and F. Ohtake (2003). 'Impact of Labor Shedding on Stock Prices,' *Japan Labour Bulletin*, January, 6–12.

Vitols, S. (2004). 'Negotiated Shareholder Value: The German Version of an Anglo-American Practice,' *Competition and Change*, 8(4): 1–18.

Yamakawa, R. (2002). '*From Security to Mobility? Changing Aspects of Japanese Dismissal Law,*' *Law in Japan: A Turning Point*. Washington, DC: University of Washington, School of Law, Asia Law Centre.

11

The Turnaround of 1997: Changes in Japanese Corporate Law and Governance

Zenichi Shishido

11.1 INTRODUCTION

Since the last trading day of the Tokyo Stock Exchange of 1989, the Japanese stock market and economy have been in decline. In 2003, the Japanese economy appeared to have hit bottom but the recovery remains fragile. People often refer to this long recession during the 1990s as the "lost decade." Business and government each made a lot of effort to end the recession but in vain. Although the situation appeared quite static, many changes were actually taking place during the lost decade. This process came to a head and became apparent in 1997. Why 1997? Although perhaps somewhat arbitrary, most students of Japan now recognize 1997 as a year of turnaround.

This article has three aims. The first aim is to explain why the traditional Japanese corporate governance system (the traditional J-model) began to malfunction and to suggest that a new Japanese corporate governance system (the new J-model) is presently emerging. The second aim is to examine the relationship between the corporate governance practice and the reforms of corporate law since 1997. Finally, the third aim is to argue that the recent history of Japan runs contrary to predominant arguments about the convergence of corporate governance systems. A growing literature predicts that corporate governance will undergo functional convergence even without a formal convergence of legal rules (Gilson 2001). Recent reforms of Japanese corporate law have, in fact, introduced substantial elements of formal convergence, whereas corporate governance continues to display functional divergence due to differences in the incentive patterns of major corporate stakeholders.

Section 11.2 will discuss trends in Japanese corporate governance practices during the lost decade and why 1997 culminated in a turning point. Section 11.3 reviews corporate law reforms since 1997 and discusses their significance for the change of corporate governance practice. Section 11.4 discusses this current history of Japanese corporate governance in the context of debates over the international convergence of corporate governance and suggests that Japan is moving toward a new J-model. Section 11.5 summarizes the main conclusions of this study.

11.2 THE LOST DECADE AND THE TURNING POINT

The traditional J-model can be described as a contingent corporate governance system based on the notion of a "company community." It is not only in Japan, but also in other countries, that the providers of human capital, i.e. management and employees, organize a kind of team and share a common interest maintaining their autonomy from the investors who provide monetary capital, i.e. shareholders and creditors, who share a common interest of obtaining stronger power to monitor the team of human capital providers. What makes the traditional J-model unique is that the human capital providers do not simply organize a temporary team, but create a long-lived community (Shishido 2000).

The common desire of the company community to keep their independence is so strong that the monetary capital providers have been forced to respect their autonomy. Actually, this is also the benefit to the monetary capital providers. Japanese firms have boards made up of insiders and normally have no outside directors. Only in the case of bad performance by the company community such as a large business loss or large declines in stock price does the main bank or major keiretsu shareholders intervene and force the company community to accept outside directors (Kaplan and Minton 1994). Such a practice is called "contingent governance" (Aoki 1994), which gives human capital providers an incentive to work hard to avoid intervention by the investors of monetary capital. Such a system worked well as long as the Japanese economy was in a phase of high economic growth.

The Japanese contingent governance system, however, ran into serious difficulties after the economic growth slowed in the early 1980s. Particularly, the traditional J-model had trouble in monitoring the use of free cash flow and firms wasted large amounts of cash during the bubble economy (Gilson and Roe 1993). In the 1990s, after the bursting of the bubble, shareholders came increasingly to the fore with their complaints about the company community, either by exit, like dissolving cross-shareholdings, or by voice, like US-style institutional investor activism (see Chapters 3 and 4, this volume).

At the same time, two important environmental changes were going on. On the investors' side, the role of the main banks was changing. Banks had acted the delegated monitors to coordinate and undertake monitoring among the monetary capital providers. However, banks lost their ability to act as effective monitors because of their bad loan problems, as well as problems in their own internal governance (see Chapter 2, this volume).

In fact, the main bank relationship itself created perverse incentives. Once a main bank gave a large loan to a specific firm, the main bank could not let the firm go bankrupt even when the firm faced serious financial distress. Many such cases existed during the lost decade, particularly in construction industries, where the main bank not only waived its own loan, but also solicited other banks to write-off their loans to the failing firm. Since company insiders providing human capital to such financially distressed firms could anticipate the bank behavior, they faced little incentive to change their moral hazard behavior even after management had clearly failed.

For employees and inside managers providing human capital, the company community also began to change during the lost decade: Employment became less secure. Although firms usually avoided outright lay-offs, they adjusted employment more quickly and frequently through early retirement or transfers (see Chapter 10, this volume). Secure jobs often came at the price of pay-cuts. As a result, employees began to feel that companies had breached implicit contracts and consequently their psychological attachment and loyalty to the company community started loosening. It should be noted that the liquidity of external labor markets still remains small, even though job change is no longer a rare case in some industries such as finance. And most board members are still promoted internally from among the company employees.

What happened in 1997? This was a very memorable year for many Japanese people. A number of watershed events happened that changed the predominant mood. It looked like an apple, which had been ripening, fell at last.

The biggest impact was made by a series of failures by major financial institutions. In particular, the bankruptcy of a major city bank, Hokkaido Takushoku Bank, and the dissolution of a big four securities firm, Yamaichi Securities, shocked the Japanese public. Most Japanese believed that the government would never let such major financial institutions fail. So first of all, 1997 was the year that the Japanese government started to let major financial institutions fail.

This change of government policy changed banks' investment policy. Japanese banks, as major players of cross shareholding networks, used to keep holding stock of their partner companies, regardless of its bad performance in the stock market. After the financial crisis, the Tokyo stock market declined further and the major decline in the asset value of such shares pushed the banks into crisis. Given the pressure of the BIS regulations, Japanese banks were forced to sell off many mochiai stocks.[1]

1997 was also the year that rapid deregulation of corporate law started. These corporate law reforms reflected market pressures. The introduction of stock options in 1997 was a particularly symbolic case, as it was the first corporate law reform initiated by a Diet member. Historically, corporate law reforms had been initiated by the Ministry of Justice after long debates at its Legislative Counsel, in which academic lawyers were very influential. But in the case of stock options, business associations lobbied the Diet and the legislation was passed very quickly. Since then, corporate law reform has become much faster, even when the Legislative Counsel of the Ministry of Justice is involved.

Lastly, in 1997, voluntary reforms of corporate governance practices were started by Sony and several other companies with many foreign shareholders.

---

[1] Interestingly, banks did not necessarily sell off low performance stocks. They sold their lowest performance stocks and highest performance stocks, keeping mediocre stocks (see Chapter 2, this volume).

Younger executive directors were demoted to "executive officers (*shikko yakuin*)" and the number of board members was decreased. This step represented an attempt to separate day-to-day management and monitoring.[2] This step did much to make the board of directors a real seat of decision-making. This type of reform, called the "executive officer system (*shikko yakuinn sei*)," has since been followed by many publicly held companies. Several leading companies even introduced outside directors and a committee system before the corporate law reform of 2002.[3]

On the whole, 1997 marked a major shift in thinking. Japanese people, particularly, members of company communities, clearly recognized that share-holders cannot be ignored and that corporate governance reform is inevitable. Since then the convergence of at least the formal rules regarding corporate governance has progressed substantially. But as shall be discussed later, such formal convergence has not necessarily resulted in the functional convergence of corporate governance practices.

11.3 CORPORATE LAW REFORMS SINCE 1997: DEMAND–PULL REFORM AND POLICY–PUSH REFORM

In a previous article, I examined the relationship between legal reforms and corporate governance practice over 100 years of Japanese corporate law by using the analytical framework of "policy–push" reform and "demand–pull" reform (Shishido 2001). Policy–push reforms are those initiated by the legislature to change market practices. The demand–pull reforms are those initiated by the business sectors to enable new practices that could not be done under the current legal rules. A key finding was that on one hand, most demand–pull reforms were strongly linked to changes in business practice, because practice was a cause of the reform effort and reform had a further effect to enable or support such change. On the other hand, policy–push reforms only rarely had a strong influence on business practice. This article extends this framework for analyzing the corporate law reforms since 1997.

Demand–pull reform of corporate law can be categorized into two types. First, some reforms are based on the interests of management or of human capital providers as a whole, particularly in order to protect their autonomy from intervention by outsid investors. The demands of the business sector for reform come mostly from the management and core employees of major publicly held corporations. They have their own lobbying organization, named Keidanren,[4] which has a seat at the Legislative Counsel of the Ministry of Justice. Second,

---

[2] Japanese boards traditionally had no concept of separation of management and monitoring except the statutory auditor, which had no voting right and was, in practice, typically an ex-employee.

[3] For example, Sony, Orix, Teijin, and Hoya.

[4] Keidanren is the major management organization for large companies.

some demand–pull reforms target the interests of shareholders and thus increase pressure on management. In either case, most demand–pull reforms take the form of deregulation of mandatory laws and thus enable new business practices.

Policy–push reform is largely developed through the legislative process that involves legal bureaucrats, who are either judges or prosecutors, and academic lawyers. These corporate law reforms can also be categorized into two types: reforms to improve the monitoring management and reforms to protect the interests of minority shareholders. Most policy–push reforms consist of mandatory regulations that prevent businesses from or require them to adopt particular practices.

11.3.1 Repurchase of Shares

The repurchase of shares by a company had once been basically prohibited with a few exceptions. Although business sectors had pushed the legislature toward deregulation of share repurchases, particularly academic lawyers had strongly resisted deregulation because it would violate some basic "principle of corporate law."

In 1994, some exceptions to the prohibition of share repurchases were added, such as repurchases for selling to employees or for stock redemption approved at the shareholder meeting. In 1997, an important exception was added to let publicly held corporations repurchase their shares for the purpose of redemption based only on the decision of the board. Finally, in 2001, share repurchases became basically unrestricted within the bounds of profit payable as dividend and subject to a few procedural rules. Even the resale of treasury stock was deregulated.

It was a typical demand–pull reform and had a huge and immediate impact on the practice of corporate finance. From April 2002 to March 2003, 1652 publicly held corporations voted to authorize stock repurchases within certain limits and 972 companies actually repurchased their own stock for a total amount of more than ¥3000 billion (Shigemi Ozawa, 'The Situation of Stock Repurchases in 2002,' Shinko Research Institute, June 26, 2003). In sum, share repurchases have become a common instrument of many Japanese corporations.

Why did management demand the power of repurchase of shares? Probably, the primary objective was to keep their companies' stock prices high during the long recession through the effect of signaling. In addition, management could have the company buy the shares that were being sold off by its cross-shareholding partners. A recent survey of companies regarding stock repurchase confirmed that around 60% of companies authorizing share repurchases did so with the intention of buying stock that was being sold by their mochiai partner (Masashi Kohara, 'The Purpose of 60% Stock Repurchasing Firms is for Taking Care of "Mochiai Dissolution",' Shinko Research Institute, September 8, 2003). Another less overt purpose for share repurchases may have been for use as a defense against hostile takeovers. While these purposes would have served the self-interest of management, they also constituted a way of returning free cash flow to shareholders other than by dividend. Thus, they were part of management response to the strong pressure of the capital market.[5] Not only in Japan, but also in the United States, management tends to prefer share repurchases over paying higher dividends because once management increases the dividend, it becomes difficult to decrease the dividend later without incurring a negative reaction by the stock market (Fried 2005).

From 1997 to 2001, two different methods of stock redemption were thus available for publicly held corporations. The formal way required a resolution of the annual shareholder meeting, but no limitation was placed on the number of repurchased stock. The less formal way only required a resolution of a board meeting, but repurchased stock was limited to 10% of issued stock. A recent study suggests that companies adopted the formal method of approval by the shareholder meeting when seeking to return their free cash flow to their shareholders, whereas companies used the informal way of stock redemption when seeking to send the stock market a signal of undervaluation of their stock (Hirose et al. 2003).

11.3.2 Stock Options

In 1997, stock options were introduced to Japan. Initially, stock options remained very restricted. For example, issuing stock options was limited either to directors or to employees. Nonetheless, deregulation of stock options introduced the concept of the equity incentive and opened a way of aligning interests between shareholders and human capital providers. In 2001, stock options were totally deregulated (e.g. no necessity of attaching to bonds) and now can be issued to anybody. As a result, stock options can also be used as poison pills although no such cases can be observed thus far.

Introduction of stock options was a demand–pull reform that had particular symbolic importance, because corporate law reform was initiated directly by members of the Diet for the first time. These Diet members were responding directly to lobbying by the business sector. Management can now use stock options to different ends. Stock options can be used to provide additional remuneration, thus serving the self-interest of company insiders. But stock options can potentially also help to resolve agency problems by aligning the interests of managers and human capital providers to the stock market. In any case, stock options have become widely used. From their introduction in 1997 through June 2004, some 1303 companies or 36% of publicly held corporations have issued stock options.[6]

Previously, Japanese companies never utilized this type of equity incentive as a scheme for motivating human capital providers because human capital providers were sufficiently motivated by the company community concept of the traditional *J*-model. Although it is too early to evaluate its effect on Japanese

[5] For example, Canon, which has more than 40% foreign shareholders, repurchased shares in 2003 for the purpose of "returning free cash flow to our shareholders." Nikkei 2003 (11/27: 1).

[6] See Nikkei 2004 (6/24: 17).

companies, several characteristics of Japanese stock options can be identified. First, stock options are given very widely, not only to directors and officers, but also to core employees. Second, for directors and officers, stock options remain only a small percentage of their total compensation. Third, the gap between option price and current price is small. Fourth, option term is relatively short, typically around four years. And fifth, companies adopting stock options are mostly market oriented and high performance companies, such as Toyota and Matsushita.

11.3.3 Corporate Reorganizations

After 1997, measures to reorganize corporate groups were rapidly deregulated and a greater variety of reorganization schemes became available for shareholders and management. These reforms were mostly demand–pull and have been used widely, although with some exceptions. Management has lobbied for wider discretion in corporate restructuring needed to change the boundaries of corporate groups. Managers have particularly been seeking convenient tools for mergers and acquisitions: Corporate reorganizations, both within a single corporate group and between different groups, have been pushed by intense product market competition and pressures of the stock market. The consequence is that in Japan, friendly mergers and acquisitions have been increasing.

Deregulation of Mergers

In 1997, procedures for mergers and acquisitions were simplified. One of the two shareholder meetings previously required to approve a merger, called the "meeting for reporting shareholders," was abolished. Requirements for notifying individual creditors were also abolished. And short-form mergers were permitted, requiring only the approval of the acquiring company's shareholders when the size of the acquired company was less than 5% of the acquiring company.[7]

Holding Companies

The prohibition against holding companies, which had a huge effect on post-war Japanese corporate governance, was also lifted in 1997. The Anti-monopoly Law had banned holding companies since 1947. The ban was introduced by the Allies, who considered *zaibatsu* holding companies to be one of the biggest evils in pre-war Japanese society.

   Obviously, the holding company structure is one of the reasonable alternatives for the governance of conglomerate firms. Big Japanese companies diversified their business, but were forced to adopt a group structure consisting of subsidiaries governed by a parent company that has its own core business (a "holding company

---

[7] Japanese short-form merger is different from American short-form merger, which is permitted if the acquiring company already owns most of the acquired company's stock.

with business"). Conflicts of interest problems often arose between the core business of the holding company and its subsidiaries. The pure holding company structure has fewer conflict of interest problems and may be a better choice in many circumstances. Nevertheless, even after the "evil" of the zaibatsu was gone, the prohibition against genuine holding company continued for 50 years.

Despite its potential strengths for monitoring subsidiaries, the pure holding company structure has been adopted less than would be expected from a typical demand–pull reform. Until September 2002, only 23 listed corporations either adopted or announced plans to adopt the holding company structure (Miyajima and Inagaki 2003). Among those multi-divisional companies with an in-house company system, the majority of companies have retained the in-house system and not yet reformed it into the formal holding company system. The major reason is probably that the concept of the autonomy of the company community in Japan tends to be applied to each corporation, even if it is a wholly owned subsidiary. In this sense, many expect the holding company to be a weaker monitor than the headquarter of an in-house company system.

Holding companies have also been used as an important means to implement mergers and acquisitions.[8] In Japan, the concept of the "company community" is still strong and members of the company community typically resist the idea that their company will be merged with another company and disappear. Merging through the creation of a holding company together is more easily acceptable by company communities.

The holding company can be expected to affect Japanese corporate governance in two ways. First, in the context of internal reorganization of a corporate group, the holding company will play a role like the venture capitalist in the Silicon Valley Model, i.e. both as a professional monitor and as a go-between for the monetary capital providers and the human capital providers.[9] Second, in the context of mergers and acquisitions, the holding company will provide the members of both company communities a framework and time to prepare for a final merger.[10]

Share-for-Share Exchanges (Stock Swaps)

In 1999, share-for-share exchanges were introduced to facilitate the creation of holding companies. This new scheme can also be used for squeezing out minority shareholders of controlled subsidiaries by giving them parent company shares without their agreement.

In fact, stock swaps now give Japanese companies a new and convenient tool for mergers and acquisitions more generally. Listed companies can acquire other companies without using cash. In Silicon Valley, Cisco Systems has grown rapidly

---

[8] Until September 2002, 18 quasi-mergers were either made or announced to be made by creating a holding company together (Miyajima and Inagaki 2003).

[9] Actually, in pre-war Japan, holding companies of zaibatsu groups played such a role.

[10] For example, two major trading companies, Nichimen and Nisho-Iwai, will merge after one year operating under a holding company (see Nikkei 2003 (12/26: 1)).

by using this method to acquire many start-up companies using a strategy called "acquisition and development." Since the 1999 reforms, mergers and acquisitions between Japanese companies have increased dramatically and involved a number of prominent cases of share-for-share exchanges.[11]

Deregulation of stock swaps is another example of demand–pull reform. Without share-for-share exchanges, creating holding companies would require very complicated procedures. Second, management has been seeking a tool for converting partially owned subsidiaries into wholly owned subsidiaries because the existence of minority shareholders creates a host of problems. And third, a tool for acquiring other companies without cash is attractive for management of publicly held companies.[12]

Corporate Divisions

In 2000, another new and convenient tool for reorganizations of corporate groups and mergers and acquisitions was introduced. The newly implemented legal scheme of corporate division (dividing the corporation), which was of German origin, could be used for various purposes: creating wholly owned subsidiaries, creating and dissolving joint ventures, American type spin-offs and split-offs, transferring a business unit to another company, etc. (Takei and Hirabayashi 2000).

In practice, corporate divisions are now frequently used for creating wholly owned subsidiaries because the new scheme can skip the notorious inspection by the court of transfers of a business to a newly created company, which is ordinarily required by the Commercial Code.

So far, however, corporate divisions have almost never been used for American type spin-offs and split-offs, which create separate companies without any controlling relationship. There are two reasons. First, such reorganizations will cause undesirable tax effects, not only on the dividing corporation by realizing a capital gain, but also on the shareholders who are considered to have received a dividend.[13] Second, they mean the division of "company community." Human capital providers in most Japanese companies still keep the team concept of the company community and would not want to divide their team even though spin-offs may increase shareholder value (Hite and Owers 1983; Miles and Rosenfeld 1983; Shipper and Smith 1983; Aron 1991; Cusatis et al. 1993; Vijh 1994).

This law reform was a demand–pull reform designed to facilitate creating wholly owned subsidiaries and creating joint ventures because management demanded a tool for bypassing formal procedures. At the same time, this reform

---

[11] A major M&A case using a share-for-share exchange was the merger of two famous photography companies: Konica and Minolta in 2003. See Nikkei 2003 (5/16: 13). Rakuten, a Japanese internet giant, looks like it is using this new scheme for "acquisition and development" like Cisco Systems. See Nikkei 2002 (10/22: 17). Kyocera, Sony, and Canon also took advantage of their high price stock for acquiring other companies. See Nikkei 2002 (5/17: 11); Nikkei 2003 (1/29: 13); Nikkei 2003 (12/27: 11).

[12] Although their companies could be targets of acquisitions, share-for-share exchanges could basically be used only for friendly acquisitions because they require a special resolution (two thirds majority) at the shareholder meeting.

[13] Chugai Pharmaceutical spun-off its bio unit, which was provably the only case of a spin-off in Japan after the law reform, and was forced to pay an enormous tax. See Nikkei 2003 (7/27: 28).

was a policy–push reform to encourage spin-offs. The legislature prepared the tool, which logically should exist and may enhance the interest of shareholders, even before management and human capital providers actually demanded. A characteristic of this policy–push reform is its enabling nature, in contrast to most policy–push reforms which create mandatory laws.

11.3.4 Accounting Reforms

Accounting rules have been also reformed and the transparency of Japanese companies has increased since the late 1990s. In 1997, consolidated accounting was required by the Securities Regulation and, in 2002, it was also required by the Commercial Code. Consolidated accounting changed the mindset of Japanese management and investors who used to evaluate the performance of management on an individual company basis. In the Commercial Code Reform of 1999, mark-to-market accounting for financial assets was also required. This reform had a significant impact toward dissolving cross shareholdings. The reform had a strong impact particularly on banks, which were forced to meet the balance sheet requirements imposed by the Bank for International Settlements (BIS). Management of non-financial companies was also forced to recognize the business reality of stock market volatility and report unrealized gains and losses on their holdings of mochiai stock.

These were typical policy–push reforms. Although management never wanted these reforms, the legislature changed the laws with a pressure of internationalization of accounting rules. These were rare cases, where policy–push reforms substantially affected the practice.

11.3.5 Corporate Governance Reforms

Limiting Directors' Liability

Since the famous reform of 1993, which fixed the filing fee of shareholder derivative actions at ¥8200 regardless of the amount of damages sought, the number of shareholder derivative actions in Japan has increased dramatically. Japanese management has complained of the "chilling effect" of the lawsuits on their business judgment and tried to decrease the volume of lawsuits. Particularly after the district court decision in the Daiwa Bank Case, which ordered directors of Daiwa Bank to pay an astronomical amount of damages, the business sector seriously lobbied for some relief. As a result, the corporate law reform of 2001 allowed companies to put an upper limit on damages for negligence of their directors by amendment of their bylaws.

Although this was a typical demand–pull reformation, the new law was a kind of compromise after bargaining between the business sector and legislature. *Ex ante* limitation, up to two times one's annual remuneration, could be put only on outside directors. Limitation of liability of inside directors, up to six times of one's annual remuneration in case of representative directors and up to four times of one's annual remuneration in case of non-representative directors, could be allowed *ex post* either by resolution of board of directors if more than 3% of shareholders did not object or by special resolution of shareholder meeting.

This reformation was significant for Japanese corporate governance in two ways. First, *ex ante* limitation of liability of outside directors opened the possibility of a monitoring system based on outside directors. Second, this reform provided Japanese management with a quasi business judgment rule because management risk could be limited where there was no illegality and gross negligence.[14]

Strengthening Statutory Auditors

The statutory auditor system was strengthened again in 2001. The history of Japanese corporate governance law reform has been the history of strengthening statutory auditors (Shishido 2001), and the reform of 2001 was the most fundamental change. This reform required Japanese large companies to have "real" outside auditors who composed at least half of all auditors after May 2005. Although outside auditors had already been required since 1993, most large companies chose ex-employees five years into their retirement to satisfy to the definition of "outside auditors" of the Commercial Code. Company communities therefore enjoyed genuine insider boards even after the reformation of 1993. The reform of 2001 was the first legislation that effectively intervened in the company community.

Of course, members of company communities never wanted to be forced to accept outsiders on the board, even if they were quasi board members without vote. The legislatures forced the business sector to accept this reform, probably as a prerequisite for the limitation of directors' liability, which was enacted at the same time. For changing the bylaws to implement the limitation of directors' liability, agreements of all statutory auditors became necessary. Therefore, the outsider requirement was a typical policy–push reform.

Although it is too early to evaluate the new law's practical effect because it is not yet effective, it will have a huge impact on Japanese corporate governance. After the new law becomes effective, a Japanese large company will have to have at least two outside auditors and probably two inside auditors because the company community would never want an outsider majority of the auditors. This means that a Japanese large company will have at least four auditors who only monitor for illegal behavior, as long as it does not become a company with committees (see the description of committees below). Two things should be expected. First, this reform will put some pressure on traditional companies with statutory auditors to adopt a board with committees. Second, this reform will make contingent governance difficult because Japanese large companies will be forced to always have at least two real outsiders (non-members of company communities) on their

---

[14] Although, in the United States, the business judgment rule prohibits courts from second guessing the adequacy of a business judgment, adequacy of business judgment is often reviewed by the court in Japan.

boards (as quasi members), even when company communities maintain good performance.

Board with Committees as an Option

In 2002, a momentous reform of Japanese corporate governance law took place. The American style board of directors, called the "board with committees" in Japan, was introduced as an option in addition to the traditional Japanese style board with statutory auditors.

The Japanese traditional board system with statutory auditors, who have no vote and are only in charge of monitoring for illegal behavior, used to fit perfectly into the Japanese contingent corporate governance system based on the company community. In the traditional system, there was little distinction between management and monitoring among board members. Directors were simply at the top of the hierarchy of management and at the same time of the company community. Therefore, a board composed of insiders was normal. Only in the case of bad performance by the company community, did the main bank or major keiretsu shareholders force the company community to accept outside directors.

There are three major characteristics of the new board system with committees as compared to the traditional board system with statutory auditors.

First, the new system is much clearer in the distinction between day-to-day management and monitoring than the traditional system. While in the traditional system, every manager must be a director, in the new system, a manager, called an officer, is not necessarily a director.

Second, outside directors, who have never been employees and officers,[15] are expected to play an important role of the corporate governance. Outside directors must be the majority in all three committees—the audit committee, the nomination committee, and the remuneration committee—whose decisions are final. Even the board of directors cannot change them.

And third, management has wider discretion than its counterpart in the traditional system. In the traditional system, the board of directors decided a lot of business decisions, such as sale of important assets and issuing new stock, because it was the managing board. However, in the new system, the board of directors can delegate many day-to-day management decisions to the management (officers) and the board can concentrate on major policy decisions, which are indispensable for monitoring management.

As I already mentioned, the board with committees is not a mandatory choice, but an option for large companies, which can stay with the traditional board with

[15] So far, the definition of outside director in Japan is quite simple. Two points are criticized. On one hand, "never" having been an employee is too extreme. On the other hand, there is no requirement for "independence," such as no affiliation and no family tie. It makes sense as a first step, however, because the company community has been so strong and the monitoring by a non-member of the company community is the most important reform in the context of Japanese corporate governance. A company community is organized by a company, i.e., legal personality, so management and employees of a parent company are not members of its subsidiary's company community (see Itoh and Shishido 1999). The protection of minority shareholders of publicly held subsidiaries, which are popular in Japan (see Egashira 1995), should be the next problem to be solved.

statutory auditors. This reform, however, being combined with the reform of strengthening statutory auditors, has a significant mandatory nature because Japanese large companies will, in any event, have to accept at least two real outsiders, either as the real board members or as the quasi board members, to their board. It means that legislatures have finally intruded into the fort of company communities.

Therefore, these reforms as a whole, which made outsiders (either as real members or as quasi members) on the board mandatory, were typical policy–push reforms. However, the nature of the reform of introducing the board with committees, which simply opened a new alternative, is a bit more complicated. Although the law reform was initiated mainly by academic lawyers, while Keidanren was indifferent toward the idea, other business groups, which had been seeking alternative board systems, welcomed the new system.[16] The reform actually had the characteristics of "demand–pull" reform, too. Since 1997, after it was recognized that contingent governance was an inadequate model, several attempts at reforming the corporate governance system, particularly, reforms of the board system, had been made by the companies with many foreign shareholders, such as SONY. They decreased the number of directors, accepted outside directors, and introduced committees under the legal system for traditional Japanese board with statutory auditors.[17] In the first year after the law reform, 55 publicly held companies, many more than expected, chose the new board system.

11.3.6 Summary

We have reviewed the reformations of corporate law since 1997 from the point of view of the distinction between demand–pull reforms and policy–push reforms. The significance of the current trend and its most salient elements must be understood.

First, most of the reformations, such as deregulation of share repurchases, stock options, and reorganization schemes, were demand–pull reforms. In other words, business sectors demanded these deregulations of what had been prohibited by Japanese corporate law, which has many more mandatory restrictions in comparison with American corporate law. Japanese management wanted to do what American management could do. As I have already pointed out in my previous article, the mandatory nature of Japanese corporate laws (as opposed to the enabling nature of American corporate law) was partly changed by the

---

[16] For example, the Japan Association of Corporate Directors was founded in 2002 by nontraditional publicly held companies, such as Orix, Sony, and HOYA, and has been active in promoting the new board system with committees.

[17] According to the survey by the Tokyo Stock Exchange (http://www.twe.or.jp/listing/cg/enquete/index.html), in November 2002, just before the board with committees was formally available, among 1363 companies, 494 (36.2%) companies decreased the number of directors, 466 (34.2%) companies adopted the executive officer system, 388 (28.5%) companies elected outside directors, 54 (4.0%) companies adopted remuneration committees, and 33 (2.4%) companies adopted nominating committees.

demand–pull reforms in 1990s. I called this "internal Americanization" (Shishido 2001). This trend in reformations is a continuation of the demand–pull reforms beginning in the early 1990s.

Second, there were several important policy–push reforms, such as accounting reforms and corporate governance reforms—new trends since 1997. The Japanese legislature introduced new corporate governance schemes colored by international, particularly American, influence during the period when the demise of the traditional Japanese corporate governance system turned out to be obvious. The historical significance of these reforms is that the legislature finally intervened in the company community centered governance system, which could not be changed to respect shareholder interests without a mandatory law approach. These corporate governance law reforms, in spite of their policy–push nature, are expected to have a significant effect on practices because they not only force company communities to change their traditional practices, but they also appear to be responding to the hidden demand of the business sector. I will call such phenomenon "a new trend of Americanization."

As a whole, Japanese corporate law, as a legal infrastructure, has been approaching American corporate law. Although there are a lot of facial differences between the two corporate law regimes, now Japanese companies can do almost as American companies do.

11.4 FORMAL CONVERGENCE AND FUNCTIONAL DIVERGENCE

11.4.1 Convergence of Corporate Governance Debates

Interesting debates on the convergence of corporate governance practices around the world have transpired in the last decade (Ramseyer 1998; Bebchuck and Roe 1999; Coffee 1999; Gilson 2001; Hansmann and Kraakman 2001). Nowadays the participants to the debates realize that they should distinguish between the formal convergence of legal systems and the functional convergence of practice. The predominant view is that even while the formal convergence is impossible, functional convergence will occur (Coffee 1999; Gilson 2001). The two main topics of the functional convergence debate are the concentration of share ownership and labor influence (Bebchuck and Roe 1999).

The concentration of share ownership is converging between the United States and Japan. Although dispersed share ownership used to be a typical characteristic of American corporate governance, institutionalization of share ownership has accelerated since the 1980s (Coffee 1991) and now, more than 50% of publicly held stock is owned by institutional investors in the United States (see Chapter 3, this volume). On the other hand, cross shareholding in Japan has been dissolved and holdings of individual shareholders and foreign shareholders have increased since the 1990s. In 2000, the difference between the institutional holding ratios (including non-financial firms) in both countries was less than 10%.

The labor influence on corporate governance, however, still looks very different in the United States and Japan. Although turnover of core employees in financial industries has increased a bit since the late 1990s, the liquidity of external labor markets in Japan is still not comparable with its American counterpart. The concept of "company community" still remains and plays an important role in corporate governance.

11.4.2 Formal Convergence of the Legal System

As we saw in section 11.3, formal convergence of corporate law to the American model (the "A-model") has nearly been accomplished via numerous law reforms since 1997. Although the vast majority of Japanese publicly held corporations still keep the traditional board with statutory auditors, the important thing is that they can choose an American type board with committees at any time. By these law reforms, not only of the board system, but also of corporate finance and mergers and acquisitions, Japanese companies now can do as Americans do. What they actually choose, and whether it means functional convergence to the A-model or not, are two different questions.

11.4.3 Functional Divergence of the Incentive Pattern

The "strong convergence" thesis argues that world corporate governance will converge or already has converged to the A-model (Hansmann and Kraakman 2001). In the A-model, shareholders, as the owners, monitor their agent, i.e. management, to run the company only in their best interest, through the mechanisms of the threat of hostile takeover, outsider super-majority boards, or performance-based compensation. Other stakeholders, creditors and employees, should be motivated through markets and should not be involved in the corporate governance, or so the argument goes. Because of such characteristics, the A-model is often called either a "monitoring model" or a "market oriented system."

Contrary to the prediction and the recognition by those strong convergence theorists, however, "there is little sign that Japanese corporate governance practices are being fundamentally transformed or rapidly 'converging' with those of the United States" (Milhaupt 2003).

In the convergence of corporate governance debate, diversity of stock ownership is usually considered to be a characteristic of functional convergence. However, the more fundamental functional aspect of a corporate governance system, which can be chosen by the players under certain exogenous conditions, is how to motivate monetary capital providers and human capital providers to invest their own capital in a company. I will call this aspect the "incentive pattern." Diversity of stock ownership (and liquidity of stock market) is rather one of the exogenous factors, which restrict the choice of incentive patterns.

From this point of view, neither the convergence of stock ownership diversity between the US and Japan, nor the choice of the American type board system by many Japanese companies[18] means the functional convergence of corporate governance. Although such superficial aspects appear to indicate the functional convergence of corporate governance in the two countries, incentive patterns are still divergent and may not be converging in the near future.

11.4.4 The New *J*-Model and the Bargaining Board

In the "lost decade," as we have seen in section 11.2 the traditional *J*-model failed. Should Japanese firms now adopt the *A*-model? Not necessarily.

First, the *A*-model, or the monitoring model, needs some exogenous conditions to be present. Liquid stock markets and labor markets are very important for the *A*-model. In addition to stock market monitoring of management, human capital providers are supposed to be motivated by the labor market. Because there is still no liquid labor market in Japan, at least so far, one of the critical prerequisites for Japanese companies to choose the *A*-model as the incentive pattern is absent.

Second, although the *A*-model may function well in an industry with little relation specific investment, such as Wall Street type financial industries, it is not necessarily efficient for certain types of manufacturing industries, in which relation specific human capital investment is indispensable. Although relation specific investment can be motivated by performance-based compensation contracts and severance contracts, these are second-best solutions. Because relation specific skill cannot be sold on an external labor market, hold up problems tend to occur.

Manufacturing systems can be divided into two categories: the "modular" system and the "integral" system. In the modular system, manufacturing companies just assemble parts, which are obtained through markets. On the other hand, in the integral system, manufacturing companies fine tune different parts for specific purposes (Fujimoto 2003). While the former system needs little relation specific investments, the latter system requires significant relation specific investment.

Japanese companies traditionally have their competitive advantage in manufacturing industries, to which the integral system is well suited. In these industries, it is necessary for Japanese companies to motivate human capital providers to make relation specific investments, for which the market approach would not work well.

If liquid labor markets are developed in the future, it is possible that Japanese companies in financial industries and the types of manufacturing industries for which the modular type system is well fit will choose the *A*-model. It is, however, not the optimal choice for Japanese companies in industries that rely heavily on relation specific investments to choose the *A*-model. They would do better to keep the relationship-oriented system, where monetary capital providers and human capital providers bargain with each other to motivate each other to invest their

---

[18] Actually, the choice of the board system has diverged even among the companies with many foreign shareholders. While Sony and HOYA, for example, chose the American type board with committees, Toyota, Honda, and Canon, for example, kept the traditional board with statutory auditors.

respective monetary and human capital. Therefore, even within a country, the optimal corporate governance system would depend upon the industry sector.

The major problem of Japanese corporate governance during the lost decade was its contingent governance aspect. The contingent governance worked best in the era of economic expansion or rapid growth, but did not work when the economic growth stopped. The contingent governance did not and does not make sense for monitoring the use of free cash flow because there are always conflicting interests between human capital providers and monetary capital providers on that issue.

I would like to propose a new *J*-model that keeps the relationship-oriented system and abandons the main bank contingent governance practice. The corporate governance law reforms since 1997 have offered Japanese firms a wonderful opportunity to achieve that outcome. Stock options can be the new scheme to motivate human capital providers to make relation specific investments. Management, as the representative of human capital providers, can obtain wide discretion on financing and reorganization to motivate monetary capital providers to invest more money. By choosing the new board system, Japanese firms could make the board a substantial place of bargaining between the team of human capital providers and the team of monetary capital providers. By encouraging institutional investors, instead of main banks, to be involved in selecting outside directors and having equal insider and outsider board representation, Japanese firms could have a real "bargaining board."[19]

Human capital providers and monetary capital providers need to bargain in any event because both sides need the other's contribution. Management, as the representative of human capital providers, and main bank, as the representative of monetary capital providers, used to bargain outside of the board, for example, at expensive Japanese restaurants for such purposes. Because of the decline of main banks and legal regulations, however, the bargaining will shift to the boardroom.

At the board meeting, human capital providers and monetary capital providers would bargain for sharing the added value. Of course, inside directors, as the representatives of human capital providers, will take initiatives, i.e. propose new projects and ways of using free cash flow. Outside directors, as the representatives of monetary capital providers would normally approve their proposals. Once, however, inside directors breach the implicit contract with outside directors, and propose a project, which is against the interest of monetary capital providers, outside directors will use their veto and reject the proposal. To keep such an efficient equilibrium of the "Folk Theorem," outside directors must be able to pull the plug on disadvantageous projects proposed by inside directors. To obtain this veto power, outside directors must constitute at least half of the board members.

The critical question becomes how to elect outside directors, who would actually represent the interests of monetary capital providers. Institutional investors would be expected to play an important role for that purpose (Black 1990;

---

[19] The bargaining board is different from the "mediating board" discussed by Blair and Stout (1999). While, in their mediating board, directors play the role of neutral mediators between different stakeholders, in our bargaining board, directors play the role of delegates of either human capital providers or monetary capital providers and bargain with each other to maximize the interests of their respective constituency and to motivate their counterparties to provide their capital.

Coffee 1991; Gilson & Kraakman 1991). In Japan, the number of institutional investors is increasing and they are becoming more activist in using their voice on corporate governance matters. They already vote against the nomination of outside directors who would not work effectively as their representatives. Furthermore, the legal rules should encourage, not discourage, institutional investors to take initiatives to elect outside directors.

11.5 CONCLUSION

The traditional *J*-model, whose characteristic was contingent governance of the company community by the main bank, began to malfunction in the late 1980s. Although the traditional *J*-model had been very effective for motivating management and employees to work hard and make relation specific investments while the Japanese economy was expanding and there were no serious conflicting interests among stakeholders, once economic growth stopped, it could not adjust itself to the new situation where conflicting interests in free cash flow use became more serious.

After struggling with this muddy situation, Japanese corporate governance came to a turning point in 1997. Deregulation of corporate law on financing and reorganization transactions and the introduction of a board system with committees, a series of changes called the Americanization of corporate law, began. At the same time, voluntary reformations of corporate governance of individual companies started.

Although the formal convergence of the legal system to the A-model has been made, the functional convergence of the business practices and incentive patterns has not yet occurred. This short history of Japanese corporate governance since the late 1980s provides a contrasting view to the predominant convergence theory corporate governance, which predicts the functional convergence even without formal convergence.

The evolution of corporate law reforms since 1997 has opened the door to creating a new *J*-model. Considering the exogenous conditions, the new *J*-model will be different from the A-model, which is the market-oriented monitoring model. The new *J*-model will not keep the main bank contingent governance regime, but will keep the relationship-oriented incentive pattern for motivating human capital providers to make relation specific investment. Instead of contingent governance, which does not require any outside directors in the ordinary course of business, the new *J*-model will have a "bargaining board," where the inside directors, who are the representatives of the human capital providers, and the outside directors, who are the representatives of the monetary capital providers, always bargain with and motivate each other to contribute their respective capitals to the company optimally.

Supplemental note

After submitting the last version of this article, a number of further changes have occurred in Japanese corporate governance that can now be recognized as another turnaround in 2005. Importantly, the era of hostile takeovers was opened by the Nippon Broadcasting case in 2005. Since then, several serious takeover battles occurred and many publicly held corporations hastily implemented poison pills. Interestingly, court cases and the governmental guideline take the Delaware type rules for defenses (see Milhaupt 2005). Shareholder activism has also turned out to be very influential. Some activist investment funds have pushed management to pay higher dividends. Institutional investors, such as pension funds, also began to vote against management proposals and even lead to the rejection of management proposals at major Japanese firms' shareholder meetings for the first time in history.

The Companies Act of 2005 separated corporate law from the Commercial Code. Although the framework and terminologies were totally changed, very few substantial changes were made in the corporate governance of publicly held corporations because major deregulation or Americanization had already been accomplished in the reforms leading up to 2001. Still, there are some important changes such as the following. First, directors may be removed through a simple majority, down from the two-thirds majority threshold previously. Second, the board of directors is required to implement and disclose a system for internal control and compliance. The 2005 Act was also followed by the securities law reform of 2006, which is called the Japanese Sarbanes Oxley Act. Third, the board of directors can decide to pay dividends, rather than the shareholder meeting. Fourth, the American type of short form merger was introduced and a freeze-out of less than 10% minority shareholders can be made through a board decision. And fifth, cash and in-kind payment to shareholders in the case of mergers and other reorganizations are allowed, while the stock of the surviving corporation may be used as tender. As a result, not only cash-out mergers, but also using parent stock for acquisition has turned out to be possible.

REFERENCES

Aoki, M. (1994). 'The Contingent Governance of Teams: Analysis of Institutional Complementarity,' *International Economic Review*, 35: 657.

Aron, D. J. (1991). 'Using the Capital Market as a Monitor: Corporate Spinoffs in an Agency Framework,' *Rand Journal of Economics*, 22: 505.

Bebchuk, L. A. and M. J. Roe (1999). 'A Theory of Path Dependence in Corporate Governance and Ownership,' *Stanford Law Review*, 52: 127.

Black, B. S. (1990). 'Shareholder Passivity Reexamined,' *Michigan Law Review*, 89: 551.

Blair, M. M. and L. A. Stout (1999). 'A Team Production Theory of Corporate Law,' *Virginia Law Review*, 85: 247.

Coffee, J. C. (1991). 'Liquidity Versus Control: The Institutional Investors as Corporate Monitor,' *Columbia Law Review*, 91: 1277.

—— (1999). 'The Future as History: The Prospects for Global Convergence in Corporate Governance and Its Implications,' *Northwestern University Law Review*, 93: 641.

Cusatis, P. J., J. A. Miles, and J. R. Woodridge (1993). 'Restructuring through Spinoffs: The Stock Market Evidence,' *Journal of Financial Economics*, 33: 293.

Egashira, K. (1995). *Ketsugo Kigyo Ho no Rippo to Kaishaku* (Legislation and Interpretation of the Conglomerate Law). Tokyo: Yuhikaku.

—— (2004). *Kabushiki Kaisha, Yugen Kaisha Ho* (Laws of Stock Corporations and Limited Liability Companies), 3rd edn. Tokyo: Yuhikaku.

Fried, J. (2005). 'Informed Trading and False Signaling with Open Market Repurchases,' *California Law Review*, 93: 1325.

Fujimoto, T. (2003). *Noryoku Kochiku Kyoso* (Competition of Ability Building). Tokyo: Chuo Koron.

Gilson, R. J. (2001). 'Globalizing Corporate Governance: Convergence of Form or Function,' *American Journal of Comparative Law*, 49: 127.

—— R. Kraakman (1991). 'Reinventing the Outside Director: An Agenda for Institutional Investors,' *Stanford Law Review*, 43: 863.

—— M. J. Roe (1993). 'Understanding the Japanese Keiretsu: Overlaps Between Corporate Governance and Industrial Organization,' *Yale Law Journal*, 102: 871.

Hansmann, H. and R. Kraakman (2001). 'The End of History for Corporate Law,' *Georgetown Law Journal*, 89: 439.

Hirose, S., N. Yanagawa, and M. Saito (2003). 'Kighonai Kyashufuroh to Kigyo Kachi: Nihonn no Kabushiki Shokyaku ni kannsuru Jishobunseki wo tsujiteno Kosatsu (Equity Repurchase and Corporate Value: Evidence from Different Legal Procedure in Japan),' *Working Paper*.

Hite, G. L. and J. E. Owers (1983). 'Security Price Reactions around Corporate Spin-off Announcements,' *Journal of Financial Economics*, 12: 409.

Itoh, H. and Z. Shishido (1999). 'The Firm as a Legal Entity: Its Importance and Implications for Corporate Restructuring in Japan,' *Working Paper*.

Kaplan, S. and B. Minton (1994). 'Appointment of Outsiders to Japanese Boards: Determinants and Implications for Managers,' *Journal of Financial Economics*, 36: 225.

Miles, J. and J. D. Rosenfeld (1983). 'The Effect of Voluntary Spin-off Announcements on Shareholder Wealth,' *Journal of Finance*, 38: 1597.

Milhaupt, C. (2003). 'The Lost Decade for Japanese Corporate Governance Reform?: What's Changed, What Hasn't, and Why,' *Working Paper*.

—— (2005). 'In the Shadow of Delaware?: The Rise of Hostile Takeovers in Japan,' *Columbia Law Review*, 105: 2171.

Miyajima, H. and K. Inagaki (2003). 'Nihonkigyo no Tayoka to Kigyo Tochi: Jigyo Senryaku, Gurupu Keiei, Bunkenka Soshiki no Bunseki' (Diversification of Japanese Companies and Their Corporate Governance: Analysis of Business Tactics, Management of Corporate Groups, and Decentralized Organizations), *Working Paper*, Research Institution of Ministry of Finance.

—— Kuroki, F. (2004). 'Gabanansu Kozo to Kigyo Pafohmansu tono Kankei ni tsuite' (On the Relationship between Governance Structure and Firm Performance), *Working Paper*.

Ramseyer, J. M. (1998). 'Are Corporate Governance Systems Converging?' *Working Paper*.

Shipper, K. and A. Smith (1983). 'Effects of Reconstructing on Shareholder Wealth: The Case of Voluntary Spin-offs,' *Journal of Financial Economics*, 12: 437.

Shishido, Z. (2000). 'Japanese Corporate Governance: The Hidden Problems of the Corporate Law and Their Solutions,' *Delaware Journal of Corporate Law*, 25: 189.

—— (2001). 'Reform in Japanese Corporate Law and Corporate Governance: Current Changes in Historical Perspective,' *American Journal of Comparative Law*, 49: 653.

Takei, K. and M. Hirabayashi (2000). *Kaisha Bunkatsu no Jitsumu* (Practice of Corporate Divisions). Tokyo: Shojihomu.

Vijh, A. M. (1994). 'The Spinoff and Merger Ex-Date Effects,' *Journal of Finance*, 69: 581.

12

The Performance Effects and Determinants of Corporate Governance Reform[1]

Hideaki Miyajima

12.1 INTRODUCTION

For much of the post-war period, the boards of Japanese firms had been composed primarily of insiders drawn from the ranks of employees who had been promoted from within; outsiders had been invited to join as directors only on rare occasions. These insider boards exhibited a low degree of separation between the management and monitoring functions, and compensated their members with salaries that were lower and less sensitive to corporate performance compared to those paid to their counterparts in the US and even compared to those paid to directors in pre-war Japan.

Although the promotion of employees to the boards of their firms was part of a historical trend, the boards that emerged after the war were shaped primarily by the post-war reforms implemented by the General Headquarters (GHQ) of the Occupation forces. GHQ had ordered a purge of incumbent managers and outside directors (representing zaibatsu families and large shareholders) from Japanese firms while encouraging the promotion of corporate insiders to boards and greater labor involvement in management (Miyajima 1995, 2004, chap. 8). The post-war board structure evolved further during the high-growth era, as boards began to expand in size[2] and include a small number of outside directors dispatched from main banks. These stylized characteristics of Japanese

[1] This chapter is based on the reports, *Waga Kuni Kigyō no Kōporēto Gabanansu ni Kansuru Ankēto Chōsa* (Questionnaire Survey on Corporate Governance in Japanese Companies), and *Shinten suru Kōporēto Gabanansu Kaikaku to Nihon Kigyō no Saisei* (Advances in Corporate Governance Reform in Japan and the Revitalization of Japanese Companies) by Hideaki Miyajima, Kenji Haramura (head researcher at the Policy Research Institute, Ministry of Finance, currently with the Financial Services Agency), and Ken'ichi Inagaki (researcher at the above institute, currently with Sumitomo Mitsui Banking Corporation). The author thanks both the Policy Research Institute of the Ministry of Finance and his two co-authors for permission to use the research results. A part of an early Japanese draft was presented at Waseda University, RIETI, Policy Research Institute of the Ministry of Finance, and the SASE Annual Conference. Comments from Naohito Abe, Katsuyuki Kubo, Shinichi Hirota, Yoshio Higuchi and Masahiro Kawai have been extremely helpful.

[2] The increase in board size can be seen as the logical outcome of long-term employment (rank hierarchies). See Miyajima and Aoki (2002).

boards had become well established by the time that cross-shareholding and the main-bank system reached their heyday around the late 1960s (Miyajima 1999; Miyajima and Aoki 2002).

This board structure had provided incentives compatible with the rank hierarchies of a long-term employment system (Aoki 1988) by allowing employees to aspire to membership on the board as an ultimate career goal. The structure was purportedly well suited to many Japanese firms because board members promoted from within could share knowledge and information acquired on the shop floor, and thus facilitate incremental (step-by step) innovation.

Insider boards began to come under increasing criticism, however, as the main-bank system and cross-shareholding started to unravel. The low degree of separation between monitoring and management had given rise to insider control problems that led to over-investment and delays in restructuring. Moreover, insider boards had tended to exhibit less concern for the interests of minority shareholders, as reflected in the fact that so many companies had scheduled general shareholder meetings on the same day of the year and had been reluctant to disclose corporate information (for more details, see Chapter 11 in this volume).

The wave of governance reforms that swept the country in the late 1990s has begun to shake up the boardrooms of Japanese corporations. The executive officer system (shikkō-yakuin sei), for example, has been widely adopted as an alternative to the traditional board structure (Figure 12.1). This system, which makes a distinction between executive officers in charge of operating divisions and board members with monitoring responsibilities, has been associated with a decrease in board size. It was first introduced by Sony in 1997, and has been introduced by many other companies in many industries. A survey conducted by the Policy Research Institute of the Ministry of Finance in October 2002 (details are provided later) found that 33.0% of listed companies (a 20%-point increase since the previous survey in 1999) and more than half of companies with capital of more than 30 billion yen (52.3%) have introduced this system (Table 12.1). In addition, according to our survey, more companies have opened their boards to outsiders—35.9% of listed as well as over-the-counter companies and approximately 50% of major companies with capital of more than ¥30 billion.[3]

Furthermore, amendments to the regulatory framework have strengthened the monitoring of corporations. The 2001 revision of the Company Law expanded the authority of the statutory auditor but did not constitute a sharp break with the previous regulatory framework. The 2002 amendment to the Company Law, however, should be considered a clear step in the direction of corporate boards patterned after the US model. The newly amended law allowed companies to

---

[3] Nonetheless, the fraction of companies that has introduced outside board members compared with the previous survey rose by only 5% points, so the pace of change in this area has been much less dramatic than the pace of adoption of the executive officer system. Furthermore, almost 40% of outside board members are from organizations that should be considered not fully independent from the company such as parent companies, affiliates, and main banks.

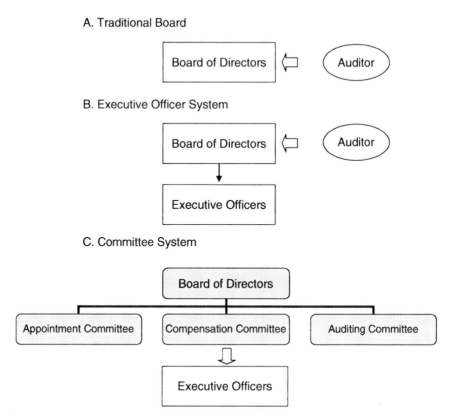

Figure 12.1 Board structure of Japanese firms

adopt the committee system (which entailed the formation of three committees responsible for appointments, compensation, and audits respectively, all with outsider majorities; see Figure 12.1).[4]

Stock options were first introduced in 1997, and the 2002 revision of the Commercial Code liberalized eligibility for stock options in principle, thus encouraging more firms to adopt them. In 2002, approximately half of all companies had introduced or were planning to introduce stock options.[5] Although actual usage of stock options is still rather limited, their availability has forced companies to rethink their incentive schemes for top managers.

The scale of the recent overhaul of the governance structure is comparable to that of the post-war reforms that transformed the pre-war corporate governance

---

[4] For more details, see Shishido, Chapter 11 in this volume, and Gilson and Milhaupt 2004.

[5] As of 2002, companies seemed to be evenly divided between those that had adopted or were in the process of adopting stock options, and those that were resisting them.

Table 12.1 Trends in Corporate Governance Reform (Unit: %)

	Exective officer system		Outside directors		Stock options	
	FY 2002 (846 firms)	FY 1999 (1145 firms)	FY 2002 (863 firms)	FY 1999 (1138 firms)	FY 2002 (864 firms)	FY 1999 (1209 firms)
Already introduced	33.0	12.8	35.8	30.1	28.1	9.5
Plan to intoduce	2.7	2.3	2.9	1.1	1.9	2.2
Considering introduction	25.8	37.4	32.7	27.3	15.2	25.6
No intention to introduce	38.5	47.5	28.6	41.4	42.7	43.7

Source: Ministry of Finance Surveys (PRI 2003b).

system that had been characterized by strong shareholder control into a system dominated by employees and financial institutions. Viewed from a historical perspective, the current wave of corporate governance reform is likely to be seen as a second important turning point in the history of Japanese business.

Unlike the changes implemented in the immediate aftermath of World War II, however, the current transformation has been voluntary and not propelled by changes in the law. Given these circumstances, Japanese companies' attitudes toward reform are quite diverse, ranging from actively receptive to very cautious. While attention is often focused on the importance of reforms based on the US corporate governance model, with three distinct reform measures—the protection of minority shareholders' rights, the separation of management from monitoring including the introduction of outside board members, and active information disclosure—seen as a single package, companies have responded in practice in diverse ways. Some have adopted only one or two of these measures; others have adopted all three. On the one hand, Canon and Toyota are two prominent companies that have been very cautious in implementing measures to separate management and monitoring but at the same time have been quite active in disclosing information about their businesses. On the other hand, a significant number of companies have introduced the executive officer system and outsiders to their boards yet have not fully embraced the idea of disclosing corporate information.

A series of questions naturally arises from an examination of the current governance reform process. First, have the recently adopted measures mattered to corporate performance? Or to put it differently, have the companies that have implemented governance reform measures actually improved their performance? If they have (to some degree at least), then which measures are most likely to improve performance? Those which separate management from ownership? Those which protect minority shareholders? Or those which promote information disclosure? Second, the question of whether corporate governance reforms improve performance or not notwithstanding, what determines a firm's decision to choose a particular reform? Has governance reform been facilitated by increasing pressures from the market but impeded by employee sovereignty, as is often assumed? And more specifically, has governance reform been hampered by employee involvement in management and the human resources practices of Japanese firms?

As a way of getting to the answers to these questions, this chapter attempts to measure the extent of recent corporate governance reforms among Japanese firms, following the methodology of Black et al. (2002a) for South Korea. As part of a project conducted for the Policy Research Institute of the Ministry of Finance, questionnaires were sent to all listed firms in December 2002. The 34% response rate yielded a sample of 876 companies[6]. Using the questionnaire results, we compiled a Corporate Governance Score (*CGS*) for each corporation.[7] The *CGS* is designed to capture the cumulative efforts of recent corporate governance reforms by focusing on: (a) protection of the rights of minority shareholders (general meetings of shareholders); (b) the extent of separation between management and monitoring in corporate boards; and (c) information disclosure.[8]

The *CGS* enabled us to determine whether recent governance reforms have influenced performance. Although our results are still tentative due mainly to the lack of a sample of sufficient size to conduct a proper assessment of post-reform performance, we can show that a high *CGS* is associated with better performance. Among the three types of governance reform measures, those which promote information disclosure were most clearly associated with better performance, whereas measures to protect minority shareholders and to promote the separation of monitoring and management have not yielded unambiguous results in terms of performance effects.

This chapter also seeks to determine what types of companies were receptive to governance reform by analyzing the determinants of reform, setting the *CGS* as an independent variable. We focus on the ownership stakes of outside investors, the bank–firm relationship, and employees' stakes as factors determining reform choices, and produce empirical evidence to verify relationships that we had predicted: namely, the higher the percentage of foreign (institutional) share-holders, and the lower the percentage of stable shareholders, the higher the firm's dependence on the capital market; and the lower the firm's dependence on bank borrowing, the more receptive it is to corporate governance reform.

---

[6] The surveys on which this chapter is based are available from the Zaimu Sōgō Seisaku Kenkyūjo (2003a, b) and http://www.mof.go.jp/jouhou/soken/kenkyu.htm

[7] In designing the questionnaire and producing the *CGS*, we referred to Black et al. (2002a, b) as well as the Tsipouri and Xanthakis (2002) study of Greece. Wakasugi et al. (2002) conducted an analysis of 159 listed companies in the First Section of the Tokyo Stock Exchange using a Corporate Governance Index (CGI). Recently, similar trials covering other countries have been conducted by Gompers et al. (2003) and Berglöf and Pajuste (2005).

[8] Recent questionnaire surveys concerning the governance structure of Japanese companies have been conducted and summarized in reports by the Japan Corporate Auditors Association (Nihon Kansayaku Kyōkai 2003), Japan Corporate Governance Forum (Nihon Kōporēto Gabanansu Fōramu 2001), Nihon Keidanren (Nihon Keizai Dantai Rengōkai 2000), and Tokyo Stock Exchange (Tokyo Shōken Torihikijo 2003), and Wakasugi et al. (2002).

Furthermore, this chapter demonstrates the impact of employee involvement in management and the wage/employment system on governance reform. A high degree of employee involvement in management and long-term employment have generally been perceived to be factors which impede board reforms that are meant to tilt the balance toward "shareholders' interests." Until now, hardly any empirical research had been conducted on the relationship between employee involvement in management and human resources practices and governance reform. Our questionnaire survey allowed us to measure how employee involvement and human resources practices impacted governance reform. We found that there was not a clearly negative relationship between employee involvement and governance reform, and, more interestingly, that there was in fact a significantly positive relationship between employee involvement and reform in firms exposed to pressures from the capital market. We also discovered that companies that retained long-term employment while seeking to shift from seniority-based to ability-based wage systems have been actively implementing governance reform measures to promote information disclosure. These results are consistent with the following observations: that when employees are aware of current trends toward greater reliance on the capital market (and of the fact that the market's evaluation of stock prices and bond ratings is playing an increasingly important role in determining the cost of capital), they are more involved in the management of the company; and that the greater a company's reliance on long-term employment, the more willing it is to implement governance reform.

This chapter is organized as follows: section 12.2 briefly explains the *CGS*; section 12.3 focuses on the relationship between governance reform and performance; section 12.4 sets the *CGS* as an independent variable to analyze the factors that determine governance reform; and section 12.5 provides concluding remarks.

12.2 THE CORPORATE GOVERNANCE SCORE (*CGS*)

We shall begin with an explanation of the *CGS* utilized in our analysis. The *CGS* gauges each company's efforts toward governance reform based on the qualitative data attained from the questionnaire survey. A higher score indicates that a company is more actively committed to introducing governance reforms. The *CGS* aggregates responses to 26 questionnaire items, and is composed of three sub-index scores that measure commitment to reform in the following areas: (a) the general meeting/protection of minority shareholders (CGS_{sh}, 10 variables); (b) the board of directors (CGS_{br}, 6 variables); and (c) information disclosure (CGS_{ds}, 10 variables). Each variable that makes up the *CGS* takes the value 0 or 1. A company that replied that it had implemented a particular reform measure was given a score of 1 for that item; otherwise, it was given a 0.

The *CGS* was computed as follows. First, the scores for all items in each sub-index were added up. Next, the sum of the scores was divided by the number of variables in each sub-index. (Variables with missing data were excluded.) Last, this quotient (the sum of scores for each sub-index divided by number of variables) was multiplied by 100/3 to equalize the weight of each sub-index score. The three sub-index scores were added together to produce the *CGS*. The value of each sub-index score could range from 0 to 100/3, and the *CGS*, that is, the sum of three sub-index scores, could range from 0 to 100. The variables comprising each sub-index are explained below.

Shareholder Sub-Index Score (CGS_{sh})—10 Variables

CGS_{sh} rates the implementation of measures to protect the rights of minority shareholders, particularly those related to general shareholders' meetings. The questionnaire data is summarized in Appendix 12.1.

The general meeting is an important mechanism for protecting minority shareholders' rights. While large shareholders have multiple means to convey their will to managers, the general meeting is often the only and last resort for minority shareholders who wish to exert influence over the company. Since the appearance of La Porta et al. (1998), researchers have begun to turn their attention to the issue of protecting minority shareholders' rights. It should be noted that the Japanese Commercial Code grants shareholders rights that are quite significant by international standards (Fukao 1995). In practice, however, the general meetings of Japanese corporations had become increasingly perfunctory occasions in recent years, drawing criticism and giving rise to calls for reform.[9]

Board Sub-Index Score (CGS_{br})—6 Variables

CGS_{br} captures the degree of separation between management and monitoring. Companies actively seeking to reform their boards of directors (by adopting the executive officer system or introducing outsiders to the board) and to strengthen monitoring received higher scores.

Among governance mechanisms, the board of directors plays a crucial role in directly monitoring the activities of management. However, in practice, prior to 1997, board members in Japanese companies had two major characteristics:

---

[9] For many years, general meetings of Japanese companies were conducted around a formulaic conversation carried on between the chairperson and employee shareholders, who replied "right on" or "done" and applauded after each of the chairperson's statements. Recently, however, shareholders' meetings have been conducted in a different manner, with management now explaining matters in a way that goes beyond their minimum obligations and is generally respectful to shareholders (*Shōji Hōmu*, 1647: 9).

a) almost all, with the exception of directors dispatched from the main bank and parent company, were employees promoted to the board from within the company, and outside directors were quite rare; and b) they were mainly engaged in managing, not in monitoring of management (Miyajima 1999; Miyajima and Aoki 2002). It is well known that these traits of board members were complementary with other institutional features of Japanese corporations such as long-term employment and the seniority-based wage system, but at the same time left the door open for an employee group represented by managers with membership on the board to exercise insider control over the company. Companies began to introduce the executive officer system and outside board members after 1997 in part to eliminate the potential for insider control abuses. Whether these board reform initiatives have yielded improvements in business performance is an important concern of this chapter.

Information Disclosure Sub-Index Score (CGS_{ds})—10 Variables

CGS_{ds} is composed of variables designed to quantify the implementation of information disclosure initiatives including investor relations activities. Information disclosure is supposed to reduce agency costs by providing information useful to current shareholders as well as potential investors. Active information disclosure efforts are an indication of the company's (managers') commitment to publicizing information (not only during periods of strong performance but also during performance downturns), and serve to keep company insiders on their toes.

In the past, Japanese companies were not active in disclosing information to investors in comparison to their Western counterparts, and few companies had departments devoted solely to investor relations. In many cases, finance/accounting departments (*zaimubu*) or general affairs departments (*sōmubu*) performed investor relations functions as side tasks. In recent years, however, Japanese companies have made great strides in sharing more corporate information with the public.[10] CGS_{ds} is used to test whether stepped-up information disclosure efforts actually affect business performance by mitigating asymmetric information problems and by disciplining managers.

Distribution of *CGS* and Attributes of Sample Companies

Our initial sample consisted of the 876 companies that responded to our questionnaire survey, but the sample was reduced to 755 after companies were

---

[10] In attempting to measure management's attitude toward shareholders, this survey found that more than 80% of the companies emphasized the importance of investor relations activities. This is an increase of more than 10% points compared to the survey conducted in 1999 (Ministry of Finance, Policy Research Institute, 2000). Also, the ratio of companies with a department specializing in IR activities has increased dramatically from 14.8% in the previous survey to 43.5% in this survey.

excluded due to lack of financial data or insufficient responses.[11] The distribution of sample companies across industries and by assets is similar to that of the 2577[12] listed companies (excluding the financial industry), so we assume that our sample does not suffer from a serious selection bias.

The average *CGS* for the 755 sample companies is 27.4 and the standard deviation is 12.9 (Table 12.2). Of the sub-indices, CGS_{ds} had the largest standard deviation, an indication of the diversity of information disclosure efforts among various corporations. The correlation coefficient for CGS_{sh} and CGS_{ds} is relatively high at 0.41. On the other hand, the correlation coefficients for CGS_{br} and CGS_{ds}, and for CGS_{sh} and CGS_{br} are relatively low at 0.26 and 0.18 respectively. These findings suggest that each governance structure reform has been implemented independently, and not as part of a package of reforms.

Table 12.2 Descriptive Statistics of *CGS* (Corporate Governance Score)

Panel 1: Descriptive Statistics

	Average	Standard deviation	Minimum value	Maximum value	Median	First quartile	Third quartile
CGS (Total)	27.4	12.9	0	68.9	25.6	17.8	35.6
CGS_{sh} (Rights of shareholders)	5.2	4.4	0	20.0	3.3	0.0	6.7
CGS_{br} (Board of directors)	10.9	5.8	0	27.8	11.1	5.6	16.7
CGS_{ds} (Information disclosure)	11.3	7.5	0	33.3	10.0	6.7	16.7

Panel 2: Correlation Matrix

	CGS	CGS_{sh}	CGS_{br}	CGS_{ds}
CGS (Total)	1			
CGS_{sh} (Rights of shareholders)	0.66	1		
CGS_{br} (Board of directors)	0.66	0.18	1	
CGS_{ds} (Information disclosure)	0.83	0.41	0.26	1

Note: For more details on *CGS*, refer to Appendix 12.1.

Source: PRI (2003b).

[11] Of the 876 companies that responded to this questionnaire survey, we eliminated 20 relatively obscure companies as well as 98 over-the-counter or newly listed companies whose financial data was not readily available. In addition, three companies were excluded because their incomplete answers prevented calculation of the *CGS*. The sample of 755 companies consists of 746 large companies (with capital stock of more than ¥500 million or debt of more than ¥20 billion) and nine medium-sized companies (with capital stock of more than ¥100 million but less than ¥500 million, and with debt less than ¥20 billion) in accordance with definitions used in the Law for Special Exceptions to the Commercial Code.

[12] Companies listed in *Nikkei Corporate Information* (Fall 2002) including the top 200 over-the-counter companies in terms of assets.

12.3 THE *CGS* AND PERFORMANCE

12.3.1 Comparison of Average Performance by *CGS* Quintile

This section addresses the relationship between Corporate Governance Scores and corporate performance. It should be noted that the *CGS* is calculated on the basis of information available as of December 2002, whereas the data for performance is based on financial data for the fiscal year from April 2001 to March 2002. Therefore, even though a firm's performance is correlated both significantly and positively with its *CGS*, we cannot rule out the possibility that our results may simply indicate that higher-performing companies were more willing to introduce reforms. The analysis below is based on the assumption that the Corporate Governance Scores computed from the survey data reflect the cumulative efforts to implement governance reforms by companies over the past several years. Nevertheless, caution should be exercised when interpreting the results.

To analyze the relationship between a company's willingness to implement corporate governance reforms and performance, the 755 companies are divided into quintiles according to their *CGS* ranking in order to observe significant differences in average performance index values for each quintile.[13] Tobin's *q* (hereinafter called *Q*),[14] *ROA*, the growth rate in sales, and the growth rate of employees are used to measure performance. To eliminate industry-specific factors, standardized *Q* is calculated by deducting the median of *Q* values by Tokyo Stock Exchange industry code from each company's *Q* value. The results are shown in Table 12.3. Standardized *ROA* is also calculated using the same method.

It is quite clear that the higher the *CGS*, the higher the average for *Q* (*ROA*) and standardized *Q* (*ROA*), although there is some variation in sales and employee growth. We also find statistically significant differences in all performance variables of *CGS* at the 1% level.

12.3.2 *CGS* and Performance Factors

Corporate performance is of course affected not only by governance structure as measured by *CGS* but also by various factors such as the size of the company, leverage, the firm's life cycle, etc. Therefore, in this section, after controlling for

---

[13] Each group consists of 151 companies. For more detailed analysis, please refer to Miyajima et al. (2003).

[14] Tobin's *q* is calculated as follows: [Stock price (at market value) × number of shares issued + amount of debt (at book value)]/ total amount of assets (only holding securities calculated at market value). The financial data is for the accounting term for the year 2001. For these calculations, the database at the Waseda University Institute of Financial Studies is used. For specific measures for calculating Tobin's *q*, see Miyajima et al. (2001).

Table 12.3 Analysis of CGS and Performance

| Index | Quintile of CGS | High | | | Low | | Testing |
		(1)	(2)	(3)	(4)	(5)	gap = (1)−(5)
1	Q	2.07	1.40	1.34	1.04	1.03	1.04 ***
2	Standardized Q	0.92	0.38	0.32	0.04	0.02	0.90 ***
3	ROA	5.01	4.17	3.38	3.15	2.75	2.26 ***
4	Standardized ROA	1.39	0.99	0.18	−0.05	−0.43	1.82 ***
5	Sales growth ratio	5.33	2.63	0.65	8.24	−1.11	6.44 ***
6	Growth rate in the # of employees	5.78	1.27	1.79	1.14	−3.06	8.84 ***

Notes: Sample companies (total 755) were divided into quintiles, (1)–(5), in terms of CGS in descending order and averages of each index for companies that belong to each quintile were calculated. The range of CGS in each quintile is as follows: (1) 67.4 ∼ 40.2, (2) 40.0 ∼ 30.5, (3) 30.5 ∼ 24.3, (4) 24.1 ∼ 17.5, and (5) 17.5∼ 0. Each index is created based on consolidated financial data at the settlement period for year 2001. Standardized Q is derived by deducting median Q for the Tokyo Stock Exchange industry category from each company's Q. ROA: *operating* profit / amount of assets × 100 (unit: %). Standardized ROA is derived by deducting median ROA for the Tokyo Stock Exchange industry category from each company's ROA and standardizing the difference in the profit ratio by industry. Sales growth ratio is the average sales growth ratio for five fiscal years from 1996 to 2001, except for those companies whose settlement data does not exist for the five years. For them, only the available data for sales growth ratio is used (unit: %). Growth rate in the number of employees is for the two fiscal years from the end of 1999 to the end of 2001 (annualized, unit: %). The column for the testing gap indicates the difference between (1) and (5), and *** suggests that it is statistically significant at the 1% level.

the above factors, a test is conducted to determine how CGS is related to a company's performance. The model for the estimation is as follows:

$$(1) \qquad P_i = F\ (CGS\ (CGS_{sh},\ CGS_{br},\ CGS_{ds}),\ SIZE,\ DAR,\ LIST,\ GSALE)$$

where P_i is a measure of performance. Tobin's q (includes future growth opportunities) and ROA (actual accounting index) are used as performance variables. Since performance measures ought not to be affected by industry-specific factors, we use standardized Q and standardized ROA as dependent variables. Hereafter, "Q" or "ROA" refer to standardized Q and standardized ROA. DAR is the debt–asset ratio, SIZE is the size of the company (natural logarithm for the amount of assets), LIST is number of years listed, and GSALE is the real growth rate in sales. Definitions of descriptive statistical variables are in Appendix 12.2, and estimation results are presented in Table 12.4.

First, let us examine the controlling variables for this estimation—namely, the coefficients for SIZE, DAR, LIST, and GSALE. Generally, the significance levels for all variables' coefficients are high (an indication of stable results), except for those for SIZE. The results suggest that a company with fewer listed years, a higher sales growth ratio, and lower debt ratio tends to perform better.

Second, corporate performance is sensitive to CGS. According to the estimation (column 1), coefficients for Q and ROA are always positive at the 1% significance level. A one standard deviation increase in CGS corresponds to an increase of 0.318 in Q (=0.024×13.034) and 0.53% increase in ROA respectively.

Panel 1

Column	(1)		(2)		(3)		(4)		(5)	
Dependent Variable	Standardized Q		Standardized Q		Standardized Q		Standardized Q		Standardized Q	
	Coefficient	t-value	Coefficient	t-value	Coefficient	t-value	Coefficient	t-value	Coefficient	t-value
C	0.132	0.14	−1.200	−1.36	−1.471 *	−1.72	0.990	1.06	0.980	1.04
SIZE	0.001	0.02	0.108 **	2.39	0.118 ***	2.73	−0.046	−0.90	−0.050	−0.95
DAR	−1.504 ***	−5.46	−1.715 ***	−6.22	−1.743 ***	−6.34	−1.316 ***	−4.74	−1.320 ***	−4.74
LIST	0.090 ***	2.73	0.105 ***	3.12	0.114 ***	3.41	0.078 **	2.37	0.080 **	2.40
GSALE	0.292 *	1.87	0.310 *	1.95	0.296 *	1.86	0.305 **	1.97	0.299 *	1.93
CGS	0.024 ***	4.67								
CGS_{sh}			0.022	1.62					−0.001	−0.10
CGS_{br}					0.016	1.55			0.007	0.75
CGS_{ds}							0.055 ***	5.85	0.054 ***	5.49
adj.R^2	0.124		0.096		0.096		0.141		0.139	
Sample number	616		616		616		616		616	

Panel 2

Column	(1)		(2)		(3)		(4)		(5)	
Dependent Variable	Standardized ROA		Standardized ROA		Standardized ROA		Standardized ROA		Standardized ROA	
	Coefficient	t-value	Coefficient	t-value	Coefficient	t-value	Coefficient	t-value	Coefficient	t-value
C	−2.611	−1.01	−4.376 **	−1.78	−5.598	−2.35	0.019	0.01	0.189	0.07
SIZE	0.148	1.04	0.293 **	2.33	0.387 ***	3.19	−0.015	−0.10	−0.004	−0.03
DAR	−4.653 ***	−5.97	−4.948 ***	−6.42	−5.040 ***	−6.53	−4.165 ***	−5.32	−4.155 ***	−5.30
LIST	0.413 ***	4.43	0.431 ***	4.61	0.456 ***	4.94	0.371 ***	4.00	0.360 ***	3.84
GSALE	1.584 ***	3.51	1.621 ***	3.58	1.627 ***	3.58	1.602 ***	3.58	1.634 ***	3.65
CGS	0.041 ***	2.74								
CGS_{sh}			0.064	1.65					0.022	0.56
CGS_{br}					−0.019	−0.68			−0.040	−1.43
CGS_{ds}							0.118 ***	4.47	0.119 ***	4.30
adj.R^2	0.134		0.128		0.125		0.151		0.151	
Sample number	638		638		638		638		638	

Notes: For more details on Standardized Q and Standardized ROA, see Table 12.3; C: Constant term; $SIZE$: Natural logarithm for total assets; DAR: Debt/asset ratio; $LIST$: Year of listing; $GSALE$: Sales growth rate. CGS: Total GGS score; CGS_{sh}: Rights of shareholders; CGS_{br}: Board of directors; CGS_{ds}: Information disclosure. See Appendices 12.1 and 12.2 for details. *** statistically significant at 1% level, ** at 5% level, * at 10% level.

Third, the sub-indices CGS_{sh}, CGS_{br}, and CGS_{ds} are used as dependent variables in place of *CGS* to identify which factors significantly affect a company's performance. The coefficient for CGS_{sh} is positive with both Q and *ROA* as dependent variables, but not sufficiently significant (column 2). The coefficient for CGS_{br} (column 3) is positive when the dependent variable is Q, but it cannot be said to be far more significant. Moreover, when the dependent variable is *ROA*, the coefficient turns negative, and its significance level is rather low.

On the other hand, estimations with Q or *ROA* (columns 4 and 5) yield a coefficient for CGS_{ds} that is significantly positive. We also confirmed that the higher the CGS_{ds}, the better the performance.[15] According to the estimation results in Table 12.4 and Appendix 12.3, a one standard deviation increase in CGS_{ds} yields an increase of 0.409 ($=0.055\times7.456$) in Q, and 0.81% ($=0.118\times 7.456$) increase in *ROA* respectively. Therefore, CGS_{ds} appears to have a strong influence on performance.

As shown above, it is clear that corporate performance is significantly and positively sensitive to a company's cumulative efforts to implement governance reforms as measured by the *CGS*, and especially to information disclosure efforts. However, it has been pointed out in many empirical studies (including Chapter 3 in this volume) that the stake of foreign shareholders and level of stable shareholders have a significant influence on a company's performance by boosting the effort level of managers. On the other hand, the magnitude of the *CGS* itself may in fact be determined by relations with other stakeholders (shareholders and banks). Hence, the relationship between *CGS* and a company's performance examined above may not reflect the impact of governance reforms per se, but rather may merely reflect the influence exerted by the composition of shareholders (in a so-called spurious correlation).

Hence, we decided to add other variables for the ownership structure and bank dependence at the beginning of FY 2000 in order to test whether *CGS* has a unique effect on corporate performance, even after controlling for ownership structure. The variables for ownership consist of the ratio of stable shareholders (*STAB*: the ratio of shares held by financial institutions plus the ratio of shares held by corporations) and the ratio of foreign shareholders (*FRG*).[16] We also introduce *BOR* (bank borrowing/assets) as a proxy for bank dependence.

According to our estimate results (not reported), the coefficient for the ratio of stable shareholders is significantly negative. On the other hand, the coefficients for the ratio of foreign shareholders and bank dependence are insignificant. But the introduction of these shareholder composition variables does not change our performance results. *CGS* and CGS_{ds} have a significantly positive correlation with

---

[15] When the estimation was conducted by using the variables CGS_{sh}, CGS_{br}, and CGS_{ds} in place of *CGS*, the coefficient for CGS_{ds}'s variable becomes positive, and its significantly positive relationship with Q and *ROA* (column 5) was confirmed.

[16] Definitions and characteristics of variables that indicate external governance structure are examined in the next chapter.

standardized Q and standardized ROA (the relationship that was confirmed in the previous section).

Thus, it is highly plausible that recent efforts devoted to governance reform by corporations have had a substantial influence on performance. When company efforts to implement governance reform are examined by specific reform category, however, neither CGS_{sh} (which measures reform efforts related to the rights of shareholders) nor CGS_{br} (which measures efforts to strengthen the function of the board of directors) are found to have a statistically significant relationship with performance. In other words, there is no evidence that protection of shareholders' rights and board reform contribute to improved performance. On the other hand, we confirmed that of the various types of governance reform, information disclosure measures including investor relations activities (CGS_{ds}) have a strong and positively significant relationship with performance.

12.3.3 Information Disclosure and Agency Costs

Why then do information disclosure efforts such as investor relations activities (CGS_{ds}) improve a company's performance? There are two possible explanations. First, active efforts to improve the firm's relationship with investors, to promote information disclosure, and to increase the transparency of the company's business may correct the asymmetry of information between shareholders and business managers, and thereby lower the cost of capital. Second, information disclosure as such may serve to keep management in check. Companies that actively pursue investor relations activities and information disclosure should be considered companies in which managers are willing to be held accountable and are committed to improving transparency. Once a company begins the process of raising its level of information disclosure, it cannot reverse course and withhold information regardless of its performance. It can be assumed that when insiders make a commitment not to conceal disadvantageous information, they are helping to discipline managers and thus improve performance.

Although it is hard to quantify the degree to which either of the above two effects influences a company's performance, both are not mutually exclusive and in fact originate from information asymmetries between shareholders and managers. To test the plausibility of the hypothesis that among the various types of governance reform, information disclosure in particular improves a company's performance by correcting the asymmetry of information, we focus on R&D investment because the level of information asymmetries in this area is assumed to be relatively high. In general, a company's R&D investment reflects its accumulation of managerial and human resources over the long term. It is difficult for outside investors to determine whether the level of investment in R&D has been reasonable or how significant the future risks and benefits of such investment are compared to the risks and benefits of real (physical) investment. As a result, managers tend to have more discretion when making R&D investment decisions than when making real investment decisions. Therefore, we can assume that a

Table 12.5 Division of Samples (High R&D and Low R&D)

Column	(1)		(2)		(3)		(4)	
Dependent variable	Standardized Q		Standardized Q		Standardized Q		Standardized Q	
Independent variable	Coefficient	t-value	Coefficient	t-value	Coefficient	t-value	Coefficient	t-value
C	0.226	0.23	−1.373	−1.42	−1.609 *	−1.75	1.139	1.13
$SIZE$	0.000	−0.01	0.106 **	2.18	0.121 ***	2.64	−0.053	−0.99
DAR	−1.406 ***	−4.61	−1.569 ***	−5.10	−1.606 ***	−5.23	−1.207 ***	−3.95
$LIST$	0.103 ***	2.84	0.117 ***	3.19	0.125 ***	3.45	0.093 **	2.58
$GSALE$	0.288 *	1.81	0.311 *	1.92	0.306 *	1.89	0.287 *	1.82
CGS	0.014 *	1.90	0.014	0.69	0.002	0.15	0.033 ***	2.61
$CGS \times HR\&D$	0.016 *	1.77	0.012	0.43	0.020	1.01	0.040 **	2.51
$HR\&D$	−0.292	−1.03	0.155	0.83	−0.022	−0.09	−0.316	−1.44
adj.R^2	0.124		0.094		0.095		0.145	
Sample number	590		590		590		590	

Notes: CGS replaced with CGS_{sh} in column (2), with CGS_{br} in column (3), and with CGS_{ds} in column (4). Standardized Q: Standardized Q; $SIZE$: Natural logarithm for total assets; DAR: Debt/asset ratio; $LIST$: Years of listing; $GSALE$: Sales growth rate; CGS: Total CGS score; CGS_{sh}: Rights of shareholders; CGS_{br}: Board of directors; CGS_{ds}: Information disclosure. $HR\&D$: Dummy variables are given value of 1 for top 50% companies with high R&D ratio and 0 for the remainder of the sample companies.
*** statistically significant at 1% level, ** at 5% level, and * at 10% level.

company with a higher rate of R&D investment will have a more serious agency problem between shareholders and managers than a company with a lower rate of R&D investment. Using the rate of R&D investment as a proxy variable for agency costs, we test the following conjecture: if a company's active information disclosure improves performance by correcting the asymmetry of information between managers and shareholders, then the higher the company's rate of R&D investment, the greater the improvement in performance.

For this test, we introduce an interaction term for the dummy variable $HR\&D$ (that gives 1 to high R&D companies) and CGS, based on the median value (0.81) of R&D ratio (R&D expenditure divided by sales amount). The interaction terms for CGS_{ds} and $HR\&D$ are statistically significant at the 5% level (Table 12.5). For $HR\&D$ companies, the influence on performance of the CGS_{ds} turns out to be twice that of low R&D companies. The above estimate result is consistent with the understanding that the higher the company's rate of R&D investment, the more likely its efforts to disclose information (including investor relations activities) will contribute to improved performance.

12.3.4 Executive Officer System, Outside Directors, and Performance

According to the analysis in the previous section, performance is positively sensitive to CGS_{br}, which measures board reform, but not to a statistically significant degree. It should be noted that CGS_{br} is calculated by using six evenly weighted variables, and thus the effect of the introduction of the executive officer system that has become central to board reform efforts since 1997 and of the introduction of outside directors may have been underestimated. Therefore, in this section, we examine the executive officer system and outside directors separately and analyze how each is related to a company's performance.

Executive Officer System

First, we examine how the introduction of the executive officer system affects a company's performance. The executive officer system adopted by Sony and other companies was not stipulated by law, and therefore different from the later committee system that has been allowed since April 2003 with the revision of the Commercial Code.[17] According to this survey, 33% of companies have adopted the executive officer system. The fraction is up 20% points from the previous survey (1999), so the pace of adoption of this system has been quite remarkable. To examine the relationship between the introduction of the executive officer system and performance, we use the following Logit model, replacing the independent variable *CGS* with *EQ*, which takes the value of 1 if a company has adopted the executive officer system.

We found from our estimate that the coefficient for *EQ* is positive, but not significant when it is calculated by making *Q* a dependent variable. When calculated by making *ROA* a dependent variable, however, the coefficient for *EQ* is negative. This result suggests that the introduction of the executive officer system as such is independent from improved performance.

Leaving measurement problems aside for the moment, one might conclude that the introduction of the executive officer system has had no impact on performance and has simply been a cosmetic reform. For instance, Nobeoka and Tanaka (2002) point out that quite a few companies utilize the executive officer system merely to reduce the number of board members, to create a buzz for reform, and to mimic companies that have already introduced the system without careful consideration of substance. Also, Miyajima and Inagaki's empirical analysis (2003) suggests that the executive officer system currently adopted by Japanese corporations may be window-dressing and may not contribute to solving the agency problem between shareholders and managers. Thus, they conclude that the introduction of the executive officer system in Japan has had a limited effect. The analysis in this section is consistent with the findings of previous studies.

Outside Directors

The introduction of outside directors has also attracted much attention due to their association with the transition to the committee system. This survey found

---

[17] In many cases, the executive officer system has been introduced to separate monitoring from management, or to reduce the number of board members and to make the size of boards of directors proportionate to the size of the company (Miyajima et al. 2003, chap. 2).

that 35.8% of listed and over-the-counter companies have introduced outside directors, as have more than half of companies with capital of more than ¥30 billion. Outside board members are thought to provide a stronger check on representative executives and advice on decision-making. On the other hand, skeptics may question whether outsiders make a positive contribution because their lack of specialized knowledge of the company's business and actual experience in it could prevent them from serving as effective decision-makers or supervisors. Furthermore, the absence of a Japanese market for business managers capable of serving as outside board members means that there is likely to be a shortage of qualified candidates.

In order to clarify how the introduction of outside board members to Japanese corporations has affected corporate performance, we conduct the following estimation, where the independent variable *CGS* in the formula (1) is replaced by the dummy variable *OD*, which is given the value of 1 when the company has outside board members and 0 otherwise.

Of the estimate sample of 609 companies, 272 companies had outside directors. However, there is no significant relationship between outside board members and corporate performance in terms of *ROA* and *Q* (not reported). As previously noted, there are problems with the estimate results—for example, this estimate does not explicitly take the timing of the introduction of outside board members into account, and the measurement of corporate performance is limited to one fiscal year, and thus should be considered tentative. But recent research has found that the introduction of outside board members does not appear to have made a clear contribution to performance.

It should be noted, however, that the above estimate counts all the companies that appoint outsiders, i.e. people not promoted from within the company, to their boards. But the nature of these outside board members varies considerably— some outside board members are fully independent but others are less so (having been dispatched from a parent company or main bank). Some companies have outside board members who are bona fide outsiders while others have appointed people who are outsiders in name only. Therefore, we have compiled a sample of outside board members (N=231), but have also compiled an index from the survey results to test the independence of outside board members and the strengthening of their function.[18]

According to the estimation results, the relationship between strengthening the function of outside board members and corporate performance is not statistically significant for both *ROA* and *Q*, although a moderately positive relationship (the t-value for the coefficient is 1.65) is found, when *Q* is used as an independent variable. In short, it can be said that the introduction of outside board members alone does not enhance performance unless the company also takes measures to ensure that outside board members can monitor management and remain independent.

---

[18] The index is calculated by extracting 11 questionnaire items concerning the strengthening of outside board members from this survey.

12.4 DETERMINANTS OF GOVERNANCE REFORM

12.4.1 The Stakeholders

The previous section looked at how governance reform affects performance and pointed out the possibility that the accumulation of reforms, as shown by a high *CGS*, and especially a high CGS_{ds} (active efforts to promote information disclosure), may improve performance. The next question to ask is, what factors have a decisive influence on the adoption of reform measures? Specifically, we will focus on assessing the significance of the influence of outside providers of capital (shareholders, creditors) and employees on governance reform.

In the past, Japanese companies had institutional characteristics different from those of US companies (Aoki 1988, 2002) and tended to be relatively homogeneous. However, as shown in the previous chapters, since the 1990s, and especially since 1997, Japanese companies have become increasingly diverse in every respect including their ties with creditors (banks), composition of shareholders, and relationship with employees. Therefore, how such diversity among companies in terms of relationships with external investors (shareholders and debt holders) and employees affects board reform is the focus of the analysis below. Previous studies have shown that companies pursuing market-based finance are also active in governance reform.[19] On the other hand, although it is widely assumed that "business management that places a high value on employee stakes impedes governance reform," not many researchers have attempted to test this view systematically.[20]

To measure the determinants of reform, we will use a simple model that regresses governance reforms on ownership, the bank–firm relationship, and employee involvement in management.

$$(2) \qquad CGS = F(SIZE, STAB, FRG, BOR, BOND, CML, EMP)$$

Here, the dependent variable *CGS* is a measure of the governance reforms explained in the previous section, and each sub-index is used as a dependent variable. *SIZE*, which is the logarithm of total assets, controls for the size of companies. The variables that test the effect of ownership structure on governance reform include the ratio of stable shareholders (*STAB*: the percentage of shares held by financial institutions and corporations) and the ratio of shares held by foreigners (*FRG*).[21]

---

[19] For a summary of the previous questionnaire survey (1999), see Ohmura and Mashiko (2000).

[20] Advances have been made recently in research into how characteristics of governance structure affect a company's choice of employment system. For example, see Abe (2002), Urasaka and Noda (2001), Tomiyama (2001).

[21] Since the ratio of shares owned by financial institutions includes shares owned by trust and banking companies (investment trusts), it should be eliminated in principle when a proxy variable

The variables introduced to capture the influence of firm–creditor relationships on the company's choice of governance reform include the ratio of borrowing divided by total assets (*BOR*), a proxy for the level of dependence on banks; a proxy for the ratio of corporate bonds over the sum of bonds and borrowing (*BOND*), which captures the degree of dependence on capital markets; and the dummy variable (*CML*),[22] which is 1 if a firm concludes a commitment line with a bank indicating that it has entered into an explicit relationship different from the previously implicit main-bank relationship. Since the concern here is to examine how much outside stakeholders influence the implementation of governance reform by managers, we use the variable for the relationship with outside investors for the period three terms prior to the most recent survey, i.e. at the end of the 1998 business year (ending March 31, 1999), around the time when the financial crisis accelerated the dissolution of cross-shareholdings and the excessive debt held by companies emerged as a problem due to the surge in non-performing loans.

On the other hand, the variable *EMP* captures the influence of employee involvement in management on the company's choice of governance reform. *EMP* is calculated from information about company–union negotiations, and negotiation/explanation agenda items at labor–management councils gathered from questionnaire surveys (details are given later). Furthermore, we attempt an estimate by replacing *EMP* with a dummy *HEMP* that gives 1 to the fourth quartile of *EMP*, and with a dummy *LEMP* that gives 1 to the first quartile of *EMP* in order to test robustness.

Stable shareholders (*STAB*) constitute 58.8% of total shareholders, and had a variance that is relatively small compared to other variables. On the other hand, the average ratio of foreign shareholders (*FRG*) is 5.7%. As emphasized in Chapter 4, the variance of *FRG* is remarkably large. While more than one-fourth of sample companies have an *FRG* less than 1%, those in the top quartile have an *FRG* of more than 8%.

The average debt ratio (*BOR*) is 19.1% (standard deviation 16.7%). Although the average of the ratio of bond dependence (the amount of corporate bonds divided by [the amount of borrowing + corporate bonds]) is 26%, the standard deviation is quite large at 33.8%. Among sample companies, 252 companies (47.7%), or approximately half were unable (or did not need) to use corporate bonds for financing. Also, a commitment line is used by 31% of sample companies (listed or over-the-counter companies).

---

for stable shareholders is calculated. As for foreign shareholders, foreign institutional investors should be differentiated from foreign companies. However, such controls are not applied in this analysis.

[22] One major feature of a commitment line is that it is based on an explicit contract, and thus is different from an existing relationship with a main bank based on an implicit contract. Also, most commitment lines take the form of syndicated loans, and can be viewed as one form of market-model indirect financing.

Employee Involvement in Strategic Decision-Making

The degree of employee involvement in the company's strategic decision-making through the labor–management council is shown in Figure 12.2.[23] A relatively large number of companies reported that an agreement between employees and the employer was required for the following situations: employment adjustments directly affecting the labor force, mergers and acquisitions, the sale of operating divisions, and extensions of stock ownership to employees that contribute to employee asset formation. Approximately half of sample companies reported that decisions related to production and sales planning, and earnings indicators were items for discussion between labor and management. But only a few percent of sample companies reported that an agreement between employees and the employer was necessary to make decisions about capital expenditures, the introduction and development of new technology, financing measures, and stock options for the board of directors and managers, and more than 70% of companies reported that these items were not discussed at labor–management councils.[24]

The index for employee involvement in management (*EMP*) is calculated as follows: two points are given for "an agreement (between employees and employers) is necessary," one point for "an item requiring explanation to employees," and 0 point for "an item not taken up at labor–management council" for the ten questionnaire items in Figure 12.2. The scores for each sample company were then added up. Since only companies that answered all the questionnaires were included in the sample, the size of the sample is 597. The index range is from 0 to 20, but the average score is 5.6, the lowest score is 0, the highest score is 19, and the standard deviation is 3.4.

We tested the relationship between the level of employee involvement in management and firm attributes such as the year of establishment, company size, the ratio of R&D, and service years of employees. Firms are divided into two groups (higher and lower) by the average value of the employee involvement in management index (*EMP*) and tested for differences. For every item, the test results of differences between the two groups' averages are significant at the 1% level. We found that the degree of employee involvement in the company's strategic decision-making rose with: (a) the age of firms, (b) the size of the company, (c) the R&D intensity, and (d) the length of service of employees. These results are consistent with conventional wisdom, and allow us to regard the index for employee involvement in management (*EMP*) as reliable.

---

[23] According to this questionnaire survey, among the listed and over-the-counter companies, 69.3% have labor unions, and the average rate of union membership is 84.5%. Although 65.3% of companies have labor–management councils, 79.8% of companies with labor unions have labor–management councils, and it is understood that in most cases, labor unions and labor–management councils are set up together.

[24] For creating questionnaire items, the researcher referred to a work by the Japan Productivity Center for Socio-Economic Development (Shakai Keizai Seisansei Honbu 1998).

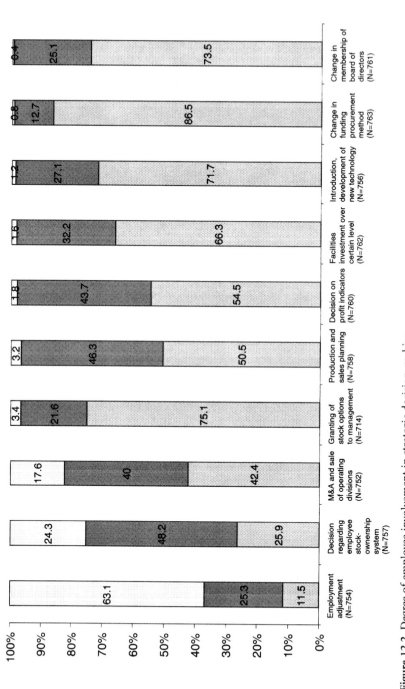

Figure 12.2 Degree of employee involvement in strategic decision-making

Notes: ☐ Not discussed ▨ Requires explanation ☐ Requires agreement.

12.4.2 Estimate Results

Outside Investors

Estimate results are summarized in Table 12.6. First, when *CGS* is set as a dependent variable, the coefficient for the ratio of stable shareholders is significantly negative at the 5% level (column 1), indicating that companies with a higher ratio of stable shareholders three terms ago tended to avoid governance reforms. When CGS_{ds} (information disclosure) is the dependent variable, much stronger results are achieved. The estimation indicates a negative relationship between CGS_{sh} and governance reform, although the results are not significant. It should be noted, however, that there is no significant relationship between stable shareholders and CGS_{br}.

Second, the coefficient for foreign shareholders (*FRG*) is positive in relation to *CGS*, and the level of significance is also sufficiently high. As expected, the existence of foreign shareholders encourages managers to implement governance reforms. It is estimated that a one standard deviation increase in the percentage of foreign shareholders would pull *CGS* up by 2.25 points. The magnitude of this influence on *CGS* is approximately twice that of stable shareholders. The same results were found with CGS_{ds}, indicating that companies with high stock ownership by foreign investors are actively pursuing information disclosure.

Third, when examining the relationship between creditors and governance reforms, one finds that the coefficient for the debt ratio (*BOR*) is negatively significant at the 1% level; the higher a company's *BOR*, the less active its pursuit of governance reforms. It is estimated that a one standard deviation increase in *BOR* would decrease *CGS* by 1.50 points. This magnitude is comparable to 11.1% of the standard deviation of *CGS*. The coefficient for the ratio of corporate bonds (*BOND*) is positively significant at the 5% level, suggesting that managers of companies heavily reliant on market-financing (corporate bonds) actively pursued governance reform. Also, the coefficient for commitment lines (*CML*) is significant at the 1% level. In other words, if a company shifts from a traditional main-bank relationship based on an implicit contract to a new company–bank relationship based on an explicit contract, it is considered to be actively pursuing governance reform.

What is clear is that the more stock owned by institutional investors and the higher the company's dependence on capital markets, the more actively it pursues governance reform, particularly in the area of information disclosure. Conversely, the higher the stable shareholder ratio and the higher the dependence on borrowing for financing, the slower the company's efforts at reform.

Employee Involvement in Management

Let us now summarize the relationship between employee involvement in management and governance reform, and examine whether the conventional wisdom

Table 12.6 Degree of Employee Involvement in Management and Governance Reforms

Dependent Variable	CGS				$CGS_{sh.}$			
	(1)		(2)		(3)		(4)	
	Coeffi-cient	t-value	Coeffi-cient	t-value	Coeffi-cient	t-value	Coeffi-cient	t-value
C	−34.29 ***	−5.46	−33.81 ***	−5.31	−7.26 ***	−2.78	−7.24 ***	−2.74
SIZE(−3)	3.61 ***	9.13	3.63 ***	9.18	0.87 ***	5.30	0.87 ***	5.28
STAB(−3)	−0.07 **	−2.41	−0.07 **	−2.45	−0.02	−1.35	−0.02	−1.44
FRG(−3)	0.29 ***	4.19	0.29 ***	4.13	0.01	0.50	0.01	0.50
BOR(−3)	−0.09 ***	−2.74	−0.09 ***	−2.74	−0.03 **	−2.02	−0.03 **	−2.02
BOND(−3)	0.04 **	2.10	0.03 **	2.05	0.01	0.87	0.01	0.81
CML	4.09 ***	4.12	4.03 ***	4.04	0.38	0.92	0.34	0.81
EMP	0.04	0.30			−0.07	−1.25		
HEMP			−0.63	−0.58			−0.67	−1.48
LEMP			−0.75	−0.68			−0.18	−0.40
adj.R^2	0.38		0.38		0.11		0.11	
Sample number	528		528		528		528	

Dependent Variable	CGS_{br}				CGS_{ds}			
	(5)		(6)		(7)		(8)	
	Coeffi-cient	t-value	Coeffi-cient	t-value	Coeffi-cient	t-value	Coeffi-cient	t-value
C	−4.67	−1.37	−3.77	−1.09	−22.37 ***	−6.45	−22.80 ***	−6.48
SIZE(−3)	0.77 ***	3.58	0.79 ***	3.69	1.97 ***	9.04	1.97 ***	9.05
STAB(−3)	0.01	0.52	0.01	0.40	−0.06 ***	−3.86	−0.06 ***	−3.75
FRG(−3)	0.06 *	1.71	0.06	1.58	0.21 ***	5.53	0.21 ***	5.57
BOR(−3)	−0.01	−0.72	−0.01	−0.78	−0.05 ***	−2.74	−0.05 ***	−2.68
BOND(−3)	0.01	0.74	0.01	0.65	0.02 **	2.42	0.02 **	2.47
CML	1.18 **	2.19	1.11 **	2.06	2.54 ***	4.62	2.58 ***	4.68
EMP	0.12 *	1.65			−0.01	−0.14		
HEMP			−0.35	−0.60			0.39	0.65
LEMP			−1.14 *	−1.92			0.57	0.94
adj.R^2	0.09		0.09		0.42		0.41	
Sample number	528		528		528		528	

Notes: CGS: Total CGS score; CGS_{sh}: Rights of shareholders; CGS_{br}: Board of directors; CGS_{ds}: Information disclosure; SIZE: Natural logarithm of total assets; STAB: Ratio of stable shareholders (%); FRG: Ratio of foreign shareholders (%); BOR: Debt ratio (borrowing/total assets (%)); BOND: Ratio of corporate bonds (Bonds/the sum of bonds and borrowing); CML: Dummy variables given value of 1 for companies that conclude a commitment-line contract with financial institution; EMP: The index for the degree of employee involvement in management, see text and Figure 12.2; HEMP: Dummy variables for third quartile of EMP are given a value of 1, and the rest take the value of 0; LEMP: Dummy variables for first quartile of EMP are given a value of 1, and the rest take the value of 0. *** denotes statistical significance at the 1% level, ** at the 5% level, and * at the 10% level.

that "governance reform favors shareholders' interests and is impeded by management that puts a stress on employee welfare" is correct.

If we look at columns 1 and 2 in Table 12.6, where *CGS* is a dependent variable, the coefficients for the indices *EMP, HEMP,* and *LEMP* are insignificant, a likely indication that governance reform is conducted independently from the degree of employee involvement in strategic decision-making. Next, when we examine the sub-indices that comprise *CGS*, in estimates that make CGS_{sh} (the rights of minority shareholders) and CGS_{ds} (information disclosure) dependent variables (columns 3, 4, 7, and 8), the significance level of coefficients for *EMP, HEMP,* and *LEMP* is still not sufficient. Meanwhile, coefficients for *EMP* and *LEMP* with CGS_{br} as a dependent variable are positive and negative respectively at the 10% significance level. These results indicate that when the degree of employee involvement in management is high, reform of the board of directors can progress.

So far, it has been shown that the conventional wisdom notwithstanding, the degree of employee involvement in strategic decision-making is independent of progress in governance reform. At the very least, it appears that governance reform that aims to solve the agency problem to the benefit of shareholders is not in conflict with "management emphasizing employee welfare."

As previously stated, a high degree of employee involvement in management is usually assumed to be incompatible with shareholder-oriented governance reform measures to protect shareholder rights, disclose information to investors, etc. However, when a company faces significant pressure from the capital market, a higher degree of employee involvement in management may in fact encourage governance reform. This is because in an environment characterized by the pre-eminence of the market, a company that sends a signal to the market by implementing measures to attenuate the asymmetrical information problem can lower its cost of capital, and thus serve the interests of employees. Therefore, the above result finding that *CGS* and the degree of employee involvement in management are independent from each other may reflect the fact that sample companies in this estimation are a mixture of two groups with different external conditions (exposed to different levels of pressure from the capital market) whose effects on reform offset each other. On the one hand, there are companies which feel little pressure from the capital market but have a high degree of employee involvement in management that has served to impede governance reform. On the other hand, there are companies exposed to strong pressure from the capital market with a high degree of employee involvement in management that has encouraged governance reform. To test this conjecture, the sample is divided into two groups—those with ratings higher than BBB, and those with ratings lower than BB or unrated, using corporate bond ratings as a proxy for market pressure. Among 528 sample companies, 150 companies (28%) had ratings higher than BBB and 378 companies (72%) did not. The key findings of the estimate results (Table 12.7) are as follows.[25]

First, when we look at the group with ratings higher than BBB in this estimation that makes *CGS* a dependent variable, we find that the coefficient for *EMP* is

---

[25] The ratings here are based on the Senior Long-Term Credit Ratings by Rating and Investment Information, Inc (March 31, 2002).

Table 12.7 The Effect of the Degree of Employee Involvement by Capital Market Pressure

Dependent Variable	CGS				CGS_{sh}			
	Rating: Higher than BBB		Rating: Lower than BB or unrated		Rating: Higher than BBB		Rating: Lower than BB or unrated	
	(1)		(2)		(3)		(4)	
Independent Variable	Coeffi- cient	t-value	Coeffi- cient	t-value	Coeffi- cient	t-value	Coeffi- cient	t-value
C	−57.07 ***	−4.37	−15.64 *	−1.88	−14.37 **	−2.55	0.48	0.14
$SIZE(-3)$	4.34 ***	5.92	2.63 ***	5.01	1.29 ***	4.07	0.41 *	1.90
$STAB(-3)$	0.11	1.51	−0.10 ***	−3.19	0.00		−0.13	−0.01	−1.00
$FRG(-3)$	0.28 **	2.56	0.30 ***	3.20	0.02	0.34	0.00	−0.05
$BOR(-3)$	−0.14	−1.32	−0.08 **	−2.35	−0.04	−0.78	−0.03 *	−1.90
$BOND(-3)$	−0.01	−0.34	0.01	0.57	−0.03	−1.52	0.01	1.57
CML	2.03 *	1.09	5.56 ***	4.72	−1.31	−1.63	1.06 **	2.19
EMP	0.52 *	1.91	−0.06	−0.40	0.12	1.06	-0.12 *	−1.92
adj.R^2	0.32		0.23		0.12		0.05	
Sample number	150		378		150		378	

Dependent Variable	CGS_{br}				CGS_{ds}			
	Rating: Higher than BBB		Rating: Lower than BB or unrated		Rating: Higher than BBB		Rating: Lower than BB or unrated	
	(5)		(6)		(7)		(8)	
Independent Variable	Coeffi- cient	t-value	Coeffi- cient	t-value	Coeffi- cient	t-value	Coeffi- cient	t-value
C	−8.02	−1.02	−4.76	−1.08	−34.68 ***	−4.70	−11.37 ***	−2.57
$SIZE(-3)$	0.67	1.51	0.81 ***	2.93	2.39 ***	5.77	1.41 ***	5.06
$STAB(-3)$	0.02	0.47	0.01	0.44	0.09 **	2.27	−0.10 ***	−5.68
$FRG(-3)$	0.08	1.26	0.08	1.57	0.18 ***	2.94	0.22 ***	4.50
$BOR(-3)$	0.05	0.80	−0.02	−1.02	−0.16 ***	−2.61	−0.03 *	−1.95
$BOND(-3)$	0.04 *	1.65	0.00	−0.24	−0.03	−1.19	0.00	0.11
CML	1.83	1.64	0.99	1.58	1.50	1.43	3.51 ***	5.63
EMP	0.35 **	2.18	0.04	0.47	0.04	0.26	0.02	0.25
adj.R^2	0.07		0.05		0.33		0.30	
Sample number	150		378		150		378	

Notes: *CGS:* Total *CGS* score: CGS_{sh}: Rights of shareholders; CGS_{br}: Board of directors; CGS_{ds}: Information disclosure; *SIZE:* Natural logarithm of total assets; *STAB:* Ratio of stable shareholders; *FRG:* Ratio of foreign shareholders; *BOR:* Debt ratio (Borrowing/total assets); BOND: Ratio of corporate bonds (Bonds/the sum of bonds and borrowing); *CML:* Dummy variables given value of 1 for companies that conclude a commitment-line contract with financial institution, and 0 for the rest; *EMP:* Index for the degree of employee involvement in management. *** statistically significant at 1% level, ** at 5% level, and * 10% level.

positive at the 10% significant level (column 1). On the other hand, in terms of the group with ratings lower than BB or unrated companies, the coefficient for *EMP* is negative although its significance level is low. Second, in the estimation that sets CGS_{br} as a dependent variable, the coefficient of *EMP* for the group with ratings better than BBB is positive at the 5% significance level (column 5). In the estimation that sets CGS_{sh} as a dependent variable, the coefficient of *EMP* for the group with ratings lower than BB is negative at the 10% significance level (column 4).

To sum up, in companies under pressure from the capital market, a high degree of employee involvement in management is in fact more likely to encourage governance reform. So in such cases, employee involvement in management is at the very least compatible with governance reform.[26] On the other hand, in companies free from pressure from the capital market, it is likely that a high degree of employee involvement in management affects governance reform negatively, and in such companies, employee involvement can be seen as acting as an impediment to reform. While further examination is necessary, it should be noted that there is a possibility that the degree of employee involvement functions in two opposing ways, depending on the company's relationship with the capital market.

12.4.3 Diversifying Human Resources Management

The previous section suggests that employee involvement in management and governance reform are not necessarily incompatible and could in fact be positively correlated if firms are exposed to a high degree of pressure from the capital market. To explore this issue further, we now look at the relationship that exists between the employee/wage system and governance reform.

Management of human resources in large Japanese companies used to be characterized by long-term (lifetime) employment and a seniority-based wage system that featured regular pay increases. However, in recent years, Japanese companies and especially major electrical component firms have been actively trimming regular pay increases, and it is often pointed out that the seniority-based wage system has started to collapse across industries. Long-term employment is also changing as the use of non-regular employees and mid-career hiring has become more common. Moreover, while long-term employment and seniority-based wages used to be seen as complementary, recent moves by Toyota and Canon indicate that companies are attempting various revisions such as ability-based pay while maintaining long-term employment. Thus, long-term

---

[26] This analysis is consistent with the results of Miyajima and Aoki (2002), who suggest that presidential turnover by insiders tends to be sensitive to corporate performance if firms are under considerable market pressure and face the need to restructure.

employment and the seniority-based wage system, once regarded as hallmarks of Japanese corporations, are undergoing significant change.

Let us begin by briefly reviewing trends in the implementation of long-term employment and seniority-based wages from our sample. *The Ministry of Finance survey* (PRI 2003b)divides companies into three types: (1) Type I—companies with long-term employment and seniority-based wages; (2) Type II—companies with long-term employment and ability-based pay; and (3) Type III—companies without long-term employment but with ability-based pay. According to Table 12.8, which presents a comparison of this questionnaire survey (conducted in December 2002, sample of 860 companies) and the previous questionnaire survey (conducted in November 1999, sample of 1,189 companies), more than half of the companies in both surveys were Type I. However, compared to the previous survey, the 2002 survey finds that the percentage of Type I companies decreased dramatically—by 15% points. On the other hand, in the 2002 survey, Type II companies increased by 9% points and Type III companies increased by 6% points. The most recent survey confirms that the number of companies with long-term employment and seniority-based wages has clearly decreased. Nonetheless, more than half of the sample companies were Type I, and more than 80% of companies answered that they maintained long-term employment. Therefore, the long-term employment system still prevails in the majority of Japanese companies.[27]

Before proceeding with our analysis of the effect of human resource management on governance reform, two points of caution should be noted. First, company questionnaire surveys concerning labor and management and employment are usually sent to the human resources departments of companies. However, for the 2002 survey, persons in charge of business planning sections were asked to respond. Consequently, the results of this survey reflect attitudes toward or knowledge of employment policy from the vantage point of the section within the company that formulates business strategy instead of that of the human resources specialists who would have a more precise understanding of the employment/wage system and would be responsible for designing it. Second, the questions about "ability pay" were not meant to probe in depth into issues such as employees' service and differences with the ability-based system. Therefore, answers to the questionnaires merely indicated that "the company is working to amend a wage system that is strongly associated with a traditional system based on years of service." The analysis below is a first attempt at understanding the relationship between the employment system and governance reform. The results should be treated as tentative at best and demand further testing.

---

[27] The interviews and statistical data found in Katoh's study (2001) support the observation that the practice of long-term employment in Japanese companies has changed little even after the collapse of the bubble economy.

Table 12.8 Governance Reform and Employment System

| Type | I | | II | | III | | | |
| | Long-term Employment and Age-Based Pay | | Long-term Employment and Adoption of Ability-Based Pay | | Limited-term Employment and Adoption of Ability-Based Pay | | Total | |
Research Point	# of Companies	(%)	# of Companies	(%)	# of Companies	(%)	# of Companies	(%)
Nov-99	826	69.5	247	20.8	116	9.8	1189	100.0
Dec-02	467	54.3	256	29.8	137	15.9	860	100.0

Source: Survey by Ministry of Finance, Policy Research Institute (PRI 2003b).

Notes: Created based on the following questions 6–6 and 6–7 (2002b) in the survey.

Notes:

Created based on questions 6-6 and 6-7 (2002b) in the survey by Ministry of Finance, Policy Research Institute.Source: Survey by Ministry of Finance, Policy Research Institute (2000) III-2- ⑭, ⑭-1

Employment/Wage Categories

Question 6-6: Is your current employment system based on a seniority-based waged system premised on lifetime employment?
(1)Yes
(2)Yes, if I had to say
(3)No, if I had to say
(4)No

Question 6-7: (Asked of corporations which chose (3) or (4) in the previous question). What type of employment system has your company adopted?
(1)Abolished lifetime employment, and have fully implemented a wage system linked to ability.
(2)Limited the scope of lifetime employment, but have fully implemented a wage system linked to ability.

Type I

(3)Limited the scope of lifetime employment, and have partially implemented a wage system linked to ability.
(4)Maintain lifetime employment, and have fully implemented a wage system linked to ability.
(5)Maintain lifetime employment, but have partially implemented a wage system linked to ability.

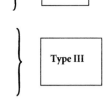

Type III

Type II

The Three Types of Employment Systems and Business Structure

In this section, preliminary observations are made from our sample regarding the relationship between the three types of employment systems laid out in the previous section, and business structure, focusing on the following three points: (a) necessity of long-term investment (R&D); (b) the degree of business diversification; and (c) business risk. As proxies, we use (a) the reporting (non-reporting) of R&D; (b) the number of business segments newly entered by a company, and the ratio of companies concentrating on specialized segments;[28] and (c) the standard deviation of *ROA* for the past decade. The relationship between business structure and the employee/wage system is summarized in Table 12.9.

First, it is expected that the higher a company's expenditures on R&D, the higher the possibility of its adoption of long-term employment. The main reason is that high R&D companies are more engaged in long-run process and product innovation. Therefore, employees working for companies with higher R&D ratios need to acquire company-specific skills, and such companies are also required to emphasize skill formation. Consistent with this view, companies that require investment for the long run tend to adopt long-term employment. Among the companies that adopt some form of long-term employment (Types I and II), approximately 70% reported R&D. However, only about 50% of Type III companies that used limited-term employment reported R&D.

Table 12.9 Typology of Employment System and Characteristics of Companies

Characteristics of Business	Substitutional Variable	Sample total # of Companies	Type I Long-term Employment	Type II Long-term Employment	Type III Limited-term
Long-term Investment	Ratio of Companies with R&D	742	68.6%	72.9%	54.4%
Business Diversification	# of Areas Entered	181	7.5 areas	9.8 areas	5.6 areas
	Ratio of Companies Concentrated on Specialized Area	181	6.2%	3.2%	19.0%
Business Risk	Standard Deviation for ROA in the Past Decade	601	1.96%	1.88%	2.83%

Notes: (1) R&D ratio is cited from Japan Company Handbook by Toyo Keizai Shinpo-sha (on the basis of account settlement at March 2000). (2) Business diversification is cited from the results of the survey by Ministry of Finance, Policy Research Institute (PRI 2003a and 2003b), and the sample size is small because we only use the data for companies that answered both surveys.

[28] For more on the number of business segments newly entered by companies and a definition of companies concentrating on specialized segments, refer to Miyajima and Inagaki (2003: 32–3, 37, 42–3).

Second, companies with widely diversified businesses tend to adopt the long-term employment system because guaranteeing stable employment to employees makes it easier to move employees to different business sections, and thus easier to diversify into new business segments. Also, companies whose business diversification is at an advanced stage are more likely to need various information-processing measures, and consequently tend to adopt long-term employment practices that help to accumulate company-specific knowledge and skills. Compared to Type III companies, those categorized as Type I and II enter more new business segments, and have lower degrees of specialization.

Lastly, because companies with higher business risk, i.e. business structures sensitive to business cycles, seek to avoid fixed costs, of which human resources make up a major part, they are more likely to adopt limited-term employment (allowing them to hire and fire employees flexibly) and ability-based pay (where wage is associated with ability/performance). As expected, business risk (measured by fluctuation of *ROA*) is higher in Type III companies.

Although the above analysis is somewhat cursory, the relationship between the companies with the employment/wage types examined in this survey and business structure were in line with our general expectations, and it is reasonable to assume that the above description has a certain degree of reliability and adequacy.

12.4.4 Human Resource Management and Governance Reform

This section attempts an estimation by replacing *EMP* (employee involvement) in formula (2) with employment/wage type in order to analyze the relationship between the employment/wage system and governance reform. Following the three categories in the previous section, the long-term employment/seniority-based pay dummy (*TYPE I*), long-term employment/ability-based pay dummy (*TYPE II*), and limited-term employment/ability-based pay dummy (*TYPE III*) are computed by giving 1 to companies in Type I, II, and III, and 0 to the rest.[29] The estimation result is summarized in Table 12.10. The effect of the debt ratio and the composition of shareholders on *CGS* is unchanged from Table 12.7. Keeping this in mind, we can summarize the relationship between the employment/wage system and *CGS* as follows.

First, compared to other types, Type I companies are negatively correlated to corporate governance reform to a statistically significant degree. For either *CGS* in Panel 1 or any estimate that uses the three *CGS* sub-indices (Panels 2, 3, and 4), the coefficient of *TYPE I* is significantly negative. Its significance level is around 5% in an estimation that sets CGS_{br} as a dependent variable; otherwise, the significance level is better than 1%. Therefore, the results here are statistically

---

[29] Basic statistics are omitted here. However, the distribution of *CGS* and other variables does not differ greatly from the samples in the previous section, though the sample sizes in the two analyses are different.

Table 12.10 Determination of CGS and Employment System

Panel 1 Dependent Variable: *CGS*

	(1)		(2)		(3)		(4)	
	Coeffi-cient	t-value	Coeffi-cient	t-value	Coeffi-cient	t-value	Coeffi-cient	t-value
C	−32.94 ***	−5.03	−34.48 ***	−5.23	−39.40 ***	−5.91	−37.33 ***	−5.66
SIZE(−3)	3.87 ***	9.69	3.77 ***	9.26	4.08 ***	10.02	3.88 ***	9.57
STAB(−3)	−0.09 ***	−2.99	−0.09 ***	−3.00	−0.10 ***	−3.06	−0.09 ***	−2.98
FRG(−3)	0.24 ***	3.38	0.26 ***	3.55	0.25 ***	3.42	0.24 ***	3.37
BOR(−3)	−0.14 ***	−4.16	−0.14 ***	−4.14	−0.15 ***	−4.19	−0.14 ***	−4.15
BOND(−3)	0.01	0.64	0.01	0.54	0.01	0.66	0.01	0.64
CML	3.36 ***	3.31	3.36 ***	3.28	3.31 ***	3.21	3.35 ***	3.30
TYPEI	−4.21 ***	−4.51						
TYPEII			3.30 ***	3.19			4.14 ***	3.91
TYPEIII					3.01 **	2.22	4.36 ***	3.16
adj.R²	0.40		0.39		0.39		0.40	
Sample numbers	512		512		512		512	

Panel 2 Dependent Variable: CGS_{sh}

Independent Variable	(1)		(2)		(3)		(4)	
	Coeffi-cient	t-value	Coeffi-cient	t-value	Coeffi-cient	t-value	Coeffi-cient	t-value
C	−8.27 ***	−3.07	−8.61 ***	−3.20	−9.97 ***	−3.66	−9.32 ***	−3.43
SIZE(−3)	0.96 ***	5.83	0.92 ***	5.53	1.01 ***	6.07	0.95 ***	5.68
STAB(−3)	−0.01	−1.03	−0.01	−1.05	−0.01	−1.11	−0.01	−1.03
FRG(−3)	0.03	1.04	0.03	1.18	0.03	1.13	0.03	1.05
BOR(−3)	−0.05 ***	−3.21	−0.05 ***	−3.21	−0.05 ***	−3.25	−0.05 ***	−3.20
BOND(−3)	−0.01	−1.00	−0.01	−1.06	−0.01	−0.98	−0.01	−1.01
CML	0.39	0.93	0.39	0.94	0.38	0.89	0.39	0.93
TYPEI	−1.24 ***	−3.22						
TYPEII			1.11 ***	2.62			1.31 ***	3.02
TYPEIII					0.64	1.16	1.07 *	1.89
adj.R²	0.15		0.15		0.14		0.15	
Sample number	512		512		512		512	

Panel 3 Dependent Variable: CGS_{br}

Independent Variable	(1)		(2)		(3)		(4)	
	Coeffi-cient	t-value	Coeffi-cient	t-value	Coeffi-cient	t-value	Coeffi-cient	t-value
C	−1.83	−0.53	−2.32	−0.67	−3.74	−1.07	−3.19	−0.91
SIZE(−3)	0.77 ***	3.62	0.75 ***	3.47	0.83 ***	3.90	0.78 ***	3.62
STAB(−3)	−0.01	−0.82	−0.01	−0.85	−0.01	−0.88	−0.01	−0.83
FRG(−3)	0.04	1.07	0.04	1.17	0.04	1.11	0.04	1.06
BOR(−3)	−0.01	−0.49	−0.01	−0.51	−0.01	−0.54	−0.01	−0.49
BOND(−3)	0.01	0.72	0.01	0.67	0.01	0.74	0.01	0.73
CML	1.05 *	1.95	1.05 *	1.95	1.04 *	1.92	1.05 *	1.95
TYPEI	−1.18 **	−2.39						
TYPEII			0.85	1.55			1.10 **	1.97
TYPEIII					0.98	1.38	1.34 *	1.83
adj.R²	0.08		0.08		0.08		0.08	
Sample number	512		512		512		512	

Panel 4 Dependent Variable: CGS_{ds}

Independent Variable	(1) Coefficient	t-value	(2) Coefficient	t-value	(3) Coefficient	t-value	(4) Coefficient	t-value
C	−22.84 ***	−6.34	−23.54 ***	−6.50	−25.68 ***	−7.04	−24.82 ***	−6.83
SIZE(−3)	2.14 ***	9.75	2.11 ***	9.43	2.24 ***	10.05	2.15 ***	9.66
STAB(−3)	−0.07 ***	−3.86	−0.07 ***	−3.88	−0.07 ***	−3.92	−0.07 ***	−3.86
FRG(−3)	0.17 ***	4.33	0.18 ***	4.46	0.17 ***	4.36	0.17 ***	4.31
BOR(−3)	−0.09 ***	−4.68	−0.09 ***	−4.67	−0.09 ***	−4.71	−0.09 ***	−4.67
BOND(−3)	0.01	1.22	0.01	1.14	0.01	1.23	0.01	1.22
CML	1.92 ***	3.43	1.92 ***	3.41	1.90 ***	3.37	1.92 ***	3.42
TYPEI	−1.80 ***	−3.49						
TYPEII			1.35 **	2.37			1.72 ***	2.95
TYPEIII					1.39 *	1.87	1.95 **	2.57
adj.R²	0.44		0.43		0.43		0.43	
Sample numbers	512		512		512		512	

Notes: *TYPEI:* Dummy variables are given a value of 1 for Type I companies and 0 for the rest; *TYPEII:* Dummy variables are given a value of 1 for Type II companies and 0 for the rest. *TYPEIII:* Dummy variables are given a value of 1 for Type III companies and 0 for the rest. *CGS:* Total *CGS* score; *CGS$_{sh}$:* Rights of shareholders; *CGS$_{br}$:* Board of directors; *CGS$_{ds}$:* Information disclosure; *C:* Constant term; *SIZE:* Natural logarithm of total assets. *STAB:* Ratio of stable shareholders; *FRG:* Ratio of foreign shareholders; *BOR:* Ratio of borrowing (Borrowing/total assets); *BOND:* Ratio of corporate bonds (Bonds/the sum of bonds and borrowing); *CML:* Dummy variables are given value of 1 for companies that conclude a commitment-line contract with financial institutions, and 0 for the rest. *** denotes statistical significance at the 1% level, ** at the 5% level, and * at the 10% level.

stable. When we look at the magnitude of the coefficient of *TYPE I* to *CGS*, *CGS* for Type I companies is lower by 4.21 points compared to other types of companies. Given that the average *CGS* is 30.54, the *CGS* of Type I companies is about 14% lower than that of other types of companies.

On the other hand, Type III companies show statistically significant results across the board (column 4 in each panel), and they are significantly more active in corporate governance reform compared to Type I companies. Since Type III companies do not practice long-term employment and are actively adopting human resources reforms such as ability-based pay, we can assume that such companies are also willing to implement corporate governance reform. The magnitude of the coefficient of *TYPE III* is 4.36 points higher than that of Type I companies, or comparable to approximately 14% of *CGS*.

The results shown above are to a certain degree expected. What should be noted here is that although Type II companies choose to maintain long-term employment as do Type I companies, they are more active in adopting corporate governance reform, and their results are more statistically significant than those of Type I companies. Even when we run an estimation that sets *CGS* as the dependent variable (Panel 1), or any estimation that breaks *CGS* down into three sub-indices (Panels 2, 3, and 4), the greater openness to reform of Type II companies is confirmed. Moreover, the significance level of the coefficient of *TYPE II* is more than 5% in an estimation that sets CGS_{br} as a dependent variable, and better than 1% in estimations that set CGS_{ds} and CGS_{sh} as dependent variables. Thus, the results obtained here are quite stable.

In sum, companies combining long-term employment with attempts to modify traditional seniority-based wage systems are actively pursuing governance reforms (by promoting board reform and information disclosure) to the same degree as those that combine fixed- or limited-term employment with ability pay. Given the results of the previous section (i.e. governance reform is likely to have a positive influence on performance), the performance of Type II companies was expected to be high. In fact, it was confirmed by simple estimation that the performance of Type II companies is higher than that of Type I companies.[30] The combination of ability/performance-based pay systems and active pursuit of governance reform suggests a new approach to reform for Japanese companies that have previously relied on long-term employment practices.

12.5 CLOSING REMARKS

The findings provided in this chapter suggest that governance reform is likely to improve the performance of Japanese companies by cutting agency costs and fostering a commitment effect among managers and employees. Information disclosure in particular is likely to boost performance because Japanese companies do business in an external environment that takes cues from the capital market. This result is consistent with the fact that some firms such as Canon and Toyota are quite wary of drawing a clear line that separates management from monitoring, and of introducing outside directors, yet are quite active in disclosing information. Thus, it is clear that promoting information disclosure is relevant to corporate governance for Japanese firms.

Second, there is thus far no evidence that efforts to protect minority shareholders and to separate management and monitoring have enhanced corporate performance. Or to put it differently, governance reforms which follow the US model including the executive officer system and outside board members are so far not necessarily associated with higher performance. This result differs sharply from similar estimations conducted for South Korea and other countries (Black et al. 2002a and b; Berglöf and Pajuste 2005). Notwithstanding measurement problems (namely, it is still not possible to obtain variables for performance

---

[30] We estimate this by adding *TYPE* dummies to the performance model in section 3 (a model that eliminates *CGS* from formula (1) and adds variables for the composition of ownership). The coefficient for *TYPE I* is significantly negative and the coefficients for *TYPE II* and *III* are significantly positive in any estimation for standardized *ROA* and *Q*.

covering terms long enough to measure the effectiveness of reforms), we should acknowledge that US-style reforms have been superficially adopted by some Japanese firms without the necessary complementary measures. For instance, Japanese firms have introduced outside directors without in fact adopting measures to strengthen their "independence." And the executive officer system was not introduced in conjunction with other essential organizational changes such as measures to decentralize decision-making.

Another interpretation is that US-style boards are not really suited to certain types of Japanese firms, especially those with relatively undiversified portfolios which remain focused on a core business, and whose competitive edge is highly dependent on incremental innovation. For these firms, the costs of reforming the board of directors may outweigh its benefits, because adopting the executive officer system or the committee system requires additional efforts to ensure that such reforms will fit their business/internal organization. This interpretation is also consistent with the view that it is more rational for companies to enhance their traditional statutory auditor system rather than reform their board of directors.

We also found clear evidence that increasing pressure from the capital market in recent years was a decisive factor in encouraging top managers to adopt reforms, i.e. firms were more likely to implement governance reforms if they had a higher percentage of foreign (institutional) shareholders and lower percentage of stable shareholders, and thus a higher dependence on the capital market and lower dependence on bank borrowing.

Contrary to the conventional wisdom, employee involvement in management is not incompatible with governance reform, or at the very least does not act as an impediment to governance reform. In fact, in companies that face strong pressure from the capital market, greater employee involvement in management is associated with a more active commitment to reforming the board of directors. Although companies that maintained long-term employment and seniority-based pay systems generally remained passive toward governance reform, companies that retained long-term employment while trying to shift from seniority-based to ability-based wages were active in implementing governance reform in the area of information disclosure, and performed better to a statistically significant degree. Combining ability-based wages and governance reform may be one way to revitalize Japanese companies that remain wedded to the practice of long-term employment.

Implications and Perspectives

Of course, not all Japanese companies conform to the patterns of behavior noted above. Many companies continue to maintain cross-shareholdings, remain dependent on bank loans for financing, and retain old hiring practices (see Chapters 2 and 4, this volume). Such companies are reluctant to implement governance reform and tend to lag in performance. The focus of revitalization efforts should be on the approximately half of all listed companies that conform to this pattern and have fallen into a state of inferior equilibrium.

The introduction of US-style boards is merely an option under the new framework created by the amended Commercial Code, not a mandatory requirement. In light of the findings of this chapter and the limited scope of the recent revisions of the Commercial Code, the governance reform process is likely to unfold as follows for these laggard companies.

First, since these companies are caught in a vicious circle of resistance to board reform and under-performance as a result of rational choices by stakeholders, there may be a need for further corrective government policies that would create additional pressure for reform under the new framework provided by the amended Commercial Code. Prodding by the government is of course not the only way to encourage reform-resistant firms to move to US-type governance structures. But given that it is highly plausible that such firms would improve their governance by strengthening separation between monitoring and management, introducing outside directors, and promoting information disclosure, some supplemental regulatory measures or slight nudge from the government may suffice to trigger reform along these lines. For example, the listing rules for the TSE could be modified to promote board reform. The M&A threat and the activities of institutional shareholders should also be considered catalysts for reform.

Second, the recent revisions to the Commercial Code may in fact have made some Japanese firms less likely to move toward a US-style governance structure by adopting the committee system, the effectiveness of which is highly contingent on a firm's core technology, organizational form, and business portfolio. Our prediction is that firms whose core technologies are integrated and which are less diversified and less decentralized will instead choose to modify their conventional boards by introducing an auditing system that can adapt to increases in pressure from the capital market resulting from information disclosure and other board reforms.[31] On the other hand, firms with modular core technologies, diversified business portfolios, and highly decentralized organizations will tend to adopt the committee system and thus move closer to the US model. These predictions are consistent with the fact that of those firms that have chosen the committee system thus far (still quite few in number), most are found in the electrical and financial sectors where business portfolios are diversified and decentralized organizational forms prevail.

---

[31] Toyota decided to introduce the executive officer system at the end of 2003 (to harmonize its board structure with world standards) but did not adopt the committee system. Toyota is still opposed to outside directors because it insists that members of its board need to have sufficient shop-floor knowledge to be effective (see Inoue 2003).

APPENDICES

Appendix 12.1 Composition of Corporate Governance Score (CGS)

Rights of Shareholders (10 items): CGS_{sh}		# of responses	# of responding companies whose answer is 1	Ratio of companies whose answer is 1
A 1	Schedule the general meeting to avoid concentrated date	750	222	29.6%
A 2	Schedule the general meeting on weekend	752	10	1.3%
A 3	Send notice for general meeting early	744	228	30.6%
A 4	Provide simultaneous English interpretation at general meeting	753	7	0.9%
A 5	Establish rules for general meeting such as number of questions, time, and how to decide the order of questions	748	51	6.8%
A 6	Encourage vigorous discussion instead of wrapping up GM in short time	745	389	52.2%
A 7	Adopt cumulative voting in choosing board members	741	40	5.4%
A 8	Attach documentation with detailed information to the notice for GM	745	203	27.2%
A 9	Notice for GM via electronic mail	749	8	1.1%
A 10	Shareholder's use of voting rights via electronic mail	749	19	2.5%

Board of Directors (6 items): CGS_{br}		# of responses	# of responding companies whose answer is 1	Ratio of companies whose answer is 1
B 1	Average attendance rate of board meetings by board members [More than 95%]	742	545	73.5%
B 2	Number of regular meetings by board members per year [More than 13 times]	751	154	20.5%
B 3	Whether the chairman of board meetings and CEO is different person or not	753	155	20.6%
B 4	Whether explicit system exists to evaluate performance by board members and to decide compensation for them	740	90	12.2%
B 5	Status of adoption of outside board members	745	269	36.1%
B 6	Status of adoption of executive officer system	730	243	33.3%

(Continued)

Appendix 12.1 (*Continued*)

Information Disclosure & Transparency (10 items): CGS_{ds}	# of responses	# of responding companies whose answer is 1	Ratio of companies whose answer is 1
C 1 Availability of business reports, etc. at major branches of the company	747	533	71.4%
C 2 Provision of annual report through the company's HP	748	365	48.8%
C 3 Hold regular meetings with analysts domestically	751	407	54.2%
C 4 Hold regular meetings with analysts abroad	751	91	12.1%
C 5 Consultation for IR activities	751	196	26.1%
C 6 Set up IR department & staff with specialized personnel	754	334	44.3%
C 7 Holding informal gatherings with shareholders	746	52	7.0%
C 8 Post board members' backgrounds on the company's HP	748	47	6.3%
C 9 Compile information brochure in English	747	216	28.9%
C 10 Status of information disclosure concerning compensation for board members or status of future considerations [Disclose either the total amount (average amount), the largest amount, or amount for individuals]	721	272	37.7%

Notes: Notation for columns 2 to 4 corresponds to the number of the questionnaire item.

Source: Ministry of Finance, Policy Research Institute (2003b).

Appendix 12.2 Definition of Variables and Basic Statistics

Variables		Definition	Source
Tobin's *q*	Q	(Stock price × number of issued shares + amount of debt in book value) / amount of assets in book value) (at settlement period year 2001)	Database at the Waseda University Institute of Financial Studies
Standardized Tobin's *q*	Standardized Q	Standardized Tobin's *q* is derived by deducting median *q* for Tokyo Stock Exchange industry category from each company's *q* (at the settlement period for year 2001).	Database at the Waseda University Institute of Financial Studies
ROA	*ROA*	Business profit / amount of assets × 100 (at the settlement period for year 2001, on a consolidated basis)	Development Bank of Japan's Corporate Financial Databank

Standardized ROA	Standardized *ROA*	Standardized ROA is derived by deducting median ROA for Tokyo Stock Exchange industry category from each company's ROA (at the settlement period for year 2001, on a consolidated basis).	Development Bank of Japan's Corporate Financial Data-bank
Size of the company	*SIZE*	Natural logarithm for total assets (at the settlement period for year 2001, on a consolidated basis)	Development Bank of Japan's Corporate Financial Data-bank
Debt / asset ratio	*DAR*	Amount of debt / Amount of assets (at the settlement period for year 2001, on a consolidated basis)	Development Bank of Japan's Corporate Financial Data-bank
Years of listing	*LIST*	The survey results (for questionnaires 1 and 2) are used; numbers are assigned as follows: [1] for prior to 1940, [2] for the 1940s, [3] for the 1950s, [4] for the 1960s, [5] for the 1970s, [6] for the 1980s, and [7] for the 1990s.	Survey by Ministry of Finance, Policy Research Institute (December 2002)
Sales growth ratio	*GSALE*	The average sales growth ratio for the five fiscal years from 1996 to 2000 is used except for companies whose settlement data does not exist for this period. For them, only available data for sales growth ratio is used.	Development Bank of Japan's Corporate Financial Data-bank

REFERENCES

Abe, M. (2002). 'Corporate Governance Structure and Employment Adjustment in Japan: Empirical Analysis Using Financial Data,' *Industrial Relations*, 41(4): 683–702.

Aoki, M. (1988). *Information, Incentives and Bargaining in the Japanese Economy*. Cambridge: Cambridge University Press.

—— (2002). *Toward a Comparative Institutional Analysis*. Cambridge, MA: MIT Press.

Berglöf, E. and A. Pajuste (2005). *What Do Firms Disclose and Why? Enforcing Corporate Governance and Transparency in Central and Eastern Europe*. Stockholm: Stockholm School of Economics.

Black, B., H. Jang, and W. Kim. (2002a). 'Does Corporate Governance Affect Firm Value?' Mimeo.

—— —— —— (2002b). 'Does Corporate Governance Matter?' Mimeo.

Fukao, M. (1995). *Financial Integration, Corporate Governance and Performance of Multinational Companies*. Washington, DC: Brookings Institution.

Gilson, R. J. and C. J. Milhaupt (2004). 'Choice as Regulatory Reform: The Case of Corporate Governance.' Unpublished paper.

Gompers, P., J. Ishii, and A. Metrick (2003). 'Corporate Governance and Equity Prices,' *Quarterly Journal of Economics*, 118: 107–55.

Higuchi, Y. (2001). Economics of Employment and Unemployment. Tokyo: Nihon Keizai Shinbun-sha.

Inoue, K. (2003). 'On the Corporate Governance of Toyota Auto Motor Corp.' *Financial Review*, Policy Research Institute, MOF, 68: 194–202 (in Japanese).

Jensen, M. C. (1986). 'Agency Costs of Free Cash Flow, Corporate Finance, and Takeover,' *American Economic Review*, 76(2): 323–9.

Katoh, T. (2001). 'The End of "Lifetime Employment" in Japan? Evidence from National Surveys and Field Research,' *Journal of the Japanese and International Economies*, 15: 489–514.

La Porta, R., F. Lopez-de-Silanes, A. Shleifer, and R. Vishny (1998). 'Law and Finance,' *Journal of Political Economy*, 106(6): 113–55.

Lichtenberger, F. R. and G. M. Pushner (1994). 'Ownership Structure and Corporate Performance in Japan,' *Japan and the World Economy*, 6: 239–61.

McConnell, J. J. and H. Servaes (1995). 'Equity Ownership and the Two Faces of Debt,' *Journal of Financial Economics*, 39(1): 131–57.

Mehran, H. (1995). 'Executive Compensation Structure, Ownership, and Firm Performance,' *Journal of Financial Economics*, 38(2): 163–84.

Miyajima, H. (1995). 'The Privatization of Ex-zaibatsu Holding Stocks and the Emergence of Bank-centered Corporate Groups,' in M. Aoki (ed.), *Corporate Governance in a Transitional Economy*. New York: The World Bank.

—— (1999). 'The Evolution and Change of Contingent Governance Structure in the J-Firm System: An Approach to Presidential Turnover and Firm Performance,' in D. Dirks, J. F. Huchet, and T. Ribault (eds.), *Japanese Management in the Low Growth Era: Between External Shock and Internal Evolution*. London: Springer Verlag.

—— (2004). *Economic History on Industrial Policy and Corporate Governance*. Tokyo: Yūhikaku (in Japanese).

—— and Y. Arikawa. (2000). 'Relational Banking and Debt Choice: Evidence from the Liberalization in Japan,' *IFMP Discussion Paper Series*, A00-07.

—— and H. Aoki (2002.) 'Change and Overhaul in the J-type Firm: Stepping Back from Bank-centered Governance and Increasing Role of Internal Governance,' in S. Maswood and H. Miyajima (eds.), *Changes and Continuity in Japan*. London: Routledge/Curzon Press.

—— and K. Inagaki (2003). *Diversification of Japanese Companies and Corporate Governance: Analysis of Business Strategy, Group Management, and Decentralized Organization*, Policy Research Institute, Ministry of Finance. (in Japanese)

—— Y. Arikawa, and T. Saito (2001). 'Corporate Governance and "Excess" Investment: Comparative Analysis of Oil Shock and Bubble Years', *Financial Review*, Policy Research Institute, MOF 60: 139–68 (in Japanese).

—— K. Haramura, and K. Inagaki (2003). 'Evolving Corporate Governance Reforms and Revitalization of Japanese Companies,' *Financial Review*, Policy Research Institute, MOF, 68: 156–93 (in Japanese).

—— K. Haramura, and Y. Enami (2003). 'Composition of Shareholders in Post-war Japanese Companies: Creation and Dissolution of Stable Shareholders,' *Financial Review*, Policy Research Institute, MOF, 68: 203–36 (in Japanese).

Nihon Kansayaku Kyōkai (2003). *Shōhō Kaisei no Taiō ni Kansuru Ankēto* (Survey on the Handling of the Revision of the Commercial Code). Tokyo: Nihon Kansayaku Kyōkai.

Nihon Keizai Dantai Rengō Kai (2000). 'Kōporēto Gabanansu ni Kansuru Kakusha no Torikumi' (Individual Companies' Approaches to Corporate Governance), *Keidanren Ikensho. Wagakuni Kōkai Kigyō ni Okeru Kōporēto Gabanansu ni Kansuru Ronten Seiri Chūkan Hōkoku*. Tokyo: Sankō Shiryō.

Nihon Kōporēto Gabanansu Fōramu (2001). *Kōporēto Gabanansu ni Kansuru Ankēto Chōsa Kekka* (Corporate Governance Survey Results). Tokyo: Nihon Kōporēto Gabanansu Fōramu.

Nobeoka, K. and K. Tanaka (2002). 'Toppu Manejimento no Senryakuteki Ishi Kettei Nōryoku' (Strategic Decision-Making Ability of Top Management), in H. Itoh (ed.), *Nihon Kigyō Henkakuki no Sentaku* (The Choice of Japanese firm in the Transitional Period). Tokyo: Tōyō Keizai Shinpō-sha.

Ohmura, K. and S. Mashiko (2000). *Waga Kuni Kigyō no Fainansu Shisutemu to Kōporēto Gabanansu ni Kansuru Ankēto Kekka Chūkan Hōkokusho* (Interim Report on Results of Survey of the Financing System and Corporate Governance of Japanese Companies). Tokyo: Policy Research Institute, MOF.

Policy Research Institute (PRI), Ministry of Finance (2003a). 'Jigyō-bu/Gurūpu Keiei ni Okeru Kōporēto Gabanansu Ankēto Chōsa' (Questionnaire Survey on Corporate Governance in Companies with Company System and Affiliate Management), in H. Miyajima and K. Inagaki (eds.), *Nihon Kigyō no Tayōka to Kigyō Tōchi* (Diversification of Japanese Companies and Corporate Goverance). Tokyo: Zaimu Sōgō Seisaku Kenkyūjo (PRI).

—— (2003b). 'Waga Kuni Kigyō no Kōporēto Gabanansu ni Kansuru Ankēto Chōsa' (Questionnaire Survey on Corporate Governance in Japanese Companies), in H. Miyajima, K. Haramura, and K. Inagaki (eds.), *Shinten suru Kōporēto Gabanansu Kaikaku to Nihon Kigyō no Saisei* (Advances in Corporate Governance Reform in Japan and the Revitalization of Japanese Companies). Tokyo: Zaimu Sōgō Seisaku Kenkyūjo (PRI).

Sasaki, T. and Y. Yonezawa (2000). 'Corporate Governance and Shareholder Value' *Security Analysts Journal*, 38(9): 28–49 (in Japanese).

Shleifer, A. and R. Vishny (1986). 'Large Shareholders and Corporate Control,' *Journal of Political Economy*, 94(3): 461–88.

Stulz, R. M. (1990). 'Managerial Discretion and Optimal Financing Policies,' *Journal of Financial Economics*, 26(1): 3–27.

Suzuki, M. (2001). 'Analysis of Management Performance and Incentives,' *Financial Review*, Policy Research Institute, MOF, 60: 169–86.

Tokyo Shōken Torihikijo (2003). *Kōporēto Gabanansu ni Kansuru Ankēto Chōsa Kekka* (Corporate Governance Survey Results). Tokyo: Tokyo Shōken Torihikijo.

Tomiyama, M. (2001). 'Main-bank System and Employment Adjustment in Firms,' *The Japanese Journal of Labour Studies*, 488: 40–51 (in Japanese).

Tsipouri, L. and M. Xanthakis (2002). *Can Corporate Governance Be Rated? Ideas Based on the Greek Experience*. Athens: University of Athens Center of Financial Studies.

Urasaka, J. and T. Noda (2001). 'The Effect of Corporate Governance on Employment Adjustment in Japanese Manufacturing Firms,' *The Japanese Journal of Labour Studies*, 488: 52–63 (in Japanese).

Wakasugi, T., A. Okumura, C. Ahmadjian, and K. Fukuda (2002). *2002 Nendo Kōporēto Gabanansu Indekusu Chōsa Hōkoku* (Report on Corporate Goverance Index Survey in FY 2002). Tokyo: Nihon Kōporēto Gabanansu Indekusu Kenkyūkai, JCGR.

Yermack, D. (1996). 'Higher Market Valuation of Companies with a Small Board of Directors,' *Journal of Financial Economics*, 40(2): 185–211.

13

Insider Management and Board Reform: For Whose Benefit?

Ronald Dore

13.1 TWO ARGUMENTS

This paper advances two main arguments. *Argument 1* is a general argument about what constitutes "good" corporate governance, and what subjecting managers to thorough and transparent external monitoring has to do with it. It is held that the importance of external monitoring varies from society to society, and that in Japan it is less important than in societies of Anglo-Saxon capitalism. *Argument 2* is that the legal and organizational changes affecting the governance structure of Japanese firms over the last decade, many of which have aimed to increase the intensity of external monitoring, have had very limited effect in promoting "good" corporate governance. Rather, they have contributed—along with other factors— to a shift in managerial objectives and priorities, specifically a downgrading of employee interests and an upgrading of shareholder interests.

Both arguments depend on a particular definition of "good" corporate governance. Large political differences exist between different normative views of the proper function of corporations in society. "Shareholder value" prescriptions suggest that corporate governance institutions should concentrate the power to decide what firms do and who gets what share of the added value from doing it exclusively in the hands of the owners of capital. "Stakeholder" prescriptions advocate that this power should be shared among a much wider range of actors— employees, the state, suppliers, creditors etc. These different views can result in very different formal institutions across countries, and are of great importance for determining the nature of social cohesion, social conflict and the distribution of income.

It is not my present concern to rehearse the arguments for or against these two normative positions, but to point out that whatever normative position people hold, they can all agree that an honest and trustworthy chief executive is better than a dishonest one. An energetic and dynamic set of top managers, capable of making entrepreneurial initiatives and able to calculate the risks involved in pursuing them is better than a group of lazy satisficers. At its core, any definition of "good" corporate governance must therefore be made in terms of institutions which provide the best chances of getting honest and dynamic managers and keeping them that way. Both arguments in the paper start from this definition.

To summarize briefly, the first argument is that there can be no universal prescriptions as to how much external monitoring is necessary for good corporate governance. The need varies as between societies depending on two sets of factors often overlooked in the corporate governance literature—namely, prevailing social values and the career patterns of corporate managers. First come the society's dominant values, especially (a) the level of "generalized trust," i.e. belief in the trustworthiness of others; and (b) the way those values direct ambitions and definitions of self-worth and hence work motivations. Second come the patterns of recruitment and promotion within business firms themselves, particularly the system by which top managers are chosen. These latter determine the strength of bottom-up internal monitoring by subordinates and peers which makes external monitoring less important. In terms of Japan, the argument is that both the motivational patterns developed in Japanese families and schools, and the lifetime employment system within large firms make for a degree and form of internal monitoring which is stronger than in Anglo-Saxon countries and important for understanding how top managers are kept dynamic and (in most respects) honest.

The second argument is embodied in a general survey of changes to the insider nature of Japanese top management in the last decade. Legal reforms of corporate governance have been wide-ranging, but for the most part these facilitate rather than mandate change. Reform has led to wider diversity across Japanese firms in the formal structure of boards and division of top managerial functions, but seems to have more limited impact on the actual way important decisions get taken and who participates in taking them. Nonetheless, a significant shift can be observed in the substantive nature of managerial objectives—a shift towards giving greater priority to service shareholders at the expense of concern for subordinate employees. This has less to do with the overt changes in the structure of corporate boards, and much more to do with the broader changes in the external environment of Japanese firms. These changes include the increased presence of foreign investors, the unwinding of cross-shareholdings, the final realization that a half century of steady asset inflation and automatic capital gains has ended, and changes in class structure of Japanese society that favor an ideological shift towards the rights of property.

The anecdotal evidence presented for these arguments is amplified by the results of a questionnaire survey carried out especially for this chapter. This questionnaire was addressed to middle managers and covered a number of corporate governance and organizational issues (hereafter called the BK survey referring to *bucho* and *kacho*—section and division heads respectively). The sample was not representative of a larger population, but the random (=haphazard) nature of its distribution may allow one to assume that it is at least indicative of more general opinions. We distributed 830 questionnaires in 14 firms via senior managers who agreed to cooperate with the survey. Another 750 questionnaires were subsequently mailed directly to names taken from the Shokuin-roku, a directory of corporation managers published by the Diamond publishing house. A total of 313 replies were received, a response rate of 20%.[1]

13.2 WHY CHANGE?

By the mid-1990s, it had become a standard journalistic cliché, repeated in the inaugural addresses of prime ministers, that "the Japanese management system" which was the source of Japanese pride and a number of bestsellers for American management gurus during the 1980s "was fine for the high-growth period, but has now outlived its usefulness." There was, however, no consensus as to why. Some said that Japanese corporations had lost their dynamism and innovative capacity as exemplified in loss of market share. Some said that the lifetime employment guarantee shackled firms' abilities to respond to shocks like the bursting of the bubble. Some pointed to a secular decline in returns to capital, but it was not always clear whether this was a matter of increasing capital/output ratio or a declining capital share of value added. But one dominant theme, and perhaps the most common justification for corporate governance reform, was the assertion that insider-dominated Japanese firms were becoming corrupt as evidenced in the frequency of scandals.

The scandals were collectively referred to as *fushoji*, which is a curious category of what seems to be peculiarly Japanese illegality. It does not, for instance, include illegal cartel behavior, nor American scandals of the Enron variety for which a different term is conventional—*fuseijiken*. There are four sub-categories:

1. Malfeasance by individuals precisely of the Enron variety, i.e., purely for their own profit, the recent scandal in a subsidiary of the Nikkei newspaper being an example.
2. Illegal pay-offs to *sokaiya*, "AGM gangsters."
3. Various kinds of false accounting by desperate managers seeking to avoid bankruptcy and keep their company afloat until the recovery of the economy "raised all boats," the most spectacular instance being Yamaichi Securities in the years before its eventual collapse.
4. Unethical or positively illegal behavior of managers, designed to profit the company at the expense of consumers (Mitsubishi Motors and Yukijirushi) or taxpayers (Nihon Ham).

The first—Enron-type managerial self-enrichment—was far rarer than the others. The other much more common forms sprang more from excessive devotion to the company, thus Hugh Patrick's quip: "In America managers

---

[1] In order to minimize (though obviously far from eliminate) the possibility that respondents would reply not with their own opinions but feel themselves speaking as representatives of their firm, the questionnaires were mailed back directly and anonymously; 43% were from firms with more than 5000 employees and 18% from those with less than 1000; 60% were from manufacturing, 17% from construction, 11% from transport and communications, 12% from commerce, finance and other services.

steal from the firm, in Japan they steal for the firm." It is questionable whether there was an increase in such incidents. It is at least a tenable hypothesis that the popular impression of a greater frequency of *fushoji* in the 1990s is a result of rising standards of expected corporate behavior and the greater likelihood of whistle-blowing and prosecution.

13.3 ORGANIZATIONAL CHANGES IN THE BOARD OF DIRECTORS

Parallel to this debate, a number of changes have taken place to the organization of the board of directors in Japanese firms over the last decade. Some of these changes have been the result of reforms to corporate law, while others have been largely voluntary changes to the less formal practices of Japanese boards.

13.3.1 Formal Changes in Corporate Law

New *facilitating* legislation over the past decade has relaxed previous prohibitions to give firms the following options: creating holding companies, buying their own shares under progressively less stringent conditions, remunerating with stock options (formerly permitted only for venture businesses), financing mergers and acquisitions with shares. Shareholders have been given the option of launching derivative suits against directors' malfeasance or negligence much more cheaply than hitherto. A new (optional) category of "Companies Establishing Committees etc." has been created. (Hereafter, following recent Japanese practice, these will be called *committee companies* and those which have not adopted the new system, *auditor companies*.) Such companies are required to have a board which establishes three sub-committees respectively for *audit*, *appointments*, and *compensation*, on each of which outside directors (defined as people who have never been employees of the firm) have a majority.

Major *mandated* changes to the board have been more limited. Mandatory changes have aimed at strengthening the function of the statutory auditors (*kansayaku*). In firms that have not become committee companies, these firms must appoint at least two outside auditors who have never been employees of the firm, (three in the case of large companies). The other major mandatory change is to require companies to consolidate their accounts and value financial assets on a mark-to-market basis.

13.3.2 Informal Changes: The Executive Officer System

Boards of directors have hitherto had a standard form, little varying across companies, which had little to do with the statutory definition of their powers. They were very large in large companies, reaching a record 58 members in Toyota.

One reason for their large size was to make appointment to the board, which usually took place when managers were in the early fifties, a feasible career objective and hence incentive for a large proportion of younger managers. The board had its hierarchy, usually of four ranks below the president—ordinary director, *jomu*, (regular director) *semmu* (special director) and vice-president. Lower-ranking members almost invariably had some divisional executive responsibility. Members could be retired at any stage according to local "up or out" conventions. The board's meetings were rather formal affairs legitimating decisions which had been worked out through normal processes of consultation, but serving to disseminate information on top-level plans and decisions widely throughout the firm. It was not a significant body either for strategic planning, major decision-taking, or monitoring performance. Those functions were usually performed by a small, much more frequently meeting group—the president, with a handful of vice-presidents or *semmu*—coopting other senior managers as required. In large companies this was formally institutionalized in what was often called a *jomukai*. Meanwhile, reformers ridiculed the Japanese system on two grounds. First, a large contrast exists between the inevitably ritual nature of these large boards, and the decisive role the board is supposed to play according to Japanese company law as well as in American practice. Second, the executive and monitoring/supervisory functions are blurred.

A widespread change which has gathered considerable momentum is to create a new non-statutory status of "executive officer" (*shikkoyaku*) and to transfer all the former lower-level directors from the board to that status. (Somewhat confusingly, however, *shikkoyaku*, as a translation of CEO, is also the title given to the president under the new committee company system.) The creation of the *shikkoyaku* position generally involves also creating a new body comprising all of them plus the internal members of the board. This new committee meets, usually monthly, and more or less duplicates the functions of the former board. Meanwhile the statutory board is much reduced in size, and may simply duplicate the former *de facto* planning group, or, commonly, include also outside directors. A further innovation adopted by some companies is to create an advisory board, usually of outsiders, which may be given a variety of powers including the monitoring of appointments and executive compensation. The concern with compliance and social responsibility has resulted in the creation of new internal monitoring mechanisms and oversight committees on which outsiders are frequently asked to serve.

13.3.3 Extent of Diffusion of Organizational Innovations

An idea of the diffusion of these innovations may be gained from a survey by the Japan Association of Corporate Executives (hereafter the Doyukai04 survey).[2] Its responses from 209 of its 864 member firms—139 public companies, 70

---

[2] 'Kigyo kyosoryoku no kiban kyoka wo mezashita koporeto gabanansu kaikaku' (Reform of Corporate Governance to Strengthen the Basis for Corporate Competitiveness) April 2004. Available at: http://www.doyukai.or.jp/policyproposals/articles/2002/020702a.html

private—is likely to exaggerate the extent of change since it is the most—forward-looking, should one say? or trend-conscious?—of executives who are most likely to be members of the association in the first place, and to be those among the members most likely to make sure that their firm should respond to the questionnaire. However, in a society where following the trend is normal behavior and bucking the trend is seen as somewhat eccentric, the degree of bias may not be very great.

Fifteen firms, 12 public and three private, or 7% of the Doyukai sample, had adopted what is generally referred to as "the American-style" Committee Company system. Given the nature of the sample, this was considerably more than the 2% of publicly traded firms which have converted—some 70 firms in total as of May 2000. Of these, nearly one half were subsidiaries of Nomura and Hitachi which had taken advantage of the loose definition of external director as "never an employee of the firm" to consolidate the core company's control over subsidiaries by appointing "external" directors from the core company. Only 11 companies converted to the committee company system in the 2004 summer's round of shareholder meetings.

As Marc Goldstein, the Tokyo representative of the American Institute for Shareholders Services, commented: "once again, the companies switching to a US-style board structure can be divided into two groups: those that make a sincere effort to improve governance by appointing independent outsiders to the board, and those that merely appoint related parties, such as representatives of a parent company, a move that does not benefit ordinary shareholders."[3] Some foreign-owned firms adopted the committee structure for exactly the same reasons as Nomura and Hitachi, since the external directors in Shinsei, D&B Holdings and Columbia Music Entertainment represent the interest of their dominant owner (Ripplewood) and those in Seiyu represent its dominant owner Walmart. Whether it was the intention of the drafters of the legislation thus to enhance the power of dominant shareholders vis-à-vis minority shareholders is questionable.[4]

Still, of the 93% of firms which had not adopted the committee company system, only 9% of the public companies and 20% of private companies were prepared to say that they had done nothing that could be classified as a change in corporate governance. (But apart from the question of the honesty of these replies, recall what was said about the bias inherent in the sample.) Among those public companies adopting reforms, 72% had adopted the executive officer/

---

[3] Marc Goldstein "Analysis: The Colourful Palette of Japan's Proxy Season." Available at: www.issproxy.com (July 2004).

[4] That the dominant shareholder's power can be abused at the expense of minority shareholders was made apparent recently. ISS notes eight transactions in 2003 which it dubbed "takeunders," "in which a parent company which already owned a majority stake in a listed subsidiary decided to buy out the minority shareholders at a price that did not reflect the fair value of their holdings. For example, Nippon Steel Corp. sought to buy out subsidiaries Nittetsu Steel Pipe and Nittetsu Steel Sheet, in both cases for a price that represented a discount to those companies' share prices at the time the deals were announced" (Marc Goldstein 2004).

executive board system, slimming down the main board. Sixty-eight percent had strengthened their auditor–auditor board system (increasing the number, increasing the number of outsiders, increasing the staff at their disposal). Fifty-four percent had appointed outside directors. Eighteen percent had created an advisory board. Nineteen percent had created committees (either sub-committees of the main board or of the advisory board or ad hoc committees) to vet senior appointments and salaries. Further proof that this sample is more innovation-prone than the whole population of companies was supplied by a broad-coverage survey conducted in August 2004 by the Nikkei newspaper.[5] It found that one Japanese company in three now had at least one external director, compared with the 54% of the Doyukai survey. In the private firms change was less common than among the public firms—except in one respect: 20% of them had created an advisory board, compared with 18% for public firms. The great majority of these changes had occurred before a previous survey in 2002: the increase since then was of a few percentage points on all counts.

It seems at the moment improbable that the committee company would become so widespread as to become the dominant form of board structure. The bureaucracy are backing it only half-heartedly, although the Koizumi–Takenaka axis in the political leadership has displayed more conviction, as evidenced by the fact that Risona Bank and Kanebo were required to adopt it as part of undergoing reconstruction under government direction. Indeed, the reformers who inspired and drafted the 2002 legislation would have preferred to make the structure mandatory, but were forced to make it optional by strong opposition from the main business federation, the Keidanren. The reformers have created a new organization to promote adoption of the new form, the Japan Association of Corporate Directors (*Nihon Torishimariyaku Kyokai*).[6] It also promotes such other innovations as ending the standard practice of promoting the former president to be chairman and bringing in chairmen from outside.

The attractions of the new structure, apart from the image presented to foreign investors—and the high score on the "Good Corporate Governance Rating Scale" run by a research institute which grew out of the pioneer reform group, the Corporate Governance Forum, founded in 1994[7]—are that it offers certain legal advantages. Responsibility for malfeasance or lack of due care and diligence is

[5] August 22, 2004.

[6] The association is very much the brainchild of Miyauchi, President of Orix and long-standing chairman of the Deregulation Commission, close to the Koizumi–Takenaka regime. As Inagami points out, however, some leading members of the JACD are on record as favoring a "welfare of all stakeholders" approach to corporate governance rather than the shareholder-value approach of the true reformers. Takeshi (2004). 'Kabunushi jushi to jugyoin jushi' (Favoring shareholders and favouring employees), I. Takeshi and M. Kyojiro (eds.), *Koporeto gabanansu tojuugyoin.* Tokyo: Toyo keizai. He cites their contributions to a publication of the JACD (2002). Torishimariyaku Kyokai (ed.), *Torishimariyaku no joken* (Being a Company Director). Tokyo: Nikkei BPsha (2003).

[7] See Japan Corporate Governance Research Institute Inc. (2003). *2003 nendo koporeto gabanansu nikansuru chosa: chukan hokoku* (Preliminary report of the 2003 Survey of corporate governance). 17 October. There appears to have been another similar rating exercise carried out by Waseda University, Nissei Research Institute, and the Nihon Keizai Shimbun. See *Nikkei Bijinesu* (2003). 1 December, 33.

individual under the new system, not collective, but liability to damages if found at fault in a shareholder derivative suit, is limited to six years' pay for a CEO, four years' for an ordinary director and two years' for an external. It is also possible, under the new system, to delegate more powers from the shareholders' AGM to the Board or its externally dominated sub-committees (approval of total expenditure on directors pay, for instance), and from the board to the CEO. As for the drawbacks, in the view of the JACD secretary-general, the major obstacle to adoption of the form was that company presidents were reluctant to lose control over the appointment of their successors to outside directors. Its secretary-general acknowledged that, in 2004, the reform movement was suffering badly from the fact that Sony, which had enthusiastically embraced the new system, and indeed already moved in that direction several years earlier, was issuing profit warnings while Canon and Toyota, which had set their faces firmly against the new system, were doing famously well.

One further advantage for smaller companies also became highly relevant in 2005 when auditor companies were required to have at least two independent outsiders as auditors and have the right to speak but not vote at board meetings. Since they are going to be present at board meetings anyway, it is a small step to make them board members, and one with advantages both for companies that wish "sincerely" (to use Goldstein's term) to expose themselves to useful outside scrutiny, and those that wish to have externals on the board for cosmetic, "image" purposes. It enables them to be "economical" with the use of outsiders—qualified people being also not too easy to find. It will be possible to have two on the main board and make both of them members, with one insider, of each of the three committees. It has to be said, a propos sincerity, that this also means that a switch to the committee company system can by the same token be a way of gaining greater protection from outside scrutiny. Auditor companies will have an audit committee of whom some will have to be full-time, with an outsider majority, whose meetings the president ordinarily will not be able to attend. In a committee company he/she or a confidant can be on all three committees, and all the members of the audit committee may be part-time.

One further straw in the wind was the May 2004 report of a stock exchange committee established to draw up a set of guidelines for corporate governance and consider their relation to listing requirements—how far the guidelines should be made mandatory à la New York, or whether listed firms should be required to comply or explain why they did differently à la London. It was chaired by Mogi a leading businessman, one of Japan's very few MBA CEOs, (Columbia Business School 1961) who was a member of reformist circles and a vice-president of the JACD. (He has, however, failed to convert his own company, Kikkoman, to Committee Company status.) The committee was sharply divided. A minority of three—the American representative of the Institute of Shareholder Services, the director of the Japanese corporate pension fund association and a well-known reformist lawyer who holds a professorship at Tokyo University and also heads an Institute of Corporate Law at Michigan University—wanted firms to be guided to adopt the committee company system and to be encouraged to move towards it at least by the London arrangement of having to say "if not why not." They lost out to the opposition from the manufacturing representatives on the committee who argued that it would be just as sensible to require firms which had adopted the committee company system to say why they had. The result was a set of guidelines with no mandatory element. They sought instead, as the last paragraph of the preface said:

To offer the basis of a shared understanding such as might be thought to be necessary if the independent efforts of individual companies to improve corporate governance and the actions of shareholders and investors demanding improvements in corporate governance can be brought together in such a way as to lead to improvement in corporate governance.[8]

The formulation of the guidelines is vague in the extreme, ruling out practically nothing and full of words like "appropriate," "timely," "adequate," and "satisfactory."

In sum, while reasons still exist for more companies to convert to the committee system in the future, it seems clear at any rate that sentiment has largely swung against the new form.

13.4 THE IMPACT ON THE INSIDER NATURE OF JAPANESE MANAGEMENT

In the light of the declared intentions of the reformers, it will be convenient to consider the effects of these changes under three heads: greater power to shareholders, more efficient decision-making and greater probity (in line with the previous definition of "the corporate governance problem" as keeping top managers honest and dynamic).

13.4.1 Shareholder Power via Voice and Loyalty

The big change for shareholders is their growing "power via exit" which will be considered in the next section. Here I consider their "power via voice and loyalty."

Until the 1990s the only shareholders who counted for most managers were their stable shareholders, for whom they organized informal private meetings. It was natural for them to look on shareholders who speak up at AGMs as troublemakers. And there was good reason to assume that most of them were indeed not just troublemakers, but potentially blackmailing troublemakers—*sokaiya*—seeking to establish themselves as a threat whose silence had to be bought. The standard defence was the *shan-shan sokai* (smooth and swift AGM), a carefully rehearsed, twenty-minute affair, with shareholder employees forming a claque which passed all resolutions by acclamation and intimidated any opposition. By the 1980s nearly

---

[8] Tokyo Stock Exchange (2004). *Jojokaisha koporeto gabanansu gensoku* (Principles of Corporate Governance for Listed Companies), May, 3

all companies held their meeting on the same June day, so that troublemakers should be thin on the ground.

In the 1990s managers had to deal with three new kinds of troublemakers. The first were the American institutional investors, particularly the larger pension funds with stakes sufficiently substantial that they could not easily unload without loss. Calpers was the pioneer in writing memoranda and sponsoring resolutions designed to enhance shareholder returns, and in recent years the actions of many of the funds have been coordinated by the recently created Institutional Shareholders' Services. Summarizing the results of the 2004 summer round of AGMs, the Tokyo representative of the ISS notes the increase in shareholder resolutions calling for an increase in dividends. "In addition to Toyota, such proposals were seen at Oji Paper Co., Keihanshin Real Estate, Yuraku Real Estate and five electric power companies. Similar resolutions were kept off the ballot at several other companies on purely procedural grounds."[9] These American examples have prodded Japanese institutional shareholders, normally entirely passive partners into a much more activist stance. The life insurance companies were reputedly afraid to lose business (pension fund management or employees' private life insurance) if they made trouble for a firm at its shareholders' meeting. Inagami cites the example of the Mizuho Trust Bank which has investment in some 1250 firms decided in 2001 to put 20 analysts on to selecting problematic firms, chose 53 for close examination and either opposed or abstained on management resolutions in some 30 of them.[10] Of much wider importance is the Pension Fund Association which acts as a custodian for member pension funds with shares in 1264 companies. In 2003 it voted quite aggressively, opposing 43% of the resolutions it voted on—directors' retirement bonuses in companies with poor results, dividend levels, appointments of directors, and changes in the articles, such as the specification of quorums and the delegation of share buy-back decisions to boards of directors.[11]

The second type of shareholder activist is the financial entrepreneur. The most prominent so far, is the Murakami Fund, run by an ex-MITI bureaucrat, said to be worth about ¥60 billion. It specializes in buying enough shares in the market to become a leading shareholder in smallish, cash-rich, and undervalued firms. The tactic is to use shareholder power—AGM resolutions or the threat thereof—to force an increase in dividends or a large-scale share buy-back, thereby raising the company's market valuation after which the Fund sells its stake. The Fund achieved great notoriety in the popular weeklies as a result of its assault on Tokyo Style, a company headed since 1979 by an apparently domineering president who shows no signs of letting go and believes in holding on to large cash reserves. He managed, however, in two successive years, 2002 and 2003, to thwart Murakami's

[9] Marc Goldstein, *op.cit.*

[10] Inagami Tadashi (2004). 'Kabunushi jushi to jugyoin jushi' (Favouring Shareholders and Favouring Employees) in I. Takashi and M. Kyojiro (eds.), *Koporeto Gabanansu to jugyoin* (Corporate Governance and Employees). Tokyo: Toyokeizai, 22.

[11] Inagami, *op.cit*, p. 20.

resolutions, presented in a spectacularly aggressive style, accusing him of excessive self-enrichment through stock options and calling on him to disgorge cash to shareholders. His supporters—the firm's three main banks, three of his cloth suppliers, Sumitomo Real Estate and Obayashi Construction, all front-rank establishment firms—rallied round and bought shares to give the president a comfortable majority to defeat any resolution, but his tactics on the second occasion provided Murakami with grounds for suing him for procedural abuse. Murakami lost the case, however. The Tokyo Style 2004 annual meeting passed without incident, but the firm has increased its dividend, and its president has reportedly been somewhat chastened by the bad publicity arising from what there was of substance in Murakami's attacks.[12]

The third type of shareholder activist is the public-spirited citizen campaigner—in American terms the Ralph Nader type. The Kabunushi Ombudsman was founded by a group of Osaka lawyers and is presided over by a university professor of industrial relations whose specialty had until recently been the study of trends in work hours. The group initially came together to bring an action over a public works bribery scandal in 1993, taking advantage of the new law which made such derivative suits much cheaper than before. It grew through the *Jusen* (mortgage loan companies), the Nomura *sokaiya* scandals, and coalesced into a permanent organization in 1996.[13] It has about 200 subscribing members and has been able to mobilize enough other shareholders of various companies to overcome the considerable obstacles put in the way of those who would sponsor shareholder resolutions.

At a recent count, the organization had sponsored 20 resolutions in six companies and got a 10% plus vote on nine of them. Their current campaign centres on requiring disclosure of individual directors' pay. In the summer of 2004, they sponsored such resolutions at both Sony and at Toyota. At Sony, where they were joined by American institutions, they got a 31% vote in support. At Toyota, they got nearly 20%, an increase over the 15% of the previous year. As the ISS comments,

shareholder interest in [the disclosure of directors pay] continues to grow, corporate resistance to such disclosure remains strong. A recent survey of top executives by Japan's leading business newspaper, the *Nihon Keizai Shimbun*, found that 70 percent are opposed to disclosing individual compensation levels. Only 6 percent believe that compensation should be fully disclosed. In practice, only a handful of companies currently provide such information.

The total effect of all these forms of shareholder activism has been to make shareholder meetings more serious affairs. Few companies any longer dare to put on a carefully rehearsed, ten-minute *shanshan sokai*, and as one small indicator of a willingness to be more open to shareholders, more companies have shifted the

---

[12] See, e.g. 'Tokyo Stairu ga hotta hakaana' (Tokyo Style digs its own grave), *Sentaku*, June (2002).

[13] This and subsequent details concerning the organization's activities from K. Ombuzuman (ed.) (2002). *Kaisha wa kaerareru* (Companies Can Be Changed), Iwanami Booklet, No. 570.

date of their meeting away from the AGM Concentration Day. This year Toyota demonstratively did so, and the ISS which covered 2100 such meetings reported that some 700 were held other than on the peak day—the highest number it had ever recorded. The Kabunushi Ombudsman also calculated that whereas in 1990 the average AGM lasted 29 minutes, in 2000 it had risen to 39 minutes, though in 2001 less than 2% of meetings lasted for more than two hours.[14]

13.4.2 More Efficient Decision-Making?

The 12 firms in the Doyukai 2004 survey which had converted to the new committee company system were asked to assess the change and given several alternatives any number of which they could choose. A half of them chose "too early to tell" and the most common choice, by nine firms, was a statement of the obvious, "it clarifies the division of roles as between the CEO and the Board." However, eight also said it speeded up decision-making and six that it led to livelier board discussions. Four said it strengthened the commitment of the CEO and three that it meant that tensions and factions within management no longer distorted decisions. Two firms chose the critical statement: "it weakens the sense of solidarity between the Board and the executive management."

The more important question concerns the effects in the majority of companies, which are auditor companies, of the two most common recent innovations—the division between an executive board of *shikkoyakuin* and a main board with supervisory functions, and secondly the inclusion of external directors on the latter. The Doyukai survey also asked the whole sample of 209 firms what they considered to be the purpose of their corporate governance reforms. "Greater transparency of decision making" got the most votes (76%) and the similar "strengthening the compliance system" got 66%. As for the quality of decision-making, 68% claimed that it was improved, but only 43% that it improved the speed with which decisions were reached. Only 19% said that one object was to prevent CEOs from going off the rails and if necessary sacking them.

The principle that the executive functions and the monitoring functions should be separated is frequently evoked by those in favor of American-style reforms. However, the firms which have taken the principle seriously, such as Sony and Hoya, are rare and mostly among those which have gone over to the committee company system. In the auditor companies, it is extremely doubtful how far there has been a real change in the relations among executives as a result of the fact that they now sit on two boards instead of one. Toyota has slimmed down its 58-member board, and the divisional heads who used to be on the board are now relegated to a new *shikkoyakkai* which Toyota, to be different, calls the *jomuyakkai*. That still leaves 27 on the board, all internal. One of the vice-presidents, in expounding its new system, quite explicitly rejects any principle of the separation of powers. Fourteen of the board members are *semmu*, who each

---

[14] *Op.cit.*, p. 5

have two or three divisional heads reporting directly to them rather than directly to the president. It is in these "hinge relations" which combine executive authority and monitoring that policy is really hammered out.[15] (The other 13 board members are an honorary chairman, a chairman, two vice-chairmen, a president, seven vice-presidents and a youngish member of the Toyota family who is the lone non-semmu "ordinary" director.) Something of this kind is common even where the board has been more radically reduced and includes external directors. The real discussions and decisions still take place in informal meetings at which the external directors are absent. How much the external directors can subsequently contribute at the formal board meeting depends on how much information they are given. In one firm they are always visited beforehand to receive background information on the items to be presented at the next board meeting. But as one external complained, this merely wastes his time since the background explanation consists of exactly what is related at the board meeting as the reasons for taking a particular decision, whereas what he wants to know, and is never told, are what were the counter arguments raised in internal discussions and why they were rejected.

How far externals on boards make a difference depends not only on how much information they are given, but also on who they are. An earlier Doyukai survey[16] asked 57 firms which had appointed one or more external directors to classify them under various heads. Fifty were from a parent firm, a business partner firm, a firm belonging to the same group or a main bank. Twelve were from another firm with which the firm in question had no business relation. Economists, consultants, journalists, and academics and officials of non-profit organizations accounted for ten, ex-bureaucrats three; there was one lawyer and one accountant. Those classified as representatives of major shareholders amounted to 12, of whom eight were from institutional shareholders, primarily life insurance companies. A Keidanren survey found a very similar breakdown a year later.[17] It also found, that, in response to a question about "what it was hoped to achieve by the governance changes" only 13 of the 99 companies said "to bring in the voice of the shareholders."

In short, in most cases the appointment of outside directors serves primarily to formalize the sort of relations which always have underpinned the system of cross-shareholding between "stable shareholders." It is a very rare president who has put himself in such a position that he can be dismissed by a board in which a majority of votes are held by external directors who are, or represent, profit-oriented shareholders with no other business relationship with the company. The president of Hoya, the spectacle manufacturer, claims that the structure he

---

[15] *Nikkei Bijinesu*, 1 December 2003: 40.

[16] *Koporeto Gabanansu kaikaku ni kansuru anketo chosa* (A survey of corporate governance reform), conducted in April 2002. Available at: http://www.doyukai.or.jp/policyproposals/articles/2003/040406a. html

[17] *'Kaisha kikan no arikata ni kansuru anketo' Kekka gaiyo* (The appropriate form for corporate governance organs), 18 February 2003.

has built up since he inherited the company from his father four years ago (his father pioneered the appointment of external directors) is exactly such and productive of a desirable degree of "tension."[18] He is quoted in a magazine article as explaining how his board turned down his stock option plan on the grounds that its incentive value would not be worth the waste of the shareholders' money.[19] One of his outside directors, however, in the course of praising his management style casts some doubt on the tenseness of the tension. "He is in his early 40s, a generation younger than any of us externals, so we can say what we feel like in a spirit of 'Now you should listen to what Mummy and Daddy tell you'."[20] Another article in the same magazine notes, however, that there has still been only one instance of external directors engineering the dismissal of a president, and that dates from 1982, when a notoriously profligate president of the Mitsukoshi department store was forced out by the representative on the board of the firm's main bank.[21]

So the changes have not improved efficiency by hanging a sword of Damocles over company presidents, but in that minority of companies which have set up compensation and appointments committees containing outsiders, exposure to evaluation may be a spur to the conscience or energies of a CEO. Similarly, it may well be the case that, where the outside directors are men of intelligence and character, they can scrutinize the proposals that come before them in useful ways, but it is clear that they nearly always do so as "friends and well-wishers of the firm"—being very frequently personal friends of the president—and not as friends or representatives of shareholders. And even for such externals, the information available to them is a crucial variable.

Sometimes external directors are hardly disinterested friends of the firm. One respondent to the Doyukai 2004 survey added a complaining note, which recalls what was said earlier about switching to the Committee system reinforcing the power of dominant shareholders. He was concerned about more widespread "tunnelling," not necessarily by parent firms:

Large firms which have an interest in another firm often send in external directors who put on pressure to make deals in their own firm's favor to the detriment of profits. The firms I'm talking about are all listed firms, among them some whose CEO is constantly appearing on television and in the newspapers saying wonderful things about compliance. Where the external is a director in his own firm he may take care to behave discreetly, but these people are often from ranks below director so that they cannot be legally charged with conflict of interest.

---

[18] On the significance of *kinchoukan*, tension, in Japanese discussions of corporate governance see, R. Dore (2001). *Stock Market Capitalism, Welfare Capitalism*. Oxford: OUP, 81–7.

[19] 'Beikokugatani tamashii wo ireru ho' ('How to Put Life into the American-Style Board System'), *Nikkei Bijinesu*, 1 December 2003: 34.

[20] *Ibid*, p. 35.

[21] 'Mezameyo torishimariyakkai' ('Wake up Board of Directors'), *Nikkei Bijinesu*, 1 December 2003: 32.

Thus improvements in efficiency of decision-making have probably all been marginal improvements in the *quality* of decision-making. But what about their speed? One of the most commonly used phrases in discussing the purpose of reforms, is the need to make decisions more *supiidei* speedy. One of the great merits claimed for the committee company system is that it is possible to delegate much more power to CEOs, and it is reasonable to assume that this could speed things up. But it is hard to see how the changes in the auditor companies could have any but contrary effects. The BK survey responses provide some indications. These middle managers were asked to compare their own situation and workload with someone in a comparable job ten years earlier. How had things changed in respect of a list of 15 characteristics? Only 7% said "now have to attend fewer meetings" compared with 36% who said "have to attend more meetings."

That survey also showed the middle managers had little expectations that external directors would contribute to toughening top managers' backbones when hard decisions—e.g. closing down divisions—had to be taken, and when we asked about hypothetical situations in which top managers had been guilty of a serious business misjudgment—would respondents think of going to an external director?—in the 155 in firms which had appointed at least one external director, 42% said absolutely no. Fifty percent said "only in extreme circumstances" and only 8% that it was perfectly on the cards. For the rest of the sample the question had to be hypothetical: would you possibly think of going to an external director if you had one? The "possibly" and the "never" answers divided 44/56.

13.4.3 Greater Probity?

Given the prominence of the scandals in prompting the reforms, it is highly relevant to ask whether recent changes have increased safeguards against their recurrence. In the Keidanren survey when firms were asked about appointing external directors and auditors, they were offered as answers "as a check on the appropriateness of the firm's actions" (chosen by 30 firms) and "as a check on legal compliance" (20 firms) This is less than the 42 and 34 respectively who chose efficiency aspects—getting an objective view and tapping specialist knowledge— but still a substantial number. Whether this reflects a triumph of hope over experience or a tendency to repeat shibboleths or is based on real experience it is hard to say. For the fact is that the likelihood of an external director or an external auditor detecting and stopping the sort of behavior exemplified in the scandals (of any of the four types listed earlier) is small. Most of those recorded over the last decade were the product of lower and middle-level decisions. Top managers were often deliberately shielded from guilty knowledge: the Mitsubishi Motors cover-up being an exception involving decisions at the very top.

Which is not to say that nothing has changed. There seems to have been a general impact on consciousness from the multiple examples of the ruination of firms whose reputation is besmirched by indulgence of *sokaiya*, mis-labeling, false application for subsidies, knowingly selling inferior products and above all not coming clean when the media get hold of the story. The "social responsibility of industry" has become a common topic for business lunches, business federation surveys, working groups and whatever, particularly after the JACE made it the theme of its annual White Paper in 2003. Half the firms in the Keidanren survey said that they had newly set up internal checking systems, often as part of the strengthening of the staff available to the (internal and external) auditors. Quite a number have set up "internal ombudsman" or "hot lines"—a move recommended in the latest ethical guidelines published by Keidanren. Those who are concerned about what they see others to be doing can inform the ombudsman under guarantee of anonymity—though a guarantee in which not all employees have faith.

Much in these responses has been rhetorical such as the publication of ethical guidelines and the like. But the greatest change must surely be in the change in attitudes, partly a response to the scandals and the manifestly devastating effects to all concerned of trying to cover up illegality as manifested at Yukijirushi and Mitsubishi Motors. It may partly also be due to a weakening of the "my company right or wrong" tightly closed community aspect of the employment relation. Our BK survey asked about whistle-blowers.

Suppose your firm had done something illegal or contrary to social norms and someone from within the firm had informed the media, which of the following best describes what would happen.

a) However much the motive was citizen conscience and public spirit he would have a hard time in the firm thereafter. Always has been the case and continues to be.
b) If the motive was citizen conscience and public spirit, he would find rather more people in the firm who would approve and back him up than used to be the case.
c) Not "rather more," "far more."

Thirty percent chose the "no change" alternative, and 17% thought there was a big change, with 52% voting for "some change." The following question asked whether the presence or absence of external directors would make any difference in these matters. "None at all" said 35%, and "Possibly somewhat," 58%. Only 7% thought it would make a big difference. These judgments of senior middle managers may not be accurate forecasts of actual behavior in actual situations, but they do suggest that any change that has taken place has been a change in the general climate of opinion, perhaps reinforced by micro-organizational changes in internal controls. But that corporate governance changes designed to reinforce external monitoring have little to do with it.

13.5 MANAGERIAL OBJECTIVES, SHAREHOLDER POWER VIA EXIT AND HOSTILE TAKEOVERS

The biggest change of all is the change in managerial objectives. "What will this do to our share price," once an insignificant consideration in managers' decisions, this has become a far more salient one. Share price trends have a far greater effect on a company's general reputation—its reputation in product markets, and in the graduate recruitment market which is generally considered to be crucial for the long-term prosperity of the firm.

The following was written in 1987:

The stock exchange has never been a very savoury place in Japan.....the corporate manager is not inclined to take his share price seriously as a comment on his "perform-ance", as a signal of "the best judgment of his best informed peers". It may be a factor of *some* consequence in his financial management, but it has no *moral* force. It is not the sort of thing that makes him feel chuffed or hang his head in shame. A semi-popular business-man's magazine has a lengthy account of Sony's stormy 1984 annual meeting which created a record by lasting 13 and a half hours. Much of the article concerns the sokaiya responsible for the relentless pursuit of managers, but it lists in detail the substance of their attacks: product development failures, loss of market share, mis-management, slow turnover growth, profits 43 percent down. But, incredibly as it may seem to anyone familiar with the British business press, the whole article contained no reference, in its accounts of Sony's bad year, to movements in its share price.[22]

Twenty years later the situation is very different. Tokyo Electric's President sent a New Year message to senior managers in 1997 telling them that the company's share price was the best consolidated index of how they were doing, and they should make a point of watching how it was moving. Hitherto they had been too concentrated on things like watching their load factors.[23]

The change is clearly part and parcel of the growing influence of shareholder value doctrines. Managers who would once have taken as much pride in how many "months-worth" of bonuses they paid to their workers as in the size of their profits, now are more likely to take pride in how tough they have been in holding down wage costs and how rewarded they have been by a rise in their share price. The reasons for the shift are complex, and they can only be listed, not analyzed, here.

- The general attention given by the media to stock exchange movements as a barometer of the health of the economy.
- The increasing use of stock options as part of managerial emoluments, particularly the recent trend to make directors retirement bonus a one-yen-a-share option to be exercised at the time of retirement.
- The striking growth of the analysts profession.
- The rapidly increasing move to publishing quarterly accounts and profits forecasts.
- The influence of the share price on bond and CP interest spreads, as well, of course, of the profitability of new share issues.
- The secular decline in union power, much accelerated in recent years by the persistent deflation. By removing the "cost-of-living increase" starting point of wage negotiations it has all but destroyed the central collective bargaining institution of the "spring offensive." Employee voice as a countervailing

---

[22] Ronald Dore (1987). *Taking Japan Seriously.* London: Athlone, 116.
[23] Keizai Doyukai, *Kigyou hakusho 13-kai* (Thirteenth Enterprise White Paper), pp. 20–2.

power to shareholder voice has been much weakened. There is hardly a large company union which could now contemplate a successful strike.

- The ideological direction given to economic-structure policy under the Koizumi–Takenaka regime, notably the belief that a winding down of cross-holdings and the facilitating of M&A is a beneficial enhancement of market discipline on Japanese firms. The strong endorsement of that position by the chief business newspaper, the Nikkei, and the absence of any concerted challenge to it from the rest of the press.

This enhancement of market discipline is so far largely a matter of managers' anxiety to avoid the desertion of shareholders and a drop in their share price. The weight of foreign institutional investors in the market—their holdings for the most part concentrated in large corporations—has added an extra element over and above rational calculation of the disadvantages of a low share price. Being deserted by Japanese speculators is one thing. But for the average manager-in-the-street, a loss of the confidence of a large American pension fund is something else. Wall Street has a different kind of aura, much affected by the whole pattern of Japanese elite attitudes towards the United States—resentment at American arrogance, to be sure, but admixed with genuine respect, fear, and even awe.[24]

The crucial question is whether this "soft power" of the potential shareholder exit will be supplemented with the "hard power" of the realistic threat of a takeover bid—whether a real market in capital control will develop. So far the prospect of trying to digest and run a large Japanese company acquired in the teeth of opposition from its management has deterred most American as well as Japanese companies. Nearly all attempts at strategic acquisitions—as in the attempts of foreign pharmaceutical firms to absorb Japanese rivals—have relied on negotiated mergers. Most of the takeover threats have come from private equity funds seeking to make a quick buck. The most consequential case was the bid made in 2004 by Steel Partners Japan Strategy Fund for two cash-rich companies with low market capitalizations, Sotoh and Yushiro Chemical Industries. Sotoh managed at first to rally enough Japanese investors to make a counter-offer but they dropped out of the bidding when Steel Partners raised their offer. Sotoh was finally forced to defend itself by disgorging its cash reserves with the promise of a ¥200 dividend. That won over their other shareholders and turned Steel Partners a nice profit without all the pain and opprobrium that goes with asset-stripping. Much the same happened to Yushiro. A magazine article[25] lists some 13 companies in which Steel Partners have acquired 5–6% of their shares, and another 30 in which other similar funds have acquired similar or even larger stakes. A large number of them—eight of Steel Partners 13—had substantially increased their dividend. The article asserts that the "bigger dividend boom"

---

[24] For a sense of the manager-in-the-street's perceptions of the New York financial community see the novel by Takashima Ryo, *Za Gaishi* (Mr Foreign Capital). Symbolically the acquaintance between the leading characters—a Japanese businessman and a tall heavily-built American fund manager—begins when the latter knocks the former down in an accidental collision while jogging in Central Park.

[25] 'TOB boeijutsu' (Defence against Takeovers), *Shukan Toyo Keizai*, 15 May 2004.

set off by these threatening investors was beginning to affect larger companies too, and the increase in shareholder resolutions demanding higher dividends at this summer's AGMs (see above) was attributed by Institutional Shareholders Services to these events.[26]

In the large corporation sector there has yet to happen anything comparable to the German trauma when Mannesmann fell to Vodaphone, but the possibility is there as noted in the Introduction to this book. Chapter 2 in this volume also documents the extent to which the banks' role in providing stable shareholders who can defend against any bid has been much reduced. The requirement that financial assets should be marked to a fluctuating market is a deterrent to their rebuilding. Nevertheless, it is still possible (see above the story of Tokyo Style) for medium-sized firms to mobilize defensive shareholdings, and would probably prove a good deal easier for large firms.

Still the major protection is "the business culture." A 1984 dictionary of economic terms lists TOB and explains that though the regulations for takeover bids were established in Japan in 1972, "the idea of taking over a Japanese company merely by the power of money seems too 'dry' [*dorai*] to us Japanese and it never happens."[27] Twenty years later, the President of Mitsui-Sumitomo Bank, a man with a reputation for a certain flamboyance, tells reporters that in response to UFJ Holdings refusal of his generous offer of a merger he is contemplating a hostile bid. The news is reported as slightly surprising, certainly not as shocking.

Nevertheless, fear of takeover seems not yet to be a widespread factor in management decision-making. In our BK survey we asked respondents to rate the extent to which their firm could count on stable shareholders, now and ten years ago. They were offered two contrasting statements:

Even if a takeover bidder were to make an offer 30 percent over our current share price, we have enough stable shareholders who would refuse, so in that sense we need not worry about our share price.

We don't have enough loyal shareholders to fend off a hostile takeover.

Respondents were asked to rate the degree to which their firm's situation approximated to the first or the second description—now and ten years' ago—counting "most certainly the first" as one and "most certainly the second" as ten. The average rating was 3.1 then and 4.5 now, a smaller shift than on three other similarly framed questions about changes in managerial objectives. Only a third of the sample gave a rating over five—i.e. said that their firm was now closer to the "no loyal shareholders" situation than to being able to count on them, and only 2% said so with enough certainty to give that answer a rating of nine or ten. A similar question about whether the firm could count on a main bank rallying round if it got into serious difficulties produced a similar pattern of response, except that the shift along the scale over ten years was smaller, from 3.6 to 4.6.

---

[26] Marc Goldstein, *op.cit.*

[27] Nihon Keizai Shimbun (1984). *Hai-Tekku Jiten* (High Tech Dictionary). Tokyo: Nihon Keizai Shimbun.

Nevertheless, as in the 1960s when capital liberalization loomed and the cross-shareholding pattern was deliberately built up as a defence against American predators, there are enough economic nationalists about to be worried and to begin to think about defences. In September 2004, Japan's Ministry of Economy, Trade and Industry announced the formation of a new working group to include academics and corporate managers. The press release (September 16) describes the background for the new initiative as lying in all the institutional changes of the last decade to facilitate M&A, which it endorses as admirable progress. But "at the same time we have urgently to consider how to prevent the excessive dissipation of firms' in-built managerial resources" by studying the various poison pill devices which American firms use to fend off hostile takeovers. The background material makes clear what the central preoccupation is: foreign investors own 20% of the Tokyo stock market, compared with 5% in 1990. Sony calculates that of the 70% of its shares in foreign hands, a half are with stable long-term investor institutions, but a half with hedge funds and speculative private equity funds. With the unravelling of cross-holdings, the average firm's reliable, loyal "stable shareholders" account for only a quarter of their shares, compared with nearly a half a decade ago. And meanwhile, it says, Pfizer has a market capitalization seven times that of Takeda Pharmaceuticals, Procter and Gamble ten times that of Kao, and Walmart eight times that of Seven-eleven.

"One more nail into the coffin of corporate governance in Japan" was the comment of the *Financial Times'* Lex column on advance news of the initiative (September 10, 2004). It is significant, though, that, as it were to soften the impression of a frontal attack on "market discipline," the other half of the group's remit is to prevent the flight of talent to other countries. Like the facilitation of M&A, the moves towards labor market mobility are admirable, says the press release, but Japan must study American personnel retention policies as well as American poison pills, both aspects of preventing "dissipation of inbuilt managerial resources."

The official title of the working group is "Enterprise Value Study Group." One hears "enterprise value" often these days, used in deliberate contradistinction to "shareholder value" to indicate a lingering attachment to the notion that Japan has a different gentler form of capitalism than that subscribed to by the FT, and believes that others besides shareholders, notably employees, have a stake in the firm. Nevertheless, it is a nice irony that the short press release justifies this effort to prepare the defences against the invasion of American capital on the grounds that "we must learn from America."

13.6 INSIDER MANAGEMENT: GOOD OR BAD

So much for Argument 2 about the extent of changes in the nature of Japanese capitalism, and the relatively small significance of those changes in promoting better corporate governance. It is time to turn to Argument 1 about external monitoring.

The best short summary of the foregoing would probably be something like the following. The micro-organizational and the macro-market changes over the last decade have given managers more options in financial matters, if largely increasing their need to take account of potentially exiting shareholders, and slightly increasing their need to take account of potential takeover predators. The appointment of outside directors and auditors and the increased reporting requirements (greater financial detail and, for example, the need to state in their annual stock exchange financial statement, and from this year on in their annual statement to the FSA, what they are doing to improve corporate governance) may have made some managers a little more circumspect, but they have made little dent in their autonomy. All attempts to make it appear that Japanese firms are as subject to external scrutiny and control as American firms, are, with a tiny number of possible exceptions, largely cosmetic.

Is that necessarily a bad thing from the point of view of our fundamental problem of making sure that top managers are honest and dynamic? In the first place a lot depends on a manager's conscience—conscience about his firm's social and legal responsibilities, conscience about putting out maximum effort, conscience about giving way to a successor when he feels he is losing momentum, conscience about choosing a successor who will do the best for the firm and not just be most indulgent to him personally when he moves on to the chairmanship. Second, much depends on how far that conscience is reinforced by the relations he/she has with the other top managers with whom he works.

It is a dominant view in the corporate governance literature that the executive and monitoring functions should be sharply separated. The "separation of powers" is seen to be as important in the micro-polity of the corporation as in the macro-polity of the state. This view rests on the "original sin" view that no-one can be trusted to monitor themselves, that conscience cannot be relied on, that "all power corrupts and absolute power corrupts absolutely." An alternative assumption is that people work better if they are trusted to have strong conscience control, though they sometimes do betray that trust and it is as well to have emergency mechanisms to cope with the situation when they do. The "institutionalization of suspicion"[28] and how far it can go without counter-productively provoking delinquency, and how far the size of the organization or community in question matters, are aspects of the transition from community to association which have preoccupied sociologists ever since the discipline acquired its name.

It is a plausible "national character" assertion that Japanese are brought up to have a stronger leaning towards the "original virtue" than towards the "original sin" position. But that is not the major reason for my assertion that the need for external monitoring is different as between Japan and, say, America. More important is the employment system. Consider two contrasting cases.

CEO A gets to the job as a result of negotiations, which can be quite protracted and tough, over salary, bonuses, stock options, pension rights etc. with a board

---

[28] See, R. Dore (1971) 'Modern cooperatives in traditional communities,' in P. Worsley (ed.), *Two Blades of Grass*. Manchester: Manchester University Press.

compensation committee which is supposedly guided by some notion of how much his/her particular talents will contribute to shareholder value.

CEO B gets to the job after several years as one of five or six colleagues—nearly all people who have been his/her colleagues for all their working life—continually under observation by superiors and peers as potential competitors for the career-culminating honor of being chosen for the top job—the resulting increase in salary being more or less fixed by precedence.

The first describes the typical (modern) American CEO. I say modern because in the 1960s a far higher proportion of American CEOs were of the B variety. Sophisticated malfeasance and greed have grown *pari passu* with the growth of head-hunting firms and external recruitment.

Japanese CEOs are still almost exclusively of the B variety, and the conventional increase in salary on being promoted from *semmu* or vice-president to president is of the order of 10–20%. In large Japanese companies, for all the talk of accelerated promotion,[29] there is no sign of any fundamental change in the bureaucratic career patterns which have become so firmly conventionalized. The new president of Kao was, according to a newspaper report,[30] selected at 54 over the heads of eight rivals all slightly his seniors. But although this was presented as unusual, it is hardly out of line with general practice. We looked at a random sample of 32 firms. The average age of appointment of the presidents incumbent in 1995 was 57.17. For those incumbent in 2003, it was 57.20. Moreover, the turnover had been considerable. In only four of those firms was it the same man in position after eight years. One of those was the president of Shinetsu Kagaku, reputedly a highly dynamic and certainly highly articulate business leader, author of several books, whom his colleagues may well think difficult to replace. Of the other three, two were family firms. Firms with recent and memorable founders often have the tradition, even after the founder's family's holding is reduced to 2–3%, of having a family member as president (as in Italy). In large firms this is usually on the clear understanding that he reigns but does not rule. This has been the case even in large firms like Toyota, and it was nearly the case in Matsushita—the appointment being in the end blocked by a critical management faction. In smaller companies, however, the "reign not rule" understanding may not be achievable and the practice can lead to prolonged inept and arbitrary management.

But in large firms it is common for a "salary man president" to serve only one four-year term, and rare for him to serve more than two. To return to the conscience question, the incentives reinforcing it for the president of a large company are formidable. His whole social world has been dominated by his connections with the company. The normal progression is for him to move on from the presidency to the chairmanship, moving on further to the position of "senior advisor" when the next president bumps him up. If he leaves the presidency with the reputation of one who has done well for the firm, he can

---

[29] The Bank of Japan recently made headlines by appointing as a section chief a man who had only been in the bank for 12 years.

[30] Available at: newsflash.nifty.com/news/ts/ts__fuji_320040413023.htm

expect the after-life of a much deferred-to elder, well supplied with secretarial help and transport on top of his pension, and, if his firm is powerful enough and he has the right personality and taste for it, a respected position in the business federations and government committees. If he leaves under a cloud his whole social world may collapse.

The big question is this: given the power given him by the convention that the president chooses his own successor, is he as much subject to the critical opinions of the senior managers closest to him as he might be. Even supposing that he is well-intentioned, does he get the right information and honest critical opinion?

There is a well-known story by Mori Ogai about two samurai who are sent by their feudal lord to Nagasaki to buy a rare stick of incense. The price is enormous. One says "The fief can't afford this. It will impoverish everybody, samurai and peasants. Our duty is to stop our lord from such folly." The other says: "Our duty is to fulfil the wishes of our lord." Which exhibits the most desirable kind of loyalty? It rather seems that Mori leans towards the latter, but the modern Japanese business man would undoubtedly side with the former. The question is: would they behave that way?

There are many attested instances of middle managers risking their career prospects to protest about senior managers' actions on the grounds not of their personal interest but because they thought that the actions were bad for the firm. A couple of decades ago it was reported in the media that younger managers at Ajinomoto had formed their own study group and issued a manifesto criticizing the strategy of top management. In another case, Okuma machine tools, the president's choice of an unimpressive nephew as a successor was thwarted by middle managers, supported by the union which threatened a strike.[31] But how general is such action?

In our BK survey we asked the following questions:

Since you became kanrishoku [the stage of career at which one normally assumes line management and has to cease to be a member of the enterprise union] have there been any occasions when you have felt that the decisions of top managers—about a big investment, starting a new line of business or closing a factory—have been mistaken?

Fifty-three percent answered "yes." They were then asked "Think of the occasion when you felt most strongly critical. What did you do?" and offered three alternatives.

I was resigned to the fact that there was nothing to be done.
I made a gushin on my own.
I made a gushin with other like-minded managers.

The word "*gushin*" is not easily translated: it means a protest, somewhat deferentially conveying advice or criticism to an organizational superior. Exactly

---

[31] Tackney, Charles T. (1995). *Institutionalization of the Japanese Lifetime Employment System: A Case Study of Changing Employment Practices in a Machine-tools Factory.* PhD dissertation, Industrial Relations Research Institute, University of Wisconsin-Madison: Ann Arbor, UMI Number: 9608158.

three-quarters of those who had thought the bosses mistaken chose "resigned," 15% said that they had protested singly and 10% in a group.

The 123 who chose "resigned" were then asked which of the following applied:

I kept my views to myself.
I made my dissatisfaction clear, but I had to be careful whom I could complain to.
The work atmosphere was such that I didn't have to be careful who I complained to.

The breakdown this time was 20% for silence, 40% for selective complaint and 41% for free and easy grumbling.

It is hard to draw firm conclusions. Some concern with whether the firm is on the right course is fairly widespread in middle management, but it is only a minority who feel strongly enough to put their necks on the line by speaking out. On the other hand the sort of repressive atmosphere in which people are afraid to criticize is not the general rule. One interesting comment on these questions from someone wise in the ways of Japanese companies:

Of course most Japanese CEOs are bottom-uppers. There really are very few presidents who make big decisions that come as a surprise to middle managers. Most decisions are the result of a long process of internal consultation. When they are finally taken most managers will already have a had a chance to exert what influence they are capable of making. They will have a good idea of which way the wind is blowing and whether there is any point in remonstrating. A lot of those who claim to have remonstrated will be exaggerating anyway: they are more likely just to have hinted at their views when they were chatting to the boss in the corridor or during a drinking session, done so in such a way that he doesn't see it as confrontational.

The view that these collegial constraints on top management are desirable and act as a substitute for external monitoring contrasts, of course, with the views of the reformers such as those of the Japan Assocation of Corporate Directors who think CEOs should show bold, confident, and decisive leadership and that they should have a greater concentration of power in their hands to change things. I asked a sample of knowledgeable people (drawn from my email address book) what they thought of these trammelling constraints. Some typical sentiments from the 23 replies:

70% good: 30% bad. Difficult to be unequivocal because the conservative bias such constraints introduce can sometimes lead to a serious failure to seize business opportunities. On the other hand every firm, if it is to achieve long-term growth, needs to have decisions at the top informed by what Hayek called the "knowledge of particular circumstances and places" that only the people at the bottom have.

There are cases where drastic reform is needed and the supervisor has to show strong willpower not to give in to resistance from subordinates. My observation of many Japanese businesses and banks is that supervisors often compromise, or, worse, voluntarily refrain from suggesting changes that are needed.

A good thing, but if the bottom-up constraint comes from more organizational forces, such as labor unions or internal factional cliques (batsu) groups, it could be a bad thing for the company as a whole.

It is striking, though, that only the last comment talked about criticism of superiors' decisions being based on subordinates' self-interest rather than on views about what was good for the firm. No-one suggested that opposition from below was almost exclusively likely to be of the former kind, and that therefore the survey question envisaged situations which hardly exist.

But it is, of course, highly probable that, if not "almost exclusively," self-interested complaint is more frequent than concern for the fate of the firm-as-employee-community. The various systems that have been set up to strengthen internal monitoring, and the "company ombudsman" and "hot line" devices to embolden whistle-blowers become relevant here. One prominent corporate law-yer who is on the end of a hot line for the employees of five firms, reports that there is a wide degree of difference among firms. From one of them he has received no complaints, which he interprets as indicating a repressive atmosphere dominated be fear. From another he receives a large volume of complaints which he interprets as a sign of low morale. The bulk of those complaints concern rule infringements, not to the detriment of the customers or society at large but to the individual complainer—e.g. "since the crack-down on unpaid overtime, my boss insists that I take work home."

My tentative conclusion coincides with that of several other writers.[32] While there are well-managed firms and badly managed firms as elsewhere, no clear correlation exists between insiderism and bad management. The absence of strong external oversight and control is not an obstacle to getting honest and dynamic managers. But it is also not clear that this will always be so. There has been little change so far in the career patterns of the most fortunate half of the work force (those who are not forced into the insecurity of "non-standard" employment). See, for example the figures cited in footnote 5. There is no sign of the development of an external labor market for executive talent. The head-hunters do the bulk of their business for foreign firms. But there are some signs of a shift in the work/life balance and a lessening of that degree of commitment to their firm on the part of managers that makes them put the interests of their firm on a par with, or even ahead of, their own. The recent spate of law suits brought by disgruntled corporate researchers who think they have been less than fairly rewarded for their inventions may be a straw in a somewhat bigger wind.[33]

13.7 GLOBALIZATION UNDER AMERICAN HEGEMONY? OR SOCIAL EVOLUTION?

It remains, briefly, to make one further point. Many of the changes described above are direct imitations of American models, their ostensible purpose being to

---

[32] E.g. Itami Hiroyuki (2000). *Keiei no mirai wo miayamaru na* (Don't get the future of manage-ment wrong). Tokyo: Nihon Keizai; Inagami Takeshi and Mori Kyojiro (eds.) (2004). *Koporeto/ Gabanansu to juugyouin* (Corporate Governance and Employees). Tokyo: Toyo Keizai; Iwai Katsundo (2003). *Kaisha wa kore kara do naru no ka* (The Company of the Future); Tanaka Kazuhiro, (2003). *Kigyo shihairyoku no seigyo* (Limiting the power of outsiders over the firm). Tokyo: Yuhikaku.

[33] See Ronald Dore (forthcoming). 'Innovation for whom,' in R. Haak and M. Pudelko (eds.), *Japanese Management: In the Search for a New Balance Between Continuity and Change.* Houndmills: Palgrave.

enhance national competitiveness. They can also be interpreted as a reflection of changes in social structure. After six generations of meritocracy—roughly three generations of social mobility limited by constricted educational opportunity, and three generations of much expanded educational opportunity and much less limited social mobility—class divisions in Japan are hardening and the intergenerational transmission of class status is increasing.

As a consequence, whatever may be happening to latent working class consciousness the effectiveness of working class leadership is diminished. The talented union leaders of the 1950s and 1960s, forced on to the shop floor by family poverty have no successors. The Socialist Party has evaporated. The managerial middle class continues to drain talent from below, but is increasingly self-recruited. The growth of private secondary schooling is reflected in the increasing polarization of educational achievement.[34] The top managers now retiring often came from large families of diverse occupational destinations and rubbed shoulders with their future subordinates in common, often rural, schools. The sense of empathetic cross-class rapport which was usual for their generation contributed a good deal to the quasi-community character of the Japanese firm. It is not being passed to younger generations. And many of that older generation had little income apart from their salaries. They built up and passed on to younger generations the financial assets, which gives their owners a strong interest in the return on capital.

Most of these social structural changes, are not one-off but progressive. They help to explain why it is that, over the last decade, Japanese firms have become more solicitous of and deferential to the owners of their capital and more inclined to treat their employees as means rather than ends. They also are grounds for expecting that trend to continue.

[34] As shown in a recent international study in *Nihon keizai shinbun*, 7 December 2004.

Part III

Diversity and Institutional Change

14

Organizational Diversity and Institutional Change: Evidence from Financial and Labor Markets in Japan

Mari Sako

Japan's economic success has been attributed largely to the nature of its national institutions, such as relational banking, lifetime employment, and relational contracting in intermediate product markets. These institutions were tightly linked to govern the Japanese economy, but more diverse patterns of organizing have become evident since the 1990s. For instance, venture capital funds and IPOs (initial public offerings) appeared alongside relational banking to finance start-ups, and non-standard forms of employment came to be a significant alternative to the lifetime employment norm.

It is clear that the Japanese business system is becoming more diverse within. But when, why and how has such organizational diversity come about in Japan? And is such diversity a sign of a gradual breakdown of the system, or has it become the very characteristic of the Japanese system? If it is the former, what is the process by which we should expect the emergence of a new system? If the latter, how much diversity can be sustained within a system?

This chapter addresses these questions with respect to specific empirical cases at the national and corporate levels. The chapter begins by developing a framework linking institutional change and organizational diversity in section 14.1. Then section 14.2 examines the timing and the extent of diversity in financial and labor markets at the economy-wide level. Section 14.3 turns to varied responses to institutional pressures at the company level in two contrasting settings. The aim here is to compare and contrast the ways in which Softbank and NTT used the holding company structure to bring about organizational diversity.

The key contributions of this study are as follows. First, the chapter advances a model of institutional change in a specific direction, namely from coordinated to more liberal, and identifies organizational diversity as a feature of such change as well as of the new emergent system. Second, the chapter identifies the late 1990s as the time when organizational diversity began to take off in the Japanese economy. Third, a comparison of Softbank and NTT shows that in both new and old sectors, there is a variety of ways in which a new organizational form—the pure holding company structure in this case—may be adopted. The ambiguity residing in the nature of institutions gives further cause for organizational diversity in the process of implementation.

14.1 INSTITUTIONAL CHANGE AND ORGANIZATIONAL DIVERSITY IN NATIONAL BUSINESS SYSTEMS

What is the link between institutional change and organizational diversity? Is it the case that institutional change is always associated with a period of increased organizational diversity? How do we gauge if increased organizational diversity is the very characteristic of a new emergent system rather than a sign of breakdown of the existing system?

Two contrasting approaches to answer these questions are outlined here. One approach emphasizes the coherence of a national business system, regards institutional change as rare and difficult, and projects a path of breakdown, institutional vacuum, followed by the erection of a new system. The other approach, which is used in this chapter, allows for the process of de-institutionalization to take a slower pace, and to involve incremental change. This latter approach enables us to incorporate the idea that incremental change is not exempt from eventual transformation in the nature of institutions (Streeck and Thelen 2005).

14.1.1 System Coherence Focus Biases Towards Radical Institutional Change

Comparative institutional analysis has become popular since the 1980s, when the Anglo-American world realized that companies originating from distinctively different institutional arrangements were challenging their own. The key analytical frameworks that range from political science, economic sociology, and economics are primarily concerned with emphasizing the internal coherence and stability of national business systems. Internal coherence provides an explanation for both the persistence of varieties of capitalism and costs of responding to forces for change. But it is precisely the specific meaning given to the notion of coherence that leads to different implications for adaptability and change. As shown below, coherence may refer to complementarity and/or to "motivational congruence." The former is a functionalist concept, while the latter is a normative concept.

Hall and Soskice (2001) present a highly stylized framework for analyzing "varieties of capitalism." This framework identifies four subsystems, namely in corporate governance, inter-firm relations, labor markets, and education and training, and directs our attention to examining the strength of complementarity of institutions within and between the subsystems. Following Milgrom and Roberts (1995) who theorized about complementarities between manufacturing practices, Hall and Soskice state that two institutions are complementary if the presence (or more) of one increases the returns from the other. Thus, institutional complementarity is an aspect of cohesion or synergy between institutions that is predicated solely on performance outcomes. By implication, piecemeal institutional change—e.g. by changing only one of the two complementary institutions—brings about sub-optimal performance outcomes. Moreover, the stronger and more widespread institutional complementarities are in a national system, greater sacrifice is made in performance through such piecemeal, rather than wholesale, change in institutions. Institutional complementarity gives rise to a tendency to see most changes as adaptive adjustments to preserve the existing system, and identify rare occasions when disruptive institutional change occur. This bifurcation in the nature of institutional change derives from a sole focus on the functionalist aspect of system coherence.

By contrast, Hollingsworth and Boyer (1997) defines their "social system of production," and Whitley (1999) identifies institutional features, by reference to more normative dimensions such as the conceptions of fairness and justice, and a society's customs and traditions that affect the notion of trust and authority. Like North (1990), these authors are concerned with institutions as both informal and formal rules of the game. Moreover, concern with informal rules compels them to give as much emphasis to what Dore (2000) calls "motivational congruence" as to "institutional complementarity" (Hall and Soskice 2001). In other words, ideas and values held by actors within the business system must be internally coherent and consistent with the incentives provided by the formal institutions. Even if formal rules are changed, the absence of "motivational congruence" may lead to no change in informal constraints, which in turn lead to a restructuring of institutions that is far less revolutionary than intended (North 1990: 91).

In these frameworks that emphasize coherence and stability, changes in practice are brought about in a discrete manner only, often under a crisis situation. So a serious decline in performance may trigger a search for alternative "templates for organising" (DiMaggio and Powell 1991: 27). But poorly performing economies may survive for a long period of time precisely because the filter of mental constructs may not change, as much as because the costs involved in switching from one set of institutions to another are higher than the benefits that result from the switch. But when the "taken for granted" nature of institutions becomes fundamentally questioned, and costs to sticking to the existing arrangement are perceived too high, then rejection by powerful actors brings about a breakdown and the adoption of an alternative "template."

Thus, the long-standing focus on system coherence, either in a functionalist or in a normative sense, has led to a view of institutional change as something that happens not too frequently but periodically, and as discrete and radical change in either formal or informal rules of the game. While this view may apply to the analysis of the impact of wars and crises, as in the case of Japan immediately after the Second World War, it is less applicable to the Japanese business system in the 1990s and beyond.

14.1.2 De-institutionalization and Re-institutionalization may be Slow and Piecemeal

A more appropriate model of institutional change for our current analytical purpose allows for slow, piecemeal, and incremental change as much as rapid, wholesale, and radical one. This analytical approach is part of the recent agenda to understand how institutions evolve through discontinuous shifts in equilibrium (Aoki 2001, 2004) or incremental changes (Streeck and Thelen 2005).

In order to develop a model of institutional change, it is necessary to identify (a) conditions for de-institutionalization; and (b) agents of change and their capacity for action. With respect to (a), we can identify, following Oliver (1992), political, functional, and social pressures that erode the legitimacy of an established and taken-for-granted organizational practice. De-institutionalization, in this sense, may occur because of a change in political power distribution, a mounting decline in the instrumental value of an institutionalized practice, or normative fragmentation caused for instance by high turnover.

Identifying these antecedents of de-institutionalization, however, is not sufficient to understand how the process of re-institutionalization may be initiated and sustained. When the legitimacy of the existing institutional structures is under attack, agents of change—what North (1990) calls political and economic entrepreneurs—have much scope to bring about transformation in institutions. These agents may be the state (e.g. the Japanese Meiji government was a "political entrepreneur" *par excellence* that commanded enormous resources and expertise to study different country models before importing appropriate modern institutions of the police, post office, and the navy from Europe (Westney 1987)). Agents may also be private sector actors such as individual entrepreneurs, corporations and associations. These actors may have varying "capacity for action" depending on the resources—economic, social, and political—that they can command to bring about change (Greenwood and Hinings 1996).

Agents in the private sector—the focus of empirical work in this chapter—may bring about institutional change in a variety of ways, in part depending on whether they are new entrants or incumbents in the scene. New entrants may create a new formal institution, which may be seen as deviant and foreign initially. The speed with which this new institution replaces the old depends on how the new and the old are related to each other. If the new institution is created without directly undermining existing institutions, both can co-exist for a long time. However, alternatively, the new institution may obtain quick support through others' defection from the old system. The former corresponds to what Streeck and Thelen (2005) call "layering," while the latter corresponds to "displacement." The more likely that the "layering" of new and old institutions might persist over a long time without triggering a "displacement" of the old by the new, the greater the degree of organizational diversity within a system.

In contrast to new entrants, incumbents, i.e. actors already in the scene, may perceive institutional change in more subtle ways. For instance, instead of abandoning existing institutions, they may attempt to adapt existing institutions marginally to serve new goals or functions. However, such "usurping of the agenda" may be a convenient way also for new entrants to use existing institutions for their own ends. Thus, as Streeck and Thelen (2005) explain, a slow pace of incremental institutional change may mask "conversion," namely the redeployment of old institutions to new goals, functions, or purposes.

For example, in Japan, pure holding company as a corporate form was re-legalized with the intention of making Japanese corporations more strategically focused and agile like their US counterparts. In reality, a new entrant, Softbank, used the holding company to build an Internet *keiretsu*, while an incumbent, NTT, created a weak holding company that had none of the strategic direction that was associated with a shareholder value capitalist firm (see later analysis for more details). This point also illustrates the variety of ways in which an existing institution may be implemented. This is in part due to the ambiguity inherent in any institution (Jackson 2005). It is also due to the contested process involved in creating any institution (Amable 2003; Sako and Jackson 2006). In unsettled times, when the legitimacy of existing institutions is under attack, such contests— e.g. between management and labor—become more apparent, leading to different resolutions in different cases. This is one reason why we might observe greater organizational diversity in unsettled than in settled times.

14.1.3 Linking Institutional Change to Organizational Diversity

Organizational diversity occurs at different levels, namely at the economy-wide level, at the level of a sector or a field, and within an organization such as the firm or the union. In linking diversity to institutional change, we focus mainly on the first two levels at which diversity occurs, although the third—diversity within organizations—may be a consequence or a trigger for diversity in the other levels.

In making a contrast between a liberal market economy (LME) and a coordinated market economy (CME), the Variety of Capitalism literature implicitly attributes greater scope for organizational diversity in the former than in the latter. This is because institutional inter-locks are much tighter in CME than in LME, thus giving limited scope for individual actors to take advantage of sub-sets of institutions in different ways. Moreover, there exist more encompassing associations and associational networks in CMEs that enforce collective action, a key force for homogenizing behavior within the system. By contrast, less complementary institutions, less investment into specific and relational assets, and greater reliance on exit rather than voice in market relations (Hirschman 1970), make LMEs conducive to tolerating diverse forms of organization. Thus, LMEs tolerate diverse forms of organization because of their specific institutions that facilitate flexible adjustments, not because organizations are less embedded in institutions in LMEs than in CMEs.

In order to link organizational diversity to institutional change, we need to move from comparative statics to dynamic analysis. The thing to note here is that the process of institutional change is asymmetric, for CME → LME shift and for LME → CME move. In particular, the ease with which actors may push for a move from CME to LME is quite different from that for a move from LME to CME.

Let us consider the move from LME to CME first. This requires actors to take concerted action through associations or through the state, in order to bring about institutions of collaboration and coordination. Thus, institutional changes are likely to be discrete and require large mobilization of resources for collective action. A new piece of legislation, like the German Co-determination Act, is a good example, as is a non-legal institution, such as the start of the Shunto spring offensive in 1955.

By contrast, a move from CME to LME is faced today by many countries, including Japan, which are implementing liberalization measures. Here, the process of dismantling the institutions of collaboration and coordination happen just as much through dissipation as through rejection. Concerted rejection may occur, but it is equally likely that the timing of exit by individual actors is uncoordinated and varied. The gradual undermining of the existing institutions would follow from such process of defection (i.e. "displacement" rather than persistent "layering"), for instance with the implementation of "side agreements" to deviate from industry-wide wage agreements in Germany. It may also follow from a process of eroding the institution at the margin in the name of defending the institution (i.e. a case of "conversion"). For example, the introduction of voluntary retirement at an earlier age, and the gradual withdrawal of employer commitment to lifetime income support may undermine the very essence of the norm of lifetime employment these changes are meant to defend (Sako 2006a). The point is that while a LME → CME move is likely to be accompanied by discrete and sometimes radical changes in institutions, a CME → LME move is likely to be accompanied by incremental changes in institutions. It is in this latter case that organizational diversity is introduced along the way. Diversity is therefore greater and more persistent with "layering" than with "displacement" or "conversion."

To summarize, organizational diversity may increase with institutional change due to three logically separable factors. First, diversity increases in a move from CME to LME because LME, with less sunk cost in building coordination and collaboration, accommodates greater diversity within the system. Second, diversity increases also because the process of institutional change may afford different timing for individual actors to defect from the old institutions, dictating the extent to which "layering" may persist. Third, organizational diversity is introduced due to different settlements that result from local contests between management and labor.

14.2 TIMING OF ORGANIZATIONAL DIVERSITY: THE LATE 1990S

The Japanese economy boomed in the 1980s with the financial bubble. The bursting of the bubble led to the so-called "lost decade" of the 1990s. However, it was not until the late 1990s that diversity in organizing became prominent. This section presents an analysis of changes in financial markets and labor markets respectively in order to interpret the reasons for this timing. In financial markets, we examine the creation of new stock exchanges for start-ups in 1999 and 2000— a case of layering—and the gradual conversion in the nature of venture capital funding from loans to investment. In labor markets, we examine the layering of temporary work onto the lifetime employment norm. A case of conversion here is the annual pay bargaining round, which had been a "spring offensive" for wage hikes led by militant public-sector unions, but increasingly a discussion forum on the macro-economy to accommodate wage restraint, pay dispersion, and diverse forms of employment (see Figure 14.1 for a typology).

The restructuring of financial markets in Japan after the accumulation of huge non-performing loans has weakened the main bank system, cross-shareholding, and other notable features of the Japanese financial institutions. Consequently, bankruptcies (notably Hokaido Takushoku, Yamaichi Securities) and bank mergers (e.g. to form the Mizuho Group) have accelerated the reduction in headcount and disruptions to lifetime employed careers. The prolonged recession more generally also quickened the erosion of lifetime employment practices in major corporations.

The weakening of national institutions in Japan resulted in an environment more conducive to the adoption of new institutional arrangements and business practices. But the functional, political and social pressures for the de-institutionalization process were present since the early 1990s. So why did it take until the late 1990s for significant institutional changes to take place? The analysis here indicates that a series of legal reforms came into effect in both financial and labor markets in the late 1990s and early 2000s, and were both forces and facilitators of institutional change. In both markets, multiple factors, some present well before the late 1990s, led to significant transformation, through "layering" in the case of the new stock exchanges and the growth of temporary

		Mode of institutional change	
		Conversion	Layering
Markets	**Financial**	Venture capital	Nasdaq Japan and TSE Mothers
	Labour	Shunto	Temporary work

Figure 14.1 Typology of institutional change

placement agencies, and through "conversion" in the case of venture capital and Shunto. The process of conversion is gradual and cumulative.

14.2.1 New Stock Exchanges (Case of Layering) and Venture Capital (Case of Conversion)

Two new stock exchanges opened in 1999 and 2000, within six months of each other, in Japan. They created a layering of equity-based corporate finance onto an existing bank-based system. It was heralded as a necessary step to enable start-ups to grow, and to induce venture capital to use Initial Public Offerings (IPOs) as a means of realizing gains from investment. Nevertheless, the new layer has not grown more quickly than the traditional financial system, despite the fact that the latter had not recovered from its problems with non-performing loans and further shake-out. Complementarity explains part of the slow growth of the new layer. In particular, there is no flexible and mobile market for technical labor and entrepreneurs, which is considered essential to create an effective demand for venture capital and new exchanges. Moreover, the slow pace of adjustment has been due to the slow conversion of venture capital industry that had existed in Japan since the 1970s. The conversion from a venture capital industry that looked more like a branch of the bank-based system to one with goals and functions that resemble those in an equity-based system was induced by both law and the creation of new stock exchanges.

The past several years have seen a dramatic change in the availability of IPOs as an option for young ventures in Japan, with the opening of the Market for High Growth and Emerging Stocks (Mothers) at the Tokyo Stock Exchange in December 1999 and Nasdaq Japan at the Osaka Stock Exchange in June 2000. Both exchanges sought to attract new and recent start-up companies particularly in high technology sectors.

Nasdaq US, as part of its global capital markets strategy, was first in approaching the Japanese Ministry of Finance, the Stock Exchanges, and various pockets of political power to lobby for Nasdaq to be set up in Japan. They faced elusive opposition, but found a willing partner in Softbank Corporation, which became a joint venture partner to create Nasdaq Japan. The creation of TSE Mothers came as a reaction to this private initiative. Moreover, Mothers suffered image problems early on as a result of suspicions of involvement by the Japanese mafia in companies planning to list on the nascent exchange. Consequently, Nasdaq Japan fared much better than Mothers (see Figure 14.2). The low points for these markets were in 2002 and 2003 respectively, reflecting a general decline in the volume of trading in stocks and shares in Japan. In fact, having not realized the sort of IPO explosion that Nasdaq US expected, it pulled out of Nasdaq Japan only after a couple of years, and the Osaka Stock Exchange came to the rescue to host the exchange as Hercules from December 2002.

The markets picked up somewhat since then, so that at the end of 2004, there were a total of 3728 listed companies in Japan, of which 1595 were in Tokyo Stock

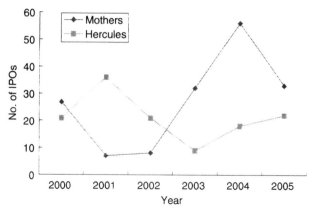

Figure 14.2 Number of IPOs in Japan's new stock exchanges

Sources: Websites of Tokyo Stock Exchange Mothers, and Osaka Stock Exchange Hercules.

Exchange (TSE) First Section, 559 in TSE Second Section, and 123 in TSE Mothers. By the end of 2005, there were a total of 150 listed companies in TSE Mothers, and 127 listed companies in Hercules. The sectoral distribution of these firms is quite similar in the two exchanges, with Information and Communication accounting for around 40% of total firms, and Services accounting for just under 30%. Of the total trading value at the two exchanges in 2004, around 80% were accounted for by individual investors, a markedly different feature from the established trading pattern (cf. only 28% in TSE First Section is by individual investors).

Table 14.1 shows the population of IPO companies at the end of June 2001, namely 55 firms in Nasdaq Japan, 31 in TSE Mothers Market, and 131 in JASDAQ. (JASDAQ as a whole was a much bigger market, but we counted only the IPOs that took place during the period December 1999 and June 2001 to provide a fair comparison with the other two marketplaces.) Total market capitalization of the three markets put together is ¥278.1 billion in 2000. The average size of the firm is quite large, ranging from 113 employees in the TSE Mothers market to 373 in the JASDAQ market. Notably, not many IPOs are start-ups as such; the average time period elapsed between the establishment of the firm and the IPO date was eight years in the Mothers Market, 14 years in Nasdaq Japan, and 28 years in JASDAQ.

One reason for the slow growth of these new exchanges generally, and the fact that IPOs were by relatively mature companies, is the nature of funding available to start-ups before they can list. Venture capital is growing but is only gradually converting from being part of the bank-based financial system to being more part of an equity-based financing system. In Japan, private venture capital grew in three phases, starting in the early 1970s when eight banks and securities houses were inspired by an earlier venture boom in the US to establish venture capital affiliates. They included JAFCO set up by Nomura Securities, Nihon Investment

Table 14.1 Characteristics of IPO Companies in Japan

	Nasdaq Japan	TSE Mothers	JASDAQ
Market opened	June 2000	December 1999	1983
No. of IPOs (as of June 30, 2001)	55	33	92*
Total capitalization 2000** (billion yen)	63.5	144.3	70.3
Employees (average per firm)	341	113	373
Average years elapsed from founding to IPO	13.7	7.4	28
Location clustering:			
No. with HQs in Tokyo	37	25	40
% located in Tokyo	(67)	(76)	(43)

Notes: * From 1 June, 2000 to 30 June, 2001 only; ** fiscal year ending in 2000 (1999–2000).

Finance set up by Daiwa Securities, and Nippon Enterprise Development (now NED) set up by Long Term Credit Bank of Japan. But soon after they were formed, the first oil shock led to a recession, forcing them to diversify into other forms of financial activity including straight lending (Clark 1987: 42). After the second oil crisis, a second phase of growth in the 1980s saw banks, securities, trading companies, regional banks and insurance companies establish their VC subsidiaries.

In the third phase in the early 1990s, venture capital funding has grown in size, preceding the timing of the legalization of stock options for all firms in 1997, the establishment of the Tokyo Stock Exchange Mothers Market and Nasdaq Japan in 1999 and 2000 respectively, and the growth of Internet-related firms. Despite the creation of these new stock markets, venture capital investment sum declined, down to an annual flow of ¥230 billion ($2 billion) (during FY 2000) and a total investment balance of ¥815.5 billion ($7.3 billion) (as of June 2000) (VEC 2001).

The Japanese venture capital industry remains highly concentrated. In the late 1990s, 64% of venture capital firms were subsidiaries of banks, securities and insurance companies, while only 12% were independent venture capitalists (Nakagawa 1999). The top four—Softbank Investment Corp., JAFCO, NIF Ventures Co. and Worldview Technology Venture Capital—accounted for 50% of total value invested in FY 1999. There are no more than 200 venture capital firms in Japan as compared to 700+ in the US, but the industry concentration at the top and the fact that the Japanese venture capital industry is only 6% of the US industry size mean that the rest of the Japanese industry is extremely fragmented.

Gompers and Lerner (1999, 2001) employ the notion of a "venture capital cycle" with three phases, namely fundraising, investing, and exiting. The following describes the slow pace of conversion in each stage of this cycle, using data from the Venture Enterprise Centre (VEC) in Japan.

Fundraising: Sources of Funds

Venture capital organizations raise money from individuals and institutions for investment in early-stage businesses that offer high potential but also high risk. In the US context, venture capitalists are financial intermediaries for external investors who prefer not to invest directly in entrepreneurial firms. Venture capital organizations are typically limited partnerships formed by several partners and associates. For each investment project, a venture capital fund is set up also as a limited partnership, with the venture capitalists acting as general partners and the outside investors as limited partners. Amongst the outside investors, pension funds, wealthy individuals, and endowments (through foundations) play a major part, each accounting for just over a fifth of total committed funds in the US (see Figure 14.3a).

In Japan, the distribution of sources of funds is quite different. For venture capital funds newly formed between July 1999 and June 2000, the sources of funds were: insurance companies/banks 32.1%, corporations 20.5%, pension funds 5.8%, venture capital 6.5%, individuals 6.1%, foreign investors and others 28.7% (see Figure 14.3b). As compared to funds formed in earlier periods (Nakagawa 1999: 9), insurance companies/banks continue to play a major role, but the role of corporations has declined, while foreign investors have increased in importance. Pension funds were non-existent until the mid-1990s, but constitute a small but significant presence by the late 1990s.

Most Japanese venture capital organizations are joint stock companies. It was only in 1998 that the Japanese government enacted the Limited Partnership Act for Venture Capital Investment (*Toshi jigyo yugensekinin kumiai ho*), which defined the legal basis for the limited liability of non-general partners in venture capital funds. The partners, be they general or limited, however, are typically joint stock companies, such as bank subsidiaries, and not individuals as in the US case.

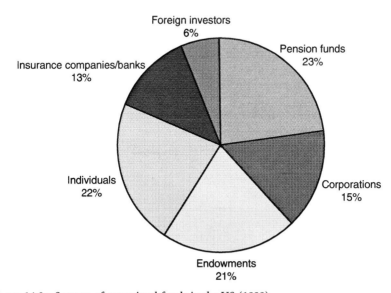

Figure 14.3a Sources of committed funds in the US (1999)

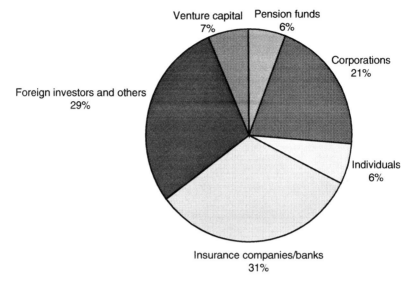

Figure 14.3b Venture capital funds newly formed in Japan (between July 1999 and June 2000)

This ownership pattern and organizational form in the Japanese venture capital industry have led to quite different modes of financing from the US mode. In particular, since the 1970s until well into the mid-1990s, Japanese venture capital firms had extended more loans than equity finance (see Figure 14.4). This is the legacy of the aforementioned attempt by early venture capital firms to survive the 1970s recession and more recently the early 1990s recession by engaging in straight lending. But a gradual conversion has been taking place since the late 1990s, preceding but continuing after the 1998 legal change mentioned above. In particular, whereas in 1990, 65% of venture capital came from loans, by 2003, less than 1% was. During the same period, the proportion of investment committed through venture capital funds rather than through own accounts (i.e. without syndication) increased from 9% to 56% (see Figure 14.3). One of the most visible signs of institutional conversion taking place in Japanese venture capital is this move towards syndicated investment funds.

Venture Investing

In the US, venture capitalists decide to invest in only a handful of entrepreneurial ventures selected from hundreds of proposals that they receive every year. Once an investment decision is made, a number of mechanisms are put in place to deal with agency problems that occur between the venture capitalist and its portfolio company. They include the syndication of investments, staging of the commitment of capital made contingent on achieving certain intermediate targets, and an active involvement of venture capitalists in the running of portfolio companies

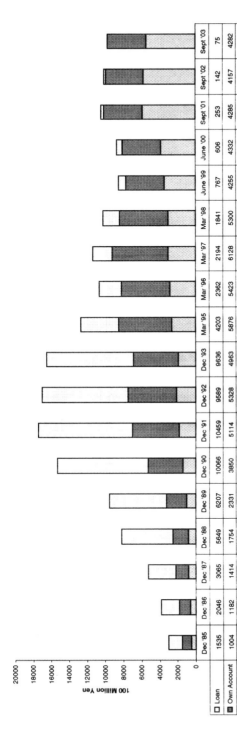

	Dec '85	Dec '86	Dec '87	Dec '88	Dec '89	Dec '90	Dec '91	Dec '92	Dec '93	Mar '95	Mar '96	Mar '97	Mar '98	June '99	June '00	Sept '01	Sept '02	Sept '03
Loan	1535	2046	3065	5649	6207	10066	10459	9589	9636	4203	2362	2194	1841	767	606	253	142	75
Own Account	1004	1182	1414	1754	2331	3850	5114	5328	4963	5876	5423	6128	5300	4255	4332	4285	4157	4282
VC Fund	524	625	825	822	967	1419	1876	2167	1978	2655	2835	3065	3092	3502	3824	5869	5820	5437

Figure 14.4 Venture capital investment and loans outstanding in Japan

Note: No data exists for 1994 because the data collection date changed from December to March.

Source: VEC various years.

often by demanding a seat on the board of directors. Venture capital firms also tend to specialize in a particular industry or a specific stage of development (e.g. early stage) in order to ease the monitoring problem. Consequently, on average, a venture capitalist commits relatively large sums of money to a small number of companies: for instance in 1997, US venture capitalists invested $4.7 million on average per portfolio company and in a total of 1298 new companies (according to the National Venture Capital Association, as quoted by EPA (2000: 232)).

In Japan, many more new ventures (2672 in 1997) receive venture capital investment, but net new investment per portfolio firm is on average about a tenth of the US sum (¥45 million, or approximately $450,000). This thinly spread nature of venture capital investment in Japan is both a manifestation and a cause of "arms-length" rather than "hands-on" involvement of venture capital firms in their portfolio firms. Until August 1995, the anti-trust law in Japan prohibited venture capital investors from taking board seats at the companies in which they have invested. But even with this prohibition lifted, it is often said that Japanese venture capital firms generally do not have the expertise to monitor and manage their portfolio companies closely. Moreover, syndication has played only a minor part in Japan until recently, and therefore risk-spreading in venture capital loans and "own account" investment has taken place by thinly spreading investment in many portfolio companies.

There is also little evidence of specialization by venture capital firms in Japan, either by sector or stage of investment. First, the sectoral distribution of venture capital investment is quite spread out, with non-high tech sectors receiving a significant proportion of funds. In the second half of the 1990s, venture capital investment directed towards the IT sector (including Internet, computers, telecommunications and semiconductor) grew to 50% of the total investment value, while biotechnology accounted for 3.8% of total investment. This indicates that venture capital is flowing into sectors without the sort of high-risk high-return characteristics that make venture capital the sole viable source of financing. Second, most Japanese venture capital firms provide funds for all stages; only a small proportion of funds goes into early stage financing. According to the 2001 VEC survey, only a few percentage points of total venture capital investment is made to support the establishment of new ventures, while around half of the total investment value is committed to ventures within five years of establishment; this implies that the other half is allocated to portfolio firms with a track record of five years or longer.

All these features of investment taken together mean that in Japan, many of the agency problems noted by Sahlman (1990) are not addressed. It is often pointed out that bank subsidiary venture capital firms make conservative investment decisions, because they obtain investing capital from their parent company and use the same sort of criteria for investment decision as for advancing loans with collateral.

Exiting

Venture capitalists need to turn illiquid stakes in private portfolio companies into realized returns. They can do so by "exiting" an investment in a number of ways, including mergers and leveraged buy-outs, but the route that has received the greatest attention because of the high return it brings, is an initial public offering (IPO). In the US, the proportion of all IPOs that are backed by venture capitalists rose from under 10% in the 1980s to about 31% in the 1990s (Gompers and Lerner 2001: 159). Gompers and Lerner also report an empirical study that found that US venture capitalists hold significant equity stakes in the firms they take public (all venture investors hold on average 34% stake immediately prior to the IPO) and control about a third of the board seats.

Until recently, it was virtually unthinkable for young ventures to go public in Japan because of strict listing requirements. As a result, venture capital firms operated in Japan without completing the venture capital cycle in the way that Gompers and Lerner envisaged. Instead, Japanese venture capital firms have realized gains mainly from interest payments on loans and normal returns on investment. But the opening of the Market for High Growth and Emerging Stocks (Mothers) at the Tokyo Stock Exchange in December 1999 and Nasdaq Japan at the Osaka Stock Exchange in June 2000 made a step change in this situation. Moreover, the Japanese government has been the main agent of institutional change, legislating for the 1995 revision of the anti-trust law that permits venture capital investors to take board seats at portfolio companies, the 1997 legalization of stock options for all companies, and the 1998 Limited Partnership Act for Venture Capital Investment.

To summarize, prior to the 1990s, the US–Japanese difference was "so great that some American venture capitalists would probably deny that the Japanese were involved in venture capital at all" (Clark 1987: 46). However, the demonstration effect of the dot.com boom in the US, and the private intervention by Nasdaq US and Softbank, followed by state action, led to a step change in the rules for new companies to go public in 1999 and 2000. However, the layering of new stock exchanges onto a bank-based system met with slow growth, in part due to the absence of supply of mobile labor (scientists from universities, professional services experts in law, finance, etc.) as a complementary institution, and in part due to the slow conversion of the Japanese venture capital industry through legal and other changes. However, the institutional conversion, with VCs turning away from loans towards syndicated investment funds, took off slowly but surely in the late 1990s. Thus, while it is too early to pronounce the mutually fueling effect of new stock exchanges and venture capital in Japan, at least we observe a case of "layered" institutional change in the Japanese financial markets.

14.2.2 Shunto Comes to Acquiesce Labor Market Diversity (Including Layering of Temporary Work)

Since the late 1990s, labor markets in Japan have become decisively more diverse and flexible, due in part to a number of changes in the law as well as in corporate strategy. Non-regular employees increased from 20.2% of the Japanese workforce in 1990 to 29.8% in 2002, and to 31.4% in 2004 (JILPT 2005: 33). In 2002, 12.6

million were part-time workers, while 2.13 million were temporary workers (Sato 2005). Of the latter, 1.79 million were "dispatched workers" (*haken rodosha*), dispatched from labor placement agencies (Morishima and Shimanuki 2005: 80).[1] In fact, the number of dispatched workers quadrupled in a decade, from 437,000 in 1994 to 1.99 million in 2003 (JILPT 2005: 37).

As in the previous discussion on venture capital and new stock exchanges, this sub-section explains the timing of labor market diversity in the late 1990s as a combination of conversion and layering of institutions in labor markets. In particular, Shunto went through a process of conversion towards new goals and functions, while exit-based temporary work—in the form of agency labor and on-site contracting—became superimposed as a new layer onto a voice-based employment system. The extent to which diversity in employment patterns might grow and stay as a long-term feature of the emergent Japanese system depends on how these two modes of institutional change—conversion and layering—plays out in the near future. The following describes the conversion of Shunto, followed by the layering of temporary work.

Shunto—the Spring Offensive—is a highly coordinated annual wage bargaining round, and is regarded as a functional equivalent of an incomes policy that contributed to the competitiveness of the Japanese economy. As the name indicates, Shunto started in 1955 when radical union leaders sought greater solidarity in bargaining, in order to overcome the shortcomings of enterprise unions (see Sako 1997 for details). Nevertheless, formal negotiations and settlements over pay and bonus take place at the decentralized level of the enterprise, leading some writers such as Calmfors and Driffil (1988) to classify the Japanese bargaining structure as one of the most decentralized in the world.

Such characterization, however, missed the key mechanisms of information sharing and coordination that ensured that Shunto settlements were compatible with good macro-economic performance and superior international competitiveness. First, at the national level, the two peak organizations, Rengo (Japanese Trade Union Confederation) and Nikkeiren (Japan Federation of Employers Association, now merged with Keidanren (Japan Federation of Economic Organizations) to become Nippon Keidanren), engage the government and the public in a debate on what pay increases Japan can afford. The resulting white papers that Rengo and Nikkeiren separately issue lay down "guidelines" for the percentage increase in wage demand and offer that they respectively perceive to be compatible with macro-economic forecasts for growth and inflation.

Second, private sector unions and leading companies in export-oriented manufacturing sectors take a lead in Shunto discussion. Unions and companies in an exposed export-oriented sector have greater incentives than those in a protected sector to be concerned about international competitiveness. Oligopolistic employers in key sectors such as steel, shipbuilding, electrical machinery, and

---

[1] Original statistical sources are *Rodoryoku Tokubetsu Chosa* (Special Labour Force Survey) and *Shugo Keitai no Tayouka ni Kansuru Sogo Jittai Chosa* (General Survey on the Diversification of Employment Status), both conducted by the Japanese Ministry of Health, Labour and Welfare.

automobiles, meet frequently not only to exchange information about their respective bargaining situation but also to agree on a specific settlement offer. At the same time, unions in the same key sectors, formally part of IMF-JC (International Metalworkers Federation—Japan Council), are pattern setters. The union leaders met to determine a specific settlement figure and generally succeeded in sticking to the agreed rate. Deviation from the agreed rate was considered impossible and a treacherous act if such deviation occurred without formal approval of the industry federation's Shunto committee.

Third, pay settlements are highly synchronized, thus eliminating the possibility of wage leapfrogging. Spring became the timing of pay settlements because new recruits start on April 1 in Japan after the academic year comes to an end in March. Over the decades, synchronization in settlement dates became more and more marked. Particularly after 1975, all key IMF-JC unions have settled on the same date, which was March 24 in 1994 for example. Other sectors settle soon thereafter, so that most settlements are completed before the summer.

Fourth, wage settlement norms diffuse in an orderly fashion from the private sector to the public sector, from leading pattern-setting sectors to follower sectors, from large to small firms, and from corporate headquarters to subsidiaries and affiliates. The social order roughly corresponding to all these dimensions is clearly not just a ranking according to the company's ability to pay, but the ranking according to the prestige of companies. Consequently, through employer coordination within corporate groups, mirrored by union coordination within *roren* federations, the focal union and the focal firm always settle first before any of the affiliates and suppliers can settle by taking account of the focal settlement.

Such diffusion mechanism is important to the extent that Shunto acts as a functional equivalent of encompassing organizations (in Olson's sense (Olson 1982)) in an age of declining union density from 34% in the mid-1970s to less than 20% by 2005. Encompassing organizations police free riders and provide members with incentives to internalize externalities (here in the form of wage-push inflation). The Olsonian logic of collective action works along three channels: first, through the organized business interests at the national and industry levels; second, through organized labor articulated from national, industry, down to enterprise levels; and third, through the institutional nexus between labor and product markets in bargaining within the corporate group. Employer coordination within corporate groups is mirrored by union coordination within *roren* federations. Specifically, labor costs are reflected in the prices of intermediate goods. Thus, affiliated suppliers' wage settlements affect the price competitiveness of the focal firm.

It is in this institutional context with a prevailing social norm of "equal pay increases for companies of equal prestige" that we examine greater dispersion in Shunto bargaining outcomes in the 1990s and the early 2000s. The Ministry of Health and Labour (MHL) conducts an annual economy-wide survey of just over 3000 firms employing 100 or more workers. The survey shows a gradual increase in the dispersion of wage settlements in the 1990s, with a marked jump in the dispersion index since 1998 (see Figure 14.5). Although it is not possible to

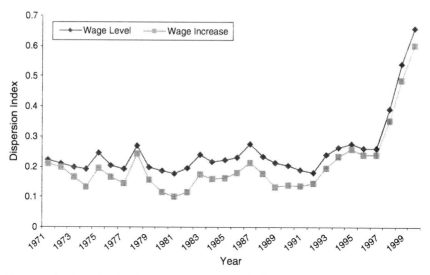

Figure 14.5 Dispersion in Shunto wage settlements in Japan

Note: Dispersion Index = $(3^{rd}$ quartile – 1st quartile$)/(2 \times$ average$)$.
Source: MHLW various years.

distinguish, in this economy-wide picture, as between dispersion within and across industries, there is evidence elsewhere that dispersion in settlements has increased within a sector such as the automobile industry in the late 1990s (Sako 2006b).

The same MHL survey reveals the reasons behind greater dispersion. This shows the increasing importance of "company performance" (i.e. the ability to pay) as a determinant in Shunto wage settlements from the employers' perspective (see Figure 14.5). Given greater within-sector variations in corporate performance, as signified by the different fortunes of Toyota and Nissan in the 1990s, it is not surprising that this factor alone has made settlement coordination more difficult. Price inflation, which was once a significant determinant after the 1973 oil shock, declined in importance to the extent that it is not an issue for most employers since the deflationary 1990s. "Social norm," i.e. setting wages according to the going rate that is seen to be socially acceptable, has risen in importance in the late 1980s and early 1990s, but has declined since. Nevertheless, comparing Figure 14.4 which shows a sudden jump in dispersion since 1998 and Figure 14.6 which shows a more gradual increase in the importance of "company performance" since 1992, it appears that the slow conversion of Shunto from a coordinated wage hike to a mechanism for legitimizing pay restraint and dispersion coincided with other types of institutional change.

Perhaps the most tangible would be labor law reforms, but the relevant ones did not come into effect until after 2000. In 2003, for example, the Labour Standards Law was revised to reassert employers' right to dismiss based on "objectively reasonable" grounds (Nakakubo 2004). Also in 2004, agency labor, hitherto prohibited in manufacturing settings, became legal (Kimura et al. 2004).

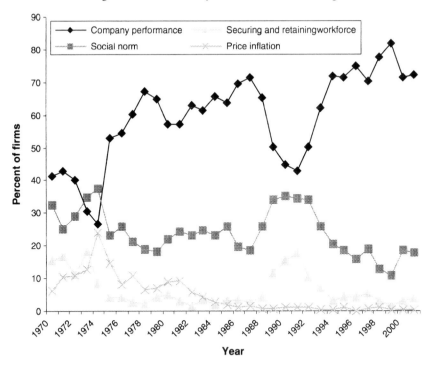

Figure 14.6 The most important factor in settling pay during Shunto negotiations

Source: MHLW (various years).

By contrast, the use of diverse forms of employment had started earlier, and these legal changes might be regarded in part as a response to employer demand for temporary placement agencies and on-site contracting. These have become layered onto the norm of lifetime employment. Thus, while part-timers and other types of non-regular workers were in use in earlier periods, the period after the late 1990s is marked by the greater use of different types of contingent workers. Whereas in the past, these non-regular workers were hired as a buffer to cope with cyclical fluctuations in demand, the prolonged recession of the 1990s has encouraged firms to use them on a continuous basis to reduce personnel costs and to turn fixed costs into variable costs (Denki Soken 1998; Chubu Sanseiken 2004). Competition from China has put extra pressure on Japanese firms to make greater efforts towards cost reduction. This also means that the recent wider use of contingent labor is prevalent on the manufacturing shopfloor, whereas the services sector (especially retailing) has had a more long-standing practice of incorporating part-time and temporary workers in their operations. Even in manufacturing, however, there are as many workplaces where regular and non-regular workers are doing the same tasks as workplaces where the two are clearly separated (Sato et al 2004: 81).

In Japan, workers who are not on a regular full-time contract are collectively known as atypical workers (*hi tenkei rodosha*). What is "atypical" or "non-standard" depends on country-specific notions of "typical" or "standard" employment (Ogura 2005). In Japan, "atypical" refer to workers who are not in full-time employment with an indefinite contract length. However, implicit in the notion of "lifetime employment" is the absence of restrictions placed on job scope and workplace location (Sato and Sano 2005: 44). In theory, therefore, "typical" employees would have no restriction on either, while "atypical" workers would have limited job scope and no expectation of re-location. In reality, however, increasingly, regular contracts have come to impose restrictions on workplace location or job scope, thus blurring at the margin the boundary of what is a typical and what is an atypical employment contract.

Despite the problem that this fact causes for data, the existing government statistics (Labour Force Survey) show clearly that the proportion of atypical workers in the total employee workforce increased from 20.2% in 1990 to 32.3% in 2005. A 1999 Survey on the Diversification of Employment Status, undertaken by the Japanese Ministry of Health, Labour and Welfare, found that 27.5% of the Japanese employee workforce were atypical, and of those, three-quarters were part-time workers, 8.4% were "professional contract workers," 6.7% were "temporary workers," and 3.9% were "dispatched workers" (dispatched from labor placement agencies) (Sato et al. 2003).

In response to employer demand, changes in labor law are likely to lead to even greater use of specific types of contingent workers. First, the 2003 revision of the Labour Standards Law extended the maximum length of fixed-term contracts from one year to three years, and this is likely to increase the use of fixed term employees (*kikankou*). At Toyota, for example, the number of fixed term employees increased from 3140 in 2000, to 9520 in 2004, constituting 25% of the total shopfloor workforce (Chubu Sanseiken 2004: 50). At the 44 supplier companies surveyed by Chubu Sanseiken, the proportion of non-standard workers to total workforce ranged from 9% to 80%. At one extreme, 6 out of the 44 suppliers had 50% or more of their workforce on non-standard contracts (Chubu Sanseiken 2004: 1). Similarly at Nissan Oppama Factory, 20% of a total of 2560 shopfloor workers were on fixed term contracts in 2003; Calsonic-Kansei's cockpit assembly line inside Oppama Factory was operated totally by a team of 35 temporary workers.[2]

Second, the 2004 revision of the Labour Dispatching Law (*haken ho*) lifted the prohibition of the use of agency labor in production areas. Before the prohibition was lifted, on-site contractors (*kounai ukeoi*)—who must provide machinery and equipment as well as supervision of labor—came to occupy manufacturing areas where employers would have preferred to hire agency labor. They are concentrated in electronic components manufacturing, automobile assembly and parts manufacturing, and telecommunications equipment (Sato et al. 2004: 30). However, agency labor is replacing on-site contractors in production areas where employers prefer direct supervision. On-site contractors are therefore being

---

[2] Factory visit by the author as part of the International Motor Vehicle Program (IMVP) plant tour, September 10, 2003.

forced to rethink their business strategy, by diversifying into labor placement agency business or by focusing on more specialist high skill tasks (Kimura et al. 2004; Fujimoto and Kimura 2005).

A wider use of contingent labor in the name of greater numerical flexibility and labor cost reduction has potentially adverse implications for work organization and industrial relations. At the level of work organization, there is a view that due to labor turnover, contingent workers cannot be expected to be as multi-skilled and problem-solving oriented as regular workers, thus making it more difficult to accumulate and transfer know-how and capability on the shopfloor. Perhaps a more immediate impact in the same direction is brought about by an increased burden on regular employees to train and supervise contingent workers (Sato et al. 2004: 100). At the level of labor–management relations, enterprise unions are "hollowed out" in two senses (Chubu Sanseiken 2004: 84). First, unless enterprise unions change their policy to exclude contingent workers from membership, a group of workers with whom the union has no contact will grow. Second, if management ignores or simply informs unions on hiring contingent workers, unions' bargaining power and voice will become weaker.

In summary, in the late 1990s, Shunto settlements have become more dispersed, revealing Shunto's conversion from an institution of coordinated pay bargaining to one acquiescing wage restraint, pay dispersion, and diverse forms of employment. Japan always had a core-periphery dual labor market, and non-regular workers had always been exempt from the Shunto norm. Nevertheless, the layering of temporary work, in the form of agency labor and on-site contracting, has become much more significant and spread to manufacturing, seriously threatening the institution of lifetime employment and enterprise unionism. Employment in Japan has become more diverse and more flexible with greater reliance on numerical rather than functional flexibility, but all in the name of paying utmost effort to making employment security for the core workforce a top priority. Nevertheless as the core of employees with secure employment and good pay diminishes over time, there would be at some stage a point at which a qualitative change would occur in the attitudes and motivation of workers as well as union leaders and managers.

14.3 DIVERSE FORMS OF IMPLEMENTING THE HOLDING COMPANY STRUCTURE

We now turn to corporate level action, to observe how agency at that level has had a hand in transforming institutions. We compare Softbank Group and NTT Group, a relatively new player contrasted to an old ex-monopoly of fixed-line telephone services. The comparison is centered around their role in bringing about institutional change and organizational diversity. In particular, both adopted a new form, the pure holding company structure, re-legalized in Japan in 1997, but to satisfy different ends. For Softbank, the pure holding company enabled it to build a *keiretsu*-like corporate group of start-up companies, in part to get around the constraint of a venture capitalist whose "exit" option was constrained. For NTT, the pure holding company was a political compromise, leading to a weak central management whose ability to introduce diversity within the corporate group was constrained by a strong union. Thus, the pure holding company structure was adopted to satisfy very different sets of goals in the two cases.

14.3.1 Softbank as a Political and Economic Entrepreneur

As mentioned earlier, the opening of Nasdaq Japan, with Softbank as a joint venture partner, represents a step change in the Japanese institutions surrounding business start-ups, and as such Softbank is a "political and economic entrepreneur" (North 1990). Softbank provides a case study of how firm-level action can lead not only to the transformation of national institutions, but also to the hybridization of business structure and strategy when working within the confines of slow-changing financial and labor market institutions.

Softbank is an archetypical business start-up, founded by a second-generation Korean Japanese in 1981. It grew rapidly from being a distributor of pre-packaged software to a Cyber Keiretsu (Whittington 2001: 106) or an Internet Zaibatsu (*Asahi Shinbun Weekly* 2000), with over 300 operating companies within two decades. The venture capital arm of Softbank Group is the largest venture capital provider in Japan, having overtaken JAFCO in ranking. By March 2001, Softbank has invested nearly ¥700 billion (US$6 billion) as venture capital in 531 start-ups, of which around 100 are located in Japan and the rest concentrated in the US: In total 32 out of the 531 have had an IPO.

However, Softbank as a venture capitalist has not had the same opportunity for an "exit option" as its North American counterparts. Consequently, in part by choice and in part due to this constraint, Softbank Group is not only a joint venture partner to the Japanese operations of Yahoo!, Nasdaq, E*Trade, Morningstar, but has pressed on with an expansionary "empire building" by retaining many companies in the Group's portfolio. The outcome was the creation of a large holding company group structure, resembling traditional corporate groupings in Japan.

The empire building has necessitated putting in place an elaborate organization structure. Within the domestic market in 1996, there was only Softbank Inc, the software distribution business, and Yahoo! Japan. By 2000, there were more than 100 operating companies in the Softbank Group. Softbank adopted in October 1999 a three-tier organization structure with a slim pure holding company employing 60 workers at the apex. It focuses on establishing a strategy for the Group as a whole, developing new business areas, and utilizing the tiered structure to manage and align the direction of each Group company. The middle-tier consists of seven key consolidated divisions, namely e-Finance, e-Commerce, Media & Marketing, Technology Services, Internet Infrastructure, Broadmedia, and Internet Culture, apart from global operations. At first, the middle-tier was intended to be product divisions, each with authority to establish strategy for its respective business domains. Nevertheless, by May 2000, Softbank decided to develop five of the seven divisions into "operational holding companies" publicly quoted in their own right: they are namely Softbank Finance, Softbank E-Commerce, Softbank Media & Marketing, Softbank Networks, and Softbank Broadmedia. In effect, a pure holding company oversees a group of operational holding companies, each responsible for raising their own finance to enable rapid business expansion (*Nikkei*, 26 May 2000).

The long tail of joint venture firms within the Softbank Group necessitates building an open architecture for the management of employees. In mid-2000, Softbank Group probably employed around 2000 workers. But it was only in August 2000 that the pure holding company instituted a system for the middle tier operational holding companies to report their workforce size. Such reporting is, however, not straightforward for the following reasons. At the operating company level, there are a variety of forms of employment, including the use of agency labor. Moreover, in joint venture companies, the employment status of joint venture managers, as to which of the JV partner is the employer, may be left undefined. Typically, it is the middle-tier operational holding companies that provide some managerial labor for new ventures. Essential expertise in financing and substantive business operations for Softbank Group ultimately comes from mid-career hiring from existing established businesses. In particular, the middle-tier holding companies hire mid-career employees for their management team, employ them for no more than 3 months, and send them out to manage newly established operating companies.

14.3.2 NTT Group[3]

NTT was privatized in 1985, and by the 1990s was pursuing a strategy of product diversification in response to technological change, deregulation, competition in global markets, and the growing importance of stock markets. It transformed itself from being primarily a fixed line telephone carrier to a telecoms group incorporating various branches of the information services industry.

Since 1999, the NTT Group has been structured around a pure holding company that controls seven key operating companies. These are NTT East and NTT West (both in fixed line business which is regulated by the government); NTT Communications (IP integration and networks); NTT Data (data communication); NTT DoCoMo (mobile communications); NTT Facilities (design, construction, and maintenance services); and NTT Comware (software). The first three were established in 1999, while the other companies were created in the late 1980s and early 1990s. The fixed line telephone business accounted for 48% of NTT Group sales in 2002, split across two regional companies (NTT East and NTT West) and one long-distance company (NTT Communications). Mobile telephone service takes up a significant part of the remaining sales, with

---

[3] See Sako and Jackson (2006) for further details.

NTT DoCoMo accounting for 41% of total group sales. Remaining sales are in various IT related fields.

The process of privatization and market liberalization involved political contestation over the strategy and structure of the former telecom monopolies. Ever since the 1985 privatization, NTT resisted the Japanese government's pressure toward an American Bell system type of break up that would separate NTT into separate regional firms (Zendentsu 1997). The holding company structure emerged as a face-saving political compromise in 1999. Politics thus explains the somewhat weak role of the NTT holding company, which only loosely coordinates investment within the NTT group and has not been able to hinder competition among group firms in new areas of business such as Internet service provision.

These changes in the strategy and structure of NTT created substantial pressures to adopt more diverse human resource systems within their corporate groups. The NTT Group has undertaken business diversification into new areas at the same time as drastically reducing employment in its older fixed line businesses. The workforce was halved from 300,000 to 150,000 in the period following privatization. However, the NTT Group maintained a uniform group-wide human resource system and relied on internal employment adjustment.

The political pressure for decentralization was great at NTT and weakened the capacity for centralized corporate strategy. Nevertheless, the NTT union maintained, until 2001, a centralized collective agreement, and made sure that the human resource system remained uniform within the corporate group. Diversity in employment conditions was introduced, however, through a number of measures to reduce costs by ¥110 billion at NTT East and ¥155 billion at NTT West in 2002/3. They included a reduction in various benefits, performance-related pay, early retirement, and the creation of 100 outsourcing companies, to which nearly 60,000 employees were transferred in May 2002. Employees aged 50 or over were asked to take early retirement, and be re-employed by the new companies at a wage up to 30% lower than in their previous jobs. The union started by negotiating for no pay cut, but ended up agreeing to the 15–30% wage reduction, with some lump-sum payment at the point of transfer to ease the pain of adjustment. These employees are doing the same job (in sales, maintenance, etc.) as before, but with pay reductions of up to 30%. This is the cost of treating employment security as the top priority under all circumstances, as both management and labor shun the use of compulsory redundancy.

14.4 IMPLICATIONS AND CONCLUSION

This chapter analyzed how institutional change is related to organizational diversity, and presented evidence from financial and labor markets in Japan. In order to do so, the analysis used a model of incremental institutional change based on Streeck and Thelen (2005), to examine what a shift from a coordinated market economy (CME) to a liberal market economy (LME) implies for organizations. Organizational diversity increases as a result of shifting from CME to LME, due to three things: (a) the specific characteristics of LME which requires less sunk cost in developing institutions of collective action; (b) the mix in the modes of shift from CME and LME, such as layering and conversion; and (c) the degree of conflict of interest between labor and management and the resolution reached at the local level.

A fourth reason for organizational diversity is highlighted in our comparison of how company-level action impacts on national institutional change. The introduction of the pure holding company form faced experimentation, and is being adopted in different ways by various companies to satisfy their own ends. In particular, Softbank not only created a new institution in the form of Nasdaq Japan, but also adopted the pure holding company structure to overcome the absence of a realistic "exit option" for venture capitalists. NTT also adopted the holding company structure but for a different reason, namely as a political compromise, and greater diversity in its internal labor markets, subverting the norm of lifetime employment, has been slowly introduced despite union resistance.

In financial markets, venture capital in Japan experienced "conversion"— shifting its goals and functions from being part of the Japanese institution of relational banking towards being more part of an equity-based finance system. New stock exchanges were created, but are layered and not directly threatening existing institutions of relational banking and stock exchanges for established public corporations. Nevertheless, the layering of the new stock exchanges and legal changes triggered a slow process of conversion in venture capital.

In labor markets, Shunto is portrayed as a case of "conversion," with its function changing from coordinated pay bargaining to a mechanism for legitimizing pay restraint and dispersion. At the same time, contingent work was identified as a case of "layering" onto the norm of lifetime employment. Although the Japanese economy had always had a dual labor market, legal changes and practices that fueled the use of agency labor and on-site contracting in manufacturing threatens the norm of lifetime employment more fundamentally than in earlier periods. Nevertheless, unlike in financial markets, in which layering triggered conversion, layering and conversion in labor markets have been much more drawn out and interactive throughout the 1990s.

In all these cases, we do not know the extent to which "layering" may eventually lead to displacement of the old by the new institution, and the extent to which "conversion" may lead to exhaustion and disappearance of an institution. Moreover, this study only implied, but did not examine, the extent to which the impact of institutional reform in financial markets depends on institutional arrangements in labor markets, and vice versa. Instead, the chapter focused on empirically demonstrating that within each sphere of the Japanese business system, institutional interaction varies in its effect on organizational diversity.

REFERENCES

Amable, B. (2003). *The Diversity of Modern Capitalism*. Oxford: Oxford University Presss.

Aoki, M. (2001). *Toward a Comparative Institutional Analysis*. Cambridge, MA: MIT Press.

—— (2004). 'Schumpeterian Innovation of Institution,' The Tenth Conference of the International Schumpeter Society, Milan, Italy, June 10.

Calmfors, L. and J. Driffil (1988). 'Bargaining Structure, Corporatism, and Macroeconomic Performance,' *Economic Policy*, 6: 13–61.

Chubu Sanseiken (2004). *Rodoryoku Tayouka no nakade no Atarashii Hatarakikata* (New Modes of Working in the midst of Labor Force Diversification: Co-existence with Non-standard Workers). Toyota City: Chubu Sanseiken.

Clark, R. (1987). *Venture Capital in Britain, America and Japan*. London: Croom Helm.

Denki Soken (1998). *Denki Sangyo ni okeru Gyomu Ukeoi Tekiseika to Kaisei Hakenho eno Taio no Kadai: Denki Sangyo ni okeru Ukeoi Katsuyo no Kittai ni Kansuru Chosa Hokokusho* (Standardization of On-Site Contracting in Electric Machinery Industry and Responding to the Revision of the Worker Dispatching Law: Report on the Survey on Utilization of Contract Workers in the Electric Machinery Industry). Tokyo: Denki Soken.

DiMaggio, P. J. and W. W. Powell (eds.) (1991). *The New Institutionalism in Organizational Analysis*. Chicago: University of Chicago Press.

Dore, R. (2000). *Stock Market Capitalism: Welfare Capitalism*. Oxford: Oxford University Press.

EPA (Economic Planning Agency) (2000). *Keizai Hakusho*, Economic White Paper. Tokyo: Okurasho Insatsukyoku.

Fukimoto, M. and T. Kimura (2005). 'Business Strategy and Human Resource Management at Contract Companies in the Manufacturing Sector,' *Japan Labor Review*, 2(2): 104–22.

Gompers, P. and J. Lerner (1999). *The Venture Capital Cycle*. Cambridge, MA: MIT Press.

—— —— (2001). 'The Venture Capital Revolution,' *Journal of Economic Perspectives*, 15(2): 145–68.

Greenwood, R. and C. R. Hinings (1996). 'Understanding Radical Organizational Change: Bringing Together the Old and the New Institutionalism,' *Academy of Management Review*, 21(4): 1022.

Hall, P. and D. Soskice (eds.) (2001). *Varieties of Capitalism*. New York: Oxford University Press.

Hirschman, A. O. (1970). *Exit, Voice and Loyalty: Reponses to Decline in Firms, Organizations and States*. Cambridge, MA: Harvard University Press.

Hollingsworth, R. and R. Boyer (eds.) (1997). *Contemporary Capitalism: The Embeddedness of Institutions*. Cambridge: Cambridge University Press.

Jackson, G. (2005). 'Contested Boundaries: Ambiguity and Creativity in the Evolution of German Codetermination,' in W. Streeck and K. Thelen (eds.), *Beyond Continuity: Institutional Change in Advanced Political Economies*. Oxford: Oxford University Press.

JILPT (The Japanese Institute of Labour Policy and Training) (2005). *Japanese Working Life Profile 2005/2006*. Tokyo: JILPT.

Kimura, T., Y. Sano et al. (2004). 'Seizo Bunya ni okeru Ukeoi Kigyo no Jigyo Senryaku to Jinzai Kanri no Kadai' (Business Strategy and Human Resource Management for Onsite Sub-contracting Service in Manufacturing Industry), *Nihon Rodo Kyokai Zasshi*, 46(5): 16–30.

Milgrom, P. and J. Roberts (1995). 'Complementarities and Fit: Strategy, Structure and Organizational Change in Manufacturing,' *Journal of Accounting and Economics*, 19: 179–208.

MHLW (various years). *Chinage no Jittai (Report on Wage Increases)*. Tokyo: Okurasho Insatsukyoku.

Morishima, M. and T. Shimanuki (2005). 'Managing Temporary Workers in Japan,' *Japan Labor Review*, 2(2): 78–103.

Nakakubo, H. (2004). 'The 2003 Revision of the Labor Standards Law: fixed-term contracts, dismissal and discretionary work schemes,' *Japan Labor Review*, 1(2): 4–25.

Nakagawa, K. (1999). *Japanese Entrepreneurship: Can the Silicon Valley Model Be Applied to Japan?* Mimeo, Asia/Pasific Research Centre, Stanford University.

North, D. C. (1990). *Institutions, Institutional Change and Economic Performance*. Cambridge: Cambridge University Press.

Ogura, K. (2005). 'International Comparison of Atypical Employment: Differing Concepts and Realities in Industrialized Countries,' *Japan Labor Review*, 2(2): 5–29.

Oliver, C. (1992). 'The Antecedents of Deinstitutionalization,' *Organization Studies*, 13(4): 563–88.

Olson, M. (1982). *The Rise and Decline of Nations: Economic Growth, Stagflation and Social Rigidities*. New Haven: Yale University Press.

Sako, M. (1997). 'Shunto: the Role of Employer and Union Co-ordination,' in M. Sako and H. Sato (eds.), *Japanese Labour and Management in Transition*. London: Routledge.

—— (2003). 'Between Bit Valley and Silicon Valley: Hybrid Forms of Business Governance in the Japanese Internet Economy,' in B. Kogut (ed.), *The Global Internet Economy*. Cambridge, MA: MIT Press.

—— (2005). 'Does Embeddedness Imply Limits to Within-Country Diversity?' *British Journal of Industrial Relations*, 43(4): 585–92.

—— (2006a) 'Japanese Industrial Relations System in the Twenty-first Century: Diversity, Flexibility and Participation,' in T. Fujimoto et al. (eds.), *Readings in Japanese Enterprise System* (in Japanese). Tokyo: Yuhikaku.

—— (2006b) *Shifting Boundaries of the Firm: Japanese Company—Japanese Labour*. Oxford: Oxford University Press.

—— G. Jackson (2006) 'Strategy Meets Institutions: The Transformation of Labor–Management Relations at Deutsche Telekom and NTT,' *Industrial and Labor Relations Review* 13: 347–66.

Sahlman, W. A. (1990) 'The Structure and Governance of Venture-Capital Organizations,' *Journal of Financial Economics*, 27: 473–521.

Sato, A. and Sano, Y. (2005). 'Introduction: Diversification of Employment and Human Resource and Personnel Management Issues,' *Japan Labor Review*, 2(2): 2–4.

Sato, H., Y. Sano et al. (2003). *Dai ikkai Seisan Genba ni okeru Jonai Ukeoi no Katsuyo ni kansuru Chosa* (First Survey on the Use of Inside Contractors on the Production Shopfloor), SSJ Data Archive Research Paper Series. Tokyo: Institute of Social Science, University of Tokyo.

—— —— et al. (2004). *Seisan Genba ni okeru Gaibu Jinzai no Katsuyou to Jinzai Bijinesu* (Human Resource Management and the Staffing Business at Japanese Manufacturing Site Volume 1). Tokyo: Institute of Social Science, University of Tokyo.

Streeck, W. and K. Thelen (eds.) (2005). *Beyond Continuity: Institutional Change in Advanced Political Economies*. Oxford: Oxford University Press.

VEC (2001). *Annual Survey of Japanese Venture Capita Investments*. Tokyo: Venture Enterprise Centre.

Vogel, S. K. (2005). 'Routine Adjustment and Bounded Innovation: The Changing Political Economy of Japan,' in W. Streeck and K. Thelen (eds.), *Beyond Continuity: Institutional Change in Advanced Political Economies*. Oxford: Oxford University Press.

Westney, D. E. (1987). *Imitation and Innovation: The Transfer of Western Organizational Patterns to Meiji Japan*. Cambridge, MA: Harvard University Press.

Whitley, R. (1999). *Divergent Capitalisms*. Oxford: Oxford University Press.

Whittington, R. (2001). *What is Strategy?* 2nd edn. London: Thomson Learning.

Zendentsu (1997). *NTT Keiei Keitai Mondai to Zendentsu no Torikumi: Bunri Bunkatsu Hantai Undo Shoushi* (The Problem of NTT's Management Pattern and How Zendentsu Tackled it: A Short History of the Movement to Oppose Divestiture). Tokyo: Zendentsu.

15

Conclusion: Whither Japan's Corporate Governance?[1]

Masahiko Aoki

In retrospect, the early 1990s can be regarded as a threshold in the post-war history of Japan's political economy. In the political domain, the half-century-long, one-party rule of the Liberal Democratic Party (LDP) came to an end in 1993. By then it also became clear that the bubble in financial and real-estate markets had burst. These two events ushered in a period of unprecedented uncertainties, as well as various trials and errors in the polity and the economy in response to them. Economy-wise, this period is conventionally characterized as a prolonged deflationary phase[2] and many have blamed the faults of the macro-economic policy for the malaise. It became the fashion among the media, and even in academia, to dub the period a "lost decade," referring to the losses of wealth, growth potential, secure permanent-employment jobs and even social morale. Challenging this popular view, I have been maintaining for several years by now that the past decade may be more properly characterized as *a decade of flux*, meaning an unfinished period of institutional change.[3]

Underlying the apparent depression, competition among firms became keener during the period and managerial responses to the challenge of deflationary pressures, as well as the rise of industrial China, the IT revolution and so on, have steadily differentiated the better performers from the laggards and losers in the industry. Through this process, economic practices have been undergoing various changes of substantial magnitude. In the political domain, the LDP eventually returned to the position of ruling party in coalition with other parties, but the continuity of its power could no longer be taken for granted without electoral support. This competitive prospect in the polity has been bringing in gradual changes in the power structures of politicians and their relationships with various interest groups and bureaucrats.[4] These changes in the economic and

[1] I am grateful to Takao Kato, Curtis Milhaupt, and contributors to the book for useful suggestions and critical comments.

[2] This popular characterization is somewhat mistaken in that the Japanese economy actually registered a positive growth rate in the mid-1990s.

[3] A series of my essays on this view were collected in Aoki (2002).

[4] See Toya (2006) for an early account of this process.

political domains have been mutually reinforcing each other. Thus, I posit that although there may not have been any single event signaling a dramatic institutional change in either the political or economic domain, the cumulative effects of incremental changes are already substantial and irreversible. This evolutionary process is still ongoing and it's likely to continue for some time, even for another decade or more, for the reasons I will soon argue.

A corporate governance institution, roughly understood as the accepted rules of the game among the corporate stakeholders governing the corporation, is not an exception. In this domain as well, there have been changes in formal laws, practices, relationships with the polity, etc., so that the old rules of the game can no longer be taken for granted, but new rules are still being sought and are in the process of evolving. However, this may be a good time for us to take stock of the cumulative changes achieved so far, and examine their implications and prospects with the help of the factual information and empirical analysis that has been assembled in preceding chapters of this book, as well as the analytical tools developed in comparative institutional analysis. This "Conclusion" provides a tentative note in that direction.

It is composed as follows: section 15.1 provides some illustrative evidence of changes that are taking place in Japan's corporate landscape. However, without a certain conceptual framework, the anecdotal evidence alone may not be sufficient for us to infer whether Japan's corporate governance is making a substantive institutional transformation; and, if it is, in which direction. Therefore in the following two sections, we make a detour into theoretical discussions. First, we discuss how corporate governance can be generally understood as an institutional equilibrium and thus its change as an equilibrium shift. Second, we present four stylized analytical models of corporate governance and try to identify the conditions that could make respective models viable (i.e. institutionalized). Then in section 15.4 we return to the Japanese scene and examine the driving forces, as well as the historical constraints, of changes in the corporate landscape. By interpreting these factors in the light of previous theoretical discussion, the last section indicates that the nature of on-going institutional change in Japan's corporate governance can be interpreted as a possible transition from the traditional bank-oriented model to a hybrid model, which is built on the combination of managerial choice of a business model, employees' human assets, and stock market evaluations in a complementary manner. External monitoring by an informative stock market would help, if not exclusively, evaluate the value of the internal linkage between a managerial business model and associated specific human assets. Stock market signals summarize a variety of information, expectations and values prevailing in the economy. However, for effective corporate governance to be implemented, a further firm-specific mechanism is needed to translate those signals into a selection/replacement of management, whenever appropriate, which constitutes the core of corporate governance. In this regard, no single mechanism has emerged as a dominant pattern, but a variety of patterns seems to be evolving for reasons that will be discussed below.

15.1 CHANGING CORPORATE LANDSCAPE: ANECDOTAL EVIDENCE

In order to highlight the changes taking place in Japan's corporate landscape in the past decade or so, let us first quote the stylized features of the preceding system—which we will refer to as the *traditional J-system* for the sake of referential convenience.[5] They are:

- Top management (the representative directors) of the corporate firm was ranked as the pinnacle of the career ladder for its permanent employees. The Board of Directors, almost exclusively composed of insiders, functioned as a substructure of top management.
- One of the main objectives of management was to provide steadily growing benefits to its permanent employees in the form of seniority wages, promotion opportunities, bonus and severance payments, fringe benefits and so on, subject to a reasonable level of profits (the so-called "*J-firm*").
- The main bank was the major supplier of funds to the corporate firm. Other financial institutions and investors expected the main bank to be a principal monitor of the firm (the so-called "delegated monitoring"). The main bank did not overtly intervene with the management of firms in excellent/normal corporate-value state. But the control right was expected to shift to the main bank in a critical corporate-value state, which was to decide whether to bail out and restructure the firm at its own cost, or liquidate it (the so-called "contingent governance").
- The government regulated the banking industry to assure rents to individual banks according to their market shares. It also intervened, if necessary, to bail out financially distressed banks or arrange for their acquisition by healthier banks (the so-called "Convoy system"). More broadly, this system is embedded in the following unique political-economy institution.
- One-party rule by the LDP was taken for granted. Under such political stability, triadic coalitions among LDP politicians, interest groups and ministerial bureaucrats were formed in parallel along various industrial, occupational and professional lines to protect mutual vested interests of the incumbents. The mediation among these coalitions was struck by LDP leaders in cooperation with top bureaucrats of the Ministry of Finance (MOF) (the so-called "bureau-pluralism" or "compartmentalized pluralism").

The traditional J-system characterized by these features started to ebb even in the 1980s.[6] However, it was only after the bubble burst that changes became evident. In contrast to the above features of the traditional J-system, we now observe:

---

[5] See Aoki (1990) and Aoki et al. (1994) for a more detailed characterization discussion of the J-system.

[6] An early account of this tendency by the author may be found in Aoki 1988, chap. 7: particularly 293–7.

- Corporate Code reform in 2002 made corporate firms choose between two options for board structure: the American-type system with independent subcommittees (on auditing, managerial compensation and nomination) or a modified traditional system with a semi-independent statutory auditor's board (Gilson and Milahaupt 2004, Shishido, Chapter 11 this volume). By 2005, more than 60 major companies (including Sony, Oryx, Toshiba, Hitachi, and Nomura Holdings) had adopted the American-type system.[7,8] Even among companies that opted for the second alternative, there seems to be some tendency toward including a greater number of outside directors, although the definition of independency of outside directors is not as rigorous as in Sarbanes-Oxley Act of 2002 in the US.
- The Boards and top management of listed companies are now increasingly exposed to the open evaluation of the stock market as a result of the unwinding of cross-stockholding (Miyajima and Kuroki, chap. 4). At the height of the bubble, the holdings of tradable stocks by financial institutions rose to almost 50% of total stockholdings. They are now down to around twenty percent. On the other hand, individuals and foreigners now hold close to 50% in a more or less arms'-length manner. Particularly, the propensity of foreign portfolio investors to trade shares more frequently strongly influences share prices and made exit a particular threat to firms (Ahmadjian, Chapter 4, this volume). A noticeable number of bank and securities company employees, as well as bureaucrats, left their permanently employed jobs and joined/ formed investment funds or other financial service companies to take advantage of their expertise.[9]
- Facing increasingly active and unpredictable stock market trading, the managers of listed companies are now much more alert to potential take-over threats. One incident, which attracted wide attention, was the take-over attempt of Nippon Broadcasting System, Inc. (NBS: No 1 in sales in the broadcasting industry) by Livedoor Co. Ltd. (LD) in the winter of 2005.[10] LD quietly acquired more than 30% of NBS's shares off the exchange floor, in lieu of open take-over bids, by taking advantage of a loophole in stock exchange regulations then. The management of NBS attempted to counteract

[7] The Japan Association of Corporate Directors, a voluntary organization of directors, academics, lawyers, accountants, and so on, is campaigning to increase the number of corporations adopting the American-type system to 300 within a few years.

[8] A dramatic example of the consequences of these changes was the Sony's Board action to replace top managements in 2005 in response to poor corporate performance, which was reported to be pushed by the active involvement of independent directors.

[9] A well publicized example is Mr. Murakami, a former bureaucrat of MITI, who founded MAC asset management funds worth several billion US dollars with aggressive American type stockholder activism. He was later indicted for insider-trading, but this incident does not seem to indicate the reversal of the trend.

[10] This company, founded by a then-college-student named Horie with ¥6 million initial capital in the late 1990s, increased its market value to ¥800 billion in 2005. But in 2006 the top management was indicted by the Public Prosecutors Office for corporate account fraud and spreading false financial information.

to the threat by issuing new equity subscription rights amounting to 150% of issued capital and assigning them to Fuji TV Network Inc., a friendly company that owned 12% of NBS. LD appealed to the court for an injunction. After widely publicized court debates, the Tokyo District Court judged that NBS's plan was "unjust." It stipulated that "the Board of Directors, which is nothing but the executive organ of the corporation, shall not decide the composition of corporate control," implicitly endorsing the doctrine of stockholder sovereignty. Although the one who elicited this stockholder-friendly court judgment was ironically LD which was indicted later for illegal stock trading, spreading of false financial information and accounting fraud, this case is noteworthy in that judgments of the court are becoming critical to settling corporate disputes.[11] Now the public debate is under way regarding whether the so-called poison pill should be legally permitted and, if so, under what conditions so as not to provide unconditional entrenchment for incumbent managers.

- In 1995 bureaucrats at the Ministry of Finance (MOF) were busy figuring out ways to liquidate *Jusen* companies (Home Financing Corporations) which suffered from non-performing loans to land speculators worth seven trillion yen. Agricultural cooperative financial institutions were major lenders to these companies, while banks were major owner-cum-lenders. The agricultural interests were able to recover most of their loans to *Jusen* thanks to the infusion of public funds made possible by the powerful lobby activities of allied politicians. Their logic was that the main banks should be the ones to assume major responsibility, not other lenders, according to the general expectation held under the traditional *J*-system. This case made the prospect of injecting public funds into the ailing financial sector enormously unpopular and the government grew timid about overtly engaging in it. Delays in injecting public funds certainly deepened and prolonged the magnitude of the financial crisis but it had the unintended consequence of making the position of the financial authorities vis-à-vis the financial industries more or less at arms' length. The Banking Bureau and Securities Bureau of the MOF, which had formed exclusive collusions with respective industries to protect the vested interests of the incumbents, were made organizationally severed from the Ministry in the 1997 Administrative Reform and were reorganized as the Financial Services Agency (FSA). The Agency became pressured to be engaged in monitoring the financial soundness of banks in arms'-length manner, sometimes even in an adversarial manner. The restructuring of the banking

---

[11] Another legal case which may be considered even more important than the case of *LD vs. NBS* in the sense of involvement of established firms is the one in which Sumitomo Trust Bank (STB) appealed an injunction of the merger of two mega financial institutions, Mitsubishi-Tokyo Financial Group (MTFG) and UFJ, in 2004 on the ground that STB had a prior agreement to be merged with the trust division of UFJ. This appeal was denied by the court, but it is said that since the incident even traditional firms have become very careful about how to draw contracts with each other in order to avoid possible law suits.

and securities industries is now largely left to the private sector. In this way, an essential feature of the so-called "convoy-system" seems to have been laid to rest.

- Some of the overt attempts by the government to bail-out distressed firms did not yield good results, as was the case of The Daiei, Inc., a supermarket giant. Direct and discretionary intervention in industrial restructuring by the government is now increasingly looked on with suspicion. In response, the Industry Revitalization Corporation of Japan was funded with public funds for the purpose of more transparent public involvement in financially distressed firms, with its management recruited from the private sector.[12] Civil Rehabilitation Law (2000) introduced a US Chapter 11-like provision and gives incentives to distressed firms to file for bankruptcy earlier. Foreign-owned equity funds, bank-related corporate revival funds and other financial services are in place and have replaced commercial banks as major players in reorganizing/rehabilitating the financially-depressed firms (see Xu, Chapter 6, and Yanagawa, Chapter 7, this volume). Markets for corporate assets are growing in a size and scope that was never seen before the burst of the bubble (Kikutani, Itoh, and Hayashida, Chapter 8, this volume). The number of M&A more than quadrupled between 1995 and 2005.
- Some major companies have gone through large-scale restructuring by reducing the number of their permanent employees without necessarily breaking the long-term employment commitment by using transfers of their employees to their subsidiaries and related firms, hiring freeze/cut, as well as early retirement.[13] Macro-wise, between 1995 and 2005, the number of regular employees decreased by 4.1 million, while temporary employees in various categories increased by 6.5 million. It seems fair to say that many Japanese firms still commit to the permanent employment system, but the core has shrunk (Jackson, Chapter 10, this volume).[14]
- In the 2005 election of the Lower House, Premier Koizumi led the LDP to a landslide victory by campaigning for the privatization of Japan Post. This one-issue platform was meant to be targeted at the so-called "reform-resisting power," i.e. coalitions between politicians (both inside and outside the LDP), specific interest groups, and the bureaucracy. He succeeded in expelling those

[12] The Industry Revitalization Corporation of Japan completed its tasks and dissolved itself in March 2007 one year ahead of schedule because its missions were considered to have been successfully fulfilled.

[13] For example, an integrated steel company reduced the size of permanent employees by more than half, although it was said to have cost them about thirty million yen per employee in severance payments and early retirement incentives. Partly through the employment reduction and partly through the recovery of markets, its market value increased fourfold in 2005.

[14] Kato (2001) contrasted the job retention rates of Japanese and US work before and after the burst of the bubble. It turned out that the job retention rates of Japanese employees did not fall significantly from the period prior to the burst of the bubble economy in the late 1980s to the post-bubble period.

politicians opposed to the privatization from the LDP. Thus the institution of bureau-pluralism seems to face a critical phase.[15]

The facts cited above are meant to be only illustrative at this point. But in taking them together, it may be hard not to have an impression of considerable changes in the landscape of Japan's corporate world and its environment. But is this impression substantiated? In other words, is Japan's corporate world in general, and corporate governance in particular, undergoing an irreversible change? If so, in which direction? Is the stock market discipline going to exercise a dominant impact on corporate management as in the US?[16] Can the management afford not to heed to the voice of the employees any more? Or, is the reduction in the size of permanent employees just an inevitable, temporary reaction to the prolonged deflation and does the old model still persist? Alternatively, is Japan's corporate sector in the process of an earnest search for a model of its own, adaptable to the evolving environment? If so, is it moving in a "good" or "bad" direction?[17] In what way are changes in the corporate domain related to changes in the political domain? To consider these and related issues, it may be helpful to introduce first a coherent conceptual and analytical framework of institutional analysis, by which several prototypes of corporate governance structure, as well as associated fitting conditions, can be identified.

15.2 HOW CORPORATE GOVERNANCE IS UNDERSTOOD AS AN INSTITUTION

An important conceptual issue was first raised in a seminal debate between Dodd and Bearle in the early 1930s regarding whether the corporation is the property of

---

[15] After the end of the one-party dominance of the LDP in 1993, a change in the parliamentary election system from a multiple-seat district system to a single-seat district system was introduced and several elections have taken place since then in both the Upper and Lower Houses. In the old system, politicians from the same party representing different interest groups were electable in tandem in each district. Thus, interest mediation within the ruling party and through the administrative process (e.g. budgetary expenditures, entry-restricting regulations) became a political focal point, leading to the institutionalization of bureau-pluralism. However, after the electoral system changed, it has become increasingly difficult for politicians representing a particular interest group to be elected. Thus the power of the prime minister in policy-making and endorsing party candidates has been gradually strengthened. The 2005 election may be regarded as a spectacular manifestation of this on-going tendency.

[16] Actually even in the US, some evidence seems to point to the rather weak stock market discipline (e.g. statistically significant yet economically insignificant pay-performance sensitivities and the "trouble with stock options"). To this end, the ongoing controversy between the optional contracting school (e.g. Murphy 2002) and the managerial power school (e.g. Bebchuk et al. 2002) may be important and informative.

[17] Such normative question is raised explicitly only by Dore (Chapter 13) in this book. Below I will not deal with the normative issue as such, but implicitly suggest ways by which evolving patterns could be improved for better corporate performance. My stance may appear somewhat at odds with Dore's critical view of the present trend, but this difference may be reduced to a difference in assessing whether the present trend is toward the American-type system (Dore) or not (myself).

the stockholders, or if the board should owe fiduciary duties to the stakeholders in general. It does not seem that this issue has been resolved yet. One view became more powerful and prevalent at one time, but then to be replaced by the other in response to emergent business landscape, particular events (such as the Asian financial crisis, the Enron scandal) and so on. Notwithstanding this unsettled fundamental issue, corporate governance was regarded for a long time as a matter of legal design. True, the kinds of recent changes in the structure and composition of board rooms in Japan, as referred to above, would not have been possible without formal changes in the commercial code. However, even if formal rules are written, there is no guarantee that they will be followed and/or enforced as the legislators intended.[18] Visions of corporate governance implicit in a law will become viable and sustainable only if it generates the proper incentives, expectations and calculations on the side of the concerned parties (stakeholders). The case of the 2005 commercial code poses the issue in a straightforward and unique way. The purpose of introducing the options in board structures, which Gilson and Milhaupt call "an enabling strategy of reform," may have been to experiment with diversity and let evolutionary selection occur. Law itself cannot implement diversity, however. It can only aid corporate firms to experiment on diversity through decentralized decisions.

We may say then in analogy with the game that the law defines the formal rules, but what we should ultimately be concerned with are the "ways by which the game is actually played," or what we may call the endogenous rules of the game. The players may not necessarily follow the formal rules of the game; the referees (law enforcers and regulators) would not, or may not be competent to, enforce the formal rules; and the spectators (public) may jeer at the players/referees in one way or another. Simplifying the game-like discussion, let us first consider only the following four generic classes of stakeholders as the players of the game: the investors who invest in financial instruments issued by firms; the employees who invest in organization-specific human assets; the manager who directs the use of these financial and human resources in "non-contractible" events,[19] but who may have interests of his/her own (e.g., income, career concerns, perks, prestige, social reputation, etc.); and the consumers who collectively assess the activities of the firm by buying or not buying its outputs (i.e. the market). Depending on its market performance (i.e. market evaluation by the consumers),

---

[18] For example, the old Japanese Commercial Code was exceptionally generous to the stockholders in that a proposal for the election and replacement of the board members could be made at a stockholders' meeting by any stockholder who owned at least one percent of the stock. However, this statutory provision provided incentives among the managers to devise countermeasures to preserve their autonomy: such as implicitly colluding among themselves to hold stockholders' meetings on the same day of each year or implicitly or secretly bribing professional trouble makers, called *sokaiya*, who collected minority shares. Such practices are now fading, however, because more stringent law enforcement and increasing public awareness of corporate social responsibility reinforce each other.

[19] The rights to control assets in uncontractible events, called the "residual rights of control," are reckoned as the essence of property rights and are made the focus of the property rights theory of contracts and governance as represented by Hart (1995).

the firm may be roughly in either of three corporate-value states: excellent, normal, or depressed. The gross value added by the firm may be distributed among the investors, the employees, and the manager according to certain rules (by contracts, conventions, discretion, etc.). Each of them may be happy or unhappy with the outcome. In response, the investors and the employees will strategically choose their actions. In particular, in the depressed corporate-value state, they may choose some punishment or non-cooperation against the manager, possibly with the help of other parties (such as the court, take-over raiders, reorganization specialists, industrial unions, the government, etc.). In anticipation of these responses, the manager will adapt his behavior and choices in the use of financial and human resources under its command beforehand.

We can then identify a firm's corporate governance mechanism with a set of rules (formal or informal) that regulate the action choices of the stakeholders contingent on the value state of the firm. In particular, the crux of such a mechanism may be in the managers' behavioral beliefs regarding the plausible strategic reactions of other parties in the depressed corporate-value state.[20] Such beliefs would in turn constrain and discipline his or her action choices *ex ante* (in other contingencies). If such a set of rules is believed to operate generally across firms, we refer to it as a corporate governance institution. This corresponds to a situation in which typical parties will not expect a unilateral deviation from it to be beneficial so they will comply with it.[21] Rules embodied in statutory law can constitute part of a corporate governance institution if every concerned party expects that the enforcer himself finds it beneficial to enforce them (fearing the loss of social reputation, punishment, public criticism, etc.). But there are self-enforcing rules not necessarily enforced by the law enforcer. Examples of these are customs, self-enforcing contracts and agreements (due to reputation concerns, trust, etc.), (digital-) technology enforcing rules, implicit collusions among a subclass of concerned parties, and so on.

I claim that this institution-as-self-sustaining-rules view has several advantages.[22] Particularly, we can identify multiple different sets of rules that are viable under certain conditions, thus a diversity of institutions, rather than enumerate them on an ad hoc basis or regard only a certain particular set of rules viable and/ or normatively correct. Certainly a set of rules to guarantee the "maximum returns to the investors" as the only "owner of corporate property"[23] could be one possibility, but it may not be the only one. Furthermore, we can identify conditions, such as the institutional characteristics of the polity, prevailing social norms, labor relations, historical legacy and so on, that fit each of the possible models

---

[20] The point that the crux of governance lies in the manager's selection is mentioned as early as Knight, who argued that "in organized activity the *crucial* decision is the selection of men to make decisions . . . all of which follows from the very nature of large-scale control, based on the replacement of knowledge of things by knowledge of men"(1921: 297).

[21] This corresponds to the "institution-as-equilibrium" view (see Aoki 2001 and Greif 2006 for this view).

[22] For more detail, see Aoki (2001) particularly chap. 1.

[23] This main-stream view of corporate governance is surveyed by Shleifer and Vishny (1997).

so that we can predict which kind of institution is likely to emerge under certain particular conditions.

15.3 FOUR PROTOTYPE INSTITUTIONS OF CORPORATE GOVERNANCE

In the literature various types of corporate governance structures are discussed and their advantages and disadvantages are compared. In this section I briefly describe four stylized models of corporate governance. All of them except for the last are derived from rigorously formulated game-theoretic models.[24] Thus all of them are bound to have unrealistic features in certain respects as a description of an actual corporate governance institution. However, they can be useful for pinpointing conditions of technology, institutional environments of corporate governance, etc., that would make them viable and efficient in the use of human and physical resources.

15.3.1 Stockholder-Sovereignty (SS Model)

This is the most widely discussed model, as well as the most widely supported, in the orthodox literature. An authoritative economic-theoretical foundation for this model can be found in the writings of property-rights theorists as represented by Hart, who argued for the inseparability of ownership and management as a starting point.[25] A crucial assumption of his is that of complementarities between the managerial ability that is malleable with his/her effort and the right to control the use of physical assets in non-contractible events. That is, the value of the manager's incremental effort is assumed to be enhanced, if he/she has discretionary rights for deciding how physical assets are to be used. If this is the case, then it follows that it is more efficient for the manager to own physical assets, provided that he/she is not financially constrained. The employees may be contracted according to the level of firm-specific skills in which they invested. The value that the firm produces net of the contractual payments to the employees accrues to the owner-cum-manager as profit. This is the case of a classical proprietor-run firm.

If the manager is financially constrained and needs to rely on equity financing, then he/she has to yield fundamental control rights to the stockholders and be subjected to an incentive contractual arrangement as an agent of the stockholders. The present value sum of expected streams of profit accruing to the stockholders is called the fundamental stock value (Note the distinction between

---

[24] See Aoki (2001: chap. 5, 11, and 12).

[25] The following is an interpretation of the main points analyzed in Hart (2005) in the present context. See Aoki (2001: 119–23).

the (gross) value-added by the firm inclusive of contractual payments to the employees and the stock value of the firm as residual after them). The fear of discharge in the job in the event of a financially depressed state (i.e., career concerns), as well as the prospect of incentive payments in the event of an excellent corporate-value state, motivates the manager to make the best effort. Under this scheme, an investor who conceives of a new business plan to enhance the stock value may take over the firm through open bids in the stock market and replace the management. This event can occur, even if the implementation of the plan induces the reduction of gross value-added of the firm and accordingly the breach/termination of (implicit) contracts with the employees. The role of the government in this model could be that of the liberal state which would not interfere with private employment contracting but only enforce private contracts as a third party.

15.3.2 Corporatism-Codetermination (D Model)

In the previous model, the employees are provided with incentive contracts for investment in firm-specific skills. Let us consider an alternative situation in which firms are situated in an institutional environment of social-compact corporatism where the wage rates are regulated according to standard job qualifications through collective bargaining between the industrial association and the industrial labor organization, while the government allows bargaining outcomes to be legally binding to all firms in relevant industries. Then an individual employer's ability is constrained in inducing the employees to acquire and use firm-specific skills with the promise of firm-specific payments. In such a situation, even if the interests of the manager and those of the employees are basically opposed in the distribution of control power over work (and the use of physical assets as a corollary), the sharing of control rights (e.g., in the form of the work council) will become of mutual interest.

A sharing arrangement can be extended to the stockholding company as co-determination in which the board members are shared between the representatives of both the investors and employees.[26] This model is reminiscent of some basic aspects of corporate governance institution in Germany (thus the D-model referring to Deutch). Contrasting this model with the previous one suggests that there are institutional complementarities between corporatism and codetermination, on one hand, and between private employment contracting and the liberal state, on the other.

---

[26] In this setting, more external financing will be made in the form of long-term debt contracts than in the SS model. This is so, because in the context of co-determination, the investors and the employees have common preferences for debt-contracts in order to control the risky behavior of the manager, while the manager prefers to limit the residual rights of control by the stockholders. See Aoki (2001: 287–91) for a rigorous analysis. A proof of institutional complementarities between codetermination and the corporatist state is also given there.

15.3.3 Relational Contingent Governance (RCG Model)

Symmetric to the assumption of an exclusive complementary relationship between managerial effort and control rights over physical assets, assume that
contributions to the gross value of the firm by the manager and the employees
are mutually indistinguishable, while the physical resources supplied by outsiders
are non-specific. In this case, an efficient governance structure dictates that the
insiders (the employees and the managers) ought to hold control rights in
excellent and normal corporate-value states, as well as receive residuals after
contractual payments to the outsiders (the investors). As contributions of individual insiders to the total value are not clearly distinguishable, however, payments to them need to be regulated by organization-specific rules (such as
payment by seniority, simple sharing, etc.) rather than as individual performance-based payments. In financially distressed state a particular monitoring agent
ought to gain control rights and decide whether firm-specific human assets
should be bailed out for continuation value or punished by the termination of
the firm in the worst case, depending on the nature and magnitude of the crisis.
Since the control rights shift between the insiders and the monitoring agent,
contingent on the corporate-value state of the firm, this model can be called the
contingent governance model.[27] As bailing out is often costly than liquidation in
the short run for the monitoring agent, some rents need to be assured for it to be
induced to assume the costs when necessary. Such rents can be guaranteed, if the
agent can expect stable fees from long-run relationships with multiple firms and/
or be insured for the monitoring costs by the government. Thus the position of
the monitoring agent in this model vis-à-vis the firm as well as the government is
relational so that the model may be characterized as the relational contingent
governance (RCG). However such arrangements may lead to a soft-budget
tendency for the monitoring agent, i.e., it may tend to bail out firms that should
be punished by the termination, because it could be less costly for them with the
government protection. Although this model is a purely theoretical construct, the
traditional Japanese governance structure emulated some basic aspects of it with
the so-called main bank playing the role of the relational monitoring agent.[28]

From the above three models, we can deduce that three factors may be crucial
in determining a viable form of corporate governance: the nature of manager/
employees' human assets and their relationships with physical assets and the
government. Namely, in the SS and D models, the individual skills of the
employees, either firm-specific or general, can be identifiable and are made
individually contractible, while in the RCG model they are not and their rewards

---

[27] See Aoki (2001, chap. 11.3) for rigorous conceptualization and proofs of various properties
claimed here.

[28] Some aspects of the relational contingent governance model may also be found in the relationship between the venture capital and the entrepreneurial firm, although it is not embedded in the
protection of the government. See Aoki (2000, 2001: 302 and chap. 12); and Kaplan and Stromberg
(2003).

can contain elements of firm-wide sharing of values/losses. Secondly, the SS model presupposes complementarities between the manager's human assets and his/her exclusive control over physical assets (that is, the manager's human assets becomes more valuable when (s)he is endowed with exclusive control rights over physical assets) through the stockholders' agency relationship, while in the other models, the control of physical assets may be complementary to both the employees' and the manager's human assets (as in the D model) or to the employees' and manager's human assets combined (as in the RCC model). Thirdly, in the former two models, the role of the government may be characterized as "neutral" in the sense of a third-party contract enforcer (the so-called liberal state as in the SS model) or that of enabling employees' and employers' organizations to jointly attain the status of quasi-state organs (the so-called "enabling state" (Streeck 1977) as in the D model). In the RCG model, the role of the government may become relational vis-a-vis the monitoring agents (banks) in assuring rents for them to make the model viable as an institution. From these observations, the following fourth model may be suggested as another possibility.

15.3.4 External Monitoring of Internal Linkage (EMIL Model)

Instead of complementarities between physical assets and managerial human assets in the SS model, consider possible complementarities between the *managerial business model* and employees' human assets. The managerial business model is a set of managerial constructs composed of such things as: organizational architectural design, marketing strategies, an organization-specific reward system, relations with the labor union, the design of work environments, and the formulation of organizational values to be shared by the employees. Complementarities in this case imply that the employees are better off through being voluntarily associated with the relevant business model, while the business model can generate greater gross value by attracting and maintaining the employees willing to develop human assets specific to it and identifying themselves with the values.[29] The function of the management of the firm can be considered as the creation and sustenance of this productive internal linkage.

Different from the SS model, the role of physical assets is regarded as secondary in that employed physical assets are composed of general-purpose machines, or relatively small in value in comparison to human assets. However, if the management lets it be known as part of its business model that a proportion of the value created by the complementary linkage accrues to the stockholders according to a certain rule and if the stock market is informative, the fundamental stock value may be constructed as a summary statistic correlated to future values of the linkage. If the board of directors is entrusted to effectively replace or appoint top management contingent on the (expected) stock value, the

---

[29] The importance of similar complementarities between the firm and the human assets are emphasized by Rajan and Zingales (2000).

management can be disciplined to create and sustain a valuable internal linkage. On the other hand, the stockholders themselves may be motivated to do a better job of monitoring if they can benefit from making good evaluative judgments. Therefore, there are complementarities between the creation and sustenance of internal linkage on one hand and the stock market evaluation on the other. Complementarities can thus be dual; external as well as internal. In this model, the board of directors ought to act not as the agent of the returns-maximizing stockholders but as the "trustees" for the stakeholders including the employees and the managers (Blair and Stout 1999). It would not force the management to increase the stock value at the sacrifice of the employees, because it would be likely to destroy the valuable internal linkage. This model will work better if the government helps infrastructural services for stock markets to process corporate information more accurately and facilitate fair and equitable stock transactions.

15.4 FACTORS TRIGGERING CHANGES IN JAPAN'S CORPORATE GOVERNANCE

As mentioned already, some stylized features of the traditional *J*-system as summarized in the beginning of section 15.1 are reminiscent of the RCG model with the main bank serving as the relational monitor. In the light of theoretical proposition in the previous section, it makes sense in that the sharing of information between the management and the *genba* (work sites), as well as among the *genba*, was an established custom within the *J*-firm facilitated by its practice of ambiguous job demarcation, job rotation, life-time internal career development, etc.[30] The RCG model-like, information-sharing practice co-evolved with the permanent employment system (the absence of active labor mobility), the main bank system, and bureau-pluralism as complementary institutions.[31] On the other hand, contrary to frequently-made casual references to the "Rhein model" (Albert 1991), the German–Japanese model of bank-oriented governance and the like, the comparison of the D model and the RCG model helps us understand that the Japanese main bank system and the German codetermination system cannot be simply lumped together in the same class of corporate governance. They operated on quite different mechanisms in terms of industrial relations, contractual arrangements, selection/replacement of management and so on, not to mention their differences in statutory legal arrangements. Therefore we expect that there have also been path-dependent differences in their responses to changes in market and technological environments that have started to accelerate since the 1980s. Let us briefly review some basic impacts of these changes on the Japanese system.

First, the gradual opening of financial markets which started in the early 1980s allowed better-run firms to rely on various financial instruments including bonds

---

[30] For information-sharing within the *J*-firm, see Aoki (1988: chap. 2, 1990).
[31] For these institutional complementarities and their historical origins, see Aoki (2001, chap. 13).

and equity issues abroad. Japanese banks steadily lost better corporate clients and failed to adapt to this new market environment. As is well known, their soft-budgeting tendency was blown up into becoming one of the major driving forces of the bubble in the late 1980s, culminating in their own crisis after it burst. However, the eclipse of the main bank system and the globalization of financial markets eased constraints for the management of the *J*-firm to experiment on various business models (see Jackson and Miyajima, Chapter 1 this volume). This is because institutional complementarities between a financial institution and other institutions (in employment, innovation, supply relations, polity, etc.) imply that a change in one of them can trigger changes in the other and create momentum for cumulative, mutually reinforcing changes—the phenomena conceptualized as dynamic institutional complementarities. The presence of institutional complementarities is one reason for the robustness of institutional arrangements, but also can become a source for generating over-all institutional adaptations if the complementary linkage is broken somewhere.[32] More on this to follow.

Second, as product markets became more mature and globalized with technological innovation progressing at an unprecedented rate, the structure of industrial competition became more complex, making the simple-minded expansion of shares in an existing market obsolete as a corporate objective as well as corporate evaluative criterion. Competition over managerial business models becomes fierce across markets, continuously creating new markets. So a new mechanism of evaluating corporate firms has become a necessity. It became evident that banks, entrenched in relational financing, could not perform a proper monitoring role in this respect. Instead, as we have noted already in section 15.1, management of the corporate firm is becoming more watchful than ever of stock market performance as an external evaluative mechanism.

Third, the progress of communication and information technology introduced dramatic impacts on the value of (tacit) information-sharing among agents within an organization, as well as within a particular collusive group. As far as a primary reason for exclusive information sharing was the limit of available information channels, it has been steadily overcome by the increasing capacity of digitalized communications and the associated social demands for information disclosure and transparency. Even some of the tacit know-how at work sites has become digitalizable through computer-aided design, computer-controlled machines and the like. People no longer need to spend most of their time communicating face-to-face with a fixed number of partners to gain useful information. Mobile phones, the Internet, e-mail and so on have dramatically changed the patterns, scope and range of communications among people. These impacts of information and communication technology can be considered as one of the most important reasons for the apparent erosion of competitiveness of Japanese

---

[32] See Aoki (2000, chap. 10) for analytical treatments of dynamic institutional complementarities and chap. 10 for their application to the Japanese economic history since the 1930s. Also, see Aoki (2007) for a summary exposition.

firms, which were able to take advantage of the value of tacit information-sharing in the pre-IT revolution era of the 1980s.[33]

In spite of all this, however, there still seems to be valuable information which cannot be digitalized, at least within a short period of time, but can be shared among a small number of people with particular common interests and complementary areas of competence, and are potentially valuable in generating new ideas (such as business strategies, technological innovation, work improvement on sites (*kaizen*), etc.).[34] The paradox is that such information sharing in a niche could become potentially more valuable precisely because it is novel and scarce in the context of the increasing amount of information widely shared in the public domain.

Indeed, we have observed divergent responses among Japanese corporate firms in this regard. The better performers often belong to the type of firm that continues to foster and utilize valuable information-sharing among its employees in combination with the complementary use of emergent information technology. This type may look superficially similar to the traditional J-firm, but there is a non-negligible difference that was shaped during the past decade or so in that the leadership of management plays a much more active role in terms of the design of organizational architecture that fits the new information technology (e.g. a flatter, modular structure;[35] spinning-off of affiliated firms rather than large integrated firms),[36] a reward system to elicit employees' cooperation and individual initiatives in a balanced way and so on. Even on-site *kaizen* (work improvement) movement has been reformed with more emphasis on the active role of the local leadership.[37] In these firms the sustenance of the permanent employment system is still regarded as important,[38] although it has been modified in terms of promotion schemes and reward systems with a certain degree of competitive elements (Jackson, Chapter 10 this volume). On the other hand, there seem to be two types of mediocre to problematic performers. Firms of the first type are composed of those that were hasty in emulating the so-called Western style reward system based on individual performance evaluation, destroying

---

[33] See Aoki (1988 and 1990) for the view that the competitiveness of the Japanese manufacturing industry up to the late 1980s was very much reliant on the use of tacit knowledge shared among the workers on the shop floor, as well as between the workers and the management, the R&D organization and the shop floor, and the prime manufacturer and suppliers.

[34] See Cowan et al. (2000) and Aoki (2001, chap. 12.1) for a taxonomy of knowledge by which some type of tacit knowledge may be regarded as economically valuable.

[35] For the innovativeness of the modular organization in a complex system, see Baldwin and Clark (2001). See also Aoki (2001, chap. 4), where the value of information encapsulation (modularization) is discussed.

[36] Kikutani et al., Chapter 8 this volume, analyze this tendency of Japanese firms.

[37] For example, field work by Kato (unpublished) shows that there is a more advanced and sophisticated case which introduced a full-time kaizen support group whose main job was to assist various kaizen teams by doing experiments for them.

[38] Consider the case of Toyota Motor Corporation that was downgraded by international bond rating companies immediately after the Asian financial crisis because of its permanent employment practices, but is still enjoying one of the highest stock values in the manufacturing industry.

the spirit of valuable information sharing.[39] Firms of the other type are led by old-fashioned managers who confine themselves to passively mediating various interest groups within an organization rather than taking the initiative in formulating a competitive business model in response to the new informational and market environments. They often try to rely on outdated collusive networks within the framework of ebbing bureau-pluralism in an attempt to hold on to losing ground.[40]

15.5 THE GRADUAL TRANSITION TO THE EMIL MODEL?

In facing the challenges described above, Japanese firms have been strenuously trying to adapt their business models, human assets, and associated corporate governance mechanisms in one way or another. As a result, the traditional RCG-type institution appears to be in eclipse as the behavioral beliefs and practices characterizing it cannot be taken for granted anymore. On the other hand, a clear alternative pattern has not yet emerged as the universally accepted rules of the game regulating the interactions of the corporate stakeholders. However, if we interpret the anecdotal evidences described in section 15.1 in the light of the theoretical models in the previous section, we may interpret the emergent pattern as the gradual transition to the EMIL model from the RCG model. In general, the presence of institutional complementarities is thought to preclude the possibility of a mixed or hybrid institution.[41] But, as discussed in the last section, the opening of financial markets has eased the constraints on institutional choice in other domains. For example, some action choices that were not supported by the traditional main bank system may become viable in Japan.

Indeed, diverse patterns are being observed, and will be observed for some time, in the areas of organizational architecture, employment practices, market strategies, supplier relations, industrial relations, and so on.[42] Those diverse business models need to be compared and assessed in terms of the values generated in possible cooperation with the employees' human assets. As a mechanism of evaluation of the value of the internal linkage between a business model and human assets, product market evaluations (thus current profit) are fundamental. However, the product market can evaluate only the present outcome of the internal linkage, not possible outcomes in the future. Also, a valuable internal

---

[39] This type is conspicuously found among laggards in the electric machinery industry, once considered the most competitive industry.

[40] Miyajima and Kuroki, Chapter 3 this volume, detected that low-performing firms tend to sustain main bank relationships with mutual stockholdings.

[41] It is because the presence of complementarities normally involves the non convexity of sustainable choice combinations. See Aoki (2001, chap. 8.3).

[42] These diversities (particularly in organizational architecture) are described and their implications for institutional change are discussed by Jackson and Miyajima, Chapter 1 and Sako, Chapter 14, this volume.

linkage takes time to build. In the previous section, I suggested that the bank may not be up to the evaluative task. Although they may still be cases in which they can monitor the corporate-value state of firms of a particular type relatively well, their time-horizon may not be far enough and their expertise may not be sufficiently nuanced in the evolving complex environments. Instead, stock markets may be potentially in a better position to predict future outcomes by aggregating dispersed information, expectations and values prevailing in the economy if they can filter noises to a reasonable degree.[43] Of course, the last condition, which I will come back to shortly, is a long way yet from being taken for granted.

Even if the stock market is hypothetically assumed to be informative for a moment, a corporate governance structure may not be complete with just that, however. One more critical question still remains to be resolved: How can a stock market evaluation of an individual firm be used effectively in the selection and replacement of management at the firm level? Remember the crux of corporate governance lies in the way in which management is selected and replaced when necessary. In the RCG-like institution of the traditional *J*-system, the control in this respect was arranged in a contingent manner. That is, in excellent and normal states of gross corporate-value of the firm, the mechanism was firmly gripped by the insiders (the top management was selected by internal promotion without any outside intervention), while in the critical state control rights shifted to the main bank. In the currently evolving situation, the insiders seem to retain effective control as far as the corporate-value state seems to be without problem. But who will exercise the disciplinary function in critical state of corporate-value? No single solution seems to have been established yet.

For small and medium-sized firms, as well as large firms with large bank loans, there may be still cases in which banks can perform major monitoring and disciplinary functions. But for large firms with rather limited bank loans, not to say those with no bank loans, the ability of the banks to correct poor management before a real crisis becomes evident is definitely limited, even if they play certain roles in arranging a bail-out or liquidation of failed firms *ex post*.[44] Further, even in this case, the banks are not embedded in the protective framework of bureau-pluralism any more, as we noted already, so that their involvement may be more passive.[45] One possible alternative to the bank's disciplinary role would be to transform the board of directors from the traditional status of a management substructure into a quasi-independent body that could discipline top executive management in critical state of corporate-value. As noted already, some firms may be heading somewhat in that direction by

---

[43] In fact, market prices cannot be completely perfect. If all information available in the economy can be immediately and completely reflected in market prices, then nobody would be motivated to collect information. Grossman and Stiglitz (1980).

[44] Xu, Chapter 6 this volume provides evidence of the tendency for banks not to bail out distressed firms until bankruptcy is filed.

[45] However, Arikawa and Miyajima, Chapter 2 this volume, detected some evidences of soft-budgeting tendency toward laggard firms in the early 1990s.

adopting a board structure with independent subcommittees or increasing the number of independent directors.[46] How it will work has yet to be seen, but an experiment is certainly worthwhile.[47] For start-up firms which are not mature yet for stock market evaluation, venture capital firms that act as sort of market surrogates in a relational manner are gradually gaining visibility.[48] For the time being, a variety of mechanisms may be tried for using stock market signals or implicit corporate values for the governance of individual firms, subject to evolutionary selection.[49]

Even if stock market evaluation progresses in Japan, it is unlikely that Japan's corporate governance institution will transit to an SS-type model reminiscent of the American system, however. For one thing, a transition from the RCG to the EMIL model would imply a shift from the practice of *sharing* of information, responsibilities, and outcomes between the management and the employees, to the development of firm-specific *complementary* relationships between the two. To repeat, these relationships presume more autonomous leadership roles of the management in designing business models than in the old RCG-like model, yet require specific employees' human assets fitting, and associated with, the models. This shift appears to be evolutionarily fitter than a shift to a clear demarcation of the management and the employees through individual contractual relationships as in the SS model.[50] Therefore, it might be quite possible that the voice of employees, implicitly or overtly, will continue to play a part in the managerial formulation of business models, if not directly in the legally specified mechanism of corporate governance as in the D-model.[51]

Finally, I will add a few words regarding the relationships between corporate governance and the polity. Needless to say, in order for an informative stock market to evolve, there must be an effective mechanism to filter the noise in processing corporate information and forming a fundamental stock value from it. For that to occur, there must be shared beliefs among market participants that regulatory rules are formulated and enforced in such a way that corporate

[46] One of the proposals that seem to be widely supported in the current discussion on corporate governance reform is that the provision of a poison pill might be allowed if the board of directors, with a majority of outside directors, approves it. Such a stipulation might provide incentives for the company to make the board more open and independent.

[47] Gilson and Milhaupt (2004) suggests that, at least as currently structured, we should not expect too much from these committees.

[48] See Hata, Ando and Ishii, Chapter 5 this volume. See also Aoki (2000); Rajan and Zingales (2000); and Kaplan and Stromberg (2003); for the nature of the corporate governance role of the venture capital firm.

[49] Another alternative is the model in which the founder family, albeit of relatively small holdings, exercises effective control over the executive management. Practices akin to this model can be found in companies like Toyota Motor Corporation and Suntory Ltd.

[50] Abe and Hoshi, Chapter 9 this volume, as well as Jackson, Chapter 10 this volume, provide some empirical support for this prediction. They find that an increase in foreign ownership does not necessarily lead to a distinctive modification of human resource management, even though there may be some modifications of certain aspects.

[51] See an interesting contribution by Sako (2006) which documents and analyzes the emergent diversity in corporate organizational structure as a result of strategic interplays between the management and the enterprise union at the firm level.

information will be disclosed transparently, but not in a way that stifles active trading among a broad range of informed participants. Furthermore, these beliefs must be supported by an infrastructure of various competent professional services (e.g., accounting, the law, system engineering, financial analysis, academic theorizing and analysis), as well as trade-facilitating, information-processing technologies. In these respects, Japanese practices still here much to be improved. Even though some reforms have been achieved in the past decade, noticeably irregular events have also emerged, such as the LD case, generated by deficiencies in regulatory rules as well as revealing the inadequacy of the stock exchange infrastructure technologies.[52] It would not be possible to entirely control the misconduct of some players who seek profits at the risk of violating the law or taking advantage of loopholes in regulatory rules in a shrewd manner. But such incidents ought not to prevent nurturing the important function of corporate monitoring by the stock market. There does not seem to be a better mechanism for evaluating and predicting uncertain corporate performances by summarizing economically valuable information dispersed in the economy, so we cannot help but try to make markets work better.

In this regard, the changes in the polity occasionally referred to above may be relevant. In the traditional *J*-system, the primary role of regulatory agencies was to assure the stability of the bank-oriented financial system. They did so by providing rents to banks in rather opaque forms of entry- and rate-regulations, as well as through backdoor agreements among parties concerned in bailing out financially distressed firms. In these arrangements, the interests of bankers and their employees, and those of regulatory bureaucrats and politicians, were intricately interwoven. But, as noted, the framework of bureau-pluralism in which such schemes were embedded is now in eclipse. In fact, the waning of bureau-pluralism in the polity and various changes in economic and social domains mutually reinforce each other, making the reversal of either one alone less likely.

Better-performing corporate firms and new entrepreneurial firms do not need the paternalistic, specific protection of politicians and the bureaucracy. The associations of life-time occupation holders (such as doctors, nurses, post-masters, contractors, etc.) are losing their organizational integrity and thus political influence, because the members of younger generations are more diverse in their values, expectations, and behavior.[53] Thus, demands for deregulating rules aimed at protecting particular interest groups are rising, as are demands for implementing rules assuring a broader spectrum of public interests and safety (e.g. pension reform adapted to the rapidly aging population, remedying public

---

[52] Immediately after the arrest of top executives at LD in January 2006, there were a tremendous number of sales bids, particularly by individuals of small holdings, which exceeded the system capacity of the Tokyo Stock Exchange and forced it to shorten trading hours for a few consecutive days.

[53] However, there is a danger that the protective framework of bureau-pluralism will be replaced by protective legislation enacted at the urging of the business community, in tacit alliance with those segments of the public who are disillusioned and indignant by some misconduct in the stock market and corporate world. I owe this comment partially to Milhaupt. Also see Rajan and Zingales (2003) for related discussion.

finance deficits, health, construction standards, child protection). The gradual transformation of the Finance Service Agency from an institutional agent of bureau-pluralism to a regulator sustaining an arms'-length relationship with the constituent industry, is nothing but a symptom of a bureaucratic response to these trends. Such tendency may be more conducive to the development of an institutional environment for the stock market to become more informative. The reason is that rules for stock market transactions, the disclosure of corporate information, and the like must be formulated and enforced in a neutral, arms'-length manner vis-à-vis concerned parties, but not by government in collusion with the incumbents in the financial market.

REFERENCES

Albert, M. (1991). *Capitalisme Contre Capitalisme*. Paris: Seuil.

Aoki, M. (1988). *Information, Incentives and Bargaining in the Japanese Economy*. Cambridge: Cambridge University Press.

—— (1990). 'Toward an Economic Model of the Japanese Firm,' *Journal of Economic Literature*, 28: 1–27.

—— (2000). 'Information and Governance in the Silicon Valley Model,' in X. Vives (ed.), *Corporate Governance: Theoretical and Empirical Perspectives*. Cambridge: Cambridge University Press, 169–95.

—— (2001). *Toward a Comparative Institutional Analysis*, Cambridge, MA: MIT Press.

—— (2002). *Unwavering Coordinates in a Decade of Flux* (in Japanese). Tokyo: Nikkei Bizinesuman Bunko.

—— (2007). 'Endogenizing Institutions and Institutional Change.' *Journal of Institutional Economics*, 3: 1–18.

—— H. Patrick, and P. Sheard (1994). 'The Japanese Main Bank System: An Introductory Overview,' in M. Aoki et al. (eds.), *The Japanese Main Bank System: Its Relevancy to Developing and Transforming Economy*. Oxford: Oxford University Press, 3–5.

Baldwin, C. Y. and K. B. Clark (2001). *Design Rules: The Power of Modularity*, Vol.1. Cambridge, MA: MIT Press.

Bebchuk, L., J. M. Fried, and D. I. Walker (2002). 'Managerial Power and Rent Extraction in the Design of Executive Compensation,' *University of Chicago Law Review*.

Blair, M. and L. Stout (1999). 'A Team Production Theory of Corporate Law,' *Virgina Law Review*, 85: 247–328.

Cowan, R. P., P. David, and D. Foray (2000). 'The Explicit Economics of Knowledge Codification and Tacitness,' *Industrial and Corporate Change*, 9: 211–54.

Gilson, R., and C. Milhaupt (2004). 'Choice as Regulatory Reform: The Case of Japanese Corporate Governance.' Available at: http://ssrn.com/abstract=537843

Greif, A. (2006). *Institutions and the Path to the Modern Economy: Lessons from Medieval Trade*. Cambridge: Cambridge University Press.

Grossman, S. and J. Stiglitz (1980). 'On The Impossibility of Informationally Efficient Markets,' *American Economic Review*, 70.

Hart, O. (1995). *Firms, Contracts, and Financial Structure*. Oxford: Clarendon Press.

Kaplan, S. N. and P. Stromberg (2003). 'Financial Contracting Theory Meets the Real World: An Empirical Analysis of Venture Capital Contracts,' *Review of Economic Studies*, 70: 281.

Kato, T. (2001). 'The End of Lifetime Employment in Japan? Evidence from National Surveys and Field Research,' *Journal of the Japanese and International Economies*, 15: 489–514.

Knight, F. (1921). *Risk, Uncertainty, and Profit*. Chicago: University of Chicago Press.

Murphy, K. J. (2002). 'Explaining Executive compensation: Managerial Power vs. the Perceived Cost of Stock Options,' *University of Chicago Law Review*.

Rajan, R. G. and L. Zingales (2000). 'The Governance of the New Enterprises,' in X. Vives (ed.), *Corporate Governance: Theoretical and Empirical Perspectives*. Cambridge: Cambridge University Press.

—— —— (2003). *Saving Capitalism from the Capitalists: Unleashing the Power of Financial Markets to Create Wealth and Spread Opportunity*. New York: Crown Business.

Sako, M. (2006). *Shifting Boundaries of the Firm*. Oxford: Oxford University Press.

Shleifer, A. and R. W. Vishny (1997). 'A Survey of Corporate Governance,' *Journal of Finance*, 52: 737–87.

Streeck, W. (1997). 'German Capitalism: Does It Exist? Can It Survive?' in C. Crouch and W. Streeck (eds.), *Political Economy of Modern Capitalism*. London: Sage, 34–54.

Toya, T. (2006). *The Political Economy of the Japanese Financial Big Bang: Institutional Change in Finance and Public Policymaking*. Oxford: Oxford University Press.

Vives, X. (ed.) (2000). *Corporate Governance: Theoretical & Empirical Perspectives*. Cambridge: Cambridge University Press.

Index